CEYLON: DILEMMAS OF A NEW NATION

Ceylon:
Dilemmas of a New Nation

BY W. HOWARD WRIGGINS

PRINCETON, NEW JERSEY
PRINCETON UNIVERSITY PRESS
1960

L.C.Card: 60-5761

Printed in the United States of America
by Princeton University Press, Princeton, New Jersey

TO SALLY
AND
DIANA, CHRISTOPHER,
AND
JENNIFER

ACKNOWLEDGMENTS

In the course of preparing this study, debts accumulated monstrously. The Rockefeller Foundation and Vassar College together made the two years of field work and preliminary drafting possible. In England the staff of the Royal Institute of International Affairs and the Royal Empire Society each helped in their special ways. Professors Carrington, Mansergh, Jennings, and Hancock and members of the Commonwealth Relations Office patiently advised a neophyte. In the United States William Holland, Sydney Bailey, Drs. Gabriel Almond, Rupert Emerson, Roger Hilsman, Henry Oliver, and Christopher Sower made valuable suggestions.

In Ceylon so many individuals gave generously of their knowledge, their time, and their hospitality they cannot all be mentioned. Many men and women in the professions, at the University, in journalism, in politics, in the public service, in education; entrepreneurs, shop foremen, union leaders, village teachers, physicians, and teaching and village *bhikkhus* contributed their share to the whole. I am deeply in their debt and trust that anything said in the following pages will not deter them from giving similarly to Ceylonese and other scholars who may be piqued by the lacunae in this study to correct and improve upon it.

Staffs of the Colombo Public Library, the libraries of the Young Men's Buddhist Association, the National Museum in Colombo, the Government Archives in Nuwara Eliya, the Associated Newspapers of Ceylon and the Times of Ceylon provided materials with utmost courtesy and readiness. To identify those individuals in retrospect who assisted most profoundly is inescapably invidious to those not mentioned. But I do wish to thank particularly those who proved willing to read and criticize parts of an early and very rough draft: Messrs. R. D. Desai, T. E. Gooneratne, J. P. Grant, D. Pieris, M. Rajendra, M. A. de Silva, Mervyn de Silva, G. H. F. Welikala, Drs. G. C. Mendis, I. D. S. Weerawardana, P. Wignaraja, and the Ven. Narada Thero. Mr. S. P. F. Senaratne, in addition to criticizing parts of the early manuscript, shared the fascination of a pre-electoral tour in Sinhalese rural districts as interpreter and anthropological consultant. Mr. Daya Perera typed his way through oceans of parliamentary debates and the first draft. Miss S. Rasaretnam assisted by clipping newspapers, filing, and preparing electoral data. Mr. B.

Aluvihare kindly assisted with reading proof. Many of their good suggestions could not be included in the text. Responsibility for the final product is mine alone.

To my Ceylonese friends I would say that I have done my best with much sympathy, and I hope some intelligence, to convey to a foreign audience the essential dynamics of social, economic, and political changes as I saw them. Those who feel dismay at what has been stressed should remember that a study of politics in any country is not necessarily a study of that country's highest philosophy or its most gentle arts. Though politics demands the highest qualities of leadership and poised judgment, it is also the study of "who gets what, when and how," which is not likely to be the field of human endeavor where the best is always revealed.

To my wife goes a particular word of thanks for putting up with her husband while he was preparing the manuscript. Without her detailed criticisms and patient editorial assistance throughout the study it would be a far less satisfactory presentation. To her and our three children, one of whom has the distinction of having been born in Colombo, this study is lovingly dedicated.

CONTENTS

MAPS AND CHARTS

Drawn by R. L. Williams

CEYLON: DILEMMAS OF A NEW NATION

CHAPTER I · INTRODUCTION: THE ISSUES

BETWEEN 1946 and 1949, over 600,000,000 people in former colonial Asia gained their independence. Ten newly independent states arose where four Western empires once ruled. Each of these states is aspiring to develop—in a cultural, religious, and economic setting unlike that of contemporary or nineteenth-century Europe—some variant of the nation state. Each is seeking to fashion a vigorous and independent social, political, and economic system suitable to its needs in the modern world. In this enterprise, leadership qualities are more severely tested by the responsibilities of domestic and international statesmanship than they were by the earlier struggle for independence.

Although each of the newly independent countries has difficulties and opportunities peculiar to itself, the first decade of independence has demonstrated that all of them face certain common fundamental problems. During the colonial period a Westernized social, administrative, legal, and economic elite developed in all these countries. Though many of the leading men were born to privilege or had unusual opportunities, they were nevertheless committed to egalitarian, democratic values. They favored representative government and reducing the gross inequalities among the people. Their economic interests, usually based on land, worked toward economically cautious policies, but their Western education led them to seek government innovations to promote economic productivity and social justice. Throughout the area, an insistent political question revolves around their future role and responsibility. Can the Westernized draw to the seats of power the growing numbers of educated, ambitious, but economically less favored citizens who now seek entry into the ruling elite? Or will the Westernized be displaced from their positions of power as new groups press forward to rule? These questions underlie the following additional domestic problems.

Religion exerts a fascination for Asian minds. In the past, respected rulers had related themselves intimately to religious values and practice. By contrast, the late colonial period created the image of a secular state. Indigenous faiths and men of religion were thrust aside by the secularizing and modernizing forces from Europe. Now, following independence, many are seeking to redress the secular influence of the colonial era and give their traditional religions a place in public affairs more in keeping with what they believe to be their due. The problems of the relation of church and state as such do not arise, for religion is not institutionalized in the same way as it is in the West, but the role of men of religion in politics and the proper approach of professional politicians toward the indigenous faiths have to be defined. In profoundly religious societies this relationship may be as important as was the church-state relationship in medieval Europe. At the end of the first decade of independence in Ceylon, religious values had been drawn to the center of political controversy.

The concept of the nation state implies a homogeneity, a unity of sentiment, and a way of life that do not yet exist. In Asia, there are plural societies, made up of a congeries of distinctive and self-aware groups. In every country there are large numbers of men and women who speak different languages and live within different cultural traditions. Racial consciousness is widespread and alert awareness of racial differences adds to the divisions. In certain countries caste stratifications and foreign immigrant communities provide other diversities. As yet, these have not been melded into a people who believe themselves to be members of a single nation. The principle of majority rule suggests that the more numerous have the right to have everything as they wish, but democratic values emphasize the rights of minorities. Each country must find a workable compromise of these new ideals in practice. This is complicated when a growing group awareness encourages each ethnic or cultural community to seek in its own past its unique qualities—a search that only accentuates the separateness of each community. In 1958 Ceylon experienced horrifying communal riots never before seen on the island, as if national disunity, not unity, were growing.

Throughout the area mass poverty is widespread. Medical science has upset a traditional balance between the hazards of life and the death rate. Certain areas are already tragically overpopulated in relation to resources and level of technology. Others still have readily available land for peasant farming or commercial agriculture, but all of them are beset with a rising population. Statesmanship must be concerned with economic development even though large groups of the population may as yet be indifferent to its urgency. Rapid economic development requires heavy investment, innovation, and organizational effectiveness. At the same time, cultural self-consciousness puts a premium on the virtues of traditional ways and national sentiment warns against the danger of collaborating with Western economic enterprises. Economic development, too, cannot avoid having political significance, for it alters the channels toward, and the distribution of, power. Ceylon's economic development efforts have succeeded in keeping only slightly ahead of the growing population, and unemployment has been growing.

In each of the colonial states, the traditional political system for selecting rulers and bestowing the legitimate right to rule did not survive the period of colonial tutelage. New political institutions, introduced gradually by the European rulers, came to be the only available means for solving the universal problem of selecting or changing leaders. The new institutions provide the devices through which important decisions of state are made. Popular elections—the occasions for confirming or replacing leadership—pose special problems in all political communities. Where the electoral experience is brief and in societies marked by pluralistic, communal differences, elections by the mass of voters present a peculiar challenge, accentuating divisions and sharpening antagonisms unless the leaders are singularly restrained.

The countries of South and Southeast Asia are beset with certain common problems in foreign affairs as well. The system of international order established by Western European empires has been dismantled. More palatable arrangements for ensuring peaceful and orderly relationships must be developed for the future. State security in the face of possible external dangers, economic relations, and movements of people across frontiers, were previously managed by foreign rulers. Only with independence has there been the opportunity—and responsibility—to make foreign policy decisions. Though relations with the "European imperialists" had been the principal preoccupation before, once independence was achieved new regional problems thrust themselves forward. Each country has had to grope toward a rationale of foreign policy, diplomatic institutions, and the skills of diplomacy. An experimental, cautious exploration has been the rule. As with the United States before World War II, statements of principle and the desire to remain aloof have marked the foreign policy of most, though not all, countries. Ceylon's statesmen moved from a very close association with the United Kingdom to a policy of "nonalignment" closely akin to India's approach to world affairs.

Pakistan, India, Burma, Indonesia, Ceylon, Cambodia, Laos, Viet Nam, the Philippines, and Malaya are all seeking the means for independent statehood. To understand their search for a viable political society requires venturing into areas beyond the normal fields of Western political science. At the risk of imperfect intellectual precision and synthesis, it has seemed preferable to develop an inclusive view of one of these new states. It is hoped that a detailed analysis of one political community—a microcosm—will assist in understanding other Asian countries. This study of Ceylon focuses attention upon certain major concerns she shares with some or all of her neighbors. It represents a case study of the growing pains and achievements of one newly independent country after the devolution of power has been accomplished.

Of the ten newly independent countries in South and Southeast Asia, Ceylon has more of the attributes of a modernized social and political system than any other, with the possible exception of the Philippines. Her population is relatively literate, roughly 60 per cent being able to read and write at the time of independence. The country has had universal franchise since 1931, receiving it only three years after the United Kingdom and fifteen years before any of her Asian neighbors. The country's citizens predominated in public service sooner than elsewhere. Her public health administration has been so dramatically successful that she has one of the fastest growing populations among the newly independent countries. Violence rarely inhibited the working of the representative political process until a protracted crisis toward the end of the first decade of independence brought about an extended emergency rule. In elections held in 1956, many members of the Westernized elite who had carried the country forward to independence were rejected by the electorate, and political power was shifted to other groups in the society. In all these respects, Ceylon was ahead of her neighbors.

To assume that other countries will follow the Ceylon example in every respect is naturally fallacious, but developments in Ceylon may suggest some possibilities for the future of other newly independent countries. Consequently, the material presented in this study is arranged topically, and with some unavoidable repetition. It should enable the serious student of Asian affairs to compare aspects of public life in Ceylon with analogous developments elsewhere.

Part I discusses the historical, social, and economic setting and the institutions and actors in politics. In order to understand the search for a viable political society, it is necessary to examine the social system providing the underlying groups, resentments, and aspirations that give direction and impetus to political activities. The economy inherited at independence and the pervasive climate of economic opinion among the articulate make up a second element setting limits to the country's evolution. The gradual introduction of Western political institutions, which provided the formative experience for many contemporary men of politics, and the way in which these institutions created the framework for political activity represent another facet of the nation's political life. Political parties, individuals, and developing interest groups are the dynamic actors on the political stage. They set the institutions in motion and give them their distinctive quality. These related, though analytically separable, elements constitute the political setting in its everyday complexity, and are analyzed in Part I.

Part II examines five of the fundamental problems that have dominated public affairs since independence: (1) the role of religious institutions, religious revival and cultural nationalism in public life; (2) the aspiration for national unity in a society still marked by traditional ethnic and linguistic differences; (3) the effort to achieve an adequate rate of economic development; (4) the practice of democratic elections as a peaceful means of changing or confirming leadership; and (5) the search for a foreign policy in Asia and toward the wider world.

On the basis of this detailed analysis of one country, the Conclusion attempts to delineate important characteristics of an Asian political society.

PART ONE

THE SETTING OF POLITICS

CHAPTER II · HISTORICAL AND SOCIAL SETTING

THE PAST, THE PLACE, AND THE PEOPLE

"The hills and valleys are beautifully ornamented with flowers and trees of great variety and beauty, the cries of animals rejoicing together fill the air with gladness, and the landscape abounds with splendour."—From a description of Ceylon in a Chinese geography of the mid-nineteenth century

I · THE ISLAND'S PAST

CEYLON is a small, pear-shaped, tropical island barely twenty-five miles to the southeast of the tip of India where the waters of the Bay of Bengal meet the Arabian Sea. For centuries, her position at the juncture of important sea routes has made Ceylon a prize for whatever sea powers held or sought control of the Indian Ocean. Arabian seafarers made Ceylon an important commercial center before the Europeans found their way around the Cape of Good Hope. Successive European sea powers have each in turn used Ceylon as one of their principal bases in the vast oceanic spaces stretching from African Mombasa in the west, the Persian Gulf in the northwest, Malacca in the east, and Australia to the southeast.

But many centuries earlier, before the coming of the Europeans—when western Europe was ruled from Rome, and the British Isles were a distant outpost of the Roman Empire—a highly productive and culturally rich civilization flourished on Ceylon. Remains of once prosperous cities, chronicles of the glories of ancient kings, and reports of foreign visitors reveal a creative, well-ordered ancient past. This civilization developed a high level of hydraulic engineering skill and massive construction, for it depended almost entirely upon artificial lakes or "tanks" to contain and store heavy but sporadic annual rainfall for use throughout the year. An extensive and finely engineered system of channels led the waters by gentle gradients across many miles of undulating dry lands to level rice fields on which the whole civilization depended for its food. Technical assistance experts from Ceylon in the eighth century A.D. advised the King of Kashmir on constructing irrigation works. The arts flourished and learning was encouraged. Pali became the language of literary and poetic expression and scholars from India and elsewhere came to learn the pure tradition of Theravada Buddhism.

Ceylon's proximity to India has been of fundamental import. Her principal racial stocks and her Hindu and Buddhist religions are of Indian origin. However much a distinctive quality developed within Ceylon's civilization, Indian influence has been profound. Particularly up to the fifteenth century, perhaps "no important change in Indian civilization has failed to leave its impress on the island."[1] To the non-Asian observer, Ceylon's culture in the broadest sense has much in common with that of India. Ceylonese art clearly shows Indian sources, although peculiarly Ceylonese qualities are also manifest. In the ruins of great cities such as Anuradhapura, where Ceylon's early kings ruled until the eighth century A.D., and at Polonnaruwa, the capital until the thirteenth century, craftsmen of Indian origin or inspiration left impressive monuments. Numerous Ceylonese kings were from South Indian royal houses. The great Indian epic, the *Ramayana*, and Ceylon's own voluminous chronicles, written by Buddhist monks, attest to the intimate association between India's culture and institutions and Ceylon's.

Indian and Ceylonese sources both confirm—as do the ruined cities—that from the subcontinent to the north came invading armies as well as religious and cultural inspiration. From the tenth to the fourteenth centuries, Ceylon was subjected to periodic invasions from South Indian dynasts. King Vijayabahu I is a traditional hero of the Sinhalese, for he succeeded in expelling the Indian Chola invaders in the twelfth century. But the new island-wide political order established by one of his successors, Parakrama Bahu the Great, was brief, and fissiparous tendencies soon predominated. A Tamil kingdom became established in the north of the island and in the south competing royal families fought one another for control, sometimes, but not always, burying their differences in the common struggle against frequent invasions.[2]

From the thirteenth to sixteenth centuries Arab traders used

1 M. B. Ariyapala, *Society in Medieval Ceylon* (Colombo, 1956), p. 1.
2 G. C. Mendis, *The Early History of Ceylon* (Calcutta, 1954), Chs. IV and V.

Ceylon as a way station in their commerce between the Far East and the thriving cities of Baghdad, Damascus, and Cairo. During the fifteenth century, Chinese naval explorations went as far as Africa. One expedition even captured a regional Ceylonese king and took him and his entourage back to China in the early fifteenth century. For nearly fifty years the Ming Emperor received tribute from the islanders who acknowledged him as suzerain.[3]

In the sixteenth century, influences from yet another source began to be felt by the people of Ceylon. Western Europeans made their first appearance in Colombo and over the next four and one-half centuries Ceylon received a more intensive impress of European influences than any other country east of Suez.[4] Even after the Portuguese forcefully established their rule in Colombo in 1517, dynastic difficulties continued and greatly eased Portugal's task of consolidating its hold on the island. For the Portuguese, the island was of key strategic importance to their enterprises throughout the Indian Ocean as well as a rich source of cinnamon and other spices. During the first part of the seventeenth century, however, Portuguese power in the Indian Ocean was sharply challenged by the growing strength of the Dutch. The Sinhalese monarch in the interior, desiring to be rid of the Portuguese, sought the aid of the growing power of Holland and, together, Ceylonese and Dutch forces ousted the Portuguese in 1655.

The Dutch were particularly concerned with trade at the outset and, although they took and retained more towns and cinnamon lands than the king expected and sought to monopolize his external trade, they did not seriously attempt to dominate the island's territory. Gradually they were tempted to consolidate their position in the coastal areas, and by 1766 had completely ringed the shores of the island, isolating from contact with the outside world the mountainous central core of the island, the Kandyan district, where a local king still ruled. Like the Portuguese, however, they never conquered the Kandyan Kingdom. In the late eighteenth century, Dutch power, like the Portuguese before it, waned in vigor and effectiveness. In Europe, Holland was absorbed into the growing realm of revolutionary France. British authorities, fearing that France would seek to add Holland's overseas possessions to those it already con-

[3] Sir Emerson Tennent, *Ceylon* (London, 1859), I, pp. 599-600.

[4] Excepted, naturally, are such foreign creations as Bombay, Calcutta, Goa, Singapore, and Hong Kong.

trolled, undertook in 1796 a preventive occupation of Dutch fortresses. Thus, the British displaced the Dutch as the Dutch had displaced the Portuguese. But the British succeeded where the other two had not. With the assistance of Kandyan notables who wished to be freed from a tyrannical king, the British occupied the Kandyan highlands in 1815. For the first time in several centuries, the whole island came under the effective sway of one government. British rule persisted for over a century and a half until 1948, when Ceylon became a fully independent member of the Commonwealth of Nations.

Thus, four hundred and fifty years of European rule came to an end only a decade ago. Different aspects of the European legacy will be discussed in detail in their proper place below. But, in general, a rough balance may be cast. The Portuguese left behind an important Catholic Christian minority so deeply rooted that efforts of Dutch and other zealots to root it out have been unsuccessful. Many family names, place names, common words, and social customs in the maritime provinces are proof of the formative importance of the Portuguese period. On the other hand, cruel religious proselytizing, harsh and repressive government, and frequent wars left the land impoverished and a particularly bitter memory to this day.[5]

The Dutch, like the Portuguese, were diligent on behalf of their religion. They destroyed Buddhist temples and by governmental and administrative means sought to convert Buddhists—and Catholics—to Dutch Protestantism. Numbers of Dutch immigrants married Sinhalese and Tamil wives and from their families has developed the Burgher community of Eurasian descent and Western cultural ways. The Dutch codified local customary law and introduced Roman-Dutch law where local law was insufficient. Their code is still the basis for much of the legal system. They promoted coconut and cinnamon cultivation, began the commercialization of the maritime provinces, and developed canal communications in the low country. Yet, their monopolization of cinnamon and every other item of profitable trade, unduly harsh and restrictive laws, the growth of corruption and inefficiency in the administration, and rigid religious intolerance provoked a growing hostility in the people. The prompt collapse of Dutch rule at the British initiative in 1796 is not to be wondered at.[6]

[5] Colvin R. de Silva, *Ceylon under the British Occupation-1795-1833* (Colombo, 1953), I, p. 4.

[6] *Ibid.*, pp. 13-14.

British reforms in the 1830's were far more revolutionary than anything that had occurred under the Portuguese or Dutch. They undermined important elements of the traditional feudal system and laid the base for an island-wide administration under the rule of law. Indeed, the British judicial system—even though it was administered in a foreign language—brought the island protection from arbitrary rule and a sense of equitable justice that is widely respected to this day. New economic modes of commerce and exchange developed. The estate pattern for large-scale production of export products also came with British rule. Political institutions permitting flexible growth and change were instituted. In 1931—fifteen years before any other of her South Asian neighbors—Ceylon obtained universal adult franchise for both men and women and sent representatives from territorial constituencies to a national state council with wide powers over virtually all domestic matters. Out of this experience, the transition in 1946 to parliamentary institutions, consciously modeled on Westminster, proceeded smoothly and full independence was obtained in 1948. Though "imperialism" was a dangerous enemy to be publicly decried, many individual Englishmen and their customs were privately held in high esteem. Racial and color consciousness, a sense of organizational and cultural superiority, and the large profits, obtained through the new economic enterprises without commensurate reinvestment in newer enterprises in Ceylon itself, are parts of the British heritage that are still indignantly recalled. It is the conservative religious groups and the political radicals who resent the British period most of all.

Ceylon has thus been faced with a double challenge from outside her shores, both emerging from her geographical situation. From early times until the fifteenth century, Indian influences prevailed. For the past four centuries, European influences have been most important. The reaction to these centuries of European control has only begun to manifest itself. And, since foreign practices from Europe influenced different groups to different degrees and in different ways, the varied reactions to this foreign impress contribute significantly to contemporary political and social instability. Underlying these and interpenetrating many social, economic, and political problems is the recollection and impact of the earlier foreign influences from India.

Yet it would be incorrect to understand the island's history as merely a succession of "periods" identified by the foreign culture or dynasty that was active at the time. For within the island itself intricate transformations of many kinds have taken place over the centuries, independent of foreign influences. These have not been neatly recorded in easily accessible, systematic reports of colonial governors to their European superiors. The indigenous history is scattered; it must be inferred and laboriously constructed from scattered bits of evidence. Earlier scholars began the work; and more interpretations from the Ceylonese perspective are appearing each year.[7]

Much of contemporary public life in Ceylon can be best understood as an effort to find a more acceptable equilibrium between the foreign customs introduced during previous centuries and the indigenous modes that are again seeking self-expression. And, insofar as foreign models are admired in certain aspects of life, there is now uncertainty as to which countries are to be preferred as sources of external influence and emulation—Great Britain, the United States, India, Russia, or China.

II · LAND AND CLIMATE

Ceylon's land and climate present remarkable contrasts which set definite limits to what her people can do. The island is roughly 275 miles long north and south and 160 miles across at its widest, encompassing some 25,000 square miles. It is thus slightly larger than the state of West Virginia and one-half as large as Illinois. In the south central core of the island, mountains rise to a height of over 8,000 feet. To the west, south, and east of this mountainous upthrust, a series of flat lands descend like steps, separated by abrupt escarpments and cut by deep, narrow valleys, leaving a border of relatively flat "low country" separating the hills from the sea. To the north a long undulating plain extends toward the Jaffna Peninsula and India beyond.

From May to September, winds from the southwest monsoon make up over the Indian Ocean and bring moisture-laden air over the island. Rising against the mountains, heavy rains are dumped onto the windward side and contribute to the characteristic monsoon climate of the southwest portion of the island. Convectional winds add further rainfall in October and April, and the northeast monsoon

[7] For examples of recent publications written from the indigenous vantage point, see: R. Pieris, *Sinhalese Social Organization* (Colombo, 1956); M. B. Ariyapala, *op.cit.*; W. Rahula, *History of Buddhism in Ceylon* (Colombo, 1956); Dr. K. W. Goonewardena, *The Foundations of Dutch Power in Ceylon—1638-1658* (Amsterdam, 1958); Dr. S. Arasaratnam, *Dutch Power in Ceylon—1658-1687* (Amsterdam, 1958).

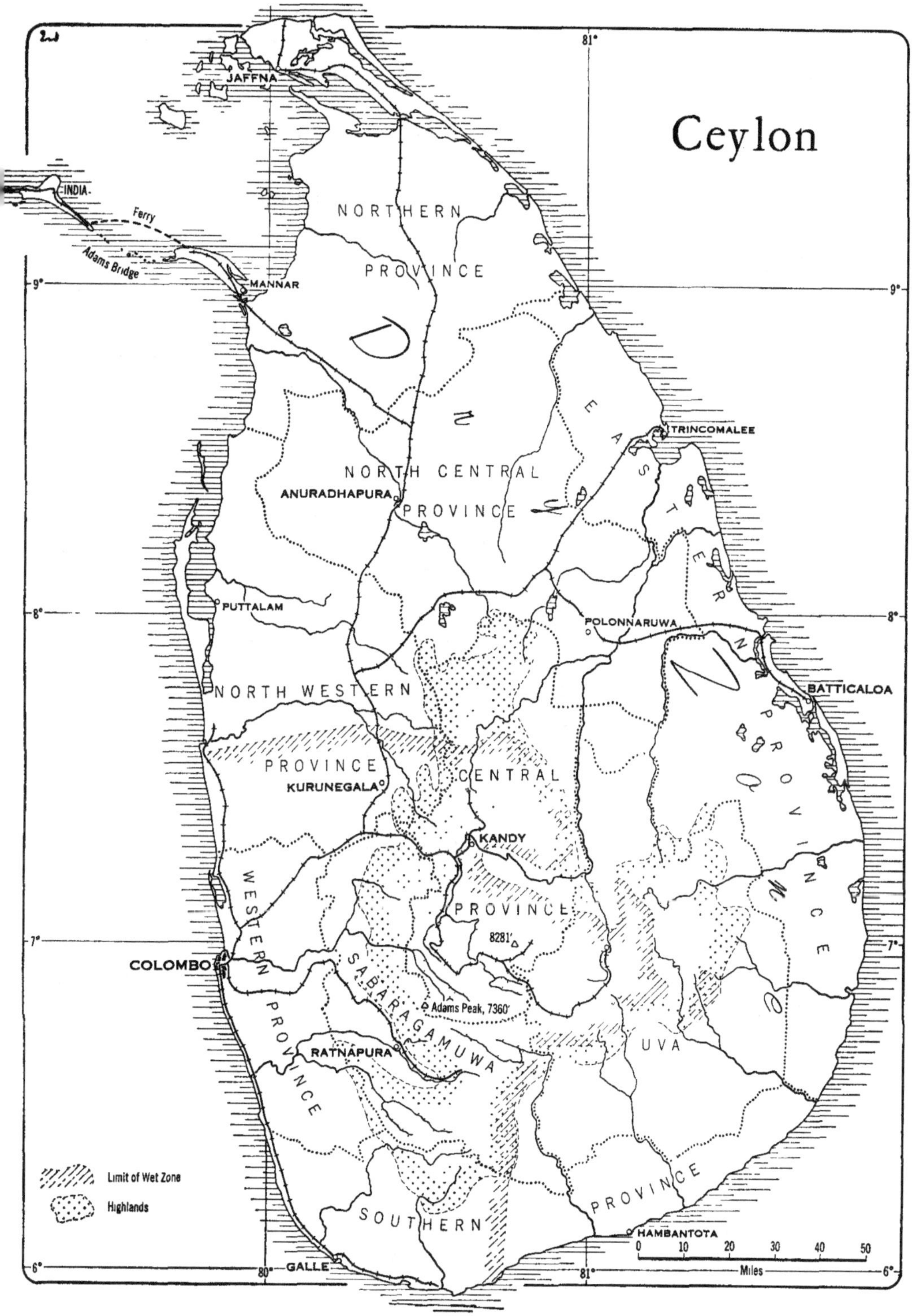
Ceylon
JAFFNA
INDIA
Ferry
Adams Bridge
MANNAR
NORTHERN PROVINCE
NORTH CENTRAL PROVINCE
ANURADHAPURA
TRINCOMALEE
EASTERN PROVINCE
PUTTALAM
POLONNARUWA
BATTICALOA
NORTH WESTERN PROVINCE
KURUNEGALA
CENTRAL PROVINCE
KANDY
8281′
WESTERN PROVINCE
COLOMBO
SABARAGAMUWA
Adams Peak, 7360′
RATNAPURA
UVA PROVINCE
SOUTHERN
HAMBANTOTA
GALLE
Limit of Wet Zone
Highlands
0 10 20 30 40 50
Miles
9°
8°
7°
6°
80°
81°

from the Bay of Bengal provides a lesser quantity of rain for the whole island in December, January, and February. Average annual rainfall in the southwest or "wet zone" runs as high as 200 inches in many places and is nowhere less than 75 inches. Particularly heavy falls of over 200 inches are recorded in the upper mountain reaches. Perhaps one-third of the land is thus generously watered.

The remaining two-thirds of the island, largely in the low-lying plains to the east and north of the mountainous core, receives much less rain and is termed the "dry zone." Rain falls mainly from the northwest monsoon of the midwinter and sporadic convectional showers. Here 50 to 75 inches are more likely, usually concentrated within three months of the year. Residents of the Temperate Zone should remember that Ceylon lies between 6 and 10 degrees north of the equator, parallel with Panama in the Western Hemisphere. The sun strikes the earth from almost overhead much of the year and evaporation is very rapid. It may require more than twice as much annual rainfall to support plant life than in more temperate climates. In the dry zone, dry winds add to the evaporation. Unhappily, as in most parts of the island, the subsoil is of an impermeable crystalline rock which precludes underground water. Wells, therefore, cannot provide water for the dry zone except in small areas of the Jaffna Peninsula. Only extensive irrigation works, storing seasonal rains or conducting water from the mountains onto the plains, can make fertile much of the land that has not been used for centuries.

A third distinctive climatic zone is to be found in the mountainous central massif. Above 2,000 feet the climate is fresh and salubrious and the rainfall very heavy from both monsoons and intermonsoonal rains. Here tea finds its favorite soil and climate; and after the 1870's British planters cleared large tracts of jungle and planted tea. Out of these mountains, deep rivers run in nearly all directions. Their flow is usually seasonal, depending largely upon the monsoon rains, rising to flood proportions during several months of the year and drying up to mere trickles at other seasons. All but one of the large rivers flow through the wet zone into the nearby sea. But one, the majestic Mahaweli Ganga, flows all the year and winds its way through the mountains and out onto the dry-zone plains to debouch on the east coast near Trincomalee.

Ceylon's subsoil mineral resources are as limited as her subsoil waters. Coal and petroleum are totally lacking. Substantial iron ore resources exist, but are widely scattered. However, Ceylon is the world's leading producer of high grade graphite. Her gemstones have been famous for generations. Ilmenite, monazite, and glass sands are found along the coast; mica has been exported for years. And her tumbling waters could supply large quantities of electric power if properly harnessed.

It was in the dry zone that Ceylon's ancient civilization once flourished before a combination of exhausting wars, civil disorganization, and disease appears to have depopulated the area and the jungle covered the ancient cities.[8] The Sinhalese population shifted to the hitherto terrifying darkness of the wet-zone jungle and the majority of Ceylon's people have been concentrated in this rich, but crowded, wet zone ever since. The migrants from the dry zone brought with them their rice cultivation which continued to form the base of the economy and society. Rice was planted on the rich alluvial valley floors and on laboriously tended hillside terraces. In addition, coconuts, cinnamon, and spices could be cultivated. Unlike the heavy investment necessary in the dry zone, no effort was required to bring in water; indeed, periodic floods were the chief impediment to cultivation. Nevertheless, the economy of Ceylon, as the Portuguese found it in the sixteenth century, in the wet-zone lowlands was far less productive than the remarkable irrigated civilization of a thousand years before.[9]

Ceylon has thus been endowed with a warm, tropical climate, well-watered in one-third of its area—the wet zone—with a topography which provides space for future cultivation if the island's water can be retained and channeled to the presently dry areas. Her subsoil resources are limited. How Ceylon supports herself and the type of economy she evolves depends not only upon the land and resources, but on the ingenuity, application, and organization of her people. Before examining the economy in greater detail as it forms part of the background to politics, it will be well to describe something of Ceylon's society.

III · THE SOCIAL SETTING: THE PEOPLE

The place men hold within the social system and their conception of their rightful claims upon it have much to do with the dreams, the resentments, and the fears that provide the energy and direction of

[8] Rhoads Murphey, "The Ruin of Ancient Ceylon," *The Journal of Asian Studies*, XVI, No. 2 (Feb. 1957), pp. 181-200.

[9] *Ibid.*, p. 183.

politics. Their sense of identification and of difference helps to define the groups that form for political purposes.

Ceylon's society is intricate, and different perspectives illumine different aspects of the whole. It may be seen first as a congeries of distinguishable groups differentiated on ethnic, linguistic, or religious grounds—a plural society. Secondly, it is predominantly rural and the structure of social influence in rural districts may suggest means of gaining political support in the countryside. Thirdly, economic classes in the traditional Marxian analysis may shed still a different light on political phenomena, particularly in the maritime western and southern provinces. These different perspectives often overlap. They serve to suggest the complexity of social analysis that must underlie political understanding. They may even provide clues to the relative fortunes of different political groups on the island.

A. A PLURAL SOCIETY

Ceylon's is a plural society, a mosaic of self-aware communities distinguished from one another along ethnic, religious, or linguistic grounds. Lacking strong parties derived from disciplined organization, from clear-cut economic or revolutionary differences, or from an intense struggle for independence, Ceylon's political life has been closely bound up with these communal and other traditional social differentiations. Until now, these traditional groupings have formed the basis of most politically significant loyalties, interests, and demands. As local political leaders have responded to the imperatives of representative politics, these differences have often been played upon and accentuated. Loyalty is still directed to the extended family clan, or to the caste, racial, religious, or linguistic group. An island-wide national sense is yet to be effectively evolved.

1. *Traditional ethnic groups.* Ethnically the population of Ceylon is diverse, yet its composition is sufficiently simple to invite invidious numerical and percentage comparisons, which a more complicated ethnic structure might preclude. The majority of Ceylon's people—nearly 70 per cent—are known as "Sinhalese," widely believed to be descended from Aryan stock of North India, probably from the Bengal region. Their language is Sinhalese, spoken only in Ceylon by some 7,000,000 people with no close contemporary linguistic relations except Bengali. They are largely Buddhist, the devout among them following the Theravada tradition also found in Burma, Thailand, and Viet Nam. The Sinhalese are concentrated in the wet zone.

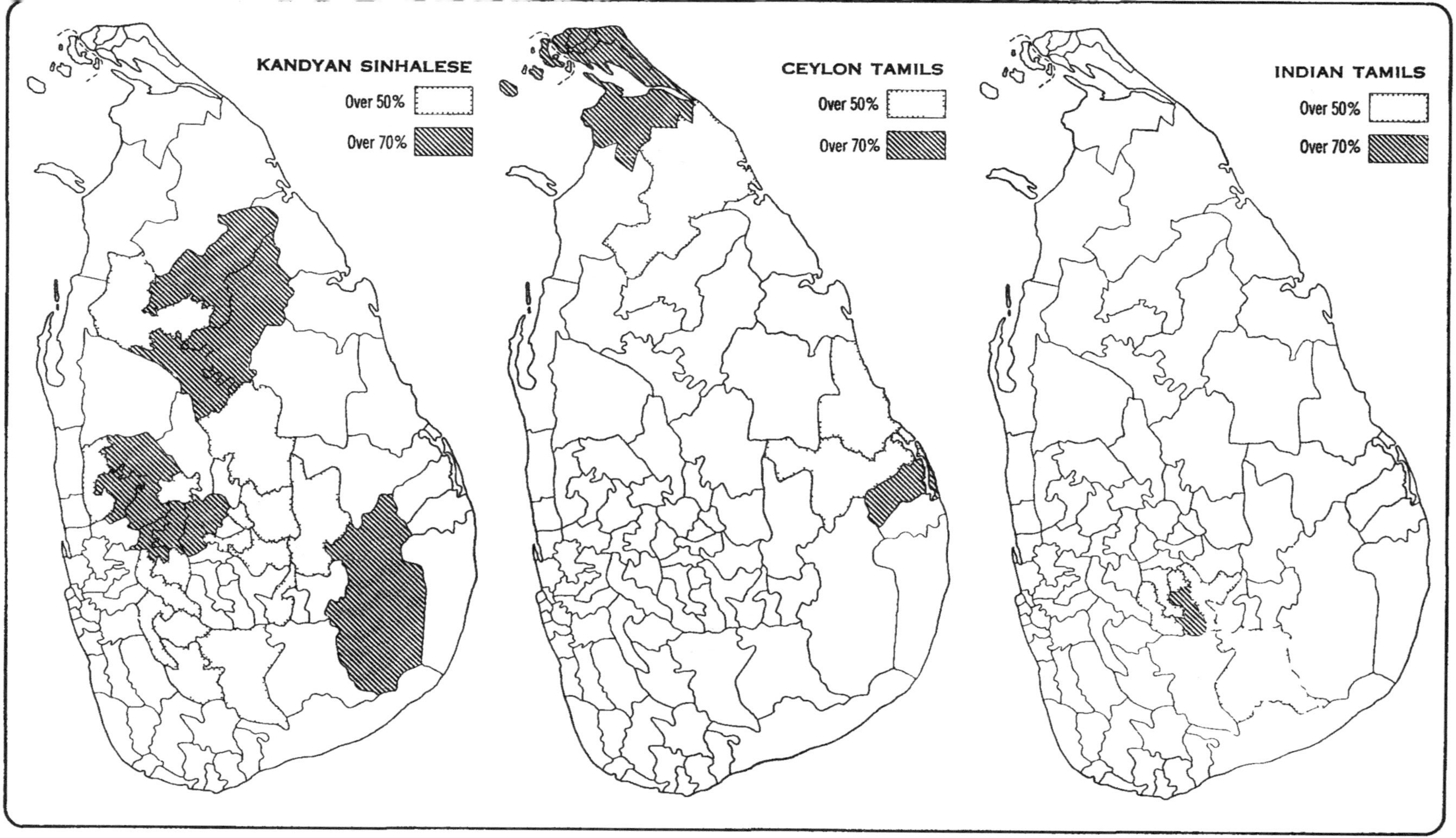

MINORITY ELECTORAL DISTRICTS, 1947

Traditionally, their civilization has been closely integrated with the production of rice, the principal staple of their diet. In the rural areas of the "Kandyan" or hill-country districts, the traditional social structure, based on a quasi-feudal stratification of reciprocal obligations and duties, has remained relatively intact. In the coastal strip, subject for many centuries to Western rule, the traditional social system has undergone profound alterations.

Those Sinhalese coming from the Kandyan areas compose roughly 38 per cent of the Sinhalese people, and those from the coastal areas, from the low country, form the other 62 per cent. Even though some low-country Sinhalese have gone to the towns and cities in the hill areas as enterprising transport, commercial, or professional men, by and large the geographical designations remain accurate. Linguistic differences between up-country and low-country Sinhalese are insignificant, but there has long been a feeling of caution and reserve between them. The up-country Sinhalese, like many rural or mountain dwellers elsewhere, consider those from the low country to be more quick-witted, sophisticated, and less trustworthy than the simpler, more conservative up-country man.

The low-country Sinhalese have had an economic and professional competitive advantage over the up-country Sinhalese since the foreigner brought to the low country his new ways of living and making a living. The low-country men were the best prepared to profit from the economic revolution that burst upon Ceylon in the middle of the nineteenth century when the plantation economy was introduced. They were the ones who already had long acquaintance with the foreigner and his strange personal, administrative, and organizational ways, and they learned his language as well. They dealt in land to good advantage and organized bullock-cart trains to provision isolated estates and take their produce back to Colombo. They knew more than the foreigner about the up-country lands where estates were being established and more than the Kandyans about the foreigner; from this double knowledge, they profited well. The up-country men, on the other hand, remained more attached to their land and were less ready to embark on the newer commercial methods of enterprise.

The largest minority group are the Ceylon Tamils, who represent 11 per cent of the total population. They are concentrated chiefly in the northern and eastern areas of the island. The city of Jaffna is still the principal center of their cultural and religious life. As a people, they are widely believed to be descendants of Tamils who came to Ceylon, in successive waves of immigration and military invasion, from Dravidian South India between A.D. 400 and 1200. Their language is the same as the Tamil spoken in South India, and they are Hindus. Life in the northern and eastern provinces is hard and agricultural resources are limited by insufficient rains. The economic opportunities which came to the wet zone with the British tea and rubber estates did not affect the already overcrowded northern peninsula. Hence, Ceylon Tamils sought opportunity in all parts of the island, and especially in the larger cities such as Colombo and Kandy. Many Tamil families have lived there for generations but retain family connections with Jaffna. Ceylon Tamils even went as far afield as Malaya and Singapore in search of new employment.[10]

Although much of Ceylon's recent political history can be understood largely in terms of the relations between the Sinhalese majority and the Tamil minority, two other groups are ethnically distinguishable: the Moors and the Burghers. Moors, of Arab descent, are to be found mainly concentrated in the western areas and along the coast in the Eastern Province, although they are found in towns in many parts of the island. Together they compose nearly five per cent of the total population, and are Muslims. They are sometimes farmers, but more often traders, businessmen, or the keepers of small shops. Although their sense of communal solidarity is high, their language varies with their surroundings; in Tamil areas it is Tamil and in Sinhalese areas it is Sinhalese. Their religious language is Arabic, and they appear to be profoundly attached to the concept of "Islam." As a group, they have not been well educated, for they were reluctant to enter Christian schools in the early period. But in recent decades this reluctance has diminished, and the growth of a nondenominational public school system is rapidly raising their educational level.

The Burghers are descendants of children of Portuguese, Dutch, and British marriages with Ceylonese. They are largely Christian, often highly educated, and have a reputation for energy, conscientiousness, and reliable workmanship. Although they compose less than one per cent of the total population, they were active in constitutional reform movements and once played a disproportionately large role in governmental and cultural life. They have adopted English as their "mother tongue" even though they often speak

[10] For a more detailed discussion of the relations between the Sinhalese majority and the Tamil minorities, see Chapter VII below.

Sinhalese; they wear European clothes and follow European rather than Ceylonese social customs. In an era of national resurgence, many Burghers are considered to be too Westernized. They are believed to have a sense of cultural and racial superiority in relation to the less Westernized Sinhalese and Tamils, and recently many have attempted to leave the island.

2. *Caste groupings.* Another way in which the island's people distinguish themselves from one another is along caste lines. The structure of caste distinctions in Sinhalese areas is much looser than it is in Tamil areas of Ceylon or in India. In the urban areas, especially, its social and political importance is diminishing. No doubt caste considerations are less significant even in rural areas than they were fifty years ago. Nevertheless, significant social and political developments cannot be properly understood without an appreciation of caste differentiations.

Closely related to the high status traditionally accorded to the cultivator—the man who tilled the soil in the Ceylonese feudal system—the highest status is generally applied to the "cultivators" or Goyigama caste.[11] As might be expected, when caste is originally derived from such a functional distinction, more than 60 per cent of the population has been in the highest caste.[12] Such a large caste was necessarily divided into subcastes, the more exclusive being closer to the ruler than the more numerous who tilled the fields. Beneath the Goyigama have been a series of service castes such as smiths, potters, barbers, tailors, drummers, and washermen, etc. Even today, when caste distinctions are far less important than they used to be, the trades of potters and carpenters or the arts of music, drumming, and the dance suffer because of their traditional association with low-caste functions.

In low-country Sinhalese districts, the caste structure is challenged more than in the Kandyan areas. New economic methods and urbanization are undermining traditional ways of doing things. Men who move to the towns and earn a good living are reluctant to defer in the traditional manner to those of "better" birth who may be no

11 For an authoritative discussion of the traditional feudal structure and the functional specialization that underlies the remnants of the caste system, see Ralph Pieris, *op.cit.* For a detailed discussion of caste in modern Ceylon, see Bryce Ryan's book of that title (New Brunswick, 1953).

12 There are no firm population statistics on modern caste strength. A census taken in 1824 recorded castes separately. At that time nearly 60 per cent in most districts were recorded as Goyigamas. Cited in Pieris, p. 192.

better off financially. Indeed, the anonymity of the urban areas is one of their attractions for village youth of lower status.

In the low country, moreover, there are certain caste groups who do not accept the Goyigama claim to be the highest caste. In the Sinhalese system, the "fisherman" caste or Karavas are considered by many to be of less distinguished standing. However, the Karavas sometimes challenge Goyigama presumptions. They claim descent from Kshatriya warriors who came in the entourage of the Indian kings who formerly ruled Ceylon, and warriors are superior to cultivators in the Indian cultural area. The Karavas were among the first to undertake estate agriculture and businesses modeled on European enterprises. Another enterprising group are known as the Salagamas or "cinnamon peelers," and they claim descent from Brahmin ancestry. The Salagamas like the Karavas had early contact with foreigners. They worked for the Portuguese and Dutch in the production and preparation of cinnamon. Both groups have had many wealthy men among them. Perhaps because of geographical concentration, access to education, and early self-consciousness as minority castes, their energy and drive have given them considerable prominence in the affairs of the country. Another active small caste is the Durava.[18] In the Tamil Hindu areas of Ceylon, caste stratifications are clearer and the position of the upper cultivator caste—the Vellala—has not yet been challenged, either by modern economic conditions or by other caste-conscious groups.

It is of course easy for an outsider to exaggerate the political or social importance of caste distinctions. There are few untraversable caste lines, except at the bottom of the social pyramid. Most people are conscious of the caste background of their friends and associates. It would appear that caste is still important, though not always decisive, where closest friends and marriage are concerned. In organizations of all kinds where castes intermingle, whether it be the public service, business houses, or education, there remains a strong tendency for men of one caste—or "community" as a caste is called—to trust one another more than men of other communities. Confidences tend to be shared within a community, and there would appear to be a subtle, but nevertheless real, informal network of camaraderie and mutual assistance based on caste loyalties.

In politics, caste considerations are important when candidates are being selected, and a candidate with origins that he feels his

[18] For a more detailed discussion, including bibliography, see Ryan, pp. 6-7, 103-111.

electorate may not like will keep the undesirable facts hidden if he can. Politicians like to choose candidates of the same caste as the majority of constituents in a particular electoral district, just as politicians in New York or Boston know in which districts an Irish Catholic or an English Protestant or an Italian Catholic must be run if he is to have a chance of winning. Serious discussions of prominent political figures often refer to their caste origins. In this respect, certain well-known families from the Kandyan districts, for instance, are considered to be of particularly high Goyigama status while even prominent low-country Goyigama men are not infrequently referred to as of lower standing. There are, nevertheless, some very prominent men of relatively low-caste origin who have distinguished themselves in public life and who carry heavy responsibilities. Accordingly, caste is relevant to politics, especially when candidates are being selected, but various trends are working to diminish the significance of these inherited ethnic and pedigree distinctions.

3. *Religious groupings.* Religious groupings are important in South Asia, since different ways of life and education, language, and often economic or professional interests are frequently associated with religious differences. Sixty-four per cent of Ceylonese are Buddhists, virtually all of them of Sinhalese ethnic background. Most of the Tamils are Hindus. Buddhists tend to draw the line of distinction between themselves and Hindus, while Hindus emphasize the view that Buddhism is merely an offshoot of Hinduism. Both have more in common than either has with Christianity, and there has been little sense of organized competition or antagonism between them on religious grounds thus far. Both are largely individual and personal religions, so that organizational interests are seldom if ever in question.

In the up-country Buddhist areas religion was the least touched by foreign invaders, and it is there that the most conservative priests and conventional temples are still to be found, drawing from the tenants of their lands the fruits of traditional obligations.[14] No doubt many in these rural areas regard the low country as the Christianized part of the country, a fact that contributes to the

[14] See, for instance, *Report of the Commission on Tenure of Lands of Viharagam, Dewalagam, and Nindagam* (Sessional Paper I—1956), particularly Part II, Chs. II and III.

reserve existing between these two groups whenever religious and political considerations are in question.

Perhaps 9 per cent of the population are Christians. Portuguese missionaries were zealous in their search for converts, and many Ceylonese became Catholic Christians in fear as well as in faith. The Dutch in the seventeenth and eighteenth centuries were less harsh, but they dealt severely with those who refused to worship in the Dutch churches and by numerous administrative devices made it expedient and safe to conform to Christian practices. The British were less directly oppressive, but their administration of schools and other matters contributed indirect assistance to the Christian churches.

In the nineteenth and early twentieth centuries, no doubt some Ceylonese were drawn to Christianity as a more "modern" or "advanced" religion. More important, schools were often run by missionary organizations and a Western education was the passport to positions in the public services. It was also the vehicle to new organizational skills, and often a competitive advantage in business or community activities went to the men educated in Christian schools. Numerically the Christian Ceylonese at present are in a bare majority in only three coastal constituencies, but they are very conscious of being a small minority, and they have been influential in Ceylonese affairs—chiefly because of their professional skills and the use they have made of educational opportunities. Of the Christians, the Catholic Church has more successfully adapted itself to indigenous practices and cultural customs than the various branches of the Protestant Church. The Catholics include many members of the poorer classes as well as the wealthy. The Protestant Christians tend to be largely urban middle class.

4. *Non-Ceylonese.* Like many other countries in South Asia, Ceylon has several foreign-background groups who retain their foreign ways.[15] They are not presently important actors on the political stage, but Indian estate labor, Indian merchants, and European businessmen and planters have great significance for the economic well-being of the island. The estate workers form 12 per cent of the population. They were brought to the island in the nineteenth and twentieth centuries to work the coffee and tea plantations in the hill lands up-country, and have been living in estate enclaves

15 For a careful survey, see Virginia Thompson and Richard Adloff, *Minority Problems in Southeast Asia* (Stanford, 1955).

in company-owned "lines" or barrack-like houses. They have been subjected to firm estate discipline, and have had little opportunity or incentive to mix with the Sinhalese peasants when they live in the same areas. The estate workers are Hindus, often in the midst of Buddhists, and they speak Tamil, not Sinhalese.

For many decades, Indian estate labor has not been allowed out of India without some guarantee undertaken by the Ceylonese government to insure adequate protection of their interests. Consequently, they have had minimum wage regulations, and medical and schooling services, often to a considerably higher degree than the neighboring Sinhalese villagers. Resentment against them has been growing as the traditional, land-based economic and social structure of the up-country village areas has been breaking down under the combined impact of gradual Westernization and increasing land pressures.

These estate workers of Indian origin—like the unabsorbed Chinese in South Asia—pose special problems. The map on p. 21 shows those districts where Indian workers formed more than 50 per cent of the population in the 1946 census on the basis of which electoral delimitation was first made. Many have retained close contact with their Indian relatives and make periodic journeys home to India to obtain wives of the proper caste and community, to pay proper respect to their elder relatives, and to keep in direct touch with their extensive families there. If they can, they send back considerable accumulated sums of rupee remittances. Unabsorbed into the indigenous life around them, there have been real doubts as to whether or not they have an "abiding interest" in Ceylon. National statehood permits no such cosmopolitan vagueness about loyalty, locale of interest, and "home."

Another economically important Indian group is the Indian commercial community. Wholesale import of foodstuffs, textiles, and other bulk goods for popular consumption has been largely in the hands of Indian wholesale merchants who came to Colombo during the British period. Because they are connected with larger commercial interests in India, they can give credit to local buyers on terms that local merchants find impossible. The Indian is thus able to retain distributors for his imports when local wholesalers cannot or dare not make such advances. Moreover the Indian merchant appears to devote his energies to business with greater vigor than do most Ceylonese. When it is considered that some 40 per cent of all goods consumed by the average family is imported, the economic power of the wholesale importer is quite clear. Some of the lesser merchants and moneylenders have moved into the towns and even some of the villages, and have occupied the usual ungracious position of moneylenders, wherever they are.[16]

The European planters and commercial people represent still another foreign community. Although previously politically dominant, they now have only the most strictly limited political rights. According to the 1953 census, there were slightly more than 6,000 Europeans on the island, the largest group being British. About half of these were to be found in Colombo commercial and banking activities; the balance were in the up-country tea districts. Their tea and rubber estates are run at high efficiency, and they contribute heavily to Ceylon's favorable trade position. However, their banking interests appear to have usually favored British enterprises, and have tended to encourage short-term commercial lending and estate investment, rather than Ceylonese business or newer industrial activities. Because of their prior organization and the capital at their disposal in Ceylon itself or available on call in London, it has been difficult for Ceylonese to enter the commercial fields customarily managed by the British. Recently, British companies have begun to sell some of their interests and repatriate their investments, but it is broadly true that "the British are still the economic leaders."[17]

It is an annoying though fundamental fact that Ceylon's prosperity and its relatively high standard of living, in comparison to any of its Asian neighbors, is due largely to the joint endeavors of two foreign populations—Indian estate labor and the British planter. In an era of national enthusiasm and of national economics, such a cosmopolitan arrangement is no longer satisfactory, however efficient it may have been. One of Ceylon's difficult problems is to work out long-range plans to insure the continued high productivity of the tea and rubber plantation industries while a larger share of profits is plowed back into new enterprises in Ceylon.

B. EDUCATIONAL STRATIFICATION

One of the far-reaching effects of Western control for so many years has been the emergence of a Western-educated elite, to whom coveted opportunities in the public service, the professions, respec-

16 Peasants often feel they have been oppressed by Indians and low-country Sinhalese "outsiders." Reported in an unpublished survey of rural education conducted by the Department of Education of the University of Ceylon.

17 Henry M. Oliver, Jr., *Economic Opinion and Policy in Ceylon* (Durham, N.C., 1957), p. 8.

table business, and politics have been readily open. In Colombo and several other principal towns, a handful of government schools, run on the English public school system, have trained students in the British educational tradition from as early as the middle of the nineteenth century.[18] Admission appears to have been generally restricted to the sons of the influential, though there were exceptions. Additional British, American, and other missionary schools, primarily in the low-country Sinhalese and the Jaffna Tamil areas, provided alternative opportunities to those parents of more modest means who did not object to sending their children to a Christian school. Gradually, with the growth of Buddhist education after the 1880's and an expanding government-financed secular school system, more ambitious students from families of lower status were also able to have a good education. In recent times, perhaps 8 per cent of the population has been trained in English.

There were many advantages open to those who carried their English education beyond the primary school level. English and training in the skills of clerkship and administration gave access to the coveted government service. For generations in South Asia, there has been no higher calling than to serve the Ruler. The deference traditionally accorded him or the foreign Raj has been directed toward the public servant. By local standards those in public service were well-paid and had a secure future. The competitive examination, by which they qualified, confirmed their mastery of the traditional values of academic learning. It was believed that only the cream of the nation's youth were acceptable. A man of standing was much more likely to be a government servant than a businessman of promise. For all these reasons, the dowry value of a public servant was high, perhaps adding to his income more than he received as salary. In the lower levels, too, government service was a channel for moving upwards—a means of gaining influence, wealth, and respectability. A knowledge of English also gave a man access to the rapidly expanding sources of Western scientific and professional information and made it possible for the ambitious to develop competence. Positions in British business firms could be had if one knew English; and English opened the doors to the newer careers of law and Western medicine. One M.P. put

18 The most famous—Royal College—was founded in 1835. For a helpful analysis of educational opportunities, see W. Ivor Jennings, "Race, Religion, and Opportunity at the University of Ceylon," *University of Ceylon Review*, II (Nov. 1944), pp. 1-13.

the situation this way: "My father did not want me to be an agriculturist. He did not want me to be a carpenter or a weaver. According to the caste system which prevails in my village, I am a goiya of the goiyas. If my parents were keen that I should get an English education, it was merely for reasons of material advancement and prosperity, which would have been out of the question without an education through the medium of a Western language."[19]

British education had further consequences than opening new opportunities to the few. In the process, those trained in the Western schools became alienated in part from the 90 per cent of the Ceylonese population, who did not have access to such an education. As they took on more and more of the skills and methods of the West, this elite grew further away from the village level. In traditional Eastern societies, the social distance between elite and masses has always been great, even though they were all within the same larger cultural matrix. Now, even that important element, binding together the social fabric, diminished as the educated turned to Greek, Roman, or European history or Western science. Intellectual association with the problems and patterns of European thought, the Western way of living, and the acceptance of Western taste by the pace-setting elite have all contributed to a marked alienation separating this group from the wider population.[20]

Largely concentrated in the towns and cities, the English-educated, regardless of social origins, came to have special prerogatives and careers open to them that the others did not. A man competent only in Sinhalese or one whose schooling had been in the traditional curriculum found himself invariably at a disadvantage unless he was an Oriental scholar, active in Buddhist or Hindu affairs, or had family wealth and could hire the Western-educated to run his business. The respected, lucrative, and secure posts were available only to the English-trained. The government was carried on in a language the Eastern-educated did not understand: even

[19] *House of Representatives*, V. 9, c. 320.

[20] An exact appraisal of this social distance is very hard to make without intensive empirical study. Intellectually, no doubt, many became more at home in Western literature, Western aesthetics, history, and philosophy than in the traditional Sinhalese or Tamil cultures. Yet beneath this intellectual surface, many who return to their family's village homes quickly slip into the more traditional ways. The democratic ideals learned abroad tended to sensitize them to this social distance and their own privileges, and sometimes induced efforts to mend the social fabric. The problem of the social distance between elite and mass is intricate and is worthy of most serious empirical investigation.

Ceylonese government servants worked, thought, and wrote in English. Except in the court of first instance, law cases were usually argued in English. To an American observer, the social distance and career advantages that separated the English-educated elite from the rest is one of the most striking characteristics of Ceylon, as it is characteristic of many other countries to the south and east of the Mediterranean.

On the other hand, the common experience of students in growing up together in a Western-education system has served to knit the social fabric in another way. Regardless of communities, Sinhalese, Tamils, Burghers, and in a few instances, the Moors, all passed through this Western curriculum, using the same language in institutions that made no distinctions on ethnic or communal grounds. Despite the diversities of their respective homes, when they entered an English school they entered a common world, and, as they moved higher, they all entered the same linguistic universe. They developed similar styles of life and recreation. Intercommunal friendships, formed in school days, created bonds of mutual trust between individuals of different communities and castes that transcend the conventional suspicions. Among the Western-educated who dominated the political and economic life of the island in the towns and cities, there developed a consciousness of a common destiny that bridged to a considerable degree the traditional communal distinctions.

Together, the men of Western education from among the Sinhalese and Tamils led the movement for political reform and eventually for independence. They were the ones who used British liberal arguments to undermine British imperial institutions. They were the proponents of a national sense, embracing all of Ceylon, and they used the slogans of a common, island-wide opposition to continued British rule. Those who did not grow beyond their traditional cultural milieu could not see the inclusive, island-wide vision. Gradually, as the British turned over more and more responsibility to the Ceylonese, it was the group of Western-educated who naturally filled the positions vacated by the British. Until the 1956 election, the political and administrative elite of independent Ceylon was almost entirely made up of the Western-educated.

To the Sinhalese-educated, opportunities appeared to be invariably open to the English-educated. It should not be assumed, however, that the English-educated group was entirely homogeneous.

There were clearly understood differences among them. Many government clerks, for instance, knew English for adequate conversation, as did many business clerks and young journalists. But because their English was limited and their education interrupted, they were inescapably in junior positions. Others failed the government service examinations and their families could not help them gain lucrative or high-status posts. On the other hand, those who came closest to British ways and whose education carried them furthest toward mastery of English and who successfully passed government examinations, or whose families could help them, obtained the better paid or most coveted positions. They lived in houses of Western design, drove cars, and appeared affluent beyond the hopes of the clerks and others lower down the scale.

Although the picture here described emphasizes distinctions, it should be clear that many of the differences depicted cut across other differences and become elements of unity. Caste distinctions cross economic and linguistic lines, so that English-educated Salagamas of upper-class position have something in common with lower-class Sinhalese-educated Salagamas. Christianity came as a divisive element during the colonial period, adding a new religion; but, unlike Buddhism or Hinduism, Christianity crosses ethnic divisions between Sinhalese and Tamils. English education also crossed this ethnic line, uniting members of various Sinhalese castes as it created a new social stratification. Thus, differences in one direction bridge differences in another. It is therefore very difficult to foresee in any circumstance which way the divisions will run—an important factor underlying the instability and unpredictable quality of Ceylonese political behavior.

C. RURAL CEYLON: THE SOCIAL-INFLUENCE STRUCTURE

Further perspective on the underlying social setting of politics may be gained from an analysis of the social-influence structure and the ways of gaining political influence in rural Ceylon. Over 70 per cent of Ceylon's population lives in rural districts and modern electoral politics must in some way come to terms with the traditional modes of influence that are best preserved in the village areas.

Rural Ceylon is diverse and varied. Villages in different geographical regions are very different in aspect, and considerably different in organization. In low-country Sinhalese areas, especially in the neighborhood of Colombo or Galle, "villages" are now often suburban residential areas sending to their nearby urban centers large numbers of daily commuters. Social mores have been changed considerably by external influences; family structure is less well-integrated, and the village has been drawn into the cash nexus of commercialized life. In new areas of government-sponsored peasant colonization, a totally different social system is developing.[21] Other regional distinctions might be cited, but the fact remains that the bulk of Ceylon's people are village dwellers.

A definitive sketch of Ceylonese rural social-influence structure is not possible here, but a tentative schematic presentation will be helpful in clarifying political developments.

1. *The family.* The basic unit of mutual obligation and interdependence is the single household of man, wife, and children. Although many families have six to ten children, the average household is nearer five persons. Each new marriage usually creates a new household, typically located in the husband's village. Thus the extended family—prevalent in India—in which many couples and their children live together within one compound, is very rare indeed in Ceylon. Nevertheless to a Western eye, the Ceylonese family system is intricate and closely knit, extending its interdependence and mutual involvement over a widely ramified family complex, including cousins, uncles, and aunts, nephews and nieces as much as the more immediate family of parents and children.[22]

Brothers and male cousins are all referred to as brothers. At marriage, the wife usually goes to her husband's village where there is sufficient land, so that a village "family" is usually a group of fathers and sons and their wives and children. They will help one another in tilling fields and other tasks that require more than a solitary member to accomplish. But if kin are lacking, neighbors are often an acceptable, though generally not a preferred, substitute.[23]

Within each family there is a clear structure of deference. There are different terms denoting an older from a younger brother or sister. Indeed, a listing of relationship terms is remarkably elaborate, suggesting that considerable attention is given to the refinements

21 See the recent careful study of B. H. Farmer, *Pioneer Peasant Colonization in Ceylon* (London: Oxford University Press, 1957), particularly Chs. 3 and 14.

22 Bryce Ryan, "The Sinhalese Family System," *The Eastern Anthropologist*, VI, Nos 3 and 4 (March-August 1953), pp. 143-163; Sydney K. Bunker, "Some Reflections on the Jaffna Family System," *The New Lanka*, I, No. 4 (July 1950), pp. 29-33.

23 Bryce Ryan, "Primary and Secondary Contacts in a Ceylonese Peasant Community," *Rural Sociology*, v. 17, 4 (December 1952), pp. 311-321.

of family relationships.[24] Age is deferred to as a matter of course, and the elder male is the dominant family figure in what is fundamentally a patriarchal system. He makes decisions on most important matters and is the recipient of reiterated and explicit deference. The wife gives obeisance which he accepts as his due, but on distaff matters and social customs, she is more likely to control the household. The children appear remarkably deferential to their father. Even adults with children of their own will follow the advice and wait upon the will of their elders in all manner of affairs.

Since blood and social status are considered closely interconnected, even in modern Ceylon, when marriages are approaching, the extended family including cousins, uncles, and aunts must be consulted, for a marriage is not merely the union of two individuals, but it is also a uniting of two family groups. At such times, the blood, caste, and social status of the other family are minutely examined to be sure there will be no depreciation of one's own status, which would jeopardize the entire family's chances for marrying their children into the proper status group. Moreover, in a diverse plural society, family background is one fundamental determinant of a couple's likely compatibility. Cross-cousin marriages are preferred above all others, for this insures status, confirms a relationship already known, and often tends to consolidate property holdings.[25]

As long as the system remained intact where family standing was so important to all its members, the behavior of each reflected upon all, and a sense of solidarity and mutual responsibility led those, who could, to care for those who faltered.[26] All were assured of a sense of belonging and a community of warmth in which each one had his place merely by virtue of having been born. Although this picture of social harmony may be somewhat idealized, it is certainly true that the village in the past looked after its own problems, and each individual, thus involved in a network of family relationships, was insured maximum personal security; and social organization as well as public order was preserved. The individual's horizon

[24] N. D. Wijesekera identified fifty-five specified differences in intra-family relationship. *The People of Ceylon* (Colombo, 1949), pp. 62-64.

[25] S. J. Tambiah, "Kandyan Marriage Customs," a paper read before the Ceylon Association for the Advancement of Science, November 24, 1956.

[26] "Gross acts of deceit and loose conduct sometimes resulted in whole families or even whole villages being treated as social outcasts. It became, therefore, the grave responsibility of each member of the family so to conduct himself that he did not risk such degradation." *Report of the Kandyan Peasantry Commission* (Sessional Paper XVIII—1951), p. 86.

was, however, considerably limited by the family in which he himself lived and the caste to which his family belonged. At the present time, family integrity is diminishing in many rural areas of Ceylon, which may explain in part the rise in incidents of homicide and other indicators of social disharmonies. Nevertheless, as one contemporary observer remarked: "the bond of common caste or family connections is one of the strongest factors and the greatest force in the social structure."[27]

Where the family plays such a fundamental part in the individual's social setting, it is to be expected that status is largely a matter of his family background—an inherited status rather than a status he has developed for himself. Especially in the rural areas, but also in the cities, Ceylonese society appears to be highly conscious of a person's inherited position. Certain village practices symbolize this status perspective. Each house or hut will have its graded seating arrangements, and everyone knows who should not enter the veranda of another's by the front steps but come around by the side. Others do not venture onto the veranda at all. Some families may enter but remain standing; others, if they come that far, sit on a low bench that is to be seen along the veranda's side entrance. Equals may enter the veranda and sit in the same type of chair that the owner sits upon, while men of superior status generally remain standing. It is considered a mark of great favor if a superior man sits in the chair apologetically offered by a social inferior. Such mores are still to be found in rural districts even near Colombo. There is no doubt that they are less marked today than twenty years ago, for the inherited status structure is no longer unquestioned, and there are newer means of gaining status other than being born into the right families. One source of social disquiet in contemporary Ceylon stems precisely from the uncertainty and the resentment of this transition from inherited to acquired status.

2. *Village influence structure.* At the base of the rural social pyramid, forming perhaps 35 per cent of the rural population, are the landless laborers who are casually employed for menial, manual tasks.[28] They work on the land periodically for planting, weeding,

27 Unpublished survey conducted by students in the University of Ceylon's Department of Education.

28 Statistical materials on Ceylonese land holding and rural occupations are not yet entirely standardized, and comparisons of data from different sources often show contradictions. Different districts show notable variations. Nevertheless, for our purposes available data will be suggestive. Final Report on the *Economic Survey of Rural Ceylon*

and harvesting; they load trucks, repair roads, work in local coconut mills, rubber factories, or repair shops. Low in social status, leading the most precarious of lives, and unorganized for any joint endeavor, they are still without significant political influence, except at voting time when their votes, too, must be secured by the aspiring politician.

Above them, forming roughly 10 per cent of the total are tenant farmers, who work the fields owned by others on a sharecropping basis. Roughly half of their crop goes to the landowner for the use of his field, but where land is particularly scarce, owners may auction off rights to sharecrop land, often raising the rent still higher. The tenant may also have to pay an additional share for the loan of buffaloes, seed rice, or even for implements. Circumstances vary widely, yet it is safe to assume that rural casual labor and tenant farmers in some districts have the poorest working conditions of any groups in Ceylon. The tenant's lot varies with the quality of the land, the regularity of water, the security of his tenure, the price he has to pay for his right to farm, the cash price he obtains for the balance he sells on the market, and the reciprocal obligations undertaken by the owner on behalf of his tenants—the latter a highly personal and variable matter.[29]

In the estate districts, workers labor for a minimum wage and a piece-rate bonus. In the tea and rubber districts, their working conditions are well regulated and supervised both by the government and well-organized unions; but in low-country coconut districts, where employment is not steady and the workers live in their own nearby villages, conditions are more dependent upon the sense of responsibility of the estate owner; although here the laborer can supplement his cash wage by his own truck garden and a few palms—a resource not available to full-time resident estate labor elsewhere.

Higher up on the scale, perhaps 15-20 per cent of total rural families (35-40 per cent of agricultural families) are owner-cultivators or peasant proprietors, who work their own fields for their own

---

1950-1951 (Sessional Paper XI—1954); *Report on the Survey of Landlessness* (Sessional Paper XIII—1952) and for the Kandyan area, N. K. Sarkar and S. J. Tambiah, *The Disintegrating Village* (Colombo: Ceylon University Press, 1957). The impossibility of accurate generalization is suggested by the fact that the *Survey of Landlessness* reports that 37.7 per cent of all families are without any land whereas Sarkar and Tambiah show that 66 per cent of families in the Kandyan district lack land (Table 3).

[29] For a discussion of rice production and the tenant's problems, see *Report of the Joint United Kingdom and Australian Mission on Rice Production in Ceylon-1954* (Sessional Paper II—1955).

profit. Only 2-5 per cent of agricultural families are absentee landholders. Statistics are inadequate to give an accurate analysis of absentee holdings. A few aristocratic families may still retain important holdings. Temples may control 15-20 per cent of paddy lands. Men influential in a district encompassing several villages may sometimes own ten to twenty acres of paddy. But the bulk of absentee riceholders are small owners, many of them government servants, teachers, physicians, or businessmen, each of whom may own no more than a few acres of rice land. Village Ceylon is not dominated by the large absentee owner controlling vast acreages of paddy land. There are no equivalents of the Zemindars. The relatively wide dispersal of village and rice-land ownership in the hands of owner-cultivators and small absentee holders is a fundamental desiderata in considering Ceylonese political development.

(a) Traditionally influential families. At the village level, the land holders are drawn from the local influential families. In each village these are not difficult to identify for they have usually been the leading families for generations. Yet the system is not entirely rigid. If the scions of a traditional land-holding family prove to be incompetent, they will be deferred to, as traditional mores require, but they will not be respected, nor will they be influential. Conversely, even though an influential family has lost most of its holdings, it will still be looked up to by the villagers because it is known as the traditionally influential family, and it may continue to earn that status by its responsible judgments on, and concern for, village affairs.

In villages where caste groups are mixed, the influential families will undoubtedly be members of the highest community or "cultivator caste." In villages inhabited by members of only one caste, this kind of distinction is unimportant. Because the influential families tend to have land where land is scarce, they have greater opportunities to purchase farm implements and buffaloes to let out to those who have little or no land. And those with less land or none will have to pay due deference to those with more, if they are to secure for themselves sufficient land to cultivate. Thus economic resources as well as traditional status contribute to the position of the locally influential. Accordingly, the village influence structure is still closely associated with the relation of individuals to the land, a matter that is itself closely tied to traditional standing.

(b) Other prominent village figures. There are others who seek and gain prestige and influence by qualifications and means different from merely holding land on traditional grounds. Small shopkeepers are established in many villages. They handle essential supplements to the villagers' production, provide the principal center for sociability for the men, and are often moneylenders when the peasant's times are hard. The peasant's margins are very slight and his ceremonial expenses, which cannot wait for a good harvest, are often heavy. The shopkeeper advances a line of credit and when the peasant cannot pay on time, a mortgage may follow. Eventually title to the land may be transferred to the local merchant. But unless he himself is from "a good family," it is unlikely that his land acquisitions will give him immediate social status. It is in the coastal areas or along the main arteries of transportation, where the cash nexus has penetrated the countryside, that tradesmen and new landowners are displacing the old, traditional landowners in social status and general influence.

In most Sinhalese areas there are other village figures who are often more influential than the new landholder. These are: the Buddhist monk, the village school master, the indigenous doctor, the Village Headman, and the elected chairman of the Village Committee. It is difficult to place the monk in this social hierarchy, for, by the nature of his Buddhist faith and his temple way of life, he is not of the village society in any ordinary sense; yet he plays a very important role in village life. Many consider the temple the focal point of the unifying forces of the village. Temple ceremonies bring the villagers together in the common celebration of Buddhist holidays. Caste and family differences, disputes over ambiguous titles to scarce land, and personal antagonisms may disrupt, but the temple wields a paternal and benign influence. The temple's hall is used for village meetings; and children play in the temple courtyard. Until secular education spread to the villages in the last few decades, it was the temple school, designed largely for the training of potential members of the priesthood, which taught the peasant how to read and write. A large proportion of the older villagers who are literate learned their lessons in the temple schools.

The head priest of the temple is widely respected as the man of the highest spiritual attainment in the village. Offering alms and meeting the bare material needs of the monks is a common responsibility and privilege. In turn the monks console the bereaved, invoke blessings for the sick, and, on important occasions, chant *pirith* or sacred verses of the religious classics. The priest is the traditional advisor on domestic affairs and sometimes the one who settles village disputes.[80]

The doctor, known as the *ayurvedic* physician, is often a "physician by descent," his special knowledge of herbs and remedies having been handed down to him from his father and grandfather. The man who can cure the villagers' ailments is greatly respected. He is a student of his patients' mental and emotional problems as well as their physical illness. *Ayurvedic* medicine considers not only the disease of the specific symptom, but more properly "the whole individual as a living organism." He is supposed to charge no fees, receiving from his patients only what they freely choose to give him. He is generally admired for his medical skill and, like the monk, he is often a repository of the lore and history of his region.

A modern interloper in the traditional village social structure is the school master. He has a triple source of status. Traditionally, the teacher has about him the aura of the religious teacher or *guru*, at whose feet the student sits as a passive absorber of the given word. Indeed, in the more isolated villages today, the students still kneel down and pay obeisance to the teacher at the beginning and end of the term. At the same time, the schoolteacher knows the world beyond the village, for he is a government servant and has in all probability come from another part of the island altogether. He has undergone specialized training in a government school which has given him ideas and techniques new and strange to village traditions. Yet the strength of his drive for innovation should not be exaggerated, since the education he received in preparation for teaching is still itself fundamentally conservative. Teacher training, hitherto, has been designed to impart the textbook knowledge necessary for passing highly academic examinations that have very little to do with the villager's life. Finally, he is respected precisely because his learning is from a different world and has little value for village life. Academic success for a village child may be one of the ways he can better himself. Passing the necessary examinations may be the open-sesame to a career in the government service, a highly respected profession even if the post be that of a minor post-office clerk or an office peon. If the child can go far enough or

[80] For a fuller discussion of the role and influence of the monks, see below, Chapter VI.

enter the proper school, he may be able to learn English, which offers the greatest opportunities. It is the village schoolmaster who thus combines the prestige of ancient learning with the respect due to the man who can help a villager's child improve his future. The teacher may also play an important extracurricular role in village development and improvement. His reputation in the village is enhanced if he participates in village endeavors.[31]

A fourth village figure is still important even though he no longer holds the dominant position that was his during the colonial period. The Village Headman is a local man traditionally endowed with the majesty of governmental authority. He is appointed by the Government Agent—a senior member of the government service who acts as the district representative of the central government much like a French prefect—from among those who have some education, financial security, and are recognized as influential in the community. The leading families are usually the source of candidates, and the Government Agent must choose among them, if there is more than one leading family. The Headman acts for a multitude of government departments as their executive agent in the village. As such, he wields real power, often confirming the position of status and wealth he held as a prerequisite for his appointment. He distinguishes himself from the villagers by carrying an umbrella in all weathers—a mark of his superior status—and his clothes, a sarong or cloth below, and a Western jacket above, symbolize that he, too, like the schoolmaster, is in touch with the wider, outside world.

In recent years, as local elective government has been developing, villages have been electing village committees, which, in turn, select their village committee chairmen. Rural development societies are being formed, composed of leading village representatives, concerned with such endeavors as improving local roads with volunteer help, raising sanitary standards, drawing upon volunteer efforts for school construction, etc. There are also several thousand rural credit and agricultural cooperatives. In these societies too, the locally influential families are still important, although in the rural development societies, village committees, and cooperatives educated and energetic younger men by their own superior initiative and organizing ability are being elected to positions of influence they could not

[31] The importance attached to education in the village is suggested by an inquiry conducted by Murray A. Strauss reported in "Childhood Experience and Emotional Security in the Context of Sinhalese Social Organization," *Social Forces*, 33, No. 2 (December 1954), pp. 152-160.

have dreamed of under the older institutions. Often the Headman, the Village Committee Chairman, and the head of the Rural Development Society will be at least cousins, sometimes even brothers. If they are getting along together, all three offices will function smoothly and effectively. If, as may often happen, different families have been able to place "their" man in these different positions, the three local leaders may cancel each other out, and little will be accomplished.[32]

3. *District influence structure.* Social structure above the village level is more complex and the manifest differences are more immediately relevant to national politics. In most areas, the hierarchy of deference and influence in the district is still based largely on the inherited family structure. It is the scions of the traditional leading families who are in general most respected and, until recently, the national political elite was drawn almost entirely from the "big families" in the different districts. They had been landowners for generations; they were the men in the countryside who usually obtained some degree of Western education for their children. They could leave the district—often for extended periods—for Colombo, Kandy, or even for education abroad, and still retain their residence and continue to be known as "men of the place." Wealth, travel, opportunity, and an inherited social position con-confirmed their high standing.[33]

In a country where land-holding was a traditional mark of wealth and status, the new economic projects, which depended upon the land, were welcome and successful. These new estate enterprises—whether coconut, tea, or rubber—reaffirmed respected families in their status and successfully projected some newcomers into more exclusive circles. In recent years, those who could afford it have been purchasing tea estates, hitherto the virtual preserve of the European planters. Such economic activities have given a good financial return. Where workers were resident on the owner's lands, estate ownership has brought status to the owner and represented a continuation of largely traditional social values within remarkably productive enterprises.

32 References to competition between Village Committees and Rural Development Societies are not infrequent. See, for instance, *Report of the Commission on Local Government* (Sessional Paper XXXIII—1955), p. 72.

33 There are, of course, exceptions. For instance, in the Kandyan and farther up-country areas, certain distinguished families are deferred to by the villagers in the best tradition even though they have lived in these districts for no more than three generations and were not even Goyigama in caste in the beginning.

4. *Change and new ways to influence.* There are many elements of change which are at work altering the traditional family, village, and district influence structure. The cash economy is penetrating farther into rural areas. The very existence of the small shop indicates that the villages are not self-sufficient subsistence units. They need goods that the outside world alone can provide; villages must sell part of their rice for cash. The government has been encouraging this trend by offering a fixed and stable price for rice delivered to the Cooperative Agricultural Produce and Sales Societies. As more impersonal relationships and cash are substituted for established reciprocal obligations of a quasi-feudal type, the way is open for replacing inherited status by status that is acquired.

Cash and mobility are closely correlated and as the countryside becomes commercialized, more peasants can afford a bus journey to a nearby town. They can observe the farming methods and ways of living in other parts of the island. They may even have a newspaper read to them, piquing their imagination with vigorous criticisms of the country's leaders, or proposals for administrative or economic reforms that might fundamentally change relationships in the conservative countryside. The assumptions of inherited status are being questioned.

The land available for peasant agriculture has been declining, while the population has been increasing. The first encroachment on village lands began several centuries ago when coconut estates were developed in the low country. In the latter part of the nineteenth century, the tea-estate areas, which had gone beyond the inhabited valleys of the Kandyan district on to the very highlands, gradually spread downward to the immediate hill lands surrounding the village areas. The highlands had been used by the peasants for shifting jungle cultivation to supplement their rice. Coming from below, indigenous and foreign rubber and coconut estates began to encroach from the other direction. Village lands became surrounded by estates, and the villages could not expand their rice or other fields as the population grew.

Land fragmentation has contributed indirectly to a changing village society. Through successive generations the land has been divided equally between the male heirs of a family, though sisters have often been included. Many tiny holdings have developed, and one man's land may be scattered through a wide valley. With these progressively increasingly smaller units, the traditional customs are no longer held in such unquestioned favor. Moreover, titles are not clear and the minute remnants of formerly adequate holdings are the source of much quarreling and litigation. There are even court cases pending over competing claims to 1-250th of an acre.[34]

Changing preferences of the old families are also contributing toward a loosening of the traditional system. Wealthy sons prefer to live in the towns or Colombo and are no longer available to perform traditional ceremonial functions or carry their old responsibilities toward their less fortunate neighbors. There is a growing protest against certain types of land tenure which require deferential and irksome services to individual land holders or ceremonial and maintenance services to the temples and shrines of local deities.[35]

Nevertheless, despite these elements of change which are no doubt weakening the integrity and vigor of traditional village life, in many areas the village social structure has not yet been seriously undermined. Isolated villages in the Kandyan areas and the North Central Province offer a clearer prototype, while the coastal western and southern provinces show profounder changes at the village level.

Changes in the traditional district influence structure are more prominent. Throughout the island, other means of gaining district prominence and influence, apart from belonging to one of the old families or drawing wealth from the land, are becoming more and more important. Already under the colonial government, new professions were opening new roads to influence. One aspect of the colonial government that was widely respected in Ceylon was the British judicial system. As time went on, it became apparent that the colonial authorities were restrained from full arbitrary rule by laws they themselves formulated. Gradually, the law-making powers were shared downward until representatives of Ceylon's people were able to participate in the law-making process. To enter the law opened lucrative careers and was one of the surest ways of being treated by leading members of the British community as an equal and worthy of respect. The intricacies of the legal system once mastered, it was possible for those who were especially skilled to turn the system against the British themselves. The law could be used to protect the best of Ceylonese traditions from arbitrary government encroachment. The subtleties of famous cases from the past

[34] For a workmanlike study of land fragmentation and other underlying difficulties in selected Kandyan villages based on intensive field investigations, see N. K. Sarkar and S. J. Tambiah, *op.cit.*

[35] *Report of the Commission on Tenure of Lands of Viharagam, Dewalagam, and Nindagam*, p. 56.

are still of great interest to the public, and there is a remarkable amount of litigation, especially on inheritance and land cases. There have been, therefore, many opportunities for a lawyer to test his mettle and show his worth before an interested public.[36] Not only the sons of the aristocracy or the wealthiest families have gone into law as a profession, but those from low-country families of modest means and status have obtained a legal education as well.

The medical profession—based on Western medical standards—was another way to respected prominence. Several political careers have been fashioned from thriving medical practices, bringing special respect apart from, and beyond, the man's inherited status. In rural areas, especially, doctors have gained high reputations. They too, often combined "good family" background with professional skill.[37]

The newer school system required school administrators, whether they were Christian, Buddhist, or secular schools. Several distinguished political careers were built by former school principals from the "old-boy net" of graduates, the high status traditionally accorded the teacher, and the organizational, intellectual, and public speaking skills required by the teaching profession.

An additional structure of influence, one that provides the most all-embracing authority is, of course, the government.[38] Traditionally, the government has played a dominant role in Ceylon's affairs that is hard for an American to appreciate. District officials from the central government—the Government Agents—have exercised throughout the island the most important immediate authority. The location of roads and drainage channels, construction of schools and clinics, supervision of markets, distribution of land belonging to the Crown, establishing in office village leaders, and supervising the administration of justice and public order in the district—these were the functions of the central authorities and the Government Agent. As representative of the Crown, the Government Agent often lived a quasi-feudal life and received the authority and deference traditionally bestowed on the feudal ruling families. During the colonial

[36] In the autumn of 1956, for instance, the full text of the famous Gampola Temple Case of 1917 was published in a Sunday newspaper, serialized in three successive issues.

[37] An outstanding member of the Communist party who has been in parliament several times is from a highest status family in Southern Province, widely known for his dedicated medical service to his constituents which contributes to his political reputation.

[38] For a brief survey, see Sir Charles Collins, *Public Administration in Ceylon* (London, 1951).

period, these officers were usually British civil servants and, with a few notable exceptions, were admired and respected for their work and their incorruptibility. Apart from some hard years following the Kandyan rebellion and in pursuit of the 1833 reforms, they tended to be neutral in their relations with the local magnates.

With the gradual Ceylonization of the service and the growing political influence of the Ceylonese, this authority structure began to provide an alternative channel to political importance. A growing trend toward a welfare "service state" was manifest and the government was expected to provide a still wider range of initiatives and services in the districts. Justice, public order, transportation, and land supervision had been the principal governmental functions; educational and public health services were now added. Village agriculture and irrigation were promoted. Since World War II even the prices paid to farmers for their rice and the "cooperative" means of collecting produce became accepted government functions.

As the scope of government activity expanded, public service in the rural districts became a profession with many opportunities to be of service to the rural populations.[39] The feudatories had long ceased to be the only ones with resources to aid the less fortunate, nor were they the only men in the district to whom the populace deferred. The Government Agent—with luck and support from various ministers at the center—could become the dispenser of public largess. If he were ambitious for elected office, he could turn progressive social policies to his own account as well. Without being "of the place," or from "the best families," or the "right community," and without substantial financial backing, he could nevertheless become "the adopted son" of a particular locality. Through public service to several districts, his repeated reelection to parliament became possible. There was even an Englishman who, as a former Government Agent, had made such a name for himself that he was returned to parliament uncontested by a Ceylonese electorate.

New forms of wealth have recently provided new opportunities for a man to become important in his district. The mining of graphite on a large scale has been essentially a new form of enterprise that gained momentum during World War I. It has provided a base of wealth for several of the island's most politically prominent families, including the first three Prime Ministers, all of whom were

[39] For a discussion of the "scope" of politics see D. A. Rustow, *Politics and Westernization in the Near East* (Princeton, 1956), p. 16.

related. During and after World War II, those who contracted for the army did well. Some became wealthy through the disposal of surplus war equipment and larger construction contracts. A group of "new rich" entering the "mudalali" or rural moneylender class has risen to considerable district influence since 1940. There is a strong drive among them to make themselves socially respected and acceptable to the upper levels of Ceylon society—an ambition that appears to have had political significance in recent years.

Whether or not social status went with managing estates, running transport services, or other economic enterprises that employ large numbers of workers, these particular economic activities are thought to give to the entrepreneurs considerable political leverage at election time. Employment is one of the greatest boons, and an employee has traditionally been expected to show quasi-feudal deference toward his employer, closely paralleling the deference due from the villager to his "better." As part of this traditional deference, it has been assumed that the employee will also vote the way the boss wishes him to, unless countervailing loyalties to labor unions prevent such traditional forms of "influence."

Another way of gaining district prominence has been through the framework of representative institutions. Elective village committees and rural development societies or in the larger centers, municipal and urban councils have provided valuable experience for many. The Colombo and Kandy municipal councils were established in 1866 and elections have been held for many years on a universal adult male franchise, and after 1931 women were also permitted to vote. Municipal elections have been hotly contested and local government institutions have been a proving ground for a significant number of parliamentarians. Those who are elected to municipal or local posts, gain political prominence and power thereby, although they have not been readily accepted into the upper social strata unless they came from there originally.[40]

A remarkable feature of Ceylonese politics is the fact that although representative political institutions based on the universal adult franchise were introduced in 1931, the bulk of political leaders embarked upon their careers from positions of traditional influence based on land or the newer professions of law and medicine which developed during the colonial period. Village middle-class influential figures

[40] Nearly half the members of the Third Parliament had been active in local politics before they entered the House of Representatives.

or locally elected individuals appeared to exert pressure on those larger owners or professional men who provided the personnel of national politics; but not until 1956 did the rural middle class assert its voice against its better-endowed neighbors. Many aspects of the social unrest and instability that have marked public life since then can be attributed to this clear shift in the locus of rural political power.

D. ECONOMIC CLASS STRUCTURE

A third method of analyzing the underlying setting of politics is through the economic class structure. The harsh facts of income differentiation form a contrasting basis for distinctive interests. For instance, over half the population earns less than Rs. 75 per month, while 88 per cent receive less than Rs. 175. The bottom 10 per cent of the population receive 1.4 per cent of total incomes received, while the top 1 per cent receive 18.2 per cent of the total income. These income differences are perhaps less sharply defined than in India, but they are nevertheless profound compared to parallel figures for an average Western country.[41]

In usual class terminology, Ceylon's society is characterized by the presence of a small wealthy upper class who own rubber, coconut, and tea estates, or engage in mining, commerce, banking, or transport activities. Beneath them is an upper middle class usually of professional people—lawyers, doctors, university faculties, staff officers of government departments, journalists, and the few, though growing, numbers of Ceylonese who are junior executives in business firms owned by others. Smaller transport owners and owners of larger stores in Colombo, Jaffna, Galle, and the larger towns should probably be included. Most of them owe their position to wealth which gave them access to advanced education or enabled them to control economic enterprises; but many have achieved this status from modest homes through superior educational performance. Beneath them, at a considerable income and deference distance, is the lower middle class—the numberless clerks in government service and business, country schoolteachers, indigenous doctors, smaller traders, the few shop foremen in automobile- and estate-servicing trades. The gap

[41] At the official rate of exchange, the rupee is worth 21 cents U.S. But this is only a rough basis for comparison since cost structures in the two countries are very different. Personal services, indigenous housing, and costs for heating, clothing, etc. are much less than in the United States, while manufactured products are generally more expensive in relation to local incomes.

between this lower middle class and the upper middle class is perhaps as great socially and economically as that between them and the working classes beneath them.

The "working class" is in fact divided into three distinct groups of relatively equal status—the urban workers, estate labor, and among the peasantry, the landless workers and tenant farmers.[42] Of all the workers, the urban wage earners have traveled farthest from the traditional social setting of rural Ceylon. Certain jobs, like scavenging, garbage collection, and taking care of latrines are reserved for the lowest castes. But in most other respects, a man in city labor is on his own and independent of any inherited status. Yet his conditions are not enviable. His teeming tenement districts are often in the least salubrious, swampy outskirts of the cities, and subject to periodic flooding. The climate imposes no imperatives of cold, but only a vigilant health service keeps disease from spreading wildly in the tropical humidity.[43] Urban workers tend to retain some ties with the countryside, much as do eastern European migrants to the city, largely for family reasons. Seasonal returns to the village family to help with the harvest are not infrequent. Employers and shop supervisors report that the worker with village ties cannot be pressed too hard to maintain production norms, since he easily throws up his job and returns to the country where his family will take him in. Principal trades—coconut manufacturing, engineering, automobile repairing and construction work, printing, cigar manufacturing, transport services, dock and harbor tending, commercial activities connected with the import and export trades, and entertainment—employ nearly 200,000 workers. Ninety thousand others work in shops and stores.[44] Wages in the organized city trades tend to be from 20 per cent to 40 per cent above those received by estate labor, but the cost of urban living is considerably higher. On a net cash basis, the estate laborer is doubtless better able to save, although life on estates is probably too restrictive for those who migrate to the city.

Mobility between the "working class" and the lower middle class and between that and the upper middle class is unusual. Statistical

[42] For a useful discussion of class divisions, see Sir Ivor Jennings, *The Commonwealth in Asia* (Oxford, 1951), Ch. IV. On earlier conditions in rural Ceylon, see his *The Economy of Ceylon*, 2nd ed. (London, 1951), Ch. V.

[43] In 1957 several cases of smallpox were isolated and the public health services proved their mettle by prompt and effective control measures, including widespread vaccination and irritating, but determined, isolation practices.

[44] *Census of Ceylon 1946* (2 vols.), Vol. I, Table 48. See also *Administration Report of the Commissioner of Labour for 1955*, Tables XV and XVI.

material for a reliable analysis of this phenomenon is lacking, but it seems a sound guess that as few rise from the lower middle class to the upper middle class as move from the laboring groups into the lower middle class.

Regardless of the perspective from which Ceylonese society is viewed, it appears to be organized along the lines of a multitude of self-aware and rather clearly differentiated groups. Past ethnic, religious, and other social distinctions persist to an important degree. The colonial period brought new divisions of religion and language, but helped to diminish certain of the other differences. The traditional, semi-feudal social structure has been significantly undermined; but new, though less rigid, stratifications of education and economic distinctions have in some measure taken their place. Each of these groups tends to live its own way of life. Each tends to look upon the political arena with a different perspective.

The challenge to statesmanship is not merely the extraordinarily difficult task of creating a sense of national unity and common destiny out of these disparate elements. The diverse demands and values of each group must in some measure be drawn into the political process, if large numbers are not to be in fact alienated from the political order.

Men do not survive on group loyalties alone, nor are their lives' purposes entirely free from the nagging necessity of finding daily bread for themselves and their families. As the older modes lose some of their persuasiveness, the standards that others live by become more plausible as yardsticks of one's own contentment. Statesmanship is tested not merely by the manner in which it contends with the different ethnic, religious, educational, class, and other groups, although these were of first importance at the outset; but the ability to cope with the economic imperatives—as these become understood by different groups of the population—becomes an important measure of the leadership's competence. A discussion of Ceylon's economy is therefore necessary.

CHAPTER III · THE ECONOMIC SETTING[1]

"Parliaments do not grow rice, nor cabinets construct irrigation works. Yet if these things are not done, the people may lose patience with parliamentary institutions and demand some alternative method of government."—Sydney Bailey, *Parliamentary Government in Southern Asia*

I · INTRODUCTION

CEYLON'S political leaders are faced with a set of economic problems which they share with the leaders of most other newly independent countries in South Asia and Africa. Hitherto, the economy has provided the people with a generally rising standard of living. Now, shortly after political independence when full responsibility for economic affairs rests upon democratically elected leaders, three phenomena converge to raise decided difficulties.

In the first place, the population of Ceylon is rising at an unprecedented rate. Nearly twice what it was before 1946, it is the highest rate of any country in Asia today with the exception of Formosa. When the British gained control of the entire island in 1815, the population was approximately one million. In the course of the next one hundred forty years, it has multiplied more than eight times and the rate of increase has been rising. Part of the increase was the result of the large-scale immigration of Tamil estate laborers brought from South India to work the tea and rubber estates in the nineteenth and early twentieth centuries. However,

1 This essay is in no sense original but is entirely derivative. Those who wish to press the analysis further are referred to the following studies: International Bank for Reconstruction and Development, *The Economic Development of Ceylon* (Baltimore, 1953); Sir Ivor Jennings, *The Economy of Ceylon*, 2nd edition (London, 1951); Government of Ceylon, *Report of the Taxation Commission* (Sessional Paper XVII—1955); Planning Secretariat, *Six-Year Programme of Investment 1954/55 to 1959/60* (1955); National Planning Council, *First Interim Report* (1957); Henry M. Oliver, Jr., *Economic Opinion and Policy in Ceylon* (Durham, N.C., 1957); B. Stein, "Development Problems in Ceylon" in Robert I. Crane and Burton Stein, *Aspects of Economic Development in South Asia* (New York, 1954). Textual references to reprint published by *The Ceylon Historical Journal*, III, Nos. 3 and 4, pp. 286-330.

the rate of natural increase has long been high and since 1946 it has leaped upward. Prior to that year, the population grew at the rate of roughly 1.8 per cent per year. Ten years later the rate was nearly 2.8 per cent. This startling increase followed the island-wide use of DDT to control malaria, which had been endemic over most of the island for centuries, and the generally improved sanitary and health services.[2] The birth rate has declined slightly; but there has been a more marked decline in infant mortality and deaths among the elderly. In 1948, when Ceylon gained its independence, there were 7,000,000 living on the island; ten years later there were 9,000,000. Such a rapidly growing and youthful population would be a source of great satisfaction to the patriots and governments of several western European countries; in the case of Ceylon it creates a most urgent problem. Educational expenses are naturally heavy, and at present some 80,000 young people seek employment annually. In thirty years the population may be twice its present size.

In the past, the economy expanded rapidly enough to give the growing population sufficient employment and a rising standard of living. This was possible because of the lush, tropical monsoon climate in the wet zone, which encouraged the growth of certain agricultural products, and because of the economic revolution that took place in Ceylon in the late nineteenth and early twentieth centuries. Foreigners invested a large amount of capital in clearing unused jungle lands and introduced new methods of cultivation and management—the large-scale, commercialized production of plantation crops for export. The foreign exchange thus earned was used to pay generous returns to the original enterprisers from Great Britain and to purchase necessary imports from areas of low-cost production abroad. Unfortunately, there is little unused land left in the wet zone suitable for plantations; foreign capital is no longer available for direct investments, and the world market for these products is highly problematical. Therefore rapid expansion of the plantation pattern seems unlikely. Unless a new dynamism is injected into the economy, more and more people will have to subsist on a relatively stable national product and compete for a limited number of job opportunities.

[2] H. Cullumbine, "An Analysis of the Vital Statistics of Ceylon" reprint by the *Ceylon Journal of Medical Science*, Section D, Volume VII, Parts 3 and 4 (December 1950), p. 12. Department of Census and Statistics, *Statistical Abstract of Ceylon 1956*, Table 37.

These developments come at a time when the people on the island have begun to expect a rising standard of living for themselves and their children. This inflation of expectations has many causes: political promises articulated by the leaders of the nationalist movement; a Westernized education made available to the elite; the rise of a critical vernacular press edited by men deeply imbued with British liberal, social, and political ideals of equality and humanitarianism. Recently, members of the intelligentsia with socialist ideals of greater social equality through governmentally managed development, and politicians of all parties attempting to win the vote by outbidding their political opponents, have given a further impetus. Western movies, available in the cities and towns and carried into the villages by itinerant entertainers, dramatize in easily understood terms the standards others live by. During World War II British and American troops stationed in Ceylon daily demonstrated that even manual laborers, mechanics, and drivers for the Allied forces lived a life of plenitude hitherto unimagined by the average Ceylonese. In addition, a growing secularization of life is reducing the persuasiveness of otherworldly religions.

This conjuncture of a rapidly rising population, a plantation economy with limits to its further expansion, and the inflation of expectations presents a formidable challenge to Ceylon's statesmen.

II · PRODUCTION

Like other countries in South Asia, Ceylon is predominately agricultural. Roughly 55 per cent of the gross national product is accounted for by growing, processing, and transporting agricultural commodities, and more than half of the gainfully employed work in agriculture and forestry.[3] Not only does Ceylon specialize in agriculture but the bulk of its agricultural activity is concentrated on producing only three products—tea, rubber, and coconut—which employ roughly 30 per cent of the work force. Large numbers of additional workers in transport, shipping, banking, and commerce also depend upon them for their livelihood.[4] These three export crops alone provide 35-40 per cent of the country's gross national product and account for 90-95 per cent of foreign exchange earnings.

Specialization has gone so far that nearly one-half of all food consumed must be imported, even though the economy is mainly agri-

[3] *Six-Year Programme of Investment*, p. 157.
[4] *Ibid.*, p. 161.

cultural. In a society traditionally centered around the cultivation of rice—where rice is the average man's staple diet—one-half of Ceylon's rice now comes from abroad. Ninety per cent of curry stuffs, pulse and dried fish important for curries, and 100 per cent of wheat and sugar are also purchased abroad.[5]

A. THE ESTATE SECTOR

Although the three principal export crops are considered to be "estate" products, their management and production differ widely.

1. *Coconuts.* Almost 30 per cent of Ceylon's cultivated area is devoted to coconuts. Coconut palms grow on over 1,000,000 acres of the coastal wet zone, in a triangle north from Colombo along the coast and inland some forty miles at its deepest; to the south a narrow fringe of palms borders the shore as far as the island's southern tip, with scattered groves on the east coast in the neighborhood of Batticaloa and Trincomalee. In the Kurunegala district the large coconut estates are impressive—mile on mile of orderly trees with glistening, quietly moving leaves above and serried rows of trunks below; the cultivation mounds and well-tended fences indicating careful maintenance and reinvestment. But these are atypical, for only 10 per cent of the total coconut acreage is in estates of more than 20 acres. Over 60 per cent is in small holdings of under 10 acres and in village and town gardens as a supplement to the family's rice and vegetables. Another 30 per cent is in the form of small estates between 10 and 20 acres. Ownership is almost entirely Ceylonese.[6]

Coconut products earn only some 16 per cent of total export values, but the coconut palm has many uses for the Ceylonese villager. Probably over one-half the total nuts produced are consumed at home in the form of coconut milk, fresh coconut meat, dried coconut, or in other ways. Easily extracted forms of the oil provide cooking fat and lighting fuel. The leaves thatch the villager's house and the trunk furnishes wood for house and roof frames, furniture, and fuel. The coconut is the offering of the host to his visitor. And from the flower of the palm, a mild yeasty toddy and the more potent arrack are extracted. When the world market price for coconut products soars, the Ceylonese consumer suffers as the grower prospers. Because of its many local uses, the coconut may have to be held off

[5] IBRD, p. 209.

[6] IBRD, p. 247; Department of Census and Statistics, *Census of Agriculture 1952; Part III—Coconut Plantations* (Colombo, 1956), p. 7.

the world market by government decision to reserve enough of this product for domestic needs. Coconuts also have a role in animal husbandry for meat and dairy products; the animals graze under the trees where grass can grow, and their manure helps to fertilize the trees This natural exchange has not yet been exploited extensively, for religious and dietary reasons.

Coconut acreage has remained relatively fixed during the past twenty years. The hard years of the Great Depression, a shortage of fertilizer during World War II, and the more recent emphasis on rice production have discouraged new planting. Nor was there an increase in yields between 1933 and 1947. Recently, however, a more thorough use of known cultivation methods and an increased application of fertilizers together raised the national yield by an estimated 25 per cent between 1947 and 1954—a considerable achievement for a seven-year period.[7] On the other hand, most of the trees are over sixty years old, an age when yields begin to decline; and replanting is now an expensive undertaking because of higher labor costs.

Coconuts require relatively little attention for considerable outturn. It is possible for one laborer to care for eight to ten acres of coconut lands for normal production. Many palms grow without any care at all in village gardens.

Some twenty-five electoral constituencies encompass the island's principal coconut districts. Although multitudinous small holders are not in a position to exert pressure in an organized fashion to protect their interests, the large number of voters directly connected with coconut production in these districts ensures their voice being heard, at least whenever elections are in prospect. The Low Country Products Association is their spokesman, heavily manned by the wealthier low-country Sinhalese estate owners. Several district coconut planters associations also speak on behalf of the small holder.

2. *Tea.* Coconuts have been grown in Ceylon for many centuries and received a major impetus toward expansion during the Dutch period, beginning in the seventeenth century. Tea-growing is relatively new, for it was not seriously undertaken until after the demise of the coffee industry in the 1870's. Acreages expanded rapidly, increasing ten times between 1880 and 1885, five times between 1885 and 1890, and from then until 1900 at a rate of some 100,000 acres

[7] *Coconut Plantations,* p. 10 compared with National Planning Council, *First Interim Report,* p. 11. The figures of total yield are necessarily estimates, since production on small holdings is not accurately reported.

every five years. After 1900 the rate of expansion slowed until by 1946 some 550,000 acres were in tea. Acreages have grown only slightly in the past decade and further growth seems unlikely.[8] The bulk of these are in the Central Province, the upper reaches of Uva and Sabaragamuwa, and the Southern Province, all within the wet zone area and above 2,000 feet. Concentrations are heaviest around Kandy (medium-grown) and Nuwara-Eliya (high-grown). Tea is the largest single foreign exchange earner, accounting for roughly 65 per cent of all export income in a typical year.[9]

Whereas the coconut groves are primarily held by small holders, only 14 per cent of Ceylon's tea is owned by individuals, virtually all of them Ceylonese. Capital requirements are such in tea that 75 per cent of tea lands is owned by share companies. Roughly half of the tea acreage is owned abroad.[10] The high-grown areas above 4,000 feet have been the longest retained by those who pioneered the industry. At present, the bulk of Ceylon's tea is grown in relatively large holdings. Nearly half of the total tea area is operated in units of more than 500 acres. Small holdings averaging less than one acre accounted for only 12 per cent of acreage in 1955.[11]

Yields on the small holdings are notoriously low and tend to deteriorate. The optimum working unit with present organizational methods appears to be between 500 and 1500 acres.[12] This is because tea is usually processed ready for consumption on the producing estate itself, and an economical factory must be able to draw on tea of controlled and known quality from an extensive acreage. At the same time, labor, housing, transport, and supervisory staff are all more costly per unit of output when applied to smaller estates.

Yields per acre, on the average, are considerably below those reported in India and Pakistan. Ceylon planters, however, consider their product more carefully plucked, culled, and prepared and Ceylon's tea is known as a high quality product that regularly fetches a premium price on the world market for most grades.[13] Tea production has increased over the past decade. From 1946 to 1958 tea production grew by nearly 40 per cent.[14] This production increase

8 Department of Census and Statistics, *Census of Agriculture 1952; Part I—Tea Plantations* (Colombo, 1956), Table I.

9 *Six-Year Programme of Investment*, p. 161.

10 *Tea Plantations*, Table VI.

11 IBRD, pp. 228-229. *Six-Year Programme of Investment*, p. 162.

12 *Tea Plantations*, p. 11.

13 *Ibid.*, p. 8.

14 *Statistical Abstract 1956*, Table 136, Central Bank of Ceylon, *Annual Report of the Monetary Board to the Minister of Finance for 1958*, p. 6.

on an acreage that expanded by only 2.3 per cent has been the result of improved cultivation methods.

Unlike coconut, the tea industry absorbs large numbers of laborers and demands close inspection, constant overseeing, and careful labor organization for good results, especially for plucking which must not be delayed. It requires roughly one employee per acre, and 65 per cent of cost is for labor.[15] Over 500,000 people work on the tea estates in all capacities, 75 per cent of them of recent Indian origin, the balance Ceylonese.[16]

Tea has little direct political representation. It is mainly concentrated in fifteen constituencies in the up-country districts and perhaps ten others in the middle-country area. Approximately half the owners are foreign, have not the franchise, and must depend upon one or two nominated members in parliament as their spokesmen. The vast majority of the laborers are also without the franchise. The Sinhalese, who have the vote, are precisely those elements in the up-country districts who are largely excluded from the tea industry. They therefore have a sense of grievance against the tea estates for restricting lands available to peasant cultivation and for employing Indian Tamils instead of Sinhalese village voters. Moreover, since tea is cultivated in large units, those Ceylonese owners who have the franchise are relatively few in number. For these and other reasons, tea is politically vulnerable although it is the backbone of the country's export economy.

3. *Rubber.* Rubber is found in the wet zone between the coastal coconut and the middle-grown tea areas, in a strip some twenty miles wide stretching northeast from Ambalangoda on the coast to Matale in the center of the island. Rubber cultivation began in about 1890; acreages expanded rapidly after 1900 until in 1935 over 600,000 acres or 20 per cent of the total cultivated land area was planted with rubber. Acreage has expanded only slightly since then, with 661,000 acres in rubber in 1955. Approximately 210,000 Ceylonese are employed in rubber production, processing, and shipping.[17]

Rubber varies in its production structure—a little more than half is held in units of over 100 acres, 22 per cent by small estates of 10 to 100 acres, and about 27 per cent in small holdings.[18] The larger

[15] *Tea Plantations*, p. 12 and Table xviii, p. 13.

[16] *Administration Report of the Commissioner of Labour for 1955*, Table xxx, p. F 109.

[17] *Statistical Abstract of Ceylon*, 1956, Table 122.

[18] *Census of Ceylon 1946*, Vol. 1, Part 2, Table 48. Six thousand added to census

estates and small holdings produce more rubber per acre than the medium sized units. In the small, owner-cultivated holding an immediate personal interest insures a good crop, and the larger estates employ trained supervisory staffs and reinvest enough for maximum results. The small estates, supervised infrequently by absentee owners, receive insufficient guidance and reinvestment.[19] Roughly, two-thirds of rubber acreage is owned by Ceylonese. The balance has been owned largely by British incorporated companies,[20] but each year a certain number of estates are acquired from the British owners.

Yields of rubber fluctuate in response to international demand. Thus, during World War II, when the trees were heavily over-tapped to meet Allied war requirements, production went up as high as 392 pounds of dry rubber per acre. In 1947 it dropped to 314 pounds per acre, and during the Korean War boom of 1950 it rose once more to over 390 pounds.[21] Tapping at such a rate does permanent damage to the trees, and such yields cannot be maintained without extensive replanting even if the market demand should again reach a comparable peak. As more than two-thirds of Ceylon's rubber trees in 1951 were over thirty years of age and new strains promised higher productivity, extensive replanting became advisable.

In about eighteen constituencies rubber is well represented and, since it includes both large estates which are organized to safeguard their interests and small holders who have a vote at the hustings, rubber interests, too, are politically protected.

B. PEASANT AND HANDICRAFTS

1. *Farming for home consumption.* A semi-subsistence, small-scale peasant agriculture has persisted along with the estate sector. In the past it was relatively independent of the cash nexus of relationships and was closer to traditional social ways. In 1955 over 1,300,000 acres were sown with rice, of which one-third was sown twice in one year. This produced roughly 50 per cent of all rice consumed on the island.[22]

---

figure to account for rubber transporters, handlers, and personnel of companies handling other products as well as those not listed separately.

19 Department of Census and Statistics, *Census of Agriculture 1952*; Part II, *Rubber Plantations*, pp. 10-11.

20 *Rubber Plantations*, p. 10.

21 *Ibid.*, Table x, p. 11.

22 Department of Census and Statistics, *A Report on Paddy Statistics*, Monograph No. 9 (Colombo, 1956), Table 11, p. 18. Acreage statistics are not entirely comparable, since one field may be sown twice in one year and statistical reports do not always

In the main, holdings of rice are small. Particularly in the wet zone, where land areas for rice growing have been progressively reduced by the growth of coconut and rubber estates and, where people have lived uninterruptedly for over 1,000 years, fragmentation has gone very far. Inheritance has divided and subdivided plots between the heirs for generations. Indeed, the median size has been estimated at roughly three-fourths of an acre; 65 per cent of the holdings are under one acre and only 4 per cent are over five acres.[23]

In the wet zone, the bulk of rice is grown by a system of rain-fed irrigation on small plots terraced on steep hillsides, with the twisting bunds breaking the water surface into graceful patterns to the sound of water running from terrace to terrace. Here every square foot of land not devoted to coconut, tea, or rubber and that has any possibility of leveling and of controlled water, is devoted to rice. On small hills or other high land are scattered huts, surrounded by garden plots of jak, coconut, pepper, papaya, or banana trees and vegetables as the householder's truck patch.

In the dry zone, peasant colonies have been established with extensive government assistance. Here cultivation depends upon elaborate irrigation systems as it did in ancient days. Some 200,000 acres have been opened to irrigated agriculture since 1945 and roughly 100,000 people have been settled.[24]

Taking the country as a whole, 55 per cent of the rice area was cultivated by the owner himself, 29 per cent was sharecropped, 14 per cent was leased, and 3 per cent was rotated successively among several owners who hold joint title to one plot. But these proportions vary widely between different districts; the large landowners are particularly prevalent in the eastern dry zone coastal areas.[25]

Yields have been notoriously low, although the methods used in the past for gathering statistics through Village Headmen have placed a premium on underreporting output. In fact yields presently appear to be averaging roughly 28 to 32 bushels per acre and are comparable to yields in India, Burma, Pakistan, and Thailand. They are still far below Japan's average and below what can reasonably

---

differentiate between actual land area sown to rice and the acreage sown in any one year. Yields, too, are imprecise because the farmer holds back a proportion for his own use, and may pay some of his obligations in kind and for other reasons.

[23] *Report of the Joint United Kingdom and Australian Mission on Rice Production in Ceylon*, p. 10. See also Sarkar and Tambiah, Ch. VII.

[24] *Six-Year Programme of Investment*, p. 179; Farmer, p. 164.

[25] *Report on Paddy Statistics*, Table 7, p. 13.

be expected, given the land and water available and the size of present rice holdings.[26]

Total production of rice on the island is still in the realm of estimate, but the most careful analysis suggests that rice crops have been rising. Statistical reporting since 1950 is considered reliable.

RICE PRODUCTION[27]

	Million bushels		*Million bushels*
1943-1944	20.5	1950-1951	22.0
1944-1945	16.4	1951-1952	28.9
1945-1946	17.1	1952-1953	21.9
1946-1947	16.7	1953-1954	31.1
1947-1948	18.7	1954-1955	35.7
1948-1949	23.1	1955-1956	26.9
1949-1950	22.0	1956-1957	30.6

If 30,000,000 bushels are taken as a conservative supply figure for the period 1953-1956, it will be seen that there has been a rise of some 50 per cent over the wartime figure. Even if part of this increase is the result of improved statistics it is unlikely to represent more than one-half of the statistical improvement. Imports of rice declined between 1948 and 1955 by roughly 9 per cent.[28] Thus, in rice production, the country more than held its own despite a 20 per cent increase in population. On the other hand, the margin remained too close for complacency. In 1957 drought and floods once more impelled larger imports and in 1958, despite a harvest close to the record of 1955, more rice had to be imported and home production was only slightly higher than imports. Fortunately, the price of imported rice was low. Otherwise, the balance of payments would have suffered severe pressure merely to import the necessities to feed the population.

Compared to their Indian neighbor, however, the Ceylonese have not known famine in any large measure. Dry zone farmers have hard times when drought reduces their water below the essential margin, or when floods drive peasants from their homes. Yet hitherto, at least, there have not been the harrowing national food crises that have periodically plagued the larger neighbor to the north. On the

26 *Statistical Abstract*, 1956, Table 133.

27 *Ibid.*, Table 137. Central Bank of Ceylon, *Annual Report of the Monetary Board to the Minister of Finance for the Year 1957*, p. 36. 1956-57 an estimate.

28 Department of Commerce, *Thirty Years of Trade Statistics (1925-54)*, Part 1, Table 20; *A Report on Paddy Statistics*, Table 11, p. 18.

other hand, since half the country's rice supply must come from abroad, the level of rice consumption depends heavily upon the continued output of the estate sector and the prices these commodities can fetch in the world markets.

Animal husbandry has not been extensively developed. Meat and draft cattle are mainly found in the low-country Christian areas. Draft cattle are also grown in the Buddhist districts, but their strain is poor and as milk or meat producers they are seriously deficient.[29] Pigs are bred in considerable numbers in the coconut districts and on the estates; and goats are raised in the Tamil areas. Poultry farming, though low in initial costs, is not well developed. Climatic conditions as well as indigenous tradition create special problems in raising healthy egg-laying poultry and in pasturage and silage for cattle. There is no religious objection to drinking milk or eating milk products but, in Buddhist areas particularly, to produce cattle or poultry for meat goes against fundamental religious convictions. It is even improper to eat fertilized eggs. Ceylon's artificial lakes provide ample opportunities for systematic fish culture; but little has been done in this field. Caste distinctions impede modern methods of fish cultivation, since trained personnel are reluctant to engage in a traditionally low-caste occupation. Offshore fishing has been a long-standing industry; but intensive research by modern Canadian and Japanese methods leave its potentialities in some doubt. The bottom plunges to the depths near most of the island's shores, and those shelves that exist are apt to be exploited by competing Indian fishermen.

The average Ceylonese diet is seriously deficient in both animal and vegetable proteins. Milk consumption is among the lowest in the world and the diet is heavily weighted by starch in the single form of rice.[30] Vegetable proteins like soya beans, peanuts, or other religiously acceptable forms are hardly eaten at all. Butter, eggs, fruits, nuts, and green vegetables are considered luxuries or delicacies. There is room for improvement in the local diet to raise energy and health levels through diversifying food crops and exploiting what is religiously acceptable in animal husbandry and fish culture. An improved local agricultural output will also reduce the country's import bill.

[29] *Six-Year Programme of Investment*, pp. 210-211; Farmer, pp. 255-258; IBRD, pp. 322-331.

[30] IBRD, pp. 734-737.

Unlike tea, the peasant sector of the economy is well represented in Parliament. Rural voters hold the majority of electoral strength. The villagers are divided along ethnic lines and the horizon of many is so limited that it prevents them as a group from exerting concerted pressure either at the hustings or in Parliament. They are not yet organized. There is no peasant party per se. Yet candidates in all but perhaps a dozen of the more urbanized constituencies must win the majority of village votes, if they are to be returned. Since most of the village districts are linked in one way or another to the peasant sector of the economy, political debates have paid much deference to subsistence agricultural interests.[31]

2. *Handicraft sector.* Peasant and town handicraft products have never been developed to the artistic and finished quality of India, Iran, or Thailand. Exports from the island before the coming of the western Europeans "consisted entirely of natural products, aromatic drugs, gems, pearls, and shells," of value in themselves but not the fruit of sophisticated or finely skilled workmanship.[32]

Nevertheless, hand-woven textiles, wall hangings, intricately worked copper, silver and ivory adornments and utensils, iron implements, steel, armor, and even guns confirm the presence of considerable artisan skills as late as the sixteenth century. The artisans were divided into hereditary communities and often received royal patronage. These occupations, often compared to medieval guilds, do not appear to have put their special stamp on the economic and social life of the island as the guild system did in Europe. And after the arrival of European goods, the artisans were unable to recast their traditional skills. Their products were too costly; taste for them declined as European products became popular; and the sons of craftsmen sought other, more promising activities in agriculture or minor positions in trade and transport. This is one reason why highly skilled artisans easily adaptable to foremen posts in industrial ventures are very rare today.[33] Although the estates brought an economic

[31] Perhaps an evidence of growing peasant self-consciousness, in February 1958 a large group of peasants came to Colombo to protest a reduction in the cash payments made under the Guaranteed Price Scheme.

[32] Tennent, Vol. I, pp. 446-447, also 525-603 and the extensive notes citing records of many travelers who visited the island before the Portuguese.

[33] For medieval period, see Ariyapala, *op.cit.*, pp. 336-338; Tennent, Vol. I, pp. 448-492. For the seventeenth century, see *Robert Knox in the Kandyan Kingdom*, E. F. C. Ludowyk (ed.), (London, 1948), "Their manufactures are few: some calicoes, not so fine as good strong cloth for their own use: all manner of iron tools for smiths, and carpenters, and husbandmen: all sorts of earthenware to boil, stew, fry, and fetch

revolution to the island, as Ceylon became drawn into the world of international trade, the artisan traditions suffered severely.[34]

C. INDUSTRY

Industrial development records no such growth as does the production of estate crops, rice, and other agricultural products during the past ten years. Considerable investments have been made in a variety of undertakings but the fruits of these have been disappointing, particularly at a time when thoughtful Ceylonese are viewing with concern the future of an economy so heavily dependent upon exportable plantation products.

It is well to remember that Ceylon had important industries in 1948. There were over 800 tea factories processing tea to its ultimate consumption form, many rubber mills, and large and small factories producing coconut oil, desiccated coconut, and other products.[35] Many thousands of workers were employed in them, and in the early 1950's some 156,000,000 KWH of electricity were consumed. According to the International Bank for Reconstruction and Development mission, "it is probable that Ceylon is proportionately far more industrialized than many other 'underdeveloped' countries." But these industrial enterprises are entirely dependent upon processing the traditional estate products for export, and from the point of view of those who press for greater industrialization, these are merely adjuncts of the plantation economy. "The real pressure, then, is not merely for an industrial payroll but for channeling local energies and resources into economical production of a wider variety of finished goods."[36]

Development of industries with even a minimum of capital, apart from traditional tea and rubber processing for export, has been very limited. According to a Census of Industry study in 1952, only 54,000 jobs were provided by "industries" employing more than five paid employees and working with not less than Rs. 3,000 capital and using some mechanical power.[37] The total net product amounted to only

water in, goldsmith's work, painter's work, carved work, making steel, and good guns, and the like." P. 156.

[34] Beautiful work is still done by elder craftsmen in the Kandyan districts in silver and brass. But they are very few and commercially their work is unimportant.

[35] Department of Census and Statistics, *Census of Agriculture 1952*, Part IV, *Agriculture*, Table XII.

[36] IBRD, p. 506.

[37] Department of Census and Statistics, *Census of Industry, 1952*, Table I.1.

some 5 per cent of the national income for 1953.[38] On the other hand, there were 300,000 workers engaged in "manufacturing" of various kinds.[39] If these and the previous figures are in any way comparable, it suggests that some 250,000 of the workers in "manufacture" are in fact self-employed or working in small shops with virtually no capital to raise their productivity or are engaged in handicraft and artisan activities at a moderate level of skill.

Intensive capital investment by the government has produced some impressive industrial establishments. The most effective of these has been the government-built cement factory at Kankesanturai on the rich coral limestone deposits of the Jaffna Peninsula, producing in most years some 80,000 tons of cement and employing 720 workers. A plywood factory, started by government during the war to make tea chests that were then almost unobtainable abroad, was reorganized after the war. Two hundred and eighty workers produce 225,000 chests, about 10 per cent of the national requirements. The total capitalized value of these and other government-built plants in 1956 was in the neighborhood of Rs. 92,000,000 and employed 1,603 workers, a ratio of roughly Rs. 57,000 per man employed.[40]

These industrial investments have absorbed valuable resources that might have been used in other ways. Nearly ten times as much capital was required per job opportunity than has been normally spent on settling a family on the land, for example. On the other hand, no doubt much managerial, technical, and other necessary skills have been learned and, at least in the field of cement and plywood, there seems every reason to expect that production will not only save foreign exchange but will be competitive as to cost and quality.

Exact data on industrial investment by private entrepreneurs is more difficult to obtain. No doubt a variety of consumer-goods industries on a small scale were undertaken during the decade of independence, though at a very moderate rate. Other industrial ventures by both the government and the private sector appear likely for the future.

38 Product in these industries from *Census of Industry*, Table 1.1. National Income from Central Bank, *Annual Report for 1954*, p. 27.

39 Preliminary analysis of 1953 census provided by the Department of Census and Statistics through the Department of Industry.

40 *Administration Report of the Director of Industries for 1956*, pp. 6-8.

III · COMMERCE, BANKING, AND FOREIGN TRADE

More important to the economy than industrial enterprises have been activities associated with foreign and domestic commerce, the professions, government, and domestic services. The International Bank for Reconstruction and Development estimated in 1952 that approximately 17 per cent of the gross national product was derived from factory and cottage industry, fisheries, and construction and government investment, while 24.5 per cent came from trade and transport, packing and shipping, finance, personal service, the professions, and government service. These proportions had not altered significantly by 1958.[41]

As in most countries in the area, the banking system is well developed for commercial and other short-term operations. These institutions, largely managed by non-Ceylonese, have tended to retain large liquid reserves in anticipation of probable fluctuations in the marketing conditions of the three export crops, which are the source of most of the funds held in these banks. They have been notably reluctant to invest in long-term activities apart from the traditional and relatively sure-return estate enterprises. Land titles are very uncertain, and banks are understandably reluctant to receive dubious titles as security in exchange for hard cash advances. There are few entrepreneurs willing to venture into new lines of business on the basis of carefully planned proposals. With a few exceptions, the personal savings of the wealthy do not go into new enterprises but are returned into land acquisition and estate activities. The lack of private capital for long-term investment in new lines and the cautious attitude of the commercial banks have led the government to take more initiative in investment enterprises than has been the tradition in certain Western countries. The government has established several banking and credit institutions of its own, notably the Bank of Ceylon, the Ceylon State Mortgage Bank, and more recently the Agricultural and Industrial Credit Corporation.

Apart from 1931 at the bottom of the Depression and 1947, when pent-up wartime demand led to heavy imports, and 1952-53 and 1957-58, Ceylon had a regular positive balance of trade. Although the average volume of her imports was one-third higher in 1948-50 than it was in 1926-30, a steady though somewhat smaller rate of

41 IBRD, p. 12, Table III.

growth in volume of exports sustained that positive trade balance.[42]

For such an economy, the terms of trade—or the amount of exports required to pay for a given amount of imports—will be just as important as the actual volume of goods exchanged. During World War II, there was a severe deterioration in Ceylon's terms of trade as export prices were held down by intergovernmental agreements, but the cost of necessary imports, especially equipment and food, rose sharply. According to official estimates, import costs rose threefold while export prices rose by only 90 per cent.[43] Since then, with the exception of 1952 and again in 1956 and 1957, the terms of trade have moved in a direction generally favorable to Ceylon.[44] In 1958 only an increased quantity of tea exports and a marked decline in the prices paid for indispensable imports prevented a serious balance of payments deficit.

The pattern of trade has been relatively simple. More than half of it has been with sterling area countries for many years and the remainder with other countries in the free world markets. The large rice imports normally come from Southeast Asia. Vehicles and other manufactured goods come from western Europe, America, or Japan; textiles from Japan and India. To purchase these necessities, Ceylon exports the bulk of her tea, rubber, coconut, and spice to western Europe and America. Though much publicized in recent years, since 1952 trade with Russia, eastern Europe, and China has been limited, apart from rubber shipments to China in exchange for rice.

Ceylon generally maintains a strongly positive balance of trade with Europe, America, Australia, and China, and is consistently in deficit to India, Burma, and Japan. She is thus dependent upon the familiar triangular pattern of world trade to balance her trade account. Invisibles are generally in deficit, because of dividend payments and repatriation to Britain of invested capital from the sale of estates and other holdings on the island, travel expenses of Ceylonese abroad, and immigrant remittances to India. Nevertheless, this deficit is usually more than made good by the positive trade account in most years.

In terms of foreign exchange, Ceylon has had a relatively favorable position over the past decade by comparison with her Asian

42 IBRD, p. 138. 43 IBRD, pp. 139-140.

44 Central Bank, *Annual Report for 1955*, Table 26. *Annual Report for 1957*, Table 29.

neighbors. As a result of her estate exports and the way the British financed their wartime purchases within the Commonwealth, Ceylon accumulated some Rs. 1,260 million worth of blocked sterling during World War II.[45] Between 1945 and 1949, heavy imports of capital goods and the satisfaction of pent-up wartime demand ran the balances down to Rs. 934 million. The boom in export commodities that accompanied the Korean War led to a new accumulation of near wartime levels in 1951. A serious deficit occurred in 1952 following the boom, when rubber prices broke sharply, but rice remained high. External assets rapidly declined from Rs. 1,185 to Rs. 836 million, a decline that continued until early 1954 when assets began to accumulate once more. Indeed, by the end of 1956, they were again at Rs. 1,179 million, though in 1957 they were down again to Rs. 950 million.[46] Inflationary movements have reduced the real value of these assets by perhaps one-half, so that the position is less satisfactory than the figures suggest. And in both 1956 and 1957, droughts and floods caused unexpectedly heavy imports of rice so that more foreign exchange was required than had been planned for, and less funds were available for development investment.

Thus, Ceylon's economy has been a virtual ideal type of plantation-export economy, in which three commercial crops are in a large part exported. Auxiliary trades and commercial exchange together with the export values account for over 60 per cent of the gross national product. In addition, a small-scale peasant agriculture for home consumption, cottage industries, handicraft work, and a few factories complete the broad picture.

IV · INCOME LEVELS, REVENUE, AND SAVINGS

A. INCOME

Like most small countries, whether they have been politically independent for centuries or only recently emerged from colonial status, Ceylon's economy is closely interwoven with the fabric of world trade. Thus involved in the world economy, Ceylon has been able to profit greatly from its unusual agricultural and climatic resources for producing high-return export products. Mainly because of this circumstance, the Ceylonese economy produces the

[45] IBRD, p. 144.

[46] Central Bank, *Annual Report of the Monetary Board to the Minister of Finance for 1958*, Chart 6.

highest per capita income of any Asian country apart from Japan. The gross national product per capita is nearly two and one-half times that of India's and Burma's.[47]

The distribution of real income compares favorably with India and all other countries in the area. Apart from Burma, contrasts between rich and poor are less sharp. Life expectancy is twice what the Indian can anticipate; there are six times as many hospital beds per thousand; many more schools and teachers per capita than in India. Transportation is relatively available. There are ten times as many vehicles and twenty times as many miles of road per capita as in India.

On the other hand, the incomes of the average Ceylonese are peculiarly dependent on the country's terms of trade which fluctuate sharply with the world marketing conditions for its three export crops and upon price movements for imported manufactured goods. Gross comparisons of one country with another are highly deceptive if they are used as a measure of contentment; but they demonstrate that in real terms the island's people are relatively well off in comparison to their fellow Asians. The casual visitor to Ceylon who knows Indian villages is surprised to note that many village huts have furniture. Medical practitioners, either indigenous or from the government service, are widely dispersed; the blue sign of the government midwife is a common sight. Large numbers of villagers are able to travel to Colombo for public fairs and religious or other occasions. Railroad stations in Ceylon are not the nightly shelter for thousands upon thousands of laborers that they are in India.

It is probably safe to say that, with the exception of the difficult years following the Great Depression and during World War II, the real income of most Ceylonese rose a certain degree each five-year period from 1900 to recent years.[48] More significant for political tranquillity, employment also expanded. Ambitious Ceylonese gradually moved into the management of coconut and rubber estates; the commercial sector expanded; and there was a relatively early replacement by educated Ceylonese of British officials in the public service. Opportunities for men of talent in professional fields offered further scope to the articulate and energetic.

[47] Ceylon's Gross National Product per capita has been calculated at $125 as compared to $59 per capita for India, $51 for Burma, and $49 for Pakistan.

[48] There were a few difficult years in the early 1930's, a malaria epidemic in 1934-35, and some months of dietary restriction during World War II.

There is still not enough statistical information for a definite conclusion about the recent years since World War II. One study published by the Central Bank of Ceylon reports that real income per capita, corrected for price changes, rose 25 per cent from 1947 to 1954. Closer analysis suggests that after a remarkable rise in 1949-50 and a further thrust in 1951, it has remained relatively stable for the succeeding years.[49] There is little statistical evidence to suggest that real incomes have risen since then. Indeed, it appears likely that any growth experienced in 1954 and 1955 was offset by a general decline in 1956 of about 7 per cent in the gross national product. The earlier unusual rise between 1947 and 1950 is presently partly discounted as the result of better statistics and may not reflect a genuine rise in real incomes.[50] As another economic specialist has reported, "Income per capita in recent years could only have been maintained constant."[51] In fact, the record for 1957 produced a net decline, although 1958 registered a slight per capita improvement over the two preceding years.

It would appear likely that at least the villagers who are not in debt—approximately 65 per cent of the rural population—are able to meet their obligations although savings are rare.[52] It is those who move to the towns and cities where cash returns are higher, but whose ambitions often outrun their incomes, who feel the pressure more sharply. As a reflection of the general income level, it is widely held that a man receiving Rs. 300 ($60.00) per month is already a "middle class" man. His way of life has been altered by his ambition for Western standards of clothing, housing, and transport. His Western clothes cost more. He prefers a cement house with a tiled roof and Western furniture. To commute to work, he must travel by bus or acquire a motor bike. If he is in government service and in the officer grade, he will hope to own a motor car. The schoolteacher's salary begins at about Rs. 150 per month and after five years may increase to Rs. 250 per month or approximately

[49] W. Rasaputram, "Gross National Product of Ceylon at Constant (1948) Prices," Central Bank of Ceylon, *Bulletin*, Vol. 6, No. 1 (January 1956), pp. 8-16, Table VIII.

[50] Central Bank, *Annual Report for 1956*, p. 27. A smaller decline was noted for 1957, *Annual Report for 1957*, p. 7.

[51] P. Wignaraja, "Some Relationships between Population Growth, Capital Formation, and Employment Opportunities," Central Bank of Ceylon, *Bulletin*, Vol. 6, No. 11 (November 1956), pp. 8-11, p. 8.

[52] Government of Ceylon, *Preliminary Report on the Economic Survey of Rural Ceylon 1950* (Sessional Paper XI—1951), p. 13. This compares very favorably with the pre-war figure of only 25 per cent debt-free families.

$52.00. Cost of living allowances supplement the salaries of those on the government payroll. The cost structure is different from America. Middle-class people can afford at least one servant. There is therefore much more leisure in the Ceylonese home than in the American. The work pace at the job is less demanding. Nevertheless, life for most of the public servants and middle class is never far from indebtedness; important savings are almost impracticable. It is therefore necessary to remember that while Ceylon's comparative position in South Asia is favorable, many Ceylonese, particularly those who are aware of how others live abroad, are conscious of being poor.

The unemployment picture is not clear. Employment exchanges registered 80,000 in 1956, a figure that passed 100,000 in 1958. But most observers consider this an understatement. Unemployment is said to be particularly prevalent among the Kandyan peasantry crowded into their restricted valleys, and among the educated youth from the expanded school system. The latter have been variously estimated at from 5,000 to 30,000.

B. REVENUE AND SAVINGS

Government revenue per capita has been at a relatively high level for Asian countries. It nearly doubled between 1945 and 1947 when progressive income taxes and export duties were raised and international marketing conditions for Ceylonese products improved. The government now disposes of nearly 25 per cent of the country's gross national product. Since 1946-47, revenue rose every year with the exceptions of 1952-54. It should be emphasized that this rapid revenue increase was not the result of a similarly rising production but was derived from increased tax rates and a generally buoyant world economy. It is therefore unwise to envisage a similar rise in the future. Since half of the revenue is from export or customs imposts and another 20 per cent comes from taxes on incomes and profits of the plantation industries, roughly 70 per cent of the government's revenue comes directly from export industries and foreign trade.

Savings and capital formation—in agriculture, commerce, or industry—have been high by South Asian standards. It has been estimated that the economy has been putting approximately 11 per cent of national income into gross capital formation.[53] Although

[53] W. Rasaputram, p. 11, averaged for five years, calculated in 1955.

investment at such a rate may be enough in an already developed economy to insure growing production and to provide increasing employment, in underdeveloped economies it is probably insufficient. It is precisely during the early developmental period that rates of investment must be higher. Heavy investments must be undertaken in such items as roads, ports, irrigation, power installations, training institutions, and other facilities that are not immediately productive. Technical experience, the knowledge of maintenance requirements, the skills and judgments requisite for effective management of new enterprises must all be learned, usually at the cost of a less effective outturn than a more developed economy would expect.[54] Dr. Wignaraja suggests that a rate of gross capital formation of at least 14-15 per cent is probably necessary (10 per cent net) if productivity is to expand rapidly enough to provide increased consumption levels and employment for the rapidly growing population. This is an increase of nearly 25 per cent over the 1956 rate of investment.[55]

Rapid rates of investment were maintained during the nineteenth century and up until the Great Depression by large-scale capital transfers from Western countries, largely Great Britain. In recent years, however, there has been a heavy net outflow of invested capital. Thus, foreign capital can no longer be expected to play the part it did before in developing Ceylon's productive enterprises.

Local rates of saving are currently insufficient. Raising the rate of domestic savings for investment presents real difficulties, for absolute income levels are low by non-Asian standards. Of the total population 95 per cent receives less than $630 per year. Highly progressive income taxes are levied on all income receivers who gross more than $1,000 annually, but less than 2 per cent of the island's income receivers have an income high enough to be taxed directly.[56] However, government loans have been subscribed to regularly. In 1952 expert outside opinion considered Ceylon's banking system to be in a strong financial position with unusually high liquid reserves in the commercial banks. These and relatively inactive funds held by insurance companies, provident funds, etc. could conceivably be available for productive investment, if sound opportunities were created.[57]

[54] W. W. Rostow and M. F. Millikan, *A Proposal* (New York, 1957), Ch. 5. For a more detailed analysis, see W. W. Rostow, "The Take-off into Self-Sustained Growth," *Economic Journal*, Vol. 66, No. 26 (March 1956), pp. 25-48.

[55] P. Wignaraja, p. 8.

[56] *Report of the Taxation Commission*, pp. 39 and 46.

[57] IBRD, p. 161.

Investment capital has been readily forthcoming when estate lands are up for sale. In the countryside, underemployment, unemployment, and extensive leisure between plantings suggest there are additional resources not being used to full advantage. Together, these and other resources, if fully mobilized, could raise the rate of investment.

In summary, although Ceylon's population has lived rather better than any other people in South or Southeast Asia, there are signs that after the initial improvement following independence, standards of consumption have leveled off. Earlier increases in national income per capita also seem to have ceased. Present rates of capital formation appear inadequate to induce a sufficient expansion of production, though all resources by no means have been tapped.

V · PERSPECTIVES ON DEVELOPMENT

There are many who conclude from these production and investment data that the economy is not expanding at a sufficiently rapid pace. They seriously question whether the present overwhelming emphasis on agricultural production is a satisfactory base for rapid expansion in the future. In the first place, nature sets rather clear limits to the future expansion of the agricultural section of the economy. Until about 1925, the area under cultivation on the island expanded more rapidly than the population. Since then there has been a contraction of land cultivated per capita.[58] This need not be a disability if new techniques can be absorbed at a rapid enough rate to increase agricultural production per capita, and if alternative employment openings in newer enterprises can be made available to the "surplus" agricultural population. In fact, production in both the estate and peasant agricultural sectors has improved per acre over the past decade, generally at a slightly faster rate than population growth, and no doubt further improvements can be registered. New land is still available in the dry zone. On the other hand, perhaps in as few as twenty-five years there will be no more new land.[59] More intensive methods and new crops will provide more men with agricultural work, but the limits here, too, are widely believed to be set by land area and water supply.

There are also social impediments. Land ownership and share-

[58] Oliver, p. 69, citing *Report of the Committee on Utilization of Crown Lands* (Sessional Paper III—1953), pp. 3, 7, 9.

[59] Farmer, pp. 340-341.

cropping practices impede the rice output. The plantation economy has raised to relative wealth a small class of large-scale estate operators who tend to hire for the coveted supervisory posts only their sons and nephews. On the other end of the scale, no educated man would think of taking to farming. Therefore, productive employment in new fields must be developed.

It is widely held that an agricultural economy is by that fact the creature of the more industrialized countries. The levels of world economic activity are decided elsewhere—in industrial countries. The agricultural countries inescapably have their prosperity and their slumps determined by other economies. In the past, political power has lain with the industrial countries, political weakness with the agricultural countries. This double weakness, then, renders an agricultural future a discouraging prospect.

The estate sector has many liabilities as the preponderant element in the economy. Its very weaknesses point to the necessity for diversification, and it is becoming more and more of a handicap to real Ceylonese interests. Estate crops, at least under present technology, can be grown economically only in the wet zone, where overcrowding is already very great and is becoming worse each year. No more land can be made available for tea and rubber except at the expense of coconut, rice, or village lands. Secondly, two of her three export commodities—coconut products and rubber—are not primarily for direct human consumption like wheat, meat, or dairy products, but are raw materials for industrial production. In the past, the demand for such industrial materials has shown greater fluctuations in the world market than the demand for direct consumption goods. In the event of a slump in the coconut and rubber markets, Ceylon has only one other major export product to depend on—tea.

Ceylon's plantation economy lacks a resiliency that other small countries have. For example, Denmark is a small country which exports her agricultural products. But she is industrialized at home and is the "dairy park" for Britain and Germany. Men require dairy products for breakfast, lunch, and supper even though they may forgo many manufactured goods when times are hard. Switzerland is another small country actively engaged in world trade, but she is an industrialized country that can switch fairly rapidly from one product, with a declining foreign demand, to another product for which the demand may be rising. By contrast, tea bushes may take five years to bear, a coconut or a rubber tree five to eight years. For a plantation to switch from one product to another is a costly process taking many years.

The future market conditions for estate products are uncertain. The rubber market is threatened by synthetics, which are becoming serious competitors in quality, use, and cost as modern industrial research and production techniques progress in the consuming countries. Demand for coconut products may decline further as synthetic detergents replace soap in the housewife's kitchen, and soya and other vegetable oils grown in consuming countries take the place of coconut oil. There is no substitute for tea in the United Kingdom and old Dominions; the tea market in Asia and Africa appears to grow with increasing cash income, and few can effectively compete with Ceylon's high-grown fine qualities. But new consumers are less discriminating and expansion in the African highlands in part with funds and skills drawn from estates in Ceylon as well as increasing output by other tea producers like India, Indonesia, and China may someday mean overproduction of tea and a decline in demand for Ceylon's quality product.

Depending thus upon three export crops to exchange for essential imports, the Ceylonese are vulnerable to adverse changes in the terms of trade over which they have no control. The island's share of these commodities in the world market and the quantities she purchases of import goods are so small that she cannot materially affect the prices of either her exports or her imports.[60] If she temporarily withholds tea from the world market, the position of India, Indonesia, China, Pakistan, and Central Africa is enhanced. Withholding rubber will favor Malaya and Indonesia; retaining coconuts will aid the Philippines and Indonesia.[61] Moreover, a country of 9,000,000 inhabitants cannot expect to influence the price of her imports by delaying purchases.[62]

Prices fetched by her exports and prices paid for necessary imports have fluctuated seriously as the shifts in her external assets suggest. This has had its repercussions on both domestic politics and foreign policy. The most dramatic instance in recent years occurred in the

60 *Six-Year Programme of Investment*, p. 236.

61 In recent years, Ceylon exported roughly one-third of total world tea supplies, coming second after India, roughly 10 per cent of world coconut and copra exports, coming after the Philippines and Indonesia, and 5 per cent of the world's natural rubber, coming after Malaya and Indonesia.

62 Perhaps only in the case of rice purchases under most unusual circumstances could Ceylon's buying policy influence the price of her purchases in the Burmese market.

rubber and rice markets after the Korean War. In 1950, before the war began, prices for rubber were in the neighborhood of Rs. 1.26 per pound. A year later they were running Rs. 3.00 per pound. The peak price of February 1951 broke abruptly. Within a matter of months, the price dropped by half to hover near Rs. 1.75 for the next year, and dollar earnings fell from Rs. 28.3 million in January to Rs. 5.9 million in April and Rs. 2.5 million in September.[63] Simultaneously, the price of Ceylon's principal imports, particularly rice, continued the war-induced rise. Whereas rubber dropped during 1951 by some 30 per cent, prices for rice rose by a similar amount. Supplies were fewer because of fighting in Indo-China and Korea, and Japan replaced its normal Korean purchases by buying in Burma and Thailand. Rice even became a dollar commodity briefly as United Nations authorities purchased rice for South Korean civilians and United Nations armies. Hence, rice took a significantly larger proportion of Ceylon's reduced foreign exchange precisely when income from rubber had rapidly declined.

The situation created a serious problem for the government, because in order to insulate the Ceylonese consumer from price changes in the world market, the government had subsidized the retail sale of rationed rice, maintaining a stable price at home regardless of the changes in price at which rice was purchased abroad. Efforts of the government to obtain American economic assistance or foreign rice at reasonable dollar prices were of little avail. Eventually, the government accepted a timely offer by the Chinese government to sell rice to Ceylon at lower than world prices and to buy her rubber at higher than world prices. This agreement eased Ceylon's import bill and strengthened her export income.[64] But it did not solve the government's financial problem, since increasingly heavy outlays were still necessary to meet the differences between the cost of rice imports and the established retail price. By 1952-53 food subsidies accounted for 20 per cent of government expenditure and at one point during the year, nearly one-third of the government's budget was being spent to subsidize the price of rice.[65] The consumer paid only one fourth of the landed cost.

[63] Central Bank of Ceylon, *Annual Report of the Monetary Board to the Minister of Finance for 1951*, p. 4. This abrupt decline in dollar earnings was in part the result of changed American stockpiling procedures, when all purchases were concentrated in the General Services Administration where Treasury views appear to have dominated long run political considerations.

[64] See Chapter x for a more detailed discussion.

[65] Central Bank of Ceylon, *Annual Report of the Monetary Board to the Minister of Finance for 1952*, p. 8.

In the spring of 1953, on the advice of the Central Bank, the subsidies were all but withdrawn and, consequently, the price of rice rose three times overnight. This was a serious disruption of the average housewife's food budget, representing nearly 20 per cent of her total expenditures.[66] A work stoppage called in protest by the Communist and noncommunist Left parties through their trade unions resulted in an almost complete tie-up of transportation and communications, loss of property, and rapidly growing public disorders. When police and army units were finally called out to restore order, ten people had been killed. The young Buddhist prime minister resigned shortly afterward and the Opposition obtained an issue of considerable importance for future partisan politics.

Thus, an unfortunate and sharp turn in Ceylon's trade conditions contributed directly to important political developments, and served to confirm in many people's minds the vulnerability of an economy dependent entirely on three export crops the prices of which fluctuate sharply on the world market.

As if there were not already enough arguments in favor of economic diversification, nationalist and Marxist views now merge to look upon the estate sector as both foreign and "exploitative." The estates were originally created on land "seized" from Ceylonese. In the past, it is held, taxes were spent and economic policies arranged to favor the estates and restrict the development of Ceylon's economy. Analysis of the earnings of the most profitable half of companies registered in Britain for estate operations in Ceylon, shows an annual return averaging 13-25 per cent over many years. During certain years, for most of these companies profit returns were considerably higher.[67] Not only Marxist Ceylonese consider these profits to have been a form of exploitation. Dividend payments and capital withdrawals remitted primarily back to Britain leave important economic decisions in the hands of foreigners and divert resources that could otherwise be used for Ceylon's own economic development. The large numbers of foreign workers, who dominate the job opportunities in the tea estates and related commercial enterprises, are now felt to deprive Ceylonese of similar opportunities.[68]

Hence, for a variety of reasons, economic diversification—in both

[66] Central Bank of Ceylon, *Survey of Ceylon's Consumer Finances* (Colombo, 1954).

[67] Fred J. Rippy, "Trinidad and Ceylon, Two Profitable British Crown Colonies," in L. W. Shannon, *Underdeveloped Areas* (New York, 1957), pp. 247-252.

[68] See Oliver, pp. 14-20, for a detailed discussion of the "exploitation" point of view.

agricultural and industrial directions—is judged imperative. Thus far, government policy has emphasized the agricultural sector of the economy, extending the area of land producing food crops for home consumption and improving yields on land already cultivated. If Ceylon can produce more of her own food, her dependence upon food imports will be that much lessened. Performance in both the estate and subsistence sectors can be improved, particularly in the latter. More intensive methods could absorb more workers. There are many other possible agricultural products that have not yet been given due attention.

There is a growing conviction on the part of many articulate Ceylonese that no matter what is done within the agricultural sector, only industrialization will provide work opportunities for the rapidly growing population. If carried far enough, it could perhaps provide the basis for a self-sustaining, expanding economy that would go beyond the limits set by nature and by world technological and marketing conditions on which the prosperity of the agricultural economy is so directly dependent.[69]

Creating an important industrial sector in tropical Ceylon presents some difficult problems. National income per capita is already so low that heavy investment at an accelerated pace will be hard. Industry requires skilled labor; skilled labor requires training. It is the rare exception among local entrepreneurs to prefer industrial venture to the easier, quick-return, and already established commercial activity or the more secure, profitable, and higher status-giving estate sector. If industrial activity is to be undertaken on any scale, many believe government-sponsored and initiated enterprises must set the pace. However, early experiments with government-managed projects have not been encouraging. Ceylon's domestic market for any one industrial commodity is bound to be limited even though the sum of her industrial imports already makes an important total. Ceylonese labor seems to prefer the slow pace and informal time discipline of the agricultural to the speed of the industrial society. At the end of the first decade of independence the Ceylonese economy had not yet been materially changed from the pattern inherited at independence.

[69] The case *for* industrialization is well set out in the National Planning Council, *First Interim Report*, pp. 165-186. Selected aspects of Economic Development are discussed in Chapter VIII below.

The central economic problem facing the Ceylonese government is how to diversify the economy and, at the same time, increase productivity. Diversification would free the country from its very heavy dependence upon three estate crops whose prices fluctuate widely on the world market and whose future is uncertain. The easiest, and politically and socially least disruptive way of achieving this objective, is to reduce Ceylon's import bill, perhaps by one half or more, by increasing the local production of food. Expanding the peasant sector or producing food crops under large, estate-like agricultural enterprises are possibilities. Although the full limit of arable land has not yet been reached, there is little conviction that even intensive agriculture could absorb the large numbers of new entrants into the labor market each year. The cost of homegrown products will probably be higher in most years than that of imported products from low-cost areas, like Burma. An alternative or additional method of diversification is to introduce and develop an industrial sector on the island to produce goods for local consumption or even for export. Such a development appeals to the educated class, which sees in it a permanent means of providing for the growing population; maintaining political independence; developing a modern economic structure; and expanding opportunities for itself as the staffs and managers of the new enterprises. Whether the mass of the population shares this vision is doubtful, and many social customs will have to be altered. Such an industrial development is likely to raise the cost of home-produced articles above that of goods from Japan, Hong Kong, or Western countries. But these considerations are outweighed by the possible benefits of industrialization.

There are, thus, a series of intricate decisions facing the island's statesmen in their efforts to diversify the economy, raise productivity, improve standards of living, open new opportunities to the educated, and free Ceylon from her dependence on three commodities in the fluctuating world market. These multiple objectives are not entirely compatible with each other. The problem of statesmanship is to find the proper balance between them and to discover those policies that will improve production in the old fields and extend it in new directions.

CHAPTER IV · CONSTITUTIONAL EVOLUTION

A COMMONWEALTH IDEAL TYPE

"The Constitutional lawyer . . . creates the legal framework for the establishment of institutions, but the institutions consist of men and women: not only the men and women who rule but also the men and women who are ruled."—Sir Ivor Jennings, *The Approach to Self-Government*

I · INTRODUCTION

CEYLON'S present governmental institutions have little in common with the island's indigenous traditions. Formerly, monarchs received their legitimate right to rule by royal descent or seized it by military usurpation. Contemporary governments since 1931 have been elected by universal suffrage. The monarchs managed their affairs with the counsel of priestly and princely advisers, and administered the nation through a network of feudal subordinates whose functions were largely defined by heredity or monarchical reward, leaving ample, though by no means unlimited, scope for whim and individual pleasure. Today, a cabinet, subject to dismissal by a popularly elected parliament, makes ultimate decisions in consultation within itself, with its professional civil servants, who are appointed after competitive examinations, and with spokesmen of different interests within the electorate. Regulations and law restrict the area of whim and pleasure within narrow bounds. Rarely did the monarch command an island-wide regime; in more recent times the central government has been able to rule throughout the island.[1]

These new institutions evolved during more than a century of British tutelage. Though the early innovations were arbitrarily applied by the colonial government, the later constitutional changes

[1] Characteristics of the old regime from S. Namasivayam, *The Legislatures of Ceylon 1928-1948* (London, 1950), pp. 169-170. For a detailed and authoritative description of the traditional system, R. Pieris, *Sinhalese Social Organization*, Part I.

were the outcome of consultations between Whitehall's officials and those relatively Westernized Ceylonese who were themselves conversant with British governmental institutions. Their task, then, was to operate these institutions within a social system and a set of cultural values wholly different from nineteenth- and twentieth-century Britain.

It was easier to define by constitutional commission the form of government than to evolve supporting institutions such as inclusive political parties or functional groups. As the intermediaries between the ambitions of specific groups within the wider, non-Westernized population, and the parliament, these supporting institutions naturally reflected more closely the cultural peculiarity and original genius of the population and were less like their British counterparts.

In this chapter, successive stages in the metamorphosis from a crown colony to fully independent status, from despotic control by officials to control by popularly elected representatives, will be described and the present constitution outlined. Political leaders, their parties and party programs will be discussed. Emerging interest groups and the Ceylonese press will be analyzed.

II · CONSTITUTIONAL DEVELOPMENT

A. THE INDEPENDENCE STRUGGLE

In the countries of South Asia, a fundamental element in the background of contemporary politics and political institutions is the nature of each country's independence "struggle." Events in Indonesia are still marked by the important role played by the army in the violent combat against the Dutch. In India, the organization of the Congress party, the position of its leaders, and their ability to command support derive in part from the way their independence struggle was organized. Ceylon is a classic example of independence and constitutional reform achieved step by step, almost entirely by constitutional means. This was a great advantage to the country in most respects, but it had one liability. Without a stern repression of either masses or leaders, there was no hardening or tempering of national solidarity in the crucible of a common and dangerous cause.

The only semblance of a mass organization found its base not in direct political agitation, but indirectly in a cultural and religious renaissance of the Buddhist religion and the temperance movement in the early decades of the twentieth century. At the time of the prohibition movement in the United States, the evils of alcohol were also widely argued in Ceylon. The temperance movement had a double use. To reiterate Buddhist advice against alcohol was to assert anew the validity and relevance of Buddhist values after years of acquiescence to the ruler's foreign values. On the political plane, the temperance movement represented a way of attacking important sources of British revenue. Although a systematically promoted boycott, like the Swadeshi or Salt March campaigns of the Indian Congress Party, was not organized, nevertheless, the lay leaders of the movement had become prominent enough as popular figures to be arrested in 1915 following the religious riots.

In 1915 Muslims and Buddhists came to blows over Buddhist religious rites that intruded drumming music on the silence of a newly established Muslim mosque. The flash of furious crowds was misinterpreted by British administrators as anti-British riots. This was during some of the most serious days of World War I, when developments in the Muslim Middle East were of prime importance. The Buddhist leaders were believed to have fomented the riots for the purpose of embarrassing the hard-pressed British, and they were promptly jailed. The government undoubtedly exaggerated the gravity of the situation; vigilante parties of nervous planters patrolled sections of the island and a number of innocent Sinhalese were executed without trial. The Buddhist leaders had had nothing to do with the riots and it was a leading Tamil Hindu who explained their innocence to the British. However, this experience brought a group of Ceylonese leaders into island-wide prominence, among them Mr. D. S. Senanayake, who later became the first prime minister of independent Ceylon.

This violent encounter between the Ceylonese and British was unusual. Nothing like it had occurred since 1848, and, shortly after the release of the Sinhalese Buddhist leaders, the tenor of peaceful negotiation was resumed. When political independence was fully achieved in 1948, few really believed that it had come or that they had contributed toward it. On the Ceylonese side, the achievement was the work of a small coterie of influential men, who had also engineered the constitutional reforms and earlier steps toward the devolution of power that had preceded it. Popular identification with a country-wide struggle for independence was lacking and a national consciousness transcending communal differences had not been created in the process.

B. SUCCESSIVE CONSTITUTIONAL DEVELOPMENTS BEFORE 1931

The transformation from a colonial, authoritarian regime to that of a parliament, elected by universal franchise and directed by a cabinet of responsible ministers, was a development of many decades. As early as 1833 a Legislative Council was established, chiefly as a result of agitation by the European business community. Its membership was set up to give the government officials, who sat in the council, a decisive majority over those British businessmen or Ceylonese private individuals who were "nominated," i.e., appointed, by the Governor. The latter were chosen as representatives of specific ethnic and special-interest groups.[2] This Legislative Council was little more than an advisory body to an Executive Council presided over by the chief officials of the government. Despite the notable economic changes that took place during the nineteenth century, these arrangements remained virtually unaltered until 1912.

The elective principle in island-wide affairs was accepted for the first time in 1912, when the franchise was opened to the Ceylonese who had received an education along European lines—roughly 4 per cent of the population. The new council had 21 members, the officials still forming a majority. Six were nominated to represent ethnic groups,[3] and four were elected to fill one European urban, one European rural, one Burgher, and one "educated Ceylonese" seat. In both these Legislative Councils, the different linguistic or ethnic communities were explicitly and separately represented. In 1912 for the first time, a member of the Karava community was given the second Sinhalese seat; and Sir Ponnambalam Ramanathan, a Tamil, was elected by the "educated Ceylonese" as their representative, with the result that Sinhalese and Tamils were equally represented.

World War I augmented nationalist agitation. The severe repression of the 1915 religious riots created a greater will for consti-

2 Reflecting the developments in the social order described in Chapter 1, the nominated Burgher was a Proctor in the Supreme Court, the Sinhalese was Chief Interpreter for the Supreme Court and the Tamil member was also an interpreter. Three other nominated members were British merchants. In 1889 a Kandyan Sinhalese and a Moor were nominated. G. C. Mendis, *Ceylon Under the British*, 3rd ed. (Colombo, 1952), pp. 75, 125.

3 One Kandyan Sinhalese, one Muslim, two Low-country Sinhalese, and two Tamils. *Ibid.*, p. 172.

tutional reform. What had been a restricted Westernized middle-class movement gained a limited degree of popular backing from those Sinhalese Buddhists who were becoming confident and active in Ceylonese affairs, even though they did not have the Westernized education of the small upper middle class. Events in India at the time also helped to set a faster pace. The proposed Montagu-Chelmsford reforms, in response to wartime agitation in India, strengthened the hands of the Ceylonese reformists. Meanwhile the Ceylon Reform League had been established in 1917 and was expanded further through the creation of the Ceylon National Congress in 1919. Tamil leaders, like Sir Ponnambalam Arunachalam, joined with such low-country Sinhalese as Sir James Peiris, Sir D. B. Jayatilaka, D. S. Senanayake, F. R. Senanayake, and members of other communities in appealing to the British for further reforms. The changes of 1920 were the result.

In the 1920 Constitution, the Legislative Council was expanded to a membership of 37, improving the position of elected members but not yet giving them a majority which remained in the hands of the government officials and nominated members.[4]

As a group the elected representatives grew in influence, but the position of the minority representatives among them became weaker. Before 1920, the Tamils had occupied as many seats as the Sinhalese, but in that year they filled only 3 seats and the Sinhalese 13. The Tamils broke from the Ceylon National Congress on the grounds that the Sinhalese had accepted an arrangement from the British that excluded a seat reserved for the Tamils in the Western Province, despite a private promise by two leading Sinhalese to the contrary before the negotiations began. The Tamils had asked for two-thirds as many seats as the Sinhalese but received less than half that many. The Sinhalese, in turn, criticized the new constitution on the grounds that it maintained representation by communities instead of the modern, Western system of representation on a territorial basis.

Future difficulties between the two main communities were inevitable. Territorial representation might be a sound principle of democratic representative practice in preference to the more divisive representation by communities; but the less numerous Tamils, as well as the Burghers and Muslims, found their political strength gradually diminished as communal representation fell into disfavor.

[4] *Ibid.*, p. 177.

The minority communities were apprehensive of the Sinhalese majority. Accordingly, they urged constitutional reforms with less vigor than the majority community. Indeed, periodically, they found themselves appearing to prefer a continuation of communal representation under British aegis to a grant of full independence with a constitution based on a wide territorial franchise. From the Sinhalese point of view, the minorities were an obstruction to independence—an obstruction which the British, with their preference for "defending minority rights," were all too ready to use as an excuse for retaining indefinite control. Continued traditional differences and the advantages British rule had brought discouraged united resistance to Great Britain.[5]

The 1920 Constitution was revised in 1923, giving still greater strength to the elected members, who now had a majority in the Legislative Council; but responsibility for governing still remained in the hands of the government officials. The elected members were thus able to criticize the government with no risk of having to hold office themselves or to put the substance of their criticisms into an effective governmental policy.[6] This was the last constitution which contained provisions for communal representation, a strictly limited

[5] G. C. Mendis summarized the political position underlying constitutional reform before the introduction of the Donoughmore Constitution in 1931:

"[The British Governor] Manning was certainly correct when he declared that social divisions in Ceylon were communal. There was little intermarriage between the various races and castes and they formed more or less separate entities. In recent times racial cleavages had been accentuated further owing to the cultural revival. Besides the various communities had not all attained to the same stage of development at the time of the British occupation, and little had been done since then to develop and educate the more backward, with the result that only those communities who were at an advantage owing to their social and economic position were able to turn to good account the new opportunities afforded by the Government. The Kandyans and the Muslims suffered chiefly because they had not had the same opportunity for education as the Low-country Sinhalese and the Tamils. The Tamils living in the Dry Zone could not benefit directly by the economic change that resulted from the establishment of the plantations, and depended on employment in the government services for their advancement. At this time openings for employment outside Ceylon in further India began to be closed to them, and in the face of competition from the Low-country Sinhalese they naturally began to be alarmed for their future. Therefore the Muslims and the Kandyans began to develop a greater sense of group solidarity in order to struggle for a share of the place and power secured by the more advanced communities, while the Tamils and the Burghers did likewise to retain the position they had already attained. During the reform debate, which was really a scramble for power, the Tamils and the minorities usually combined against the Sinhalese; and when the Sinhalese and the Tamils united, the minorities joined hands with the officials against them." *Ceylon under the British*, pp. 182-183.

[6] Government of Ceylon, *Report of the Special Commission on the Ceylon Constitution* (Colombo, 1928), pp. 18-21.

franchise, and the Legislative Council. The Donoughmore Constitution of 1931 which replaced the 1923 arrangements marked a revolutionary break with all of the earlier constitutions. It provided the immediate background for the present institutions of government.

C. THE DONOUGHMORE CONSTITUTION, 1931

The royal commissioners who visited Ceylon in 1927-28 examined the electoral system with a view to establishing sound principles of representation. They observed the diversity of the population. "Not only is the population not homogeneous, but the diverse elements of which it is composed distrust and suspect each other. It is almost true to say that the conception of patriotism in Ceylon is as much racial as national and that the best interests of the country are at times regarded as synonymous with the welfare of a particular section of its people."[7]

The commissioners expressed the belief that it was the majority community which sought to eliminate those representative devices which the minorities considered to be their chief safeguards. Nevertheless, despite the Tamil and other minorities' preference for continued communal representation, they rejected such a principle. "We have come unhesitatingly to the conclusion," they wrote, "that communal representation is, as it were, a canker on the body politic, eating deeper and deeper into the vital energies of the people, breeding self-interest, suspicion and animosity, poisoning the new growth of political consciousness and effectively preventing the development of a national or corporate spirit. . . . There can be no hope of binding together the diverse elements of the population in a realization of their common kinship and an acknowledgment of common obligations to the country of which they are all citizens so long as the system of communal representation, with all its disintegrating influences, remains a distinctive feature of the constitution."[8] They therefore recommended that communal electorates be abolished and that territorial constituencies be used instead. In order to allay the fears of the minorities, however, they recommended that the number of elected seats be raised to sixty-five and that twelve members be nominated to speak for interests otherwise unrepresented.[9]

[7] *Ibid.*, p. 31. [8] *Ibid.*, p. 39.

[9] These numbers were reduced by the Secretary of State for the Colonies in London to 50 elected members and 8 nominated members, thus reducing significantly the minority representatives. Namasivayam, pp. 59-60. These arrangements closely parallel

The commissioners then examined the franchise problem. They found that although the spokesmen of political reform urged that full responsible government be passed to the Ceylonese, many of the island's leaders were not yet prepared to accept the implications of political equality. "The various social strata have been for so long definitely marked off, the transition from the lower to the higher has been practically impossible, and no one has questioned the supreme right of one or a few to dominate the lives of the multitude."[10] They argued that a broad extension of the franchise would induce Ceylonese leaders to listen more sensitively to the needs of the populace, especially the industrial workers and the agricultural laborers. They recommended universal adult franchise for all men over 21 and women over 30, a proposal amended by the Secretary of State Lord Passfield (Sidney Webb) to allow women also to vote at 21. The only restriction pertained to residence—a restriction necessitated by the large number of estate workers of Indian origin, many of whom came and went as virtual migrant labor. For the first time an Asian country was to have universal suffrage without income, property, literacy, or sex qualifications.

Finally, they examined the nature and powers of the representative institutions to be established. Because there were no effective political parties, a parliamentary system along British lines would only sharpen communal or other divisions and would be inimical to the best interests of Ceylon. They therefore recommended the creation of a State Council to replace the old legislative councils of the previous constitutions. It was to have 65 members elected on a *territorial* basis, 3 nonvoting government officials, and up to 12 nominated to represent otherwise unrepresented groups.[11]

The State Council had both legislative and executive functions. Three government departments remained under the direct control of colonial office officials, who could debate but had no vote. Other government departments were divided among seven standing Executive Committees made up of the other members of the State Council. These Executive Committees had the power to direct the different departments under their charge, and each committee elected its chairman who controlled a number of government departments. The

those in the Montagu-Chelmsford proposals, where the case against communal and interest group representation was made in greater detail. Cmd. 9109, 1918, pp. 185-90.

10 *Report of the Special Commission on the Ceylon Constitution*, p. 83.

11 Later reduced to 61 members by the Secretary of State for the Colonies.

three colonial office officers, or "official members," and seven ministers together formed a Board of Ministers, roughly equivalent to a "cabinet."

Reserved to the three official members were such powers as the management of the public service, defense and foreign affairs, the administration of justice and legal matters, and the handling of revenue and supervision of departmental expenditures. All other powers were transferred to the Executive Committees.[12] At the same time, in view of the sweeping changes proposed, the governor was given wide powers to veto the decisions of the council, although he was not normally expected to exercise them.[13] Certain financial reservations were also retained by the governor, but significant financial and revenue powers were placed in the hands of the proposed Ceylonese legislature. Members of the State Council, as members of the different Executive Committees, were responsible for preparing annual and supplementary budgets for each department. These estimates were then to be considered by the Board of Ministers and, if accepted, they were to be sent on to the State Council for approval, amendment, or rejection.

When the Donoughmore Constitution was originally debated in the Legislative Council it was ratified by a margin of only two votes; the Tamil and other minority representatives and one Sinhalese voted against it. For its duration until 1946, the Donoughmore Constitution was the object of vigorous and unremitting criticism.[14] The powers of the governor rendered the reforms less than full independence. The new institutions were cumbersome and represented another example of divide and rule. In addition, the executive committee system impeded the development of party solidarity. Each Minister had his own immediate political "constituency" in his committee members; and each committee member had his special responsibilities to his "constituency of friends." There was every incentive to take advantage of the government revenue and virtually no inducement to think except in the most parochial terms. The govern-

[12] For instance, powers over the police, agriculture, education, local government, public health and sanitation, public works, ports and railways, posts and telegraph were all transferred.

[13] *Report of the Special Commission on the Ceylon Constitution*, p. 54.

[14] It is beyond our scope to attempt a detailed evaluation of this unusual expedient in colonial constitutions. Two comprehensive studies have already been published on the question. The more detailed is by I. D. S. Weerawardana, *Government and Politics in Ceylon (1931-1946)* (Colombo, 1951). The more conceptualized is S. Namasivayam, *op.cit.*

ment was ineffective, lacked action, and was unable to coordinate a government-wide program. The annual budget—the only measure for which the Board of Ministers was collectively responsible—proved inadequate for the task of integrating the projects of each minister and his committee.[15]

Certain characteristics inherent in the American governmental system parallel those in the Donoughmore plan. American congressional committees have wide powers over public policy and the detailed routine of departments as the Executive Committees had in Ceylon. Details are often the congressman's principal means of grasping the complex matters upon which he is passing judgment. His party is more like a shifting set of coalitions that alter with the issues than the disciplined British party. Since his term is fixed regardless of how many of the administration's measures are rejected, no fear of an early election need chasten his criticism. In contrast to the Donoughmore scheme, however, the American political system has a powerful office at its center—the Presidency. If the chief executive uses the conventional powers at his disposal, he can, under most circumstances, enlist enough support to approximate cabinet rule. But the Ceylonese system lacked a strong Ceylonese executive as well as the elements of government that give strength and direction to British institutions. As Governor Caldecott put it in his famous reforms dispatch of 1938, there was "no determining, coordinating, eliminating, controlling or designing force behind the administrative machine. Everything depends upon bargaining and compromise. As a result, there can be no fixation and concentration, either of policy or of responsibility."[16]

Constitutions set limits to what men can do; the range of possible accomplishment within them varies widely. The manner in which the Donoughmore Constitution was operated by the Ceylonese politicians and British officials from 1931 up through World War II belies Caldecott's severe strictures. The public service became thoroughly Ceylonized. The poor social conditions that had prompted the commissioners to urge universal franchise improved markedly. Federal aid for education, health, unemployment, and relief increased rapidly. Government allocations for schools more than trebled during the period; the number of schools doubled; and

[15] For evaluations of the Donoughmore Constitution, see Weerawardana, *ibid.*, Ch. XI; Namasivayam, Chapter VI.

[16] Sessional Paper XXVIII—1938, pp. 5, 6.

medical allocations rose by 30 per cent. Comprehensive measures of social and industrial legislation related to trade unions, workmen's compensation, maternity benefits, etc. were also passed.[17]

The Donoughmore Constitution had mixed results in the distribution of communal power. The minorities had proportionately fewer representatives than under previous constitutions. On the other hand, through the Executive Committee system, power within each committee was diffused enough for the members of even the minority communities to gain their share of the "pork" for their constituencies.[18] One development that the minorities have not forgotten was the all-Sinhalese Cabinet of 1936 from which the minorities were excluded; and not until 1942 were any Tamils again admitted into the ministry. The Sinhalese justify the all-Sinhalese Cabinet on several grounds. They consider the Tamils had only themselves to blame, since they were not originally enthusiastic about the Donoughmore Constitution, and Tamil politicians in the north had boycotted the first elections. Sinhalese politicians also believed, if further reforms were to be pressed at that time, a cabinet of like-minded men would be more likely to reach the unanimity the British required than a ministry reflecting divergent constitutional views.[19] Subsequent political campaigners have frequently referred to this Pan-Sinhalese Cabinet as an example of the Sinhalese ambition to dominate the minorities. On the other hand, it is also clear that many significant problems were solved on a noncommunal basis.[20]

The Donoughmore Constitution provided the framework within which the agitation for constitutional reforms was carried on; resolutions were passed and protests made through the State Council. During the critical war years, the civil affairs of the country were almost exclusively in the hands of Ceylonese ministers. Such intricate and easily corruptible matters as food collection and distribution were handled efficiently. Rubber and coconut exports were government regulated. Important policy decisions were reached through the prescribed constitutional procedures; deadlock was effectively avoided. By the time the war was over and constitutional reform

17 Namasivayam, pp. 112-113.

18 *Ibid.*, p. 114; Weerawardana, *op.cit.*, p. 172.

19 In 1934 a Muslim and an Indian who were in the Ministry disagreed with the Sinhalese majority in the Cabinet on constitutional matters. Jennings, *The Commonwealth in Asia*, p. 72; Sydney D. Bailey, *Ceylon* (London, 1952), p. 147.

20 Namasivayam, who has made the calmest study of the communal implications of the Donoughmore Constitution, concluded that communalism did not increase during the period of its operation, pp. 64-68.

was again on the agenda, Ceylon had a large number of experienced parliamentarians and ministers, well versed in the practice of government. The committee system had given hardworking backbenchers ample opportunities for useful service and to build independent political careers not normally available under a strict party system. A constitutional arrangement that permitted so much was far from the "proved failure" Governor Stubbs had called it. Indeed, in view of all that was accomplished during the period, and the consolidation in practice of both universal franchise and territorial constituencies, it is fairer to call it a marked success. The customs and methods developed under its aegis have persisted and help explain many of the characteristics of politics today.

III · THE PRESENT CONSTITUTION

A. THE SOULBURY CONSTITUTION AND THE ATTAINMENT OF INDEPENDENCE[21]

Early in World War II the Ceylonese protested the vague British promises for constitutional reform, and in 1943 the British government declared that the postwar examination of constitutional reforms would be directed toward the "grant to Ceylon . . . of full, responsible government under the Crown in all matters of internal civil administration." Defense and external affairs and certain classes of bills, however, were to remain reserved to the governor. The Ceylonese Board of Ministers was invited to draft a plan which, if approved by three-quarters of the members of the State Council, would be examined by a suitable commission or conference after the war.

Accordingly, the ministers formulated a draft which, in its fundamentals, formed the base for the present constitution. The executive committee system had been thoroughly discredited in the eyes of the public and the politicians. Indeed, anything differing from the parliamentary cabinet system patterned on Westminster was *ipso facto* less than full home rule and felt by the Ceylonese to be "derogatory to their status as fellow citizens of the British Commonwealth. . . ."[22] Only the Westminster model would do, even though

[21] There is no benefit in discussing in detail the development and final passage of the present constitution; more competent analyses have been given by those actually engaged in the drafting process. See particularly Sir Ivor Jennings' numerous writings on the subject. Most detailed is his *The Constitution of Ceylon*, 3rd ed. (London, 1953); also his more succinct, interpretive essay in *The Commonwealth in Asia*, Ch. VI.

[22] Colonial Office: *Ceylon: Report of the Commission on Constitutional Reform*, Cmd. 6677 (London, 1945), para. 412.

there were important elements of minority opinion who had their doubts.

The ministers' proposed constitution was put forward in 1944 and the British sent the Soulbury Commission to Ceylon to study the draft and consult with other interests on the island not represented on the Board of Ministers. Due to a misunderstanding, the Ceylonese ministers considered such a commission an impairment of their own powers and officially boycotted its investigations.[23] Nevertheless, the island cooperated and the conferences with the minorities and other interests served to insure that all relevant groups were given a hearing.[24]

Among the electoral schemes submitted to the Soulbury Commission, was a proposal that the Sinhalese should receive half the seats in the proposed House of Representatives and the minorities—Indian Tamils, Ceylon Tamils, Burghers, Muslims, and Europeans—should control the other half. Thus no one community could dominate the others. This proposal—known as the "fifty-fifty" scheme—was urged on the "principle of non-domination," one which, it was argued, had long been recognized in India and Ceylon. It became a symbol to the Sinhalese of the vaulting ambitions of the Tamils, although its original significance has become misrepresented in recent years. The main objection to the "fifty-fifty" scheme was that it was "communal representation" under another name.[25]

As Sir Ivor Jennings described the problem of representation: "It was impossible not to recognize that most of the communal groups wanted to be represented by members of those groups. The Ministers did not want Tamils, Muslims, and Indians to be elected as such, but they recognized the need for sufficient numbers of Tamils, Muslims, and Indians to be elected. They were prepared for any compromise which gave the minorities adequate, or more than adequate, representation, provided that they were elected as representatives of the people and not as communal representatives."[26] The solution to the problem was an ingenious delimitation formula that took into account area as well as population. Thus one seat assigned to a population of 75,000 and one seat for every 1000 square miles gave the

[23] Namasivayam gives a detailed discussion of the difficulty, p. 124.

[24] Cmd. 6677, pp. 90-91. Namasivayam, p. 125.

[25] Bailey, p. 149; the case for it was ably argued by Mr. G. G. Ponnambalam in his *Presidential Address, First Plenary Session*, The All-Ceylon Tamil Congress, November 27, 1944. The Soulbury Commission's evaluation, Cmd. 6677, para. 254-264.

[26] Jennings, *The Commonwealth in Asia*, pp. 75, 76.

Muslim and Tamil minorities, living in the scattered communities of the dry zone, a higher number of seats than they would receive on the basis of population alone. In the Legislative Council before 1931, the Ceylon Tamils were represented in the ratio of 1:2 in relation to the Sinhalese. The Donoughmore Constitution gave them representation in the ratio of 1:5. The new proposals were expected to yield for the minorities 37 seats out of 95 elected representatives, giving all minorities representation of 1:3 Sinhalese.[27]

In its report in 1945 the Soulbury Commission accepted the essentials of the proposals put forward by the Ceylonese ministers. Its central recommendations were as follows: (1) universal franchise was to be retained; (2) representation would be on a territorial basis; communal electorates were not restored, but the proposals called for a delimitation of electorates that would help the minorities secure more seats; (3) a governor general would have full powers relating to external affairs, defense, and certain other matters explicitly reserved to him and Westminster; (4) a cabinet of ministers presided over by one of its members—the prime minister—would be responsible to an elected legislature; (5) ninety-five elected members and six representatives of special groups, would form the House of Representatives with full powers in all domestic matters, including finance; (6) The Soulbury Commissioners added a second chamber—a senate —to be filled by fifteen members elected by the house of representatives and fifteen members nominated by the governor general.[28]

After lengthy debate, the Ceylon State Council overwhelmingly accepted the commission's proposals and the Soulbury Constitution came into effect in May 1946. Ceylon thereby gained a government modeled on cabinet rule with full and responsible self-government in all matters of civil internal administration; only defense, external affairs, and a limited power to reserve certain types of bills were retained by the United Kingdom.[29]

As independence for India and Pakistan approached in 1947, it

[27] Cmd. 6677, para. 270. In fact, in the 1947 elections the minorities acquired 27 seats, 13 going to the Ceylon Tamils, 7 to the Indian Tamils, 6 to the Muslims, and 1 Burgher. This gave the Ceylon Tamils 1 representative to 4 Sinhalese and the Indian Tamils 1 to 10 Sinhalese. These were fewer than the Soulbury Commission anticipated but matched closely the estimates contained in *The Report of the First Delimitation Commission* (Sessional Paper XIII—1946), para. 70.

[28] The Ceylon Ministers considered the Second Chamber too controversial and unlikely to win approval of the necessary 75 per cent of the State Councilors. Bailey, p. 150; Cmd. 6677, Chapter XIV.

[29] Cmd. 6677, Chap. XVII and Namasivayam, p. 132.

was impossible for Britain to withhold similar rights from Ceylon. Ceylon, after all, had sought reforms and independence by constitutional methods in sharp contrast to the civil disobedience and mass campaigns in India. She had also loyally mobilized all her energies during World War II to help the Allies. And in the world of states, Great Britain and other colonial powers had agreed to assist their colonial peoples to attain self-government. In June 1947, the Secretary of State for the Colonies announced that Ceylon should be given responsible status within the British Commonwealth as soon as the necessary agreements had been concluded. Although this signified the achievement of dominion status, the term was not used for to some it implied continued overlordship.[80] Ceylon's leaders, like the Indian and Pakistani, preferred to remain within the Commonwealth, and agreements on foreign affairs, defense, and civil service matters were duly signed in November 1947. The Ceylon Independence Act of 1947 extended to Ceylon the provisions of the Statute of Westminster, conferring on the Colombo parliament full legislative powers and depriving the United Kingdom of all powers and responsibility for Ceylon's affairs.

B. THE 1948 CONSTITUTION

The 1948 Constitution was not a new creation, for the conventions of British cabinet government had been defined in detail by the terms of the Soulbury Constitution, which was in turn based on the Ceylonese ministers' draft of 1944. The "new" constitution of 1948 was not new at all; only a few, though fundamental, substitutions and special agreements relating to particular affairs were added on to what had been. Instead of marking a radical break with the past, the achievement of independence represented a culminating step toward full representative and responsible instruments of government. The first Legislative Council in 1833 took nonofficials into consultation; the Constitutions of 1912, 1920, and 1923 introduced a limited franchise and progressively greater responsibility in legis-

[80] Bailey, p. 152. Her constitutional and legal status as a dominion is not set forth in a single document. It rests on several documents which in turn are based on other statutes and understood conventions. The three most important documents are (1) The Ceylon (Constitution) Order in Council, 1946 as amended by subsequent Orders in Council; (2) Ceylon Independence Act, 1947 and (3) three agreements signed on behalf of the United Kingdom and Ceylon Governments relating to external affairs, defense and transitional matters concerning the Public Service. These are conveniently available and exhaustively discussed by Sir Ivor Jennings in his *The Constitution of Ceylon.*

lative affairs. The Donoughmore Constitution of 1931 included such bold features as universal franchise and territorial representation, and furnished experience in running the country's public affairs during critical depression and war years. The Soulbury Constitution came into effect in 1946 and provided a system of cabinet government. In 1948 it was revised to give the island full political independence and remove from the London government any powers in regard to Ceylon.

1. *The governor general.* At the apex of this Ceylonese system of cabinet government is the governor general. His role and powers are explicitly like those of the British monarch. He is to summon, prorogue, or dissolve parliament. He appoints the prime minister, but, in accordance with British conventions, he normally selects the leader of the party with the largest following in the lower house of parliament. He appoints other ministers "on the advice of" the prime minister—according to the prime minister's instructions. He can declare war and make treaties on the advice of the prime minister, as the British monarch does.

In Ceylon's short history of independence, the governor general has already had to make a difficult choice in regard to the prime minister. In 1952 the first prime minister, leader of the United National Party, Mr. D. S. Senanayake, was thrown from his horse and killed. The country was immediately faced with the problem of succession. The deputy leader of the ruling party was Sir John Kotelawala, who, according to convention, would normally have been selected as prime minister. On the other hand, there were important members of the party who preferred the late prime minister's son, Mr. Dudley Senanayake, a less experienced man but one with more popular support. It is generally believed that Governor General Lord Soulbury fulfilled an agreement reached with the former prime minister, before his death, and responded to party pressures by appointing Mr. Dudley Senanayake instead of Sir John Kotelawala. This incident clearly revealed the tensions within Mr. D. S. Senanayake's United National Party. It demonstrated the important role the governor general can play when there is disagreement about the leadership of the party commanding a majority in parliament. In times of national emergency, he can also exercise extraordinary powers. In 1958, when communal riots threatened the personal safety of thousands of Tamils and brought civil power into question, the governor general became the center of government authority during the crisis days of a ten-months' emergency. But these are the exceptions. Under normal circumstances his role is formal and advisory. He is no longer a governor who acts on instructions or on behalf of the United Kingdom and Her Majesty, but he is a governor general, as in other commonwealth countries, acting according to the will of the prime minister.[31]

2. *The legislature.* A second chamber was provided for in the 1946 Constitution in order to enlist men of nonpolitical stature to contribute their experience and judgment to national affairs. One half of its members are elected by the lower house, and the governor general appoints the other half, on the advice of the prime minister, to form a senate of thirty members. They sit for a term of six years. Although its powers were severely limited from the outset, it was hoped that the senate would be a place where hasty and controversial legislation could be examined in an atmosphere detached from the imperatives of partisan debate. As yet, however, its members appear to have been closely bound by their sense of indebtedness to the party responsible for their selection. They tend to recapitulate the arguments of the house of representatives and seldom provide detached and nonpartisan judgment.[32]

The house of representatives, the principal legislative body, was originally composed of 101 representatives, six being appointed by the governor general on the advice of the prime minister to represent groups otherwise unrepresented, while 95 were elected from territorial constituencies on the basis of universal adult franchise for those 21 and over. All electoral districts were single-member constituencies except four, where the caste, communal, and religious composition was so complex as to warrant multi-member representation to ensure a voice for the minorities.[33] As indicated earlier, delimitation was based on a principle of combining the size of the population with the territorial extent of a constituency. Thus, the minorities living in the dry zone received more representation than they would have if delimitation had been based on numbers alone. At the same time, the delimitation of 1946 gave strength to the less developed Kandyan districts where populations were less concen-

[31] Namasivayam, p. 132, referring to *The Independence of Ceylon* (Sessional Paper XXII—1947), p. 7, para. 13.

[32] For a careful analysis of the working of the Senate see I. D. S. Weerawardana, *The Senate of Ceylon at Work* (Colombo, 1955).

[33] For a meticulous examination of the problem of delimitation, see *Report of the First Delimitation Commission*; also Jennings, *The Constitution of Ceylon*, pp. 51-59.

trated than in the densely settled Western and Southern Provinces. The number of voters that each parliamentarian represented varied considerably. In the 1952 election, for example, the average constituency in the Western Province contained 46,000 voters, while in the North Central and Uva provinces the constituencies averaged only 15,000. As a result of the disenfranchisement of the Indian estate workers in 1948, the Member of Parliament for Talawakele had only 3,000 voters to worry about, but his counterpart from Colombo Central had to look after 58,000.[34]

In an effort to give the more populated areas of the country a fairer share of parliamentary power, a new Delimitation Commission recommended redistricting in 1959, apportioning 151 seats in such a way that Sinhalese voters in the more urbanized coastal area proportionately improved their position.

Elections to the house must take place at least once in every five years. The prime minister can choose the time to appeal to the country unless he loses his majority, in which case dissolution is the expected rule.

The house of representatives has broad legislative powers. All earlier restrictions pertaining to the governor's power to reserve bills for the "signification of his Majesty's pleasure," or those reserved to the United Kingdom concerning foreign affairs and defense, were expressly removed by the 1948 revision of the constitution. Its power to legislate for the peace, order, and good government of the country is limited in these respects only: no law may,

(a) prohibit or restrict the free exercise of any religion; or
(b) make persons of any community or religion liable to disability or restrictions to which persons of other communities or religions are not made liable; or
(c) confer on persons of any community or religion any privilege or advantage which is not conferred on persons of other communities or religions;
(d) alter the constitution of any religious body except with the consent of the governing authority of that body.[35]

[34] I. D. S. Weerawardana, "The General Elections in Ceylon, 1952," *The Ceylon Historical Journal* II, Nos. 1 and 2 (July and October 1952), pp. 111-178; p. 117 and Appendix II.

[35] Ceylon (Constitution) Order in Council 1946, Section 29 (2); Jennings, *The Constitution of Ceylon*, pp. 276-277 for discussion.

It was against British tradition to include such a generalized statement of rights, but the minorities argued that even these clauses did not provide sufficient guarantees in a country of religious and linguistic diversity like Ceylon.

The formal procedures of the house follow the rules of Westminster, enforced by the speaker who is elected by the house. The Donoughmore Constitution discouraged a dialectic of debate on principles and tended to focus attention on the details of different measures. After independence and especially during the first eight years when the U.N.P. was never in doubt as to its majority, the government had little need to "marshal an effective case," and the Opposition itself was divided. Several members of the Left attacked the government's endeavors wholesale, but with few exceptions, Opposition members followed the Donoughmore tradition of attacking details and criticizing the government on particulars.[36] It is still probably correct to say that the search for consensus on matters of public policy takes place more in the corridors of the house or on private verandas than through serious confrontation and debate in the house.

3. *The cabinet.* The core of the constitutional system is not the house of representatives but the cabinet, and the constitution is explicit regarding its composition, powers, and functions.[37] The cabinet is to be appointed by the governor general "on the advice" of the prime minister. Unlike the Board of Ministers, the "halfway cabinet" in the Donoughmore Constitution, ministers were now to be collectively responsible to a parliament that would be dissolved if the minister's proposals were not supported. Parliamentary secretaries were to assist the ministers and to act for them in parliament when the ministers were away temporarily, if the ministers were members of the upper house, or if they were otherwise unable to attend sessions. The cabinet was charged with "the general direction and control" of the government. The prime minister himself was to be in charge of defense and external affairs in addition to his other duties.

Cabinets have a decision-making or a representative function; in practice, these purposes merge into each other, but they can often conflict. Seen from the point of view of making decisions, a cabinet

[36] Jennings, *ibid.*, pp. 86-88.
[37] Ceylon (Constitution) Order in Council, Sections 46-50.

should be small, made up of men with identity of purpose and harmony of view. A homogeneous population with moderate demands facilitates the matter. A prerequisite for such a cabinet is a party well enough organized and widely representative enough to insure parliamentary support for cabinet decisions. On the other hand, the representative function of the cabinet invites an increase in the number of cabinet members, and diversity of view is apt to diffuse the cabinet's sense of purpose and direction. During the first years of independence, the cabinet was used as much as a device to ensure widespread support for the party and constitution as it was a source of vigorous decisions. From 7 members on the Board of Ministers under the old constitution, in 1947 the new cabinet was increased to 12 ministers and one minister without portfolio. In addition, 10 parliamentary secretaries made a total of 23 posts in the government out of a house of 95 elected members. Geographical and minority support were insured by including 2 Tamils, 2 Kandyan Sinhalese, and 1 Muslim in the first cabinet in addition to 7 low-country Sinhalese including the prime minister. The 1952 Cabinet of Mr. Dudley Senanayake and the 1953 Cabinet of Sir John Kotelawala retained approximately the same proportions.

Under the conventions of the British cabinet system, major policy is the affair of the cabinet as a whole and not of any one minister. Collective responsibility implies that all stand together in defense of the policies that have been accepted jointly as sound for the country. But there appear to be impediments in the way of transferring this set of practices to Ceylon. The Donoughmore constitutional experience—the apprenticeship for most of Ceylon's contemporary leaders—did not encourage the conventions of collective responsibility. To the contrary, dispersion of responsibility was its hallmark. The representative role assigned to the cabinets since 1947 has added to cabinet divisions. Moreover, where political parties are not well-developed and lack reliable organization, parliamentarians cannot count on cabinet loyalty to ensure them enough party support to contribute decisively to their re-election. In many cases, only outstanding behavior can separate a minister from a widely unpopular, but necessary, policy. Resignation is the Westminster way of accomplishing this end. But resignations in Ceylon on specific issues are still rare. Indeed, there is often political kudos to be gained from remaining in the cabinet and resisting a prime minister from that prominent position. From such a vantage point, a minister may better demonstrate to the country that he has bigger and better ideas on all important national issues than his other cabinet colleagues. If his ambitions are for the highest office, he can, from his cabinet position, enlist the support of backbenchers and weaken the strength of his cabinet rivals. As the cabinet seeks to define its fundamental policy preparatory to submitting legislation to the house, the threat of public disagreement can be a bargaining gambit for a cabinet member who does not have enough other means of influencing the cabinet's inner circle.

Political expediency alone, however, does not entirely explain the persisting public disagreements among cabinet members. Traditional social ways may also play a part. In a traditional society, status considerations are of great moment. A man of higher status can normally expect that his associates of lower standing will acquiesce in his views, not so much out of conviction but as a concomitant of acknowledging their subordination. To agree with another, therefore, has status implications, putting the one who agrees below the one who puts forward the idea in the first place. Hence, among members who wish to confirm their mutual equality, there are social incentives to public disagreement that add their weight to political calculations.

For these and other reasons, Ceylonese cabinets are more like the exciting American cabinets of the early New Deal period than the staid and publicly homogeneous Westminster model. Since independence, it has not been uncommon for cabinet ministers to disagree with one another in public regarding important government policies. Under the U.N.P., the Minister of Health and Local Government openly disagreed with the prime minister on a broad range of policies—he later became prime minister himself by defeating his former party at the hustings. The Minister of Trade openly argued against the known trade views of the Minister of Finance and ran against him successfully at the next election. Considerable progress was made toward a collective financial policy as the U.N.P. developed, and towards the end of the U.N.P. regime, a young and relatively inexperienced Finance Minister was able to carry through his not entirely popular budgetary prescriptions without public disagreement from other cabinet colleagues. In 1956, however, the Minister of Agriculture and Food in the new M.E.P. government had no compunctions in appealing directly to port labor on a specific issue, and he put forward radical proposals for land reform prior to collective decision by the Cabinet. The Minister of Education was similarly independent in public.

In a country where personalities play such an important role, cabinet loyalty has been enhanced where the widespread popularity of the party's leader becomes, to some extent, a substitute for a party organization and program. No doubt in the three elections in independent Ceylon, certain M.P.s have been brought to parliament on the coattails of the three elected prime ministers. This was true in the popular upsurge of emotion toward Dudley Senanayake in 1952 and S. W. R. D. Bandaranaike in 1956. There are relatively prominent men who are likely to be cabinet material in any event, but it is a significant fact that there are those who have entered parliament and even become ministers primarily because of their close association with the prime minister rather than from any other identifiable source of political strength.

4. *The public service.* In 1881 the Ceylon Civil Service, i.e. the upper echelons of the public service, was manned by 84 British and 7 Ceylonese. By 1949, it was almost exclusively Ceylonese.[38] The public service has always had a high reputation for integrity and the impersonal application of the rule of law. Although the family claims on Ceylonese public servants are no less insistent than in other South Asian countries, it has shown the greatest resistance to corruption and nepotism of any service in the area. A career in the public service has been the object of ambition for the nation's most highly educated and intellectually talented youth. Young men in the public service, particularly the civil service, which requires rigorous entrance examinations, have a higher dowry and social status, even though their salaries may be considerably lower than those in banking, commerce, and other forms of business. The public service has provided important career opportunities for many men of talent, and members of the Tamil and Burgher minorities have been especially drawn toward it. These groups were afraid that the new political arrangements might mean that the majority community could use its stronger political position to restrict their opportunities in the public service.

A public services commission had been provided for under the Donoughmore Constitution. It was not only obsolete but it has been suggested that political considerations had influenced its decisions.[39]

[38] Namasivayam, p. 94.

[39] *Ibid.*, pp. 103-104, 153.

Accordingly, a new Public Service Commission was established under the 1946 Constitution, consisting of three men appointed by the governor general, one at least of whom "shall be a person who has not, at any time during the period of five years immediately preceding, held any public office or judicial office."[40] Senators and members of parliament were expressly excluded and it was hoped that the commission "was given all the independence that a constitution makes possible."[41] Their duties involved supervising the service, deciding on promotions, and other career matters.

The relationship between the government departments and parliamentarians was also changed in an effort to avoid some of the abuses that had developed under the Donoughmore Constitution. Previously, the government departments were under the direct supervision of one of the Executive Committees which allowed full rein to the members' interest in the details of departmental functions. Under the present scheme, each department has at its head a permanent secretary appointed by the governor general on advice from the prime minister.[42] The permanent secretary supervises the government department for his minister instead of the minister functioning directly as a virtual department head. Ministers and parliamentarians find it impossible to resist the temptation to blame public servants in public for many of Ceylon's difficulties when the minister in question should be challenged. By convention and by administrative order the public servant cannot reply to these attacks. It was hoped that under the new constitutional arrangements, the ministers would be concerned with matters of broad department policy, but ministerial attention is still concentrated to a great degree on detailed matters such as transfers, appointments, promotions, and discipline.[43]

5. *The legislative process.* The cabinet defines the fundamental purposes of the government and the direction of legislation. It is the source of most legislation and the final arbiter of its intent. The inner core of the cabinet filters the particular demands of various groups in and out of government, articulating the selected alter-

[40] Section 58 (1); Ceylon (Constitution) Order in Council.

[41] Jennings, *The Constitution of Ceylon*, p. 229.

[42] Section 51 (2). There have been increasingly vocal criticisms of the arrangement since, it is argued, the permanent secretaries are just one more layer of administrative machinery between the cabinet and the bureaucracy.

[43] Jennings, *The Constitution of Ceylon*, pp. 133-135. Cmd. 6677, para. 366. These practices persist, *Morning Times* (Colombo, December 21, 1956), Attila's column.

natives or compromises into a policy proposal. It oversees the specific form of the proposed legislation and submits it to the parliament for passage. Party voting is sufficiently regular to assure a majority for every measure submitted by the government.

The public service is a source of much specific legislation as experienced officials, familiar with the details, see the need for altered legislation. The bureaucracy also influences legislation by the advice it gives regarding the feasibility of a cabinet proposal or by the actual drafting which is usually done by the ministry concerned. By comparison with India, however, the smaller Ceylonese bureaucracy carries less responsibility for policy initiative. At budget time, government departments press the first claim on the government's limited resources to continue or extend activities already under way. Only a margin of uncommitted funds can be made available for unencumbered allocations.

Party organization has been weak and the party's influence on M.P.s or cabinet members is commensurately slight. In the absence of strong parties, the cabinet itself is subject to direct pressure from specific interest groups. Backbenchers express their doubts in an overt, independent way that would astonish their more disciplined British counterparts. In the absence of real party sanctions, they may even resort to public disagreements if the inner circle of the cabinet neglects their demands.

Once in the house of representatives, legislation passes through much the same procedures that have developed in Great Britain. The speech from the throne at the beginning of the session, formulated by the cabinet and read by the governor general, defines broad policy intentions. The budget speech a few weeks later gives a more concrete form to the government's program. Debate on the budget items gives the parties of the Opposition their principal opportunity to challenge government policy, criticize its execution, or to formulate alternatives. In return, the government has to justify its specific measures. In the autumn and spring sessions, supplementary appropriations, motions of no confidence, and occasional private member motions extend additional opportunities for criticism.

Debate regarding the government's proposals is often detailed and usually very critical. Debate is generally orderly and after the style of Westminster with a speaker insisting on due propriety and relevancy. Few can argue that they do not have an opportunity to raise a critical voice.

As a result of one hundred and fifty years of British rule and the Ceylonese elite's reaction to it, the constitutional forms now instituted are closely modeled on the London example. It is the cabinet rule of responsible ministers who must retain a majority in the parliament if they are to continue to govern. Despite the fissiparous tendencies of Ceylonese cabinets, and certain differences in parliamentary style, the recognizable constitutional channels closely resemble their British counterpart. It is in the realm of parties and interest groups that the contrasts are more marked and where the peculiar bent of indigenous values and modes will be seen most clearly.

CHAPTER V · THE ACTORS OF POLITICS

POLITICAL PARTIES AND INTEREST GROUPS

"The party system is not closely knit, nor are certain parties either well-disciplined or strong. Even now, persons are sometimes more important than policies. The opposition is not strong enough to make the government close its ranks, and personal rivalry has yet too much importance in Ceylon politics."—I. D. S. and M. I. Weerawardana, *Ceylon and Her Citizens*

I · POLITICAL PARTIES

POLITICAL parties are the principal means for defining a majority consensus on important issues before laws are submitted to the House and passed or rejected by it. Through parties, political leaders are selected as candidates for public office and stand or fall in contest at the hustings. In societies of rapid transition, like those of South Asia, parties can also perform an important social function, providing status, role, and purpose as partial substitutes for the traditional social customs that are breaking down. They can provide new and broader loyalties than the loyalty to smaller, exclusive communal or other groupings. They can also provide a means for reasserting one's loyalty to the traditional ethnic or social divisions of the society.

Implicit in much that follows is an idea of what a stable, effective, yet representative, party that seeks a broad national consensus on fundamental problems might be. This concept does not exclude the fact that South Asian societies are pluralistic, largely rural, marked by the social and cultural gaps between the Westernized elite and the masses as well as by sharply stratified class distinctions among people who are undergoing rapid social changes. The parties in such a society are bound to be different; their development is so new and the direction of their growth is so uncertain that it is impossible to project the eventual outcome. The rapid changes in these societies tend to make recent observations obsolescent, particularly when the environment itself is such that personal rather than formal institutional relationships are paramount. All the parties are stamped by the idiosyncrasies of their dominating personalities. With but one or two exceptions, no party institution is well enough established to resist the characteristics and peculiarities of its leaders. Hence the parties themselves cannot be understood without applying adequate attention to the party leaders and their often rapidly changing and ephemeral personal relationships.

Ceylon has already evolved a multiparty system showing significant parallels with India, in which one large party forms the government and is faced by an opposition of relatively small, splintered, and competitive parties.[1] In the first election held under the new constitution in 1947, the United National Party secured 42 out of 95 seats in the House. The six appointed members and a significant proportion of the 21 "Independents" voted regularly with the U.N.P. In addition, the Tamil Congress returned 7 members, 5 of whom eventually joined the government party. Hence the U.N.P. could always count on a clear majority of never less than 60 votes, although it lacked the two-thirds majority needed for constitutional amendments.[2] As a result of the same election, the Opposition was made up of four significant parties. Two self-styled Trotskyist parties—the Lanka Sama Samaja Party and the smaller Bolshevik-Leninist Party—together gained 15 seats. The Communist party took 3 and the Ceylon Indian Congress, supported by Indian commercial interests and estate labor, took 6 seats.

In the 1952 election, the U.N.P. strengthened its own position by winning 54 seats outright and, with the 6 appointed members and certain of the "Independents," was sure of an even larger majority. The Opposition was again divided between the Trotskyists, the Communists, a Sinhalese communal party, two Tamil parties, and two insignificant "splinter" parties. In the General Election of 1956, although the U.N.P. was swept from office, obtaining only 8 seats, the overall picture was in some ways the same. The new government party—the Mahajana Eksath Peramuna or M.E.P.—had a clear majority as long as its membership was loyal and was faced with an Opposition splintered into six distinguishable groups, none of which held more than 14 per cent of the seats in the House.

1 Myron Weiner, *Party Politics in India* (Princeton, 1957).
2 Jennings, *The Constitution of Ceylon*, p. 30.

A. THE UNITED NATIONAL PARTY

1. *Leadership and sources of strength.* The dominant party for most of the first decade of independence was the United National Party. Despite its clear electoral victory in 1947 and the prominent role in national life that its leadership had played during the previous ten to fifteen years, it would be misleading to suggest that the U.N.P. was a well-organized and disciplined party.[8] It was, and remained, more a coalition of distinguishable political groups. In this respect the parallel is closer to American political parties or to British parties in the early nineteenth or late eighteenth centuries. Nevertheless, it did represent a notable step forward from the preindependence period and for nearly a decade it was a broadly representative, all-island party.

It was brought together in 1945-46, under the leadership of Mr. D. S. Senanayake. Many members joined the U.N.P. from the Ceylon National Congress, an association founded in 1919 on the model of the Indian National Congress. The Ceylonese congress lacked the organizational roots in the countryside and among the lower classes in urbanized areas that its Indian counterpart developed, but it was manned by the same type of Western-educated, upper middle-class, and upper-class leadership. Tamils and Sinhalese leaders had cooperated in the congress at the outset in the common struggle for independence, but disagreements over communal representation led to a withdrawal of the Tamil members, leaving it predominantly a Sinhalese organization. The Ceylon National Congress, however, concentrated on island-wide considerations and the eventual achievement of independence. After the Nazi-German attack on the Soviet Union, the Communist party, then following a "People's Front" policy, sought entry into this national movement. Although an important group of younger congressmen favored accepting Communist members, Mr. D. S. Senanayake refused to and resigned on the issue. This demonstrated his influence in the congress, for after his resignation it never regained its previous vigor. Several years later, in 1945, when the United National Party was formed to include all communities in a democratic, island-wide party to manage Ceylon's affairs under the proposed constitution, almost all of the Ceylon

[8] A wag has said it was neither "united" nor "national" nor a "party" but rather a precarious association of Sinhalese relatives, and it was widely known as the Uncle Nephew Party.

National Congress, except its Communist members, went over to it.

Two other groups that joined virtually en bloc, were the Ceylon Muslim League and the Sinhala Maha Sabha. The latter organization, founded in 1937, represented Sinhalese and Buddhist interests and was led by Mr. S. W. R. D. Bandaranaike.

Apart from these identifiable political organizations that antedated the formation of the U.N.P., Mr. Senanayake could count upon a considerable following of his own. For many years under the Donoughmore Constitution he had been Minister of Agriculture and Lands and he had labored to improve Ceylon's peasant agriculture. He had wide personal support in village areas, and the reputation for being a simple, direct man, not alienated from Ceylon's village life by an advanced or foreign education. He was known as a devout Buddhist, which appealed to the Buddhist majority elements, both urban as well as rural, and his nationalist efforts toward self-government and independence won him the direct support of many of the more educated nationalists. Insofar as Mr. Senanayake had a direct charismatic appeal, these were its principal elements. Moreover, he articulated clearly the vision of one Ceylonese nation, embracing all the communities of Ceylon. Although he excluded Indian estate workers from this concept, a large number of Ceylon Tamils had sufficient confidence in his inclusive national vision to join or support the party. Even the leader of the ardent Tamil Congress Party entered the Cabinet and assumed the duties of the Minister of Industries in 1948. Hence, the U.N.P. combined a variety of traditionally diverse elements into one political party.

Locally influential notables were the source of much political support for the U.N.P. The elder Senanayake had tried to encourage middle-class candidates from the Kandyan districts, but in the end the U.N.P. was not able to find as spokesmen many substitutes for the exclusive aristocracy in that area. Elsewhere it was generally true that the intermediaries between the U.N.P. and the mass of voters were the wealthy and the upper middle class. Even though Ceylon has had universal franchise since 1931, it is the writer's impression that until the 1956 election, the workers and peasants were prone to vote the way their employers wished, unless the labor unions or other similar groups were able to exert a countervailing influence. In effect the workers transferred into their wage-earning role elements of quasi-feudal deference. In return for the use of land, or the bullocks lent or rented, or emergency aid in time of family crises, or a chit to a doctor or lawyer, the peasant gave his vote. Wage earners in the countryside employed on estates or in the towns, driving trucks and busses, were expected to vote the "boss's" ticket. It would be incorrect to infer intimidation or bribery; to vote as their employer wished was expected and accepted. The U.N.P. counted on this employee vote in the 1947, 1952, and 1956 elections, and only in 1956 did it fail them.

The leaders of the U.N.P. government were already well-known. Apart from the two Tamil members and a young nephew of Mr. D. S. Senanayake, every member of the 1947 Cabinet had been prominent during the days of the State Council. Indeed, out of the seven members who composed the Board of Ministers before independence, five retained office in the first Senanayake cabinet. Such continuity had the virtue of experience, but this and succeeding U.N.P. ministries could not escape being held responsible for whatever had happened over many years, whether it was good or bad.

Party discipline was relatively lacking in the U.N.P. Each member of parliament was virtually on his own and dealt with legislation and with his colleagues almost exclusively with an eye to his local constituency. In the 1947 election, a candidate on the U.N.P. ticket "depended more on his race, his religion, his caste, his family and his 'influence' than upon his party label."[4] Where the party's assistance was not an essential ingredient of electoral victory, there was no harm—indeed, there might be much advantage—in distinguishing oneself from the party's line in debate. Unless the party developed an effective "grass roots" organization in each constituency, capable of assuring at least a significant bloc of votes, the parliamentarian had to decide his public response to each measure on the basis of party backing or nonparty support in his constituency. In this connection, it is necessary to distinguish between voting in parliament, participation in debates, and speeches on public platforms. An analysis of voting records would show a high degree of party regularity at division time—a phenomenon any American party leader would envy. On the other hand, absences on controversial bills or on challenges to the government were marked, and public speaking in the constituency was often ingeniously indirect or sometimes even quite direct in differentiating the member of parliament from the party's line in parliament.

[4] Jennings, *ibid.*, p. 29. See also his more detailed discussion, "The Ceylon General Elections of 1947," *University of Ceylon Review*, VI, No. 3 (July 1948), pp. 133-195.

Not unrelated to these observations was the notable fact that even though the leader of the Sinhala Maha Sabha became a vice president of the U.N.P. and was made leader of the house, his organization was not officially or effectively dissolved. According to the constitution of the United National Party this was not necessary, for it was expressly provided that members of political organizations existing prior to the formation of the U.N.P. could become members of the party while retaining their earlier affiliation if that organization agreed to accept the program, principles, and policy of the U.N.P.; to conform to its standing orders and constitution; and to be bound by all decisions arrived at regarding party discipline, appointments, and financing of elections, etc.[5] Insofar as the Maha Sabha conformed to the letter of the U.N.P.'s constitution, there could be no constitutional objection. On the other hand, if an integrated, nation-wide party had been one of the objectives at all, it was anomalous for a constituent part of the party to continue its independent existence. As late as four years after the formation of the U.N.P., the Sinhala Maha Sabha was still holding annual sessions in which its position was hammered out and widely publicized prior to a thorough discussion of its position with the U.N.P. leadership. As the *Times of Ceylon* put it, "Expediency dictated that the structure of the U.N.P. should be as loosely knit as possible at the outset. Today, the old reason is no longer valid. On the contrary, the existence of forces pulling in different directions within the party prevents its consolidation and holds it up to justifiable ridicule. It has also led to an unhealthy rivalry and the unseemly maneuvering for power . . . if party politics are to develop on sound and progressive lines, the anomaly of parties within parties must be ended without delay."[6]

There were other differences within the U.N.P. It is the price of holding public office in Ceylon (as elsewhere) that differences between associates are exposed, perhaps inflated, and eagerly interpreted by a knowing press or interested public. It is significant, however, that on the island plausible explanations of cabinet diver-

[5] Articles 3 and 9 of the party constitution in *The Manifesto and Constitution of the United National Party* (Colombo, 1947).

[6] May 18, 1949. Moreover, delicately in parliament and more directly on public platforms, members of the Sabha clearly advocated policies on linguistic and religious matters that were not always consonant with U.N.P. principles. See particularly the controversy preceding and following Mr. Bandaranaike's withdrawal from the party in July 1951. Hansard, *House of Representatives*, Vol. 10, *passim*. There were reiterated references to the Sabha as late as 1950. *Times of Ceylon*, January 25, 1950.

gence under the U.N.P. centered around alleged family and social status differences or competing personal ambitions. That there should be honest disagreement between informed and thoughtful men regarding the merits of a policy appeared implausible.

One fundamental rift within the U.N.P. sprang from the problem of succession. When the Sinhala Maha Sabha was brought into the U.N.P., it was generally understood that Mr. Bandaranaike, as leader of the second largest component of the U.N.P., would succeed Mr. D. S. Senanayake who was expected to step down from the party leadership in the near future. But Mr. Senanayake did not step down. It became clear as time went on that Mr. Senanayake was not sure that his post should be reserved for Mr. Bandaranaike. On the contrary, it became evident that he was grooming his nephew, Major John Kotelawala, for the post instead. These maneuvers were explicable as part of a long-standing family competition between the Senanayake and Bandaranaike family clans.

The following interpretation is not atypical of explanations used to describe other political relationships. The Bandaranaike family has a long history of prominence on the island. Indeed, this family was one of the earliest Sinhalese low-country families to become associated with British rule. Mr. Bandaranaike's ancestors were titled by the British as Mudaliyars, and they acted for the British in the more remote areas of the low country. They were of highest Goyigama status in the coastal area and were Christians in faith. S. W. R. D. Bandaranaike's father was knighted and distinguished himself as a host to British royalty. He was not active in the independence movement; his social interests and his position of influence perhaps depended too closely upon the British. At the same time, one group of leaders of the independence movement—nationalists like the Senanayakes, the Kotelawalas, and the Jayewardenes, all related in various and intricate ways—was allegedly considered by the elder Bandaranaike as of lower standing.[7] The younger Bandaranaike realized that his father's ways were inappropriate to the changing times; and on his return to Ceylon from Oxford in the early 1930's, he set about learning Sinhalese. He, too, joined the congress and was active in promoting the independence movement, at the same time building up his own Sinhala Maha Sabha following. But the Sena-

[7] For instance, if public affairs required that any of these nationalists should visit the Bandaranaike estate, it was reported to the writer they would be treated as inferiors on the Bandaranaike veranda and would not be asked to sit down.

nayake-Kotelawala-Jayewardene families continued to feel that the younger Bandaranaike, like his father, considered them of inferior social status. There was little trust and confidence between them. Hence, when the U.N.P. was formed with Mr. D. S. Senanayake as the dominant figure, it was not surprising to those who knew the family background of these men that Mr. Bandaranaike should have been unwilling to subordinate himself to the elder Senanayake. On the other hand, Mr. Bandaranaike and others came to feel that the elder Senanayake did not trust Mr. Bandaranaike. It appeared that Mr. D. S. Senanayake kept foreign policy matters to himself, a circumstance already formalized in the constitution in which the portfolio of External Affairs was merged with the Office of the Prime Minister.[8] With this interpretation in mind, it was not surprising that the Sinhala Maha Sabha was not dissolved; nor was Mr. Bandaranaike's resignation from the cabinet in 1951 unexpected.

When Mr. Bandaranaike crossed the floor and formed the Sri Lanka Freedom Party in the Opposition, this left the U.N.P. cabinet consolidated and in many ways the party and cabinet task of the prime minister was simplified.[9] But family rivalries had not been eliminated entirely, for the remaining cousins would not check the competition between themselves. It is widely believed that Mr. D. S. Senanayake, Sr., began to build up his son, Mr. Dudley Senanayake, as a possible successor even though his nephew, now Sir John Kotelawala, was leader of the House and in the ordinary course of events likely to succeed him. Moreover, another nephew, Mr. R. G. Senanayake, showed promise of considerable independence. When Mr. D. S. Senanayake died in March 1952, less than one year after Mr. Bandaranaike crossed the floor, these family rifts became as open as their former disagreements with Mr. Bandaranaike. Mr. Dudley Senanayake was called to, and finally accepted with reluctance and after much indecision, the office of prime minister. Sir John Kotelawala, later persuaded by the young prime minister to return to his old post in the cabinet as Minister of Transport and Works, did not appear to give whole-hearted backing to the difficult decisions Mr. Dudley Senanayake had to make. The supporters of the prime minister did not trust Sir John's known ambitions, nor did they consider his political judgment entirely sound.

[8] The only apparent exception was when Mr. Bandaranaike represented Ceylon in New Delhi at the Indonesian conference called in 1949.

[9] The Sinhala Maha Sabha was dissolved with the formation of the Sri Lanka Freedom Party.

Mr. Dudley Senanayake resigned as premier, when several workers were killed during riots that followed a sudden rise in the price of rice. His health was poor, and he lacked genuine support in his own Cabinet. Sir John Kotelawala then became Ceylon's third prime minister.

During the Kotelawala regime, which lasted until the General Election in April 1956, these differences persisted. Indeed, Mr. R. G. Senanayake carved himself a memorable niche as the one member of the U.N.P. cabinet who pressed in public a policy of intimate trade relations with Communist China. He became known as "China Dick" and resigned after a vigorous open disagreement with the policy of other cabinet members. In the 1956 election he ran in two constituencies as an "Independent," defeating in one of these his cousin, Mr. J. R. Jayewardene, the Minister of Finance. Mr. Dudley Senanayake, for his part, resigned from the U.N.P. and "withdrew from politics" prior to the 1956 election, when the U.N.P. was thoroughly defeated. He did not return to active political life until February 1957 when he rejoined the U.N.P. with a mandate to "clean up the Party." The understanding in this case was that Sir John Kotelawala would step down as party president in a year, when Mr. Dudley Senanayake would take his place.

These elaborated comments on the intricacies of intraparty maneuvers at the top of the United National Party are necessary for an understanding of the fundamental party structure. As a reflection of these involved developments, and in part a contribution to them, each one of the principals had a considerable personal following within and without the party. These followings were not merged in a solid bloc of party members loyal to the party as a whole. As long as the commanding figure of Mr. D. S. Senanayake was there, the defection of Mr. Bandaranaike had been a source of strength. When he was gone, the heirs could not agree to back any one of their number, and the projection of family quarrels into the public arena contributed significantly to the disintegration and subsequent defeat of the U.N.P.[10]

As a comment on this family spirit, the U.N.P. was widely known as a "caste-bound" party. The charge was not entirely true, for many

[10] Myron Weiner has observed similar phenomena in India. He writes: "How important the leader is as a unifying link and symbol for the party factions is indicated by what has happened upon the death of various leaders. While the loss of the leader was not the only factor involved, in at least three of the case studies . . . it was a major element in subsequent splits." P. 242.

non-Goyigama men voted for it and participated in party activities and one of its principal officers was not a "G." But it is certainly correct that the leadership came to be virtually limited to the Goyigama community, and ambitious young men of other communities felt that they could never attain positions of policy-making responsibility within the United National Party. At the outset, many wealthy members of the Karava community voted with the U.N.P. and gave it financial support, for the caste exclusiveness had not yet been tested, and the financial interests of the wealthier among them seemed to be adequately protected by the party's policies. But as the party's exclusiveness became clear, many fell away despite what were believed to be their common economic interests. An indication of this party characteristic was the fact that in no U.N.P. cabinet were more than 3 of 11-12 Sinhalese posts given to men of non-Goyigama castes.

2. *Organization.* At the top of the United National Party was a working committee composed of from 10 to 15 of the party's most active and influential members. Within this body a small, inner core of officeholders dominated the party's affairs: the president, general secretary, and the most important vice-presidents. According to the party's constitution, the working committee was elected by the executive committee, a larger body composed of 25 members elected at the annual conference by the party's M.P.s, and by members representing each electoral association or party branch. Over a thousand delegates, (in theory) sent by the different party branches, attended the annual conference each year. Its decision-making powers were small. In only one instance has a real disagreement been aired at the annual conference.[11]

Since the U.N.P. was founded only in 1946, it is not surprising that there was not a real structure of effective party branches or organizations related to the party. The Youth League confined its activities to enlisting young men to appear at public celebrations and to cheering at political meetings; and there were only a few full-time party professional workers. By the 1952 election, the local organizations had improved. Some of them appeared to be well-financed and they controlled a large amount of transport—an important part of any voting day in Ceylon. These achievements, how-

[11] In 1954 a leading party figure proposed that it adopt a plank in favor of prohibition. Another member opposed the motion and it was lost. Apart from this instance, the conference has accepted the proposals put before it by the working committee with virtual unanimity.

ever, were not so much the work of an integral party mobilized to support a national program as an association of influential individuals who brought their own resources to bear at a particular time of year.[12] In certain places, such as Kotte, younger party men sought energetically to organize local party branches that had a live program of recreational and political activities. On the whole, the party's members of parliament resisted efforts of the central party staff to organize active local branches. With few exceptions, most M.P.s preferred to depend upon their own "influence" rather than develop an organization which they might not always be able to control. From the M.P.'s point of view, if the U.N.P. lacked a local organization, the M.P. himself would remain indispensable to the party; no other candidate would be selected. It was also argued that a local organization would be filled by office seekers and others whose interest was jobs and favors rather than hard work on behalf of the party. Nevertheless, the working committee was able to increase its powers enough to select candidates in several districts, sometimes despite the wishes of local party supporters.[13]

As Sir Ivor Jennings has pointed out, the U.N.P. had an easy passage during its early years.[14] As long as Mr. D. S. Senanayake survived, his stature in relation to all his party colleagues was such that faction was kept to a minimum. The times were prosperous during his regime. Resources accumulated during the war were still available and export prices were generally buoyant. Dramatic irrigation projects were undertaken that appealed to the popular imagination, and more immediate benefits resulted from the government's welfare policies. Equally significant from a political point of view was the fact that the Opposition was divided and did not present an effective parliamentary challenge. The 1952 election itself only served to strengthen the U.N.P.'s position. There was therefore little incentive to the party leadership to find other sources of strength or to get down to the hard, painstaking, drudgery of building an effective political organization at the local level. Quite the contrary.

Moreover, for the party in power, there were alternative approaches

[12] For a discussion that lays stress on the party's organization as distinct from its more direct appeal to the voters, see I. D. S. Weerawardana, "General Elections in Ceylon, 1952" *Ceylon Historical Journal*, II, No. 1-2 (July-October 1952), pp. 111-178.

[13] Before the 1956 election, certain districts, Matara for one, protested that they had not been adequately consulted before a candidate was named.

[14] Jennings, *The Constitution of Ceylon*, p. 30.

for ensuring political support that seemed easier. The public administration in Ceylon is highly centralized and represents by far the largest single enterprise on the island. Every district has its officials, from the government agent through the district revenue officers to the headmen in the local villages. Their actions are supervised closely from Colombo and they can be subjected to "influence" for enlisting political support. The school system is equally centralized and teacher transfers are not outside the province of an M.P.'s influence. It would be incorrect to suggest that these administrative alternatives to the ward and precinct political organization were in any sense decisive in the 1947 or 1952 elections. The smashing U.N.P. defeat in the 1956 elections is perhaps one answer to the exaggerated allegations hurled against the U.N.P. for its "corruption of the public service." Nevertheless, it does seem clear that the U.N.P. was not disinclined to use its command over the public administration in the hope of gaining political support, nor is it to be expected that other parties in power will be any more self-restrained in this regard.

It was also characteristic of the U.N.P. that during its period in power there was a generous "bonanza" of cabinet posts to reward the faithful and to enlist additional support among key groups of voters. It has already been pointed out that D. S. Senanayake's government contained 12 ministers and one minister without portfolio. In addition, there were 10 parliamentary secretaries. Thus, out of a house of 101 members, 23 held office. It is no doubt excessive to have such a large government for a small country; yet the extreme diversity of the island's people, the multiplicity of interests to be represented, and the tendency for followers to rally around an individual rather than a party suggests that it was an expedient move at the outset. Unfortunately, it has set a precedent that only a prime minister who is exceptionally strong in his own right can now repudiate.

The U.N.P.'s financial support came largely from the island's wealthy who saw their economic interests bound up with those of a moderately conservative government such as the U.N.P. appeared to be. Politically, they had nowhere else to go. Most of the U.N.P. leaders were themselves men of some wealth who owned or managed estates or other lands, graphite mines, commercial enterprises, or transport services. Expensive advertising in U.N.P. publications brought funds to the party from business houses, and the widely alleged sale of imperial honors, such as knighthoods, etc., appears to have added further to the party's resources and supporters.

A loose organization served admirably for the period following independence, for in most areas the local influence structure remained relatively stable. However, as other parties gradually developed competing sources of local support and changes in the social influence structure became more significant, the position of the local notables who made up the bulk of the U.N.P. candidates became politically less secure. Since the party lacked effective subsidiary branches, there were relatively few occasions to test new, young people and increase their opportunities for responsible party work. This institutional difficulty showed up clearly in 1957 after the party's debacle the previous spring: there were no new faces among the newly elected party officers. All the vice-presidents were older men long prominent in U.N.P. circles, even though the party's problems were vastly different in the Opposition from what they had been in power. Only in late 1958 did new men begin to come forward in the party.

3. *The U.N.P. program.* In an age and in an area where doctrinaire ideologies play a significant role in political debate, the program of the U.N.P. appeared eclectic and lacking in specific direction. Nevertheless, it did come to stand for certain discernible policies and values. The U.N.P. argued that parliamentary democracy as developed in Western countries, particularly in Britain, provided the best framework for political competition in Ceylon. Against those who stood for revolutionary upheaval, it claimed that democracy permitted a stable and lawful government. Important social, economic, or political changes could be effected through the constitutional processes for which the U.N.P. claimed to stand. It was determined to defend the democratic way of life and the freedoms of speech, assembly, and association. It stood also for freedom of religion in the sense that all religions should be treated equally and no one should be given a special status. And the party argued that protection of all religions was required against those who stood for anti-religion, i.e. the Leftist parties.[15]

The U.N.P. was explicitly an intercommunal and interfaith party, seeking to draw Sinhalese, Ceylon Tamils, Moors and Burghers,

[15] The latter argument was put forward with particular vigor in the 1952 election.

Christians, Buddhists, and Muslims into common collaboration. The U.N.P. was on record as wishing to demote the English language from its previously predominant place. Legislation introduced by party figures before independence called for restricting the use of English in the educational system and insisting, instead, that children of Tamil parents learn in Tamil and Sinhalese children in Sinhalese. They also held in principle that the language of the government should be changed from English to "swabasha," or the two indigenous languages. For a variety of complex reasons, the pace of the changeover was to be gradual.

These were all nationalistic policies. Moreover, the U.N.P. was the party that had successfully negotiated for independence from Great Britain. Although few had made the kind of personal and group sacrifices that had been associated with the Indian Congress Party's struggle in India, the party leaders could rightly claim the accomplishment of independence. Nationalist perspectives entered their economic policy as well. They wanted a substantial transfer of income and economic power from foreign hands to Ceylonese. By market controls and taxation policy they sought to substitute a considerable measure of governmental decision for private-sector decision; particularly at the beginning of their rule.[16] Certain resources and industries were reserved as the exclusive domain of the State. Other aspects of the economy, such as trade with defeated Germany and Japan or with new trading partners like the Soviet Union and China, were reserved to Ceylonese nationals. And foreign businesses were required to take larger numbers of Ceylonese into their employment and into corporate responsibility.[17]

In general, the party sought a mixed economy, in which the state would manage certain sectors; state regulations would bend the activities of some segments of the private sector to national purposes; and private entrepreneurs, if given the proper environment, were expected to do the rest. Foreign capital was to be encouraged to bring new enterprises and techniques to the island under proper safeguards. Direct government investment went into extensive and costly irrigation projects and certain "basic" industries like cement, plywood, ceramics, paper manufacture, and coconut oil processing.

[16] Oliver, p. 23.

[17] For an extended and thorough discussion, see Oliver, Chs. 2 and 4.

Government price support schemes sought to encourage the production of rice. The government was expected to ensure full employment and sufficiently rapid economic development to give a rising standard of living to everyone. A series of "six-year plans" were published, although doubts were expressed as to the seriousness with which these "plans" were either prepared or used as a basis for policy.

Although their early economic programs were originally termed "socialist," the exact meaning of the term remained somewhat obscure. In Ceylon, every political party is to some extent "socialist," a plus term with connotations primarily of social justice and equality, although a more "rational" and planned management of the economic life of the country is also implied. Nationalization of foreign estates and other enterprises was not pressed under the U.N.P. Instead, the party acknowledged the importance of the estate sector to Ceylon's economy, and, by raising taxes on company and individual profits and by heavy export duties, sought to skim the excess from these productive enterprises. The increment to government revenue thus obtained was directed by the government into social and productive investment.

High social welfare objectives were expressed by the U.N.P. from the beginning. Their goals included a rapid expansion of the school system based on the principle of universal free education, increased medical services, a continuation of wartime food subsidies as a means of restricting the cost of living for the masses, and wages and hours legislation. Expenditures from the government's budget on these items were large and absorbed approximately 30 per cent of the budget during most years of the U.N.P.

In terms of foreign policy, the United National Party stood for independence from British political control although it was prepared to remain within the Commonwealth. It permitted the British to retain the naval base at Trincomalee and the airforce establishment at Katunayake, near Negombo. They spoke of Asian solidarity and of following a third way, associated neither with the Western powers nor with the Communist "camp," although diplomatic representation remained limited to non-Communist countries.[18]

Taken in its entirety, this moderate but welfare-conscious program was a complex and varied whole. The efforts to invite foreign capital aroused more political criticism than most other aspects of the

[18] For a detailed discussion of foreign policy, see Chapters x and xi below.

economic program, though few new foreign investments were made. Production increased in the agricultural sector of the economy. Although considerable investments went into laying parts of the foundation for future industrial development, tangible results in terms of jobs or outturn were disappointing. The school system's rapid expansion and the consequent increase in the numbers of students graduating in the indigenous languages satisfied some ambitions but contributed new social pressures among the articulate educated middle classes. The rapid rate of population growth, mainly the result of health measures undertaken or consolidated under the U.N.P., contributed further social pressures that will be felt in the near future. The party's defeat in 1956, however, is attributable not so much to inadequacies in the party's program itself as to the manner of its promotion and execution, the personality of its later leadership, and to political forces mobilized not on programmatic but on other grounds.

B. THE SRI LANKA FREEDOM PARTY

1. *Leadership and sources of strength.* The newest of the important parties prior to the 1956 elections, the Sri Lanka Freedom Party, was the personal creation of one man and a few devoted followers. When Mr. Bandaranaike crossed the floor in June 1951, he dissolved his Sinhala Maha Sabha which had voiced Buddhist and Sinhalese aspirations since its founding in 1937. In its stead, he created the Sri Lanka Freedom Party, or the S.L.F.P.

Born in 1899, Mr. Bandaranaike was groomed for a public career from his youth. Brought up in an atmosphere of aristocratic ease on a large estate in Ceylon's low country, he learned his classics and his gentleman's sports from an English tutor. His family mingled with royalty and was titled. His father's statue—in morning coat and top hat—still stands outside the Colombo Turf Club that he was instrumental in founding. At Oxford the young Bandaranaike showed his flair for verbal brilliance and became secretary of the Oxford Union, a distinction no other living Ceylonese equalled except the leader of the rival Communist party, Mr. Pieter Keuneman, who was president of the Cambridge Union fifteen years later. In the early 1930's the young Bandaranaike returned to his country at the time of the Donoughmore Constitution and the institution of universal franchise. He was imbued with liberal political ideas, and on public platforms he openly disagreed with his father by discussing "the masses," "socialism," and "independence." Instead of following his father's ways, he studied Sinhalese assiduously and became an accomplished orator in that language. Although born a Christian, he lost interest in its teachings and found greater satisfaction in the Buddhist faith.[19] His opponents accused him of a change in religion with the change to a representative constitution. Mr. Bandaranaike was therefore an aristocratic product of British education who came to lead a national and religious revival.

His road to the premiership was not an easy one. In 1931 he ran successfully for the State Council, and in 1936 he was returned again when he became Minister of Local Government. He later took the portfolio of Health and combined the two. Both of these cabinet positions gave him opportunities for building a following in the rural areas, an endeavor to which he devoted much time and effort. Outside of the parliament and in part through his administrative duties he developed the Sinhala Maha Sabha. It will be recalled that the Sinhala Maha Sabha was not dissolved during the days of the U.N.P. When the elder Senanayake's reluctance to give him full responsibilities within the U.N.P. became clear, he resigned from the party. Just eight months before Mr. Senanayake died in 1952, Mr. Bandaranaike crossed the floor and became leader of the Opposition.

As a U.N.P. minister in parliament he was at pains to distinguish himself from the whole-hearted endorsement of the U.N.P. government policy. As early as 1949 he managed to convey the impression that while others might disagree with him, he, for himself, was prepared to consider a socialist answer to Ceylon's economic problems, with a greater measure of government planning and social justice than was then provided for. On other occasions his references to his own independent line were also carefully worded, distinguishing himself more by suggestion and implication than by the less seemly open disagreement.[20] In this exercise he showed his remarkable mastery of the English language, finding in elaborate sentences the exact shade of meaning he sought to convey. In most speeches he was concerned with immediate details and not making political capital on virtually every possible occasion, as did the Left Opposition.

Mr. Bandaranaike sought the support of those local district nota-

[19] See his interesting explanation: "Why I became a Buddhist," *The Buddhist*, v new series (May/June, 1934).

[20] For instance, *House of Representatives*, V. 16, c. 1009, 1013-1014.

bles who were disgruntled with the U.N.P. for a variety of reasons. He began to build his popular following upon already existing religious associations and Sinhalese professional groups with specific grievances which he espoused. These tended to represent lower middle-class rural voters who themselves were influential in their own limited areas. Mr. Bandaranaike knew the village committee chairmen from the time when he was Minister of Local Government, and for many years he was president of the All-Ceylon Village Committees' Conference. Addresses to the association's meetings often set the keynote of his campaigning. In 1951, for instance, before crossing the floor, he argued that Sinhalese and Tamil should be made the official languages immediately, instead of waiting for the gradual and easy transition, which the United National Party had advocated.[21] As Minister of Health he was one of the early English-trained ministers to speak well of *ayurvedic* medicine and to press for greater appropriations for *ayurvedic* services. The bent of his effort was to prove that he was the better friend of the indigenous doctors than either the Marxists or the U.N.P. He was one of the first to speak with respect and deference of the "swabasha" teacher, the village schoolteacher whose training had been in Sinhalese or Tamil and who was limited to teaching in one vernacular language. Before he was a member of the Opposition, he courted Buddhist opinion by protesting against the government's neglect of the Buddhist religion and Sinhalese culture.[22] At the time, he publicly proposed making Buddhism a state religion, but both Buddhist priests and laymen objected.[23]

2. *Organization.* Only ten months after leaving the United National Party, Mr. Bandaranaike had to face the 1952 General Election. The elections found the Sri Lanka Freedom Party with only nine members in parliament. Forty-eight candidates ran on the party ticket, but virtually without organized backing. Mr. Bandaranaike himself provided the primary element of unity and, although several of his most loyal followers performed prodigies of travel in efforts to drum up support, the party depended almost entirely on the following he could gather around himself. There was no central

[21] Reported in *Ceylon Observer*, March 3, 1951; April 1, 1951. *House of Representatives*, V. 10, c. 1136, June 26, 1951.

[22] Speech at Young Men's Buddhist Association, *Ceylon Observer*, March 3, 1951. Parliamentary references to this interest of his were not infrequent. For instance, V. 10, c. 1425, 1537.

[23] Interview with priests who were attending a large meeting when the proposal was made.

party organization.[24] Contributions appear to have been limited. In the election, his party polled some 360,000 votes, or 16 per cent of the total popular vote, giving the Sri Lanka Freedom Party second place among the parties. This demonstrated the remarkable and widespread support he could command. But he gained only nine seats—the same number held previously—since his votes were spread over too many constituencies for real strength in any but a few, such as his family seat, Attanagala.[25] It was clear that in 1952, the S.L.F.P. commanded limited influence in the face of the U.N.P.'s better organization and the party's popularity following the death of Mr. Senanayake.

3. *Program.* Mr. Bandaranaike's 1952 program was designed to appeal to Sinhalese national sentiment, combining a clear rejection of British and Western influence with an assertion of indigenous Sinhalese cultural, religious, and traditional village values. He urged a constitutional convention to formulate a truly indigenous constitution to replace the constitution negotiated *in camera* between the Senanayake government and the British. He promised to cancel the defense agreements with Britain and to take Ceylon out of the Commonwealth; he hoped to retain and develop friendly relations with all countries. Indigenous languages were to be promoted immediately to official status. State aid was to be given to religious institutions and to indigenous medicine. The administration, under the control of the "old gang" for years, would be cleaned up should the S.L.F.P. be returned to power.[26]

On economic policy, he placed first emphasis on promoting peasant agriculture and solving other problems of the Sinhalese peasants. He declared himself in favor of repatriating the Indian estate workers in order to open estate jobs to Sinhalese villagers. He promised to expand village lands at the expense of estates, to introduce laws to increase the tenant's security on the land he tilled. Large estates and basic industries, like transport and banks, were to be progressively nationalized with compensation to the owners. He promised to tax the rich and to solve the unemployment problem.[27]

He carefully distinguished himself from the Marxists—both Trot-

[24] I. D. S. Weerawardana, "The General Elections in Ceylon, 1952," p. 144.

[25] Mr. Bandaranaike there gained 38,000 out of 45,000 votes cast.

[26] I. D. S. Weerawardana, "The General Elections in Ceylon, 1952," p. 122.

[27] For a discussion of the economic program sketched before the 1956 election, see Oliver, pp. 58-59. Many of these measures were part of the S.L.F.P.'s program defined for the 1952 election, although the formulations had become more precise by 1956.

skyites and Communists—and from the United National Party, the capitalists. His was the "middle way" of political democracy, embracing the classic freedoms of speech, assembly, press, and freedom from arbitrary arrest—values denied by the Marxist parties. Economically, he argued for a "socialist" way which alone could solve the economic problem and insure economic freedom, such as freedom from want, from ignorance, from disease, and the nagging fears of insecurity that plagued inhabitants of Asian countries. The United National Party could not solve the country's economic problems, and the Marxists would deprive the people of their political freedoms. On the cultural plane, he urged a revival of Sinhalese values.[28]

Until just prior to the 1956 election his party's platform and organization remained much the same, and he continued to cultivate the same elements in the countryside. As a debater in parliament and speaker in public he continuously pointed out the limitations and failures of the U.N.P. Together with the Marxist members in the Opposition he managed to place the U.N.P. in a defensive posture.

In 1955, language and communal issues came to play an increasingly important part in the Sri Lanka Freedom Party's program. Mr. Bandaranaike more openly courted the support of the Sinhalese majority by pressing the case for making Sinhalese the sole official language. Sinhalese fears of Tamils were reawakened, Mr. Bandaranaike's opponents were made out to be friends of the Tamils or dominated by Christians. The fires of communal and religious conflict were ingenuously fed for short-run political advantage. As leadership of the U.N.P. shifted away from Senanayake hands, the S.L.F.P. took up with greater enthusiasm rural values and argued that the U.N.P. had been corrupted by urban life, and intimate association with Westerners and Christians. As a new General Election for 1956 became evident, the S.L.F.P. drew into close association with a faction of the Marxists and with vernacular enthusiasts. Mr. Bandaranaike began to endorse the rising movement among Buddhists to reform Ceylon's society according to the more traditional religious precepts, an ambition which could not be fulfilled, it was argued, unless Buddhists gained a greater measure of political influence. The 1956 election finally projected Mr. Bandaranaike into

28 A. P. Jayasuriya, *Sri Lanka Freedom Party-First Anniversary Number* (December 1952). As early as 1949 he argued for "democratic socialism." *House of Representatives*, V. 6, c. 889, 1009-1010.

the Prime Ministership and gave the S.L.F.P. stalwarts, who had stayed with Mr. Bandaranaike, cabinet positions they had not had before. It also gave the few members of the non-Communist Marxist Left, who had collaborated with him, two important portfolios.

C. THE NON-COMMUNIST LEFT AND THE COMMUNIST PARTY

1. *History of disunity.* In the first Parliament the U.N.P. faced a divided Opposition of three Marxist parties: the Lanka Sama Samaja (L.S.S.P.), the oldest party on the island, founded in 1935; a short-lived Bolshevik-Leninist Party related to the B.L.P. of India; and a small Communist party. Nearly all the leaders of these three Marxist parties had been active in Left politics on the island from the early thirties. With the exception of Philip Gunawardena, they had become imbued with Marxism in their student days in London. Mr. Philip Gunawardena was the then *doyen,* having learned his Marxism in the United States at the University of Wisconsin and in New York, where he had been active in the Socialist movement in the 1920's. He went to England in 1928 and there met Harry Politt, Palme Dutt, and others of the British Communist party. Other Ceylonese were studying at the time at the London School of Economics; outstanding among them were: N. M. Perera, Colvin R. de Silva, Leslie Goonewardene, and Dr. S. A. Wickremasinghe.[29] All of these men were low-country Sinhalese, and all of them were able to finance an expensive foreign education. They met together in study circles and developed a general line of thought whose economic philosophy was vaguely socialist and whose political credo was to wrest Ceylon from British political and economic control.

They were at the center of the "capitalist world" during its worst period of economic depression, at a time when nationalist movements in the colonies were gathering momentum. The writings of Marx and Engels, and Lenin's writings on "Imperialism," gave Lenin's creation in Russia a moral rightness and a special relevance to the rising "colonial" peoples of South Asia. The steadily expanding economy of the Soviet Union contrasted markedly with the stagnation of depression-ridden Britain and the United States in the early 1930's. Harold Laski's brilliant fluency amazed and charmed them. His Marxist analysis and collectivist prescriptions, which were

29 Dr. Perera has said that the three men who most influenced him during his lifetime were Mahatma Gandhi, who taught the meaning of national independence, and Harold Laski and Leon Trotsky, who taught the fundamental tools of Marxist analysis of history.

never brought into real harmony with his fundamentally liberal democratic faith, affected them profoundly. A study of their public statements in the 1950's suggests that these earlier emotional and intellectual experiences made a decisive impression on them.

They returned to Ceylon in the early 1930's and formed their first organization, the Suriya Mal or "Sunflower Movement." The sunflower symbolized their hostility to the British ruler whose "poppy-movement" raised money for veterans of World War I. Their early activities were largely propagandist, but a serious malaria epidemic in 1934-35 gave the Suriya Mal organization its opportunity to work with dedication to aid the fever victims. The beginning of Dr. N. M. Perera's political career is still attributed to his care for the Ceylonese workers during this epidemic.

The Lanka Sama Samaja Party was officially launched in 1935. Independence was its first plank, socialism the second, including "state ownership of the means of production." In the 1936 elections Philip Gunawardena and Dr. N. M. Perera were elected to the State Council.[80] From 1936 to 1939 was a period of growth, although the party organization developed few organized links with the working class.[81] It could claim some credit for its agitation for free meals for children in schools and for the formation of the Estate Workers Union, but it was not yet a force capable of influencing national politics.[82]

In most countries, when the Nazi-Soviet Pact precipitated a profound split in Left parties, it was usually the Stalinists who ejected the non-Stalinists from the Communist party; in Ceylon it was the Stalinists who were expelled! Even while the students were meeting in London, a few known as the "T" group sometimes met separately to study the writings of Trotsky in more detail. Mr. Philip Gunawardena and Dr. N. M. Perera and others came to believe that Stalin was betraying Lenin and the Revolution. As they saw it, the Soviet State, originally a workers' and peasants' government, was now controlled by an oppressive Stalinst bureaucracy. In the late thirties in Ceylon, those of the "T" Group dominated the L.S.S.P.

80 Dr. Wickremasinghe and Leslie Goonewardene lost their seats. Dr. Wickremasinghe then went back to London, where he came under the influence of the Communist party during its United Front phase.

81 A. Vaidialingham, *Samasamajism* (Colombo, 1940) pamphlet.

82 It suffered from identifiable weaknesses. Some of its members "knew their Marxist-Leninist theory" but were unable to use the "insights of the fathers" as a "guide to action"; still others were "council worshippers," so preoccupied with running for office that they indulged in communal appeals and other electioneering compromises. *Ibid.*

and in 1939, when Dr. Wickremasinghe pressed the L.S.S.P. to affiliate with the Third International, they refused to do so. The Nazi-Soviet Pact of August 1939 precipitated a vigorous intraparty debate, but the bulk of the leaders remained opposed to affiliation. The minority were ejected, including four members of the Executive Committee and roughly 10 per cent of the party membership.

The leadership of the L.S.S.P. argued that no affiliation was possible, since each national Communist party within the Third International had to subordinate its policy to the foreign policy needs of the Soviet Union. Overnight switches of fundamental policy lines left the workers confused and revealed the subservience of the Communist party to Moscow.[38] They reaffirmed their solidarity with the Soviet Union, "the first worker's state," though they dissociated themselves from Stalin's regime.

Events in World War II led to overnight switches for the Communist party: when Russia was attacked by the Nazis in 1941, the Communist party had to change from a policy of opposing the British war effort to full cooperation with the British. For its part, the L.S.S.P. regarded the war as an imperialist war and adhered to its fundamental policy of "revolutionary defeatism," i.e., opposing the British war effort in order to further the revolution in Great Britain. The L.S.S.P. was therefore banned in Ceylon and its leaders were arrested. Eventually in 1942, Dr. N. M. Perera, Colvin R. de Silva, Philip Gunawardena, and Edmund Samarakkody escaped to India where they strengthened the Indian-Bolshevik Leninist Party and remained in hiding for most of the war period. The L.S.S.P. in Ceylon emerged from World War II with its organization disrupted and its union base diminished. Many unionized estate laborers went over to the Ceylon Indian Congress. But its leaders could claim for themselves an unusual asset in Ceylonese politics—a myth of heroic sacrifice in the struggle. With the exception of those arrested at the time of the riots in 1915, which gave nation-wide stature to such men as D. S. Senanayake, virtually no Ceylonese leaders have been jailed for their activities. The leaders of the V.L.S.S.P. and the N.L.S.S.P. can make such a claim, and the party rank and file can romanticize the days of the clandestine struggle. This mystique has a particular appeal for the younger intelligentsia, though it is losing its political utility as World War II recedes into history.

38 For instance, L. Goonewardene, *The Third International Condemned* (Colombo, March 1940), particularly pp. 3-4.

After the 1940 split in the L.S.S.P. when the Stalinist group was ejected, the followers of Dr. Wickremasinghe formed the United Socialist Party in 1941, which became the Ceylon Communist party in July 1943. Dr. Wickremasinghe became president and Pieter Keuneman, a former president of the Cambridge Union, its secretary-general. The Communist party's policy was full cooperation with the British in an anti-Fascist People's Front during the war. They aided the British war effort on the basis of a "United-Front-from-Above" tactical line discouraging strikes and urging greater productivity. They used their wartime opportunities to develop a party organization and had some success in taking over selected port and transport unions hitherto organized by the L.S.S.P.

The L.S.S.P.'s years of proscription not only prevented the party from open action, but party leaders became adept at the nice theoretical points and different shadings of argumentation. When its leaders were released from prison in 1945, a new split occurred; the faction led by Colvin R. de Silva became the Bolshevik-Leninist Party, which won five seats in the first General Election. Dr. de Silva is a brilliant lawyer and one of the principal propagandists and party theoreticians.[34] In 1950 the largely personal difficulties that precipitated the 1945 split were resolved, and Colvin R. de Silva and several members of his group were drawn back into the L.S.S.P. But Philip Gunawardena, who had remained with Dr. Perera in the L.S.S.P., did not approve of taking back some of the more independent intellectuals, and he himself departed. Thus one rift in the Left was repaired, but another occurred immediately. The larger segment, under the leadership of Dr. Perera, then came to be known as the Nava (New) Lanka Sama Samaja Party or N.L.S.S.P.

Mr. Philip Gunawardena took with him several of the younger L.S.S.P. stalwarts and formed the Viplavakari (Revolutionary) Lanka Sama Samaja Party or V.L.S.S.P. In the 1952 elections, the V.L.S.S.P. and the Communist party formed a United Front, contested 19 seats in Parliament and won 4. The N.L.S.S.P. contested 39 and won 9. Efforts to draw the N.L.S.S.P. together with the Communist party, or with the temporary combined front of the Communist party and Mr. Philip Gunawardena's group, all failed. Negotiations between

[34] For instance, *Outline of the Permanent Revolution, A Study Course* (Colombo, 1955) or *Their Politics—And Ours* (Colombo, 1954). His two-volume history, *Ceylon under the British Occupation, 1795-1833* (Colombo, 1942), a doctoral thesis for the London School of Economics, is perhaps the most detailed and well-balanced study of that period.

the two were undertaken periodically, particularly in 1953. However, as a condition for unity, the Communist party refused to allow the N.L.S.S.P. to continue to criticize the Soviet, Chinese, or eastern European governments or Communist parties anywhere—a key element hitherto in N.L.S.S.P. polemics. For its part, the N.L.S.S.P. suspected the Communist party of seeking a "United Front" in order to absorb or "take over" the N.L.S.S.P.[85]

Shortly after the 1952 election, Mr. Philip Gunawardena of the V.L.S.S.P. broke from his United Front with the Communists and in 1956 joined with Mr. Bandaranaike's party to fight the General Election. He and his followers gained five seats and, for the first time in Ceylon's history, a leader from the Left entered the cabinet. He received the portfolio of Food and Agriculture and a close associate, the younger P. H. William Silva, became Minister of Industries and Fisheries. Another former member of the L.S.S.P., Mr. T. B. Subasinghe, became Parliamentary Secretary to the Ministry of Defense and External Affairs. Thus members or former members of the Left parties achieved cabinet rank—not through a concerted working class movement, but by means of one faction associating with a self-styled Socialist party that rode to power on largely nationalist and religious issues.[86]

Although the number of seats which the principal Marxist groups have contested among themselves has been small, their antipathy to one another has worked against them in the eyes of the uncommitted voter.[87] Despite this competition, in 1947 they surprised the U.N.P. by winning together 18 per cent of the seats, although the party with the largest number of seats, the L.S.S.P., had been illegal until only two years before the election. In the 1952 election, following the death of D. S. Senanayake, the Marxists won only 13

[85] The Communists argued that the N.L.S.S.P. sought merely a limited agreement on a few specific issues for common parliamentary effort, thus "keeping the working class divided," while the Communist party claimed it sought wide working-class unity by defining a common stand on many issues. Each asserted that the other's rank and file were misled by a group of self-seeking politicians who refused to risk their positions of prominence for the sake of working class unity. For an example of the "unity" polemics, see Leslie Goonewardene, *Differences between Trotskyism and Stalinism* (Colombo, 1954) in contrast to P. Keuneman, *The Fight for Left Unity* (Colombo, 1951).

[86] See Chapter IX for a detailed discussion of the 1956 General Election.

[87] It seems probable that at least three constituencies were lost to the Left because of conflict between Communist candidates on the one hand and those of the L.S.S.P. and B.L.P. on the other. Jennings, "The Ceylon General Election of 1947," *The University of Ceylon Review*, VI, 3 (July 1948), pp. 133-195.

per cent. In the 1956 elections, they managed a considerable degree of cooperation, contesting only two electorates between themselves and gained nearly 25 per cent of the seats. A variety of factors were at work in the 1956 elections, and the large percentage may be somewhat deceptive. For example, less than a year later, in the 1957 Municipal Elections the N.L.S.S.P. and Communist party experienced such a serious setback that even Dr. N. M. Perera lost his seat on the Colombo Municipal Council.[38]

2. *Leadership and sources of strength.* The sources of strength of the three Marxist parties, until recent years, were much the same. At the top of each have been upper middle-class intellectuals from well-to-do families. Each one of the leading figures in these parties owes his repeated return to parliament in some degree to the respected position of his family in the districts in which he runs. This is true for instance of Dr. Wickremasinghe in Akuressa, Mr. Pieter Keuneman in Colombo, Mr. Philip Gunawardena in Avissawella, Dr. N. M. Perera in Ruwanwella, Mr. J. C. T. Kotelawala in Badulla, and Mr. P. H. William Silva in Ambalangoda-Balapitiya.[39] The position of these men, and a few others with similar backgrounds, is strengthened by the fact that they step out of their expected class or social status roles to be friendly with the people and treat them as equals. They receive double credit for this precisely

[38] Dr. Perera had been tending this ward for some twenty years. The wife of the Communist party leader also lost.

[39] Dr. Wickremasinghe, it is said, would gain a seat despite his party label. He was disqualified on an election petition at one time and his brother ran as an independent in his stead, joining the Communist party after he entered parliament. In the 1952 election his British-born wife ran for him and was elected.

Mr. Keuneman is the son of a Puisne Judge, a wealthy burgher who gave his son "the best of everything." Despite his social skills and his ability to meet "the best society" as a social equal, of all the Marxists he has perhaps best identified himself as a "friend of the people."

Mr. Philip Gunawardena is from a low-country landed family. Several of his relatives have also been active in Left politics.

Dr. N. M. Perera is the son of a wealthy land-owning family who has been more skillful than some of his other Left colleagues in managing more than a thousand acres of rubber to good advantage. He is an expert on British parliamentary practice and is perhaps the most insistent of all parliamentarians that these conventions be adhered to for the benefit of all, especially the minority parties. His economic erudition is widely respected.

J. C. T. Kotelawala is the scion of a low-country family which has been influential in an up-country tea district for several generations. Voters are said to pay traditional feudal deference to him before they vote, despite the fact that he has been an outspoken critic of feudal land and social remnants in Ceylon.

P. H. William Silva is the son of a wealthy professional and land-owning family who studied in London from 1935-40.

because they come from "good" families. No doubt this is a waning asset, but for these first and, to a certain extent, second generation Marxists, their personal influence and followings are partly derived from this traditional influence base.

The leaders of the Marxist parties have a growing reputation as the only political leaders who understand economics—a claim which they have not been hesitant in making about themselves. In Ceylon, as in other countries in the East, the esoteric academic specialist—the Oriental scholar or Doctor of History or Economics from London—receives a deference wholly unfamiliar to the American scene. When Dr. N. M. Perera analyzes one of Ceylon's economic problems, he receives an immediate hearing far beyond his party's ranks. In contrast to the occasional words of caution issuing from the business community, the Marxists have an elaborate diagnosis of today's needs and project a promising future of industrialization and a diversified economy. A self-propelling growth, sparked by the energetic and experimenting entrepreneur of Western political economy and economic analysis, does not now exist as an alternative. There is no body of non-Marxist economic doctrine which provides a similar appeal.

Enthusiastic intellectuals have been an important source of strength for these parties. Education has gradually alienated them from their family associations unless the family was of the educated, Westernized elite. In a society that still puts great emphasis on deference to age when these young men think they can solve the problems of the day, few older people take them seriously and there is no opportunity to experiment with responsibility in their homes, their schools, or at the university. Their liberal arts education has made them keenly aware of the discrepancy between the social, economic, and political reality and the ideal defined in the democratic or communist West.

To many, Marxism appears more applicable to Ceylon's society than to America's. Class distances and rigidities are marked; the intermediary middle class is small; the few wealthy live well; the many poor do not. High profit margins withdrawn from the estate and commercial sectors employing hands at very low pay invite the identification of profit with exploitation. Marxism's prescription of "industrialization" is appealing, for it promises modernization, economic "independence," and a rising standard of living for all. The ideological content of Marxist shop talk provides concepts that readily identify the heroes and villains of local politics. Manipulating the concepts opens new intellectual horizons to many and receives the ready recognition accorded to verbal facility and intellectual agility.

The intensity of group competition between followers of the Trotskyists and the Communist party at the University of Ceylon suggest that social needs as much as ideological issues may be at stake. In societies that are emerging from the traditional, family-bound social system, there are few indigenous organized outlets such as Boy Scouts, sports clubs, debating societies.[40] The monastic emphasis in Buddhism has retarded the development of a network of Buddhist youth organizations with their own sports programs and social activities. Hence, political parties of the Left, which make a particular point of combining meaningful social activity with their political organization, provide an important substitute for the intricate network of family-defined relationships which the student leaves behind when he goes to the university. Similarly, party agitational activities in strikes, public demonstrations, or speeches provide analogous social purpose to uprooted young men in the city. This is particularly true among the lower middle classes and clerks, who cannot afford club memberships and whose living conditions cut them off most effectively from wider family connections. The N.L.S.S.P. leaders have not ignored this aspect of the party's potential appeal. May Day celebrations are marked by bicycle races and other sports events, and the members of both the N.L.S.S.P. and the Communist party attest to the inclusive social relationships that come to center around party activities.

Hitherto, the proportion of young people who hold revolutionary convictions after leaving the University has probably been small. The working conditions, the skills required, and the social and economic scene being commented upon appear to encourage the continued use of Marxian concepts in journalism more than in most other fields. This gives public debate in the press a distinctively Marxist cast, particularly when economic policy is in question. The "Marxism" in question is often of a moderate variety. For example, among many government servants, publicists, professional groups, and businessmen there seems to be a fairly solid conviction that there would be little difference between an N.L.S.S.P. government led by the "Trotskyist" Dr. N. M. Perera and the British Labour Party. It was

[40] D. A. Rustow, *Politics and Westernization in the Near East*, p. 33.

the Labour government in Britain, self-styled socialist, based on a wide trade union movement, which proved humane and liberal. The Labour government gave independence to six hundred million Asians, and its program of nationalizing key industries in Britain did not affect civil liberties materially or the right of anti-government parties to protest. Moreover, many years of N.L.S.S.P. polemic against the excesses of Stalin's regime gave the N.L.S.S.P. an aura of being a democratic socialist party very much like the British Labour Party.

Personal factors also enter into the appeal of the Left parties for Ceylonese intellectuals. Everyone knows Dr. N. M. Perera, and Dr. Colvin R. de Silva is a popular colleague in the court buildings as well as an "old boy" of Royal College, one of the distinguished schools on the island. Dr. Perera, as Mayor of Colombo in the early 1950's, showed himself an able and serious administrator whose term of office contrasted most favorably with the largely ceremonial approach of other mayors. The Communist party can make no such claim to Western democratic respectability as the Trotskyite N.L.S.S.P. But its suave and personable spokesman, Mr. Pieter Keuneman, and its President, Dr. S. A. Wickremasinghe, have both been successful in overcoming their upper middle-class backgrounds and are known among the mass voters as "friends of the people." At the same time, there is a tendency among the influential people not to take their political talk too seriously. Everyone realizes that politicians must make speeches, and their public polemics regarding the "class struggle," "dictatorship of the proletariat," and so on are often dismissed as mere words.

As in many other countries of South and Southeast Asia, political parties have been organized before the development of a strong trade union movement. The Marxist parties, as was to be expected, have sought to insure their own "mass base," and to "forge links with the masses" through organizing party-controlled unions. The challenge of drawing workers away from an organizing rival appears to be more stimulating, to call for greater organizing efforts, and prompter attention to workers' grievances than occurs when there is no competitor. Unfortunately, however, politically inspired competition does more harm than good to the labor movement as a whole.[41] In some areas of the economy, there may be as many as three different unions representing essentially the same laboring interests, but com-

[41] Comments of Victor Feather, British trade union organizer, *Ceylon Observer*, February 11, 1957.

peting with each other for party followers. In the port of Colombo, for example, where some 8 to 10,000 workers are employed, there have been three principal unions. The All-Ceylon Harbour and Dock Workers Union, under the leadership of Mr. Philip Gunawardena, has, since 1946, been successfully fighting the Communist-dominated Colombo Harbour Workers Union. More recently, following Mr. Gunawardena's break with the Lanka Sama Samaja Party, Dr. N. M. Perera has developed the rival United Port Workers Union.[42] Control of the port of Colombo is the coveted labor prize, for the party that controls the harbor workers could effectively hold the country to ransom should the political situation become ripe for such uninhibited pressure. There have been real grievances about the quality of free midday meals, pay scales, and hours of work. The longshoremen have sometimes had to work around the clock on alternate and even consecutive days.[43] Basic pay has risen considerably since independence, but time and a-half for stevedores working overtime is a relatively recent innovation. Occasional strikes were justified, but jurisdictional quarrels and strike irregularities became so frequent and flagrant that in November 1956 the government declared the port an "essential service," and strikes could therefore not take place until 21 days after the declaration of intent to strike. In the fall and winter of 1957, strikes were even more numerous and serious. The port was running at less than one-quarter capacity for several months; ships were avoiding Colombo and unloading, instead, at much less well-equipped South Indian ports.[44] In August 1958 the port was nationalized. Serious strikes persisted as unions tested the government's determination, and by December long queues of ships remained anchored outside the harbor. The record in 1959 was no better.

Similar but less dramatic strife is found in the engineering, metal-

[42] Other small but strategic harbor unions are the Tally Clerks Union and Colombo Harbour Boatmen's Union.

[43] "These are instances of an attitude of thoughtlessness which has tended to affect the mood of the dock labourer adversely and has caused him to be misled more easily by trouble-makers." *Report of the Commission of Inquiry on the Working of the Commercial Sector of the Port of Colombo* (Sessional Paper 11—1957), p. 9.

[44] An American reader should not forget the jurisdictional disputes and wild-cat strikes that have tied up New York or West Coast harbors during recent years. There is a difference, however, for these strikes are not linked to a political party and its desire to seek control of the country's government. With but few exceptions they are directed toward harbor issues and the gravy from shakedowns; eventual control of the country's political life is not in question.

working, transport, and other industries.[45] When rival unions combine, they can wield great power in key spots, particularly in the Western and Southern Provinces. This was demonstrated in 1953, when a widespread popular grievance over the cost of living was utilized to call an extensive work stoppage or "hartal." With the end of government subsidy on rice, the price of rice—the key staple in every household—rose three times overnight, provoking a widespread protest. Through agreement between the Marxist parties and with the tacit approval of the S.L.F.P., railway workshops, transport, communications, and harbor workers and sections of the government clerical staff went out on a day-long work stoppage. Commuters could not get to their jobs, and services dependent on road and rail transport were interrupted. The bulk of employees stopped work and disorders became widespread. Tardy but draconian steps by the police resulted in the death of ten people.[46]

The largest single "trade" in Ceylon is the estate workers'—mostly in tea and rubber. In 1958, there were nearly 285,000 workers in two principal estate workers' unions that had not been adjuncts of political parties. Of the Marxist parties, the N.L.S.S.P. claimed 70,000 and the Communist party, 12,000. In all, over 360,000 estate workers were claimed by different unions.

The geographical distribution of Marxist strength shows a well-defined concentration in the Western and Southern Provinces and the western part of Sabaragamuwa. The map on page 137 shows the constituencies won by Marxist parties in 1947, 1952, and 1956. Seen geographically, 1952 was an aberration but 1957 reasserted the pattern of 1947 with an important increase in Marxist strength. It is significant that the corridor of Left strength that runs inland toward Kandy follows generally the main arteries of communication from Colombo to the interior.

In a fundamental sense, the areas of Marxist strength are the most Westernized. They have been in touch with the outside world longer than any other regions. Decades of accessibility, of relatively easy movement to and from Colombo, of the penetration into the surrounding countryside of urban customs, and the cash and contract basis of relationships have transformed these areas more than the

[45] In the autumn of 1956, for instance, one large metal-working shop in Colombo was tied up for six days before the union leader—a leading political figure—could define the labor issue for which the strike presumably had been called.

[46] The Marxists claimed twenty had been killed while official reports insisted no more than ten. *House of Representatives*, V. 15, c. 593, 607.

others. Educational statistics show a significantly higher proportion of children in school in the Western and Southern and Sabaragamuwa Provinces than elsewhere.[47] The only exception is Northern Province, which is traditionally highly literate, but for religious and other reasons, generally resistant to Marxist organizational work.[48] Although Western Province contains about 25 per cent of the island's population, it buys 75 per cent of the island's newspapers. Automobile registration is also proportionately higher in that province, and there are other indications of social mobility. The total picture is one in which new demands have been created as city customs penetrate the countryside and actual incomes and development have not kept pace with rising expectations. Equally important, in these areas the quasi-feudal village network of familial relationships and mutual responsibilities has been undermined by the urbanizing developments. The subjective comfort of the all-embracing family system no longer exists in these districts; and a cash-based livelihood leaves little room for taking in a relative who is temporarily down on his luck. In the Western and Southern Provinces, too, the mobility of persons and ideas has more clearly revealed the contrasts between the wealthy, living a conspicuously comfortable life, and the rest. Social inequality conflicts more sharply with modern egalitarian ideas, but in the up-country districts, where the feudal network still prevails to a greater degree, the legitimacy of the stark contrast has not yet been challenged.

The political importance of the Christian (mostly Catholic) element in Western Province is difficult to assess. Christian educational

[47] Percentage of the Total Population in Schools by Provinces

Provinces	*Total Population*	*No. in Schools*	*Percentage*
Western Province	2,353,000	501,868	24.2%
Central Province	1,430,000	232,943	16.3
Southern Province	1,205,000	253,505	21.0
Northern Province	601,000	141,880	23.2
Eastern Province	382,000	60,335	16.5
North-Western Pro.	919,000	175,213	19.1
North-Central Pro.	257,000	45,752	17.8
Uva Province	496,000	73,261	14.7
Sabaragamuwa Pro.	944,000	168,863	19.8
	8,587,000	1,653,620	19.1% average

Source: Population statistics from *Statistical Abstract 1955*, based on 1953 census; children in school from *Administration Report of the Director of Education, 1955*, Table III.

[48] An exception to this in the north is Point Pedro, where caste issues are said to be particularly close to the surface.

and organizational modes have contributed to a weakening of the traditional family system and to a sharpened awareness of the contrast between the social ideal and social reality. This has no doubt aided the Left parties. In North-Western Province, where the Christian minority is also extensive, Catholic organization has been firm since Portuguese times. British influence has not disturbed, and urbanization has not gone far among, the fishermen, small coconut holders, and workers who form the Christian minority.[49] The Marxist parties have therefore made less progress here than in Western Province.

Apart from the Tamil areas of the north and east, Buddhists form a majority in all but three constituencies of Western Province. However, in the face of the superior organization and wealth of the Catholic Church along the coast, many Buddhists feel that they are a minority community. Hence, anti-Catholic attacks by Marxist parties are likely to draw Buddhist votes in the low country, even though the Marxist parties are fundamentally antireligious and basically critical of the "obscurantism" and "conservatism" of Buddhist thought. It is possible that the Marxists may have drawn as many votes from Buddhists as from Christians in the low country. The situation is therefore not an exact parallel to Travancore-Cochin, but there are no doubt fundamental similarities.

Caste status plays a certain part in Marxist strength in the Western and Southern Provinces, although the Left parties explicitly repudiate caste as a "feudal remnant." Members of non-Goyigama castes are more numerous in the Western and Southern Provinces than in most of the other Sinhalese areas. Unlike lower caste groups elsewhere, these coastal groups have been able to gain enough wealth and education to go into professional and business careers and to express in effective action certain caste resentments that have nothing to do with party ideology. Though not the only outlet for these resentments, the Marxist parties are the principal parties of protest in coastal communities and have, no doubt, drawn support on caste grounds.[50]

Apart from the tea and rubber estate areas, the bulk of the wage earners are in the Western and Southern Provinces and it is therefore to be expected that these provinces constitute the areas to which the Marxists would be most naturally drawn. On the other hand, it is

[49] In Western Province, Christians represent 17 per cent of the population, in North-Western 16 per cent and in Northern 14 per cent.

[50] For greater detail see Bryce Ryan, *Caste in Modern Ceylon*, pp. 199-200, 300-302.

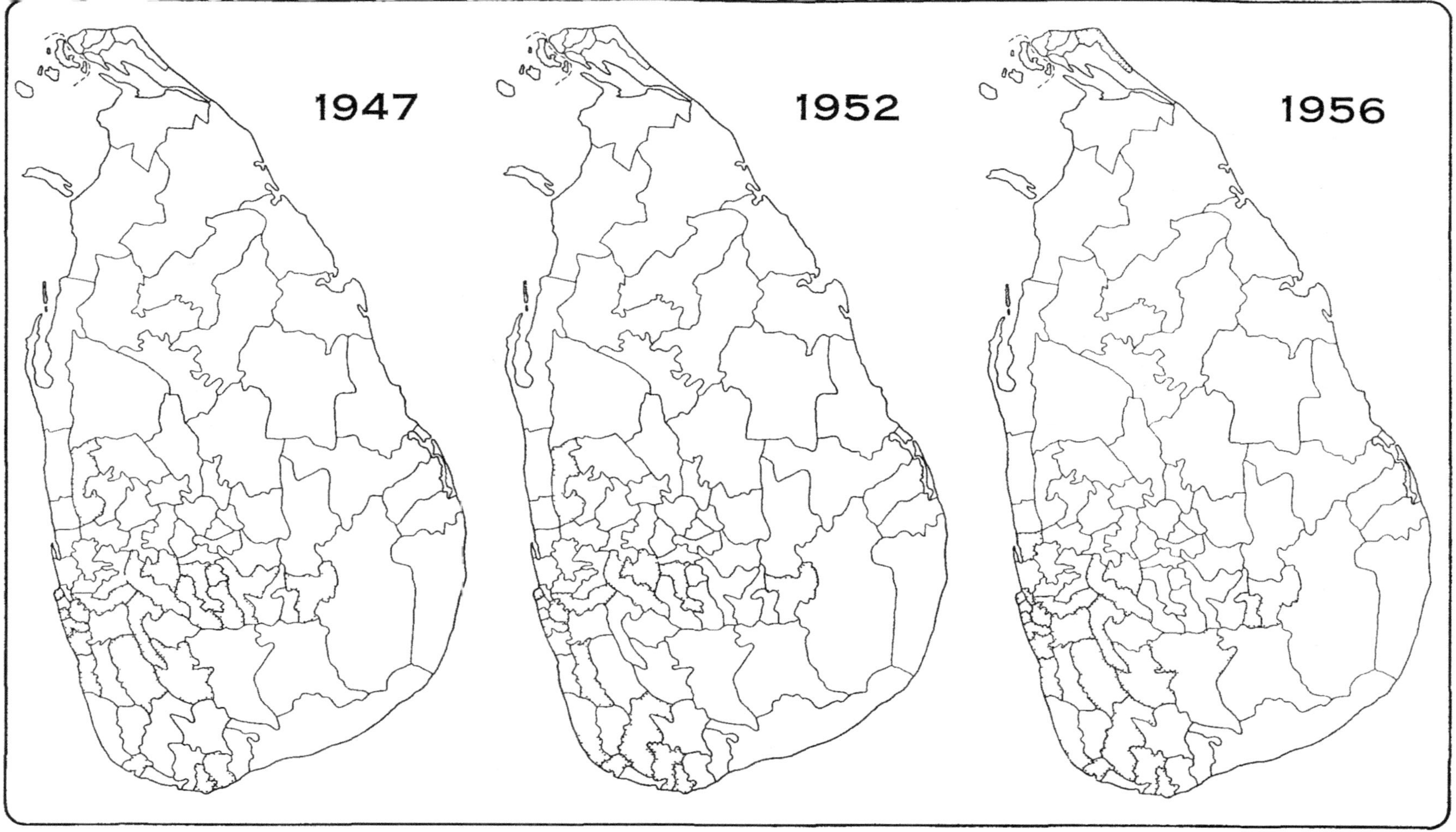

DISTRICTS SENDING "LEFT" PARTY MEMBERS TO THE HOUSE OF REPRESENTATIVES

well not to overlook other more personal or organizational factors behind the concentration of Marxist strength. It is precisely in these coastal belt areas that the Marxists have made their most intensive organizational drive. With few exceptions, the leaders who went to London were from these areas where their families were long resident. Their natural strength, apart from ideology or party, lay along the coast. Marxist parties have attempted greater organization in depth than the other parties, and these areas with their better transport, easier accessibility to Colombo, greater literacy, and easier access to propaganda and other types of agitation, were the most convenient for organizing.

For all these reasons, the new delimitation of 1959 will probably result in increasing the proportion of Parliamentary seats within the reach of Leftist candidates.

3. *Organization.* The organization of the Left parties seems to be similar. Each has a Central Committee, or equivalent, which effectively dominates policy. In the case of the N.L.S.S.P., the intellectuals that lead, such as Dr. Perera, Dr. de Silva, or Mr. Doric de Souza, appear to control more by their intellectual kudos and talent for debate than by the "iron discipline" for which the Communist party strives. There are, indeed, instances where the rank and file have been sufficiently resistant to a policy line to induce the leadership to change it.[51] Questions are aired and argued within the party with considerable vigor. However, unlike the U.N.P. when it was in power, these differences are not taken to the public. To the outside world, the N.L.S.S.P. presents a united front of mutual solidarity and support—an unusual achievement in Ceylonese politics. Life within the N.L.S.S.P. appears to be one of considerable enthusiasm and serious purpose under respected leadership. It is disciplined, but not rigorously so. The N.L.S.S.P. Youth League in Colombo is well organized and tends to attract lower middle-class clerks in government and commercial firms as well as workers in N.L.S.S.P. unions.

The Communist party is a "hard" organization. Full-time dedication is expected of party activists; leisure time outside the party is discouraged and those who break with the party have as much difficulty in picking up the threads of normal, disinterested, easygoing

[51] As reported in the *Times of Ceylon,* January 25, 1950. On ideological and internationalist grounds, the leadership was reportedly in favor of free immigration. Under rank and file pressure, the party became in favor of restricted movement of Indian immigrants.

friendship again as their counterparts in the United States, Britain, or France.[52] Their loyalty to, and influence from, the Soviet Union is not only obvious but admitted.

Proceedings of the party congresses of both the N.L.S.S.P. and the Communist party are not open to the public, but are secret party conclaves. It is therefore difficult to know to what extent these parties have esoteric policies and private party intentions that diverge considerably from the publicly announced aims. If the Ceylonese Communist party is at all like its counterparts elsewhere, the private aim is very different from the publicly announced tactical lines. In the absence of public sessions, comparisons are difficult, but according to reasonably reliable sources there is considerably less genuine discussion of the party's policy within the Communist party congresses than at N.L.S.S.P. sessions. "Discussion" seems to follow the familiar path of leadership expounding the party's line in the convenient form of agitation themes and slogans. Any "discussion" is in the form of "resolving of doubts" about the particular line. The line is not open to serious challenge from the rank and file.

It would also appear that loyalties within these parties as well as in their trade unions are largely based on a personal following for a particular leader rather than out of respect for the institution as such. This is symbolized by the common reference to a union as "Philip's union" or an individual as "N.M.'s man." It is the writer's impression that the Communist party has been able to transmute this personalization to a somewhat greater extent than the N.L.S.S.P.

Both the Communist party and the N.L.S.S.P. have made some organizational efforts in the countryside. Their small membership works hard at improving village conditions. Evening meetings are called to discuss the problem of improving housing conditions or repairing a bridge—practical, detailed, and personally important issues that draw a gathering. A discussion of village difficulties can easily swing into national political talk, and the extent to which national issues sometimes divert village committees from their immediate responsibilities is striking.[53] Youth fellowship groups for

[52] Descriptions of life in the party given to the writer by former members suggest a close parallel with accounts of life in the party in other countries. See, for instance, Gabriel Almond, *The Appeals of Communism* (Princeton, 1954), Chap. IV or A. Rossi, *A Communist Party in Action*, trans. W. Kendall (New Haven, 1949), or Philip Selznick, *The Organizational Weapon* (New York, 1952).

[53] In 1956, for instance, the Bandarawela Urban Council passed a resolution condemning the role of France and Britain in the Suez Canal crisis. Other examples could

sports and games have also been organized. So far, electoral results from these endeavors have not been remarkable; for the Marxist parties are mainly phenomena of the coastal belt and their program designed largely for the urban voters has not been able to enlist much of a village following.

The financial resources of the Marxist parties have been relatively limited. The N.L.S.S.P. has been a member of the Fourth International, a poor organization that can hardly afford to help its constituent elements. The N.L.S.S.P. leadership is wealthy and no doubt contributes heavily from its own resources.[54] It is probable that until 1957 the Communist party received little outside aid although several prominent members married wealthy British party members. Nevertheless Communist party leadership is wealthy, too, and during the days of urgent need the Communist party probably subsisted on these large personal sources and the small contributions of the rank and file. However, since the opening of diplomatic relations and the establishment of Russian and Chinese embassies in Ceylon, the Communist countries have had a greater incentive and easier channels for increasing the financial resources available to the Ceylon Communist party.

4. *Program.* The program of the Marxist parties has been adept and insistent in its criticism of the U.N.P. ever since the first independence Parliament of 1947. Those Marxists remaining in the Opposition during the M.E.P. regime continued to criticize the government. The lines of parliamentary attack on the governing party, drawn in 1947, were used over and over again during the next nine years.

One of the basic tenets of the N.L.S.S.P. was that the government could not solve the problems of Ceylon within the framework of a capitalist economy. They attacked the U.N.P. for its corruption, its nepotism, and personal patronage; they held the government responsible for growing unemployment in the cities and landlessness in the countryside; they accused the government of dictatorial aspirations. The N.L.S.S.P. program urged withdrawal from the Commonwealth, abrogation of defense agreements with the British and warned of

---

be cited in which competition between the Marxist parties takes the form of conflicting resolutions regarding Soviet foreign policy.

54 Funds for publications and organization come from countless small donations, it would appear. Contributions of cars and other electoral services come from upper middle class supporters and the voluntary efforts of their lower middle class unionized followers.

becoming entangled in the war plans of Anglo-American imperialists against the Soviet Union, China, and their allies. At the same time they pressed for mutual friendship pacts with India, Pakistan, North Viet Nam, and mainland China.

On the side of the domestic economy, they promised to confiscate and run as government enterprises all estates of over twenty-five acres and to nationalize the bus system and foreign-owned banks. They would establish a state monopoly of the export and import businesses. No monthly income should go above Rs. 2,000 (roughly equivalent to $400) and the forty-hour week and worker control of all industrial establishments should be instituted.[55]

The Communist party followed a similar program, but with the special differences which their interest in the Soviet Union demanded. They held the government responsible for the "subhuman" conditions of peasants and fishermen and for the spread in Ceylon of "the uncultured, sub-human American 'culture.'" They sought "real independence," i.e. withdrawal from the Commonwealth, and the abrogation of defense agreements with Britain. Their domestic program demanded the nationalization, without compensation, of all estates, banks, and factories "belonging to foreigners and their Ceylonese collaborators," and advocated wage increases and land to the landless. They urged that the post of Governor General be abolished, that the senate be abolished, and that the vote should be given to everyone over the age of 18.[56] They, too, were for Swabasha, the use of national languages as the official languages instead of English.[57]

The parties naturally differed vehemently regarding the attitude to take toward the Soviet Union. The Communists made no reservations in their adherence to the Moscow line, but the Trotskyist N.L.S.S.P. has been as sharply critical of the Russian party line as of American or British foreign policy. In this respect, there are close affinities between the N.L.S.S.P. and Titoism.[58] China has been rising

[55] Leslie Goonewardene, *L.S.S.P. Manifesto* (Colombo, 1951); Weerawardana, "The General Elections in Ceylon, 1952," pp. 119-121. *House of Representatives*, V. 1, c. 917-951; V. 3, c. 1558-1594; V. 8, c. 1184-1199.

[56] It was 21 until 1959 when it was lowered to 18.

[57] Dr. S. A. Wickremasinghe, *The Way Ahead* (Colombo, 1955), also *House of Representatives*, V. 10, c. 217; 1952-1953, V. 13, c. 1833-1842, 2349-2367; Weerawardana, *ibid.*, pp. 119-121.

[58] These distinctions were particularly marked during the simultaneous Egyptian and Hungarian crises in the autumn of 1956. The Communist party adopted the Moscow line throughout while the N.L.S.S.P. used the Hungarian events as an object lesson in what happens to countries that become subjected to "Soviet bureaucratic

in importance in Asia and a response to the Chinese party and state has become imperative. Thus far, the Communist party has been the principal public admirer of Communist China, and the N.L.S.S.P. has been somewhat cautious in its references to China. The Hungarian crisis of 1956 provoked bitter criticism from the Trotskyist leader but the Communist party leader accepted Moscow's interpretation from the beginning.

On fundamental constitutional issues, the Marxist parties have been ambiguous. Both the Communist party and the Trotskyist N.L.S.S.P. are clearly prepared to manipulate "democratic forms" and employ the parliamentary platform to "raise the political consciousness" of the people and to press forward toward power. Dr. Perera himself is perhaps the best informed M.P. on parliamentary conventions and democratic practice. He contends that his conception of the dictatorship of the proletariat includes the notions of multiparty competition for votes, the existence of an unfettered political opposition, and, like the British Labour Party, if the majority of the voters reject the N.L.S.S.P., it will step down. Although the N.L.S.S.P. does not accept the notion of the "seizure of power," "the class struggle" is still indispensable as a basis for progress toward socialism.[59] It is doubtful whether the other leading members of the N.L.S.S.P. entirely agree with Dr. Perera's liberal political principles. The Communist party has made no such concessions to traditional democratic practice. But it has been following a line closely paralleling that of the Indian Communist party, arguing for a broad coalition of all national forces in favor of "real independence from economic domination by the Western imperialists" and "for peace."[60]

Thus far the Marxists have preempted the field of public economic debate in Ceylon. They have faith in the congenial idea of directing the economic and social development of the country through the government according to a prearranged plan. With the exception of those who joined the M.E.P. coalition in 1956, they have avoided communal issues, which are issues fundamentally dependent upon perpetuating past divisions. Instead, they appear to grasp issues that

---

rule." Compare Pieter Keuneman in the *Ceylon Daily News*, November 17, 1956 with Robert Gunawardena in the *Ceylon Daily News*, November 13, 1956.

59 Colvin R. de Silva as reported in the *Ceylon Daily News*, March 12, 1957.

60 For an excellent discussion of developments in India which show close parallels with the lines adopted by the Communist party in Ceylon, see J. H. Kautsky, *Moscow and the Communist Party in India* (New York, 1956). The line of the Communist party in Ceylon is close to that described by Kautsky as "Neo-Maoist."

point to the future. On the other hand, their perspective is oriented toward a redistribution of the existing economic pie rather than the expansion of Ceylon's economy. The arduous efforts necessary in a production-oriented economy are seldom debated—at least in public. Economic matters are discussed in a vocabulary that is drawn from Fabian and Leninist literature. In political discussion there is almost ritualistic use of the slogans: "nationalization," and "industrialization." Leading Marxists have themselves acknowledged that they are so preoccupied with their private careers or constituency responsibilities that they do not have time to work out detailed economic plans of their own. There has been little serious analysis in their literature of the practical management of production and marketing problems that must be solved regardless of the pattern of ownership; neither have they attempted a careful analysis of the production and social problems peculiar to rural tropical Ceylon.[61]

D. TAMIL PARTIES

Chief among other political groups are the Tamil parties, drawing their strength from the Ceylon Tamils, who are heavily concentrated on the northern and eastern coasts and in the Western Province cities. The more than half a million inhabitants of Northern Province are 90 per cent Ceylon Tamils, and in Eastern Province slightly less than half the 350,000 residents are Tamils. Here 38 per cent are Ceylon Moors and another 8 per cent are Sinhalese—all three communities living closely intermingled. The Jaffna Peninsula is an area of highly concentrated population, equipped with good schools, and a literate and hardworking population. Its concentration lends itself to intensive political organization, unlike the eastern and Sinhalese areas outside Western Province. Professional associations of lawyers, school and college teachers, and doctors have been the principal articulators of political demands until recently, when certain semi-industrial and agricultural working class groups have begun to be

[61] A few rather careful pamphlets have been written by the Communist party president, Dr. Wickremasinghe, particularly calling attention to soil erosion and calling for rapid investment in multipurpose projects similar to those in Communist China that have been widely publicized or in basic industries. They show some effort in the direction of economic development, but the estate political enemies are so clearly identified as the villains of an otherwise technical piece that the argument loses some of its strength. *The Way Ahead, An Economic Policy for Ceylon* (Colombo, 1955). His earlier pamphlet, *The Economic Crisis* (Colombo, 1953) is so oriented toward the foreign policy needs of the Soviet Union and vigorous criticism of the ruling U.N.P. government that it contains virtually no recommendations on how to achieve an expanding economy.

organized by Marxist parties. Virtually all of their political leaders as well as those professional men who work in other parts of the island are of the highest cultivator caste.

Tamil politics are notable for the intensity and public nature of personal rivalries as men of local influence contend with one another for the Tamil vote. Tamil politicians, on the whole, have been brilliant individualists who have found it difficult to pool their energies and cooperate effectively with one another.[62] Genuine differences of judgment regarding proper policies have also divided them. For the Tamil leaders have been preoccupied with one overriding problem—how best to cope with the consequences of the fact that the Ceylon Tamil community is a perpetual minority representing only 11 per cent of the population. After working in relative harmony with the Sinhalese during the early days of constitutional reform, when the common opponent was the British, the Tamils broke from the Ceylon National Congress after the 1920 Constitution was instituted. As the principle of representation by territory rather than by community was advanced, the Tamils found themselves less and less enthusiastic about the trend of constitutional reforms. They boycotted the first elections after the Donoughmore Constitution came into effect, and from 1936 to 1942 there were no Tamils in the ministry. A Tamil Congress was founded in 1944 to make sure that new constitutional reforms did not injure Tamil political, economic, or cultural interests. The Congress pressed the Soulbury Commission to adopt their principle of "balanced representation" by which the minorities together would be assured of a number of seats equal to those obtainable by the majority. It will be recalled that certain safeguards were included in the 1946 Constitution. Weighted voting, a limited "Bill of Rights," the establishment of a more apolitical Public Service Commission, and the governor general's power to nominate six members of the house, for interests not otherwise represented, were all designed in part to allay Tamil and other minority fears.

Mr. Ponnambalam, as President of the Tamil Congress, had pressed the proposals for "balanced representation"—the fifty-fifty scheme—and was one of the more brilliant, if supple, Tamil politicians. His political strength was well consolidated in a detailed ward and pre-

[62] For example, in 1947 an Independent Tamil spent more time during the debate on the Address in attacking members of the Tamil Congress than in discussing the Address itself. *House of Representatives*, V. 1, c. 130-131. Or the persisting polemic exchanges between the members for Jaffna and Vavuniya, V. 7, c. 408, etc.

cinct organization centered on Jaffna and its environs. Within the Tamil Congress, a second group led by Mr. Chelvanayakam argued for a more fundamental revision of Ceylon's constitutional development than there had been since the 1833 Colebrook Reforms first brought the whole island under one centralized administration. Mr. Chelvanayakam believed that only if Ceylon were organized as a Federal State would the minority Tamils have sufficient regional autonomy to protect their own interests. A marked characteristic of political debate in Ceylon is the intense feelings that can be mobilized around proposals that are left essentially abstract and therefore ambiguous. The polemic over "federalism" is an example. Few of the proponents of the scheme, for instance, ever troubled to present in sufficient detail the economic aspects of the federal "solution" to say nothing of delineating the specific powers that might be retained by the central government and those that would be devolved upon the component states.[63] Lacking such precision, the proponents had to play on the fears of the minority while the Sinhalese opponents were left a free hand to allege that Mr. Chelvanayakam's proposal would be the first step in the disintegration of Ceylon. In the 1947 election, both Mr. Ponnambalam and Mr. Chelvanayakam ran together on the Tamil Congress ticket and won 51 per cent of the votes in the Northern and Eastern Provinces; they filled 8 out of 9 seats in Northern Province and 1 out of the 7 in Eastern Province.

Tamil politics have also been characterized by a greater propensity toward independent candidacies than in Sinhalese areas. In 1947, one third of all seats contested in Northern Province were won by independents. No doubt this reflects the fact that the social structure is relatively unchanged in the Tamil areas and individuals can depend upon traditional sources of influence that are independent of party considerations.

During the premiership of D. S. Senanayake two Tamils were drawn into the Cabinet. One of these, Mr. Suntharalingam, who ran on an independent ticket, was a man with manifestly unmatched local influence in the sparsely settled Vavuniya. He resigned from the Cabinet in 1948 when the U.N.P. government pressed its policy of defining citizenship in such a way as to deprive many Tamil-speaking Indian estate workers of the franchise. Mr. G. G. Ponnambalam was persuaded to join in his place and became Minister of Commerce

[63] An exception is George Livingston's pamphlet, *The Tamilians in Ceylon and a Federal Constitution* (Colombo, n.d.).

and Industry. There were anxious conclaves over this step of Mr. Ponnambalam, for he had been an outspoken protagonist of the "Tamil cause," warning of Sinhalese domination and the demise of Tamil rights and Tamil culture. Several Tamils joined the government side at the same time but Mr. Chelvanayakam's small but determined following remained in the Opposition and formed the Federal Party shortly thereafter.[64]

Although Mr. Ponnambalam, in joining the predominantly Sinhalese Cabinet, temporarily weakened his own organizational following in the Jaffna area and brought down upon his head the charge of "traitor to the Tamil cause," the fruits of cooperation with the Senanayake government began to make themselves felt. Irrigation projects, a paper and a cement factory were established in the north. Many came to feel that the United National Party was a better defense against "Sinhalese domination" than were any of the other primarily Sinhalese parties. To be part of a national party gave promise of a fruitful participation in national affairs instead of being cramped and cribbed in the arid and overcrowded Jaffna Peninsula.

In the 1952 election, Mr. Ponnambalam's followers in the Tamil Congress fought against Mr. Chelvanayakam's in the Federalist Party. Both argued in public that they were true defenders of the Tamil cause. But Mr. Chelvanayakam saw safety only in a policy of confronting the Sinhalese with an intransigent Tamil minority whereas Mr. Ponnambalam was, in fact, prepared to cooperate with the Sinhalese as long as positions of influence were available to Tamils. Several leading Tamils even ran directly on the U.N.P. ticket, arguing that only by working in closely organized cooperation with the Sinhalese majority could Tamils expect justice and a place in Ceylon's public affairs—the cooperators won the day. In Northern Province, the U.N.P. and Tamil Congress won 40 per cent of the vote and the Federalists only 27 per cent, in Eastern Province the U.N.P. itself won 40 per cent and the Federalists only 4 per cent.

Some argue that Tamil Congress victories were largely a result of the "influence" the Congress was able to wield because it held office within the Cabinet, and that the defeat of the Federalists was not a true reflection of Tamil anxieties about Sinhalese dominance. Nevertheless, from the point of view of parliamentary and party politics, the rift between Tamil and Sinhalese at the political level appeared

[64] *House of Representatives*, V. 9, c. 1679.

to have been considerably narrowed. A national party existed that gave many Tamils a personal interest in cooperation, an interest that extended to their own followings as much as to themselves. Where communal interests were still influencing voting, it was no doubt salutary to have the cooperators rather than the parochial receive political recognition and satisfaction.

The collaboration of many Tamils with Sinhalese continued until the eve of the 1956 General Election when the United National Party broke its tradition of intercommunal cooperation and, by yielding to pressures from the southern part of the island, adopted a policy of advocating Sinhalese as the only state language. This change of front on the part of the U.N.P. radically undermined the position of those who had sought to cooperate with the Sinhalese. In the 1956 election, all the Tamils who had worked with the U.N.P. were defeated except for Mr. Ponnambalam. The Federalists under Mr. Chelvanayakam returned in great strength, gaining 47 per cent of the votes in Northern Province and 33 per cent in Eastern Province. Although the numerical strength in the north was greater, the swing of opinion toward the Federalists was more significant in Eastern Province where relationships with the Sinhalese were more sensitive because of the new language policy. During 1957 the Federalists continued to be the principal spokesmen for the Tamils. Through a policy of extraparliamentary organization on Gandhist lines, they induced the prime minister to agree to a measure of decentralization that if implemented would give the Ceylon Tamils some assurance that their own language and cultural interests would be protected.[65]

E. THE PARTY SYSTEM

Ceylon parties are like many of their Asian counterparts and the parties of eighteenth- and early nineteenth-century Britain. Like the early "moderates" in India or the post World War II A.F.P.F.L. in Burma, the two parties that have dominated Ceylon's life since independence have been more like coalitions of distinguishable political groups than parties. In effect, prominent men have been brought—or have come—together, drawing with them into some degree of intimacy and common effort their own followings. These may derive from the traditional standing possessed by certain leading families in their districts. Sometimes the associated member draws his strength from his presumed capacity to

[65] For a detailed discussion of language politics, see Chapter VII.

speak on behalf of a regional bloc of voters, or ethnic, cultural, religious, or other groups.

As in neighboring India or Burma prominent men in all political parties were from the same separated strata of society—those with a Westernized education. More often than not they were men of wealth from families that were already affluent enough to provide a special education for their sons. It is therefore possible to look upon party politics during much of the first decade of independence as competition between groups of men in the same social strata, each seeking to acquire, at the expense of the others, support of the voters and thereby the legitimate right to rule. Only toward the end of the decade of independence was there an extensive recruitment of men of different status into prominent party positions.

Within the dominating parties, there was little basic party structure. The U.N.P. had a constitution and certain formal institutions, but important party problems were not in reality solved by these means. Election of officers and defining party policy were largely the outcome of bargaining between the leaders of the constituent groups. For the party in power, the prospect of losing majority support in parliament no doubt acted as an important deterrent to allowing party differences to go too far. The first U.N.P. government, though composed of men of great vigor and of strikingly different personalities, nevertheless retained a good measure of solidarity under the dominating personality of the first prime minister. The successors were less successful, as personality, age, family, and policy differences were more marked. The Opposition itself had no incentive toward unity until just before an election when steps would be taken toward cementing a coalition out of the disparate Opposition splinters. The diversity within the M.E.P. after the 1956 election placed an almost impossible burden of compromise upon the fourth prime minister. Less firm as a person, he had to compose the more diverse, better organized, and more determined interest groups that had developed during the decade of independence.

All the parties, including the Left, revealed the difficulties experienced in Ceylon when individuals of relatively equal standing are called upon to cooperate effectively with one another. Struggles for the succession marred the U.N.P.; remarkable public disagreements over policy and personalities punctuated its rule and that of its successor. On the Left the differences were cloaked in doctrinal niceties, but the same trouble persisted. The role of *primus inter pares* is difficult to fill. Power and deference tend to be drawn away from the equals into the hands of the outstanding leader, a fact which makes it all the more important to succeed to his place. Disputes between colleagues could often be resolved only by the party leader himself. He became the dramatic focus of organizational loyalty and public interest.

In all the parties, whoever was conceded to be the leader was given a wide scope for policy initiative. The rank and file did not presume to have views that counted; by their competition, members of the entourage, including cabinet colleagues, ensured that the prime minister had the last word.

In the dominating parties, there was an inner circle formed on family grounds, or the shared experience of being excluded from the inner circle of the opponent, or by proven loyalty to the party leader. On the Left, a London education and being among the "founders" appeared to be the prerequisites for leadership. Channels for approaching the party inner circle were not clearly defined or readily opened. The assumptions of traditional society seemed to be reflected in the parties' approach to renewal. Few younger men could expect opportunities to experiment with responsibility or to test their political mettle, though opposition parties offered more scope than the party that brought independence.

Lacking grass-roots organization, the dominating parties were more than usually dependent on intermediaries between themselves and the mass voters. In the case of the U.N.P., these tended to be relatively unorganized, but nevertheless influential district figures, leading families, or men of traditional standing in the different ethnic communities. The S.L.F.P. sought to enlist professional and other groups in the countryside of lesser standing. The Left parties sought to depend upon their own urban labor unions, lower middle-class public servants, and educated intelligentsia. Because the ruling parties were readily susceptible to interest-group pressures, a brief examination of these will be necessary.

II · THE PUBLIC SERVICE AND THE ARMY

In certain other South and Southeast Asian countries, the problems of government have been so intricate, or the competition between political parties and individuals has produced so much political instability, that the bureaucracy has become the effective center of governmental initiative and the source of fundamental objectives pursued by the state apparatus. It is true in Ceylon, too, that the bureaucracy contains a much higher level of experts on most public issues than the majority of parliamentarians. In one sense, in Ceylon, too, the political struggle is carried on on the surface of affairs while the business of running the country proceeds unobtrusively in the hands of the officials.

Yet by comparison with her neighbors, Ceylon's bureaucracy does not play as dynamic a role in policy definition as in India, for instance. Nor does the army, as in Pakistan, Burma, Indonesia, and Thailand, have an important role in politics.

Because of the small size of the country, the average parliamentarian can grasp the dimensions of his country's problems without defaulting to the bureaucracy. Vast India and divided Pakistan pose many more intractable problems to the parliamentarian. There he must depend upon the bureaucracy to inform him. In Ceylon the M.P. can investigate the matter himself. Moreover, experience under the Donoughmore Constitution gave many parliamentarians a sense of competence and understanding, and defined for the parliamentarian an independent, policy-oriented role. The executive committee system brought to elected representatives administrative experience their counterparts elsewhere did not have. The orderly transition to independence favored the influence of the parliamentarian; national emergency did not foreclose his right to formulate and dominate policy.

The army has remained aloof from politics and has loyally served whatever governments the electorate have chosen. The army itself is small, probably not more than 4,500 men at the outside. Less than 5 per cent of the government budget goes to defense. Ceylon's army has no great tradition of combat, either in colonial wars alongside of Britain, as in India and Pakistan; in a national liberation effort as in Indonesia; or in guerilla combat against an invader or in suppressing insurrection as in Burma. This is not to say it is ineffectual. When it was called out in the 1958 communal riots, it promptly mastered the disorders and reestablished public peace. But no recollections of past grand missions tempt its leadership to dominate affairs. Moreover, while its officer corps no doubt has that firm disdain for the men of politics that is common to many army professionals, they nevertheless have been men deeply imbued with British ideas of the limited place of the military man in public life. If public disorders became frequent and if the men of politics appear chronically incapable of effective government, some leaders in the army might become persuaded that they were indispensable in the domestic political arena. But matters would have to be dire indeed before this lurking temptation would become a political reality.

III · INTEREST GROUPS AND THE PRESS

A. INTEREST GROUPS

The pattern of interest groups is not well defined and their concerns are not expressed in a stable manner. A group will become active as its emotions are stirred, interests challenged, or competition for leadership brings on a temporary increase of activity. A year or so later it will be quiescent again and other groups will thrust themselves forward. Issues that excite the public may give a group a temporary importance it will lose when public interest is turned in other directions. Nevertheless, interest groups and the parties together are the essential intermediaries between the Western constitutional structure and the bulk of the Ceylonese who live in rural villages. It is the interest groups which draw together—and sometimes so artfully evoke as almost to create—the latent, half-expressed anxieties, frustrations, and ambitions of countless, nameless individuals, and make them articulate and politically "visible." It is the parties that then take up these different particular interests—or are importuned until they do—and attempt to mold them into a series of inclusive issues and programs which will then attract sufficient votes for success within the imported institutions of popular elections based on the universal franchise.[66]

Ceylon's interest groups show as wide a variety as the society itself. Four types, however, can be discerned. Some are relatively highly structured, with disciplined and stable membership, wielding much economic power or power to disrupt public order. Business associations and certain trade unions like the Ceylon Indian Congress are of this type. But even the more established trade unions found it difficult to organize procedures for bestowing legitimate leadership or retaining a stable membership. Indeed, many trade unions and professional groups shade over into a second, intermedi-

[66] See G. Almond, "The Comparative Study of Interest Groups," *American Political Science Review* (March 1958), pp. 270-282, for a basis of comparison.

ate type where membership, though recognizable and disciplined, is often shifting and unreliable. Organizational channels to leadership or the expediency of the policies they seek to implement do not appear to be important. Leaders depend upon their personal standing—their charisma. In a third type, masses of people are drawn along a common line by a group of spokesmen often formally unrelated to each other, each of whom responding to his sense of disquiet and frustration finds a popular hearing. There may be no question of establishing a permanent organization with a grassroots membership. The purpose is to mobilize large numbers of people in order to influence voters on behalf of particular candidates, to press a specific issue, or to awaken communal consciousness. Perhaps the least organized in a formal sense, though highly, often rigorously, organized in a social sense, are groups of a fourth type based on caste and familial influence systems. Becoming less important as the traditional social system changes, and as more visible, formal organizations gain in effectiveness and membership, nevertheless, they are still significant. Concerned not so much with public policy as with the distribution of office and of opportunity, they work quietly and informally with whomever comes to power as protective societies for their own members.

Of the modern, relatively stable interest groups, business associations were the first to be established and were once influential in political and administrative affairs. Electoral politics nowadays, however, leave them very little influence at election time. Business firms no doubt contributed generously to the campaign chests of the U.N.P. and there is considerable evidence that during the 1956 election they contributed to the other democratic party as well. Especially among businesses with unorganized labor, it is likely that they were able to influence the vote of their workers. On the other hand, unionization in the Colombo area, Kandy, and other larger towns has now proceeded far enough so that the larger businesses do not automatically command the vote of their employees. Bus and transport operators are important because they provide vehicles on election day and Ceylonese voters expect a free ride to the polls. It may have been true that the transporter helped the voter to decide his vote in the first two elections, but in 1956 this was certainly not the case.

Certain economic interests undoubtedly have considerable influence between elections. Productivity and the orderly transport of estate products are naturally of value to the company that produces and sells those commodities; they are also of importance to the country whose revenue depends so heavily upon the export trade. Hence, government consultation with the European Association and Low Country Products Association served a useful purpose. These leading estate organizations and other less prominent spokesmen for low-country rubber and coconut growers maintained close touch with the government servants dealing with their particular concerns. Apart from the European Association, representing largely foreign-owned tea, which controlled no votes, the other organizations were scrupulously attentive to M.P.s from the planting districts and relevant cabinet ministers. The very size of Ceylon favored such contacts, many of which were informal, social, and not always distinguishable from family relationships.

A network of relationships persisted between the foreign banking firms and estate management houses through which estate supplies were channeled into the island, disbursements made in Ceylon itself, and profits remitted "home." Yet there is little evidence to show that this economic influence has been used to affect the government's policies toward investment or economic development. In the early days, when the British dominated politics, the commercial and planting communities employed state resources for the development of roads and railroads of use primarily to their interests. But the charge cannot be applied to government policies since the end of World War II.

The Ceylon Employers Federation of commercial and retail business centered chiefly in Colombo was largely made up of British firms, although a large number have been purchased recently by wealthy Ceylonese. Taxation policies have seriously cut into their former profit margins and Ceylonization has changed their personnel policies. They are not ignored when commercial policies are under discussion, but the scope of foreign-owned firms is becoming more limited as various segments of foreign trade have been taken over by government trading or by Ceylonese firms. Union action against the firms in the Ceylon Employers Federation is still understood by the union rank and file as being directed against the "foreign interests" even though more and more owners are Ceylonese.

More important for electoral politics are trade unions and various middle-class professional organizations. All unions in Ceylon cannot be considered as merely interest groups, for many of them are well known adjuncts of political parties. By 1958 some 700,000 workers were claimed by labor unions, a fourfold increase over the figure for 1947, one that jumped rapidly forward after the new government of Mr. Bandaranaike came to power in 1956.[67] Seventy-five per cent of these were in the largest single trade—tea and rubber estate labor. The remainder, 177,000, was divided among transport, clerical, professional workers, and the 60,000 who were in "industrial" unions.

At the beginning of 1959, the estate workers were divided into four principal unions. The Ceylon Workers Congress, the largest union, had organized roughly 190,000 workers until a split occurred in 1956, when the leaders fell out with one another. In 1959, the smaller group of estate workers of about 45,000 was under the leadership of Mr. A. Aziz, and was said to have definite communist leanings, though direct affiliation was not clear. The larger group of about 235,000 was led by Mr. V.E.K.R.S. Thondaman, the son of an estate "kangany" or work gang supervisor, who became successful and owned several estates. His union appeared to be more truly indigenous to the estate workers and without noticeable external affiliations. It was independent of long-standing political commitments. The Communist and the Lanka Sama Samaja parties have developed small estate unions of their own, but these together had a membership of probably less than 80,000. All four unions have been competing against each other for membership and the ultimate control of the whole estate worker population. After 1948 the estate workers were without the franchise and therefore without direct electoral significance. Despite union differences, they would probably be able to exert considerable direct pressure on the economy for a period of several weeks. A protracted strike would be likely to create great tension and considerable defection within the unions, since union funds are limited and laborers' savings meagre. Moreover, estate administrations have often provided basic food supplies. One-day industry-wide demonstration strikes or extended strikes on a few estates are more likely than an industry-wide extended walkout.[68]

Of the other working class employees who were organized, perhaps half were in party-dominated unions. The Marxist parties vied

[67] *Administration Report of the Commissioner of Labour for 1957*, p. 58. In 1955, the total unionized strength was 360,000.

[68] These figures represent the author's best estimates, inescapably imprecise because of the natural tendency of every union leader to exaggerate his membership.

with each other for control, an ambition that led to a number of jurisdictional conflicts. Personal rivalries between union leaders also led to competitive strikes and to the splitting of unions into rival forces aligned behind leading individuals. Those uncommitted to a leader drifted from one union to another, depending on which one seemed to be most effective in obtaining short term benefits. In the words of the Commissioner of Labour, as a result: "trade unions lacked cohesion and stability and the fundamental basis of trade unionism—unity—was forgotten in this wrangle for power among a number of unions catering for the same categories of workers."[69] There are signs that the union movement may be reaching that stage of maturity where individuals who have risen through the labor movement itself are now coming into positions of greater union influence, thus helping to free the unions from political dominance. But by 1959, political parties appeared to still control large segments of the union movement and politically motivated strikes were as likely as strikes concerned exclusively with wages and conditions of labor.

Despite labor conflict, however, the unions are so distributed in the commercial, industrial, and transport trades that they could effectively and rapidly tie up the country's economy if their leaders could agree among themselves on important strike issues that have widespread support from their rank and file. By concerted strike action, they could, for example, materially influence the composition of a cabinet, the distribution of portfolios, or the direction of a government's policies. A response by the government to restrain union activity could turn the burden of opinion against a "repressive" government. Electorally, the unions' influence is likely to be less important, since, apart from the large estate unions whose Indian members were deprived of the franchise, the bulk of the unions is concentrated in a relatively few urbanized and suburban constituencies of the Western and Southern Provinces and Kandy town.

Another set of interests was centered around professional and career groups. There were 30,000 Sinhalese teachers on the island, organized into two large associations, one representing those in government schools and the other more independent group representing those in the assisted schools. The latter, the Jatika Guru Sangamaya, was at one time Communist dominated, but when the Communist party adopted a policy opposed to Sinhalese as the State

[69] *Administration Report of the Commissioner of Labour for 1957*, p. 23.

Language, even the Communists within the organization broke with the Communist party. Their return to the party appeared to depend largely on the Communist line on the language question. On the whole, these were not disciplined organizations and there were rivalries and differences of various kinds within them. Nevertheless, they were capable of provoking a fairly standard response among their followers on professional issues such as salaries, conditions of work, and retirement benefits and these on occasion could be turned to political purposes. *Ayurvedic* physicians, of whom there were an estimated 10,000 on the island, were also organized in several associations. Their differences were derived from contrasting views on the difficult technical questions of indigenous medicine. Both the teachers and indigenous doctors hold respected positions throughout the island, particularly in rural areas. They are believed to be politically influential, and it is clear from the politicians' behavior before elections that they consider these two groups to be important.[70]

Religious interest groups are also important though less firmly organized than most trade unions or professional associations. Of these, the Catholic Church was the first to organize in an effective fashion. It owned considerable land and had many good schools on the island—two important sources of "influence." For many years Catholics and other Christians received better education than non-Christians and hence were found in influential positions. Many Buddhists came to believe that the network of Christian Catholics and Protestants scattered in the government service and parliament ran the public system for the benefit of Christians. It was widely believed that they had resisted the universal educational proposals since World War II, lobbied for taxation legislation that protected their interests, and influenced the restrictive provisions in the constitution that protected religious bodies from reforms they did not themselves accept. There is no doubt that the Catholic Church openly opposed the Marxist parties in each General Election, sometimes from the pulpits, sometimes less obtrusively in the parishes. And in many instances, Catholic votes were openly solicited for Catholic candidates.

Another group developed around Buddhist and cultural considerations. *Bhikkhus* or Buddhist monks have canvassed in all three elec-

[70] See Chapter IX on the 1956 General Election for greater details on these organizations. See also relevant parts of Chapter VI.

tions though not necessarily supporting the same candidate. Before the 1956 election, they were not well organized and acted more as individuals than as disciplined electoral agents.[71] The ruling party until 1956 seemed to consider the up-country Buddhist clergy politically influential in the more conservative Kandyan areas, sensitive to traditional Buddhist leadership where the temples owned large tracts of land. Later, certain groups of Buddhist laymen and clergy entered the political arena more actively, forming for themselves explicitly Buddhist interest organizations. These were mainly composed of low-country Sinhalese professional men and *bhikkhus* who, for a variety of reasons, had grievances against the ruling social and political elite whose values they deplored. A small number of energetic, single-minded men financed and controlled these organizations which aired the grievances and eventually sought to influence voting behavior. Organizational structure was informal; there were few devices for rank and file influence; and the leaders tended to dominate. When leaders disagreed, the organizations would split into factions. The holy year of Buddha Jayanti and the General Election in 1956 evoked their maximum energy.

Ill-organized cultural interest groups used language and communal appeals to press their claims for political influence. Language enthusiasts, largely would-be spokesmen of middle-class Sinhalese, organized meetings, buttonholed political leaders, and attempted to express their influence through ephemeral and shifting political pressures. Their impact on sensitive political leaders was very real, even if they did not often develop firm, readily identified organizations.

In addition and equally influential, have been groups that derived from regional loyalties, community, or family attachments. For instance, throughout much of recent Ceylonese history, the Kandyans have played an important role. The Kandyan uplands were least touched by foreign influences. Relatively few Kandyans learned English and they remained isolated from the modernizing currents of the coastal, more Westernized, areas. A peculiar set of Kandyan rights—religious, civic, and customary—were guaranteed when Britain, by treaty, obtained control over the kingdom in 1815. These often form the core of essentially Kandyan claims to this day. Kandyan art and culture represent the purest of Sinhalese traditions.

[71] I. D. S. Weerawardana, "The General Elections in Ceylon, 1952," p. 129.

The names of leading Kandyan families are known and respected throughout the island.

In recent years the trials of their peasantry have been given wide public attention and a special commission investigated their grievances.[72] Influence exerted by the Kandyans contributed a great deal to the defining of policies toward the Indian estate workers who have been concentrated in the mountainous districts. Kandyan organizations argued vigorously for reserving business and career opportunities to Sinhalese-speakers and for promoting the use of the Sinhalese language.

The homogeneity of this interest group has been in doubt, for it contains both aristocracy and peasant. Yet the ruling U.N.P. found Kandyan spokesmen insistent on a variety of questions and the party tended to respond. In the 1956 election all the leading families lost their seats in parliament, but other less prominent M.P.s quickly took up again the cause of "protecting the interests" of the Kandyan peasant or Kandyan cultural and religious interests.

Other groups drew together to promote or to defend the interests of this or that minority community—the Moors, the Burghers, the Ceylon Tamils. By no means were all of these traditionally defined interests adequately expressed through the parties that dominated the political landscape. The men of influence in these communities might not be active in the political arena but they would visit the political leaders and personally communicate their desires to them. The political leaders would, in turn, reciprocate according to the weight of influence of his visitor. The usual means of winning political support, well-known in American politics, would be put in motion—a job granted, a promise made, a piece of pending legislation revised.

Caste groups, too, could not be ignored. How prominent members of different caste or community groups fared at the hands of this minister or that party was expected to enter the balance of voting behavior. Sensitive politicians in the Opposition or in the government would necessarily be alert to these currents of opinion. Family loyalties came into play. A man well-rewarded might be counted upon to attempt to enlist the votes of his ramified family. The family and caste incentive more likely worked in a defensive sense. Should a man of one family or community be hurt by police, dismissal, or publicized scandal, his family and community were more likely

[72] *Report of the Kandyan Peasantry Commission* (Sessional Paper XVIII—1951).

to rally behind him against those who had harmed him than they might support those who had contributed to his success.

There was a subtle interplay between the interest group and the parties. Spokesmen for the particular interest could argue vehemently on behalf of their own following; the political party could itself argue the same case to win the group's support. This, in turn, might raise the consciousness and expand the ambitions of the group in question. This process was more than usually marked where the pressure group came to articulate the interests of one of the traditional ethnic or communal groups. During the first part of the independence decade, the ruling party encompassed many of these traditional communal interests. Toward the end of the decade, interest groups became sufficiently articulate on behalf of exclusive communal issues and political leaders sufficiently responsive to them so that most parties lost what intercommunal characteristics they had and became essentially expressions of traditional community ambitions. By the end of 1957, labor union organization had proceeded to such an extent that its strength was more clearly felt in the political arena.

Where political parties remained only loosely organized and leaders remained dependent upon a cluster of semi-independent groups for their support, the art of political survival depended heavily upon the skill in maneuvering and manipulating a congeries of distinguishable interest groups. This gave the articulate spokesmen of particular group interests a prominence in political affairs they might not have otherwise had. This tendency was enhanced by the fact that in few of the interest groups did the rank and file have regularized access to, or check upon, the spokesman's successive positions. Since internal procedures for defining the group's position often did not exist, disagreements were aired in public. These were often defined in personal terms. Contending leaders within any one interest group might dramatize their own greater dedication to the group's interest than their rivals' as a means of promoting their own position within the group in question. The personal followings of the contenders would precipitate the organization's breaking up into factions. Thus, characteristic processes discernible in the political parties could also be seen in the interest groups.

Out of the intricate interplay of interest group and party, the peculiar interests and aims of specific groups were redefined, sharpened, or softened to merge with the altered specific demands of other groups to eventually form a large enough following to win a majority of votes in any one constituency. The instability of parties and interest groups contributed to that unexpected quality that lends such excitement to political activity in Ceylon—and makes prediction of the future so difficult.

B. THE PRESS AND COMMUNICATIONS

Of all the countries in South and Southeast Asia, Ceylon has the most active press with the largest circulation. For a population of 9,000,000 there are ten daily newspapers selling over 350,000 copies a day and eight Sunday papers with a total circulation of 450,000. Indeed, two of the Sunday papers, the *Silumina* and *Irida Lankadipa*, both in Sinhalese, have the first and second largest circulations of any papers in South and Southeast Asia, the former running over 150,000 copies each week. Although roughly 75 per cent of the circulation of the Sinhalese and English language papers is concentrated in Western Province, there has been a rising circulation in the rural inland districts. The principal publishing houses have well-organized distribution systems and even in remote villages there are the familiar yellow and black signs of the newspaper venders.

There have been two principal newspaper publishers. The Associated Newspapers of Ceylon owns five dailies and three Sunday papers in three languages, and the Times of Ceylon, Ltd., publishes two dailies and two Sunday papers in two languages. These papers, however, have not always followed the same editorial policies. The papers of the Associated Newspapers of Ceylon, particularly, are stamped with the special emphasis given them by their editors who are permitted a large scope to express their personal views or to slant their policies in the direction of a particular audience. Tamil, Sinhalese, and English-language papers frequently follow significantly different editorial policies on the same public issue. Hence, there is less homogeneity of view expressed than might be expected of such concentrated ownership. The Trotskyist party has a paper of its own, the *Samasamajist*, and there are other weekly papers of much smaller circulation. The *Tribune* is known for its well-written and often detailed articles on public issues, although the vigor of its attacks is often stronger than the accuracy of its charges.

In marked contrast to many Indian journals, Ceylon's newspapers are frankly, often brutally, critical, constantly exposing the weaknesses of men in high places and cutting them down to an all-too-human size. Many press men conceive of their role as the vigilant protectors of the public from the ambitious and corrupt official and politician. Inconsistencies and faults of the public administration, the divisions between leading cabinet personalities, and allegations of corrupt practice and misappropriation of funds are frequent elements of their crusading enterprise. Few countries can boast of a similarly skillful critical press. Political cartoons have been developed to a fine and devastating art.

Newspaper men actively seek out grievances and give publicity to any group that raises its voice. Letter columns have been readily open to many individuals and small groups with a special view to air. It is sufficient for three or four individuals to associate together, to make up a name, and to present to the public a bold project to protect its interests, for the columns of the press to publicize their program. The more serious protests of the groups of unemployed students, dispossessed tenants, disgruntled port workers or postal employees could easily find expression.

The press has an additional role to play. Men in high places, inside or outside of the cabinet, in the professions or in politics, often take their views directly to the press. Men in a minority within an organization can also publicize their arguments. Sometimes they will use the "calculated" leak—a device dear to the American capital—to drum up support for their project; sometimes a bold accusation against an opponent or a prospective ally will be publicized in the hope that the person attacked will come to terms in private in order to call off his accuser. Because of its tactical utilities and its fundamental critical bent, to view Ceylonese affairs merely through the press gives a highly distorted perspective.

Scanning the press over a period of ten years, gives the impression that the English-language press, at least, became more accessible to the voices of protest. During the 1947 and 1952 election campaigns, for instance, the large newspaper houses appear to have supported the government not only in their editorial policy but also by limiting the coverage given to the Opposition candidates. By 1955, however, this appeared no longer to be true, and penetrating criticisms of the government were perhaps as frequent as criticisms of the Opposition.

Thus, a critical press plays an important part in Ceylon's affairs. Its propensity for discrediting men in public life, exposing the government's weaknesses, and devoting space to reporting public disagreements is no doubt useful. The voicing of grievances is essential. Perhaps at some time the press will be able to play a more directly constructive role.

Without a specialized study, it is difficult to characterize the wider communications system. As a small island, rural areas are in much closer contact with urban areas than in India or Pakistan. With better roads, more public vehicles than any neighboring country, and a more complete telephone and telegraph establishment at their disposal, the Ceylonese are in closer touch with one another than any other people in the area. On the other hand, the underlying familial and communal structure, and the language and educational differences induce communication within the communities rather than from one to another. A visitor is struck with how little comprehension one group has of another. Personal experience that crosses the communications barriers is rare enough to allow the most implausible generalizations about "the other" to go unchallenged, whether the educated man is generalizing about the peasant, the village Sinhalese about the Tamil, the entrepreneur about the union man, or vice versa.

CONCLUSION: THE SETTING OF POLITICS, A CHARACTERIZATION[73]

Like all its Asian neighbors, Ceylon is a society in which political groups still form on the basis of shared ethnic, religious, or cultural distinctions. Few can conceive of a Ceylonese nation, united in its multiple diversity. A vision of "the public interest" encompasses not the citizenry as a whole, but only those who belong in one individual group. As in Burma, the ethnic, religious, and linguistic composition of the people is such that one "community" makes up a clear majority of the citizens, and a number of small minorities, the remainder. An underlying theme of political life is the search for a relationship between the majority community and the minorities within a representative political system.

Social rigidities and inherited stratifications are more marked in Ceylon than in Burma though less sharply drawn than in Pakistan or India. Educational contrasts are not only great but clearly visible.

[73] See Lucian W. Pye, "The Non-Western Political Process," *The Journal of Politics*, xx, 3 (August 1958), pp. 468-486 for propositions based on Southeast Asian experience that are similar to some of these.

Status consciousness and group comparisons are widespread. Opportunities for wealth and responsibility at the national level have for many years been the prerogative of the Westernized, who have usually been the men of privilege and wealth from a previous generation. Though called a "stagnant society" in political polemic, nevertheless important social and economic changes have gained momentum. A cash economy penetrating the countryside and an expanding educational system are undermining traditional modes of influence. As elsewhere in the area, various aspects of the legacy of the colonial period are being challenged, including the assumed position of the Westernized and the role of important minorities.

The economy is narrowly based like that of Burma, Pakistan, and Malaya. All of these countries are seriously affected by adverse and abrupt changes in their terms of trade with other countries. Hitherto, Ceylon had provided a standard of living probably two to two and one-half times as high as India's or Pakistan's, the highest in the area with the possible exception of Malaya. Unused irrigable land is still available for the traditional types of farming or newer commercial crops, if heavy capital expenditure is possible. Yet a population that can double itself within the next thirty years threatens to change Ceylon's relatively favorable position. Her economic problems may become more urgent, like those of her less fortunate neighbors.

As in India and elsewhere in the area, the present type of economy does not offer the educated enough opportunities; the plantations do not provide openings that they find desirable; and peasant farming is beneath all but the less educated sons of peasants. Only a relatively few, usually from caste or ethnic minorities, find commerce or business activities congenial. Many assume that only a dramatic alteration can set a new expansive economic thrust in motion. Yet the conservatism of the peasantry and of the numerous rubber and coconut small holders, together with the social distance separating them from the Westernized elite impedes the adoption of the new techniques that must come to the economy through the Westernized elite.

Unlike any other country in the area, the transition to representative, constitutional government and then to independence in Ceylon was accomplished without bloodshed or mass involvement. The Westernized who managed the transition from the Ceylonese side, like their counterparts in other British colonial areas, adopted the Westminster model of government. They instituted a cabinet responsible to a parliament of which the lower chamber was elected by universal franchise on the basis of territorial constituencies. Elections based on universal suffrage have been practiced since 1931, the assumption of the secret ballot and the freely expressed voter choice becoming more generally accepted with each experience. The parties were creations of leading personalities, often drawn together by considerations other than broad public policy. By comparison with Pakistan, Burma, or Indonesia, Ceylonese parties have developed certain contrasting party commitments, although dramatic changes in a party's position on controversial matters are not unknown. As in all these countries, personality differences and public disagreements have marked cabinet deliberations as well as party life. The factional difficulties that followed the death in 1952 of Mr. D. S. Senanayake, a man politically comparable to Mohammed Ali Jinnah or Mr. Nehru, confirmed the importance of a dominating personality during the formative years.

The extent of the commitment to the constitution is difficult to appraise. It is among the Westernized minority that the clearest understanding of the constitution is to be found. But the constitution suffers in the eyes of the masses by its close association with the privileged and wealthy who introduced the system under British auspices and have been operating it since the late 1930's. Because the Westernized constitutionalists were the ones with access to economic and political advantages, the non-Westernized—and the Marxists—can question the sincerity of their attachment to "democracy." Recent policies pressed by the majority community have alienated the principal ethnic minority from the constitution. The astonishing public disorders of 1958 in Ceylon, and the suspension of the constitution in Pakistan and Burma have raised doubts in other minds as well. Even the prime minister has publicly questioned the appropriateness of the Ceylonese constitution and has called for widespread discussion of possible alternatives.[74]

Certain interest groups have been well organized for a number of years or even decades and are well able to press their claims. Others, however, remain latent and inchoate, yet vaguely sense—or are ready to be persuaded—that they have been kept from the centers of influence. As new interest groups develop, representing the resentments and the aspirations of the non-Westernized, it cannot be as-

[74] Text in *Times of Ceylon*, April 19, 1959.

sumed that they will share an underlying constitutional sense or will be aware of the limits beyond which it disrupts the body politic to push their particular demands.

These general characteristics of the social, economic, and political system will be more clearly seen in the following chapters where specific problems of public affairs are examined in detail.

PART TWO

CHARACTERISTIC PROBLEMS OF DOMESTIC POLITICS

CHAPTER VI · RELIGIOUS REVIVAL AND CULTURAL NATIONALISM

"When the Guide of the World, having accomplished the salvation of the whole world . . . was lying on the bed of his nibbana, in the midst of the great assembly of gods, he, the great sage, the greatest of those who have speech, spoke to Sakka who stood there near him: 'Vijaya, son of King Sihabahu, is come to Lanka . . . together with seven hundred followers. In Lanka, O lord of gods, will my religion be established, therefore carefully protect him with his followers and Lanka.' "—*The Mahavamsa*, or The Great Chronicle of Ceylon

I · INTRODUCTION

RELIGIOUS traditions and values are closer to the source of behavior in Asia than they have been in Western countries for many centuries. The man of religious bent and his efforts to find tranquility are widely admired. During the declining years of life it is not uncommon for a man to seek a closer understanding of his religious tradition by separating himself from his family and living with scholars or ascetics. Religious spokesmen retain a moral authority over the private thoughts and inner recesses of the mind in a way that is now strange to Western life, although medieval Western man would have needed no effort to understand these things. Many in the Westernized elite, like their European, American, or Russian counterparts, are religiously skeptical, if not downright anti-religious, because of the conservatism and "archaic" qualities now attributed to anything religious. But rural Asia is still profoundly moved by religious symbols and belief. There is no indigenous tradition of the separation of church and state that has done so much in western Europe to promote the notion of Caesar's province as distinct from the realm of religion. In Asia the two have not been different worlds but they interpenetrated and merged with one another. Traditional religions provide the source of values and justifications that help to distinguish these peoples from their former Western rulers. Existing bonds between the elite and masses are most likely to be found in the traditional cultural and religious spheres. Hence, it was logical for the devout and the religiously committed to expect that under the new dispensation to come with independence, religion would play a more important role than it had when foreign Christians ruled. Disappointment in these hopes has created politically significant grievances.

Religious values can therefore be expected to play an important role in politics to a degree rarely found in contemporary Western politics. In India, Gandhi evoked profoundly Hindu values in the course of the independence struggle, and since independence the Nehru government has had to emphasize its secular character to counter the insistent pressures that bring religious communities into conflict. In Pakistan, religious belief and affiliation were the primary distinguishing justifications for separate statehood, and the role to be played by religion formed a central theme of politics.[1] The leaders of independent Burma have stressed the Buddhist inspiration of their purpose and their rule. It is difficult for outsiders to grasp the elements of these phenomena and to assign them proper weight in considering political developments. With the exception of Pakistan, there are none of the organizational structures of authority familiar to Western Christendom. There are no clear-cut doctrinal definitions of belief. The structure of influence within the religious community is diffused, informal, unobtrusive.

Toward the end of the first decade of independence in Ceylon, religious concerns and grievances played an increasingly prominent role in public life. This Buddhist "revival" can be seen as an effort of religious spokesmen to accomplish a reformation of religious organization and outlook. It was clearly linked to political developments, though the two were distinguishable. Accordingly, connections between Buddhism and Sinhalese culture and between Buddhist revival, political independence, and the Holy Year of Buddha Jayanti are relevant.

A gross outline of Buddhist belief and ethic may help to understand the problems of religious organization, the relation between monk and layman, and the application of the Buddhist ideal to social practice. In order to highlight the contrast between the days of Buddhist glory and the present, the traditional relation between church and state and the role historically played by the priesthood are examined. The legacy of foreign rule and efforts to correct some

[1] Keith Callard, *Pakistan, A Political Study* (New York, 1957), Ch. VI.

of the internal difficulties within the priesthood contribute to contemporary Buddhist activity.

A. BUDDHISM AND SINHALESE DISTINCTIVENESS

The national independence movement had been relatively secular, led by Buddhists, Hindus, and Christians of Western education who were generally persuaded that a state detached from religious concerns was the appropriate model for a country of religious diversity such as Ceylon. Feeling themselves under no imperative to create a mass movement in order to wrest power from a reluctant Raj, the political leaders of all Ceylonese communities had no need to appeal to religious sentiment in order to mobilize a following. The temperance movement of the 1880's and 1890's had stressed the essential Buddhist precepts regarding alcohol while encouraging protests against the colonial government's handling of liquor licenses and its related revenue policies. The leaders of the movement in the twentieth century became prominent enough to have been arrested briefly by the British during the religious riots of 1915. These men sought political independence, but they experienced no need for a radical religious or cultural transformation. They respected the Western civilization they had come to know in their schools; they were not aliens in the Colombo which they, as well as foreign officials and businessmen, had created. On ceremonial occasions they appealed to the memory of Sinhalese kings of the past, but few professed to find real inspiration in this for contemporary guidance. Aristotle, Rousseau, John Stuart Mill, and Thomas Jefferson were their mentors, not Parakrama Bahu I or even Buddhaghosa, the great Buddhist commentator. Some were deeply versed in Ceylonese history and many understood their religious traditions; they carried on religious, educational, or other voluntary activity. But religious identifications and protest were much less important to Ceylon's political life than they were in undivided India, in Burma or Indonesia.

Only recently, during the decade of independence itself, did religious concerns become of importance politically. A delayed cultural revival, a turning back to precolonial days in search for identity, brought Buddhist values into greater prominence. The distinctiveness of Ceylon in the world of states was gradually found to have been the result of its unique association with Theravada Buddhism.

After the great Indian Emperor Asoka, Buddhism rapidly declined in India. Had it not been for the welcome accorded to Buddhism in Ceylon, it was argued, Buddhism might not have survived at all.[2] According to the *Mahavamsa*—the Great Chronicle—written by Buddhist monks to glorify those rulers who properly fulfilled their obligations to the faith, even the founding of Ceylon was the occasion for the most notable miracles. As the Buddha lay dying, it reports, he knew that Buddhism would be established in Ceylon and he besought the gods to protect Vijaya, the legendary founder of the Sinhalese race who was at that very time landing on the island that was to become the fountainhead of his "Way."[3] The Buddha's message was preserved in its purity by Ceylonese monks who were the first to commit it to writing. Buddhaghosa came to Ceylon in the fifth century A.D. in search of the authoritative source for the original teaching.[4] A most sacred relic—the eyetooth of the Buddha —has been in the safekeeping of Ceylon's rulers ever since the fourth century.

In the minds of a growing number of articulate and politically active people in Ceylon, the Buddhist religious culture has been the preserver and carrier of the national heritage—its source and seed. It is held that Buddhism produced the civilizing influence which made its culture and government great at a time when Britain was merely an outpost province of the Roman Empire.[5] The Sinhalese alphabet and writing derive from the Pali of Buddhist scripture. Just as the efforts of European Christian monks contributed fundamentally to the important place Latin holds in European languages, so the industry and scholarship of Buddhist monks provided the Sinhalese with a literary and linguistic foundation. As a result of their activities, Ceylon is one of the few countries to possess a continuous chronicle from the very beginning to modern times. A grow-

2 Buddhist Committee of Inquiry, *The Betrayal of Buddhism*, in English, abridged (Balangoda, 1956), p. iii. The role of Asoka in the development of Buddhism has been likened to that of St. Paul in Christianity. F. Harold Smith, *The Buddhist Way of Life* (London, 1951), p. 80.

3 Wilhelm Geiger, trans. *The Mahavamsa or The Great Chronicle of Ceylon* (Colombo, 1950), pp. 54-55.

4 Christmas Humphreys, *Buddhism* (London, 1954), p. 63.

5 Pliny recorded that the Sinhalese ambassador from the court of Anuradhapura sat on the right of Claudius Caesar when two kings from Britain were among the captives paraded past the Roman Emperor. D. C. Vijayavardhana, *Dharma-Vijaya or The Revolt in the Temple* (Colombo, 1953), p. 92. *The Revolt in the Temple* cannot be taken as authentic history at every point, but it can be properly used as a source for attitudes that had considerable currency between 1954 and 1957. We also assume some of its criticisms of certain segments of the priesthood to have been reasonably accurate. In no instance, however, was this study considered a sufficient source in itself. Corroborative interview evidence regarding the Sangha was obtained on all points cited.

ing number of Sinhalese saw their cultural debt to Buddhism as they became more conscious of Lanka's contribution to Theravada Buddhism.[6]

B. BUDDHA JAYANTI

Particular events contributed to a growing self-awareness among Buddhists. In 1947 Buddhist relics formerly taken from India to Great Britain were returned to Sanchi by a circuitous and triumphal journey through many Buddhist countries, awakening a widespread popular enthusiasm. More important, according to Buddhist belief, the Buddha's Way, philosophy, or religion was to grow and develop for 2,500 years. The 2,500th anniversary of his death was to mark the apogee of Buddhism. It was to be a year of public commemoration of this great Buddhist milestone. Personal rededication to Buddhist values in that year would have special meaning. In Theravada countries the crucial year was from June 1956 to May 1957.[7]

Buddha Jayanti year had a peculiarly Sinhalese significance. The coincidence of the landing of Vijaya and the death of the Buddha made it possible to see the year 1956 as a unique, three-fold event—the completion of 2,500 years of Buddhism, of the life of the Sinhalese race, and of Ceylon's recorded history.

Buddhist consciousness grew as the Burmese government convened a great conclave of Buddhist monks and laymen in 1955 to revise the sacred texts, as great councils had done in centuries past. Lavish expenditures on behalf of this Buddhist enterprise and the manifest deference paid by Burma's political rulers to the Buddhist faith set a high example for other Asian leaders. As Buddha Jayanti ap-

[6] "Theravada" Buddhism is the term used in Ceylon to describe their Buddhism. Another term used outside Theravada countries is "Hinayana" Buddhism, meaning literally "the Lesser Vehicle" and therefore carrying pejorative implications. It was used originally by a group of Buddhists who developed, as they affirmed, the real meaning of the Buddha's teachings and called their interpretations the Mahayana or "Greater Vehicle." Theravada Buddhism is at home in Ceylon, Burma, Thailand, Cambodia, and Laos. Humphreys, pp. 61-66; Bhikkhu J. Kashyap, "Origin and Expansion of Buddhism," in Kenneth W. Morgan, *The Path of the Buddha* (New York, 1956), p. 39.

[7] Theravada Buddhists, following the Ceylonese tradition, accept the year 544 B.C. as the death year of the Buddha and on that basis celebrated the 2,500th anniversary in 1956. But there is considerable uncertainty about the exact date, and there were variations in belief as to whether Buddha Jayanti in 1956 celebrated his death, his enlightenment, or even his birth. For discussion, see Hajime Nakamura, "Unity and Diversity in Buddhism," in Morgan, p. 365. May is the sacred month, when his birth, enlightenment, and death all took place, giving great importance to the Vesak celebrations of that month each year. See also E. A. Burtt's introduction to his *The Teachings of the Compassionate Buddha* (New York, 1955), pp. 20-22.

proached, the government of Ceylon responded by promoting various religious activities—translations into Sinhalese of the sacred books, the beginning of a Buddhist encyclopedia, and restoration of Buddhist holy monuments. These activities connected with the sacred year provided an impetus toward Buddhist solidarity and collective effort unusual in the recent Buddhist past.

II · SOME BASIC BUDDHIST PERSPECTIVES

In the Buddhist house there are many mansions. Beliefs vary greatly in different countries and between different schools. Because it is a highly individualistic belief system in which each person is responsible for his own enlightenment, it tolerates a wider diversity of views than is to be found within any single Christian sect or church, and perhaps even greater variations than are encompassed by all Christian denominations together. It is therefore difficult enough for a Buddhist to generalize about his own faith.[8] It is doubly difficult for an outsider to make observations that will be both fair and sound. Yet, an endeavor must be made to discuss various aspects of Buddhist faith and organization which have a bearing on political and social development in Ceylon.[9]

The traditional canonic literature in Theravada countries stresses the value of detachment, aloofness, and non-involvement in worldly affairs or preoccupations. In the Buddhist cosmology, one is involved in a succession of births and rebirths, each of which brings us into a world where all is fleeting, painful, and sorrowful. For most people this life is one of "quiet desperation." The attachments we form to other men and women are inescapably transitory in any cosmic sense; the loved one changes and finally dies, and the attraction we had for the other is said to be merely lust, the admired object tarnishes even as the lovely lotus fades. Men and women become old, they lose their faculties. The average person, it is held, spends his life in a tragically vain endeavor to gratify the essentially insatiable demands of his senses. The fundamental aim of man therefore is to find the way of release from this world of sorrow and futility. Despite the

8 For an interesting collection of essays by Buddhists designed for a Western audience, see Kenneth Morgan's *The Path of the Buddha.*

9 The observations that follow must be taken as one person's exploratory effort to understand. They should not be considered in any way as definitive. The writer wishes to express his thanks to the *bhikkhus* of different nikayas and temples who have explored patiently with him many facets of Buddhism. Naturally only the writer is responsible for the particular interpretation given.

stress on the pain and sorrow and sadness of this world, to many of its devotees Buddhism is a faith of optimism and hope, for the Buddha's teaching is held to provide a method, a "Way of Liberation," from this infinite sorrow. If one lives rightly, if one lives the Way, one can expect to find release. Release may be in this life to the most adept, in the next rebirth for the very skilled, and some time within the next half a dozen births if one is seriously seeking.

To "live rightly" is to achieve self-mastery, to gain control of errant moods and feelings and thoughts; to "walk watchfully" is to keep guard over perceptions so that any tendency toward craving the sad and transitory things or feelings of this world may be nipped in the bud. Not entirely unlike some psychoanalytic schools in the West today, the self is seen as a field of forces in tension or balance one against another. Through will and training the individual can intervene in this inward process to inhibit, offset, or undercut unwanted feelings or to promote desired feelings and actions. The nature of the desired feelings and the technique of control in the two systems of thought are quite different, but the hypothecated processes in both have much in common.

Karma is the Buddhist conception of cause and effect. In essentials it appears to mean that what I am in this life is in considerable part the result of what I have thought and done in past lives. What I am is only in part what I am given; I am also what I make of what I am given. My future is what I make of myself today. There are thus two aspects to karma. One is the idea that we are fortunate in this life because we have created "good" karma for ourselves in preceding births. If we are unfortunate, it is because we did not act and think rightly before. On the other hand, it is distinguishable from fatalism, the feeling of helplessness and not caring, because the full doctrine avers that it is possible to lead a sufficiently correct life in word, thought, and deed now, today, in order that our lot in this life may be improved and our situation in the next life markedly better. It is not entirely dissimilar from our common sense view that we as adults are a peculiar and original combination resulting from those qualities we inherited at birth and from what happened to us in our early childhood and adolescence; elements over which we had no control, and yet curiously and rather mysteriously molded and given form by our own, often hard, efforts to "overcome" this or that "handicap."[10]

10 See, for instance, the important Maha Mangala Sutta, recently republished with a

Where it differs from this Western view most significantly is the emphasis the Buddhist puts on the all-powerful quality of thought and inward motivation. In the view of many Buddhists, the subjective, inward reality is as important as the action it may lead to. Indeed, it is frequently argued that mind, thought, and feeling are all determinants of action; that the distinction between the subjective state and external behavior is difficult, if not impossible, to make in any functional sense. The motive behind action is more determining of the full quality of the act than the consequences of the action in the world of behavior. Ideas and feelings toward another contribute as much to the ineluctable network of cause and effect that binds us all as does action itself. In 1956, when the island was riven with communal discord, one of the leading Buddhist scholars and laymen who showed an awareness of the minority's anxieties appealed to all Buddhists to fast, to visit places of worship, offer flowers, light incense at shrines, to engage in thoughts of love and compassion to all beings, and fervently wish for peace and harmony in the world and especially Sri Lanka.[11] Similarly, some Christian monks and nuns have regarded the "work of prayer" as primary and far more important and religiously relevant than aiding the sick or actively comforting the fearful.

Thus the mind, motives behind action, the inward state are the primary causative elements according to the Buddhist way of thought; their mastery is the true challenge of life. If this were strictly so, there would be no need to distinguish between different ways of living this life in order to achieve different degrees of Buddhist enlightenment. But in the texts that are generally considered to be close reflections of earliest Buddhist thought, a clear distinction was made between the life of the *bhikkhu* and the way of life of the layman. The layman, bound as he was by the inescapable commitments of family and occupation, could not expect to gain the degree of detachment or enlightenment that could be achieved by the *bhikkhu*.

The *bhikkhu* retired from the world precisely to lead a life of full-time, disciplined, professional search for enlightenment and re-

contemporary commentary by the Burmese Ven. U. Nana Dicca under the title, *The Thirty-Eight Blessings for World Peace* (Rangoon, 1955), or a different commentary, *Mangala Sutta Vanna* (Penang, 1956), by the Mahanayake Thero of Malaya and Singapore.

11 *Times of Ceylon*, June 7, 1956.

lease.[12] His mode of life has been defined minutely in the *Vinaya Pitaka,* a set of rules which fill four volumes of texts. As might be expected, Vinaya rules concern not only the details of his simple dress, prescribed ways of sustenance, of greeting others, the daily schedule, and texts to ponder, but are important instructions regarding the proper thoughts and feelings that he should train himself to experience and those he should repudiate. His days are supposed to be filled with reading and the study of the canon, committing to memory the classic words of the Buddha as well as the various commentaries on Buddhist texts. In addition, much vigorous endeavor should be applied to meditation, to the willful concentration of all the mind's strength and energy on a particular point, cutting out the usual sensations that distract us, in a systematic effort to perceive further into the "Cloud of the Unknowing." Thus study, meditation, and self-training are the primary tasks of the good *bhikkhu.* If the monk has time, in addition, then he has the duty to teach religious philosophy and the sacred literature to all those who come to him. He must be accessible and welcoming to the laymen who may seek his advice on many matters and he may perform certain understood ceremonial and intercessory functions. But he has no such obligations toward the laity that a Christian churchman has. He is not responsible for the spiritual well-being of a congregation. If laymen come to him, he must help them as he can. His primary religious obligation, however, is to the life of meditation and piety.

In the classical canon, life among the *bhikkhus* is depicted as a model community composed of self-less individuals who work and live together in harmony, preserving "kindness of action, speech and thought"; "dividing without partiality and sharing in common with their upright companions" whatever may come to them; "gathering in concord and rising up and carrying out their duties in concord." It is a society where life is ordered by the self-restraint and inward discipline of each member. It requires no external sanctions and no structure of authority because the devotees are presumed to know the importance of preventing their own potentially expansive and destructive appetites from intruding on the peacefulness of others

[12] "Bhikkhu" or "bhikkshu" is the Pali word for "monk," "recluse," or "religieux." The word *bhikkhu* is sometimes rendered in English as priest, but the *bhikkhu* claims no priestly powers. The use of the term monk is not accurate either, for it implies obedience to the rules of an order. *Bhikkhus* do not yield obedience to an organization or a human superior in this sense, though they do follow the Vinaya rules of discipline to the Buddha's "Way." The term *bhikkhu* will therefore be used throughout this study.

as well as on their own serenity. It is a life lived by blameless men who impinge on others as little as possible.[13]

The "Sangha" is the order of monks who are attempting to lead such lives of perfection. But it is deceptive to apply analogies with Christian religious orders. There is no Superior who orders the monk's behavior. The Buddha did not appoint a successor to himself. He held, on the contrary, that each man and each *bhikkhu* had to be himself the lamp to guide his own footsteps. Each monk is himself attempting to achieve enlightenment or release and he himself must be his own judge. There are group confessionals periodically in which each *bhikkhu* must tell where he has erred from the path of watchfulness, and he must make amends according to the Vinaya rules. But the emphasis is on loose organization and the slight structure of authority of one over another. One senior, or more learned, *bhikkhu* may ordain another, but this fact gives him no special authority. "The obedience expected of a *bhikkhu* is to the Dhamma (or the Way of Buddha); to his seniors in the Sangha he owes only a respectful submission."[14] Gradations within the order are not so much on the basis of authority of one over another, but on the mastery of the lessons of the Buddha, the knowledge and ability to follow the Buddha Dhamma or Dharma, the "Way."

The Dhamma or "Way" that applies to the *bhikkhus* is the ultimate ideal for the good Buddhist layman, too, even though the layman cannot achieve the fullest perfection because of his involvements with his family, in gaining wealth, and living in this world. The following eight rules for interpreting the manifold passages of the Teachings of Buddha suggest the essential bent of this standard of perfection. Buddhists are admonished to choose that interpretation of the Dhamma or Way that will:

> "eliminate pleasure in anything;
> eliminate attachment to worldly things;
> not make you accumulate sins or worldly things;
> make you moderate in your desires;
> make you satisfied with what you have;
> will make you like solitude;

[13] For the most succinct description of this "ideal society," see Dighanikaya, Sixteenth Discourse, Maha Parinibbana Suttanta, Dialogues of the Buddha in *Sacred Books of the Buddhists*, T. W. Rhys Davids, ed. (London, 1910), III, pp. 82-84.

[14] Ananda Maitreya Nayaka Thero, "Buddhism in Theravada Countries," in Morgan, p. 125.

will make you persevere, be diligent to attain Nibbana;
will make you easy to feed, will keep you from requiring luxuries."[15]

This is essentially an ascetic ethic, not because the good Buddhist feels it is "good for his soul" to deprive himself, but because by cultivating simplicity of wants he can achieve the detachment and enlightenment which are the ends of his strenuous endeavor. The good layman should strive to develop for himself the kind of life which will require utmost simplicity, a generosity that stems from his own inward mastery of greed, and a consideration for others that follows from the unimportance he attaches to himself.

These requirements are defined for the layman in a series of "Sila," principles or precepts for practical morality. The Five Precepts or "Pancha Sila" require the Buddhist to (1) abstain from taking the life of any sentient being; (2) to abstain from taking what is not given; (3) to abstain from improper or excessive sexuality; (4) to abstain from false, disruptive, argumentative speech; and (5) to abstain from intoxicants since they cloud the mind and make "mindfulness" impossible. From time to time the devout Buddhist will "take sil," that is, renew his vows to follow these and other precepts in his external behavior while carrying out the inward, mental or emotional disciplines that alone give the external behavior its true meaning.

Although Theravada Buddhism is usually interpreted by those philosophically oriented in the West as being concerned almost exclusively with the monastic life of the professional recluse, there are specific "Suttas" that define the householder's proper code of behavior in greater detail than the Five Precepts. The Sigalowada Sutta, for instance, sets forth the rules and prescriptions for the good life of the layman in a moral code not unlike the Confucian. Characteristic relationships are identified, and the proper approach to each is defined. Parents are to love and care for their children while they themselves are to be revered and cared for in their old age; teachers are to give their best knowledge and help their pupils grow, while they are to receive in return an eagerness to learn, deference, and adequate fees; wives and children are to defer to their husbands and fathers and receive from them care and protection; friends should reciprocate affection, protect each other, and share useful information. Servants and work people should rise before their masters,

[15] *Ibid.*, p. 127.

retire after they retire, serve them devotedly and well, and receive from their masters gentle treatment, care, and protection. Within this nicely balanced code of interrelated services and dependency, the emphasis is one of a vertical vision where the strong looks down from his higher position to those weaker ones below whom he nevertheless loves and protects. The only relationship of equality is that between friend and friend.[16]

The Sigalowada Sutta also includes a list of vices that a good person should not indulge in, six possible ways of dissipating one's wealth, and five additional virtues. One should strive to be wise, to rise early, and avoid sloth; one should make friends easily and work well with others; one should give good counsel when one's friends require it. One should be generous and openhanded, living a life of service to others.[17] A great deal of Buddhist literature contains five ways to achieve this and six ways to attain that, a tradition that greatly aided memorization.

III · THE BUDDHIST TRADITION

A. INTIMACY OF CHURCH AND STATE

This benign and gentle faith or philosophy in its early form became firmly established in Ceylon about the third century, B.C. when Mahinda, the son of the Indian emperor Asoka, came to convert the island. The rulers of Ceylon actively promoted Buddhism thenceforward for many centuries. Monarch and Sangha were intimately interlinked.

The rulers were guardians of the sacred relic—the tooth—and possession of the relic was a symbol of the legitimate right to rule.[18] The monarchs, admired in the Great Chronicle, erected magnificent "stupas" or reliquary mounds in which precious Buddhist relics were enshrined. They saw to the proper care of the Sangha, building large and costly residences and bestowing land upon the temples. Those who farmed the lands paid rent in kind or in services to main-

16 This is pointed out by C. A. R. Rhys Davids' introduction to the Sigalowada Sutta in T. W. Rhys Davids, ed., *Sacred Books of the Buddhists* (London, 1921), IV, p. 172. The balance of the discussion is from pp. 180-183.

17 For useful discussions of these problems, see Dr. O. H. De A. Wijesekera, *Buddhism and Society* (Colombo n.d., c. 1954), and *Buddhism and the Moral Problem* (Colombo, 1945).

18 Mendis, *The Early History of Ceylon*, pp. 58-59. There is here a parallel, though short-lived, between the legitimacy deriving from the tooth relic and that inhering in the Crown of St. Stephen in Hungary.

tain the temples. Care for sick *bhikkhus* was particularly worthy. By tradition, the king paid the Sangha both deference and reverence. Several notable kings even offered their kingdoms to the Sangha. The white umbrella, sign of royal sovereignty, was not infrequently bestowed upon the Sangha as a reminder that the State was believed to be run for the good of Buddhism.[19] It was not unknown for leading monks to have the final word in selecting a king when the succession was disputed.[20] Conversely, the priesthood appealed to the king when it became divided on doctrinal or other matters. Without an apostolic succession or some device for giving the men of the yellow robe supreme authority over one another in internal matters, there was need for outside assistance. Periodically the kings lent their authority to revisions of the discipline and to conferences called to clarify disputed matters of doctrine.[21]

The individual *bhikkhu's* advance to the grade of "Thero" or elder and to "Maha Thero" or senior elder is accomplished by an "ordination ceremony" carried out by senior members of the Sangha who accept into their company those who have progressed far enough in years and in knowledge to be deemed worthy. In the eleventh century A.D., following invasions from South India and other grave disorders, there were not enough *bhikkhus* of the higher ordination and King Vijaya Bahu had to renew the priestly succession by bringing monks from Pegu in Burma. In 1603 the Ceylonese king performed the same service by bringing monks from Aracan. The present Siam Nikaya was founded as recently as 1753 by the same means—ten *bhikkhus* were imported by the king from Ayuthia in Thailand.[22]

As individuals, the monarchs were supposed to exemplify Buddhist values in their private lives and public acts. Three rulers in particular have been honored. King Asoka of India (270-233 B.C.) occupies a position in Buddhism similar to that of St. Paul in Christianity. He sent missionaries to the distant reaches of his empire and beyond. He set an example of devotion by his good works, organizing hostels for the needy and the sick, by his tolerance of all religious faiths, and by his admonitory Pillar Edicts. Duttha-Gamini of Ceylon (161-

19 Rahula, *History of Buddhism in Ceylon*, p. 75; Geiger, p. 218.

20 Geiger, p. 229; Ariyapala, *Society in Medieval Ceylon*, p. 55.

21 Geiger, p. 270; H. W. Codrington, *A Short History of Ceylon* (London, 1947), p. 64; Ariyapala, p. 228. For Asoka's reign, see B. M. Barua, *Asoka and His Inscriptions*, 2nd ed. (Calcutta, 1955).

22 Codrington, pp. 57, 109; Morgan, p. 128.

137 B.C.) drove out the Indian invader, Elara, with the cry "not for kingdom, but for Buddhism." Repenting of the slaughter on both sides of this struggle, he sought to exemplify the Buddhist virtues by building temples and leading a life of gentleness and piety.[23] The reign of Parakrama Bahu I (1153-1196 A.D.) marked the zenith of Sinhalese grandeur. He constructed the largest tank, "the Sea of Parakrama," and one thousand other smaller water tanks.[24] Parakrama Bahu I also built temples and monastic residences as well as parks and pleasure gardens for the populace. He restored Buddhist shrines at Anuradhapura and reconciled three sects of monks. The Mahavamsa summarized the virtues of good monarchs in these terms: "men of good understanding, who have conquered pride and indolence, and have freed themselves from the attachment to lust, when they have attained to great power, without working harm to the people, delighting in deeds of merit, rejoicing in faith, do many and various pious works."[25]

In the Buddhist tradition the ruler promoted the Way of Piety, nurtured the Sangha, and was himself guided by the precepts of the Sangha and the Buddha's Way. Church and state were closely knit. The otherworldly preoccupations of the Sangha and the natural tendency for religious chroniclers to describe only the devout kings may partly account for the very few recorded instances where the temporal or religious interests of the Sangha clashed with the temporal interests of the king or vice versa. The contrast with western Europe is sharp, and conclusions drawn from European history would not apply to Ceylon. In a period of growing national self-awareness the tradition of harmony between the Buddhist church and the royal state, and the influence exerted by the Sangha when it received full secular support provides an alluring image of a future possibility.

B. THE SANGHA'S ROLE IN THE VILLAGE

The Sangha had a fundamental role in the villages. The *bhikkhu* was usually the most highly educated member of a community; in many instances, he was the only one who could read and write. He was the teacher who brought to the villagers the wisdom of the Buddha as well as the skills of writing, language, and a knowledge of literature. Although it was against the Vinaya rules, some *bhikkhus*

[23] Rahula, p. 79.
[24] Codrington, p. 64; Ariyapala, p. 330.
[25] Geiger, p. 245.

practiced medicine, and it was to them that the villagers went for the relief of their ailments. The villagers also came for advice on domestic troubles or to present before the *bhikkhu* two sides of a village dispute for settlement. He controlled the village temple, the only public gathering place.[26]

The temple and its ceremonies and festivals provided the color and excitement for the otherwise tranquil and monotonous village life.[27] In a society which had no weekly congregational worship, public religious ceremonies were important. And Buddhism in Ceylon developed several ceremonies of great beauty and impressiveness. One of the most important Buddhist festivals is "Vesak" which celebrates the Buddha's enlightenment. Another popular festival is often held to celebrate the preaching—or *bana*—of a special "sutta" or sacred text.[28] The *perahera* is an elaborate ritualized procession in which Buddhist and other relics are carried on the backs of elephants from one temple to another by the light of a full tropical moon, flaming torches above, whirling flares beneath, to the accompaniment of the conch shell and drumming. Although traditionally it had little to do with Buddhism, in recent centuries it has become an occasion for honoring the Buddha. There were private or family ceremonies at which the *bhikkhu* preached or he chanted sacred verses or *pirith* (which means literally "protection") in order to drive out a disease, to protect a patient from evil spirits, or to cleanse a new house about to be occupied.[29]

The *bhikkhu* did not have a monopoly in all these village roles, for the villager's life was, and still is, profoundly influenced by deities that have nothing to do with Buddhism. In any logical sense, the folk religions are antithetical to Buddhism, for they emphasize the existence of a multitude of supernatural beings and religious manifestations the Buddha himself criticized. On the other hand, Theravada Buddhism in Ceylon has long since come to terms with these beliefs just as in Burma it has come to terms with Nat-worship. The deities and parts of folk rituals have been "converted" to Buddhism in the sense that their original meaning has been changed. It is difficult to say how far this conversion has gone, for the indigenous gods and demons still help the villager to cope with the immediate urgen-

[26] Ariyapala, pp. 271-272; Humphreys, pp. 137-138.

[27] The importance of Buddhist ceremonies to village life today is well brought out in *Report of the Kandyan Peasantry Commission*, pp. 80-81.

[28] Rahula, pp. 267-268.

[29] *Ibid.*, pp. 277-280; E. R. Sarathchandra, *The Sinhalese Folk Play* (Colombo, 1953), p. 4.

cies which beset him. Village rites usually begin with deference and offerings to the Buddha before the serious immediate business of exorcism or intercessory appeal to Kataragama, Pattini, or another deity is made.[80] In spite of the persisting problems posed to the Sangha by the indigenous cults, Buddhism remains the ideal path to follow and it is the *bhikkhu* who teaches the fundamental moral lessons and explains the answers to ultimate questions of existence.

Members of the Sangha have been the principal figures in the educational, ceremonial, and religious life of the village. At the same time, the Theros and Maha Theros were advisers and teachers to the kings, the objects of royal veneration, and the recipients of royalty's lavish generosity. For the village *bhikkhu* and the leading Theros, this image of the past contrasted sharply with their present position.

IV · CONTRAST BETWEEN TODAY AND YESTERDAY

A. THE CHANGE IN STATUS AND INFLUENCE

With the withdrawal of the foreign Christian powers in 1948, the Sangha might have been expected to return to the esteemed position they had held at the time of the great Ceylonese kings. But the Sangha was not elevated; its advice was not sought. When its counsel was proffered, the modern leaders of Ceylon did not take it seriously. To the devout, the government seemed to be carried on through institutions that had no parallel in the traditions they knew and understood.

A few Buddhist temples retained their wealth on the basis of their hereditary endowments or contemporary pilgrims' alms, but wealthy Christians went on building impressive temples with money from abroad. In the early days, the members of the Sangha had been the bearers of traditional culture and perfecters of literary language. They were now faced with a language foreign to their knowledge, their religion, and their culture. They watched helplessly while this alien culture encouraged elements which the Buddhist tradition regarded as false and destructive, and lured young and old from their kindly and traditional oversight. Even in the village areas, to which the Buddhist religion had retreated from foreign rule and Christian organization, responsible laymen experienced more and more diffi-

80 For a discussion of the contemporary adjustment between Buddhism and the indigenous practices, Sarathchandra, pp. 2-5.

culty in obtaining services for the upkeep of their temples. Fewer villagers came to the temple for counsel and advice on their worldly and spiritual problems. The present was full of signs of distress and their discontent was not unlike the malaise of those who lived ". . . at the time of the Buddha and also immediately after his death, (when) there was a strong body of opinion that good men belonged to the past, contemporaries were unsatisfactory, and future generations would be corrupt beyond hope. . . . Influenced by this idea, monks in ancient Ceylon too, were naturally dissatisfied with the contemporary state of affairs."[81] It was clear that the public culture was infused with ideas and worldly standards from overseas. The Sangha itself was no longer the preceptor of youth or of power. By recreating the conditions of the glorious Sinhalese past, perhaps they could again guide the rulers and create a society where traditional religious values would have their due place.

B. EXPLANATIONS FOR THIS ALTERED POSITION

There are many explanations for the altered status and function of both the Sangha and of Buddhist values. Scholars are not of one mind regarding the beginning of these unfortunate developments. Dr. Ariyapala, for example, suggests that as early as the thirteenth century the Sangha "had lost much of its purity . . . the *bhikkhus* seem to have been lax in discipline and corruption set in."[82] Professor Mendis points to the difficulties experienced during the thirteenth, fourteenth, and fifteenth centuries attending the recurrent invasions from South India and the disorders stemming from dynastic struggles at home in Ceylon.[83] A more popular view, one which fits better the requirements of a nationalist awakening following the withdrawal of a European power, attributes the difficulties experienced by Buddhist institutions to the coming of the European Christians in the sixteenth century and to the succeeding centuries of European control.

Under the Portuguese and Dutch, temples were destroyed, *bhikkhus* persecuted, and laymen coerced into religious practices in the invaders' churches. Under the more subtle British, it is held, many disabilities developed. The intent of the nineteenth century administrators is understood to be revealed by Lord Acton's famous passage: "The religion and manners of the Orientals naturally sup-

[81] Rahula, pp. 203-204.
[82] Ariyapala, p. 227; Rahula, pp. 182-184.
[83] G. C. Mendis, *The Early History of Ceylon*, p. 107.

port one another; neither can be changed without the other. Hence, the pioneer of civilization has to get rid of the religion of India to enable him to introduce a better culture, and the pioneer of Christianity has to get rid of the Indian culture before he can establish his religion."[34]

It is often held against the British that they did not abide by the terms of the Kandyan convention, the treaty that gave them control of the upland, Kandyan provinces in 1815. It was then agreed that "the religion of the Boodhoo . . . is declared inviolable and its Rites, Ministers and Places of Worship are to be maintained and protected." At first, a British Resident in Kandy undertook the necessary official functions in lieu of the Kandyan monarch who had been displaced. But in the 1830's, under pressure from Christian missionary organizations in England, the London government decided it was inappropriate for a British official to bear responsibility for maintaining property, confirming officers, and generally overseeing the affairs of Buddhist temples.[35]

Finding an alternative arrangement proved difficult. The Governor of Ceylon proposed a central Buddhist committee to carry on these functions, but the law officers of the Crown advised against it as tending to "give the most dangerous force and unity" to the Buddhists.[36] In consequence there was now no official means of confirming lay trustees of particular temples. Lacking official standing, it was argued, neither temple incumbents nor laymen could make good a claim in court, and they were unable properly to defend their temple lands or other rights. A more decentralized arrangement was attempted, but according to Vinaya rules, the *bhikkhus* were not allowed to deal with temporal and money matters, and rural lay trustees were not scrupulous in their management of finances.[37]

The religious corporation is the usual legal form for the Christian churches, combining all churches in one sect into one perpetual,

[34] Quoted in Buddhist Committee of Inquiry, p. 2; also Dr. G. P. Malalasekera, "Buddhism in Ceylon" in A. W. P. Guruge and K. G. Amaradasa (eds.) *2,500 Buddha Jayanti Souvenir* (Colombo, 1956), p. 134.

[35] Buddhist Committee of Inquiry stresses this explanation for the Sangha's present plight, particularly Chapter I, section 5.

[36] A young lawyer active in the Buddhist movement has laid stress on this exchange of correspondence. For instance, C. D. S. Siriwardane, "The Buddhist Problem Today," *Law College Buddhist Annual 1955-1956*, pp. 2-6. It is also a central theme in the report of the Buddhist Committee of Inquiry.

[37] See G. C. Mendis' understanding discussion, *Ceylon under the British*, pp. 81-82. Reports of a *Commission Appointed to Inquire into the Working of the Buddhist Temporalities Ordinance, No. 8 of 1905* (Sessional Papers XXIV—1920; XII—1923) discuss the difficulties.

centralized organization managed by a board of self-selected trustees who have authority to invest funds, and to transfer funds from one part of the sect to another. In the Buddhist community, on the other hand, each temple remained a separate entity administered by a group of lay trustees under the general supervision of a Public Trustee, a government official. Incomes from temple lands could be utilized only as allowed under specific ordinance; gifts go to each temple, not to the sect as a whole; and each individual temple controls its own property.[88]

Certain temples, usually in the up-country areas, are heirs to royal grants of land made prior to the British. They are relatively wealthy in contrast to the low-country temples that are generally without land endowments. The decentralized organizational form perpetuates this difference. In contrast to the Christian churches—organized around the congregation with a more disciplined tithing system, receiving some assistance from abroad, and with centralized management—most Buddhist organizations have fewer ready resources. Lacking sufficient capital in "church" hands, the Buddhist community has been relatively ill-provided with those institutions that foster religiously motivated social service and educational work.

The British are also accused of taking land from the temples without proper recompense. In the 1860's, 1870's, and 1880's, where land titles could not be confirmed, large quantities of land were taken by the Crown and sold to British planters for coffee and tea estates. Much of the land was above the line of habitation in highland jungle areas where cultivation was irregular and title difficult to justify by European legal standards. Many acres of temple property are said to have been among the alienated lands. Reliable data on the magnitude could not be obtained. One report claimed 800,000 acres of temple lands had been confiscated, but interviews with officials suggested the figure should be much lower.[89]

The British are also criticized for their educational policies. Following the reforms in the 1830's, an English curriculum was advanced in selected government schools. Schools organized and operated by Christian missionary societies received generous government support. Temple schools organized on traditional lines declined; the

[88] C. D. S. Siriwardane, pp. 4-5.

[89] Vijayavardhana, p. 106; Buddhist Committee of Inquiry, pp. 6 and 7. The statistical difficulty is real since traditional land calculations were not based on area but on the likely product of the land and records were scant. In the writer's discussions with *bhikkhus* up-country, few expressed resentment against alleged land confiscation.

new method of education, which included foreign languages, geography of the outside world, European history, and more systematic ways of instruction and organized group activities, was alien to the *bhikkhu* instructors in the temple schools. *Bhikkhus* were naturally reluctant to recast their traditional practices to meet the new demands and showed little enthusiasm for following this strange, new system of education. Parents did not wish to send their children to traditional schools when they could send them to the better-equipped, foreign-managed institutions which emphasized the new languages, social ways, and newer skills that were at a premium in the colonial society. Later, when the Buddhist community opened its own schools, they were modeled on the secular and missionary schools in the British tradition and did not, as a rule, adopt the traditional modes as their pedagogic ideal.[40]

In the end, it was the foreigner's ways and the foreigner's culture that received state support. The educational system became oriented toward a foreign curriculum and the language of instruction in the best schools, and in official government dealings, was English. As the traditional teacher of the youth, the Sangha found itself progressively deprived of its principal means of approach to the lay community; it was cut off from influencing the adult of tomorrow in the Buddhist way of life. The majority of village *bhikkhus* considered the alienation of the Sangha from the laity, and the latter's defection to the educational innovations of the nineteenth century, the most deleterious result of the colonial period. The *Buddha Jayanti* summarized the view of the evil consequences of the foreign cultural invasion when it wrote: "The most important factor in the present condition of the common people is the absolutely alien social system imposed on them by the British, which is still functioning. It is a system which prevents the generality of the Buddhist population from coming into close contact with the monasteries and the monks, and (which has) estranged the people to a great extent from the traditional culture of a Buddhist nation; it is a system unsuited to the genius of the great majority of the inhabitants of this island and is destructive of the basis of friendliness, compassion and sobriety essential to the happy and peaceful life.[41]

The emotions involved in the contemporary Buddhist nationalist revival cannot be understood without reference to the Christian

[40] G. C. Mendis, *Ceylon under the British*, pp. 46, 61, 82; particularly pp. 163, 165.

[41] Editorial, "The Present Discontent," *Buddha Jayanti*, September 10, 1954, Vol. 1, No. 18.

efforts to convert Buddhists to Christianity. Christians were committed to the notion of zealous missionary effort and they introduced hitherto unknown organizational methods. Many believe that these organizational innovations gave the Christians an altogether unfair advantage, especially when they received state assistance for one of the instruments of Christian proselytizing—their schools. Many Buddhists have an image today of an all-seeing, tightly knit Christian religious organization—particularly Catholic—wielding political influence out of all proportion to its numbers, rapidly enhancing its wealth by virtue of its autonomy and disciplined organization, and slowly but surely winning Buddhists from their traditional ways, even though outright conversions may no longer be numerous.[42]

C. INTERNAL PROBLEMS

There is no doubt that the coming of the Europeans had an adverse affect on the status of the Sangha. There are those who argue that of all the still identifiable groups in Ceylon, it is the Sangha that has suffered the gravest disadvantages as a result of colonial policies. Other Buddhists stress certain internal limitations which have contributed to the decline in the status of the Sangha. Some of the most vigorous criticism comes from the Sangha's most devout well-wishers.

Bhikkhus are sometimes charged with being overly preoccupied with their own spiritual purity to the exclusion of effective thought and action on behalf of other human beings. The Sangha's stress on detachment may lead to fatalism, a passive acceptance of man's lot on earth, whereas Buddhism is a positive doctrine which requires a driving out of sloth and the energetic pursuit of enlightenment.[43] The *bhikkhus,* it is said, assume that real progress in this life along the Way is possible only to members of the Sangha; but in the time of the Buddha, laymen could achieve Arahantship in this life through diligent effort in the right direction.[44]

As in all orders of professional *religieux,* the range of intellectual training and philosophical sophistication varies enormously—from the highly cultivated *bhikkhus* of the Vajirarama in Colombo and the Vidyalankara Pirivena (training seminary) in Kelaniya to the

[42] For instance, the 1953 census shows that the Buddhists formed 64.3 per cent of the population in that year while in 1946 they represented 64.6 per cent, a reduction of only .3 per cent in 7 years. During the same period the Christians declined by 2.2 per cent.

[43] For instance, Vijayavardhana, pp. 292-312.

[44] *Ibid.,* pp. 581-583.

relatively untrained *bhikkhus* in the more isolated parts of the island. Admission standards have been loose, often subject to the wish of a novice's parents; many join the order who are really without vocation for the life of a recluse. Some of the older Theros are distressed by the educational level in the Sangha. Pirivena education has degenerated into rote-learning and cramming for examination papers, and the essential spirit of the "Way of Life" goes unnoticed. Two thousand years ago a development of the skill of memorization was essential to preserve and to hand down the unwritten Buddhist tradition. But for many centuries this skill has not been necessary. Some *bhikkhus* believe they should turn their attention to the interpreting of Buddhist precepts for the contemporary layman's life.[45]

Ceylon's Theravada Buddhism gives rise to organizational difficulties. Buddhist laymen are their own spiritual counselors, and do not depend on the Sangha as Christians depend on their priests for absolution or mediation between the individual and God.[46] The faith itself is wary of the vested interests, the ambitions, and the presumptions of authority of man over man that are the inescapable accompaniments of human organizations. The fundamental Buddhist search is a lonely, personal endeavor. In comparison, Western religions appear to be regimented and mechanized. It is difficult for Buddhists to believe that religious growth can be affected by the clock on a Sunday morning. To them religious insight depends fundamentally on the individual's mastery of himself and of his own impediments toward enlightenment.

In village areas, where the majority of the *bhikkhus* live, the *bhikkhu* can lead his exemplary life and be an advisor to the villagers without organization. His services to the villagers—teaching Sinhalese, instructing in the Dhamma, and officiating at ceremonies—require no organization. Village *bhikkhus* are not unduly concerned with it. The city Buddhists, seeing the need to prevent the young people from being drawn away by competing religions or political parties, urge the organization of the Sangha and the laity. They see organization as the means of obtaining state assistance for Buddhist social work; it is important for enhancing the role of Buddhists

[45] Interviews with *bhikkhus*.

[46] Humphreys discusses the lack of internal organization and its implications, pp. 132-139. On the lack of special provisions for close relations with the laity, see Dutt, N., *Early Monastic Buddhism*, 2 vols. (Calcutta, 1941), II, p. 107. Mendis, *Ceylon under the British*, pp. 82, 108.

in education or for influencing legislation designed to favor a Buddhist way of life.

That the Buddhist community has not developed institutions to meet its own educational or charitable needs, is not true. As long as the Sinhalese equivalent of the feudal system survived, an elaborate organization of temple maintenance and management remained intact. Recently, Buddhist laymen became organizationally active under the enthusiastic efforts of Colonel Olcott, the Theosophist, who encouraged the Buddhist community to develop its own lay institutions. The Buddhist Theosophical Society was founded and was active in the establishment of many Buddhist schools. The Maha Bodhi Society was created in 1891 to revive Buddhism in India and to carry its message elsewhere. The All-Ceylon Buddhist Congress is more recent in origin. Charitable institutions, orphanages and homes, have been opened; there are young men and young women's Buddhist organizations, modeled after the Y.M.C.A.; and Buddhist newspapers and pamphlets are published. However, many of these organizations are unrelated to each other or compete with one another for funds and personnel. By comparison, the Catholic Church and the Church of Ceylon (Protestant Episcopal) have highly elaborate institutions for performing a host of activities in a systematic fashion.

Apart from the lack of an organizational armature within the Buddhist religious community, there are divisions that prevent cooperation. In the old days, "The religious status of a person [was] sought to be determined by the state of purity and all-round spiritual advancement, and not by birth, or family, or any outward sign."[47] Yet the Sangha in Ceylon is organized on a caste basis today and has been for several centuries. Most of the 15-18,000 *bhikkhus* in Ceylon belong to one of three principal sects or "nikayas." The largest and oldest is the Siam Nikaya, founded in the middle of the eighteenth century. Its center is in the Central Province of Ceylon, in the up-country districts surrounding Kandy. By far the wealthiest sect, it has retained title to many of the lands given to its predecessors by the Sinhalese kings. It has an estimated 12,000 members or approximately 65 per cent of the Sangha. Higher ordination in this sect is restricted to members of the higher levels of the Goyigamas. The Siam Nikaya has been traditionally dominated by the up-country elements who control, through family succession, title to the temples

[47] Barua, p. 243.

and their lands, although many of its most learned members are said to come from the coastal area.[48] A second sect, the Amarapura, was founded as recently as the early nineteenth century with the intention of purifying the Sangha. One of its principal targets was the caste-consciousness of the Siam Nikaya. It is open to members of the Karava, Salagma, and Durava castes. About 20 per cent of the *bhikkus* belong to this sect. A third, the Ramanya, is more recent in origin, and was founded by some previous members of the Siam Nikaya who desired ordination under more rigorous and disciplined leadership. They now comprise almost 15 per cent of the Sangha.

Younger *bhikkhus* in all three Nikayas have shown reformist tendencies, but the Amarapura and the Ramanya have set a higher example of discipline and have been more active in criticizing the government for non-Buddhist characteristics. The Siam Nikaya tends to be conservative and the Ramanya has had a reputation for effective public discussion derived from its earlier promotion of debates between Buddhist *bhikkhus* and Christian missionaries. But these differences do not appear to be crucial to the separate existence of the sects. The significant distinctive criterion is that of caste differentiations.[49] Their continued divisions prevent them from having the influence they might have on Ceylon's life.

D. THE COST OF SOCIAL CHANGE

Others regard the social and economic changes of the last fifty years as key factors in isolating the *bhikkhu* from the contemporary currents of city life. Reference has already been made to the new importance of English and the missionary educational institutions and English ways that come in its train. With the advent of the Western technology of transportation and standards of consumption, individuals began to move from their villages and seek opportunities in the towns. Country visitors to the cities learned new modes of living, eating, and entertaining themselves, and new ways of making a living.[50]

Where the Buddha was specific in regard to the layman's ethic, in the Sigalowada Sutta, for instance, he gave guidance for practical behavior within a traditional, family-oriented, and "feudal" society. The Sigalowada Sutta does not in itself provide specific precepts for

[48] Vijayavardhana, p. 585.

[49] *Ibid.*, Ryan, pp. 38-42; H. de S. Kularatne, *The Essence of the Buddha Dhamma* (Galle, n.d., c. 1955), p. 123; Mendis, *Ceylon under the British*, p. 44.

[50] N. D. Wijesekera, *The People of Ceylon*, Ch. xxv, for instance.

the special problems faced by individuals living in a semi-urbanized or urban society. Buddhist scriptures do not, nor could they be expected to, provide concepts which are directly applicable to a situation where relations are becoming more and more impersonal on a contractual basis within a cash economy. Except in its highest philosophical principles, it makes no specific and vivid provision for the notion of a lay "community" that is limited enough to be comprehensible and yet larger than a family or village, that may even include those of other ethnic or religious backgrounds. In its fullest, most perfect expressions, the Buddhist ethic calls for a selfless life profoundly sensitive to the needs of all others in its mastery of self. But since each Buddhist is expected to work out his own destiny, there have not been many contemporary efforts to mediate between the perfectionist demands of the classical canon and the hard, perplexing choices that individual laymen must face each day in a society that is very different from the Buddha's.[51]

V · NEW BUDDHIST ACTIVISM

A. ORGANIZATIONAL INNOVATIONS

Although Buddhists compose nearly 65 per cent of the total population, many of them feel that the life of their country is dominated by non-Buddhist forces. Even though Ceylon has been fully independent for ten years, Buddhism has not been given "its rightful place." Some of the deleterious influences have emanated from the Western world, whence came both imperialism and Christianity, the two principal causes of Buddhist decline. Non-Buddhist minorities were also believed to have contributed indirectly to the lack of prominence of Buddhism in public life.

Individuals and groups in Ceylon who represented these non-Buddhist influences have been singled out and Buddhists have been warned of their unhappy influence. They may be Sinhalese who have become particularly Westernized, especially those educated in English-language schools, and have loosened their ties to their Buddhist origins. Often they are members of the wealthy upper and upper middle classes living an urban European life. Indeed, the city itself and those who were most marked by it became an object of Buddhist criticism. Christians of various sects were also in this group, and not only for religious reasons. Devout Sinhalese Buddhists believed that

[51] Exceptional in this connection have been the lectures and writings of Dr. O. H. de A. Wijesekera already referred to.

when a person became a Christian, he paid no heed to Sinhalese ceremonies, gave up his traditions, and was less modest and sober in his way of life. During the colonial regime, Christians and Ceylon Tamils obtained higher education proportionately more often than the Buddhists. More Christians and Jaffna Tamils entered the public service relative to their numbers than Sinhalese Buddhists, though Sinhalese Buddhists have always held a majority of positions. Many years later, these groups have been identified by some of the most articulate spokesmen of the Buddhist cause; the positions they occupy have been regarded as unfair, and legislative and administrative measures were thought necessary to redress this imbalance.

In order to strengthen Buddhist institutions and the place of Buddhism in Ceylon's life, some laymen and *bhikkhus* came to believe that the Buddhists had to wield political influence, bringing pressure to bear upon ministers and parliamentarians to pay more attention to Buddhist needs and less attention to the better-organized Christians and the more closely knit Tamil minority. Shortly after independence, the United National Party encouraged this idea by seeking the assistance of the Sangha and devout Buddhist laymen as a group whose support in the majority community would insure success in the U.N.P.'s political competition against the extreme Left. Deference was paid to the leading Theros and funds were made available. As Buddha Jayanti approached, an official organization was established and large sums appropriated by the governing party to encourage an impressive celebration of this great event. The flattering attentions given to the Buddhist leaders did more than win them temporarily to the United National Party banner; it encouraged an awareness of their own possible political importance. As they grew in political consciousness, they articulated more precisely a sense of their own difficulties and grievances.

Certain organizations developed to advance Buddhist interests in public life. One began as an effort to organize the Sangha more effectively. It was the work of a handful of middle and upper middle-class Buddhist government servants, teachers, and lawyers, some of them wealthy, most of them highly Westernized themselves. It is significant that the most active of its members were from the Karava community, a group that has traditionally been heavily Christianized. In one sense, perhaps, these men were a religious minority within their caste group which itself was not accorded equal standing by the Goyigamas. They endeavored to awaken the rural *bhikkhus* to a more acute awareness of their responsibilities to live strictly according to the Dhamma, to know their Dhamma better, to preach the Dhamma more effectively to their neighboring laymen. They sought to draw the differing sects together regardless of caste and combined the widely-dispersed *bhikkhu* associations into one congress, the Sri Lanka Maha Sangha Sabha.[52] This became an important interest group that articulated Buddhist grievances and quietly mobilized *bhikkhus* first for combined action in connection with Buddha Jayanti celebrations and then to encourage rural voters to cast their ballots against the U.N.P. in the 1956 General Elections.

A leading Buddhist scholar developed the All-Ceylon Buddhist Congress that held periodic conferences of leading *bhikkhus* and laymen. In an effort to clarify for the Ceylonese public the unhappy state of Buddhism in Ceylon and to find government-sponsored remedies, the Buddhist Congress appealed to the government to establish a Commission of Inquiry into the state of Buddhism on the island. The government of D. S. Senanayake and his successors refused the request, foreseeing that such an investigation could cause religious disharmony. Eventually in 1954 a Buddhist Committee of Inquiry was set up without government sponsorship under the aegis of the All-Ceylon Buddhist Congress. It was composed primarily of vice-principals of some of the leading *bhikkhu* training colleges in the low-country and the most articulate Buddhist lay educators. There were two Theros from the up-country Siam Nikaya although the heads of the two principal Siam Nikaya chapters—the Malwatta and Asgiriya Chapters—dissociated their sect from its enquiry. The Buddhist Committee was to "Inquire into the present state of Buddhism in Ceylon and to report on the conditions necessary to improve and strengthen the position of Buddhism and the means whereby those conditions may be fulfilled."[53]

For two years members of the "Commission," as it became known, toured the Buddhist areas of Ceylon. It was ceremoniously received wherever it gathered testimony, partially because of the local *bhikkhu* associations already established by the younger laymen and other committees that were being set up in preparation for Buddha Jayanti. It was clear to those who were active in its endeavors that considerable resentment against the government was being expressed and generated through the public hearings of the commission. The report

[52] *Buddha Jayanti*, Vol. III, No. 15, August 17, 1956.

[53] See foreword to *Report of the Buddhist Committee of Inquiry* for terms of reference.

itself was not published until February 1956, shortly before the Prime Minister called for a new election.

The report was an extraordinary document, not so much as a balanced or thorough rendering of the causes of the present state of Buddhism, but because it provided for the first time a brief for the Buddhists. It was argued that the days of Buddhist glory were the days when it received state support and that its decline coincided with the colonial regime's support of Christianity.[54] Its fundamental aspiration called for strong state support of various kinds to come to the rescue of Buddhism. Its recommendations urged that the legal status of Buddhist properties be revised to bring them in line with Christian institutions against which the Buddhists have had to compete. Inspired in part by institutions developed in Burma, it recommended the establishment of a central body—the Buddha Sasana Council—made up of laymen and members of the Sangha to carry on the prerogatives of the Buddhist kings with respect to Buddhism that passed to the British in 1815. It suggested that an annual sum be paid by the government to the proposed Council in compensation for the income lost to the Sangha when temple lands were expropriated during the colonial period. Extensive reforms in the country's educational system were proposed, ensuring that Buddhist children would be educated in schools run only by Buddhists and reducing commensurately the role of Christian organizations in operating schools that have been patronized heavily by children of other faiths. Other recommendations concerned the social conditions of Ceylon and urged measures to ensure that obscene books or films should not be imported, that film censors should have an intimate understanding of the national culture, and that intoxicating drinks and ill-practices, such as horse racing, should be banned.

The commission's report assumed throughout that progress could be achieved in the religious and social world through proper legis-

[54] As a leading member of the Committee put it when the report was completed: "The Buddhists wish—and quite rightly—that in this country where they form 70 per cent of the population, Buddhism should be recognized as the predominant religion of the people. In the rest of the world, Ceylon is regarded as essentially a Buddhist country, and they want this claim established here as well. . . . They will not be content to remain in the position of inferiority to which they have been reduced by 450 years of foreign occupation. . . . They have no desire to make Buddhism the State religion—in spite of the cry raised by self-seeking politicians—but they want the State to help them rehabilitate themselves and undo some, at least, of the injustices perpetrated against them during the days of their subjection." Dr. G. P. Malalasekera, President of the All-Ceylon Buddhist Congress. Text of speech reproduced in *Times of Ceylon*, January 15, 1956.

lative, financial, and institutional reforms. As such, it was a document impregnated with modern Western attitudes and represented a revolutionary departure for Theravada Buddhist laymen.[55] Its interpretation of past and present merged Buddhist considerations intimately with Sinhalese nationalistic sensitivities. Apart from the proposed Sasana Council, some discussion of Buddhist land problems, a reference to the need for stricter training of *bhikkhus* and means of settling disputes between temples, the Sangha itself was scarcely referred to in the report. The economic problems of Ceylon were only briefly alluded to.[56] The principal problem as seen by the commissioners was the position of Buddhist institutions in comparison with Christian bodies, all other questions being either less important or more difficult to agree upon.

During 1955 while the commission was at work, language reform was the principal issue for those Buddhists who were publicly concerned over the state of their religion.[57] Large numbers of Buddhist laymen and *bhikkhus* came to feel that as long as English was the official language of Ceylon, those who were adept in Sinhalese—usually the Buddhists—would not have an equal opportunity to contribute their special qualities to the people of Ceylon. Others saw it in a more complex fashion. As long as English remained the effective language for government administration, business, and higher education, the most energetic and ambitious young people would seek education in English, and in this process they would become half-cosmopolitan, part Christian, and wholly alienated from their cultural and religious roots. Buddhist *bhikkhus* and scholars had remained the most adept in classical Sinhalese and oriental languages, and if Sinhalese were made the official language, they would receive a wider hearing in the country's affairs. Similarly, the religious culture and philosophy of which they were a part would receive greater respect on the part of large numbers of Ceylonese. It was possible even to look ahead to a time when the youth of the country would seek their intellectual and business future through a knowledge of the indigenous language and when that happened, those who were skilled in it would no longer be considered backward and

55 Thoughtful articles by G. C. Mendis, *Times of Ceylon*, October 1 and 2, 1956.

56 Wealthy Buddhists were urged to lead less extravagant lives as a means of conserving foreign exchange and making available capital for industrial and other investments in order to raise the standard of living of the poor. Land rents, too, were to be reduced for the benefit of the poor farmer.

57 See Chapter VII for a discussion of the language problem in greater detail.

old fashioned. The widening gap between *bhikkhus* and laymen might also be narrowed if not entirely bridged through language reform.

Mr. Bandaranaike himself, in his efforts to ensure a large following in the rural areas, "generally agreed" to implement the recommendations of the Buddhist Committee report.[58] As the General Election of 1956 approached, politicians of different parties began to canvass the support of the Sangha, especially in rural areas. And two associations of *bhikkhus*, the relatively new Sri Lanka Maha Sangha Sabha and the older All-Ceylon Bhikkhu Congress led largely by *bhikkhus* from the low-country areas, joined together to form the Eksath Bhikkhu Peramuna.[59] The leadership and majority of *bhikkhu* members were from the Amarapura and Ramanya sects. Laymen active in the Buddhist Congress or in the earlier rural *bhikkhu* associations threw their energies and organizing abilities into the E.B.P. The Siam Nikaya as a sect remained aloof although Siam Nikaya priests from the wealthy Kelaniya and important Kotte temples in the low-country were influential in its councils. The combined efforts of the Sangha associations, developed in the countryside by Buddhist laymen, the work of the All-Ceylon Buddhist Congress on behalf of the hearings, the publication of the Buddhist Committee's Report and the activities of the central association of *bhikkhus*—the Eksath Bhikkhu Peramuna—contributed materially to the final electoral result. Their activities are discussed later in connection with the general election.

Following the election of 1956 which, for a time, strengthened the will and enlarged the ambitions of ardent Buddhists, several distinct areas of Buddhist activity could be identified. These suggested possible fields of future Buddhist developments. In the first place, there were renewed efforts to develop a centralized organizational armature for the Sangha; secondly, the country's educational institutions came under concerted criticism from Buddhist sources; and thirdly, Buddhist organizations continued to exert considerable pressure on the new government. Fourthly, and most difficult to document, more Buddhists tended to dedicate themselves to the Five Precepts, the Noble Eightfold Path, and to the endeavor of leading a good Buddhist life.

[58] The Sinhalese version of these commitments left no such room for doubt on all the recommendations of the Report as the English word "generally" suggests.

[59] For greater detail, see Chapter IX on the 1956 General Election.

B. EFFORTS TOWARD UNITY IN THE SANGHA

The Report of the Buddhist Committee of Inquiry had recommended establishing a Buddha Sasana Council on the lines of a similar body in Burma: ". . . to which may be entrusted all the prerogatives of the Buddhist kings as regards the Buddhist religion assumed by the British Crown in 1815. The Buddha Sasana Council should consist of representatives of the Sangha and laity selected by election and nomination."[60]

Efforts to develop a central Sangha Council were pressed by *bhikkhus* and laymen for a wide variety of reasons. Some felt that if the Sangha and laity were brought into closer working intimacy, the laity might be more profoundly touched by the Buddha's message. There were those who believed that only a united organization of *bhikkhus* and laymen could influence members of parliament and the public administration as a counter to the Catholic hierarchy's influence in certain areas. Others felt that a central body into which all resources of the Buddhist community could be channeled would permit the poorer temples, Buddhist social service, and educational enterprises to operate with greater resources. Finally, a central Sasana Council could consider carefully an appropriate stand for individuals on such matters as birth control, business ethics, or even economic development.

Some of these activities would be unusual innovations in the Buddhist community. A central pooling of funds, for instance, would go directly against one of the fundamental traditions. A hierarchy given the power to define the Buddhist position on a host of problems would be strange indeed for the highly individualistic Theravada Buddhism of Ceylon. Yet many were concerned enough about the state of Buddhism to insist on greater organizational strength.[61]

As the proponents of organizational change pressed their case, underlying differences became discernible. The low-country sects were the younger ones in a civilization where status and respect normally adhere to elders. They were the poorer ones without landed endowments, the more energetic, often of non-Goyigama caste, and the ones most in touch with the non-Buddhist world and the prob-

[60] Recommendation 6, Chapter 1, Buddhist Committee Report, p. 41.

[61] Other justifications for a Sasana Council were argued by C. D. S. Siriwardane in articles in the *Ceylon Observer*, October 9 and 11, 1956 and "The Buddhist Problem Today," *Law College Buddhist Annual*, 1955-1956. Other justifications and reservations are from interviews with *bhikkhus* and laymen.

lems it posed to the Buddhist community. These circumstances confirmed both the up-country Siam Nikaya elders in their belief that the newcomers had little right to press for such innovations and the low-country sects in their belief that their up-country elders were backward and selfish.[62]

Many were of a divided mind, feeling the need for greater organizational unity, yet not wishing to push so fast as to divide the Sangha or to draw *bhikkhus* further into the public controversies publicized by an eager press. As often happened whenever groups were beset by serious differences, the Prime Minister himself was appealed to. His attempts to draw the contending parties together were not notably successful, but in October 1956 the Government announced it planned to set up a commission to examine the problems of implementing the Buddhist report. Once again, the Siam Nikaya showed its fundamental distrust of secular organizations of all kinds. Their spokesmen declared: "If a Sasana Council was actually established, it was bound to be a failure because personal ambition, greed for power, and self-interestedness were bound to reign within it."[63]

In early February 1957, the membership of the long-proposed official committee of inquiry was announced. Roughly half the members were carried over from the early Buddhist Committee of Inquiry; three of the remaining seven new members were of the Siam Nikaya, although the Maha Theros made it clear that these *bhikkhus* were serving as individuals.[64] The commissioners were to look into the various recommendations of the Committee of Inquiry, and any other matter that might be necessary "for the purpose of according Buddhism its rightful place in Ceylon."[65]

Thus, after many years of agitation an official commission had finally been appointed by the government to look into the state of Buddhism on the island.[66] The Siam Nikaya Maha Theros appealed to the governor general to prohibit the new committee from inquiring into the affairs of the Siamese sect, arguing that the Siam Nikaya had not sponsored any nomination to this commission and

[62] *Morning Times*, July 20, 1956; *Times of Ceylon*, July 21, 1956.

[63] *Times of Ceylon*, January 7, 1957. So firm was their opposition that the President of the All-Ceylon Buddhist Congress himself requested the Minister of Cultural Affairs to defer the appointment of the proposed Sasana Commission. *Ceylon Daily News*, January 9, 1957.

[64] *Ceylon Daily News*, February 4, 1957; March 12, 1957.

[65] Text of Gazette reproduced in *Ceylon Daily News*, March 6, 1957.

[66] In the end, the E.B.P. was not consulted on the personnel of the new commission. *Ceylon Daily News*, March 4, 1957.

the commission therefore had no power to inquire into their concerns.[67]

At the outset, it appeared to be preoccupied with internal problems of the Sangha, such as those conditions which impede the *bhikkhu* from leading an ideal life, types of social service work they might do, what should be done to get the best incomes from temple lands, and similar matters. It was clear that as the new commission pursued its inquiries, there would be other disagreements within the Sangha, but out of the discussions might come a renewed sense of dedication to the traditional Vinaya code. Innovations designed to bring the Sangha into closer relation to the laity and to permit the Buddhist community to exert more influence on Ceylon's affairs might also emerge from the commission's efforts. It seemed likely that as the Buddhists saw their problems less in terms of short-run political agitation and more in terms of extended effort at group reorganization, more moderate voices could take the initiative. The more strident ones that contributed much to the original thrust of the Buddhist movement—and raised many fears among Christians and Tamil minorities by virtue of their vigor and impatience—would be less necessary and would not have the field to themselves as they have had so frequently in the past. It remained unclear whether the fears of the traditionalist *bhikkhus*—and the minorities—were to be fulfilled. By 1959, no concrete steps had been taken to establish the controversial Sasana Council.

C. THE PROBLEM OF EDUCATION

One of the main grievances against the colonial government was that its educational system deprived the Sangha of its principal channel to the lay community. *Bhikkhu* "preceptors of youth" were compelled to look on while Christian schools, it was held, undermined the beliefs of Buddhist children. Educational facilities were an important theme in the Buddhist Committee report, and the commissioners sought to show that the youth of the country received little knowledge of their national traditions and preferred to ape foreign ways largely because of the existing school system, which was considered dominated by Christians. Extensive reforms were proposed in their final report designed to ensure that Buddhist children would be educated in schools run by Buddhists.

The denationalization of Ceylonese youth and their departure

[67] Text of the resolution reported in *Ceylon Daily News*, March 12, 1957.

from traditional Buddhist ways were regarded as the causes of a number of social ills and generalized discontent within Ceylon. The civilization of Lanka was said to be a denationalized hybrid. The sons and daughters of Lanka had no true sense of values. They were too impressed with the flashy, the glamorous, and that which comes from the noisy, hurried West. They ignored or rejected the real values of Ceylonese life—the simple, calm, detached, poised, and serene life of the good Buddhist society. Only as the youth of the country recaptured the ancient virtues that are at the center of the Buddha's teaching would Lanka's society be again happy and peaceful; and until such time as Ceylon's society developed its own genius, the Ceylonese would not achieve true freedom. "In this country now, although there is no visible foreign yoke in the form of a colonial government we are as subject as we were before we broke loose from the British bonds a few years ago, to the invisible yoke of evil, unenlightened teachings, practices, habits, customs and views, fostered by the British. Thus we are still in moral bondage to the West."[68]

The school system has been blamed for this situation, and active Buddhists have been deeply concerned as to how to set the matter right. They saw it largely in terms of school management and comparative school resources. They noted that the present arrangements were not merely a legacy of the colonial past but also a legacy of the missionary past, from a time when the church's educational—and therefore proselytizing—activities were financed largely by the foreign state.

The school system is divided into a set of English-language and vernacular schools, some of them managed by the state and the others run by private bodies with state assistance. The English-language schools have long been accorded the highest standing and were the coveted channels to an education that opened opportunities to status and income. Although only 35 per cent of all assisted schools are run by Christians, they manage probably nearly 70 per cent of the English-language schools.[69] Moreover, the amount of assistance per pupil each school receives from the state depends upon its classification. A well-equipped school with known high standards of training receives considerably higher allowances than a poorly equipped institution with less rigorous standards. Particularly among

[68] Editorial, "True Freedom," *Buddha Jayanti*, August 13, 1954. Vol. I, Nos. 16, 17.

[69] Estimate from interviews in the Department of Education. Reliable published figures were not available. Other statistics from *Administration Report of the Director of Education for 1955*, Table I (A).

educators, therefore, there is resentment against the fact that many of the Christian schools, having been in operation for many years and benefiting from donations collected abroad, have been able to construct superior buildings and install better equipment—an original capitalization that enables them to receive more assistance from the government in order to maintain their high standards. The bulk of Buddhist schools, by contrast, it is said, receive less.

The private bodies or denominations themselves are responsible for the management of their schools within broad rules laid down by the Ministry of Education. The government's policy regarding the language of instruction and regulations on curricula, examinations, and the like are followed by all assisted schools. Since 1952 there has been a strict conscience clause, and Christianity cannot be taught to Buddhist children attending a Christian school unless their parents request it explicitly. Despite this clause, many argue that the Christians are still determined to make as many converts as they can, even if their methods are now more indirect. Or if they do not actively proselytize and convert, they do make Buddhist children into "bad Buddhists." It is also held that even if instruction in the Christian schools is in the native languages, these are nonetheless insidious channels for Westernization and the subtle intrusion of Western cultural and social patterns. Girls trained through Christian schools are said to emerge as models of young British girls, undisciplined and unwilling to pay due respect to their parents or to the Sangha.

Another aspect of the educational problem concerns the predominant position of Christians in the administration of educational institutions, either through their positions as heads of schools, in the Ministry of Education, or in supervisory positions at the University of Ceylon. It is argued that Christian ideas and curricula are promoted at the expense of the Buddhist curriculum. A more incisive issue hinges on employment opportunities; as long as Christians control so many schools, there are disproportionately more jobs open to Christians. Among Christian educators themselves there is a widespread awareness of the anomalies in matters of educational administration. One solution was argued by the Buddhist commissioners; to wit, that every school that had over 50 per cent of students of one faith should have a principal of that same faith. Thus many Christian principals would have to resign and Buddhist or Hindu principals would be appointed in their places. This reform has not been pressed successfully, in part, it is argued, because there are not enough trained Buddhist school administrators. Christians have pre-empted this field in the past because they have been able to train their people in institutions abroad. Now that there is more wide-spread interest, it should be easier to find funds for training Buddhist educators perhaps with state assistance.

More recently, as this proposal has not been carried out, one group of Buddhist educators and laymen has been pressing for the abolition of the whole system of assisted schools, arguing that all of them —Buddhist as well as Christian—should be taken over by the state. Many responsible Buddhist educators will acknowledge that state-managed schools provide an inferior training to that received in most assisted schools. The disciplinary and intellectual standards of assisted schools tend to be more rigorous; educational innovations take place more often in the assisted schools than in government-managed schools, and since the teachers in assisted schools are not government servants, they are known to be more independent in their demands on the government. In spite of all these considerations, which sound very much like the arguments for and against private and public schooling in America, there are those who are willing to accept a decline in standards if only they can be rid of "the foreign educators."[70] Better to have a Sinhalese Buddhist education first, even though its specific training is not as "high" by curricular standards than have this continuing "hybrid education" that takes children from their national and religious roots.

This argument had an appeal to some Buddhist laymen and *bhikkhus* because the principal Buddhist educational organization, the Buddhist Theosophical Society, had fallen upon evil days and was fraught with faction and public dispute. Efforts to refashion its constitution and change its leadership met with little success, and the prospect of the state taking over all assisted schools might be expected to speed desirable changes within the Buddhist Theosophical Society as well as ousting the Christian assisted schools.[71]

In 1959 probably the majority of Buddhists believed the proposed remedy to be worse than the disease. If all religious schools were

[70] By far the majority of the "foreign educators" are now in fact Ceylonese who manage and teach in Christian schools, and what is meant truly is those who have come under the influence of foreign educators.

[71] See, for instance, "The Tragedy of Buddhist Education," C. D. S. Siriwardane, *Times of Ceylon*, September 24, 1956, and earlier reports of the difficulties within the Buddhist Theosophical Society in August 1956. Also P. de S. Kularatne, *Ceylon Observer*, May 5, 1957.

brought under the direct management of the state, and the government should change, bringing into power those who have no respect for religion, would not Buddhism be even worse off? The state was already overburdened with its own educational commitments and the costs to the state would increase since part of the costs of the denominational schools are borne by the societies that manage them.[72] Nevertheless, it remained anomalous that the "best schools" continued to be run by minority religious bodies, largely at state expense. Only careful action by the religious bodies and the Department of Education would lead to correction without serious loss to the country's scarce educational resources.

One aspect of Buddhist educational arrangements that had deep status implications concerned the educational recognition to be accorded to the *bhikkhu* training colleges—the *pirivenas*. For many years there had been a desire among ardent Buddhists to have them given the same recognition accorded to the national university. Finally, in 1959, two of the leading *pirivenas* were accorded university status and Nayake Theros became vice-chancellors of the famous Maligakanda and Peliyagoda *pirivenas*.

Another problem that deserved fullest consideration by Buddhist educationalists concerned a Buddhist curriculum. What are the human values Buddhist schools should stand for that would give them a peculiarly Buddhist stamp? It was becoming recognized that technical education was needed in Ceylon. Have there been studies made to see how best to combine a more wide-spread technical education with the desire for a deeper and more integral Buddhist atmosphere? What careful and detailed thought has been directed toward curricula for different age groups proposing fundamental changes in curricula, in the organization of leisure time, the use of work camps, meditative practices, or a dozen other possibilities?

Dissatisfaction has been growing with other anomalies in the rapidly expanding school system. An overly academic curriculum does not fit young men and women for the hard tasks ahead. The school system itself has nearly doubled in the last decade and this expansion presented serious staffing problems. It was therefore not surprising that one of the first lay institutions to be identified as the proper subject for thorough Buddhist reform should be the country's school system.

[72] Interviews with Buddhist educators. Also, for instance, *Ceylon Observer*, April 20, 1957; *Morning Times*, April 30, 1957; *Ceylon Observer*, May 4, 1957.

D. NEW INTEREST GROUPS IN POLITICS

Buddhist organizations were especially active during the Buddha Jayanti year. Some of them appealed for total prohibition; others urged that the Red Cross symbol on lottery tickets of the national hospital sweepstakes be replaced. The more articulate argued against certain appointments made by the new Prime Minister on the grounds that the appointees were Roman Catholics instead of Buddhists.[73] The most political of the Buddhist organizations was the Eksath Bhikkhu Peramuna. It did not restrict its activities to pressing for the establishment of a Sasana Council or for educational reform. Shortly after the 1956 election, it challenged the Communist and non-Communist Left parties, arguing that they were not supporting the new government in its policy of promoting the Sinhalese language as the one official language. They held that because the Marxist parties had had electoral agreements with the party that formed the new government, they should either follow the new government's policy on language reform or else test their own popularity in competition with the victorious party they refused to support.[74] In subsequent language debates, the Eksath Bhikkhu Peramuna was one of the most articulate single interest groups working to make Sinhalese the only state language.[75]

The E.B.P. also threatened to take direct action—whatever was contemplated by this was never made clear—if the government refused to take immediate steps to stop the Tamils in the north from refusing to carry a Sinhalese symbol for "Sri" on their automobile license plates.[76] Some *bhikkhus* urged Sinhalese to boycott Tamil shops to protest against the Federal party's activities in opposition to the 'Sinhalese Only" legislation of the government.[77]

The leaders of the Eksath Bhikkhu Peramuna tended to identify themselves with "the people" and any action which displeased the E.B.P. was action taken against "the people."[78] On another occasion, they also appealed to the public to send in reports on all known cases of corrupt practices that could be substantiated in order to keep the administration clean and to help the people.[79] As one commenta-

[73] Mr. Mettananda textual statement, *Ceylon Daily News*, July 30, 1956. He particularly criticized the Minister of Finance, who was not a Buddhist, and the Prime Minister himself had to reply to criticism because his daughter was attending a Catholic school.

[74] *Ceylon Daily News*, May 7, 1956.

[75] See Chapter VII for a fuller discussion of the language question.

[76] *Ceylon Observer*, January 27, 1957.

[77] *Morning Times*, March 13, 1957.

[78] *Ceylon Observer*, March 17, 1957.

[79] *Ceylon Observer*, March 24, 1957.

tor put it, no doubt exaggerating: "All the reports add up to the fact that the E.B.P. has assumed upon itself the role of a supra Cabinet. . . . Stalwarts of the E.B.P. claim that Ministers and even high government officials are at their beck and call; that they promptly reply to any summons from the E.B.P. headquarters; that they are often put on 'trial' at E.B.P. headquarters where they explain their actions and attitudes toward national problems."[80]

A large part of the E.B.P.'s activities was carried on through resolutions, press releases, and public statements in efforts to publicize its own endeavors and enlist public backing. Official visits to the offices and homes of ministers and government servants were not infrequent, intended to persuade them that it was worth their while to pay attention to its members. These activities gave a certain flamboyance to the organization that was not entirely in keeping with the essence of the Buddha's Way. Many Buddhists were in sympathy with the E.B.P.'s objective of promoting legislation and government decision that would inspire more Buddhists to lead a life according to the Dhamma. But they were deeply disturbed by the methods adopted that projected *bhikkhus* into the world of publicity, public disputes, and worldly ways detracting materially from the *bhikkhu's* traditional role as the highest example of the good Buddhist. Until more moderate Buddhists came forward to devote time and energy to the Ceylonese community, the field was left to these enthusiasts who were not necessarily representative of the community they professed to protect.

There have been no serious moves to give the *bhikkhus* in Buddhist Ceylon the powers that the mullahs sought to acquire in Muslim Pakistan shortly after the state was established. Efforts to have Buddhism declared the state religion have failed thus far. Most intelligent *bhikkhus* and laymen do recognize that Ceylon is a multiple-religious state, in which more than one-third of the population are not Buddhists. Those who fear that ardent Buddhists may make such a claim in the future remind the visitor that the Sinhalese language is spoken by only 65 per cent of the population, even if it has been made the sole state language. Cannot the same forces be roused to make Buddhism "the established Church" of Ceylon? Ambitious political leaders may someday use such an issue to gain or retain the votes of the rural masses or of those city voters who suffer the anxieties and frustrations of a new urban life. But it seemed

[80] *Times of Ceylon*, March 24, 1957.

more likely that the emotional upsurge focused on Buddhist symbols during the years 1956-57 would subside as Buddha Jayanti receded.

E. THE GOOD BUDDHIST LIFE AND CONTEMPORARY SOCIETY

It is difficult to document a widespread concern for Buddhist values, but by 1957 more individuals were finding their way back to the temples to "take sil," to meditate, and to seek the teachings of the leading *bhikkhus.* Many observers agreed that in the urban areas, there had been an increase in temple going. There was more interest in temple matters, especially among the English-educated who had been the social and political elite and, in many respects, still set the tone of public life. Public servants who previously would have felt somewhat out of place in a Buddhist temple had been returning more regularly. Some hitherto secular intellectuals were deriving new satisfaction from exploring with the better-trained *bhikkhus* the significance of traditional Buddhist values. No doubt the Buddha Jayanti celebrations invited a reconsideration of one's personal way of life, even though the ceremonies stressed the side of public display.

But many were disappointed that these increased manifestations of religious interest did not appreciably affect the country's murder rate, labor unrest, or other indications of social malaise. Some Buddhists argued that the bulk of the people remained uninterested and led lives that were virtually devoid of ethical inspiration.[81] To the extent that this was so, they held, another approach might also be required. The Buddhist devotees had sought to replace one group of political leaders by another, to obtain legislation reorganizing the school and taxation systems, or to create for the Sangha and laity one organizational armature. Some Buddhists felt these efforts did not touch the core of the problem which was, as they saw it, to give the Buddhist ethic a renewed immediacy and relevance for the people living in contemporary Ceylon.

It is incorrect, as some Western and Eastern critics declare, that Theravada Buddhism in Ceylon is entirely otherworldly, preoccupied only with the *bhikkhu's* mastery of self. There are clear principles set forth for the layman's guidance, and these have been given concrete application in the canonical literature. Perhaps where the fundamental, timeless principles were expounded in detailed applica-

[81] Dr. O. H. de A. Wijesekera, *Ceylon Daily News,* June 23, 1956; Mr. Dudley Senanayake, *Ceylon Daily News,* May 2, 1957.

tion to the problems of daily living, they have been defined for the type of life that can now be led only in those villages where traditional social relations and economic modes have been relatively undisturbed. Today's requirements, it was held, were now very different. In a contract money economy, men must work in intimate yet relatively impersonal cooperation with one another. This requires that men apply precepts hitherto often reserved to members of their immediate family or traditional social community to others with whom they have little in common except their daily work or the fate they share as common citizens of a political state. Buddhist laymen and clergy, therefore, had a rare opportunity to contribute to the Buddhist revival precisely by taking semiurbanized and urbanized social and economic life in contemporary Ceylon as their point of departure and then dramatizing the good Buddhist choices as distinct from those thought inappropriate. Perhaps, what was required was a Sigalowada Sutta for mid-twentieth-century, pluralistic Ceylon—a contemporary model of applied Buddhist ethics.

Buddhist heroes have not been solely otherworldly nor has the Buddhist ethic called for subjective purity alone. Asoka, Duttha-Gamini, and Parakrama Bahu had combined such private benevolence with public acts of piety. According to tradition, they became adept at living the subjective requirements of the Buddhist ethic while in their policies they energetically promoted what now would be considered very worldly enterprises. Asoka's public order, his rest houses, and irrigation projects were by no means only otherworldly in intent or result. The tanks, dams, and channels of the Ceylonese kings were pious works—they were also investments essential to the well-being of their people and to the "economic development" of ancient Ceylon.

Classic precepts call upon Buddhists to show "dauntless energy in wealth" or "mindfulness in keeping what is earned"—precepts which could have a bearing on Ceylon's productivity and investment rate.[82] The Buddhist Committee report though devoting only 3 out of 125 pages to Ceylon's economic situation, urged upon the wealthy a puritanical simplicity of life worthy of early Calvinist preachers as a means for furthering development. Buddhist belief, therefore, need not exclude concern for action on behalf of such mundane matters as economic development.

82 Sigalowada Sutta as discussed in Morgan, p. 134.

CONCLUSION

The Buddhist revival, therefore, was a complex phenomenon. No doubt it was encouraged by the desire of Ceylon's secular politicians to ensure themselves of the Buddhist majority vote. But it was more than this. It revealed profound emotions and a foundation of ideas and aspirations in its own right. It represented a rural, fundamentalist reaction to the city's worldly ways, a middle- and lower-class protest against the wealthy and influential elite who had been educated by a foreign curriculum away from Sinhalese social ways and religious practices. The desire to restore Buddhism to its "rightful place" in the affairs of the country underlay the movement. In one sense, it looked to the past, casting back to the times when Buddhist monarchs ruled a realm that was believed to have been happy and serene, the perfect embodiment of the Dhamma. In another sense, it was revolutionary. The attempt consciously to alter relations between laity and Sangha and between the individual and his faith in an effort to counter denationalizing Western influences, has no historical model in recent centuries. Some of the more active lay Buddhists were concerned to effect changes in Buddhism on an institutional plane—by legislating financial and other state assistance to Buddhist endeavors, by insuring through legislative and administrative action that sufficient schools were manned by Buddhists, and by developing a central Sasana Council, uniting all groups of *bhikkhus* and laymen alike. These efforts tended to pit low-country sects against the wealthier and higher-status up-country Siam Nikaya. A few saw the need for a contemporary applied Buddhist ethic for laymen which would come to terms with the ethnic and religious pluralism and the semiurban and urbanized life in a Ceylon that is undergoing rapid change. The appropriate role for the priesthood in a representative government remained to be defined as newly organized Buddhist interest groups sought to influence public policy. Confronted with rising communal discord and secularizing forces emanating from urbanization, political ideologies, and social change, Buddhist leaders—laymen and clergy—faced a formidable challenge.

CHAPTER VII · THE PROBLEM OF NATIONAL UNITY

> "So long as an alien power governs a Southeast Asian country, the situation is relatively simple—a very small minority controls other larger minorities, as well as the dominant indigenous people. But when this foreign imperialism comes to an end, or when it genuinely begins to share its power with the nationalists of the country, readjustment in relationships between the various ethnic groups becomes imperative."—V. Thompson and R. Adloff, *Minority Problems in Southeast Asia*

I · INTRODUCTION

NATIONAL UNITY is a mysterious phenomenon. In nineteenth-century Europe, Ernest Renan posed the fundamental question, "Qu'est-ce qu'une Nation?" The people of South Asia are now deeply engaged in a search for their own answers to this universal question. For many statesmen, publicists, and voters, the growth of national consciousness involves a widespread desire to rid themselves of all vestiges of the colonial era and to create or revive their own distinctive culture. The vision of a modern nation state almost inescapably includes the aspiration for a unified, homogeneous people.

The very nature of the population groups within their own boundaries has impeded this endeavor. Diverse groups of people—speaking different languages, living in different ways, looking back on contrasting histories in which their ancestors often fought against one another—are living side by side. Religious differences and narrow regional loyalties add to the diversity and contribute to the absence of common cultural values. In Ceylon, too, the people are a mosaic of distinguishable groups divided on the basis of traditional family, caste, ethnic, linguistic, and religious differences. Most groups could unite in opposition to colonialism and help to modernize their country, but they have few cultural values or historical memories in common to offset their other differences.

During the colonial regime different ethnic groups developed special responses to British rule. Some adjusted to it and grasped its opportunities, others held aloof. In using opportunities, some retained their own individuality, others found their culture and way of life eroded by the outsiders' ways. When the foreigners withdrew, a certain degree of ethnic competition could be expected as groups sought to retain positions gained or seized at opportunities hitherto neglected or inaccessible. Ceylon's peculiar location—a small island of 9,000,000 people close beside a massive subcontinent of 400,000,000 —greatly influenced her approach to a minority that came to Ceylon under British aegis. It also conditioned to some extent the majority's position toward the Ceylon Tamils. A keen political sense led to an elaborate political evaluation of legislative proposals as they seemed likely to favor or hinder the interests of different ethnic groups.

There were class implications in the problem of national unity. The social influence structure inherited at independence saw the elite culturally and socially alienated from the indigenous population by its Western language and culture, its administrative and legal skills. When the foreign power withdrew, the Westernized elite suddenly found itself face to face with its own people. Toward the end of the first decade, the distance between the two was projected into the center of the political arena as the Ceylonese sought to decide which language or languages should be given official status. Simultaneously, the Ceylon Tamil minority found its position severely challenged by the proposed language policy. Consequently, communal antagonisms were sharper than they had been for many generations.

The government's approach to the Indian minority will be discussed first. The problem of relationships between the Ceylon Tamils and the Sinhalese will receive more extended treatment.

II · INDIANS IN CEYLON

Most of the newly independent governments of South Asia have faced the difficult problem of redefining the economic and political rights acquired by the important ethnic minorities that migrated to their country during the period of foreign rule or earlier. Burma, Malaya, Viet Nam, and Indonesia had "overseas" Chinese to cope with; Ceylon, like Burma, Fiji, and other countries within the former British Empire, had a large number of Indians.

More hours in parliament have been spent discussing the proper status for Indians resident on the island than any other single subject.[1] And it is not difficult to see why this should be. By their sheer numbers, recent immigrants from India to Ceylon are important, forming roughly 10 per cent of the total population. Awareness of, and anxiety about, economic competition between the "foreign" minority and the indigenous majority have been rising in Sinhalese rural districts. The estate population lives a life apart and does not assimilate the cultural ways or adopt the language of the majority island community. As exclusive national sentiment rises, such cosmopolitanism is considered a threat to national unity. In the past, the political activities of their leaders have not always been calculated to conciliate the fears of the majority. The political interests of prominent Sinhalese added further incentive to examining with a critical eye the political and economic rights already achieved by the Indians under British rule.

A. BACKGROUND CIRCUMSTANCES

1. *Population and population movements.* At the 1953 census, there were 990,000 individuals of recent Indian ethnic origin in Ceylon.[2] Of these, some 800,000 were estate laborers and their families living in the high-country tea areas and to a lesser extent in the rubber and tea estates in the middle country. Over 50 per cent were concentrated in upper Central and Uva provinces. Ever since the coffee boom in the middle of the nineteenth century, foreign operators have depended upon these immigrants for the monotonous and unremitting work of maintaining and harvesting the estate crops.[3] Although Sinhalese labor appears to have cleared much of the land in the beginning, the peasant villager preferred the casual schedule of the rice cultivator to the disciplined estate labor where there could be no delay in the tea-picking cycle.[4] The supervised life in estate, barracklike "lines" did not compare with his traditional village ambiance. South Indian laborers, on the other hand, less generously endowed with land and water, were eager to improve them-

[1] *House of Representatives*, V. 22, c. 275-276 (June 22, 1956). A column count would no doubt confirm this assertion up to mid-1956. After that into 1957, the "language question" would have taken first honors.

[2] *Statistical Abstract*, 1956, Table 15. Although 6,000 of these are now considered to be of Pakistani origin, they are here all referred to as "Indians."

[3] For an exciting romantic novel based on careful research on the coffee period and its demise, see Christine Wilson's *The Bitter Berry* (London, 1957).

[4] Picking the fresh young green leaves must be done on the proper day, the "flush" taking from 10 to 14 days to mature. There can be no delay in this operation; hence the need for a constant and disciplined work force.

selves by coming to Ceylon even though they lived under company discipline and were always on call to meet the needs of the estate.

Another group of Indians came to Ceylon as the city of Colombo, government services, and trading opportunities expanded. Many of the harbor workers, conservancy, and street cleaning laborers, the staff of the railroads and Public Works Department were from South India.[5] Since 1939, the Indians have been gradually replaced by Ceylonese in the harbor, railroads, and public works departments, but they are still active in low-caste occupations of a service or soiling nature, such as street cleaning, laundry, barbering, or scavenging.[6] Indians entered commerce, too, and many Indian traders, shopkeepers, and money lenders have penetrated into the countryside. At the top of the economic ladder are Indian merchants from Madras, Bombay, and Calcutta, retaining commercial links with large Indian establishments, who import many goods for mass consumption. Until recently, their establishments dominated important streets of the wholesale district.[7] Indians in these non-estate activities have been estimated at a little less than 200,000.

During most of the British period, as necessary hands on the tea estates and as British subjects, Indian laborers had no difficulties put in their way if they desired to work in Ceylon. Periodically, the government of India sought to ensure that Indians working overseas in Ceylon as elsewhere were protected against unfair indebtedness, received fair working conditions and appropriate political rights in the colony.[8] An elaborate organization, established by the estate interests and operated from a tax on estate products, saw to the recruitment of workers in India and eased their travel back and forth whenever they wished to return for brief family or other visits. During periods of economic distress, excess laborers were aided to go back to India.

Immigration from India contributed materially to the rapid growth in Ceylon's population in the nineteenth century. Between 1871 and 1881—during the coffee boom—24,000 new immigrants arrived each year and again, between 1891 and 1900—when tea planting expanded very rapidly—34,000 more came annually. These migrations added

[5] *House of Representatives*, V. 10, c. 1483. For a detailed discussion, see *Report of a Commission on Immigration into Ceylon*, known as the Jackson Report (Sessional Paper III—1938), pp. 8-23.

[6] *House of Representatives*, V. 18, c. 1335.

[7] *House of Representatives*, V. 4, c. 1738-1739.

[8] C. Kondapi, *Indians Overseas 1838-1949* (New Delhi, 1951), pp. 52-62, 74-78, 351, 396-415.

10 per cent to the total population during these decades, exceeding the natural increase by a large amount. From 1901 to 1911, 18,000 new immigrants each year added 5 per cent to the population, less than half the natural increase.[9] Subsequently, as the rate of natural increase accelerated, immigrants contributed less to the rate of growth. From 1923 to 1928, the booming rubber plantations attracted some 60,000 new workers each year, but they added less than one-fourth of the natural increase. With the Great Depression, there was a net outflow of Indians, 9,000 more returning to India each year between 1931 and 1940 than arrived.[10]

Before World War II, Indian leaders became critical of certain policies of the Ceylonese government that appeared to discriminate against Indians. Delhi therefore imposed a ban on new emigration to Ceylon despite the desire of Ceylon's plantation interests to again increase its estate labor force. During the early war years, there was a further net outflow from Ceylon of nearly 185,000. Particularly during 1942-43, when the Japanese fleet approached Ceylon's exposed shores, many non-estate Indians left for the more spacious India. The Indian emigration restrictions meanwhile having been eased, more estate workers arrived to man the crucial rubber estates during the later war years. And from 1946 to 1949 heavy immigration again made up for the wartime losses, virtually all of the immigrants having been former workers in Ceylon. Not until 1950 was there a renewed net outflow as Ceylonese government regulations virtually forbade new entrants, and retiring workers and other categories did not have their permits renewed and had to return to India. But the fact of sheer numbers does not in itself provide an adequate explanation for the important place in public life the "Indian question" has occupied since independence.

2. *Fear and economic competition.* One of the intractable elements of the problem is a pervasive fear which has been articulated in up-country Sinhalese areas. The peasants in the Kandyan districts, especially, are caught between two worlds; above them are the thousands of tea workers on the hilltops speaking another tongue, living an alien life and down below are the alien low-country city people who seem to be more dynamic, intrusive, and stronger than they. It is hard to say whether the fear of being "swamped" is the creation of

[9] *Statistical Abstract 1956*, Table 37.

[10] From Ferguson's, *Ceylon Directory*, 1956, p. 64; Jennings, *The Economy of Ceylon*, pp. 3, 4; *Administration Report of the Commissioner of Labour for 1955*, Table xx; Kondapi, pp. 37-39, 301, 352-353.

highly nationalistic spokesmen or whether it is the more spontaneous emergence from the villager's own world, but the fear is very real. As one M.P. put it: "I am not certain about the Government, but I am myself inspired by a fear complex. One of the first things that a person should be in possession of is freedom from fear. But believe me we are afraid, and that is why we feel that we have to restrict the composition of our nationals—of our population in this country. It may be that we may not be able to follow the examples of other countries. We have to consider our own citizenship rights according to our own circumstances. . . ."[11]

Immediacy of fear stems from some hard realities too. Land is becoming more and more scarce in the Kandyan districts. There is little question that as the estates moved downward from the high country, they encroached on village lands; first the villager's highland for transient jungle cultivation was absorbed, and then the land proximate to the village itself.[12] As the Kandyan Peasantry Commission reported: "The village area is comparatively densely populated. The villages are hemmed in on all sides by plantations and are found as a rule in a cluster at the bottom of the hills. Many tanks and 'pathahas' which provided irrigation for the sowing of paddy, the main item of diet, have been partly silted up by soil erosion or absorbed by estates. The paddy area has not increased with the increase of population. The garden land available is not sufficient to meet other requirements. . . . The peasants are landless and the main problem is landlessness."[13]

It is no doubt stretching historical truth to blame the estate laborers for the landlessness among the Sinhalese peasantry, for they were merely employees of the estate enterprises.[14] "Landlessness" is growing in seriousness because of low death rates, of relatively unintensive use of the rice lands available, and an unwillingness, until

[11] *House of Representatives*, V. 4, c. 1771 (Aug. 19, 1948). Another example may be cited. "To them (the Sinhalese members) it is a life-and-death question, seeing that the Indian settlers who are perched on the hill tops are a menace to their future. They have nothing but dread for their future. They fear the extinction of their race, the disappearance of their religion and their language." V. 16, c. 3065-6. As another put it, "It is really becoming now a stark question of survival." V. 16, c. 2888.

[12] The chena land often went by default and became Crown Land, since no one occupied the lands regularly nor were there any but customary titles. Lands nearer villages that went to the estates may have been purchased from a local notable, taken in lieu of unpaid debts and sold to the estates by store keepers or money lenders, or by other means.

[13] *Report of the Kandyan Peasantry Commission*, p. 4.

[14] As pointed out by one of their spokesmen, *House of Representatives*, V. 10, c. 338.

recent years, of many to migrate to other parts of the island, although opportunities elsewhere were admittedly limited. Chronic underemployment of large Sinhalese families, who possess very small plots of land as a result of successive subdivision by inheritance, adds resentment. What exacerbates the "landlessness" problem is the fact that the Ceylonese economy has not enough alternative methods of production and is wanting in intensive systems of agriculture to absorb large numbers of people in activities other than rural rice growing in the traditional mode. And for that method of production, there is not enough land available.[15] Then, too, the Indian laborer has a reputation for harder work, for being willing to live on a lower standard of living, and for accepting lower wages than the Ceylonese.

It is therefore natural that the Sinhalese peasant and laborer should be envious of those who hold thousands of regularly paid estate jobs and afraid of their unfair competition. Sinhalese peasant spokesmen claim that they are now as capable of working the tea estates as the Tamils, and estate managers consider them adequate labor though less willing to pluck during heavy rains and more liable to absenteeism. Some 100,000 Ceylonese work mostly in low-country tea estates as compared to the 400,000 Indian Tamils in middle- and up-country enterprises. In the rubber districts, where work is less demanding, there are as many Ceylonese as Indians employed.[16] Competition for scarce jobs is rendered more acute because the Indian Tamil population on the estates is already producing its own "surplus" of young men and women for whom there are no more jobs available on the estates. These are swelling the ranks of the rural population.[17] These developments have led some Ceylonese leaders in good faith and out of sheer perplexity to argue that the only solution to the problem of rural employment is for a good part of the Indian estate population to return to India.[18]

Those who speak for the Sinhalese up-country areas voice other grievances against the estate workers than competition for scarce

[15] For a study of population pressure as seen by a specialist in population problems, see N. K. Sarkar, "Population Trends and Population Policy in Ceylon," *Population Studies*, IX, No. 3 (March 1956), pp. 195-216. For a carefully worked empirical study, see N. K. Sarkar and S. J. Tambiah, *The Disintegrating Village*.

[16] *Report of the Commissioner of Labour for 1955*, Table XXX.

[17] The fear of this development was voiced some time ago. As early as 1938 the Jackson Report examined the problem and found it was not yet of serious proportions. But by 1956 estate labor unions were making an issue of this growing difficulty, insisting that estate managers register all estate youths for jobs.

[18] *House of Representatives*, V. 16, c. 2891-2892, 3204.

jobs. For some years before independence, estate workers received a more secure cash income and, in most instances, better medical and more widespread educational services than those available to the neighboring Sinhalese villager. To be sure, the price support scheme for rice introduced during World War II enhanced cash incomes in many rice villages. Since independence, medical services, the school system, and other government services have been improved for the Sinhalese peasants. The divergence between the estate labor and the villager may have all but closed in many areas.[19] Nevertheless, recollection lingers on and past privileges recalled are more persuasive than today's reality.[20]

3. *Assimilation*. These invidious economic comparisons and their attendant competitive ambitions and anxieties are real enough. Where competition for coveted and scarce jobs exists and wherever there are also identifiable minorities, distinguishing themselves by their language, religion, way of life, color, or dress, group consciousness and intergroup tensions are bound to grow. In Ceylon, economic and other fears have been accentuated because the "Indians" have not become assimilated into the nation's life.

The Indian laborers are isolated in their estate enclaves, living in "company towns." They are strongly bound within an Indian familial, caste, and religious-cultural community. They have had traditionally little possibility or incentive to become assimilated into the Sinhalese village culture in those areas where there were indigenous inhabitants already. Further up in the mountains there was no local culture at all except that which the immigrants themselves brought with them. Traditionally, Ceylon's plural society, that mosaic of different cultural elements living in mutual tolerance, though not deeply interacting, left room for divergence. But the newer nationalism, modeled on the Western notion of a state of homogeneous cultural design, leaves less room for such cultural diversity. Particularly when language or other "cultural" issues are the focus of public attention, the position of unassimilated minorities is challenged.

Some emphasize that assimilation has not taken place in a political or residential sense. It is held that the Indians in Ceylon are pri-

19 Indicative of this change is the fact that before 1947 infant mortality rates on the estates never exceeded the island's average. Since 1947, however, estate rates have remained relatively stable but the island-wide averages have markedly declined. As reported in *House of Representatives*, V. 10, c. 1562.

20 For characteristic invidious comparisons, see for instance, *House of Representatives*, V. 5, c. 543, also c. 440-441; V. 10, c. 328-329.

marily birds of passage who come when times are good and flee back to India when times are hard. The ebb and flow of movement across the Palk Strait has already been described, dependent as it has been, to some extent, upon prosperity or depression in the estate industry. And each year, large numbers move back and forth for essentially private reasons. Some return to see their families, to seek a bride of proper status and caste in the communities from which their ancestors originally came or to make pilgrimages to holy places. That family links are retained by many is confirmed by the remittances that flow from the estate workers to South India. This is a movement of payments very much like the immigrant remittances from the United States to Ireland, Italy, Germany, and earlier to eastern Europe.[21] The economic significance of this outflow has been exaggerated, for it averaged less than 5 per cent of Ceylon's annual foreign exchange remittances and .24 per cent of annual payments. But it is held to be symptomatic of their continued attachment to their families in South India.

In quantitative terms, the number of individuals who go back and forth each year is impressive and, like travelers everywhere, these movements are conspicuous. In 1939, for instance, 156,000 individuals left the island while 130,000 entered. In 1946, 283,000 came to the island and 226,000 departed.[22] Proponents of restricting the movement of Indians cited such figures to contend that the Indians were merely transients who did not make their home in Ceylon. The heated question of when does an Indian overseas really make his home in the country where he resides cannot be definitively answered. But it is a fact that only about one-fourth of those who passed back and forth between India and Ceylon were estate laborers. In 1946, for example, less than 80,000 out of 240,000 Indian immigrants were estate labor. In 1954, 100,000 immigrants were reported in all, but only 27,000 of these were estate labor.[23] For the years 1944 through 1950, roughly 55,000 estate laborers on the average traveled to and fro each year. This is roughly one-seventh of the adult estate population. Some maintain from this that the estate population visits India once every seven years. Others, closer to the estates, hold that perhaps 50 per cent of the laborers hardly ever

[21] After 1948, government regulations rationed the amount of Rupees each family could send abroad. Between 1949-55, the average outflow was in the neighborhood of Rs. 3,177,000 per year.

[22] Ferguson's *Ceylon Directory*, p. 64.

[23] *Administration Report of the Commissioner of Labour for 1955*, Table xx; Ferguson's, p. 64.

go to India and that the 55,000 annual average during those years represents the mobile individuals who do travel back and forth every two or three years, the remainder being considered as "permanent residents."[24] The other Indian travelers not from the estates are from among the estimated 200,000 engaged largely in commerce and in service trades in Colombo.

4. *Limitations on Indian rights.* Already before independence the Ceylonese had taken specific measures to protect their peoples' economic opportunities from the energetic Indians. During the depression, Indian daily paid government workers were let off first. Ordinances regarding the disposal of Crown lands were so drafted as to virtually prohibit those of Indian origin from acquiring Crown land. Indians on the island were in fact prevented from fishing in Ceylonese waters and Indian entrepreneurs could not obtain autobus franchises.[25] During the war, the government took over the import of essential foodstuffs and through government-sponsored cooperatives distributed essential foodstuffs and collected home grown rice from the countryside. These measures were designed to prevent profiteering in scarce food supplies. But they also eliminated the Indian trader as middleman. Subsequently, port labor and other government and municipal laborers have been largely replaced by Ceylonese. Thus, the free scope of economic activity for Indians has been gradually restricted.

More hotly debated was the restriction of Indian political rights. In 1931, the Donoughmore Constitution gave wide political powers to a legislature elected on the basis of the universal adult franchise. To many Sinhalese, giving the right to vote to Indian estate laborers was tantamount to giving the franchise to a transient population so numerous in certain districts as to threaten to "overwhelm" the long-term Sinhalese residents. The commissioners considered that those who had been in residence for at least five years had shown evidence of having an "abiding interest" in the affairs of the island and, therefore, the franchise was made contingent upon a residence of five years. But the electoral provisions putting into effect the Donoughmore Constitution required Indians to apply for a special certificate of permanent settlement or show evidence of being domi-

[24] Interviews with estate union leaders and managers. The Jackson Report of 1939 used a figure of 60 per cent "as illustrative" of the proportion who were permanent residents and there is little evidence to suggest that mobility has increased since then. The presupposition would be to the contrary. (Sessional Paper III—1938), p. 26.

[25] Kondapi, pp. 301, 352-353.

ciled on the island, and the procedures for obtaining either document were elaborate enough to discourage many from applying. As some Indians saw these measures, either step meant an alienation from the rights Indians should have enjoyed in Ceylon as British subjects and were measures that were in reality discriminatory against Indians, since they were by far the largest group to which these measures applied. The national franchise was in fact widely accessible to Indians and in 1939 some 225,000 Indians had the vote, although a stricter application of the laws in 1943 reduced the numbers to 168,000.[26]

The Indians contend that ever since the Sinhalese obtained a commanding majority in the popularly elected State Council their political rights have been progressively whittled down.[27] In 1937, for example, village franchise rights were not extended to Indians although they were extended at that time to other minorities. Some Indians appear to have wanted it this way since they would thus remain free from village taxes. However, the protests of other Indian spokesmen were not stilled when Sinhalese resident labor on estates was also explicitly debarred from exercising the village franchise.[28] This removed any formal legal discrimination against Indians as Indians but confirmed the government's unwillingness to enfranchise the Indians. Despite these political restrictions, the Indian estate laborers were able to develop effective union and political organizations and came to play a significant and distinctive role in Ceylon's national politics.

5. *Indian political organization and activities.* Since the founding of the Ceylon Indian Congress in the late 1930's, estate workers have been gradually organized. In 1947, some 130,000 were joined in unions, of whom 116,500 were claimed by the Ceylon Indian Congress labor union. Leaders of the Lanka Sama Samaja Party and the Communist party have also supported their cause on the grounds that the estate laborers are proletarians and, if organized, could exert very real economic pressures on the body politic.[29]

The Ceylon Indian Congress nominally represented the interests

[26] Weerawardana, "The General Elections in Ceylon, 1952," p. 113; Kondapi, pp. 398-402.

[27] The most thorough compilation of Indian grievances is to be found in Kondapi, *Indians Overseas.* Unfortunately for the scholar, there is no such convenient and thorough presentation of the Sinhalese point of view.

[28] Kondapi, pp. 410-412.

[29] *Administration Report of the Commissioner of Labour for 1947,* Table III. By 1957, some 360,000 were claimed by four different unions.

of all the Indians on the island; it directed its attention more consistently to the estate workers of Indian ethnic origin for purposes of trade union and political action. Most of the time their actions were concerned with normal trade union matters of hours, wages, and conditions of work. Occasionally, however, important political issues attracted their attention. In 1946, for example, they organized a "hartal" or work stoppage in protest against the Soulbury proposals for constitutional reform and called out over 290,000 Indians and 50,000 non-Indian laborers.[30] They had expressed themselves on various political issues before, and this was a notable example of their willingness and ability to use their strength for essentially political purposes. Since it was rumored that at least one of their leaders was a close follower of the Communist party line, even if his union was not formally affiliated, there were many who viewed their political endeavors with some misgivings.

The peculiar concentration of estate workers of Indian ethnic origin in certain electoral districts gave them clear majorities in six constituencies and, as an ethnic minority relatively well organized, they tended to vote in a bloc. Leaders of the Congress acknowledged that they sometimes held decisive influence in as many as twelve to fourteen additional constituencies in up-country areas.[31] The Delimitation Commission expected that the estate workers of Indian ethnic origin could return seven representatives to parliament.[32] In the 1947 election they put forward seven candidates in the estate areas and returned six persons of Indian ethnic origin, most of whom had been among the party workers and organizers of the Congress. Analysis of voting results suggests that where Congress candidates themselves were not running, the estate population generally voted for the Marxist candidates.[33] It may be that they did so because of the attraction of Marxist class appeals; but more likely because, of all the political parties running candidates in their area, the Marxists had worked the hardest on their behalf. They had attempted to organize the estate labor force, opposed restrictive immigration and other similar measures, and stood up against the ardent Sinhalese communalists.

Because of their voting strength, the strong political organizations

[30] *Administration Report of the Commissioner of Labour for 1946*, p. 18.

[31] Interviews with some leading Congress organizers.

[32] *Report of the Delimitation Commission*, para. 70.

[33] For a detailed analysis and commentary see Sir Ivor Jennings, "The Ceylon General Elections of 1947," *University of Ceylon Review*, VI, No. 3 (July 1948), pp. 133-195.

among them, and their minority position, it was not difficult for Sinhalese leaders to point to them as wielding a balance of parliamentary power. As one government M.P. put it:

"Suppose the entire Kandyan area is represented by Members returned by general electorates composed of both Indians and Kandyans, and suppose that, as happened in the last elections but one, the vast majority of the Members so returned are non-Ceylonese, what would be the result? These members can bargain with the various parties.

"To the UNP they can say, 'We are prepared to support you provided you concede these things to us.' The UNP can carry on the Government forever with that support.

"Or the members so returned can tell the SLFP, 'We will give one hundred per cent support if you concede these things to us.' The SLFP would regard that as a windfall as with all the Indian representatives going over to their side they can control the future of the country.

"Or let us say that Indian members go to the Communist Party and say, 'We are with you provided you give us these concessions.' The Communist Party would be very happy to accept that aid in their efforts to do away with capitalism and various other things. All this could happen if such a controlling voice is vested in non-nationals of the country."[34]

If they were considered insufficiently assimilated, having only a doubtful claim to an "abiding interest" in the island, and were actually organized under radical Left auspices for purposes of class warfare, then it was possible to argue that their continued franchise posed a threat to Ceylon's new parliamentary system.

The temptation to act on the basis of such an argument was no doubt strengthened by the fact that the political fortunes of the ruling United National Party were not unaffected by these political calculations. If the government could restrict the citizenship and franchise of the Indians, a large bloc of Marxist representatives would be eliminated from parliament and the U.N.P. could expect to win, in return for its action, firm support among the Kandyan elements of the Sinhalese. The party's position in the conservative Central Province would be strengthened because small and easily canvassed

[34] *House of Representatives*, V. 16, c. 3027-3028. Statement made during the debate on the Indo-Ceylon Pact of 1954. Although made several years after the original citizenship legislation, it well states one view of the political considerations underlying the original legislation.

constituencies would be virtually reserved to Sinhalese politicians, and the presence of unrepresented Indians could always be used as a recurrent threat with which to frighten voters away from the Left parties who usually supported the case of the Indians.[35] More generally, those political leaders who sought to strengthen their support in the majority community could weaken their opponents by charging that they were not sufficiently vigorous in defending the Ceylonese from Indian competition. The image could easily be evoked of tiny Ceylon being inundated by a flood of poverty-stricken Indians. And for the communally conscious, the linguistic affinity of the estate workers with the Ceylon Tamils raised in some minds the possibility of a Tamil alliance for concerted political action against the Sinhalese community should communal divisions emerge as politically important in the future.

B. CITIZENSHIP STATUS

In view of the problems the Indian estate workers presented of an economic, cultural, and political nature, it is not surprising that the Ceylonese leadership promptly set about limiting the political rights of the Indian population. They developed three legal strategies for dealing with the problem. Firstly Ceylon citizenship was so defined as to limit it to those who could prove that their ancestors have been in Ceylon for several generations. This tended to exclude all but Sinhalese and Ceylon Tamils and other indigenous groups like Ceylon Moors and Burghers. Secondly special legislation was provided to define how Indians and Pakistanis who were resident on the island should apply for and be registered as citizens. And thirdly by a series of regulations and enactments directed against the European as well as the Indian business community, economic activities were to be progressively Ceylonized. There was little objection to legislation directed toward Ceylonizing various economic activities but the other two strategies were hotly contested.

The Citizenship Act No. 18 of 1948 (operative September 21, 1948) provides two ways by which a person may acquire Ceylonese citizenship, by descent or by registration. To acquire it by descent,

[35] This interpretation appears to have been confirmed by Mr. Nehru when attempting to explain in the Lokh Sabha why the Ceylonese were not prepared to give full rights to all Indian residents. He then declared: "The reasons . . . are obvious. It has no rational element in it at all. The reasons are that the political fortunes of certain parties were likely to be affected by it and it is not for us to argue about it—and they laid stress on this." *Government of India, Council of State,* Vol. VI, No. 5, p. 484.

that is automatically without going through specially provided procedures, a person born on the island before September 21, 1948 had to be able to prove that his father before him was also born in Ceylon or that both his paternal grandfather and paternal great-grandfather were born in Ceylon. If born outside Ceylon before the appointed day, he had to prove that his father and his paternal grandfather were born in Ceylon. If born after September 21, 1948, he could receive Ceylonese citizenship if his father was then a citizen; if born outside Ceylon his birth had to be registered with an appropriate official. Such provisions for citizenship by descent were notably restrictive, designed to prevent automatic granting of citizenship to anyone whose family had not been living on the island for at least two generations. This effectively debarred the Indian and Pakistan community.

The 1948 act also provided for citizenship by registration, available to a person who "is and intends to be ordinarily resident in Ceylon." In addition, not more than twenty-five persons in a year may be granted citizenship because they have rendered distinguished service or are eminent in professional, commercial, industrial, or agricultural life or have been naturalized as British subjects in Ceylon.[36] Having thus created a category of "citizen of Ceylon" which was controllable by the legislature, the franchise laws were then revised so as to provide that no person shall be qualified to have his name entered or retained on a register of electors if he is not a citizen.[37]

The Indian and Pakistani Residents (Citizenship) Act No. 3 of 1949 specifically defined the terms under which persons of Indian or Pakistani descent may become citizens by registration. They must have been in residence continuously since January 1, 1946 and have been in residence prior to that for ten years in the case of an unmarried person or seven years in the case of married persons. Documentary proof of residence during these periods was required and special commissioners were appointed to investigate and pass upon the applications that must be submitted. In practice the administration of this act has had the effect of seriously limiting the numbers of Indian residents who can qualify as citizens. The courts have not been entirely satisfied with the equity of the act's administration,

[36] For a discussion of these provisions, see Jennings, *The Constitution of Ceylon*, pp. 40-43.

[37] Ceylon (Parliamentary Elections), Amendment Act, No. 48 of 1949; Ceylon (Parliamentary Elections), Order in Council, 1946.

and the politicians have claimed that the administration has been too generous.[38] Appeals to higher courts have sometimes led to a reversal of the administrator's decision, although an appeal to the Privy Council in an effort to have the whole legislation declared contrary to Article 29 (2) of the Constitution failed.[39]

The Ceylonese government has been beset by conflicting pressures in its approach to the Indians. Political leaders responsive to the anxieties of the Sinhalese sought to restrict immigration. The planters, on the other hand, Ceylonese and foreign, tried to retain and, on occasion, increase their labor force from India.

The civil status of Indians accepted as Ceylonese citizens has also posed difficulties. In order to diminish Kandyan opposition to giving resident Indians citizenship, the Kotelawala government established four special seats in parliament to be filled by elections among those of Indian origin who had become Ceylonese citizens by registration. This measure was never put into effect and in 1959 it was superseded by constitutional amendments giving all citizens by registration full voting rights in the constituencies where they resided.

C. INTERGOVERNMENTAL RELATIONS

The status of Indians in Ceylon raised perplexing problems for the Indian government, too. Even during the days of British rule, the government of India sought to protect the welfare of its sons and daughters overseas. Independence increased Delhi's sense of responsibility for her own nationals. It was clear to the Indian government that it was not in a position to welcome back to India all of the more than 4,000,000 Indians in Ceylon, South Africa, Fiji, Malaya, and elsewhere in the former British Empire. In order to improve the conditions of Indians overseas, the Indian government had to remain on friendly terms with the governments concerned. Yet to insist on better conditions for Indians often ran contrary to the political or other interests of these same governments, and, if pressed too far by the Indian government, only added difficulties to the lot of overseas Indians. India's concern for its expatriates left an Indian hostage in the host country. In the case of Ceylon, however, India had another way of exerting influence in the mat-

[38] See, for instance, editorial supporting the Supreme Court in *Morning Times* (Colombo), November 23, 1956. Kandyan spokesmen have argued to the contrary that the act has not been administered severely enough. For instance, *House of Representatives*, V. 17, c. 1275.

[39] Mudanayake v. Sivagnanasunderam (1952), 53 N.L.R.25.

ter. Whenever drought plagued the Carnatic coast of South India, large numbers of Indians would try to cross the straits to the lusher island of Ceylon. Only the Indian administration could reduce to a minimum the numbers who attempted to leave India, a matter of interest to the Ceylonese. Only the Ceylonese administration could insure fair treatment to the Indians in Ceylon, a matter of concern to Delhi. Hence, in this matter the two governments were deeply interdependent despite their divergent views as to the ultimate "solution" of the problem.

The Indian government considered that Indians had to decide for themselves whether or not they wished to adopt their present country of residence as their homeland. Mr. Nehru was explicit about this, advising the expatriates to make up their own minds. The Ceylonese government, on the other hand, sought the repatriation of very large numbers of the immigrants and its citizenship provisions were not always administered in such a way as to give a fully free choice.

In 1941, representatives of the two countries met to attempt tc define satisfactory principles for the control and supervision of emigration, and political and economic rights. In 1947, as the Ceylonese government began to draft its citizenship legislation, Mr. Nehru and Mr. Senanayake met again.[40] The actual legislation as finally drafted was thoroughly unsatisfactory to Mr. Nehru, for it clearly restricted Ceylonese citizenship to those who had resided there for several generations, and the special procedures set up for Indians and Pakistanis to opt for Ceylonese citizenship were considered cumbersome and discriminatory.

The Ceylonese officials appear to have assumed that all "Indians" who were not accepted as Ceylonese citizens would automatically then become citizens of India.[41] But when the Indian Constitution was adopted in 1949, Article 8 so defined Indian citizenship as to set up a special selective procedure on the Indian side. In any event, the Indian administrators in Ceylon appear to have been highly selective in accepting applicants qualified for Indian citizenship. As a result of the caution of both the Ceylonese and Indian administrators, a large body of individuals with neither Indian nor Ceylonese nationality has been emerging. Diplomatic representatives

40 *Correspondence Relating to the Citizenship Status of Indians in Ceylon* (Sessional Paper XXII—1948).

41 See, for instance, letter of Mr. D. S. Senanayake, June 22, 1948, SP XXII—1948. Also *House of Representatives,* V. 20, c. 1006.

and the heads of both states have met many times to attempt to solve the problem of stateless Indians at another level of administration. Their conferences and negotiations have been without success. By 1959, for example, only 100,000 had been accepted as Ceylonese citizens, leaving a stateless residue of over 600,000.[42]

CONCLUSION

Some ten per cent of Ceylon's inhabitants are presently without civic status, with neither citizenship nor the right to vote. They are in fact, if not yet according to the Ceylonese government, "stateless people." They have been considered a social, economic, and political threat to the safety and wellbeing of Ceylon. Some argue that they are a potential Indian fifth column, a strategically placed south Indian Tamil bridgehead in the middle of the island should the Indian government one day decide to engulf Ceylon. Yet the measures taken against them are precisely those which would lead the estate population to welcome Indian intervention and they are measures most likely to vindicate Delhi should there be a radical revision of Indian foreign policy after the death of Mr. Nehru.

No doubt some practical measures can eventually be devised. For example, if a fair retirement scheme were developed with a retirement bonus and reduced return fares to India, many of the older workers would stop work right now and leave openings for the younger ones. If the same facilities were granted to the younger ones, their representatives argue, perhaps half of the Indian population would leave the island. It would then be easier to cope with the problems posed by the remainder. Much depends upon the relationship which the popular leadership of the unions can develop with the government and the confidence they can inspire in the Sinhalese that their ambitions have limits and their intentions are bona fide.

III · CEYLON TAMIL-SINHALESE RELATIONSHIPS

A. INTRODUCTION

Compared with her neighbors—India, Pakistan, or Burma—Ceylon has been remarkably free from ardent communal strife. Until 1958 the undercurrent of communal antagonism had never reached

[42] See Chapter x for a discussion of the foreign policy implications of the problem of stateless Indians.

the point of violent hostility of the partition years in India or more recently over Indian language problems. The national movement toward independence did not have the same religious cast that Gandhi's intensely Hindu appeals evoked among his followers. No Mohammed Ali Jinnah arose with a vision to insure a religious ambiance for the minority community by seeking an independent state. Minorities did not try by insurrection to assert their independent character, as in Burma.

Communal divisions cut through Ceylonese society and have been preserved by differing languages and religions and by the reluctance of families and their children to marry across communal lines. The underlying attitudes of members of one community toward members of another have been unflattering at best. There has been keen competition between them for economic and political opportunities. On occasion, political leaders of each community have called upon the sentiments of communal solidarity to ensure a following at election time. Successive constitutional reforms have evoked vigorous communal politics to make certain that the reforms would not infringe on each community's separate interests. The present constitution, modeled on the views of the Ceylonese ministers themselves, provides for certain safeguards to ensure that communal politics will not be accented and that the special interests of the minorities will be protected.

Communal hostility in Ceylon was held in bounds by circumstances and conscious choice. The leadership that achieved independence held to the concept of a diverse Ceylon encompassing in its continued variety Sinhalese, Tamils, Moors, and Burghers, each with an assured and acknowledged place within the whole. The British insisted that reforms toward independence should be acceptable to the minorities—a policy that strengthened the will of the majority's spokesmen to resist the extreme claims of some of their followers. By and large there were enough careers open to the talents and ambitions of those who graduated from the school system. It was also important that the political leaders, competing with each other for the popular vote, were neither so short-sighted nor so desperate as to push to extremes whatever communal arguments they knew were within their reach.

Unhappily for communal harmony, the end of the first decade of independence saw this conjuncture of favorable conditions change and the new combination of forces produce such communal outbursts as the island had not known in centuries. Underlying attitudes of each community toward the other, economic competition between their educated members, and the growing communal self-consciousness resulting from a cultural revival will be examined. The specific problems that emerged from the growing agitation for more rapid language reforms serve as further background to a discussion of the political forces that brought to a head these communal differences.

B. BACKGROUNDS TO COMMUNAL TENSION

1. *The moderate experience.* Sinhalese and Tamils have been living on the island together for a thousand years. Sinhalese and Tamil kings fought one another, particularly between the tenth and fourteenth centuries, but, in so far as evidence is available, the people subsisted on the land as best they could without conflict.[43] In some predominantly Sinhalese areas, Tamils entered and gradually adopted Sinhalese customs; in areas largely Tamil, Sinhalese lived with the Tamils. On the whole, however, the two populations did not intermingle.

After the decline of Polonnaruwa in the thirteenth century, the Sinhalese gradually shifted the center of their activity to the wet zone jungle areas to the south, and the Tamils fell back on to their center in the northern Jaffna district and the dry zone eastern coast, leaving a relatively uninhabited territory in between. Except along the coasts in two provinces where intermingling continued, language, religion, territory, and cultural ways divided the two peoples.[44] Centuries of mutual separation accentuated their differences.

Under the British, the island became a single administrative and economic unit, and once again Tamils and Sinhalese began to mingle. There were three principal points of encounter, each with a different effect upon communal relationships. At the upper levels of the society, Tamils and Sinhalese began to go to "the best schools" together where no communal distinctions were made. From this experience the cultural diversities were in many ways bridged. Intimate friendship and a substantially common view of life, public purpose, and private enjoyment came to be shared by many English-educated in both Sinhalese and Tamil communities. A second point

[43] G. C. Mendis, "The Causes of Communal Conflict in Ceylon," *Ceylon Historical Journal,* I (April 1943), pp. 41-49.

[44] Northwestern and Eastern Provinces.

of encounter, the public service and the professions, produced less clear results for communal peace. The mutual knowledge that came from solving problems in concerted judgment and effort brought men of both communities closer together. But competition for openings and advancement in professional fields is sharp in any land. Where professional positions were not alone the fruits of individual effort but also the instruments and symbols of comparative community success, the communal consequences were bound to have been mixed. A third encounter occurred in certain village areas where Ceylon Tamil traders and storekeepers brought to the villages the services and the resentments that come with the small shopkeeper and money-lender in Asia. No doubt more Sinhalese low-country storekeepers penetrated rural Sinhalese districts than did Ceylon Tamils, and many of the Tamils were Indians. Nevertheless, the consequences of this encounter were detrimental to communal solidarity.

Where members of both communities had lived together for generations as neighboring peasants and villagers, there developed a reasonable degree of understanding and mutual tolerance.[45] They were self-conscious about their differences, and mutually suspicious, but they were not intensely hostile prior to the language agitation of 1955-56.

2. *Group attitudes.* Before this period of growing animosity in 1955-56, members of each community had developed clearly defined and unflattering ideas about the other. Such opinions are the primary ingredients of intergroup prejudice analogous to the ideas of one another held by first generation minorities in America. In Ceylon these prejudices remained latent and did not become politically important for a long period. Later, under appropriate stimulus, they contributed to hostile action of great political consequence.

It is difficult to define the exact contours of these prejudices or "stereotypes." One way of exploring the problem is to ask individuals to list those terms they spontaneously associate with the words "Tamils" and "Sinhalese." Only a few such studies have been made. The samples are so small as to make it hazardous to draw general conclusions. However, the studies available confirm that group consciousness was already well-developed before the communal agitation began in 1955.

[45] Mendis, *ibid.*

For example, when a sample of seventy Sinhalese children in a government school in Colombo was asked to characterize themselves and the "Tamils," and the words they used are arranged in order of their frequency, they revealed clearly differentiated images of each group.[46] The first fifteen words in order of their frequency compared as follows:

Sinhalese self-conception	*Conception of Tamils*
kind	cruel
clever	clever
rich	poor
brave	diligent
jealous	cunning
proud	rich
good	kind
religious	black
farmers	intelligent
poor	thrifty
courageous	ugly
lazy	arrogant
honest	business minded
patient	dirty
educated	proud

The Sinhalese students considered themselves predominantly kind; many believed the Tamils cruel. Both groups were considered by the Sinhalese equally clever and equally rich, although the Tamils were also considered poorer. Sinhalese considered themselves twice as lazy as the Tamils. Tamils were seen as markedly more thrifty than the Sinhalese, more diligent, and more arrogant. They were also considered clannish, mathematically minded, self-centered, living simply, and talkers. The Sinhalese considered themselves efficient in the past, fair-minded, good at language, and helpful to each other. If the descriptive terms used were classified as socially acceptable or unacceptable, the Sinhalese gave themselves more acceptable qualities than they attributed to the Tamils.[47]

An analogous study among Tamil children from Jaffna produced similar results. They considered themselves cultured, intelligent, and

[46] Less than 5 per cent were English-educated.

[47] All references are to an unpublished paper, "Sinhalese Children's Stereotypes of Sinhalese, Tamil, Burgher, and English," by Professor T. L. Green, formerly of the University of Ceylon. It is to be expected that if the terms applied to both groups are classified as socially acceptable or socially unacceptable, children will apply to themselves a higher proportion of favorable terms than they apply to others. But Sinhalese gave themselves less favored qualities than they assigned to the British.

industrious and the Sinhalese lazy, proud, and bold. Sinhalese were more selfish than the Tamils although the Tamil children believed that both shared equally the quality of superstitiousness. Tamils were thriftier than the Sinhalese, but the Sinhalese were more friendly than the Tamils. The Tamils gave themselves as many undesirable as desirable traits, but the Sinhalese were given mostly undesirable characteristics.[48]

An analysis of the opinions held by university graduate teachers who returned to the University for refresher courses after five to ten years teaching experience tells the same story, suggesting that the prejudices identified in children are not merely ephemeral youthful ideas. The Sinhalese among the teachers showed evidence of attributing to Tamil teachers more qualities that would make the Tamils effective in their professional field than the Sinhalese attributed to themselves. In contrast—and typical of such studies—regarding characteristics other than those concerned with "levels of performance," the Sinhalese teachers showed a clear preference for their own ways over those of the Tamils.[49]

Although too much importance should not be attached to elaborated analysis of such limited data, these careful studies lend empirical confirmation to the clear impression a visitor might receive—that Tamils and Sinhalese see each other as different peoples; they tend to be mutually critical, and each tends to prefer his own approach to life rather than the other's; it is clear that their prejudices are undisguised. Where one group—the Sinhalese—rated itself lower than it rated the other, it was in the field where anxieties over competition for career opportunities and professional jobs could easily be given a communal interpretation.

3. *Economic competition.* A principal source of contention between these two communities has been the secure, influential, and relatively well-paid opportunities in the public service. Invidious comparisons have been frequent, sometimes cast in numerical terms to indicate that this or that community has not had its "fair share" of such positions. There have always been more low-country Sinhalese than Tamils in the public service. But in relation to the total numbers of each community in the population, there have been

[48] Unpublished paper, Professor T. L. Green, "Tamil Stereotypes of Sinhalese, Tamils, English, and Burghers." Like their Sinhalese compatriots, they attributed to the British more socially positive traits than they gave to themselves.

[49] Unpublished paper, Professor T. L. Green, "Studies in Stereotypes held by Ceylonese; Group Attitudes of Adult University Graduate Teachers."

proportionately more Tamils and many more Burghers than Sinhalese.[50]

It was the peoples from the north—the Tamils—who first experienced the pressures of overpopulation and limited local resources. Hence, the growing public service presented itself as a career for which they were well suited by virtue of another historical circumstance. More missionary schools in relation to the population had been established in Tamil areas than in Sinhalese areas. Tamil children were good at figures and their parents goaded them in their academic work for fear of unemployment or hard labor as the price of failure. In addition, their religious beliefs allowed them wide latitude in adopting foreign ways for work purposes without disturbing their fundamental Hindu traditions. Their schools prepared them for government service and teaching posts, and they found jobs in many parts of the island.

In the south where the Sinhalese lived there was more watered land; there were estates and commerce. The economic innovations introduced by the British were centered largely in this area and those with means could participate directly in the plantation enterprises and others with ambition could find opportunities supplying the estates or transporting, preparing, and shipping estate products. It was not until much later, perhaps the second or third decades of the twentieth century, that population pressure became acute in Sinhalese areas. Although missionary schools had also been developed in the Western and Southern Provinces, education was not as proportionately available elsewhere in the south until the nineteen thirties when the state school system expanded. Even now in many Sinhalese areas, especially in Central Province, educational facilities are still noticeably inferior to those in the northern and western maritime provinces.

Sinhalese parents of most communities demand less of their children than the sterner Tamil disciplinarians. The Sinhalese family system is less closeknit and fewer familes scrape together all their resources to send the family "bright boy"—perhaps a distant cousin—to a good school and beyond. It may be that the more conservative Goyigama community did not find the public service as uniquely a rewarding occupation for their sons as did the northern Tamils.

[50] For the most detailed historical analysis, see S. J. Tambiah, "Ethnic Representation in Ceylon's Higher Administrative Services 1870-1946," *University of Ceylon Review*, XIII, Nos. 2 and 3 (April-July 1955), pp. 113-134.

Until recently, proportionately fewer Sinhalese directed their ambitions toward government jobs.

The proportion of Sinhalese and Tamils in the public service has become a public issue, as competition between the two communities grows more open and direct. The most authoritative data available are as follows: a service-wide census taken in 1951 showed that out of a total of 123,194 reported as employed directly by the central government, those with Sinhalese educational backgrounds represented 81,374 and those with Tamil backgrounds represented 21,768. Of the remaining 20,000 who had had an exclusively English educational background, it would be plausible to assume that 10,000 were Sinhalese, 5,000 Burghers, and 5,000 Tamils. This would make a total of 27,000 Tamils out of a total government strength of 123,-000 or roughly 22 per cent. If, however, the entire 20,000 are added to the Tamil numbers—an operation quite inaccurate and only for the sake of argument—it would raise the Tamil representation to 42,000 making the Tamil proportion still no more than 34 per cent of the total.[51]

Figures as high as 60 per cent of government posts being held by Tamils have been used. A possible explanation for this exaggeration is that as a minority, they are therefore visible. It may also stem from the fact that there are many Tamils in certain parts of the service whose work is widely scattered throughout the country—such as the engineering and lower levels of the Public Works Department.[52] Another charge is that once they gain positions of prominence in a department, they promptly fill new posts with relatives or those to whom they are in some way indebted. The statistical data referred to suggest that the extent of this practice among Tamils has been exaggerated.

The educational reforms since World War II added to a growing sense of competition between the communities for the middle-class jobs which had always been the coveted fruits of education—government service, teaching, and the professions. Growing numbers of Sinhalese—speaking only Sinhalese—began to graduate from the

[51] Department of Census and Statistics, *Report of the Census of Government and Local Government Employees 1951* (Colombo, 1952). Table 7. Tambiah's analysis of the Civil List, i.e., those in upper level positions entered by examination, shows 20 per cent being Tamils in 1946, p. 133.

[52] It was reliably reported that a department like the Public Works Department has a high percentage of Tamil overseers and laborers employed, perhaps reaching the 60 per cent figure in *certain specified categories.*

higher levels of the school system. Unable to find job openings deemed suitable to their educational attainments, they were naturally resentful and attributed their failure to the Tamils, who had a reputation for acquiring good positions and for good performance once established. The growing competition for a limited number of careers contributed to intercommunal tension.

4. *Community self-consciousness with the cultural revival.* There have been other grounds for communal self-consciousness and invidious comparison. The national cultural revival and the repudiation of Western cultural patterns inescapably lead back into a Sinhalese past, a Tamil past, or a Muslim past, each distinct from the other. As one M.P. put it, no doubt exaggerating: "The three major communities in Ceylon are today living in three water-tight compartments; the Muslims do not know the Buddhist point of view, the Tamils do not know the Muslim point of view; the people of each community want to . . . imbibe their own culture and move within the confines of their own closed communal compartment."[53]

As the self-conscious Tamils view their culture, it has a sound integrity, the strength of immediate life, and the vistas of thousands of years. Less touched by Western ways than the Sinhalese culture, it is felt to be linked inextricably through continuous centuries of creative art, dance, and literature to earliest times. This sense of cultural continuity goes back to the dawn of civilization. Some Tamil spokesmen contend that their culture goes back to Mohenjodaro and the Indus Valley civilization of 5000 B.C. that antedated the coming of the Aryans to India.[54]

The Tamil Hindu religion has an absolute and inclusive quality to it. Just as their sense of time seems to approach the timeless, the mythology and philosophy of Hinduism is thought of as all-embracing. Hindus believe that nothing is strange to their capacious faith and view of life. Buddhism is often seen as a phase of its own wide development and Christianity as merely a young religion. Hindus take a profound satisfaction in the wide range of belief and practice and in the rich ceremonial that is intimately bound up with their family and social life. Indian classical dancing is closely related to Hindu religious themes and is a vivid and beautiful reminder of the unity of their art and religion. Just as English is often thought of as

[53] *House of Representatives*, V. 9, c. 1755.
[54] Xavier S. Thani Nayagam, *Tamil Culture* (Colombo, 1955), p. 5.

"the language of commerce," Tamil is regarded as the language of devotion, especially suited for mystical and poetic expression.

There is an unconscious and not always unexpressed pride and self-confidence in the Tamil's approach to his tradition. He looks down on the culture of his Sinhalese neighbors in much the same way that certain European intellectuals have a quiet disdain for American cultural creations. Geographically, Tamil culture in South Asia extends beyond the 27,000,000 people who speak Tamil in South India. Tamils from South India have gone to Madagascar, Malaya, Fiji, West Indies, Indonesia, Mauritius, and South Africa as well as Ceylon.[55] When they have settled on foreign shores, they have retained a core of direction and inspiration which is distinct from the native culture of the lands in which they live. Wherever they go, they can look to a large cultural area in South India, to Madras as a center of Indian classical dancing, to the ancient temples of South India as places of pilgrimage or to thriving Indian universities.

As the Sinhalese view their culture they are keenly aware of being only 7,000,000 people in all the world and solely on the island of Ceylon. Their culture is unique and differentiated, and they cannot depend on others to help them perpetuate it. Many centuries with little evidence of creative endeavor separate them today from the flowering past when ancient monarchs concentrated the resources of their kingdoms to create stupendous monuments and public works and to encourage the labor and piety of the scholars and *bhikkhus* at Anuradhapura and Polonnaruwa.

The richness of the ancient culture cannot be denied. Anuradhapura, the capital for over a thousand years, is still impressive. It was "begun at a time roughly contemporary with the conquest of Alexander the Great and his successors, and continued throughout the period of the Roman Empire. . . . The palaces of such monarchs as Tissa and Dutthagamini, as described by the ancient Sinhalese writers, would have made Diocletian's palace seem a poor thing by comparison; their great *dagobas*, artificial hills of masonry supporting shrines and reliquaries, were sometimes over three hundred feet high, and can be compared with the pyramids of Egypt. Their hydraulic engineering has no parallel save in the nineteenth and twentieth centuries; for example, the artificial lake of Mineria, created

[55] The figure of 40,000,000 Tamils in South India is popularly used in Ceylon polemics. On the contrary, India contains 27,000,000 Tamils.

in the third century A.D., by Maha Sen, had a circumference of twenty miles. . . ."[56]

The earliest surviving structures are "stupas" or *dagobas*, as they are called in Ceylon. To King Duttha-Gamini and his brother Saddha Tissa goes the credit "of being the first rulers to appreciate the grandeur of the effect of an enormous white dome, far greater than anything of the kind previously erected in Ceylon or India, and admirably adapted to an expression of stability, and permanence and inaccessibility, such as the purpose of its construction demanded."[57] The Thuparama *dagoba* or dome (244 B.C.) was built by Tissa and contains various relics of the Buddha. It is an architectural form which is still used, and it is as familiar and beautiful in its simplicity as the white spired church in New England. Fifth-century frescoes on the side of the rock at Sigiriya match those of the famous Ajanta caves in India. It is evident that, even though the painters of Sigiriya shared the ideals of Indian classical arts, there is an air of "conscious gravity" and slightly differing accentuations of the human form which are exclusively Ceylonese.[58]

In the first decade of the eleventh century the greater part of Ceylon was subject to the mighty Chola empire of India. When the Sinhalese regained their independence, the old capital of Anuradhapura was abandoned in favor of Polonnaruwa, the former headquarters of the Chola rulers. In the twelfth century Polonnaruwa witnessed a brilliant period under King Parakrama Bahu (A.D. 1156-86). The paintings on the walls of the Tivanka Image House, the lofty Lankatilaka, the rock-cut images of the Gal Vihara, and the Audience Hall within his palace attest to this monarch's grand conceptions and artistic taste and achievement.[59]

Polonnaruwa has two outstanding examples of sculpture: the huge rock-cut statue which was traditionally thought to be a representation of Parakrama Bahu the Great, and the colossal Buddha images which suggest such supreme tranquility. Along with the famous figure of Buddha on the Outer Circle Road at Anuradhapura, these pieces of sculpture evoke feelings of great calm. As one observer

[56] Leonard Cottrell, *Lost Cities* (New York, 1957), p. 133. See also Vincent Smith, *History of Fine Art in India and Ceylon* (Oxford, 1930), pp. 109ff. and 142ff.

[57] Henry Parker, *Ancient Ceylon* (London, 1909), cited by A. K. Coomaraswamy, *History of Indian and Indonesian Art* (New York, 1927), p. 161.

[58] UNESCO, World Art Series, *Paintings from Temple, Shrine and Rock* (New York, 1957), pp. 13ff., preface by W. G. Archer.

[59] Arts Council of Ceylon, *Art and Architecture of Ceylon Polonnaruva Period* (Colombo, 1954), introduction by S. Paranavitana, pp. 23ff.

phrased it: "Ceylonese art is elegant and gentle, somewhat idyllic, and perfectly human. . . . Some of the Buddhas are among the finest ever rendered; there is no dryness, no sophistication. The art is completely natural in its approach both to the sublime and the earthly; so that, though it mirrors various phases of the Indian tradition, it has transformed the continental impulses into a smooth, harmonious expression of its own, and in this sense it is comparable to the art of Java."[60] Sinhalese metal castings dating from the fifth to the twelfth century are still another aspect of this creativeness.[61] These were the outstanding periods of cultural efflorescence. By the eighteenth century Sinhalese art had become a provincial folk art, and the society itself had changed to such an extent that the same cultural forms were a lost art.

Today, despite the impact of Westernization, Sinhalese dancing and theatre are impressive for their vigor and tradition. The Kandyan dance, though clearly of Indian origin, has, in its present form in Ceylon, a justified reputation for its vigor and rhythm, the strength of its dance forms, and exciting accompaniment. Low-country Sinhalese dancers, though less publicized, show "a remarkable standard of dazzling, pyrotechnical body movements" and the ability through mime and dance to tell a story and create a mood.[62] Dance and theatre are interwoven in these rural functions. Traditional themes provide a wide repertoire of village stories, closely bound with legends surrounding favorite dieties that have little to do with the Buddhism of the purer faith but are fundamental to life in rural Ceylon. Faubian Bower considers the Kolam masks used in village drama and dance "probably the finest examples of wood carving still being executed for the theatre in the modern world." In view of these manifestations of dance and drama, he concludes that "Ceylon . . . has, in fact retained a surprising degree of cultural consistency and steadfastness."[63]

Despite this cultural heritage many Sinhalese are keenly sensitive to the ebb and flow in their own creative energies. More than five centuries separated the late Polonnaruwa period from its predeces-

60 Heinrich Zimmer, *The Art of Indian Asia*, 2 vols., Joseph Campbell, ed. (New York, 1955), I, p. 366.

61 Smith, pp. 150-156; Coomaraswamy, 166ff.

62 Faubian Bowers, *Theatre in the East* (New York, Edinburgh, 1956), pp. 85, 102.

63 *Ibid.*, p. 102. In 1957 a contemporary production of the traditional story of *Maname* combining theater, dance, and drumming set on a modern stage drew very large crowds from nearly all segments of the population.

sors and another five hundred years intervened before the Kandyan kingdom put its stamp on the culture of the central highlands. The coming of the Europeans, it is felt, all but destroyed many aspects of indigenous culture. Many Sinhalese, therefore, consider their culture fragile, requiring unusual defenses if it is to survive in proximity to the vigorous Tamil culture and in the face of insistent European influences. Lacking a strong culture, the people, too, are considered vulnerable. "For have not certain societies where traditional cultures were abandoned become extinct within our living memory? Some of the South Sea Islands have become depopulated. The Tasmanians are no more. The ancient cultures of Mayas and Incas have died out. The modern tribes of India are on the point of extinction. Why? . . . No colonial people have contributed to human progress nor have they progressed themselves. All of them without exception were on the point of losing their soul and self-respect because of the suppression of traditional cultures and the imposition of alien cultures on unwilling minds . . . what is native, what is tradition and what mattered were exchanged for the novel and the foreign."[64]

Quite apart from the intrinsic merit of reviving Sinhalese culture, this endeavor has political implications. It has been the vehicle for expressing antagonism against the ruling, Westernized Ceylonese elite who are held to be in part responsible for this cultural weakness. Uncritical use of Western art forms in the pace-setting urban schools deprived school curricula of their inspirational and artistic educative function. The social and political elite developed a taste for Western modes and looked down on local creative efforts. This cultural snobbery has been turned against them for political purposes.

Most sophisticated students of the problem of cultural revival see many difficulties that must be overcome, but none will deny that state patronage is indispensable.[65] It is popularly held that since Tamil culture is so strong, it needs no state aid. There has therefore been a growing pressure to use the resources of the Ceylonese state for nurturing a purely Sinhalese art. Politicians have sought favor in their constituencies by urging the use of state funds to promote a cultural revival. The debates surrounding this budgetary issue have stirred community self-consciousness. Understandable

[64] N. D. Wijesekera, "Dynamism of Traditional Cultures," in R. Pieris ed. *Traditional Sinhalese Culture* (Peradeniya, 1956), pp. 21-22.

[65] R. Pieris, *ibid., passim.*

Tamil reluctance to allow all cultural funds to go to Sinhalese cultural development has caused irritation among Sinhalese.

The widespread use of the *Mahavamsa* as a well-rounded record of Sinhalese history has also helped to exacerbate communal feelings. Sinhalese *bhikkhus* kept a record over thousands of years in this document—part legend, part history—which glorifies the monarchs who supported the Sangha and criticizes those who did not. Its historical inspiration defines the one significant community as the Sinhalese, a community that gained its glorious history and its grandeur by virtue of its ancient wars with the distant ancestors of the Tamil community. Only conscious efforts to distinguish between the ancient invading Tamils and the contemporary Ceylon Tamils could offset the effects of reviving and popularizing the traditional story. Unhappily, this has not been the custom in recent times. Certain Tamil politicians have contributed to this very identification by tactless references to the Tamil victories in these wars. Active proponents of the Sinhalese cause, including Buddhist laymen, have also not made this distinction.

Hence, although group relations tended to be moderate, particularly in those areas where Sinhalese and Tamil villagers and peasants lived as neighbors, underlying invidious attitudes provided one set of ingredients for potential communal antagonism. Among the more educated middle classes, competition for public service and professional career opportunities added an economic ingredient. Cultural revival, particularly among the Sinhalese, led them to identify the greatness of Lanka with the Sinhalese alone and to feel that their culture was threatened by the presumably more vigorous Tamil.

C. PROBLEMS OF LANGUAGE POLICY

1. *Language reform: the significance of language.* These ingredients of communal antagonism were precipitated into open conflict toward the end of the first decade of independence by heated differences over language reform. When language is taken for granted, as it is in the United States, where nearly everyone speaks the same language and aspires to become part of the wider American culture, there are few emotions that adhere to language and it is difficult to appreciate the excitement that can be provoked over linguistic politics. In South Asia, however, where a multitude of languages exist within the same political boundaries, language policy has

created more difficulties than almost any other single issue of public affairs.

Language is of profound significance to an individual. It is the person's mode of contact with his social world. A challenge to an individual's language is a threat to this personal net that saves him from the abyss of loneliness. An individual's values and life purposes are expressed through his language. When the means of knowing a panorama of culture is brought into question the values of this culture are thereby threatened. Some cultures attach great importance to fluency, grace, and precision of expression, and consider skill in the use of language as the mark of the educated man.

Language is often the dominating symbol of group distinctiveness. In an age of cultural revival and nationalist sentiment, language may become part of the cultural background that must be revived and defended if the group is itself to gain a sense of integrity and standing. The example of Eire in contemporary Commonwealth affairs presents a close parallel. The problems posed to, and by, linguistic minorities were well demonstrated in the Succession States in eastern Europe after World War I. Efforts to assimilate ethnic and linguistic minorities through enforced language policies provoked passionate resistance. And the resentments of these unassimilated minorities speeded the disintegration of these states when large neighbors became aggressive.

Language may also serve to set off one social class from another. *Pygmalion* has its egalitarian message in almost all societies where different usage and accent reveal a person's origin and education and provide clues to the proper treatment to be accorded him. In countries where aliens have ruled, the alien's language becomes the means to advancement. Proficiency in the foreigner's tongue gains access to jobs, to social equality with the rulers, and, often, to opportunities to become influential oneself. Conversely, language in many circumstances may be a stigma, a means of relegating to menial positions those who are not adept. It can therefore be one of the keys to social and economic standing.

Language has all these meanings in Ceylon. Until recently, there was an interplay of three languages—English, Tamil, and Sinhalese.[66] At the top of the last two communities, there was the small but influential and relatively wealthy group who also spoke English with

[66] Moors and Muslims sometimes spoke all three languages. The Burghers considered English as their "mother tongue," though some of them spoke fluent Sinhalese, fewer spoke Tamil.

great fluency. As one M.P. put it: "My friend . . . spoke of two nations, the Sinhalese and the Tamils. There are also two other nations —those who speak English and those who do not, in this Island of ours."[67] Universal franchise had been granted in 1931, but the language of 8 per cent of the population remained the language of government until 1956.

The foreign ruler's language was the instrument for learning about the technology and civilization of the outside world. It was the passport to professional careers in government or for material advancement and prosperity more generally. English was the mark of high social status, and pride, if not arrogance, went with its mastery. By contrast, the man who knew only Tamil or Sinhalese was generally relegated to a minor position or had more difficulty in gaining employment. There were all kinds of disabilities put in the way of the majority of the population who spoke only Tamil and Sinhalese. Lower status was even accorded in such simple matters as affixing a signature in Sinhalese or Tamil; two witnesses were required to attest to its correctness, but an English signature required no such confirmation.

It is safe to say that the cultivator cared little about language problems. The vernaculars, Sinhalese or Tamil, were sufficient to serve his purposes. As educational opportunities increased, however, more families sought for their children positions traditionally open only to the man with a higher education, to the man who knew English. The growing demand for English could not be met, owing to a shortage of English teachers.[68] In their disappointment they looked upon English as a barrier to their own advancement. Their numbers were growing and they were only too eager to do away with a language which made them second-class citizens.

Specific middle class professional groups in both town and country came to a clearer awareness of invidious linguistic distinctions. They became more conscious that standing and opportunity were in part defined by a person's own language and that their language—closest to indigenous tradition—was given second class standing. *Ayurvedic* physicians, teachers in the vernacular schools, village elective officials, each in their own way, became more sensitive to the social and career implications of language skills and opportunity. These men were believed to influence opinions in rural areas; political leaders

[67] *House of Representatives,* V. 20, c. 2042.

[68] T. L. Green, "Education and Society in Ceylon," *The Educand,* II, No. 3 (Nov. 1956), pp. 49-65, p. 54.

were particularly sensitive to their aspirations and in seeking to identify themselves with these groups no doubt further sharpened the growing awareness of invidious distinctions that had not concerned them seriously before.

Accordingly, a considerable part of the language agitation that developed in Ceylon was attributable to the desire to promote indigenous languages at the expense of English, to open wider opportunities to men educated in the vernacular languages, and to diminish the advantageous position of the man educated in the foreigner's tongue.

Just as the governments of India, Pakistan, and other countries in South Asia were faced with difficult decisions in regard to language, the new government of independent Ceylon had to face the questions of what should be the language of instruction in schools and what should be the official language of state. Apart from these two major policy decisions, there were many subsidiary questions that required an answer. What should be the language or languages of parliamentary debate, of legislation? Should local government be in the vernacular? What about examinations for the public service? Should court cases be tried in the language of the litigants if they were the same or in English if they were different? Should legal sources be translated? These were all difficult problems in and of themselves. To find the answers that maximized justice to all and contributed to a knitting together of all the communities and classes that were differentiated on grounds of language would have taxed the highest statesmanship.

2. *Language reform and the school system.* One of the first decisions to be made concerned the languages to be used as a medium of instruction in the school system. English had the advantage of giving Ceylonese students access to world knowledge and to the latest scientific, technical, and intellectual developments. Professional educational advice, however, indicated that to teach children through the medium of foreign languages slowed down their learning in the important early years. It alienated them from their homes and traditions and left them uncertain of their identity. English had been the language of the colonial power, and anyone who supported English could readily be tarred with the brush of being friendly to "imperialists." Hence, it was decided that "the medium of instruction" should be in the "mother tongue" or Swabasha. Tamil families would send their children through a Tamil "stream" of education,

Sinhalese families would send theirs through a Sinhalese stream, and the Burghers and others of "European origin" would send their children to English medium schools. English was to be the universal "second language" in the way American or English children learn French or German.

There was considerable debate over whether or not parents should have a choice of through which stream to send their children. It was recognized that because of the preferential status given to those who had acquired English in the past, many parents would opt for English. It was therefore decided that parents would have no such choice.

At the same time that the "mother tongue" principle was accepted it was agreed that the school system was to be extended. Universal education up to 14 years was adopted as an objective and schooling was to be free. These liberal measures were passed by the State Council in 1945. In fact, the school system expanded rapidly. In 1947 there were slightly more than 1,000,000 pupils attending school but in 1951 nearly 1,456,000 attended, a rise of 50 per cent.[69] By 1955, the total had risen to 1,650,000, a further rise of 20 per cent over the 1947 figure.[70] The curriculum remained relatively unchanged, however, and it was soon apparent that the schools were educating their pupils into white collar capacities for which there were no jobs.[71]

There were other consequences of these reforms besides merely producing "more of the same." The schools which were most affected by the new policy of education in the "mother tongue" were the best schools in the principal cities. The bulk of the island schools had already been using the vernacular for generations and had not deviated from the indigenous tradition far enough to teach in English. The English language schools in the larger cities had been the creators of the all-island elite which had grown beyond communal limitations through a common educational experience in one language. Instead of the schools melding the different communities, Tamil children henceforward had to be segregated into a Tamil language stream, the Sinhalese into a Sinhalese, and those of European descent into an English stream. In the name of the egalitarian and democratic principle of reducing the gap between the elite of each community and the bulk of its members, Sinhalese children learned

[69] Ministry of Finance, *Economic and Social Development of Ceylon* (a survey), 1926-1954, Table XVI.

[70] *Administration Report of the Director of Education for 1955*, Table III.

[71] See, for instance, *House of Representatives*, V. 9, c. 239; V. 16, c. 1560.

to be aware of their Tamil playmates as a different racial group and vice versa. Numerically, this did not appear to be serious. In 1955, for instance, less than 300,000 students were involved in this change compared to the more than 1,250,000 students already in Sinhalese and Tamil schools.[72]

This change influenced intercommunal relations in several other ways, however. Firstly, the division of the former English-speaking group into two communally based school-going populations promptly led to a significant increase in communal consciousness within the one group in the country which had been virtually devoid of it before. Secondly, administrative difficulties incident to such a rapid expansion and change in the school-system aroused communal anxieties. For example, parents of the minorities were legally entitled to have their children taught Sinhalese as a second language, if they wished. But Tamil schools often had difficulties in obtaining from the government qualified Sinhalese language instructors. Some argued administrative and financial impediments; others attributed these difficulties to a more sinister communal intent—to deprive Tamil children of those skills which would permit them to participate in Ceylon's wider affairs, thus relegating them to work only in the Tamil-speaking areas of the island. A few incidents where Tamil children were abruptly asked to withdraw from a Sinhalese school and to transfer to a nearby Tamil school gave substance to Tamil anxieties. Only later was it explained to the parents that in this way alone would their children have sufficiently large classes for adequate training.[73]

The change-over from English to the vernacular languages has been the subject of extended discussions in parliament, as if a regular topic of debate in the state legislatures was detailed argument on the curricula of American schools. In these debates the governing party emphasized the difficulties of the change-over—textbooks were scarce and of poor quality, teachers competent in mathematics and science were scarce even though the change-over was proceeding gradually. A favorite mode of attack against the U.N.P. was the charge that the government was not promoting the vernacular languages rapidly enough. If the textbooks were so poor and teachers were not trained to teach science in the vernacular languages, it was

[72] *Administration Report of the Director of Education for 1955*, Table 1 (A).
[73] *House of Representatives*, V. 16, c. 756, 758, 762-766, 772.

an indictment of the non-English schools in general and of those responsible for the educational system—the ruling party.

There was considerable agitation in favor of a similar transformation at the University of Ceylon. In the past, only those with adequate English could enter the university, where English was the medium of instruction. Those who had an education limited to the vernacular language could not go further than the rough equivalent of junior high school. The questions posed with regard to using the vernacular languages at the university were similar to those used at lower levels of education. Opening the university to the vernacular students would bring additional talent into the world of advanced education. Already certain university subjects could be taught adequately in Sinhalese and Tamil. The sciences and modern technological subjects, however, presented difficulties. The university could grow closer to the community at large, at least the Sinhalese part of it, but in consequence the university would find it increasingly more difficult to acquaint its students with the scientific, technological, cultural, and philosophical developments in the outside world. These were difficult matters to judge on their academic merits.

University reform also had implications for Tamil-Sinhalese relations. If English were replaced, would the university then have two language streams within it, Sinhalese and Tamil? Would this not perpetuate differences to an indefinite future? If, on the other hand, it became a center for instruction and learning in the majority's language alone, Tamil students would be at a disadvantage and Tamils aspiring to academic positions would have great difficulties. Hence, the future of higher education for the Tamils on the island was brought into doubt by agitation on language reform at the university.

3. *The language of government.* The question of what language or languages should replace English as the "official language" or language of state business was even more disturbing. Once English became officially dethroned, the discussion then turned to the relative importance to be officially given Sinhalese and Tamil. Values important to both communities became identified ultimately with diametrically opposed solutions to the "language problem." Questions of comparative political standing, honorific respect, and career opportunities for members of both communities became inextricably linked with the matter of official language. When these issues became

actively canvassed as part of electoral competition for votes, the consequences were bound to be incendiary.

(a) From "Swabasha" to "parity." At first, however, the object was to replace English by the two vernacular languages—Sinhalese and Tamil.[74] The term "Swabasha" or "mother tongue" had been applied to this aspiration to replace English with the national language. In many circumstances it suggested that "both Sinhalese and Tamil" would replace English, but when used on political platforms in Sinhalese areas it could just as well convey the idea that Sinhalese alone would become the official language. In Tamil areas it meant that Tamil as well as Sinhalese would receive official status. The ambiguity of terms employed during the language debate was extraordinary. As one leading politician later admitted: "Our minds were really fixed at that time on the question of English versus swabasha. We did not bring our minds to bear—maybe it was a fault on our part—on the question of Sinhalese versus Tamil. . . ."[75] By including the two languages under one generalized term of reference, future contingencies were not discussed. It had the utility of enlisting both Sinhalese and Tamil communities in the task of removing English from its position of high standing. At the same time it avoided a host of future—and foreseeable—difficulties.

In 1944, a resolution was placed before the State Council designed to displace English from its position of official language. In order that this should be done, the mover of the resolution believed that school instruction, public examinations, and the business of the State Council should be in Sinhalese.[76] It is reflective of the public mood at the time that during the debate, which culminated in 1944, Sinhalese members as well as Tamils urged that Tamil should also be made an official language for purposes of instruction in the schools, public examinations, and the business of the State Council. In 1944 Ceylon legislators agreed that both vernaculars would become official in the place of English.

In September 1945, a select committee was appointed to look into

[74] As early as 1932 a member of the State Council urged that the Council's proceedings be conducted in the national languages. Reported *House of Representatives*, V. 9, c. 1352. Also *Report of the Select Committee of the State Council on Sinhalese and Tamil as the Official Languages* (Sessional Paper XXII—1946), p. 6.

[75] S. W. R. D. Bandaranaike, *House of Representatives*, V. 23, c. 676.

[76] A commission was also urged to see to the translation of important books into Sinhalese and another to report on all steps necessary to make the transition from English. Reproduced in Debate on the State Language, *House of Representatives*, V. 23, c. 595-596.

the question of replacing English by the two indigenous languages.[77] The members were clear that Tamil should be given official status along with Sinhalese, but they acknowledged greater concern for the Sinhalese language on the grounds that it had no home other than Lanka. Nearly 30,000,000 people in South India spoke Tamil, "one of the best developed and most copious of Indian languages." They further argued that, until recent years in secondary or higher education, Sinhalese had not even been treated as a living language. It was not being used in everyday life, in business, commerce, in the courts, or in government administration.[78] Language itself came to have a virtual life and purpose of its own, a life that in the case of Sinhalese had to be "saved" or "resuscitated" by government action. They concluded their survey with a detailed recommendation regarding the gradual change from English to the indigenous languages. They foresaw a ten-year transition period and specified what changes should be effected within two five-year periods.[79]

The report of the select committee was accepted by the State Council. The government began to implement its recommendations and a series of interim commissions studied the difficulties of language transition as they became evident through practice.[80] Mr. D. S. Senanayake himself urged caution in the matter of speed and carefully avoided committing his party to a deadline for making both Sinhalese and Tamil official languages.[81] However, each time legislation came up for specifying new school grades that were to

[77] The committee was composed of both Sinhalese and Tamils. The report gave a detailed analysis of the difficulties involved, but the commissioners were determined to strengthen the two languages. The nature of their work ahead was stated as follows: "It is argued that the national languages cannot be made the media of administration and instruction because they are not sufficiently developed. They cannot develop unless they are made the media of administration and thus become of economic value to those who use them." (Sessional Paper XXII—1946), p. 11.

[78] Sessional Paper XXII—1954, p. 11. For the original article on which the commissioners based much of their analysis, see J. de Lanerolle, "The Future Official Languages of Ceylon," *University of Ceylon Review*, IV (Nov. 1945), pp. 35-43.

[79] Their recommendations included a transition from English to Swabasha in the departments of government, in examinations for entry into public service, in the State Council's proceedings and records, in the courts and educational system. They discussed technical problems of improving typewriters, translating and codifying the complex legal system combining Roman-Dutch, Kandyan, British, and Tamilian law; translating textbooks and similar problems.

[80] Government forms were more regularly printed in Swabasha as well as English, the Clerical Service began to appoint clerks on the basis of skill in Sinhalese and Tamil and larger numbers of letters received were replied to in the indigenous languages. *House of Representatives*, V. 11, c. 643.

[81] He was also cautious regarding the transition at the university, *House of Representatives*, V. 10, c. 1545-1547.

switch from English to Swabasha or other curricular matters, and in each appropriation debate, the language policy of the government came under heated attack.

It is difficult to specify exactly when the Sinhalese and Tamil languages became pitted against each other in a competitive search for the "final" solution to the "language problem." When this happened, the dispute took on a more embittered tone and led to sharpened communal tension. It is evident that the ground shifted gradually. Key decisions of a fairly technical nature became slogans for public debate. Careful analysis of inherently intricate and delicate problems became more difficult as ardent Sinhalese whittled down the position of the Tamil language, and the Tamils sought to defend their own position and status as these became involved in the status of their language.

It is evident that a change had taken place when the technical term "Swabasha," however imprecise, became employed less frequently and the comparative term "parity," one of the key slogans of the year 1955, appeared more often in public debate. "Parity" implied that both Sinhalese and Tamil should be recognized as official languages of the country. This had been the original position of those in the Select Committee on Language Reform, and the United National Party had based its language policy on the proposition that both languages should become "official" when English was displaced. This was also the position of the Left opposition and of the Sri Lanka Freedom Party until 1955. "Parity" meant to the Tamils that there would be full "equality before the law"; that individual Tamils should have equal opportunity and status with Sinhalese throughout the island. Some Tamils refused to rally behind the slogan of "parity" for it had been popularized by the same politician who had made the "fifty-fifty" constitutional proposal for distributing parliamentary seats. No effort was made to find a clearer term that would reach across the growing rift separating the two communities. In Sinhalese areas publicists sometimes even gave "parity" the misleading connotation that all Sinhalese would have to learn Tamil or that it was a device to make it necessary for the government to appoint two government servants to every post—one Sinhalese and one Tamil!

Gradually, in the rising tide of mutual distrust the prospects of "parity," of giving Tamils equal status with the majority, came to have a fearful connotation to many Sinhalese. Some argued, as did a leading member of the Sri Lanka Freedom Party, that Sinhalese must be assured by government fiat. "If parity of status . . . is given to both languages, I can assure you that in a couple of years the Sinhalese language will cease to exist."[82]

The details of the Sinhalese case for making Sinhalese the sole official language were clearly delineated during the 1956 election campaign and will be elaborated later in a discussion of the election. The Sinhalese awareness of the vigor of Tamil life north of the Palk Strait was sharpened as they explored the problems of revivifying the Sinhalese language. Many honestly believed that their language needed the kudos of official standing as an inducement to young Sinhalese to learn and to perfect it. Official status would compensate Sinhalese for the past neglect of their language. Specific pressure groups no doubt foresaw enlarged opportunities for the Sinhalese middle class if their language became the official language of the government. And it was evident that, since the Tamils were quick and had willingly learned English when it had been the official language, they could easily learn Sinhalese now instead.

In fact, many Tamils with ambition for public service careers began to learn Sinhalese before the language agitation became acute. But once their community's relative position became identified with language reform, they showed themselves noticeably reluctant to continue. Status goes with "recognition by government" in Ceylon. By the same act of recognition which excluded Tamil, Tamil would be thrust into a lower status position than Sinhalese. Such a tacit admission of its inferiority was unthinkable. Just as the Sinhalese came to think that it was essential to make Sinhalese the sole language of state, Tamils came to feel that to acquiesce in learning Sinhalese was to acquiesce in giving Sinhalese superior recognition. Learning English had had no such comparative downgrading implications, for both Sinhalese and Tamil together had been accorded secondary standing. Moreover, learning English had opened cultural horizons to the wider world. Sinhalese was spoken by only 7,000,000 people. Once the issue was posed in terms of Sinhalese alone, career implications were brought to the fore. If it were necessary for Tamils to learn Sinhalese before they could participate in public affairs or the professions, they would be at a perpetual disadvantage in competition with the young Sinhalese entering their careers in the tongue they had known since infancy.

[82] *House of Representatives*, V. 24, c. 1374.

Hence, the Sinhalese argument excluded giving Tamil the official status accorded the minority language in Canada, for instance, a position that would have gone far to reassure the bulk of articulate Tamils. Had the Tamils been willing to learn Sinhalese for professional and career purposes, there need have been little communal strife. As it was, for each partisan of this developing dispute, the other's view became more and more unthinkable.

Underlying the arguments for and against parity was the intractable fact that the Ceylonese majority community of 7,000,000 Sinhalese was a small minority in the face of the hypothetical combination of Ceylon's Tamil population and the 27,000,000 Tamils in South India. Indeed, both groups were beset with acute minority feelings, the Tamils believing that they were destined to be a perpetual minority in Ceylon itself, which the majority was determined to dominate by every means, and the Sinhalese believing that they were a language minority in the shadow of India.

(b) Interest group activity. By 1954, there were a number of indications of growing pressure for "Sinhalese Only" as the official language. At a public ceremony receiving the Queen of England, the Finance Minister astonished his cabinet colleagues by addressing her in Sinhalese, a gesture that angered the Tamils in the Government and the country at large. Pressure groups that had hitherto sought to ensure special interests of their own began to press in common for language reform. Meetings of Swabasha teachers, *ayurvedic* physicians, and *bhikkhus* urged the adoption of "Sinhalese Only." The Tri Sinhala Peramuna openly spread anti-Tamil propaganda in the Kandyan districts and pressed for "Sinhalese Only." A prominent educationist, member of the Buddhist Committee of Inquiry, was reported to have declared that: "If the present Government did not make Sinhalese the State Language before the Buddhist anniversary of 2500 years of the birth of Buddhism, he would openly and vehemently oppose the Government. 'We must demand from the Prime Minister of Ceylon in no uncertain terms that this should be done and done forthwith.' "[88]

The commission which was to report on the problem of Higher Education in the National Languages was not careful to keep within the terms of its appointed reference. Some of the commissioners were particularly concerned over the fact that there were virtually

[88] Reported in *Times of Ceylon*, February 1, 1954.

no Sinhalese science and mathematics textbooks, but ample Tamil textbooks that had been developed in South India. They stated in a rider to the 1954 report: "A situation will be created placing the Sinhalese-speaking students at a disadvantageous position and rendering it almost impossible for them to attain the same standards as the Tamil-speaking students in those subjects. *Of course this difficulty will not arise if there is only one official national language.*"[84] During the subsequent proceedings, the majority commissioners went against usual procedures and released to the press parts of their conclusions indicating that they were in favor of making Sinhalese the language of instruction at the university as well as of government administration, thus calling for a reversal of the government's policy of giving official status to both vernaculars.[85]

Simultaneously, Tamil politics in the north exaggerated the problem. The Sinhalese agitation in the south strengthened the hand of the ardent Tamils and led many to seriously consider supporting the Federalists. Other Tamil politicians, attempting to outdo the Federalist leader, denounced in ringing words Sinhalese ambitions and cried defiance, not always neglecting to remind their hearers of Tamil victories over the Sinhalese in the past.

In the vicious circle of deteriorating relationships, the cries of one community—even if defensive—tended to mobilize the defensive consciousness of the other. In each camp gestures toward solidarity and expressions of determination to defend its rights were used within the other to solidify the ranks. Each one's defensive efforts provoked further anguish and defiance on the part of the other. This process was accelerated by the fact that the Tamils and Sinhalese lived within two different systems of communication and their newspapers gave widely differing versions of the same events. Understanding diminished as each came to feel the other's behavior to be more and more unreasonable and alarming. Hence, once conflict between the linguistic communities was evoked, it became difficult for the two communities to come together once again.[86]

(c) Emerging political image. As mentioned earlier, the common

[84] *Final Report of the Commission on Higher Education in the National Languages, July 1956*, p. 217. Italics author's.

[85] *Morning Times* (Colombo), July 19, 1955; editorial, *Times of Ceylon*, July 20, 1955, July 29, 1955.

[86] For a discussion of this phenomenon in India, see Gardner Murphy, *In the Minds of Men* (New York, 1953), p. 60.

prejudices about personal, intellectual, and moral characteristics were spontaneous and undirected. As the tension mounted, it became possible to discern a "political image" in the view of each toward the other. The political image centered on reviving past political grievances and seeing all attributed characteristics of the other in the light of calculations regarding the future distribution of political power. However, no one political spokesman expressed all elements of the emerging political image, and to that extent its representation here is somewhat exaggerated. But, on the whole, the characteristics attributed to the other by the politically articulate in each community took on a clear form. Ordinarily, few held such politically oriented conceptions of the other. As communal tension rose, the political image became widespread within each community and overcame any other basis for judging policy or persons.

The Sinhalese political image of the Tamils had various components. The Sinhalese consider themselves of Aryan descent from North India and look down on the "Dravidian" Tamils with a disdain that includes the fact that the Tamils are often darker than they. The Tamils were and had always been a threat to the Ceylonese state. In the ancient past "they" invaded and destroyed. They were the ones who regularly resisted constitutional reforms except those which preserved their preferential position gained during the British period. Even now, they signified their defection from the Ceylonese state by flying black flags on Independence Day. Their leading party went so far as to propose a federal form of government, a device which was merely the first step in dismembering Lanka and subjecting the whole to India. They looked to India for cultural inspiration and their admiration for Indian leaders showed that their affections and loyalties went to the north.

They were fundamentally suspicious and they therefore refused to trust the majority. They had always sought special privileges for themselves. For instance, they wanted the whole island to be open to them for jobs in the public service, but when a few Sinhalese families were settled in agricultural colonies in so-called Tamil areas, they raised a bitter protest. Not only were they deemed a nuisance with their suspicious natures and their perpetual reference to rights, parity, and so on, but they were determined to retain their own individuality in their personal lives. They did not want to join wholeheartedly in the formation of a unified state.

The Tamil image of the Sinhalese was more obvious and no less deep-seated. The Sinhalese have always tried to dominate them. The pressure for universal franchise was cited as an example of this desire, since it gave the Sinhalese majority a commanding position in Ceylon. Soon afterwards they formed a ministry which excluded all Tamils. They did not give the minorities a proper place on the new flag. They have already deprived Indian estate workers of citizenship and political rights as a first step toward discriminating against all Tamil-speaking peoples. Government-sponsored settlement schemes revealed a clearly thought-out strategy of introducing a wedge of Sinhalese peasants to split up traditional Tamil areas. The Sinhalese had always wanted to relegate the Tamil minority to the arid and cramped land of the northern peninsula. Sinhalese efforts to make their language the only official language were directed solely toward excluding Tamils from effective participation in Ceylon's life. They hoped, in this way, to force the Tamils to abandon their own precious cultural tradition and to lose their identity in the larger Sinhalese whole.

As the crisis of 1956 approached, the political image each group held of the other became more widely accepted. Partisans on each side tended to take the extreme statements of their opponents as representative of the attitude of all the others. Thus, bitter attacks on the Tamils by one or two communal organizations in the south were taken by Tamils as representing the "Sinhalese view" of the Tamils, and extreme spokesmen of Federalism in the north came to represent "the Tamil view" to more and more Sinhalese.

Different conceptions of the type of state that should be developed in Ceylon provided another source of misunderstanding and distrust. What concepts did the two peoples have in mind in thinking about their country on a level above communal fears and ambitions? In colloquial Sinhalese, there was no clear distinction between "nation" and "race." "The Ceylonese nation" referred to the "race of Ceylon," but in Sinhalese areas this was understood to mean the Sinhalese race. The nearest word for "national feeling" connoted "race consciousness" rather than a sense of solidarity encompassing all the communities inhabiting the island. A nation made up of several different racial communities, therefore, was popularly almost unthinkable. Only the conscious searching for other words and serious popular discussion of a multiracial state would have offset this oversimplified view of Ceylon's ethnic and linguistic reality. Naturally the Tamil view of the proper state was one of racial and linguistic multiplicity, a state that encompassed more than one race and language, but to which all owed allegiance and in which each had a respected part to play. The Sinhalese considered France a congenial type of state while the Tamils looked to Switzerland, Belgium, or Canada as the ideal and natural model.

There were differences in this respect, too, depending in part on education. The Sinhalese with a Western education could see more clearly the vision of a state with more than one linguistic and religious community within it while the Sinhalese lower middle class with an exclusively Sinhalese education found the unitary cultural and linguistic state more natural. As Sinhalese leaders from the former group identified themselves more closely with village areas they came to voice the more popular conception.

Hence, with alternative models in their minds, members of both communities could seek with full sincerity alternative types of state. The efforts of each to evolve communal relations on the basis of his preferred model only angered the other, however logical and inevitable his own image of appropriate relationships might have seemed.

(d) The parties change their stands. Effective communication between the leaders of the communities began to diminish. Social intercourse between prominent elite members of the communities grew less frequent. Few institutions bridged the communal gap apart from the public service itself, the Christian churches and certain, though by no means all, labor unions. The United National Party and the Left parties continued to warn against adopting communalist arguments for the sake of short-term political gain. There were still large numbers of moderates who deplored the growing rift between the two communities. Both Sinhalese and Tamils in parliament warned of the risks of fanning communal flames.[87]

There were many others who privately regretted the growing communal antagonism that developed as a byproduct of agitation over the matter of state language. But like moderates everywhere, they were slow to express their views in public. The language agitation had a certain socio-economic significance which induced many of them to hold their peace. To press for displacing both English and Tamil and giving sole place to Sinhalese as the official language

[87] *House of Representatives*, V. 19, c. 550-551; V. 23, c. 603.

had egalitarian significance. The earlier agitation against English had in part been politically oriented against those Sinhalese and Tamils who had become most Westernized and who had come to expect the gradual disappearance of communal differences. They felt themselves under attack and more than a few of the sensitive among them felt a sense of guilt that they had allowed themselves to ignore their own traditional culture and language. They were no longer sure that they or their parents had been right in so completely adapting themselves to British ways. They therefore found it wiser to remain on the sidelines rather than expose themselves to vigorous polemic attacks which many had come to believe they partly deserved.

In an effort to reassure the Tamils, Prime Minister Sir John Kotelawala visited Jaffna in September 1954.[88] Since Sir John was considered by many Tamils to be one of the Ceylonese politicians who stood firmly for a united nation, he was warmly received.[89] At the Kokuvil Hindu College, the anxieties of Tamils, in connection with the report of the Interim Commission on Higher Education in the National Languages, and other developments in the south, were discussed. Various leading Tamils urged the prime minister to pass a constitutional amendment which would state that "both Sinhalese and Tamil should be official languages of Ceylon and that a citizen should have a statutory right to transact all his business with the government at all levels in his own language."[90] Sir John was reported to have declared, in reply, that he would see that the constitution was changed accordingly.[91] The democratic opposition, particularly the spokesmen for the Sri Lanka Freedom Party, seized upon this incident and soon Sinhalese rural districts were aware that Sir John Kotelawala—that friend of the Tamils—had sought to give the Tamils equal constitutional status with the Sinhalese.[92]

[88] Tamil opponents of those Tamils who were then collaborating with the U.N.P. government had been painting the Sinhalese Prime Minister as an arch communalist who refused to give fullest satisfaction to the more extreme Tamil demands. *Times of Ceylon*, September 20, 1954.

[89] He was communally tolerant and often expressed himself to the effect that "I always maintain that this country belongs to all of us. Every one of us has got equal rights in this country, and every one of us must respect each other if we wish to be respected." *House of Representatives*, V. 19, c. 553.

[90] S. Handy-Perinbanayagam, "Principal's Address of Welcome to the Prime Minister," *Kokuvil Hindu College*, December 1954, p. 9.

[91] Reported in *Times of Ceylon*, September 30, 1954. Sir John later asserted that he had been misreported. His detailed explanation is to be found in *House of Representatives*, V. 21, c. 485-486.

[92] From interviews in widely scattered rural areas of Sinhalese wet zone.

The U.N.P. and the N.L.S.S.P. maintained their stand in favor of making Tamil and Sinhalese official languages. Occasionally, individuals within the U.N.P., and even some cabinet members, issued statements in support of the Sinhalese objective, particularly as the end of 1955 approached. Earlier in the year the Trotskyite group under the leadership of Mr. Philip Gunawardena began to argue in favor of making Sinhalese the sole state language.[93] The Sri Lanka Freedom Party continued to attack the government for its delay in changing to the vernacular languages. In the autumn of 1955, it adopted a policy of formally advocating that Sinhalese alone should be made the official language and that Tamil should be made the language of administration in Tamil areas.[94]

Before the end of 1955 it was clear that certain local branches of the U.N.P. were dissatisfied and desired a change in the party's traditional stand on language. In late October, one group within the party called for a special session of the U.N.P. to adopt "Sinhalese Only" as its platform.[95] In January 1956, anxious Tamil members of the party asked that the party debate an alternative to the "Sinhalese Only" motion then rumored in preparation for the Annual Congress in February. They recommended spelling out the fundamental constitutional rights guaranteed to all inhabitants of Ceylon which would be in stronger language and more detailed than the "Bill of Rights" provisions of the constitution. The U.N.P. Agenda Committee decided against debating such a motion and the Tamil-speaking members of the U.N.P. resigned from the party.[96]

In mid-February 1956 at the party's Annual Congress, the "Sinhalese Only" policy was accepted unanimously. Because this was a complete reversal of its traditional stand on the "language question," the prime minister requested an immediate dissolution of Parliament and called for a general election in which the new language slogan was to play a fundamental part.[97]

[93] Other members of the party added that Tamil should be made the language of administration in Tamil areas, but only one language should be official for the country as a whole. *House of Representatives*, V. 21, c. 1304, for instance.

[94] Reports of the S.L.F.P. change of line appeared in the press in February 1955, *Morning Times* (Colombo), Feb. 29, 1955. The decision was confirmed in September, *Morning Times* (Colombo), September 24, 1955. The party's annual session formally adopted such a policy in December. *Ceylon Daily News*, December 19, 1955.

[95] *Ceylon Daily News*, October 25, 1955.

[96] *Ceylon Daily News*, January 18, 19, 1956.

[97] *Ceylon Daily News*, February 20, 1956; Party Manifesto, *Ceylon Observer*, March 21, 1956. The U.N.P. no longer included any reference whatsoever to giving a "due place to Tamil." Its principal opponents under the leadership of Mr. Bandaranaike

During the heated and bitter campaign the tensions developed over the past two years came to a head. Tamil sentiment swung sharply against those who had collaborated with the U.N.P. and supported instead the Federal Party as the only consistent and determined defender of the Tamil cause. In the south, an unexpected and varied coalition led by Mr. Bandaranaike fought in common contest against the U.N.P. that had ruled since independence.

As the discussion of the 1956 election will make clear, language was not the only issue that led to the defeat of the U.N.P., but it was used by the Opposition to undermine the U.N.P.'s strength in the countryside. As long as the leader of the U.N.P. bore the Senanayake name, it had a strong direct following in the rural areas and a firm group of supporters in the rural district notables. Mr. Bandaranaike saw in the lower middle class an alternative channel to the village vote. By 1955 the language issue had become an ideal instrument for enlisting the support of this important strata in the countryside, and the former Minister of Health and Local Government was in a good position to win its backing. For many years he had helped to clarify the grievances and espouse the cause of identifiable groups for whom the position of their language was a source of humiliation and class inferiority. Even if it did not solve some of their fundamental problems they believed that a change in the official language would improve their status. For these groups the speed with which the official language was changed over to Sinhalese became a touchstone for judging the different politicians and parties. A vote for the party of Mr. Bandaranaike implied a judgment against the sincerity and wholeheartedness of the U.N.P.'s new language policy.

D. "SINHALESE ONLY" LEGISLATION AND COMMUNAL STRIFE

The first legislation submitted by the new government of Mr. Bandaranaike was designed to implement his pledge to make Sinhalese the sole official language. The drafting of this legislation showed clearly the forces that were pressing upon the new prime minister through nonparty interest groups mobilized on linguistic issues. The first draft bill was prepared by a subcommittee of the parliamentary party and certain leading supporters not in parlia-

---

recognized that although they were for an immediate grant of official status to Sinhalese, they did not wish "the suppression of such a minority language as Tamil, whose reasonable use will receive due recognition." Joint Program of the *Mahajana Eksath Peramuna*, p. 2.

ment. At the outset their draft contained a series of provisions designed to specify in great detail the role that the Tamil language should play in public life in the future.[98] There were clauses ensuring that individuals trained in English or Tamil could enter the public service through examinations conducted in these languages; that local bodies had the right to decide for themselves the language of their business; and that individuals could communicate with the government in their own language.

Such explicit legislative guarantees would have gone a long way to reassure the bulk of Tamils, but the reactions of extremists among the Tamils and the Sinhalese were decidedly unfavorable.[99] A group of Buddhist *bhikkhus* connected with the Eksath Bhikkhu Peramuna protested against the inclusion of a clause permitting individuals who had been educated in English or Tamil to take public examinations in that language until 1967 and urged the government to press ahead more rapidly with language changes. Their rally on the steps of the house of representatives culminated in a fast by a prominent university lecturer.[100] Through this dramatic step and the agitation of those in the priesthood and laity who supported his stand, he was invited to present his case to the parliamentary party group

[98] Section 3 entitled the "Use of Languages other than the official languages" provided, among other things that "the language or languages to be used for the transaction of business of each Chamber of Parliament . . . shall be determined by the Chamber" through the normal procedure for altering the Standing Orders, thus implying the use of other languages beside Sinhalese in parliament. Paragraph ii of Section 3 proposed that "The language or languages to be used for the purpose of conducting the proceedings and other business and keeping of records of any local authority shall be determined by that authority." Paragraphs iii and iv provided that the Tamil or English languages could be used for communicating with officials, for any religious purpose, for carrying on any trade or business, and for unofficial speech or writing. A final set of specifications explicitly stated that a person who had been educated through either Tamil or English and who was to be appointed to the Supreme Court, Commissioner of Assize or any other judicial officers, or as a public officer should be "Required to have only such proficiency in the Sinhala language as is reasonable, taking into consideration the fact that he was not educated through the medium of the Sinhala language" and would be allowed to take the necessary examination in the language of his education until July 1, 1967 or ten years from the passage of the proposed legislation. Text as reported in the *Ceylon Daily News*, May 18, 1956.

[99] *Ceylon Daily News*, May 17, 1956. Even moderate Tamils considered it highly inappropriate that the Sinhalese should give them "concessions" merely because they formed a majority. One of the most outspoken Sinhalese educationists protested against allowing citizens to communicate with the government in either Tamil or English, for this, it was held, would discourage them from learning Sinhalese. *Ceylon Daily News*, May 16, 1956.

[100] Though the *bhikkhus* in question at the time were reported to be active members of the Eksath Bhikkhu Peramuna, in September a leading member of the E. B. P. denied the organization had supported the activities on the steps of Parliament. *Ceylon Daily News*, September 6 and 7, 1956.

who were, it would appear, profoundly influenced by his views. He was opposed among other things to the principle of giving local bodies the right to decide the language of their business, arguing that Leftists and Tamils could join together in opposition to Sinhalese—an argument particularly persuasive to Kandyan ears.[101]

Many political opponents of the U.N.P. and some spokesmen for it painted the "Tamil threat" in such lurid colors for electioneering purposes that communal tensions were higher than they had ever been, except for the communal riots in 1915. Antagonism became so great that a Tamil sit-down demonstration, near the house of representatives, called by the Federalist leader the day the controversial legislation was submitted to parliament, led to bitter riots in which over 100 people were injured. In a few days they spread to Eastern Province, where Tamils and Sinhalese lived intermingled; in Batticaloa and the Gal Oya valley there was such violence that between 20 and 200 persons were killed, depending on which side was doing the tallying.[102]

In an effort to balance the diverse and contradictory forces harassing him, the new prime minister urged the support of a short bill, which would put the policy of making Sinhalese the one state language beyond a doubt, but leave the specific detailed provisions to be worked out later when passions would have subsided. In its final draft the bill was clear and brief.

Official Language Act, No. 33 of 1956

L.D.-O. 14/56

AN ACT TO PRESCRIBE THE SINHALA LANGUAGE AS THE ONE OFFICIAL LANGUAGE OF CEYLON AND TO ENABLE CERTAIN TRANSITORY PROVISIONS TO BE MADE

(Date of Assent: July 7, 1956)

Be it enacted by the Queen's most Excellent Majesty, by and with the advice and consent of the Senate and the House of Representatives of Ceylon in this present Parliament assembled, and by the authority of the same, as follows:

1. This Act may be cited as the Official Language Act, No. 33 of 1956.

[101] *Ceylon Daily News*, May 25, 1956; May 26, 1956; May 29, 1956.

[102] Interviews with eye-witnesses *Times of Ceylon*, June 15, 1956; *Morning Times* (Colombo), July 4, 1956. An official commission to investigate was finally appointed, but it was subsequently dissolved as likely to arouse communal passions once more.

2. The Sinhala Language shall be the one official language of Ceylon:

Provided that where the Minister considers it impracticable to commence the use of only the Sinhala language for any official purpose immediately on the coming into force of this Act, the language or languages hitherto used for that purpose may be continued to be used until the necessary change is effected as early as possible before the expiry of the thirty-first day of December, 1960, and, if such changes cannot be effected by administrative order, regulations may be made under this Act to effect such change.

3. (1) The Minister may make regulations in respect of all matters for which regulations are authorized by this Act to be made and generally for the purpose of giving effect to the principles and provisions of this Act.

(2) No regulation made under sub-section (1) shall have effect until it is approved by the Senate and the House of Representatives and notification of such approval is published in the Gazette.

The debate on the Language Bill proceeded and after five days the Sinhala Only Bill was passed by a vote of 56 for and 29 against. All members present from the M.E.P. and the U.N.P. and the appointed members voted for the bill. The Tamils and the Left parties voted against it. As was amply borne out during the language debates, the nature of the bill, as drafted, reposed full responsibility in the prime minister for personal oversight of the application of the bill. As one English-language newspaper put it: "The sense of fear and grievance under which the Tamil-speaking people labour today is very real. Their fears have only been confirmed by the signal failure of the Bill to provide any guarantees of the protestations of goodwill and fair treatment toward the minorities heard from the Government benches during the Language debate. . . . We have not the slightest doubt that the Prime Minister himself means what he says when he assures minorities, and especially the Tamil-speaking group, that no disabilities will be forced upon them as a result of this Bill. We are not so sure that the intentions of the ultra-nationalist pressure groups that have attached themselves to his party are quite so sincere."[103]

During the last half of 1956, the government made considerable progress in changing the official language of communication between different government departments, and proponents of changing the language of government were rapidly advanced within the public service. In the house of representatives indigenous languages were

[103] Editorial, *Morning Times* (Colombo), June 15, 1956.

Courtesy of the *Ceylon Observer*

The cartoonist depicts the real alternatives facing future students at the university—to learn in English will lead to a void, to learn in Tamil will lead up a tree. Only Sinhalese will lead to opportunities in the desired professions

more frequently used in place of English. But the government made no moves to allay the Tamil fears.

There were other signs of further rapid changes that were watched anxiously by the minorities, both Tamil- and English-speaking. The Minister of Education argued in public that the English medium for the schools should be abolished in 1958, although English could be continued as a noncompulsory second language. In the last months of 1956 it was announced that one of the leading teacher training colleges would be reserved to Sinhalese teachers only and that there would be 500 Swabasha scholarships open to competitors on the basis of a six-to-one quota ratio as between Sinhalese and Tamils.[104] To the minorities it appeared that, through legislative enactments on language reform and such administrative measures, the majority community was reserving to itself the right to decide on what terms members of the different communities would compete for state-supported educational opportunities.

Meanwhile, Tamil leaders had not been awaiting various restrictions without response.[105] In June 1956 the Federal Party held an important meeting in which they confirmed their objective of establishing an "autonomous Tamil linguistic state within a Federal Union of Ceylon" as the only way of protecting the "cultural freedom and identity of the Tamil-speaking people." They also urged all Tamils to refuse to learn or to speak Sinhalese and to transact all their business in Tamil or, if necessary, in English.[106] A wider meeting demanded a new federal constitution for Ceylon, made up of areas where Tamil-speaking people are in the majority and Sinhalese areas, each with the "widest autonomous and residuary powers consistent with the unity and external security of Ceylon." They demanded the restoration of the Tamil language, the substitution of simple residence requirements for the elaborate restrictions of the present citizenship law—a gesture seeking to gain the support of the Indian Tamil estate workers—the cessation of all Sinhalese colonization in areas that were "traditionally" Tamil-speaking. "They warned that unless the Government took measures to constitute a Federal Union in Ceylon within a year the Federal Party would undertake a campaign of non-violent direct action (*Satyagraha*) to achieve its objectives" in August 1957.[107]

In terms of actual power the Tamil position was relatively weak. Most of the Tamil political leadership and the educated middle-class groups had fundamental financial or career interests in the richer southern area. The Sinhalese community commanded a two-thirds majority of seats in parliament and, if united, could pass any kind of legislation it desired. The Federalists alone had a parliamentary following among the Tamils, and yet they had not settled down to the hard task of specifying in concrete terms the type of consti-

104 *Morning Times* (Colombo), December 28, 1956; *Times of Ceylon*, November 29, 1956.

105 As early as May 1, 1956 the small Tamil Congress urged Tamils to stop learning Sinhalese. *Times of Ceylon*, May 26, 1956.

106 *Times of Ceylon*, June 25, 1956.

107 *Ceylon Daily News*, August 20, 1956.

tution they sought or how the economy of the Tamil areas might be self-sustaining. Of the national parties, only the N.L.S.S.P. had consistently advocated a policy of giving equal status to both languages and seemed to provide an alternative for younger members of the Tamil community to participate in political affairs throughout the island. Tamil educators noted a growing interest among Tamil students in seeking careers in business as opposed to government service.[108]

Members of Mr. Bandaranaike's cabinet adopted differing attitudes toward the Tamils. Not all were prepared to push the Sinhalese advantage to the full. Others, however, responded readily to Sinhalese encouragement and sought to emphasize the new position acquired by the Sinhalese language. The Minister of Transport and and Works, for instance, introduced a Sinhalese symbol on automobile license plates representing a word that has religious and cultural overtones for both communities. In late January 1957 Tamil M.P.s altered their license plates to Tamil letters in defiance of the law, and the movement gained momentum in many Tamil areas as an expression of protest against the government's policy toward the Tamil language.[109]

In April 1957, nearly one year after the original language legislation, the prime minister indicated on behalf of the government that steps would be taken to ensure the reasonable use of Tamil and to give it a proper place in the country's affairs.[110] As the threatened *Satyagraha* campaign of the Tamils approached, the Federalist leader and Mr. Bandaranaike entered a series of protracted negotiations to clarify the position. The Tamil leader sought above all specific assurances in the form of legislation to define Tamil rights beyond ambiguity and doubt. The hitherto verbal assurances given by the prime minister and other government spokesmen were felt by anxious Tamils to be insufficient. The Federal Party continued its preparations for a *Satyagraha* campaign in August.[111] The government itself was beset on its Sinhalese flank by the ardent spokesmen of the Sinhalese cause, such as the Eksath Bhikkhu Peramuna and the Sri Lanka Sangha Sabha which made their views

108 Interviews in Jaffna as early as March 1956. See also Senator Sir Sangarapillai Pararajasingam, *Morning Times* (Colombo), October 13, 1956.

109 At this time the government did not prosecute those who illegally altered their license plates nor did it go back on the Minister's decision. *Times of Ceylon*, January 18, 1956.

110 *Ceylon Daily News*, April 26, 1957.

111 *Ceylon Daily News*, July 22, 1957.

clearly known in favor of a firmer stand on behalf of the Sinhalese language.[112]

Toward the end of July, agreement was finally reached between the prime minister and the Federal leaders regarding the legislation to be submitted to the house. The proposed legislation was to recognize Tamil as the "language of a national minority in Ceylon." Administration in Tamil areas in the Northern and Eastern Provinces was to be in Tamil, although the interests of Sinhalese-speaking populations there were to be fully protected.[113] Legislation then under consideration proposed to establish elected regional councils to correct the overcentralization of Ceylon's administration. Mr. Bandaranaike had long favored such a reform in local government institutions and administration. If the regional councils were strong enough, they might go far to meet the Tamil objective for a degree of regional autonomy without going all the way toward the federal constitution the Sinhalese appeared to fear. As Tamils saw the doors to professional careers closing on them, they became even more concerned to ensure access to irrigated land for their people. In these discussions, the powers of the proposed councils were extended, including certain powers over the selection of colonists for the government land settlements in the dry zone.[114]

The *Satyagraha* campaign of the Federalist Party was consequently called off, to the relief of an increasingly tense population in both Sinhalese and Tamil areas. Some ardent Tamil politicians criticized the Federalists, declaring that the agreement was a "complete and abject surrender" to the Sinhalese. In Sinhalese areas, leading Theros and laymen behind the Eksath Bhikkhu Peramuna, the Kandyan Tri Sinhala Peramuna and other ardent Sinhalese threatened their own *Satyagraha* campaign unless the prime minister repudiated the agreement.[115] The Kandyans were particularly concerned to assure their people of access to government colonies. Mr. Bandaranaike was at pains to reassure them, indicating that no new government policy was in prospect as a result of this clarification of the position of Tamil embodied in the agreements.[116] The United National Party, now agitating in support of solely Sinhalese aspirations, pro-

[112] *Ceylon Daily News*, July 26, 1957; July 27, 1957. Among other aims, they tried to have Sinhalese made the compulsory language of all education above the 14-year age of "primary" classes. The prime minister referred to their demands in a long statement in August justifying the more moderate policy he had followed.

[113] *Ibid.*

[114] *Ibid.*, July 27, 1957.

[115] *Ibid.*, August 5, 1957.

[116] *Ibid.*, August 13, 1957.

tested against the concessions made to the Tamils. The agitation on the opposite flanks of both the Sinhalese and Tamil leaders revealed the narrow margin left for further maneuvering.[117]

Serious floods in December temporarily submerged communal differences in the common task of caring for flood victims and reconstructing the damage. This disaster was followed by a series of strikes in Colombo Harbor. Both crises distracted the prime minister from promptly considering the legislation desired by the Federalists. But as draft legislation neared completion in late March, a fleet of new buses operated by the National Transport Board and marked in Sinhalese lettering was sent by the government to Jaffna to replace outworn vehicles. In the absence of the promised legislation, the Sinhalese markings symbolized to the Tamils a denial of their claim to use Tamil in their dealings with the government. Federalists began to deface the buses, tarring over the Sinhalese lettering and substituting Tamil symbols. Over one hundred and fifty Tamils were arrested. In retaliation in the south, Sinhalese gangs smeared tar over Tamil lettering on stores run by Tamils. The police were slow to restore order, unsure of the backing they would receive from the cabinet in view of the vehement public criticism directed against the police by certain cabinet members. Spokesmen for Sinhalese interests used the occasion to protest to the prime minister against making any concession to the Tamils regarding the powers over land settlement to be delegated to the regional councils. Many *bhikkhus* participated in a mass sit-down demonstration in front of the prime minister's residence. The next day he abrogated his agreement with Mr. Chelvanayakam arguing that because of the Federalist activities in Jaffna, the Government was no longer bound by the terms of this agreement.[117]

Two weeks later a new wave of strikes diverted public attention. Large numbers of government workers struck as the Communist leaders tried to increase their labor union strength at the expense of growing Trotskyist unions.[118] An atmosphere of imminent public disorder developed as police and then the army patrolled Colombo; demonstrations were banned and army personnel maintained essential government services. Union protests led to a withdrawal of army units, after a dozen workers were seriously injured in a baton charge,

[117] The following paragraphs are based on an article by the writer published in the *Far Eastern Survey*, March 1959. For a vivid and detailed discussion by a Ceylonese, see Tarzie Vittachi, *Emergency '58* (London, 1958).

[118] *Ceylon Daily News*, April 26, 1958.

and the police received strict orders of restraint. Coming on top of the public criticism and political interference in the promotions and transfer of officers, these orders seriously demoralized the police. Most of the workers returned to their jobs on May 5, although some non-government workers remained on strike.

The crisis of June 1958, therefore, drew near with the government's law-enforcement agencies weakened. As yet no end to communal tension was in sight. The one effort to reach a compromise solution that would reassure the minority had miscarried.

The Federal Party's annual public meeting was called for late May. The conclave was to decide whether or not to undertake a *Satyagraha* campaign now that the prime minister had withdrawn his support from the agreement he had endorsed a year before. The outbreak of violence began when a train, presumed to be carrying Tamil delegates to the meetings, was derailed and its passengers beaten up by ruffians. The next day Sinhalese laborers set fire to Tamil shops and homes in nearby villages where they lived intermingled with Sinhalese. Police stations were surrounded by large crowds and their communications cut so that effective protection to scattered Tamil residents could not be assured despite many instances of police heroism. Arson and beatings spread rapidly to Colombo. Gangs roamed the districts where Tamils lived, ransacking and setting fire to homes and cars, and looting shops. Individual Tamils were attacked, humiliated, and beaten. Many were subjected to torture and some killed outright. The outbreaks threatened to become religious riots when a Hindu priest and temple were burned and a Buddhist temple demolished. Some ten thousand Tamils were reported to have fled their homes to seek safety in improvised refugee camps established in requisitioned schools and protected by police and army units. Many fled to the north by sea. About two thousand Sinhalese in the north similarly sought camp protection.

The troubles had begun on May 23. After three days of terrifying disorders, the prime minister broadcast a message to the people, urging them to remain calm. But his reference to a prominent Sinhalese who had been killed in Batticaloa only incensed the Sinhalese masses the more and the riots grew in intensity. On May 27, the prime minister finally made his decision and asked the governor general to declare a state of emergency. The toll during the days of disorders included an estimated 300-400 killed, over 2,000 incidents of arson, looting, and assault, and 12,000 Ceylonese transformed into homeless refugees.

The governor general then became the effective center of government. The armed forces received orders to shoot if commands were not obeyed. Groups in the streets were to be disbanded. Houses could be entered without a warrant. A strict curfew was imposed and the most stringent censorship of the press introduced. The Tamil Federal Party and the most extreme Sinhalese group (the small, but incendiary, Jatika Vimukti Peramuna) were both proscribed and their members placed under house arrest. The troops methodically set about clearing out the trouble spots of the capital.

The Federalist leaders and a few Sinhalese leaders were held under house arrest from June until September. During that period, legislation was finally passed concerning the "reasonable use of Tamil." Tamils were assured that they could continue educating their children in Tamil and that they could use their language in corresponding with the government and in local government affairs. Tamils could compete for government service examinations, although they would have to develop proficiency in Sinhalese if they were to continue in the service and be promoted. However, since the Tamil spokesmen were not in parliament when legislation concerning them was brought forward, all but two members of the Opposition walked out. The bill that passed, therefore, lacked the sanction of a fully representative house. From the Tamil point of view, it also fell short of the Federalist requirements—and the Bandaranaike-Chelvanayagam Pact—for it made no reference to the proposed developments of regional councils and promised no assurance of greater regional autonomy in cultural and administrative matters.

The tragedy of these events is heightened by the realization that if these safeguards of Tamil interests—all of them included in the preliminary draft legislation proposed by the M.E.P. parliamentary party in 1956—had been passed two years before, both the 1956 and 1958 riots might have been avoided.

Before the National Emergency of 1958 was officially brought to an end in March 1959, the government obtained from parliament wide powers to permit it to declare a state of emergency in a limited area of the island instead of throughout the country as had been required before. Politically motivated strikes could henceforth be declared illegal. The new powers would strengthen the hand of a decisive premier if he had to face communal conflict in the future, and would also limit the scope for misuse of the trade union movement by Opposition party leaders. Whether such powers would infringe on the organizing opportunities for legitimate trade unionists remained to be seen.

CONCLUSION

Underlying group prejudices accentuated by awakened memories of past conflicts aroused communal consciousness and antagonism. Concern for cultural survival and language reform induced members of the majority community to fear the greater vigor of the minority's culture in itself and also because of its association with the culture, language, and tradition of the more spacious South India. These language reforms had profound status and opportunity implications and were seen as both the symbol and the guarantee of future wealth and standing. As long as popular nationalist and egalitarian purposes could be served by demoting the English language, communal tensions were not acute. Once this was accomplished, the very effectiveness of the minority in coveted middle-class and upper middle-class positions led to a growing number of newly educated Sinhalese looking upon the minority as a serious impediment to their own frustrated ambitions. The interests mobilized to assert Sinhalese rights of status and opportunity were not ready to take into account the needs and objectives of the Tamils. The readiness of political leaders to use these frustrations as a means of enlisting interest group support to obtain a rural political following, and the efforts of Tamil politicians to outbid one another as "defenders of the Tamils," sharpened communal tension still further.

In the event, the majority community succeeded in obtaining the language reform legislation its ardent spokesmen sought. The alarming riots of 1958, unparalleled in the island's history, were the direct result of these reforms and of government reluctance to insist that public order be maintained and individuals protected. The memory of these events will retard the creation of a unified, modern nation-state commanding the allegiance of all communities.

CHAPTER VIII · TOWARD ECONOMIC DEVELOPMENT

> "Capital investment per se does not originate anything other than the capital expenditure itself. It is people, who, if they possess the disposition, aptitudes, experience and knowledge and if they find suitable environmental opportunities alone can originate anything at all."—S. H. Frankel, *The Economic Impact on Under-Developed Societies*

I. INTRODUCTION

POLITICS during the first decade of independence were dominated by communal, linguistic, regional, and cultural-religious issues. Economic considerations, however, were likely to be of greater importance for the future. Toward the end of the period, economic margins were narrowing as the population rapidly expanded. Educated, articulate young men experienced increasing difficulties in finding jobs commensurate with their ambitions. Land pressure in certain rural districts was on the increase. Mounting communal strife further complicated the problem of achieving maximum productivity. Failure to show visible economic progress could be an additional element of public life threatening the continued influence of elected leaders and the representative institutions established at independence. A study of political phenomena, therefore, inescapably calls for the examination of economic development possibilities and policy.

There has been an underlying agreement among the educated and articulate concerning the goals of economic policy, even though there were manifest differences in the means thought appropriate for achieving these goals. "Everyone" was in favor of "transforming a colonial economy into a national economy." There were, however, more specific subsidiary objectives. The economy, it was thought, must be rendered more stable and less fraught with periodic "boom and bust" imported from beyond the seas. It must produce higher standards of living and expand productive employment opportunities for the rapidly growing population. For these objectives, the economy must become more diversified. Instead of concentrating so heavily on three export products, food crops for home consumption and additional export commodities must be grown in larger quantities. An important industrial component must be added. The fruits of the economy must be more equitably shared. The gap between the high privilege of the few and the poverty of the many must be narrowed. Finally, Ceylonese themselves must obtain a greater command over the country's product and resources.

In the eyes of many Ceylonese, political independence may have been obtained, but Ceylon's economy remained essentially dependent on the outside world and on the decisions of nonnationals. Prices received for estate exports and the cost of essential imports were determined abroad, and the Ceylonese could exert no influence over them. Foreigners "continued . . . to make a high percentage of business decisions, as managers, directors, and shareholders of plantation, commercial manufacturing, and financial enterprises. Foreigners also continued to derive incomes from salaries, profits and dividends. . . ."[1] The majority of the best tea estates, a good share of the rubber estates, most of the important importing, exporting, and engineering trades deriving from the estate business, were still largely owned and managed by British personnel. All banks, but one, and most insurance firms were foreign. The wholesale importing of consumer goods was dominated by Indians.

So long as this state of affairs continued, it was widely believed, the country's economic bondage would persist. Nationalists expected no harmony of interest between these foreign businesses and the Ceylonese. Foreign entrepreneurs could not operate in such a way as to achieve Ceylonese objectives. It was held that the basic interest of nonnationals impelled them to perpetuate estate agriculture and high-profit commerce whereas Ceylon required diversification, more consumer agriculture, and industrialization. The desire of foreign firms to repatriate high profits inescapably meant low wages, persisting economic inequality, and sweated labor. Their continued control of large shares of Ceylon's capital assets and annually repatriated dividends retarded investment in the directions desired by many educated Ceylonese. Some went further and inferred that because foreigners still made the major economic decisions, political control still rested in foreign hands.

Almost all were agreed in principle that a large role should be

[1] Henry M. Oliver, Jr., *Economic Opinion and Policy in Ceylon*, p. 21.

assigned to the state in fulfilling the objectives of economic development. As generally understood, the government's task was not merely that of performing the function of law and order; providing an incorruptible public administration, fiscal, and monetary system; and supplying adequate communications and basic welfare services.[2] The state had to make the fundamental investment decisions. It had to direct the bent of new development. Initiating and managing the country's "basic" industries and maintaining government-operated food collection and distribution systems were also part of its responsibilities. The aspiration for greater economic equality as well as faith in a centrally planned development underlay this broad consensus on the extensive role of the state. In the first budget speech of independent Ceylon, the Finance Minister epitomized this view when he argued that "Today the State can by legislative acts control production as well as distribution, decide the location of the factories and compel the employer to attend to the welfare of the workers."[3]

This dynamic role assigned to the state for promoting desirable economic changes was not a new idea. In Ceylon, as in most parts of the British Empire, it was the colonial government that had held the initiative in providing basic service investments, such as railroads, roads, and communications. Only after the Ceylonese began to use the apparatus of state power to reclaim dry zone areas did they make genuine progress in extending peasant cultivation. World War II initiatives by the Ceylonese government in industrial ventures, food production, and distribution showed what could be done. Those nationalists who referred to the pre-European periods for indigenous precedents could recall the indispensable role of monarchical initiative and management in the hydraulic society of ancient Ceylon.[4]

Japan was an example of an Asian people modernizing through the conscious efforts of its leaders so successfully as to confound the European power of Imperial Russia. Fabian Socialist theory brought back by students from Great Britain, and the examples of western European governments facing depression or wartime emergencies, showed Ceylon what states might and could do when the political will was clear. Russia's rise to industrial power through centrally

[2] S. H. Frankel, *The Economic Impact on Under-developed Societies* (Oxford, 1953), p. 71.

[3] *House of Representatives*, V. 3, c. 1046; also cited, Oliver, p. 51.

[4] K. A. Wittfogel, *Oriental Despotism, a Comparative Study of Total Power* (New Haven, 1957).

planned, state-managed development was widely admired as an economic *tour de force* though the human costs were often deplored. Independent India's planning effort in a mixed economy and China's centrally directed endeavors added the encouragement of contemporary experience to the arguments that had appeal on other grounds.

Among those public servants and publicists who contributed to the climate of opinion, there has long been the conviction that the public service attracted the best brains of the country and provided the best experience in administering large enterprises. The prerequisites for entry were thought to cull out the mediocre and leave only the best for government service. Others who went into business or other lines of endeavor were usually considered less capable.

There was the widespread conviction that entrepreneurs were too few or not sufficiently capable or trustworthy instruments for developing a truly independent national economy. They were considered either too cautious, too closely identified with foreign entrepreneurs, or too bent on quick returns and high profits. Savings derived from the normal working of the market were generally considered insufficient. Only the government, it was thought, through its capacity to tax incomes and external commerce and to raise state-backed loans could command sufficient resources for the heavy investments necessary for economic growth and development.[5] Hence, for a variety of reasons, the Schumpeter model of development through the private enterpriser seemed foreign and even irrelevant by comparison to experience and models drawn from economies developed in significant part by state initiative.

Although most politically active men shared to a great extent the views just defined, considerable political debate surrounded each economic policy adopted. There were widely divergent degrees of distrust of the foreign entrepreneur. Views differed on the proper role to be assigned to "the government" or to the "private sector" in development or the proper balance between agricultural and industrial investment. Opinions varied on the proper proportions between welfare expenditure and investment in productive enterprises, and of raising the necessary resources. But certain policies provoked little dissent, particularly efforts towards "Ceylonization" and a rapid expansion of government expenditure for education, health, social services, and food subsidies.

The factors or propensities that promote or impede economic

[5] For a detailed analysis of opinions toward the role of the state, see Oliver, Ch. 3.

development cannot be identified here in detail. In general terms it may be said that in considering development in South Asia, Westerners tend to argue that economic and social institutions and social ways impede development, while Asians themselves lay stress upon the lack of capital resources and insufficient political direction. In efforts to expand productivity and to diversify the Ceylonese economy, many aspects of Ceylonese life come into play. The following discussion of development resources and policy is by no means exhaustive. Only certain problems will be closely examined. Many less explored phenomena excite the curiosity, but their analysis would lengthen the discussion and digress too far into the realm of speculation.

Natural, capital, and human resources for development will be discussed before policies toward Ceylonization and welfare, agricultural, and industrial development are described. Foreign assistance and certain connections between economic development and political power will then be suggested.

II · RESOURCES FOR DEVELOPMENT

A. NATURAL RESOURCES

It has been indicated in Chapter III that the land area fit for estate agriculture has nearly reached its limit. In the case of rubber perhaps there is more uneconomic acreage already planted than there are possible new rubber areas. Peasant overcrowding in the wet zone precludes expanding acreages there for either estates or rice. The dry zone, however, contains many square miles of land that, with costly irrigation works and proper conservation techniques, could again be productive. Irrigation investments in village tanks and water courses could bring in additional acreage. Rainfall, temperature, and other natural elements are such that, with irrigation and proper techniques, many other crops can be grown, apart from the traditional subsistence or export products, oil seeds, tannins, hard fibers, lighter tobaccos, sugar cane, and cotton among them.

So far as is now known, industrial metals are rare. In widely scattered deposits there is iron ore. Coal appears to be entirely absent, but hydroelectric potentials are considerable. The central core of the island has heavy rainfall coursing down steep descents. Storage areas above these descents are limited in size and often are inundated at the expense of productive tea land. Lower catchments could be more extensive but they provide shorter drops, and surface evaporation in the lowlands is very heavy—six to ten degrees from the equator. Rainfall varies sharply over the year and between one year and another. Despite these difficulties, however, much still can be done to develop hydroelectric power.

Other known subsoil resources include top grade graphite which has been exported for many years, monazite, silica, and ilmenite sands. Kaolin clay is also present in commercial quantities. Gem stones have drawn visitors to the island since long before Sinbad's day. But since a modern geological survey has not yet been made much still remains to be learned.[6]

B. FINANCIAL RESOURCES AND INVESTMENT

With the possible exception of Malaya, Ceylon has command of larger foreign exchange resources per capita than any other country in South or Southeast Asia. Her need to import consumer goods is unusually great, but in most years until 1955-56 her resources were sufficient. At the end of World War II accumulated external assets, mostly sterling, amounted to over three times her budgeted government expenditure for the year 1945-46. By 1950, heavy capital imports, pent-up wartime consumer demand and a sluggish rubber market reduced these assets by one-third while rising government spending brought the external assets about level with annual government expenditure. Since 1952, external assets have been roughly 80 per cent of government expenditure, a not inconsiderable figure despite the heavy essential imports that must be met from these foreign exchange resources. The relatively less favorable position toward the end of the first decade is, however, noteworthy.

The external financial resources readily available for development have varied considerably over the years, depending upon the level of foreign assets, the terms of trade, and the output of domestic consumption agriculture, all of which have been subject to marked fluctuations. This circumstance complicated forward planning by both the government and private business. The large accumulated wartime balances available to the government were a great asset at the beginning of independence. There was a rapid fall in the terms of trade following the Korean boom, and in 1956-57, droughts and floods reduced domestic rice production which necessitated larger imports, reducing the sums otherwise available for development.

[6] IBRD, p. 527.

Nevertheless, in every year of the independence decade but three, government investment expenditures increased.[7] They rose from Rs. 118 m. in 1947 to Rs. 462 m. in 1958, ranging between 25 per cent and 30 per cent of all government expenditures during the first decade.

The government depended to a considerable degree upon revenue —income taxes and import and export duties—for investment resources. Shortly after independence, progressive income tax rates and export duties were sharply raised, bringing the government revenues three times their 1947 figure. In this way, an equivalent of nearly 25 per cent of the country's gross national product came under the control of the Ceylonese government. In the early years, the government annually was able to call upon up to $6,000,000 of additional resources, by means of long-term, low-interest rate loans promptly purchased by institutional savers and those who preferred secure, low-interest, government loans to savings in more traditional forms. Government borrowings from the banking system provided an additional one-third of domestic development resources.[8] In 1956, 1957, and 1958, however, there were serious governmental budget deficits.

Apart from $5,800,000 worth of development assistance in various forms provided through the Colombo Plan, Ceylon's development from 1947 to 1954 proceeded entirely on its own resources. Earlier, Ceylon had received large inflows of investment capital directed toward the estate and commercial sectors, but, with the Great Depression, these virtually ceased. After World War II, on the contrary, large amounts of private capital were withdrawn from the island and only small amounts were invested in new activities. Indeed, Ceylon was a net loser of private foreign capital by about $6,000,000 per year.[9] In 1954 the government floated a loan for £5,000,000 on the London market, an issue that was promptly taken up. In that year, too, the International Bank for Reconstruction and Development opened a line of credit at 4¾ per cent to the amount of $20,000,000 in the aggregate to finance the external costs of a large hydroelectric scheme. These measures reinforced the country's external finances

[7] All but 1952/1953, 1953/1954, 1956/1957. S. Kanesathasan, "Export instability and contra-cyclical Fiscal policy in Under-developed Export Economies—A Case Study of Ceylon since 1948." International Monetary Fund, *Staff Papers*, V. VII, 1 (April 1959), 41-74, p. 59.

[8] *Report of the Taxation Commission*, pp. 23, 26, 32.

[9] Average for the years 1950-1956, calculated from Table 24a, Central Bank of Ceylon, *Annual Reports*, using 1957 exchange rate for all years.

and helped the government to maintain the level of investment decided upon in earlier years when Ceylon's external assets had been more plentiful.

The pace of a country's development is significantly influenced by its rate of capital formation in both the public and private sectors. Though probably somewhat lower immediately after independence, as indicated in Chapter III, gross capital formation has been estimated at roughly 11 per cent with a probable net rate of 7 per cent.[10] By 1958, the Central Bank reported over 13 per cent of G.N.P. was being invested.[11] Assuming with the Planning Secretariat that for every added increment of production 2.5 units of capital are required, such a rate of net capital formation would add enough productive capacity merely to keep pace with a population rising at the rate of 2.8 per cent per year. A rate of capital formation more nearly 15 per cent or even 16 per cent of gross national product is probably necessary for rapid growth unless most productive increments can be obtained through transfer of techniques and other factors that require relatively little capital.[12] The proportion of this total investment provided by the government rose considerably during the decade as the government greatly expanded its outlays and the private sector came to depend almost entirely upon domestic resources. Although private investment in 1947 was estimated to be four times government capital formation, by 1958 the government provided more than 60 per cent of total national investment.[13]

Raising the rate of capital formation beyond its present level presents obvious difficulties. One-third of government expenditures have been committed to welfare expenditures and the political costs of reducing these would be great, as the U.N.P. discovered in 1953 when the rice subsidy was slashed. The atmosphere and symbols of

10 Wignaraja, p. 8.

11 Central Bank of Ceylon, *Annual Report of the Monetary Board to the Minister of Finance 1958*, p. 11.

12 For a discussion of the 2.5:1 capital output ratio see Planning Secretariat, *Six-Year Programme of Investment* 1954/55 to 1959/60, p. 497. The I.B.R.D. preferred a 4:1 ratio. The uncertainties of the proper figure within an economy like Ceylon's are obvious.

13 Central Bank of Ceylon, *Annual Report of the Monetary Board to the Minister of Finance 1958*, p. 11. Errors are quite possible in these calculations if they are being used as a basis for estimated *productive* capital investment. Small scale investment by peasant farmers, handicraft workers and small workshop operators may be quite productive though not easily accounted for. Expensive housing may enter the private sector account but not be equivalently productive in any economic sense. Government expenditure, too, may not necessarily be any more economically efficient than many expenditures by, say, American municipalities.

representative government as practiced in Ceylon, genuine commitment to humanitarian beliefs, and a populace expecting tangible welfare benefits from the government combine to deter a high rate of government investment. Such a small proportion of the population are eligible for the privilege of paying income taxes that a more austere style of life by the country's wealthy would not add greatly to Ceylon's investable savings though a more equitable distribution of austerity may have merit in the eyes of political leaders. Some portion of savings is still "held in the traditional forms of consumer durables, land, buildings, jewelry and cash hoardings."[14] The low living standards of the masses and traditional, though by no means Calvinist, savings habits make it difficult to achieve higher rates of capital formation. All the greater, therefore, are the imperatives to *invest Ceylon's capital development funds to the best productive* advantage.

C. ORGANIZATIONAL AND HUMAN RESOURCES AND PUBLIC ORDER

In view of the important role in economic development assigned to the government, Ceylon is fortunate in having a public service of many highly qualified men. The service is nationwide; few are the villages too remote for effective liaison with representatives of the Colombo government. Public servants may lack certain kinds of initiative; interdepartmental coordination may be difficult; treasury regulations framed for an earlier period may still dominate internal accounting and personnel procedures; the service is not cheap; it absorbs nearly one-third of the government budget. Nevertheless, few countries in the area can boast as capable a service. In all probability, few large American cities could boast as honest a service.

Ceylon was already equipped with many of the basic capital investments that other countries must still make. Her road system was already well developed, though new trunk and feeder roads were required in parts of the dry zone, many villages in the wet zone needed road connections, and roads were narrow. Most parts of the island were already accessible by rail with haulages of no more than four hours to the rail head though equipment was out of date and badly run down during the war. Although hydroelectric production was low, even by Asian standards, and heavy investment continued to be necessary to bring arable lands under cultivation in the dry

[14] *Report of the Taxation Commission*, p. 26.

zone, basic elements of the economic infrastructure of Ceylon were well developed in comparison with other Asian countries.

The government's school system was already extensive in 1948, but many villages were still without schools ten years later and school curricula seemed inappropriate for maximum economic development. Facilities for practical technical education, for example, were still rare. But Ceylon had a more extensive educational system, with higher general standards in all but the most advanced work, and it was better equipped with schools and teachers per thousand inhabitants, than any of her Asian neighbors.

Literacy alone cannot make an economically productive people. But under suitable cultural and economic conditions literacy can greatly facilitate technological improvement in agriculture, ease the problem of maintaining machinery in industry, and open to the literate a horizon of innovation and experiment.[15] Ceylon's rate of literacy at independence was roughly 50 per cent, higher than any other country in the area. Ten years later nearly 60 per cent were literate.

It is difficult to evaluate the characteristics of the population which impede or accelerate economic development. As in the remarkable German economic recovery, individuals in some economies are oriented primarily toward production; in others toward consumption. Some achieve high levels of consumption because of high productivity per worker—a combination of many subjective, capital, and technological factors.[16] In Ceylon production orientation appeared to be limited, incentives toward maximum productivity per capita or manpower factor were weak, and innovation tended to lag. Few of those with money or education tried to convert what capital was available into new types of productive activity. The pull of ready markets was obvious; a look at the import list showed what was needed; but the enterprising impulse, applying imaginative effort and poised business judgment to meeting this local market demand with available capital through the creation of new business activities, was rare indeed.[17] Entrepreneurs preferred to retain within

[15] The word "innovation" is used throughout in its common sense meaning, not according to its technical meaning in economic literature. Any process or technique that has not hitherto been used in Ceylon but which is introduced and used in Ceylon is "innovation" for the Ceylon economy, whether it is technically "borrowed" from some other country or "invented" for the first time in Ceylon.

[16] Henry C. Wallich, *Mainsprings of the German Revival* (New Haven, 1955), pp. 30-31.

[17] B. B. das Gupta, "The Theory and Reality of Economic Development," Central Bank of Ceylon, *Bulletin*, v, 11 (Nov. 1955), pp. 5-10.

their own family firms whatever profits were not spent on spacious living. To invest in stock company ventures was unusual.

Many appeared to be experiencing personal frustration and distress. The murder rate and increased communal antagonism suggested discontent with things as they were. But apart from Western educated public servants, publicists, professional men, and politicians, there were relatively few in the city or countryside who appeared eager to grasp new techniques or exchange familiar ways for the relatively impersonal, impatient, hurried life of the more productive countries.

Technical skills were still rare, but Ceylonese were clearly adept at manual skills when given proper incentives and training. Japanese textile technicians and Americans who supervised workers at the Gal Oya project confirm that Ceylonese workers were innately dextrous.[18] They do not lack the capacity for skilled performance in machine manipulation or in skilled handicraft work. The level of verbal performance or prodigies of memory suggest additional gifts among the people—whether educated or uneducated—that are much more highly prized in Ceylon's culture. The traditional culture and the high status attributed to foreign supervisors who seldom did manual work have led to an under-evaluation of the manually skilled. Men are rare who combine supervisory status with a willingness to descend to the working level of the man at the bench or the workman in the irrigation ditch. Such manual activities are still considered soiling and beneath the dignity of the man with a degree training. Manipulative skills have received little attention in school curricula and are not rewarded in economic or other ways.

An economic pattern that has changed little over the past sixty years has not encouraged experimentation or innovation. The experience of striking out in new directions after the responsible calculation of risks, the process of exploration, was usually carried on by foreign businessmen or government servants from abroad. In a society where the family elders retained the balance of influence, younger men with new ideas were not encouraged. In their homes and in schools or other associations, they have had few opportunities to experiment with responsibility or to try new ways of doing things.

Although the larger cities are growing, village ties remain strong. Working for hire is still considered debasing in the traditional

[18] Interview evidence confirmed by research conducted by Professor T. L. Green, Department of Education, University of Ceylon. Brief reference to it in his article, "Education and Society in Ceylon," *The Educand*, v. 2, No. 3 (Nov. 1956), p. 59.

value system, but may be acceptable when land pressures are too great. Heavy physical labor is avoided by Sinhalese workers, if at all possible. In the Sinhalese low-country, especially, tropical climate discourages effort, and the proximity of village and family connections induces more absenteeism than is desirable. On the other hand, though preferring his own pace, the Ceylonese worker learns new skills easily if work, social, and other conditions are considered appropriate. He has the added virtue of remaining in a job once it proves satisfactory and if security of tenure is assured.[19]

Increasing labor productivity is therefore not merely a matter of providing better capital equipment, though equipment at all levels—from subsistence farming to textile looms—leaves much room for improvement, but a problem of social, political, and economic organization, training and the development of incentives. Some firms that have introduced more sensitive incentive systems report good returns.[20] Labor-management relations have not always been of the best as many employers have persisted in resisting unionization. The unions themselves have often been more politically than economically oriented and have not been concerned with productivity or encouraging regularity. In 1957, for example, over 800,000 man days were lost through strikes.

Until 1958, when vicious riots drove thousands of Tamils to seek safety in the north and Sinhalese from the north fled south, Ceylon, unique among her neighbors, had not suffered internal disruption. There was nothing like the flight of millions in India and Pakistan, military occupation followed by armed rebellion in Burma, or incipient and recurrent insurrection in Indonesia and Malaya. No armed bands ranged the countryside holding peasants to ransom and preventing the nation's products from reaching the nation's markets. From 1947 to 1957, police and defense forces together consumed less than 6 per cent of total government expenditures. Until 1958, the days of personal insecurity from public disorders could be counted on the fingers of one hand. In no other country in the whole of South and Southeast Asia, from the Persian Gulf to the arc of Indonesia had there been such public peace. The imminence of violence diverted neither men nor materials from more productive uses.

On the surface, it would appear that Ceylon's resources are par-

19 IBRD, pp. 53-57; Farmer, pp. 71, 72, 96.

20 Interviews with selected industrial firms in the Colombo area.

ticularly suited to a diverse and productive agriculture. Switzerland and Hong Kong are both reminders of what an energetic, skillful, and thrifty population can do with adequate financial resources when effectively organized for, and adapted to, productive purposes. But as yet, it is the exceptional tropical country that has been able to develop a rapidly expanding economy based on incentive values and organizational modes drawn from the temperate zone. These considerations define the challenge facing the people of Ceylon.[21]

III · GOVERNMENT POLICIES TOWARD "CEYLONIZATION," ECONOMIC POWER, AND SOCIAL EQUALITY

A. CEYLONIZATION AND ENHANCED COMMAND OVER ECONOMIC RESOURCES

One of the important objectives of "transforming a colonial economy into a national economy" has been to ensure Ceylon's nationals of a greater share in the making of important economic decisions. Ceylonese have long argued that their entrepreneurial activity has hitherto been slight not so much for the sociological or cultural reasons which foreigners use to explain this phenomenon but because the foreign entrepreneurs entered the most lucrative fields first. Then through a network of interlocking banking, agency, and managerial relationships, the foreigners successfully prevented all but a few Ceylonese from entering these fields. Independence brought with it the chance to redress this imbalance of opportunity. The Finance Minister stated this objective as wishing to "ensure a higher percentage of participation by the nationals of the country in trade, commerce, and industrial activities as regards management, labour, and finance."[22]

Since independence, foreign firms have had to employ progressively more Ceylonese in subordinate and managerial posts. These beginnings of Ceylonization were accomplished more by administrative measures and pressure from certain ministries than by legislation. The large foreign firms that still operate, such as the Shell Oil Company, now apply regularized European promotional procedures, high remuneration for high performance, and offer wide scope for personal capacities not previously to be had by the Ceylonese in

[21] Douglas H. K. Lee, *Climate and Economic Development in the Tropics* (New York, 1957).

[22] *House of Representatives*, V. 3, c. 1047.

government service or commercial firms. Appointments in estate agency houses, in the import-export trade, and in banking have also been opened. Ceylonese are gaining training in foreign business methods, access to new promotional opportunities and their economic influence will be enhanced in the long run.[23] Numerically, however, the openings have not been large, for few of the foreign firms have been expanding their activities on the island.

Many Indian importers and retail shopkeepers have been permanently displaced as the result of government activities developed during World War II. The government-run Cooperative Wholesale Establishment was not only designed to ensure regular imports of extremely scarce commodities but also to eliminate Indian middleman profiteering. It continues to distribute essential foodstuffs, such as rice, flour, and sugar and has warehouses in each province at key distributing points. Other government-sponsored "cooperatives" to encourage the home production of rice and to replace profiteering village shopkeepers are responsible for purchasing country rice and other products from the peasant at a guaranteed price.

Part of the agitation to replace Indian wage labor was a desire to open wage employment to Ceylonese. Regulations also restrict the employment of Indians in many categories, and residence permits are administered with an eye to reserving employment opportunities to Ceylonese in domestic and hotel service fields, just as the Port of Colombo and many other government departments had been Ceylonized some years earlier.[24]

Efforts have been made to limit to Ceylonese trade with certain countries or in specific commodities. Import and export licenses ensure that Ceylonese firms alone trade with Germany and Japan. The same is true of trade with Poland, Czechoslovakia, and Russia. The rubber export business had been predominantly a foreign activity until the trade agreement with China led the government to reserve rubber shipments to Ceylonese citizens.[25]

With the exception of the rice-rubber trade with China and imports from Germany and Japan, exchanges with these other countries through 1957 remained unimportant though widely publicized. They did, however, provide a preserve for Ceylonese into which several thousand wholesalers sought entry at the outset. The Ceylonese,

[23] IBRD, p. 77.

[24] See Chapter VII above. Also Oliver, p. 242; Stein, "Problems of Economic Development in Ceylon," p. 314; IBRD, pp. 77-78, 198.

[25] Oliver, pp. 23, 24; IBRD, p. 149; Stein, p. 314.

who tried to participate in the export-import trade and found it difficult to compete against the more established foreign business houses oriented toward European and American commerce, formed a potentially important group with a clear vested interest in diversifying Ceylon's exports toward nondollar, nonsterling area markets. Nationalist economic politics and the urge to find more diversified markets could be expected to support them in their endeavors.

The government has also made credit easily available for the purchase by Ceylonese of foreign estates, and exchange control has been so administered as to allow British sellers to repatriate their capital. Numerous tea estates have been purchased by Ceylonese with government assistance and considerable numbers of commercial firms, including several of the larger retail establishments, have come under Ceylonese ownership. In the short run, these acquisitions merely use liquid capital to transfer ownership or management when these resources might have been alternatively invested in opening new estates or in industrial ventures. They will, however, reduce foreign exchange dividend payments in the future and enhance Ceylonese managerial opportunities.

Perhaps the most important measures increasing government control over its own economy have been in the field of tax policy. And these policies in turn have materially influenced the amount of resources available to the government for purposes of welfare expenditure or economic development. In 1938-39, import duties accounted for nearly 60 per cent of revenue, income tax for 20 per cent, and excise duties 9 per cent. The tax structure and rates have greatly altered since then. Import duties that used to place the burden of taxation on all consumers now account for only one-third of the revenue and are imposed predominantly on luxury goods, although some mass consumption articles, such as cotton cloth, must hurdle significant tariffs in order to favor domestic production. Income taxes, now with steeply graduated rates in the upper brackets, continue to account for roughly one-fifth of the revenue. Export duties, reinstated during the war, now account for another one-third of the revenue compared to a mere 4 per cent before the war.[26] Indeed, export duties bring the government nearly 15 per cent of tea export values, largely at the expense of tea company margins that are substantially foreign owned or managed, and of foreign tea consumers. In addition a profits tax adds some 7 per cent more to the government revenue.

[26] *Report of the Taxation Commission*, p. 10.

As a result of these tax and other financial measures, the government now controls nearly one-fourth of the gross national product. Since a substantial proportion of this revenue is derived from the economic activities of non-Ceylonese, these revenue measures are materially altering the balance of economic power in favor of the Ceylonese parliamentarians and government servants who decide how the government revenues should be expended. In comparison to Burma, Indonesia, or even India, these policies have been moderate. Nevertheless, as Henry Oliver concludes, "they have altered the significance more than the appearance of foreign economic power."[27]

B. GENERAL BUDGETARY DESIGN

Policies toward Ceylonization do not show up on the expenditure side of the government budget, but most other policies are reflected there. Before discussing the government's policies toward the other objectives within the broader aim of "transforming a colonial economy into a national economy," a general description of the government budget will be useful.

Taking 1954-55 as a typical year, if expenditure for both current payments and for investment be combined for different categories of expenditure, the distribution of government spending can be shown as follows:

Administration	13.0%
Social services	33.6
Economic services	30.8
Pay'ts to gov't enterprises	6.9
Grants-in-aid, pensions, other transfers	7.1
Interest on public debt	2.6
Acquisition of financial assets and other misc.	6.0
	100.0[28]

Alternatively, the direction of government expenditure on capital account can be shown separately from current expenditure. On the average for the first eight years of independence, expenditure on

[27] Oliver, p. 22.

[28] From Table 20, Government Finance, in Central Bank of Ceylon, *Annual Report of the Monetary Board to the Minister of Finance for 1957*. "Administration" does not include all government salaries and pensions. These together amount to nearly 30 per cent of all government expenditures. No doubt some proportion of "Payments to Government Enterprises" and of "grants-in-aid to local authorities" belong under "economic services" for our purposes.

capital acquisition, formation, and maintenance came to nearly 29 per cent of total government spending.[29]

The distribution of these capital expenditures for two characteristic years was as follows:

		1948/1949		1953/1954
Administration		5.5%		6.4%
Social services		15.0		21.5
Health	3.4		5.7	
Education	6.2		5.4	
Housing	5.4		10.4	
Economic services		79.5		72.1
Rural development	1.5		4.9	
Public utilities	37.1		32.0	
Agriculture, irrigation, fisheries	35.7		34.4	
Manufacturing, industry, commerce	5.2		.8	
		100.0		100.0

It will be noticed that over one-third of total government expenditure went to social services and that slightly less than one-third went to economic development. Of the capital budget, which itself absorbed one-third of government spending, economic development activities accounted for over two-thirds, and social services slightly less than one-quarter. It will be well to retain these gross proportions in mind during the discussion of expenditure policies that follows.

C. POLICIES TOWARD GREATER SOCIAL EQUALITY AND WELFARE

The need to ensure a voting majority and an egalitarian political faith have both combined to induce policies designed to share more widely some of the services and opportunities hitherto reserved to the wealthy. In anticipation of independence, the State Council adopted the principle of "universal, free education," financed by central government appropriations. Under this program, the government pays the total staff salary costs and provides grants for equipment and maintenance for nearly all the schools on the island from the primary grade up through the University of Ceylon. "Primary education" extends from age five through fourteen and is compulsory in principle although numbers of children still cannot go for lack of

[29] From Table 20, Item 21, Central Bank of Ceylon, *Annual Report of the Monetary Board to the Minister of Finance for 1957*.

sufficient teaching staff and rural school buildings. At 14 students pass a so-called "fitness test" which eliminates many from pursuing the coveted "academic" courses. Those rejected at the fitness test can go forward to vocational and technical schools, which are still rudimentary and scarce; those who pass go on with a liberal arts training which leads, after a further hurdle, to the university.

This educational program covered tuition expenses. It did not include the costs of paper or lunches at school. These additional expenses have been more than some families could bear, particularly when school meant that the family had to forego the earning power of their children.[30] Hence, in addition to increased costs for expanded school staffs and new construction, heavy political pressures developed in favor of free school lunches, government payment of facilities fees, and other kinds of subsidy. The government's educational budget doubled between 1946 and 1948 and doubled again by 1956.

Ceylonese government practice has usually been to consider education, health, welfare, and food subsidies "welfare expenditures."[31] For the first decade of independence, there would have been considerable justification for that practice. No doubt, part of the educational budget could be properly chargeable as "development expenditure." School building is accounted for as part of the gross capital investment. Literacy and educational standards have been cited as positive contributions to economic development. Nevertheless, a study of debates on education in parliament and an analysis of school curricula in practice strongly suggest that the educational budget has thus far been more an investment in answering the demand for equality of status and welfare than it has been designed to increase productivity and speed economic development. The curriculum used has been largely oriented toward producing candidates for jobs that provided high social status and secure incomes rather than encouraging the skills of productivity, mechanical ingenuity, and the bent of mind and interest to apply agricultural and technical knowledge to expanding production.[32]

Health services too have received extensive appropriations. A system of free medical care was undertaken shortly after World War II.

[30] T. L. Green, "Education and Society in Ceylon," p. 54.

[31] For instance, *Report of the Taxation Commission*, p. 17; *Economic and Social Development of Ceylon (A Survey) 1926-1954*, Section VI.

[32] Particularly, T. L. Green, "Looking for Status rather than Work," *Manchester Guardian*, October 4, 1954.

Outpatient treatment is free for most services and free hospitalization is widely available. Efforts have been made to increase the number of doctors, and nurses' training institutions have been established. There are many rural clinics, financed by the central government or sponsored by a local benefactor. Urban hospitals have been built beyond the capacity of local personnel to staff them. Malaria has been all but eliminated—an achievement that also contributes to agricultural development although it is covered by the public health budget. Government expenditures on these health items have mounted from Rs. 38 million in 1946-47 to Rs. 105 million in 1955-56, an increase by three times.[33] Consequently, the death rate has been nearly halved and the rate of population growth has plunged forward. Debilitating diseases are still prevalent, however, particularly hookworm and enteric infections from fouled drinking water. Poor sanitary conditions and a diet low in proteins and vitamins contribute to a large daily turnout at clinics and add otherwise avoidable demands on the state health services. A Department of Social Services provides limited allowances and family services to the many needy.

A final important item in the government's measures toward social equality and welfare purposes has been the food subsidies that became an accepted policy during World War II. These have served to keep down the cost of living of the masses on their basic food staple—rice. Until 1953 the cost of rice to the consumer was held relatively stable despite wide fluctuations in the world's price. In that year, the difference between the high world wholesale price and the low domestic retail price became such that over 20 per cent of the government revenue was being spent to meet this gap. Under acute financial pressure, the government withdrew the subsidies. Subsequent disorders led to organized riots, the death of ten, the resignation of the Prime Minister, and incidents that were effectively used against the ruling party at a general election three years later. The new government of 1956 restored the subsidies, absorbing roughly Rs. 100 million, or some 10 per cent of planned government expenditure.

Together these important social welfare programs accounted on the average for over 35 per cent of the government's expenditure for the first ten years of independence. The high point was reached

[33] Government of Ceylon, *Estimates of the Revenue and Expenditure of the Government of Ceylon for the Financial Year 1st October 1956 to 30th September 1957*, p. 15.

in 1951-52 when the food subsidy item pushed the welfare account to 45 per cent of total government spending.[34] Even if food subsidy costs were eliminated for the years 1950 to 1953, when they were highest, health, education, and welfare have regularly absorbed as much as one-third of the government's budget.

IV · POLICIES TOWARD INCREASING PRODUCTIVITY AND DIVERSIFYING THE ECONOMY

A. DOMESTIC FOOD PRODUCTION AND LAND SETTLEMENT

In the first budget of independent Ceylon, roughly 18 per cent of total government expenditure was identified as directed toward "Development of National Wealth."[35] As the Finance Minister put the priorities then: "The first step in our plans must be to produce our own food. To be self-supporting in essential foods and in articles necessary for clothing and housing is one of the main tasks we have to devote our attention to."[36] Over one-third of all development funds were assigned to agriculture, irrigation, and fisheries.[37] Very large allocations were made for irrigating and settling the dry zone, less went to small-scale village irrigation projects, often in the wet zone, and to improving the output on presently tilled land. In the category of nonagricultural investment expenditure, 22 per cent of development funds were directed toward transport and communications, particularly development of Colombo Harbor; 8 per cent assigned to power development, largely hydroelectric; 6 per cent to government-financed industrial investment; and another 27 per cent to social capital, including housing, health, and education investment.[38]

[34] Calculated from the *Report of the Taxation Commission* for years up to 1952/53, pp. 18-19, after that Central Bank of Ceylon, *Annual Reports of the Monetary Board to the Minister of Finance*. Pensions for Government Employees and Rural Development items were withdrawn as inappropriately classified for our purposes, giving thus a lower welfare proportion than the Taxation Commission calculated.

[35] *House of Representatives*, V. 3, July 20, 1948, Appendix J. [36] *Ibid.*, c. 1036.

[37] Commonwealth Consultative Committee, *The Colombo Plan for Co-operative Economic Development in South and Southeast Asia, 1950*. Cmd. 8080, Table 14, p. 29.

[38] A comparison with India's first plan submitted to the Colombo Plan Council follows (Cmd. 8080, p. 13):

	Ceylon	*India*
Agriculture	37%	33%
Transport/communication	22	38
Power/fuel	8	3
Industry/mining	6	10
Social capital	27	16

1. *Settlement and irrigation.* As much as 25 per cent of all development funds since independence went to irrigation and colonization. Irrigation—as much a prerequisite for opening new lands as jungle clearance—has received much government attention for many years. By 1956, some 562,000 acres were under irrigation, of which slightly more than half were developed and operated under major schemes for which central government capital and operational resources were essential.[39] The other half were less exclusively the responsibility of Colombo since many were "village tanks" and small scale irrigation works that village authorities themselves could maintain, although cash and material inducements were usually necessary to reconstruct them at the outset. Between 15 and 20,000 acres had been irrigated each year during the early years of independence, a figure that moved forward when the Gal Oya lands were brought in. Future plans beyond 1957 called for extending irrigated acreage by roughly 20,000 more acres per year.[40]

Since the 1930's, the government has sought to settle peasant cultivators on lands opened by irrigation. Reversing the colonial government's previous policy of making large grants of Crown land available to the highest bidder—a policy that had promoted the estate industries but which deprived poorer villagers of access to the land they could not hope to compete for—the government sought to promote local production of food grains and to provide with new land the land-hungry peasants in the densely populated districts of the wet zone and the arid, crowded north. Needy peasants were selected by government officials from the applicants and given tentative title to a plot of land on condition they improved, irrigated, and fenced it and maintained production to an acceptable standard. At that time relatively large allocations of five acres of rice lands and three acres of "high land," for gardens and houses, were made in order to lure peasants into what were then the malarial areas of the dry zone. The government also provided many services, including clearing the irrigated plots, building a house, and running irrigation ditches and roads to the peasant's own land. After the payment of a small land rent for a number of years and continuous satisfactory cultivation, permanent title devolved upon the peasant cultivator. In order to prevent land fragmentation, land could be left by inheritance to only one descendant.[41]

39 Planning Secretariat, *First Interim Report, National Planning Council*, p. 33.
40 *Ibid.*, p. 33.
41 For a convenient discussion, see Farmer, pp. 159-160, and Ch. 14.

The virtual elimination of malaria in the dry zone and increasing land pressure in the wet zone together have produced many more applicants for these allotments than there have been available plots. Costs for the assistance given by the government have run in the neighborhood of Rs. 12,000 per family, of which irrigation costs have been only Rs. 3,000.[42] Five acres of rice lands proved to be too much land to work intensively. Accordingly, levels of government assistance have been lowered recently and allotments reduced to three acres of rice lands and two of highlands.

Many acres have been developed in the shadow of ancient dams now restored and beside reopened channels dating back before the twelfth century A.D. New projects, such as the Gal Oya River Valley Scheme, have also been undertaken. This development is based upon a complex of dams begun by American contractors that control the runoff from a catchment area of 770 square miles in the dry zone. It is operated by an independent Valley Development Board, administratively likened to the T.V.A. During the first five years of the Board's activities, 65,000 acres of land were cleared, irrigated, and developed. Peasant allotments have been distributed to nearly 5,000 families, and village services, such as schools, clinics, and co-operative stores, provided.[43] Blocks of irrigable land have also been assigned for pasture land, government and entrepreneurial development of sugar cane and for experiments with cotton.

Unfortunately, because of insufficient planning and incomplete soil analysis, it has since been discovered that the Gal Oya soils have a low clay content for rice and yields have been markedly lower than those in other colonization schemes closer to the repaired ancient tanks such as at Polonnaruwa.[44] Costs for peasant allotments at Gal Oya have been considerably higher than elsewhere because of the captal works, but part of these costs, at least, can be charged off to flood control and the production of electricity as the island's grid develops and draws on its hitherto unused hydroelectric power.

From 1945 to 1955, nearly 200,000 acres of dry zone lands had been opened for cultivation and some 100,000 people had found

[42] IBRD, p. 386. Farmer is inclined to accept these estimates, though rightly stressing the great variation in costs as between the different colonies, p. 318.

[43] Government of Ceylon, Gal Oya Development Board, *Annual Report, 1954-1955*, pp. 4, 11.

[44] Gal Oya averaged roughly 27 bushels of rice per acre compared to Polonnaruwa's 40 to 45 for both seasons during the years 1954-1955. Gal Oya Development Board, *ibid.*, p. 15; Farmer, pp. 246-247; Department of Census and Statistics, *A Report on Paddy Statistics* (1956), Table VIII.

new homes.[45] The Planning Secretariat estimated in 1957 that approximately 95,000 additional acres would be opened to irrigation by 1960 and some 15,000 more families settled, the limit being set by lack of technical personnel, such as engineers, supervisors, and skilled workers for irrigation and development construction.[46]

2. *Increasing yields.* One objective of peasant colonization had been to increase rice acreages; improving rice yields received less pressing attention. Village rice production faces certain institutional and other difficulties. Successive division at each inheritance has carried fragmentation to an extreme, particularly in the Kandyan and coastal areas of the wet zone. Plots are now minute, over 30 per cent being less than one-half an acre. The median holding of farming families for all agricultural purposes being four-fifths of an acre.[47] Land worked by a family may be scattered in different parts of one valley, necessitating time-consuming transfers of plows and animals and deterring rational and concerted use of water. Titles are uncertain; in the coastal areas, where differing Portuguese, Dutch, and British practices were superimposed upon customary Sinhalese rights, land titles are indescribably confused. Individual owners are reluctant to improve their land for fear it will awaken a hitherto dormant claimant; banks are reluctant to offer regularized credit where security in land is unclear, forcing the cultivator to turn to the usurious shopkeeper if a government-sponsored credit cooperative is not at hand. Costly and time-consuming litigation over titles is frequent, even to the extent of mortgaging clear land to fight a claim for 1/250th of an acre.

The nonowning tenant cultivators, roughly 20 per cent of agricultural workers, have little incentive to improve the land they work, for their tenancy is not assured and improvements may only induce a higher rent, often determined by auction among competing sharecroppers. Rents are high; as much as one-half the rice crop may go to the landlord, merely for the right to use the land; additional rents may be charged for buffalo, seed, and fertilizers, though these are sometimes included in the basic rent.

One measure designed to increase paddy production was begun during World War II when rice supplies had to come great distances and depend on wartime shipping. A guaranteed price scheme

[45] *Six-Year Programme of Investment*, pp. 178-179; Farmer, p. 164.

[46] National Planning Council, *First Interim Report*, pp. 27-39.

[47] For a thorough study, see *Report of the Joint United Kingdom and Australian Mission on Rice Production in Ceylon* (Sessional Paper II—1955).

assured the paddy farmer a minimum price for his product, and the policy was continued after the war. There were administrative anomalies in the program and the cash incentive did not produce all the results expected. Nevertheless, it contributed to improved rice production.

Land reform received some official attention in 1953 when a bill was enacted designed to give tenants greater security of tenure over a five-year period. It called for written agreements between landlord and tenant, setting out the conditions of the tenancy. Primarily due to the large numbers of peasants seeking to farm, owners were under no economic compulsion to reach the agreements and government administrators themselves were unable to induce compliance. Hence, few agreements were entered into. Its experimental application in the Hambantota and Batticaloa districts, where conditions were admittedly among the worst for tenants, proved a failure.

In 1958, after bitter political controversy that dramatized the differences within the new M.E.P. government, another and more detailed paddy lands bill was passed. It was intended to provide security of tenure to tenants, to limit the rents that could be charged, and to bring unused paddy land into cultivation. An elaborate scheme of rural committees was provided presumably to assist the government in administering the new law. Some opponents feared these committees would be misused as political instruments to improve the political fortunes of the Minister of Agriculture. Others saw lands belonging to Buddhist temples as a principal target of the land reformers. In practice, the first area to be tackled was the largely Moorish districts in the south which the other bill had not been strong enough to deal with.[48]

Data on absentee owners is scarce, but it is clear that with exceptions, notably in the Batticaloa and Hambantota areas, rise absenteeism is largely, though not entirely, "middle class." The village schoolmaster, the *bhikkhu*, and Headman, the government servant and village storekeeper, as much as the rural notables, the temples or urban wealthy, are the absentee landlords.[49] With ownership thus dispersed, radical land reform will not be easy, and the resulting holdings will be, for the most part, widely scattered small parcels.

[48] *Paddy Lands Act, No. 1 of 1958*. For the debate, *House of Representatives*, V. 30, Nos. 21, 22, 23, and 25; December 12, 13, 17, 19, 1957.

[49] Sarkar and Tambiah, *The Disintegrating Village*, Table 10 and p. 16, give unusual empirical evidence to confirm this widespread impression.

It has generally been assumed that greater permanency of tenure would induce greater output, but in fact, in the Kandyan districts at least, the sharecropper, with relatively assured access to capital items like seed and bullocks provided by the owner, produced more per acre than his peasant proprietor neighbor.[50] The need for rural credit available to the small farmer has long been recognized, and various means have been tried. Either defaults have been heavy or credit has not been readily accessible to those who needed it most. In 1959 efforts of the Minister of Agriculture to promote a new rural credit scheme brought on a cabinet crisis. Many members of the M.E.P. coalition—and other parties, too—were in favor of a similar credit proposal, but they were afraid that the minister would misuse his proposed credit powers for political ends. The Prime Minister himself took responsibility for its administration. In mid-May, the controversial Minister of Agriculture and his close political associates withdrew from the cabinet and the coalition. Only a hasty realignment allowed the government to retain a slender majority in parliament.

An agricultural extension service has broadly dispersed facilities in many parts of the island with more officers per rural inhabitant than the United States has county agents. The Department of Agriculture distributes pure-line seed and attempts in other ways to raise the level of rice technology. These efforts have borne some fruit, but not as much as had been hoped.[51] A rural development organization sought to establish local committees in each Headman's district to encourage villagers to employ their spare time for village improvement activities, such as building roads or school buildings, meeting halls, water supplies, deepening irrigation channels, etc. Some of these received government assistance for materials, others operated on an entirely voluntary basis. By 1953-54, assets worth approximately Rs. 12.8 million had been created at an estimated expenditure of Rs. 4.8 million.[52] Considerable experience had been gained by villagers in themselves providing what their village needed rather than waiting upon a government department to provide it for them.

In the new colonies or older villages, however, the peasants had not yet found the incentive for maximizing their agricultural output. Farmers still preferred to sow broadcast rather than to trans-

[50] *Ibid.*, pp. 43-44.

[51] Murray Strauss, "Cultural Factors in the Functioning of Agricultural Extension in Ceylon," *Rural Sociology*, Vol. 18, No. 3 (September 1953), p. 250.

[52] *Six-Year Programme of Investment*, p. 276.

plant according to the Japanese method, a process that demands a number of additional procedures that must be exactly performed for good results. Fertilizers were not regularly applied to more than one-quarter of the acreage; only one-eighth of the fields was weeded;[53] water was not used efficiently; even in the colonies, perhaps one-third to one-half of the water was wasted; and rotation was not often practiced. On colonization schemes, where maximum government efforts have been undertaken through extension services and close supervision, yields did not appear to have been much better than in the surrounding villages.[54]

This discouraging conclusion suggests that more sociological research is necessary before government-sponsored innovation in agricultural techniques can be effectively transmitted to the Ceylonese peasant farmers.[55] Devices involving more intensive cultivation and known to promote greater yields are not adopted, even though there is manifest underemployment in rural areas. The peasants are not lazy in any ordinary sense; great energy can be applied when it is thought worthwhile within their value system. Individual farmers will perform prodigies of labor in clearing single-handed a jungle plot that can be tilled for only a few years. Many farmers may not bother to weed their rice fields regularly, but will go thirty miles in the heat of the dry season, carrying babies, fuel, and food to a Buddhist festival.[56] This does not mean that they are "otherworldly" in a profoundly mystical sense, for the festival may also be part fair and part family reunion. When extra cash is acquired, villagers promptly spend it on articles that derive from customary needs or to satisfy newer tastes, such as bicycles and flashlights, or for transporting themselves and their families to places of pilgrimage. Their lack of understanding of the growth process and their faith in astrology and woodland deities leads them to undervalue such mundane matters as weeding and fertilizing. At the same time, their very susceptibility to religious and traditional symbolism, if properly harnessed to productive purposes, might release remarkable energies. The political results obtained by striking these chords suggest the possibilities.[57] More empirical research is necessary before the largely Western trained administrative and political elite can be expected

[53] *Statistical Abstract, 1956*, Table 134. [54] Farmer, p. 247.

[55] Farmer, pp. 293-294; Murray Strauss, *ibid.*

[56] Farmer, Ch. 14, for a discussion.

[57] Farmer suggested, among other things, the possibility of utilizing religious motivations more sensitively, pp. 293-294.

to understand with full sympathy the peasant's motivations and know how best to enlist his energies and desires toward greater production.

At the same time, there are often rational economic reasons for peasant resistance to innovations recommended by government authorities. Not infrequently insufficient preliminary laboratory or applied research lies behind the new policy. As B. H. Farmer suggests, for tropical agriculture many of the right technical answers are not yet known and applying the logic and solutions from the temperate zone may only bring more difficulties. After all, the peasant's methods have permitted him to wrest a living, however low, from the same land for nearly a thousand years.[58] Where the margin of survival is so narrow, failure from a mistaken innovation may be far more costly to the peasant, who runs the risk, than to the noncultivator administrative official who advocates the change.

Despite these manifest and persisting difficulties, total rice production improved between 1947 and 1956, perhaps by 30 per cent.[59] Heavy investments in opening new lands, government efforts to demonstrate and communicate newer and improved techniques, cash incentives provided by the Guaranteed Price Scheme, all contributed to this end.[60] Although the growing population absorbed most of the increase during the period, the imports of rice, in fact, declined somewhat until natural disasters in 1956 and 1957 required additional rice imports once more.

During the next decade rice yields may rise considerably as new skills and knowledge become more widely diffused among the peasantry. These are problems of communication, of motivation, of extension service skills, and small scale but dispersed and responsible credit facilities. They do not necessarily require a large capital outlay unless new lands continue to be opened.

Other food crops apart from rice, such as onions, chillies, and certain curry requisites, have been encouraged by the Guaranteed Price Scheme with some success, especially in the Tamil areas, where peasant farmers appear to be more prepared for intensive cultivation and are somewhat more flexible in their approach to land use. There are, no doubt, many possibilities in this direction as well.

Plans to produce cotton and sugar cane on a commercial scale

[58] *Six-Year Programme of Investment*, p. 201.

[59] Though greater improvements are sometimes claimed, these are probably due largely to the use of improved methods of collecting data.

[60] The evidence regarding the distribution of the fruits of the Guaranteed Price Scheme is mixed. For a critical—and empirical—view see Sarkar and Tambiah, pp. 42-43.

in large units are already in progress. By 1957 5,000 acres had been planted in cotton.[61] The broad commitment to the ideal of independent peasant proprietors has raised considerable resistance to alienating Crown lands for large-scale exploitation of such commercial crops. Political incentives have added the excuse of expediency to accustomed practice. Each new settlement brought new voters indebted to the parliamentarian, minister, or party which promoted the project. Large-scale undertakings using agricultural wage labor perpetuated the estate design of employment—in bad odor as foreign enterprise—and ran counter to agricultural traditions; at the same time doing nothing to relieve the pressure of landlessness among land-hungry peasants in the Kandyan or maritime districts. Hence, alternative uses of Crown lands ran into longstanding political difficulties quite apart from the research and experimentation still required.

B. EXPORT CROPS

Although peasant agricultural activities depended heavily upon government action and expenditure, policy toward the estate sector in general was quite different. Tea, for instance, was widely expected to look after its own development. A Tea Research Institute, financed by a tax on tea, has carried on research for many years on diseases, fertilizers, and pruning and has been developing newer strains of tea that promise to raise production by 50 to 100 per cent if increasingly costly replanting can be accomplished. Tea production increased by 35 per cent from 1945 to 1955, although acreage remained virtually the same. This increase was accomplished by more effective control of blister blight, improved fertilizing, pruning, and soil conservation practices. Some new and ultra-modern tea factories have been constructed, but on the whole estate companies have raised their output without plowing back heavy capital resources because of the obvious uncertainties of future government policy toward ownership and capital repatriation.

Rubber, however, has received considerable attention from government policy. During the pre-Korean depression in the rubber market, a thorough study of the industry was made under parliamentary auspices.[62] Methods were found to be conservative, tapping equipment out of date, tappers working fewer trees per day than

[61] *Administration Report of the Director of Agriculture for 1957*, p. 11.
[62] Government of Ceylon, *Report on the Rubber Industry* (Sessional Paper XVIII—1947).

in neighboring competitor countries. Much of the rubber is obsolescent, nearly 70 per cent being over 30 years old. Roughly one-quarter of the rubber acreage was classified as uneconomic on grounds of wages, yields, or net selling prices.[63] In 1947, careful recommendations were formulated for replacing older trees with new, high-yielding strains and transferring uneconomic rubber acres into other types of production. With the Korean boom thoughts of taking land out of rubber quickly faded, but rubber replanting had hardly begun when prices fell once again. The five-year Rice-Rubber Agreement concluded with China in 1952 thenceforth provided a relatively stable and profitable price for a substantial part of the rubber output.[64] A tax on these steady and predictable sales permitted the government to subsidize replanting, providing relatively complete grants to cover costs for small holders with a declining scale of grants for progressively larger acreages. Replanting proceeded at a rate of roughly 13,000 acres a year until by 1957, some 65,000 acres had been renewed with high-yielding clones at very little expense to the government.[65] Yet this represented only one-tenth of the rubber acreage renewed in five years, a rate of renewal which may well not be keeping pace with competitive developments in Malaya and the growing versatility and cheapness of synthetics.

Coconut production has also been the beneficiary of government attention, but it is suggestive of a widespread lack of interest in the problems of coconut growing that data on this third most important crop, and one that produces nearly 5 to 8 per cent of the gross national product, is remarkably imprecise. Even the size of coconut plots is unclear, the ages of coconut trees have not been surveyed in detail although many of them are already beyond their peak capacity. Estimates of annual production vary widely.[66] Considering that one-half the coconut crop is retained for domestic consumption, over 1,000,000 seedlings—or enough to replant 16,000 acres—will have to be planted each year to maintain the present export level and meet the rising home demand.[67]

Since 1948, the Coconut Research Institute has received an annual grant from the government to subsidize the sale of seedlings from high-yielding palms. In 1953, seedlings sufficient to plant 6,000 acres

63 *Ibid.*, and IBRD, p. 239.

64 *Six-Year Programme of Investment*, p. 164.

65 *Ibid.*, also *Administration Report of the Rubber Commissioner* for relevant years.

66 The IBRD disagreed with the Coconut Commissioner on the distribution of different sized plots. IBRD, pp. 245-247.

67 IBRD, p. 250.

were made available to the public, a figure that nearly trebled by 1956.[68] After independence, there was a marked rise in coconut production, attributed mainly to increased use of fertilizers.[69] In 1955 the government established a subsidy scheme to promote fertilizers and reportedly fertilizer deliveries trebled during the first year.[70] Output estimates suggest an increase of 20-25 per cent between 1947 and 1956, a not inconsiderable improvement.[71] Yet it was barely keeping up with the population growth during the period.

Hence, in terms of improved agricultural output, the one-third of the government's development expenditure that went for agricultural purposes can be said to have done slightly better than keep pace with the growing population. This has neither materially freed Ceylon from dependence upon imports, nor has the national agricultural product per capita noticeably increased. There are still many ways of improving the yields of traditional crops on present acreage. Cultivated lands can be expanded. Agricultural diversification can also be undertaken if new crops are tried. Cotton, sugar cane, peanuts, jute, hemp, cashew nuts, cacao, spices, and other crops for domestic food, for industrial raw materials, and for export can all be introduced or production greatly increased. These can reduce Ceylon's import bill, provide a wider range of export products, make the island less vulnerable to foreign fluctuations in prices for her three major products.

C. INFRASTRUCTURE INVESTMENT

Irrigation and agriculture received the largest development appropriations, but transport, communications, and other necessary "infrastructure" facilities were not neglected. Nearly one-fourth of development funds went to these purposes. Though impressive to the eye and essential for middle- and long-run development, their short-run contribution to productivity is often relatively slight.[72]

Ceylon was already well endowed with a transport network at independence. Nevertheless, arrears of expenditure during the depression and war years had to be made good. Parts of the country

[68] *Six-Year Programme of Investment*, p. 167. National Planning Council, *First Interim Report*, p. 14.

[69] Census of Agriculture, Part III—*Coconut Plantations*, p. 10.

[70] National Planning Council, *First Interim Report*, p. 13.

[71] Census of Agriculture, Part III, p. 10, compared with its own figures elsewhere and National Planning Council, *ibid.*, p. 11.

[72] 25.5 per cent of estimated investment expenditure under the Six-Year Programme were allocated to the Ministry of Transport and Works, p. 24.

outside the Jaffna Peninsula, the wet zone estate areas, and the Colombo district needed new roads. Roads also needed widening and a new bridge across the Kelani Ganga constructed with Colombo Plan assistance was expected to alleviate serious congestion at the outskirts of the capital. Railroad rolling stock needed renewing, roadbeds had to be reconstructed, new rails and railroad signal systems installed. Although private bus operators had rapidly extended bus services, profits were high, actual service poor, and popular resentment against the bus operators widespread. Fulfilling a pledge made during the 1956 election, the Government of Mr. Bandaranaike nationalized the nation's bus lines in early 1958. Schedules were regularized and heavy investment made in new equipment, but costs outran income and an annual subsidy proved necessary.

The Port of Colombo received heavy investments. Reflecting its central position in the Indian Ocean and its heavy import and export traffic, Colombo Harbor has often handled larger tonnages than any other Indian Ocean port, topping Bombay often and Singapore, Calcutta, Madras, Cochin, and Rangoon regularly.[73] Though providing a safe artificial harbor for over fifty ocean-going vessels, Colombo Harbor at independence had to load and unload all cargoes and passengers by means of lighters and launches. Only oil tankers had quay-side facilities; all others anchored in the roadstead. As a result, when import, export, and transit tonnages rose rapidly after World War II, the port became seriously congested. A French construction firm contracted to provide a dozen alongside berths for freighters and passenger vessels, with nearby warehouses facilitating rapid loading, unloading, and turnarounds. These should eventually lead to a removal of a 25 per cent freight surcharge for Colombo consignments and reduce heavy annual expenditure of foreign exchange on overtime demurrage on delayed cargoes.

Despite delays, by late 1956 much of the basic investment in deep-water berths and related warehouses was completed.[74] Unfortunately, the port handled less cargo in 1956 and 1957 than in previous years because of a series of strikes precipitated by competing unions and justified grievances of the work force.[75] Competing lighterage and stevedoring firms and divided responsibilities in the port's administration added difficulties. In August 1958 the port was nationalized,

[73] IBRD, pp. 610-611.

[74] IBRD, pp. 611-620.

[75] For a recent government report, see *Report of the Commission of Inquiry on the Working of the Commercial Sector of the Port of Colombo* (Sessional Paper II—1957). *Administration Report of the Commissioner of Labour for 1957*, pp. 23-24.

but strikes and disorders continued, and a long queue of ships continued to grace the entrance to the harbor. In the spring of 1959, however, there were signs that the port was once more operating at greater efficiency and freight and demurrage costs were likely to come down.

The largest single allocation for capital improvements for Transport and Works under the Six-Year Programme of Investment—roughly one-third—was directed toward power development, mainly hydroelectric. The core of immediate development was the completion of the Laksapana works in the lower reaches of Central Province. Begun in the 1920's, the project was halted during the depression and work was not resumed until after World War II when Laksapana received relatively high priority. The International Bank for Reconstruction and Development has advanced a loan covering foreign exchange costs of part of these improvements. Altogether, when this multiphase project is completed, some 300,000,000 KWH will be brought in, more than twice the output of 1957.[76] In addition to the Gal Oya powerhouse, that could provide perhaps 40,000,000 KWH if costs of linking to the national grid are warranted, and to a thermal plant to be constructed at Grandpass, there is under discussion the picturesquely named Seven Virgins project in the same district as Laksapana. This would produce between 420,000,000 and 600,000,000 KWH, depending upon the rain conditions, at a probable cost of Rs. 225,000,000 initial investment.[77] Several multipurpose river valley projects are also being investigated. Hence, a considerable increase in power supply can be foreseen for the next decade as long as sufficient technical and financial resources are applied to the task.

Apart from the construction let under contract for part of the Colombo Harbor development, specific segments of the Laksapana hydrel scheme, irrigation works, and the Kelani Ganga bridge, the bulk of Ceylon's capital investments were constructed by the Public Works Department. Like public works departments throughout South and Southeast Asia, demands made upon the P.W.D. grew enormously as development investment gathered way. Not only were the normal responsibilities of the P.W.D.—road and bridge construction—carried forward at an increased tempo, hospitals, school

[76] For a detailed discussion, see IBRD, pp. 473-476.

[77] For proposals as of 1957, see National Planning Council, *First Interim Report*, pp. 107-108.

construction, the University of Ceylon's new site, buildings of all kinds, a water supply for Colombo, and sewerage disposal systems were all undertaken by the P.W.D. Much of the designing and actual work had to be done by the department's own administration, since contractors lacked the heavy equipment and often the skilled personnel required for some of the projects.[78]

It is therefore not to be wondered at that loan fund expenditures for construction often fell far behind schedule. Underspending throughout the government on loan funds amounted to roughly 37 per cent on the average during the first seven years of independence, a good part of it probably because of difficulties in the heavily overloaded Public Works Department.[79]

At the end of the decade of independence, despite arrears in completing projects, economic infrastructure in the basic fields of communication, transportation, of government building for necessary services, and harbor development were well along. The needs outstanding were in the fields of power development, in providing safe water and sewerage disposal, and the assured access to power, water, and industrial sites that underlie factory growth.

D. INDUSTRIAL POLICY

1. *Government effort.* Policy toward industrialization has been less steady and fewer resources have been allocated to the truly revolutionary enterprise of establishing in agricultural Ceylon a large industrial component. Although there has been a great deal written and said about industrial development—in the press, in magazines, in parliament, and at the university—only 6 per cent of the proposed government expenditure was directed toward industrial enterprises under the government's investment program submitted to the Colombo Plan organization in 1950.[80] After that there was no further increase in industrial expenditure until 1957-58 when the new M.E.P. government decided to raise the loan fund expenditure for industrial investment. It is too soon to fully appraise the results of this decision.

Wartime shortages of essential imports gave an impetus to the market side of government-sponsored industrial enterprises, though up-to-date machinery was often unobtainable and the plants had

[78] IBRD, pp. 655-657; *Six-Year Programme*, p. 58.

[79] *Six-Year Programme*, p. 55.

[80] Cmd. 8080, p. 29; *Six-Year Programme* industrial allocations accounted for 4.5 per cent of total planned expenditure, p. 32.

to operate with a good deal of improvisation. Factories to produce plywood, acetic acid, pharmaceuticals, rolled steel, ceramics, glass, and leather goods were started. To those Ceylonese who argued the urgent necessity of industrialization, mostly on the Left at the outset, these plants appeared to be the forerunners of the future. During the war, political consensus developed in favor of continuing and expanding the government-managed industrial sector.[81]

The first budget speech of the independent government in 1948 furthered this concept. Seeking to "reorganize" the wartime factories "on more modern lines," the government had already begun to construct a large cement factory and proposed to establish steel, caustic soda, hydrogenated coconut oil, textile, paper and sugar factories. It was expected that employment would be provided for 18,500 people and imports of these items would be reduced by Rs. 100,000,000, by the investment of an estimated Rs. 130,000,000.[82] It was held that "basic industries," such as steel and cement, and "industries which supply the necessities of life," should be state-owned. As for the private sector, the government invited the investment of private capital—Ceylonese or foreign—and agreed to provide industrial research, establish pilot factories, and "whatever help is necessary for private capital to increase the national wealth."[83]

As long as wartime conditions prevailed, foreign goods remained scarce and state-operated factories collectively showed a net profit. But already by 1947 the government was reviewing their operation with the idea of modernizing and reorganizing them because of recurring deficits in almost every case. A few years later a Parliamentary Commission investigated these extended wartime enterprises. Costs were found to be high not merely because of the improvised equipment, but many administrative anomalies impeded their functioning. Procurement regulations hindered prompt replacements in response to production breakdowns. Traditional Treasury personnel regulations made it difficult to reward unusually good performance and protected time-servers. Remarkably small contingency funds were the rule. Cost accounting was rare, largely because of a lack of cost accountants on the island. Budgeting was often grossly unrealistic.[84] It seemed probable that the low esteem attributed to

[81] Oliver traces these developments of economic opinion in detail. Chs. 3, 4.

[82] *House of Representatives*, V. 3, c. 1043-1044 and Appendix D to No. 16.

[83] *Ibid.*, c. 1045-1046.

[84] *Report of the Commission on Government Commercial Undertakings* (Sessional Paper XIX—1953), pp. 21-26.

commerce explained the niggardly Treasury provision for sales and promotional activities. Few government servants appeared to become readily identified with "their" product or were prepared to engage in the seemingly undignified activities associated with effective commercial promotion.

Quality weaknesses were also marked. Importers were required by the Industrial Products Act to purchase a quota of government-produced articles as a prerequisite for having their import licenses renewed. They tended to conceal the home-produced article in the back of their stores, covering their additional costs by higher mark-ups on their imported and readily saleable articles. Sufficiently rigorous quality control proved difficult to administer.

These data refer to the commercial undertakings begun during the war under emergency conditions, when machinery was lacking, and staffs were recruited hastily and overworked. Difficulties were to be expected and losses likely when peacetime conditions returned. Unhappily, during the decade of independence, the record of newer government enterprises was not much better. Despite the announced policy of developing government basic industries, progress after 1947 was discouragingly slow. By 1952, five years after the policy had been adopted in principle, "the only post-war factory the government had completed was the cement plant initially scheduled much earlier and begun in 1946."[85] The paper factory was then under construction, and contracts had been let for the caustic soda plant and the coconut oil mill. The proposed steel mill and the textile factories were still in the planning stage.

By 1956, though output lagged behind promise for the cement and certain reorganized wartime factories, production figures were not negligible. The cement plant, for instance, produced roughly 60,000 tons of cement in 1952, a figure raised to 83,000 tons by 1956. The plywood factory produced in 1956 over 7,400,000 square feet of plywood for 10 per cent of the national requirements of tea chests and for other purposes at improving efficiency and technical quality. The reorganized leather products industry produced 23,000 pairs of shoes and 270,000 lbs. of tanned leather.[86] These instances show a not unsatisfactory relation between capital invested and annual output

[85] Oliver, p. 83. For detailed discussion of different industries, see IBRD, pp. 531ff.

[86] *Administration Report of the Director of Industries for 1956*, pp. 6-7. A ceramics plant reportedly produced 250 tons of utility crockery, but glazes continued to give difficulty and sales figures were not available.

values. Together, the three industries identified provided work opportunities for 1,000 workers.

But these three productive enterprises were the exception, representing less than half the funds expended. Three other plants originally committed on a policy basis in 1947 and scheduled for completion by 1952—paper, caustic soda, and coconut oil milling—were not yet in commercial operation by 1956, although over Rs. 57,000,000 had been already incurred on their behalf.

A variety of factors contributed to the generally disappointing results of these government industrial efforts. Capital works were behind schedule, delaying the preparation of sites and construction. The International Bank for Reconstruction and Development Mission itself contributed to retarding the activation of the paper plant and the coconut oil mill, by advocating further research into raw materials for paper and the improvement of existing facilities for coconut oil milling in preference to proceeding with a new and already redundant enterprise. Lack of clear political continuity at the top deterred vigorous action when construction and operation difficulties were encountered. There was no permanent head of the Department of Industries during much of the period and there were four Ministers of Industries in the course of five years.[87] External difficulties, too, stood in the way. Rapid industrial expansion in countries normally supplying the capital machinery for the proposed plants delayed deliveries and rising equipment prices abroad necessitated frequent revision of plans.[88]

The International Bank for Reconstruction and Development called attention to another difficulty which applied to both industrial construction and operation. "What is not yet fully appreciated is that the application of industrial technology in all its forms is deficient in Ceylon for historical reasons . . . technical knowledge is the very essence of industry, extending all the way from top planning and administration down to the daily duties of supervisors and skilled workmen."[89] Academically trained engineering graduates, themselves numerically insufficient, found it difficult to translate into concrete acts the theoretical knowledge they had learned at foreign universities and were learning in Ceylon. Practical information already available in certain government laboratories was not com-

87 *Report of the Commission on Government Commercial Undertakings*, p. 84.
88 *Economic and Social Development of Ceylon*, p. 48.
89 IBRD, pp. 520-521.

municated to designers, planners, and plant managers.[90] Because the concrete knowledge of designs, transport and operating costs and practical possibilities was limited to a relatively few, there was a congestion of decisions at the top. Successive foreign advisers sometimes gave conflicting advice, necessitating altered plans and further delays. The widespread lack of qualified managerial personnel necessitated importing technicians from abroad who took time to become acclimated and to learn the fine art of manipulating an intricate government apparatus on behalf of novel industrial undertakings. In government agricultural programs, almost all higher civil servants, and many government workers in intermediate grades, themselves had some personal, though often rudimentary, knowledge of the agricultural or irrigational activities they were administering. But a working understanding of industrial problems permitting the use of practical judgment at all levels of administration was not frequently encountered. Such a deficiency could not be overcome merely by the application of capital or the drawing up of plans.

Hence, for a variety of political, technical, and administrative reasons, government-sponsored industrial ventures during the postwar era were disappointing, although the cement factory and the plywood factory were successes.

2. *Private industrial effort.* In the beginning, government policy called for the encouraging of private enterprise to participate in the economic development of the country in less "basic" lines, but there was some uncertainty whether departmental practice actually worked toward that end. Sporadically the Ministry of Industries announced its intention of itself entering a wide variety of activities, thus discouraging prospective private entrepreneurs from even considering those specific fields. The wartime plants were kept in operation under subsidy in competition with several struggling private ones, particularly in the tannery business. Even before public funds were invested in the coconut oil mill, the country was already supplied with milling capacity sufficient to process the whole of the island's available coconut crop.[91]

Uncertainty came, too, from the government's policy toward foreign industrial capital. One important incident with a foreign shoe firm left a deep impression on local enterprisers. With official

[90] IBRD, p. 543. *Report of the Commission on Government Commercial Undertakings*, p. 88.

[91] IBRD, pp. 512-513, quoted with apparent approval in the *Report of the Taxation Commission.*

support from the Ministry of Industries and capital participation by several leading public figures, a group of local entrepreneurs opened a shoe factory. Shortly thereafter an agreement was reached with the Bata Shoe Company to open a branch factory near Colombo. The capital and machinery at the disposal of the Bata works from abroad were superior to those resources the local men could command and the managerial staff more experienced. Accordingly, the sums invested by local enterprisers had to be written off. A substantial number of individuals had participated, and the effects of their losses in this one project appear to have discouraged them from new ventures.

Despite these governmental disincentives to private entrepreneurship, other aspects of policy favored local industry. The government's tariff policy was basically designed to protect "infant industries." Although, according to the International Bank for Reconstruction and Development Mission, the Industrial Products Act deterred high quality performance, it guaranteed a market for most locally manufactured goods. Tax incentives for investors were also provided.[92]

Institutional limitations were notable. The deficiencies in technology that dogged the government enterprises also slowed entrepreneurial activity, though the entrepreneur, once embarked on a venture, had more urgent incentives for finding answers to technical difficulties than his government servant counterpart. Facilities for obtaining medium- and long-term credit were inadequate. Commercial banks concentrated on short-term, import-export lending. Contentious land titles and insufficient real assets reduced possible loan collateral.[93] Occasionally, short-term overdrafts for industrial raw material imports were allowed. But for capital equipment and industrial investment more generally, the International Bank for Reconstruction and Development reported that "the island now has no agencies whatsoever from which a local industrial operator can get the long-term credit he needs."[94]

Even if such institutional deficiencies were remedied, many doubted that entrepreneurs would come forward in large enough numbers and with sufficient vigor to open enough new and hitherto untried industrial ventures. The Ceylonese have a reputation for being cautious and unadventuresome.

[92] *Report of the Taxation Commission*, p. 228, though a higher rate was urged.

[93] *Six-Year Programme of Investment*, p. 265.

[94] IBRD, p. 518. The Bank of Ceylon and a government credit institution were not in themselves sufficient.

There were, of course, good economic reasons why this should have been so. What liquid investment funds were available went into agricultural investments, the acquisition of estates, and participation in estate share companies. Though part of this may be attributed to customary preferences for land holding, estate investment can return up to 20 per cent per year. Levels of return have been high for decades, with only a few extended periods of difficulty. Share participation began in reliable foreign estate companies and the pattern has been taken over to a limited extent in reference to Ceylonese estate companies, too.

The management of tea and rubber estates offers few unfamiliar problems. Local owners are well able to judge the competence of estate supervisors; technology has not changed so rapidly as to put mature owners "at the mercy" of young technicians. By comparison, industrial investment is economically risky, technologically uncertain, and operated on a relatively rapid production sequence that may require prompt decisions on the basis of unfamiliar criteria. Individuals who make good through industrial enterprise often transfer a large part of their capital into estate activities where security is higher and where higher social status is given the man who owns estates. Even entrepreneurs who have already arrived in a social sense, and therefore are not seeking social acceptance, tend to retain the bulk of their resources in estate enterprise and use only part of their resources for industrial activity.

Commerce, too, is a preferred activity. If social (or sometimes political) contacts are right, it is relatively easy for a person to establish himself as an agent for the import of some foreign product such as tractors, motor cars, radios, or other equipment or consumption articles. Profits are high—up to 20-25 per cent. Returns on a specific outlay are quick and such business activity requires a minimum of intimate, prolonged, and technical supervision for maximum profit.

Corporate financing for industrial or commercial activities is rare, in part because of considerable distrust in the business community. Family firms tend to be the overwhelming norm.[95] But it may be that the personal qualities associated with entrepreneurship are the essentials, regardless of the form of business organization or whether such individuals are to be found in the business house or government office. Japanese and Indian experience, for instance, suggests that family firms can become highly productive when in-

[95] *Report of the Taxation Commission,* p. 80.

fused with a dynamic, exploratory attitude, and a readiness to bear the responsibility for the calculated risks. The International Bank for Reconstruction and Development reported that in Ceylon, on the contrary, there were "far too few businessmen with that initiative, resourcefulness and daring which leads to the search for new productive opportunities and to their successful exploitation."[96]

From the government's point of view, there were certain political hazards in attempting to provide all the incentives necessary to lure private entrepreneurship into those channels most desired by the politically articulate. The local capitalist suffers by his association in the public eye with the usurious village money lender or the foreign "capitalist exploiter." The notion of maximizing profit is frowned on from the standards of both the traditional Buddhist culture and Marx's more recent analysis. Often, the "capitalist" enterpriser has thoroughly adopted a Western style of life. In Ceylon and in other countries that have not experienced a full industrial development, the most active entrepreneurs are frequently members of minority communities. Karavas, Salagamas, and Duravas among the Sinhalese, and Ceylon Tamils formed the bulk of the business and entrepreneurial community. Measures designed to induce entrepreneurship tended in the short run to favor members of these communities who were more eager to seize the opportunities provided than was the majority Sinhalese community.

Nevertheless, despite these characteristics that appear to limit the effectiveness of the entrepreneurs and the possible political liabilities of giving them greater incentives, the U.N.P. government in 1954 changed the emphasis of its industrialization policy. No doubt the growing awareness of the government's difficulties in initiating and running large-scale industrial ventures and its greater financial stringency led to a closer scrutiny of government expenditures and a search for more economical ways of achieving industrial growth. Perhaps the entrepreneurial community itself was able to press its case with greater persuasiveness after the searching reports of the Commission on Government Commercial Undertakings, the Taxation Commission, and the International Bank for Reconstruction and Development. For whatever reasons, the government sought to relieve its administrators of managerial functions in the heavy industry field and to encourage private initiative.

[96] IBRD, p. 773; see also B. B. das Gupta, "The Theory and Reality of Economic Development," Central Bank of Ceylon, *Bulletin*, v, 11 (Nov. 1955), pp. 5-10.

Whereas earlier policy had emphasized capital-intensive "basic" industries built and run by the government, the new policy sought to promote a variety of relatively small-scale enterprises with an eye to creating more employment opportunities out of limited capital factors and raising rural incomes through more cottage industries. Consumer industries were to be encouraged by government sponsorship and share participation in cooperation with private entrepreneurs, by government loans, or by guaranteeing bank credit.[97] Several of the hitherto government-operated industrial enterprises were reorganized to enable their gradual transfer to private hands. The plywood, caustic soda, cement, leather, ceramics, paper, and coconut oil factories were set up as semi-independent public corporations relinquishing to private Boards of Directors the management responsibility.[98] Following the advice of the Taxation Commission, tax exemption allowances for initial plant costs were increased, bonus share issues were exempted from taxation, import duties on capital goods and raw materials were reduced. Efforts to lure foreign capital had not proved successful, not merely because of the shortage of investment capital abroad but also because of a certain ambiguity in government policy and previous administrative delays in processing applications. An authoritative cabinet statement on government policy in respect to private foreign investment in Ceylon was presented to Parliament in May 1955, setting forth the general principles by which foreign capital would be welcomed and the procedures investors should follow in presenting their requests.[99]

The International Bank for Reconstruction and Development had emphasized technical and credit deficiencies. Accordingly, in 1955 the government established the Ceylon Institute of Scientific and Industrial Research analogous to similar technical research institutes in Central and South American countries. It was designed to pursue problems of applied technology of utility to government and private industry. The Development Finance Corporation was also founded to encourage and speed investment in new industries. These were, of course, long term in their intent, and results could not be expected promptly. By 1957 requests to the Institute of Scientific and Industrial Research had more than doubled over the previous

97 *Six-Year Programme of Investment*, pp. 238-241.

98 *Administration Report of the Director of Industries for 1956*, pp. 6-8.

99 Ministry of Finance, *Government Policy in Respect of Private Foreign Investment in Ceylon* (July 1955).

year and the Development Corporation had a handful of worthwhile projects already under consideration.

During 1955 and 1956, there were certain apparent results of these policies, though some of the new activities had been contemplated somewhat earlier. British, Danish, and Japanese firms cooperated with Ceylonese firms in joint ventures in the chemical, food processing, and clothing industry. Ceylonese firms began manufacturing new types of building material, aluminum ware, and bicycle frames.

Such evidence of entrepreneurial readiness suggested that there might be more possibilities in this direction than doctrinaire critics had been prepared to admit. And the testing period for these policies was admittedly short. Compared to the rising population, however, these new enterprises were few in number and the opportunities they opened for productive employment gave little promise of solving, in the short run, the manifest problem of insufficient employment opportunities.

In any case, developments after the 1956 election tended to create an atmosphere to discourage rather than speed entrepreneurial venture. Although the Prime Minister and the Minister of Finance sought to encourage foreign investment, other ministers publicly urged the nationalization of the tea and rubber estates. Numerous and extended strikes reduced effective man-days of work and added further uncertainties.[100] Days lost in industrial disputes more than doubled between 1956 and 1958. Communal disorders and tardy emergency police measures weakened confidence and disrupted civil life. Natural events—droughts and floods—by upsetting home production, increased import requirements, reducing proportionately the foreign exchange available for capital imports.

Apart from the talk of "nationalization" which added special disquiet to the private sector, the other sources of uncertainty that marked 1957 and 1958 affected government, as much as private, enterprise. Only a continued rise in tea output and a bumper crop of rice in Ceylon and in supplying countries in the Indian Ocean area prevented these difficulties from precipitating grave financial dislocations in 1958.

Despite the disappointing progress in the field of industrialization

100 Economic Commission for Asia and the Far East, *Economic Survey of Asia and the Far East 1957*, p. 19.

PLANTER'S WIFE

Courtesy of the *Ceylon Observer*

The Minister of Finance seeks to lure British capital to the island while the Minister of Agriculture scares it away by talk of nationalization.

so far, there are no doubt many possibilities for replacing imports of construction and consumption goods. Cement, hollow bricks, quality tiles on the construction side; salt, sugar refining, textiles, kaolin clay, flashlight batteries and electric bulbs, bicycle frames, metal containers, kitchen utensils, and simple but improved farm implements, etc. can all be produced for the domestic market. Though the cash sale price may be somewhat higher than the imported article in many instances, the additional costs may be more than offset by the long-run reduction in foreign exchange costs and the aggregate opportunities for putting hitherto underemployed or unemployed workers into productive activities. The national profit or loss will depend in large part upon the ingenuity with which capital and supervisory overheads are held down and worker effort and regularity can be enlisted.

Additional export industries, such as manufacturing rubber products, processing peanut, cashew, and other vegetable oils, food canning, mining ilmenite and monazite sands, can be foreseen. Perhaps industries processing imported materials and utilizing Ceylon's advantageous location in relation to Indian Ocean markets, might eventually be undertaken. Success in industrialization will depend upon Ceylonese developing the necessary motivation and acquiring greater managerial, technical, and marketing skills. These human elements are as important as the more easily measured and controlled direction and rate of capital investment. In these respects, perhaps as much can be learned from Japan and India as from the industrialized Western nations.

V · PLANNING

These policies designed to promote economic development in its various aspects were undertaken without the elaborate and inclusive Five-Year Plan that has become *de rigueur* in most underdeveloped countries seeking through government initiative to speed economic development. Early U.N.P. governments spoke much of planning. Indeed, in all sectors of the political spectrum, "planning" was a universal plus term that no one seriously questioned. The Indian Five-Year Plans were often referred to as models of what should be done. Until 1959 no detailed, inclusive plan had been elaborated. Technical, political, and other impediments appeared to stand in the way.

Systematic planning was hampered by a widespread feeling that, as a small island vulnerable to all manner of outside influences, Ceylon was at the mercy of economic and other forces that could never be controlled. The fall and rise and fall again of foreign assets after World War II and the Korean boom confirmed the pre-war recollection of instability, of an unpredictable and rapidly altering future. Many felt that planning exercises would prove illusory, that good times should be used to accumulate large liquid reserves for the unpredictable but inescapable hard times that were bound to come again. The firm advocates of planning argued to the contrary, that precisely because Ceylon's economy remained so susceptible to fluctuations originating from outside, planning was essential. It represented an indispensable ordering of priorities and of all too scarce resources if development toward greater productivity, diversity, and equality was to be successfully accomplished.

During the early days of independence, Ceylonese leaders were aware of the obvious tasks before them—land needed to be cleared, agriculture needed encouragement, Colombo Harbor had to be rapidly improved, a multipurpose river valley scheme was obviously worthwhile. There was money for all these endeavors and all were embarked upon, in addition to expanded school and health facilities. The first prime minister, Mr. D. S. Senanayake, appears to have had little faith in elaborate intellectual preparations before undertaking the manifestly necessary. The difficult problems of priority in the use of scarce resources were not sharply posed during his premiership. A subcommittee of the cabinet was established as early as 1948 to draft a plan for the country's economic objectives and resources. But nothing resulted from that committee.[101] There was a six-year plan submitted to the Commonwealth Consultative Committee of the Colombo Plan in September 1950, setting gross targets for Ceylon's capital investment program, but this was in no way comparable to India's detailed proposals.[102]

Continuing the practices developed under the Donoughmore Constitution, each minister evolved his own proposals as he saw fit, asking for much and allocating funds received to the best economic or political advantage. Each minister was said to push his own favorite schemes by trying to do "everything at the highest possible level," i.e. with the prime minister himself.[103] As long as the prime minister retained the principal coordinating function without elaborate advice from a planning secretariat, in addition to taking such economic counsel as he chose from the Minister of Finance or the Central Bank, he was relatively free to trim the proportions of the budget as the political winds required. In a plural society, with universal franchise but without disciplined parties, the prime minister's ability to hold a minister to his side or to ensure the support of a whole community might depend in considerable part upon the direction of impressive allocations. The ordinary government M.P., too, believing that his political future might well depend upon his ability

[101] Referred to by both D. S. Senanayake and S.W.R.D. Bandaranaike in *House of Representatives*, V. 10, c. 1553; V. 16, c. 1135.

[102] Cmd. 8080, Ch. VI.

[103] *House of Representatives*, V. 8, c. 1593. For greater detail, with considerable polemic intent on both sides, see V. 10, c. 1402 and 1553, exchange between Mr. Bandaranaike and Mr. D. S. Senanayake.

to obtain a better hospital, school, or an improved irrigation channel for his constituents, might well be dubious in private though publicly in favor of more "planning."

The second prime minister was intellectually more sympathetic to "planning" than the first, but his term of office was beset with economic difficulties culminating in the "hartal" and his cabinet was divided. Had he mastered the cabinet divisions and remained in office another year or two, more elaborate planning might have been undertaken. In the spring of 1953 a planning committee of the cabinet was established, but there was insufficient time or solidarity for it to produce results.

Under Sir John Kotelawala, a planning secretariat was finally established with four public servants as its complement. In 1955, a *Six-Year Programme of Investment* emerged. It was frankly a limited document. It claimed only to describe the details of investment made by the government sector. The investment programs of the different government departments were listed, compared, and discussed; the total costs were computed in relation to probable resources available. It was largely a passive document, drawing together in a single presentation departmental proposals. It did not define objectives and specify means in such a way as to inspire extra effort by the general public or the public service. Yet it did attempt to justify the bent of government development policy. Avoiding the clichés of both Marxist analysis and the free enterprise enthusiasts, it included a first class economics dissertation on the problems of developing Ceylon's economy and alternative possible approaches to their solution.

Hailed by the press on its publication, within a year it suffered the fate of the government that had sponsored it and was liberally criticized for its limitations. In April 1956, when the U.N.P. was swept from power and the M.E.P. set up a new government, the cabinet repudiated the investment program of its predecessor. Five months later a planning council was established, composed of five ministers and seven leading citizens. The prime minister was nominal chairman, but was so deeply engaged in communal difficulties that the parliamentary secretary to the Minister of Defense and External Affairs acted on his behalf. Prepared by a series of committees drawn from activists in the public service, the business community, and the university, a first interim report appeared in July 1957. This document analyzed the possibilities for development in such fields as export industries, rice, and other domestic food production, power output and industrial development. Though less inclusive than its predecessor, the technical, human, budgetary, and other problems and specific productive goals in the chosen fields were more closely examined and requirements specified.

By 1957, a growing body of opinion appeared to favor more effective planning for its broader public implications. It was argued that if business and public servants participated jointly in the preparation of a plan, the former would think more in terms of the national economic challenge while the latter would consider more realistically and sympathetically the aims and needs of those not "in the service." Perhaps as important, it might provide a rationale for resisting the parochial demands of electoral districts, influential individuals, or pressure groups. By its more specific definition of means it might contribute to greater national solidarity. In times of communal tension, of growing competition between groups for status and income, a plan might provide alternative purposes and give a sense of hope for the future that would reduce antagonisms. Differences as to how development should proceed might impede agreement on a specific detailed plan and might precipitate divisions of a doctrinal, ideological kind. Administered by government officials used to the supervisory and accountable functions of a "law and order" government, a detailed plan might in fact impede and constrict effort rather than promote and release it. In 1959, a more ambitious Ten-Year Plan was published, but specific short-term operational programs had not been made public. It remained to be seen whether it would have sufficient manifest merit to be defended from political storms. Would it be implemented with vigor?

VI · FOREIGN AID

From 1950 onwards, Ceylon received comparatively large numbers of technical experts through the Colombo Plan and United Nations. Of all the countries participating in the Colombo Plan, Ceylon was the most eager to obtain technical experts. Between 1950 and 1956, the government applied for 322 experts and received 211.[104] Ceylonese officials were entirely used to working with British technicians in the government service. Officials in the Finance Ministry concerned with the search for outside assistance were unusually adept

[104] By comparison, India sought 180 and received 110. The Colombo Plan, *Report for 1955-56 by the Council for Technical Cooperation in South and Southeast Asia,* November 1956, Appendix I.

at communicating departmental needs to likely foreign countries where such experts might be found. The small size of the departments favored applications for experts, since the men in touch with the foreign governments could easily discuss their needs directly with departmental personnel. The larger India and the less organized Pakistan inevitably had more difficulties defining the skills required and presenting firm requests to those charged with seeking outside assistance. But to some observers, officials in certain areas of government seemed unduly prone to look abroad for help in solving a problem that was already well within their own grasp.[105] The experts demanded were mainly in the medical and health fields, engineering, fisheries, industry, trade, and education.

From 1951-52 to 1956-57, Ceylon received roughly Rs. 99,000,000 worth of grants through the Colombo Plan. These were for technical experts; for capital assistance in developing medical facilities; a fish freezing and processing plant and railroad equipment from Canada; tractor stations from Australia for extensive areas in the dry zone; high tension wires and standards to connect the Gal Oya generators to the national grid; and a Canadian aerial survey team for mapping land use. Part of these funds were allocated to meet the costs of over 700 Ceylonese who received technical training overseas.[106]

American assistance was limited to its share in the United Nations Technical Assistance Program. Through the United Nations more than thirty experts were active in Ceylon at one time and a number of Ceylonese were studying abroad. Ceylon itself was being used as a training ground for South Asian administrators to study public health administration, particularly malaria control, low-cost housing and the development of cooperatives.[107]

Substantial American aid did not begin until 1956. A General Agreement for Technical Cooperation had been reached between Washington and Colombo as early as 1950, but only a few health technicians were assigned before the "Battle Act" precluded the American administration from making further assistance available. By 1955 political developments within the United States permitted the government to consider Ceylon as again eligible for American aid despite its continuing trade with China. Preliminary negotiations were undertaken and in the early months of 1956 a $5,000,000 aid

105 Interviews with Ceylon government servants and visiting experts.

106 Rupee figures from Table 20, Central Bank of Ceylon, *Annual Report 1957*. Number of trainees from Colombo Plan, *ibid.* Appendix I.

107 UN Technical Assistance Board reports, unpublished.

program was announced for that year. This was increased by 1958/1959 to $25,000,000 including $20,000,000 of food transfers under Public Law 480 authorizations, a $3,250,000 loan by the Development Loan Fund and $1,400,000 in technical assistance.

American technical and capital assistance concentrated on a limited number of projects designed to inject technical skills and capital at crucial places. It assisted the Irrigation Department in developing an expanded repair shop for training technicians in the care and operation of earth-moving and engineering equipment, and loan funds were made available to help complete irrigation projects planned or already under way. Other activities included an improved railroad signal system to ease commuter congestion and modernizing the P.W.D.'s equipment and procedures. The School of Engineering at the University of Ceylon was expanded and through contract agreement with an American engineering college, a more immediately applicable curriculum was being applied. A rapid graduation of practical engineers and of agricultural and machine technicians should promote both agricultural and industrial development. Agricultural research, a thorough survey of physical resources, and science training in the schools have been receiving attention.[108] In 1957 it was decided to survey the Mahaweli Ganga river valley as a possible site for a multipurpose project harnessing Ceylon's greatest river for dry zone irrigation, flood control, and electricity production.[109] Through CARE, flour and milk from American agricultural surpluses were distributed to all school children, a renewal of the free school snack eliminated in 1953. Larger transfers of flour and rice went into normal supply channels for commercial distribution against counterpart accumulation.

In late 1956, foreign assistance from Communist countries began. A trade agreement with Czechoslovakia provided a long-term, low-interest credit for the purchase of capital equipment. A cement plant proposal, surveyed by Czech engineers at the request of the Minister of Industries, was to be supplied with Czech machinery on the basis of an eight-year 3 per cent interest capital loan.[110]

The Rice-Rubber Agreement with China was renewed in 1957. It called for sharply reduced deliveries of Ceylonese rubber at world market prices. But the Chinese agreed to grant aid in the form of

108 *Ceylon Daily News*, June 29, 1956.

109 *Ibid.*, May 3, 1957; January 28, 1958.

110 Central Bank, *Annual Report of the Monetary Board to the Minister of Finance for 1956*, p. 10; *The Wall Street Journal*, October 8, 1957.

commodities exported from China at world market prices to the amount of Rs. 15 million annually for five years, the proceeds from counterpart sales to be earmarked to help finance the Rubber Re-Planting Subsidy Scheme.[111] In early 1958, the Soviet Union agreed to provide a $30,000,000 line of credit at 2.5 per cent for capital equipment purchases.[112]

In response to the serious floods that disrupted agricultural production in many areas during December 1957 and burst through important dams and irrigation works under construction, assistance of many kinds flowed to Ceylon. India, Great Britain, and the United States were the promptest, bringing by ships, planes, and helicopters needed relief, and medical and food supplies. Supplies in smaller quantities arrived from other countries, too.

Thus, by the end of 1957, in addition to Colombo Plan assistance, Ceylon was receiving substantial aid from outside the Commonwealth in the form of food supplies, technical assistance, capital equipment, emergency aid, and long-term credits. These aggregates of foreign resources could be expected to ease her balance of payments position and speed the pace of development in key sectors of the economy, particularly in the fields of infrastructure investment, technical skills, and administrative management.

VII · DEVELOPMENT AND POLITICAL POWER

Most of the literature on economic development tends to assume a political vacuum. Economic development, however, has implications for the distribution of domestic political power. To exercise the spending power of government is bound to influence the following of the man responsible for disbursing funds. This is especially so in a country where men live close to the margin of poverty and where traditional modes of relationship give prominence and a sense of indebtedness to a leading person rather than to a public institution. Government activities that offer careers and opportunities to the able and ambitious will in themselves create a following. These consequences of government-sponsored development activities are inevitable. At the same time, economic development can introduce new systems, alter the traditional means of gaining fortune or social

[111] Central Bank, *Annual Report of the Monetary Board to the Minister of Finance for 1957*, p. 23.

[112] *Ceylon Daily News*, February 12, 1958.

status, and thereby have an indirect effect upon the distribution of domestic political power.

Given the present documentation on Ceylonese politics, it is impossible to disentangle cause from effect in these matters. But certain observations can be made. For example, Mr. D. S. Senanayake assuredly had a popular following before he undertook the use of state resources for extensive land development projects. At the same time, the fact that he was able to direct the use of large appropriations for such purposes no doubt enhanced his own political following in the countryside where the balance of Ceylon's electoral strength has lain since 1931. His political strength then made it possible for still more funds to be spent in that direction. It would be incorrect to attribute his political strength solely to his activities as the Chairman of the Executive Committee on Lands from 1932 until 1947 when he became Prime Minister. But these development activities enhanced his own position.

Similarly, the fact that Sir John Kotelawala was Chairman of the Committee on Communications and Works for a decade before he became Minister of Transport and Works under the 1946 constitution helped him to develop a following of loyal and enthusiastic supporters within an important segment of the public service and in those elements of the business community who were particularly concerned with construction. This is not to say that the following was bought through bribery or by distribution of contracts only to those who provided assured political support to Sir John. But, as Minister of Transport and Works he became associated with those large endeavors, and found jobs for many men. Being ultimately responsible for the priorities with which construction programs were undertaken, M.P.s and interested individuals found it prudent to remain on friendly terms with him.

The "social service" functions conducted with state funds in the departments of public health, social service, and local government helped Mr. Bandaranaike bring to his ministership in the 1948 Senanayake Cabinet an important political following. This, in turn, probably helped persuade Mr. Senanayake to decide to allocate extensive resources to Mr. Bandaranaike's Ministry, even though there were additional social and political reasons for doing so. These same social service expenditures strengthened Mr. Bandaranaike's position for the 1956 election, for some of his supporters came from the very groups who were most assisted by him during his period in office.

Again, within the cabinet formed by Mr. Bandaranaike in 1956, the course of economic development materially affected the political position of different ministers—and conversely their political position influenced the course of development policy. If, for instance, land development continued to receive as much prominence in the future as in the past, then the Minister of Lands would be likely to develop an extensive nationwide following in his own right. On the other hand, there was a shift in governmental emphasis. Although large sums were still expended on opening new lands, the M.E.P. stressed the use of improved agricultural techniques on lands already under cultivation through improved extension services, highly organized "cooperative" facilities in the countryside, and land reform legislation. These could be justified on economic grounds insofar as greater productivity might well be achieved with an expenditure of fewer capital factors. But not entirely incidental, the Minister of Agriculture would probably increase his own influence at the expense of the Minister of Lands. Because of his "hard" Marxist background, he was considered likely to use to best long-run political advantage whatever opportunities the altered development policies presented to him. Appropriations for loan fund expenditures by the Ministry of Industries were greatly increased. This was justified as a correction of previous policy, when, it was held, too few resources were directed toward industrial development. No doubt these increased allocations would redound to the political advantage of the Minister of Industries.

Similarly, alternative patterns of development alter the distribution of political power in its larger conception. Peasant colonization had political merit for representatives of both the overcrowded districts and the sparse areas of new settlement. Peasant cultivators might be expected to be conservative in their voting and less easily caught up in the radical agitational appeals of the far Left, though in 1956 they clearly did not retain a sense of loyalty to the U.N.P. that had spent so much on their behalf. A policy of reducing colonization and increasing, instead, the effort to improve cultivation techniques in the wet zone may favor representatives from these areas, if the new outturns are achieved by methods the peasantry find acceptable and in keeping with their values. Those in the Western and Southern Provinces, who were already adept at organizing a "working class" following, were the most interested in developing the industrial sector of the economy which would, in turn, promote their political fortunes as well as contribute to the desired "diversification" of Ceylon's economy. Opposition to rapid industrialization was often discredited on the grounds that the critics really feared an increase in Marxist power.

In private conversation such connections were often made by men of widely differing persuasions. Ceylonese discussions of economic development thus often proceeded against a background of intense and elaborate political calculation. The direction of development allocations was expected to alter—as well as reveal—the balance of political power within a cabinet. Capital programs were expected to materially change the distribution of political power for electoral purposes in the not too distant future. Hence, considerations of productivity, maximum productive output for minimum capital input, even social equality or economic independence were only part of the criteria used to judge policy alternatives. Political considerations were also of great importance.

CONCLUSION

The net results of Ceylon's development efforts during the first decade of independence are not easy to assess. Agricultural production increased in quantity over the period slightly more, in the aggregate, than did population. Bad weather during 1956 and 1957 sharply reduced outturns once again though 1958 showed a near record production in rice and a record output of tea. The rate of industrial growth was more difficult to gauge with accuracy. Taking long-run trends into account, it was concluded in 1956 that " 'real output' per capita is probably not so very much greater than in 1926 or 1938."[113] Ceylonization, progressive income and profits taxes and export duties redirected some resources from foreign hands to Ceylonese and from higher income receivers to those in lower brackets, particularly in the agricultural settlements and in urban areas. Extensive "social capital" programs have also redistributed real incomes. As yet, neither of these nor more direct capital investments have materially contributed to increasing the national product available for each inhabitant.[114]

It may be that the political elite is changing certain of its economic perspectives. During the early years of democratic government in Ceylon, from the introduction of the universal franchise

113 Oliver, pp. 12-13.

114 See Oliver, Chapter 6, for a more elaborate analysis.

in 1931 to the middle 1950's, the imperatives of representative politics led ministers to press for a more equitable distribution of service functions throughout the country. Ceylon's population received schools, hospitals, rural development cooperatives, and other government-sponsored service activities to a high degree. In consequence, Ceylon's population has been better serviced than any other people in South Asia. The opening of new lands also gave some, though limited, outlet to overcrowded wet zone landless peasants. But, more recently, as a rapidly growing population presses down upon a relatively stable resource base, more political leaders and members of the intellectual and other elites were seriously considering how service-oriented political imperatives were to be translated into production-oriented activity. The political and economic leaders faced many intractable problems, including resource, technological, managerial, and capital limitations. Their populations did not yet appear eager to be caught up in the disciplined, relatively impersonal and time-delimited life that marks modern industrial or other highly productive societies. In the countryside, the rural population was relieved to be spared the rigors of hunger, malaria, and drought and had more sarongs, bicycles, cooking utensils, and flashlights than ever before. But experience during the first decade suggested they were not yet ready to adopt the recommendations of the political or administrative elites as to why and how they should maximize their agricultural output. It was therefore not surprising that the political returns from production-oriented activities were not yet compelling to Ceylon's political leaders. For the future, it remained to be seen whether political advancement could be as well served by efforts to increase the nation's productivity as welfare distribution had served their political purposes in the past.

The gap between the elite and the mass of the population, noticeable in more directly political phenomena, was perhaps as fundamental to progress toward economic development as it was to national and cultural unity. The role of political leaders was no doubt of great importance. If any members of the ruling elite had an incentive to understand the thought, the feeling, and deeper dreams of the laboring millions—in paddy field, coconut grove, or city repair shop—it was the men of politics. They set the tone of public aspiration. They helped to define the ambitions and ideas of what people could legitimately expect of their government and of one another. They identified the targets of hostility, the villains of the public drama and the heroes, too. For political survival they must know the symbolism that moves their constituents. Their own activities contribute powerfully to that symbolism. In Ceylon, they were sufficiently cultivated in intellect and moving close enough to the national view to be able to bring their knowledge of aspirations to bear upon the economic development effort.

To enlist popular support in the social and value changes implicit in economic development remained to be accomplished. Yet, a noticeable shadow of Malthus was on the horizon, already larger than a man's hand. Failing more rapid improvement in national—and inescapably in individual—productivity, the approaching cloud might well bring darkness to the land.

CHAPTER IX · THE GENERAL ELECTION OF 1956

CHANGING POLITICAL LEADERS

> ". . . democracy . . . is by no means only a type of political structure. Far more significantly it is a state of mind and a basic social pattern enabling men to live together in equality and freedom. It rests upon that elusive but fundamental concept of the dignity of the individual human being, and upon an all-pervading sense that the ordinary man of the street and the village has rights which must be respected. . . . The continued functioning of democracy demands as much wise restraint in the exercise of power as it does readiness to use power to achieve goals which seem of immediate and pressing importance."—Rupert Emerson, *Representative Government in Southeast Asia*

I · INTRODUCTION

PRECEDING chapters have discussed prominent issues of public policy as they became defined during the decade of independence. Although each issue owed something to the politicians who sought to use it, each had a *raison-d'être* apart from electoral competition; each emerged from some aspect of the colonial legacy of class, cultural, or religious resentments, or the personal or group search for opportunity and advancement. The following discussion centers its attention upon the political process more directly as these and other issues came into play in the General Election of 1956.

Legitimacy acquired at the hustings is very different from the tradition of inherited status and influence. The given or usurped right to rule has become subject to recall by the electorate. The rulers are periodically put to the test of acceptability. Leaders, drawn largely from Westernized, relatively urbanized layers of society, and for the most part from wealthy families, have had to seek the approval of culturally indigenous villagers.

The 1956 election was remarkable in that of all the elections held in Ceylon since 1931, and in India and Burma since independence, it alone resulted in a marked transfer of political power from one segment of the population to another. This shift in the locus of power was accomplished without bloodshed, mass corruption, or intimidation of the electorate by violence. It was not the elective confirmation of a *coup d'état,* but a genuine change in leadership effected by the cumulated choice of hundreds of thousands of individual voters.

The consolidation of opposition forces, the issues of the campaign as these evoked interest-group activity, the campaign itself, and the results will each be discussed in turn.[1]

II · CHANGING POLITICAL LEADERSHIP

The composition of the House of Representatives changed more radically in the 1956 General Election than the American House of Representatives did in the 1932 landslide election of Franklin Delano Roosevelt. A coalition of hitherto divided forces representing Sinhalese nationalists, Buddhists, and Marxists swept into power behind Mr. S. W. R. D. Bandaranaike, gaining by election 51 seats and 6 additional seats filled by prime ministerial appointment. The United National Party, which had controlled the country's affairs since independence, obtained only 8 seats. Ten ministers from the U.N.P. government lost their seats and only two U.N.P. ministers were returned. For the first time in Ceylon's electoral history, all the parties of the Opposition in the Sinhalese area were drawn together in a series of no-contest agreements. They had little in common with one another but the shared desire "to throw the rascals out."

After every other election, cabinet faces were familiar as the same men returned to office. After the 1956 election, however, only the new prime minister and one minister had held office in previous cabinets. Instead of the house of representatives resembling the "Mother of Parliaments' " in dress, speech, and ceremony, for the first time, all members of the new governing party appeared for the opening of parliament in Sinhalese national dress. Deference was paid

[1] For a detailed discussion of the 1952 General Election, see I. D. S. Weerawardana, "The General Elections in Ceylon, 1952," *Ceylon Historical Journal,* II, Nos. 1 and 2 (July, Oct. 1952), pp. 111-180. Also Sir Ivor Jennings, "Additional Notes on the General Election," *Ceylon Historical Journal,* II, Nos. 3 and 4 (Jan. and April 1953), pp. 193-208. For the 1947 election, see Sir Ivor Jennings, "The Ceylon General Elections of 1947," *University of Ceylon Review* VI, No. 3 (July 1948), pp. 133-195.

to one of the island's languages by many speakers presenting their views in Sinhalese. Indigenous cultural values were stressed by using traditional Sinhalese music to open parliament instead of the Western fanfare. Yellow-robed Buddhist priests occupied seats in the visitors' gallery, symbolizing their important role in the recent campaign. Large numbers of village and lower-class people thronged the public galleries as they had never done before.

The defeat of the U.N.P. was as astonishing to the victors as it was to the vanquished for all indications seemed to point toward a strong return of the ruling party, although with a slightly reduced majority. The Prime Minister had recently returned from a world tour where he had been received by many of the world's leading statesmen and his ideas on foreign affairs had been widely quoted abroad. Independence and equal status in the world of nations was dramatized as recently as December 1955 when Ceylon entered the United Nations. Unique among South Asian countries, Ceylon's decade of independence was without civil war or protracted public disorders. Health services had improved spectacularly. The school system had expanded over the decade, and the school-going population had nearly doubled. Ceylon's practice of universal free education was more extensive than any other country in South Asia. Over a dozen quayside berths had been provided to improve the Port of Colombo and the cumbersome and costly system of lighterage could be eliminated. The Gal Oya project, modeled on the T.V.A. in the United States, could show a river tamed, turbines producing more electricity than could yet be completely tapped, and thousands of families settled on new and well watered land. The island's staple food, rice, was being produced in much larger quantities than eight to ten years previously; tea and coconut production had increased as much as 30 per cent and 15 per cent respectively. Improved capital assets and increased productivity, internal peace and political stability had all been achieved during the years of U.N.P. rule.[2]

The record of the party thus appeared worthy of respect. Its influence in the country also seemed assured. The party had become rich, and not only because of the wealthy men among its members. In Ceylon, the government has a widely diffused power that penetrates many aspects of economic and professional life, and attracts those whose interests might be furthered or ruined by alternative

[2] The U.N.P. stressed these accomplishments as the principal justification for their return to power. Text in *Times of Ceylon*, March 21, 1956.

Courtesy of the *Ceylon Observer*

The "snap" election had been well-advertised in advance and many believed the U N P had ensured a favorable response from the voters.

government actions. In rural districts the U.N.P. supporters were generally considered the wealthy or the traditionally influential. Both of these were thought to influence the rural vote, for traditional standing or employment obligated a man to deposit his vote as the notable advised or the employer wished. The U.N.P. had also been able to consolidate its position in the public service by rewarding the faithful and punishing the disloyal. The political loyalty of the police and the army were not in doubt. In short, the U.N.P. entrenched itself by its wealth, the way it distributed patronage, and by its solicitude for the public service, the police, and the army.[3]

[3] Such matters proved difficult to document. It was the writer's impression that

The overwhelming defeat was all the more astonishing since, according to British practice, the U.N.P. had chosen the time for election and had even selected the issue on which the election was presumably to be fought. There was no constitutional need to hold the election until the summer of 1957, five years after the opening of the second parliament. But the ruling party chose to go to the people more than a year earlier than necessary. Indeed, the early date and the issue selected were virtually the only suggestions from the U.N.P. side that they were anxious about the trend of events in the country.

That certain Buddhist groups espoused the cause of "Sinhalese Only" was a factor in the timing of the election. The long-awaited sacred year of Buddha Jayanti was to begin in May 1956. It seems plausible that the U.N.P. high command considered that waiting until the end of Buddha Jayanti for the election would have given the ardent Sinhalese among the Buddhists more than a year during which to mobilize Buddhist opinion on behalf of radical language legislation. It also became apparent that the more ardent Buddhists would agitate against the U.N.P., for the tenor of the meetings called to prepare the Buddhist Committee Report could not have escaped the party leadership. Internal party difficulties added their weight to the decision. During the autumn and winter of 1955 it was thought that Mr. Dudley Senanayake might leave the party and attempt to form a third democratic party. Issues of personal opinion and public policy were both in question. To have postponed the election for a year longer might have given this contingency time to mature.

The U.N.P. leadership chose to fight the election on the language question, and adopted a proposal that "Sinhalese alone should be the State Language of Ceylon and that immediate action be taken to implement this decision."[4] The seven Tamil M.P.s who were members of the U.N.P. had all resigned in protest and the proposal for "Sinhalese Only" was unanimously endorsed by the Eighth An-

---

larger and more handsome central schools were built in U.N.P. constituencies and that lesser buildings were judged sufficient for other districts. Roads in loyal constituencies were frequently better; medical services more heavily capitalized. On the other hand it is easy to overstate the case. In certain dry zone constituencies, for instance, heavy irrigation and other capital expenditures appear to have been made in constituencies where the M.P. was a vigorous critic of the government. On balance, however, the argument appeared to have some validity.

[4] *Ceylon Observer*, February 19, 1956, Report of the Eighth Annual Conference of the U.N.P.

nual Conference of the U.N.P. held in February 1956. Declaring that this was a radical departure from the U.N.P.'s previous policies, the prime minister asked the governor general for the dissolution of parliament. This was done as of February 18, and the election was called for a time to be fixed between six and seven weeks later.[5]

III · THE OPPOSITION CONSOLIDATED

The leaders of the several Opposition parties and groups had begun to form a coalition as early as November 1955.[6] A series of false starts finally culminated in an announced agreement a few days after the dissolution.[7] Four politically distinct groups agreed to fight the coming election as a single Front on the basis of a common program of opposition to the U.N.P. and promising to make Sinhalese the sole official language.[8] This Front took the name of the Mahajana Eksath Peramuna (People's United Front). Mr. Bandaranaike's Sri Lanka Freedom Party contributed the largest number of candidates to the M.E.P., 41 in all. The V.L.S.S.P. of Mr. Philip Gunawardena joined the M.E.P. with five candidates. The Basha Peramuna (or Language Front) also joined, a group associated with the ebullient M.P. from Galle, Mr. Dahanayake.[9] In addition, a group of Independents under the leadership of Mr. I. M. R. A. Iriyagolla brought eight more to complete the M.E.P. total of sixty candidates. Never before had the U.N.P. had to face so many candidates running on a single ticket.

The coalition was an implausible combination. Mr. Bandaranaike was an aristocrat with vaguely socialist ideas, especially sensitive to Sinhalese religious and cultural aspirations. His support came from rural middle-class professional people, active Buddhists and others concerned with Sinhalese cultural and linguistic matters as well as some rural notables dissatisfied with the U.N.P. Mr. Dahanayake had the reputation of "friend of the common man," and was only recently converted from Marxist polemics to ardent lan-

[5] *Ceylon Observer, ibid.*

[6] *Ibid.*, November 11, 1955.

[7] *Ceylon Daily News*, February 23, 1956.

[8] The distinction between a political front (*peramuna*) and a political party (*pakse*) was not discussed in public, but it was widely understood that a *peramuna* was looser, less disciplined, and drawn together for a relatively specific purpose.

[9] Originally, some six individuals were identified as Basha Peramuna candidates, but all except Mr. Dahanayake himself ran ultimately as M.E.P. candidates or as Independents. After the election, Mr. Dahanayake, too, joined the M.E.P.

guage reform. Mr. Gunawardena was known as an able and determined Marxist who had contested the previous election in a common front with the Communist party and who meanwhile had taken up the issue of language reform. This combination would no doubt find it easier to agree on the double platform of reducing the power of the U.N.P. and reforming language policy than to define a common program of social and economic development.

Even before the formation of the M.E.P., Mr. Bandaranaike as head of the Sri Lanka Freedom Party had reached a no-contest agreement with the Communist party and the N.L.S.S.P. on the single issue of weakening the United National Party. It was agreed that wherever the U.N.P. was contesting, these three parties would not compete against each other but would all throw their combined influence behind one mutually agreed candidate who would run on the ticket of his own party. This agreement carried over when the M.E.P. was formed, although it presented special difficulties to the Communist party and the N.L.S.S.P. where Mr. Philip Gunawardena and his five supporters were contesting as M.E.P. candidates. This was so because for many years, the Communist party, the N.L.S.S.P., and Mr. Gunawardena's group had been competing against one another, each attempting to win for itself the others' "working class" support.

But there were also difficulties in maintaining the agreement with Mr. Bandaranaike's candidates as well, for the Communist party and the N.L.S.S.P. agreed with the M.E.P. on only two issues—ejecting the U.N.P. from power and diminishing Ceylon's ties with the British "imperialists." On the language issue, these two had been committed to a policy of giving equal status to the Tamil and Sinhalese languages. They were thus diametrically opposed to the principal M.E.P. plank. Their position with respect to Buddhism was ambiguous. The Left parties could sidestep the religious issue per se by aligning themselves with at least one current of the Buddhist movement—identifying the Catholic Church as a creature of Western imperialism, representing, it was argued, the interests of the upper levels of Ceylon society where influential Christians were largely to be found. This satisfied traditional Leftist polemic requirements without alienating ardent Buddhists.

In view of these ideological and other differences between the component parts of the Mahajana Eksath Peramuna and the Communist party and N.L.S.S.P., the effectiveness of the no-contest agreement was a remarkable achievement. In hard-bargained interparty negotiations, many local party hopefuls had to withdraw from the running at nomination time and support instead long-standing local rivals. The no-contest agreement held in every constituency but eleven in contrast to the previous election, when the opposition to the U.N.P. split the vote in twenty-five single-member constituencies, outside the Northern and Eastern Provinces.[10]

In all previous elections the U.N.P. dominated the field to the extent that few voters could have seriously believed they were lodging more than a mere protest vote when they voted for any of the opposition parties. In 1952 for example, the U.N.P. put up 81 candidates to return 54. The nearest contender, the S.L.F.P., put up 48 and returned 9. Since all the other parties were contesting against each other as much as against the U.N.P., there seemed to have been little hope that any one of them could form a government. But in 1956, the M.E.P. with its 60 candidates was a fair numerical match for the U.N.P.'s 76 candidates. Assuming that the M.E.P. was a seriously effective political "front" it was just conceivable that the M.E.P. might form an alternative government. Hence the desire to cast a ballot for a winner for the first time could lead individuals to vote for the chief opposition contender.

With less competing opposition candidates, fewer candidates ran as Independents. Whereas in the 1952 election 64 Independents outside the Northern and Eastern Provinces sought election, in 1956 only 41 entered the lists.[11] Contests were thus simplified and there was more opportunity for the voter to express an effective party choice.

In spite of these assets, Mr. Bandaranaike's chances appeared so slim that many qualified men, when asked to run on his ticket, turned him down on the assumption that it was pointless to go to all the trouble and expense of a campaign only to be defeated. Indeed, two M.P.s who had been leaders of Mr. Bandaranaike's own party deserted him on the eve of the campaign and ran as U.N.P. candidates. Hence, his slate presented many inexperienced men. Fifteen of his 42 candidates had never contested a national election before, 7 had had experience in local politics only and 4 of his

10 Weerawardana, "The General Elections in Ceylon, 1952," p. 131.

11 Northern and Eastern Provinces are excluded from these comparisons because the U.N.P. ran no candidates there in 1956 as a result of the language agitation. These two provinces put forward 23 Independents in 16 constituencies compared to the 41 Independents who ran for 79 seats in the rest of the island.

candidates were 30 or under.[12] Some of these younger men decided to try their luck to gain experience rather than with any real expectation of success.

In the Northern and Eastern Provinces where Ceylon Tamils formed the majority of voters, the political trends were different. Whereas in the first general elections under the present constitution, the U.N.P. ran candidates in these largely Tamil provinces, this time no candidates contested on the U.N.P. ticket. The party's abrupt abandonment of its traditional intercommunal policy made it impossible for any Tamil politician to run as a U.N.P. candidate. Indeed, the party's adoption of "Sinhalese Only" as its main platform put in jeopardy the re-election of any Tamil politician who had previously collaborated with it, so strong was the Tamil feeling against the proposed language reform. During the 1952 election, for instance, in the Northern and Eastern provinces, eight ran as U.N.P. candidates in sixteen constituencies. In 1956 there were no contenders.[13] For the first time since independence, Tamil politics were proceeding in a system quite distinct from that in the Sinhalese areas. Only the Left parties had organized connections in both the Tamil and Sinhalese areas, the Communist party running four candidates and the N.L.S.S.P. running two in the Northern and Eastern provinces.

The largest grouping of Tamil candidates ran on the Federal Party ticket under the single-minded direction of Mr. Chelvanayakam. He had long been the most outspoken and consistent Tamil political leader to warn of Sinhalese domination and he had refused all offers of office made by the U.N.P. in the past. Ever since the first independence Parliament he had maintained that the present unitary constitution was inappropriate to a country of mixed population, that only a federal constitution could protect the rights of the Tamil-speaking minority. When the Tamils began to feel seriously threatened by the Sinhalese language reform that would clearly be to their disadvantage, they naturally turned to a man of known integrity.[14]

[12] Of the candidates 30 or under, one had just finished his secondary schooling, one was a part-time journalist pursuing his law course on the side, one a teacher in a Government Central School, and one a former government clerk who had lost his job as a result of unionizing activities.

[13] In 1947, 7 ran as U.N.P. candidates. After both the 1947 and 1952 elections, several successful candidates who ran as Independents then joined the U.N.P.

[14] Although he had been elected in 1947, he lost in 1952 as the cooperators swept the board. In 1956 the cooperators were in a weak position and Mr. Chelvanayakam's possibilities were thereby strengthened.

IV · CAMPAIGN ISSUES

A. TIME FOR A CHANGE

Although the most insistent polemic concerned "the language question" at the outset of the campaign, in retrospect it is apparent that another fundamental issue was the right of the U.N.P. to continue to rule five more years. The otherwise implausible coalition of ardent Buddhists, Sinhalese cultural enthusiasts, and Marxists and the no-contest agreement between parties with diametrically opposed policies on the language question suggested the overriding importance of this issue.

The very sources of U.N.P. strength were turned against the party as clear evidence of its desire to misuse political power. A film of petty financial scandal and public cynicism had settled over the U.N.P. regime. The wealth of the party, the privileged position of its known supporters, and the widespread belief that U.N.P. funds were raised through sales of honors and citizenships worked to its disadvantage. The alleged misuse of the public service, and the fact that close relatives of the prime minister himself were appointed to lucrative and prominent posts regardless of competence, did much harm to the U.N.P. Several years before the election, when the outcry against bribery had been loudest, a Bribery Commission was established with special powers of investigation. It was then asserted that the prime minister used the powers of the Bribery Commission to gather damaging evidence against individuals who would therefore be forced to keep quiet by the threat of exposure.[15] Several public cases of graft in high places had been given wide publicity.[16]

Often the results of the government's policies appeared to fall short of expectations. The social welfare measures as administered never seemed to provide the relief the poor had been led to expect. Municipal housing projects were undertaken, but they were not made as visible in a political sense as the spacious new homes of

[15] A well-known case of a Tamil politician who when a minister had allegedly attempted to obtain kick-backs on some fishing trawlers lent credence to the story since it was reliably understood that evidence against him was held in the vaults of the U.N.P. and the party had thus been able to silence the hitherto critical voice of that politician.

[16] A former governor of the Central Bank was forced to resign on the grounds of unduly large overdrafts from member banks in order to build himself a house. It was widely argued that this was not surprising, since "everyone" in the top levels was said to be doing just the same. The case did not clear the governing party of an atmosphere of petty scandal and brought criticism against the party itself on grounds of "personal revenge" and even of caste-thinking since the man in question was not a Goyigama.

the wealthy that many understood to have been financed by government housing loans. Increased rice production was nearly cancelled out by the growing numbers of mouths to feed. The Gal Oya project was in a remote section of the island and only a relatively few families had profited from it. Colombo Harbor's new equipment and quay-side berths were not dramatized in ways which the mass of voters could understand. Shortly before the election, the U.N.P. government established a Ceylonese national airlines with services between Colombo and European capitals, permitting the wealthy and the government officials to fly in comfort. For the man in the street, bus service in Colombo remained poor and the bus owners as wealthy as ever. This contrast was indicative of a seeming lack of awareness of, and care for, the small man's needs. The Opposition successfully pinned on the U.N.P. charges of special privilege and crass unconcern for the mass of voters.

There was a growing popular feeling of irritation and impatience at the U.N.P. leadership in general and Sir John Kotelawala in particular. The leaders of the U.N.P. had been in power for a long time. Even before the formation of the party in 1946 many of the same men had been prominent in the government during the later colonial period. The press helped to build a picture of U.N.P. leaders as more concerned with public ceremonies and official missions abroad than worrying about, and solving, the immediate problems at home. An air of lethargy and lack of enthusiasm had settled over the ministries. There was much talk of economic development but there were few tangible results that produced jobs. During the year preceding the election, two prominent members of the U.N.P. who belonged to the distinguished and generally respected Senanayake family no longer supported the Party; this defection only confirmed the mass of voters in their worst suspicions. While the moral position of the U.N.P. was being questioned, there were several incidents of police irregularities and abuse of police power.

The government of Sir John Kotelawala became less and less attentive to Opposition criticism. Assured of its majority in parliament, it allowed attacks to go by default and merely carried the day in the voting. The personal predilections of the prime minister were important in this respect, for Sir John tended to be impatient with debate and discussion. He considered himself a man of action. He was often abrupt and shortened or dismissed debate. His military background, his special security measures, and the resources devoted to housing and caring for the police, together with his apparent impatience with parliamentary procedures, gave his critics grounds for labeling him an incipient dictator.

B. THE LANGUAGE ISSUE: SINHALESE AS THE SOLE OFFICIAL LANGUAGE

Much of the electoral discussion on the official language of Ceylon had an unreal quality, since both the M.E.P. and the U.N.P. promised that "Sinhalese Only" would replace English as the official language.[17] The question for the voter to decide was which party was most likely to give him what he wanted. To the language enthusiast this choice required a judgment as to the sincerity of each party and the promptness with which either might implement its language program. In this contest Mr. Bandaranaike and the M.E.P. party had several advantages, among them Mr. Bandaranaike's greater vehemence on the matter prior to the election, his longer history of advocacy, and his freedom from the taint of past responsibility. Many therefore were drawn to him on this issue and were dubious of the U.N.P., a Johnny-come-lately convert to "Sinhalese Only" under the pressure of mounting public excitement.

The language agitation aroused deep communal and class emotions among the people, no doubt causing many otherwise disinterested voters to vote for the M.E.P. In addition, specific identifiable interest groups could unite in common opposition to the U.N.P. on the language issue though they might not agree on anything else.

The teachers in Sinhalese day schools numbered some 35,000 or roughly 70 per cent of all the teachers on the island. They were organized in two principal associations, one for government teachers and the other for those employed in assisted schools. The teachers believed that they were being treated as second-class professionals

[17] "Immediate provision must be made in the Constitution Order in Council declaring Sinhalese to be the only Official Language of the country, and immediately thereafter the necessary steps taken for the implementation of this provision. This will not involve the suppression of such a minority language as Tamil, whose reasonable use will receive due recognition." *Joint Programme of Mahajana Eksath Peramuna* (Colombo, March 10, 1956), p. 2. The U.N.P. declared simply that "Our Party . . . registered an unanimous vote accepting Sinhalese only as the State Language of Ceylon. This substantial change in our policy must now be endorsed by the electorate. We also require a two-thirds majority to alter our Constitution to this effect. In all other respects we shall preserve intact our present Constitution. We shall resist all efforts to divide the country. Even if we are unable to amend the Constitution our first act will be to pass legislation to make Sinhalese the State Language." Text in *Times of Ceylon*, March 21, 1956.

by a Westernized Colombo government. Comparison of teachers' pay scales showed that an English trained teacher began at a salary nearly twice as high as a Sinhalese or Tamil teacher and the gap between them was never closed throughout their careers. There has been some justification for a different salary scale, since a longer training period has been required of those teaching in the English schools but the disparity of 100 per cent pay difference at the start was excessive.[18] The status of the Sinhalese teachers was also affected adversely when the students who obtained a Senior School Certificate in Sinhalese found it difficult to obtain jobs.

Other grievances grew from the fact that the English schools of Colombo and other cities have traditionally received the best equipment and their students come from the best families. The social and economic status of the principals and teachers was also high. A teacher in the Sinhalese schools knew that his future held no hope of promotion into the first-rate schools. For many years teachers in the English language schools have been able to enter the supervisory staff of the Ministry of Education and become school inspectors but Sinhalese teachers could not do so until recently. There were anomalies in administration, too. Many Swabasha teachers found that they were required to teach a wide variety of subjects with very large classes in poor facilities while the English language schools permitted a teacher to specialize in two or three subjects. Specialization indicated not only more prestige and higher status but left the English teacher more leisure.

Most of these disadvantages would disappear, it was argued, if Sinhalese were made the sole official language. All the status that previously adhered to English when it was the "official languge" would become associated with the Sinhalese language and thence to Sinhalese teachers. They were, after all, the experts in Sinhalese culture and language, and if their proficiency received state recognition, naturally they themselves would rise in status. If Sinhalese were made the state language, differential pay, educational facilities, and job opportunities would no longer favor the English speaking elite. And, as it was seen from the village, vast numbers of govern-

18 Most of the English teachers teach in cities and towns where the cost of living and the style of life expected of an English teacher are higher than is the case for largely rural village Sinhalese teachers. However, the village school teacher, living within the village social system, is expected to fulfill certain ceremonial and social functions.

ment jobs would immediately be opened to their students if English were displaced and Sinhalese promoted.[19]

The unemployed students themselves were vocal in presenting their dilemma, and as a group they were the most ardent enthusiasts of "Sinhalese Only." Three factors made their position increasingly difficult: the rapid expansion of the education system, the language reforms of the 1940's which resulted in more students receiving high-school education through the Sinhalese or Tamil medium, and the fact that government jobs were still virtually reserved to the English-educated. Never before had there been so many with competence in Sinhalese seeking white-collar jobs, particularly the high status posts in the public service. Had they been able to take their advanced work in English, they could have found jobs as clerks in the public service. So long as much of the work in government offices was in English, they saw few opportunities befitting their educational achievement. With time on their hands, they were able to agitate forcefully on behalf of whatever party was able to enlist their support. The airing of their grievances also contributed to the conviction of many parents that the U.N.P. was not doing enough to expand employment opportunities.

Many of the *ayurvedic* physicians on the island concluded that their position would be enhanced if Sinhalese became the language of the government. There are between 7,000 and 10,000 practitioners of the traditional herbal medicine with widely varying standards of training and competence. For some time their problems had given rise to public controversy. Most of the political parties active in Sinhalese areas had been seeking their support, for the physicians are strategically placed, occupying positions of respect in widely scattered villages. Backing from different political parties unfortunately tended to encourage factionalism among them. Seeking support, each party encouraged practitioners who differed from those already allied to competing political parties. Disagreement was all the easier because there are very difficult policy alternatives facing the profession. These involved the advisability of preserving their tradition against the newfangled Western medicine or the need to accept revolutionary Western medical advances.[20]

[19] The writer acknowledges with thanks the time and thought of some 40 Swabasha teachers in Western, Sabaragamuwa, Central, and Northwest Provinces whose kindness helped in the preparation of this section.

[20] Some argued that the *ayurvedic* tradition should be kept "pure" and intact, insulated from the theories and medicines from the West. Others believed that there

The grievances of the indigenous doctor had been mounting during the past years because their relatively distinguished traditional social status was being threatened both by innovations from modern medicine and present day health services. Enteric diseases are endemic in rural Ceylon, and the new antibiotics reduce fever in a much shorter time than traditional medicines. But the desire to retain the *ayurvedic* tradition is strong, and the difficulties are real in finding the correct *via media* that combines the fundamentals of the old system and enough of the new so as not to be dangerous. There has also been a great increase in rural health services during the past ten years. A map of government-run dispensaries and clinics shows most areas of the island dotted with facilities. In the country the red cross of the government dispensary or the blue sign of the government midwife are familiar sights. The indigenous doctor, suffering from the onslaught of modern technical developments, sees the government as the agent of attack since it has expanded modern practice and given relatively little support to the traditional system.

The government has undermined the doctor's position in other ways. It has restricted his access to certain drugs such as opium. It has given the midwife, who has had only a brief training in Western medicine, a higher status than he himself received. On the other hand, the doctor believed that poor village patients would continue to patronize him if the government paid his fees as it subsidized the free service that patients received in Western clinics. If the government would scientifically test his many herbal medicines, and promote the growth of needed herbs—as it spent state resources for the importation of costly Western drugs—the profession would not need to bring in to its traditional wisdom the relatively new and untried prescriptions from outside.[21]

Since their *ayurvedic* knowledge is embedded in the Sinhalese cultural tradition, their profession suffers because their culture has been put on the defensive by the high official status given to English. If Sinhalese were raised to its proper place and English demoted, it was argued, then the respect and resources available to *ayurvedic* medi-

---

should be a careful mingling of the two systems, that anatomy should be taught at the College of Indigenous Medicine and the use of penicillin and other antibiotics explained.

[21] The search for tranquilizers in Western countries also adversely affected his position. One of the basic herbal components, long known in the *ayurvedic* tradition as a specific against hypertension, was becoming too expensive for his slender purse as a result of growing export demand for the product!

cine would increase and Western practice would no longer virtually monopolize government medical expenditures.

There is a thread of egalitarianism in both the demands of the teacher and the physician. Raising the status of Sinhalese education, opening up by law avenues of employment hitherto closed to its students, and raising the status of native medicine are all devices designed to level away privileges formerly reserved to the wealthy Sinhalese or to those who managed access to a Western education regardless of their wealth.

Active Buddhist laymen and certain Buddhist priests were among the most articulate advocates of "Sinhalese Only" and the most effective opponents of those who sought a place for Tamil alongside of Sinhalese. They saw in the continued use of English in most governmental matters the dead hand of a destructive foreign past. If the language of their culture were fully recognized, Buddhist culture and the Buddhist Way of Life would be restored to their former greatness. So long as English occupied such a high status in the land, the most talented would seek education in English. And in this process, they argued, the youth of Ceylon would be alienated from its cultural and religious roots.

The language issue drew members of another group to Mr. Bandaranaike, especially in the coastal areas. In recent years numbers of businessmen had made money through transportation services, wartime contracts, and wholesale dealings in estate products. They had enough money now to be treated as socially equal to the more established English-educated strata, but because their culture and their language did not give them social or political access to the ruling group around the U.N.P., significant numbers of them turned to support Mr. Bandaranaike. He was prepared to be socially approachable and politically attuned to this source of potential opposition to the U.N.P. leadership. For them language reform symbolized a revision of the social order permitting entry into official circles that had hitherto been barred to them.

Opinion within these groups was by no means unanimous. There were some teachers who claimed that administrative practices were really to blame for their plight, some physicians who believed that more English was necessary in order to improve their practice of medicine, and many *bhikkhus* gave priority to an inner spiritual transformation of individuals. But it was safe to say that the most active within all these groups believed the matter of state language to be of basic importance, and the speed with which the official language was changed over to Sinhalese became their touchstone for judging the different politicians and parties.

The language issue, used to undermine the U.N.P. position among the Sinhalese voters, raised serious communal problems. In efforts to weaken the U.N.P., its opponents charged it with being a friend of the Tamils. When the opposition was able to point to Sir John Kotelawala as "a friend of the Tamils" it was then only necessary to reawaken the Sinhalese fears of the Tamils in order to weaken the U.N.P.'s electoral position. This temptation was too much for many candidates to resist. Tamil resentment at the proposed language change mounted rapidly with the Sinhalese agitation. Each politician in the north sought to prove that he and not his opponent was the best friend of the Tamils. This served to further arouse the ardent proponents of Sinhalese in the south. The net result of electoral agitation over the language issue was to raise communal self-consciousness and antagonism to a new high and promised to render the task of the new government, whichever it was to be, more difficult.[22]

C. THE STATE OF BUDDHISM

Although the language agitation probably had little impact on the peasantry, the question of Buddhism had deep political importance for them and many other groups as well. Coinciding with the great year-long celebration of 2,500 years of Buddhism were widespread anxieties among the Buddhists over the state of their religion. In anticipation of this great event, a number of Buddhist laymen began to organize *bhikkhu* associations as early as 1953. Committees were formed in rural districts by those concerned for the welfare of Buddhism in Ceylon. For these men, this was a spiritual problem that did not have political implications at the outset. Their organizational work continued for several years until perhaps seventy committees or Sabhas were formed. These associations combined to form the Sri Lanka Maha Sangha Sabha. Each of these Sabhas attempted to encourage its members to live more dedicated Buddhist lives. Members of all the different *nikayas* participated in its activities, although its religious leadership was usually considered to be from the low-country sects.

Eventually the Maha Sangha Sabha bent its efforts to arrange the

[22] See Chapter VII for a more detailed discussion.

hearings of the Buddhist Committee which had been organized in 1954 to inquire into the state of Buddhism on the island. There is some evidence to suggest that the committee's final report—*The Betrayal of Buddhism*—became primarily a political document designed to discredit the U.N.P.[23] At the time of the 1956 election campaign, the activities of these groups of organized Buddhists received little publicity. Few professed to know that the network of Sabhas was actively promoting the downfall of the U.N.P. Its leaders were able to carry out their work unobtrusively, for many of the Sabhas were also preparing local Buddha Jayanti celebrations so that the correspondence and comings and goings that were necessary for such widespread agitation could be explained away on other grounds.

Meanwhile another association of Buddhist *bhikkhus* developed under the leadership of two leading *bhikkhus* in the low-country—the All-Ceylon Congress of Bhikkhu Societies. It was understood to be largely political in inspiration.[24] Shortly after the publication of the Buddhist report and before the campaign began, these two organizations came together to form the Eksath Bhikkhu Peramuna, a "front" within which the two *bhikkhu* organizations were to continue their separate existence but work together to fight the U.N.P. in the forthcoming election.[25]

Those seeking to mobilize the *bhikkhus* for active political work in this campaign faced several obvious difficulties. The sects were divided and had had no recent experience of active cooperation. There was a strong tradition of monks remaining aloof from organized political activities. Until the 1956 election, and for many centuries, there had been no organized armature of Buddhist monks and laymen. Never before had there been energetic and capable laymen so dedicated to the task of drawing all together with a single common political purpose—a change of government.

23 Interviews with some who were active in its preparation. Supporting this view is the fact that there was a serious effort made to postpone the election, as one informant put it, "because we were not yet ready for the campaign." In the end, the Buddhist Committee Report was hastily edited and rushed through the press in order to have it ready for the campaign. It was published on February 4, 1956 ten days before the dissolution of Parliament but after the U.N.P. plan to dissolve Parliament was widely known.

24 One of these was wealthy in his own right, the incumbent of the important temple of Kelaniya. He was known to be in open conflict with one of the leading ministers of the U.N.P. who himself represented the Kelaniya district in parliament. The basis for this quarrel was obscure.

25 Based on interviews. The chronology follows a detailed letter to the *Ceylon Daily News* by one of the prime movers, September 4, 1956.

Brought together for the election itself, the Eksath Bhikkhu Peramuna had no politically trained party workers such as a well-developed political party might have. Discipline could not be expected to assure reliable followers. Other means were needed. A ten point check list was drawn up and publicized by which devout Buddhists were expected to test the various candidates. These points fell into three categories; dedication to Buddhist values in their private lives; trustworthy commitment to make "Sinhalese Only" the state language and acceptance of the Buddhist Committee report. These criteria for judging political candidates could hardly be said to have been devised without thought; they could only apply to one man—Mr. Bandaranaike.

Until the 1956 election there had been no succinct exposition of Buddhist grievances and relatively simple prescriptions for its rejuvenation. The Buddhist Committee report provided just such a brief for those who wished to use it. The report argued that the days of Buddhist glory were the days when it received state support from Sinhalese kings. The decline of Buddhism began with the Indian-Tamil invasions and was climaxed by the years of Christian inquisition and colonial rule. Christian groups had been permitted to occupy a position vis-à-vis the state that made them absolutely free from state control.[26] They had expanded their activities into fields other than religion until "Ceylon, bound hand and foot, has been delivered at the foot of the Cross."[27] The Report set forth a series of recommendations on organizational, educational, legal, and other matters of prime concern to the Buddhist community.

The Sinhalese edition of the Buddhist Committee report found its way into every temple. Excerpts were read at services, especially the historical chapter which purported to describe what happened to Buddhism during the period of foreign domination and the chapter that argued that missionary education—largely Catholic—was at the root of Buddhist difficulties.

In addition to *The Betrayal of Buddhism*, the promoters of the new Buddhist activism published their own newspaper—the *Rodaya*—a small paper in Sinhalese that had an extensive circulation among Buddhist *bhikkhus* and those susceptible to Sinhalese cultural and religious appeals. *Rodaya* stated their case against the U.N.P. as follows: "A majority of our ruling party do not know the first thing

[26] See Chapter VI.

[27] Buddhist Committee of Inquiry, pp. 23ff., and p. 31.

about Buddhism. They do not know their history. The only thing they know is how to live like Westerners. If democracy is the Government of the majority, this country should be ruled by the demands of the majority."[28] As the election approached, it called on all *bhikkhus* for specific action: "The *bhikkhus* should be present in every polling booth. They should explain to the people how to use the vote correctly. A keen interest should be taken because the Buddha Jayanti celebration is close by. A Government that will work for the country, religion and its culture should be elected. The end of the Sasana will not be very long if we remain in silence. . . . We appeal to *bhikkhus* to visit every Buddhist home and to direct them on the right path. You may have to confront many difficulties. But be ready to sacrifice your life to restore a Buddhist Ceylon."[29]

Even before the formation of the M.E.P., as leader of the Sri Lanka Freedom Party, Mr. Bandaranaike had received the support of some of the more ardent Buddhist spokesmen.[30] The manifesto or platform of the M.E.P. explicitly endorsed the recommendations of the Buddhist Committee report but reassured non-Buddhists of continued religious tolerance.[31] The manifesto of the U.N.P. reviewed the concrete measures it had taken to forward the cause of Buddhism such as restoring the sacred Temple of the Tooth at Kandy, the translation of the Tripitaka, or sacred books, into Sinhalese, the compilation of a Buddhist and Sinhalese encyclopedia and its general efforts on behalf of the Buddha Jayanti celebrations. The manifesto declared that the Party "welcomed the exhaustive report" of the Buddhist Committee of Inquiry and promised to "give our most earnest attention to the committee's recommendations at the earliest opportunity."[32] But despite its many activities and heavy expenditures for the Buddha Jayanti celebrations, in the eyes of ardent Buddhists the

28 *Rodaya*, April 1, 1955.

29 *Rodaya*, February 25, 1956.

30 One week before the Prime Minister requested dissolution, for instance, a large gathering of monks was urged to support Mr. Bandaranaike in the forthcoming election campaign. Reported by the Political Correspondent of the *Ceylon Daily News*, February 18, 1956.

31 Paragraph 3 of the MEP manifesto read as follows: *Religion*: "While recognizing the position of Buddhism in this country as the faith of a large majority of the people, we guarantee the fullest freedom of worship and conscience to all, and accept the position that there shall be no discrimination on religious grounds. We generally approve the recommendations of the Buddhist Committee of Inquiry." There was subsequent disagreement over the exact extent of the commitment implied by "generally approve," particularly since the Sinhalese version of the manifesto carried no such qualification as is implied by the word "generally."

32 Text as reported in *Times of Ceylon*, March 21, 1956.

U.N.P. lacked the aura of sincerity and religious conviction. Although the U.N.P. retained its effective relationships with the leaders of the up-country chapters of monks who attempted to forbid the younger men in their chapters from participating in politics, Mr. Bandaranaike had much closer personal working relationships with the active Buddhist laymen and *bhikkhus* than Sir John Kotelawala.

Many Buddhists had several specific grievances against the U.N.P. Ever since independence in 1948 the U.N.P. had refused to appoint a commission to investigate and report on the state of Buddhism. *The Betrayal of Buddhism* was therefore the product of impatient men who had to do for themselves what the U.N.P. had not done for them. Numerous *bhikkhus* had protested against the decision of the U.N.P. to hold its elections so near the beginning of their holy year and warned the U.N.P. that if it went ahead with the election, the party would be ignoring the advice of the priesthood, a fact that would seriously undermine the party.[33] Shortly after the dissolution of parliament a *bhikkhu* fast took place on the steps of the house of representatives to dramatize the fact that the U.N.P. did not listen to the advice of the monks.[34]

The prime minister also contributed to the case against himself. Before the election Sir John Kotelawala's memoirs were published. They depicted him as a playboy of Western European capitals rather than a serious-minded statesman who weighed his words and thought over his policies carefully as a Buddhist ruler in the great tradition should. Chapters of his memoirs were read by priests at Temple preaching evenings to show how unfitted the prime minister was to rule Buddhist Ceylon. As early as a year before the election certain priests in the more strict Ramanya and Amarapura sects had openly criticized the prime minister for his un-Buddhist style of personal life. As Ceylon was about to enter the Buddha Jayanti year, strict Buddhist *bhikkhus* had traditional ethical grounds for censure, but Sir John responded with a vehemence that surprised even his friends. Whether or not he was quoted accurately, his reputation for tough talk made it possible for the most vigorous remarks to seem plausible and numerous *bhikkhus* came to fear that the Sangha might actually be in danger if Sir John was returned to power.

Family quarrels within the U.N.P. also played into the hands of the opposition. The relative weakness of Sir John as a representative of a Buddhist country has just been mentioned. The Senanayake

[33] *Times of Ceylon*, February 16, 1956. [34] *Ceylon Observer*, February 26, 1956.

element in the U.N.P. might have strengthened the party's case in Buddhist circles. The elder D. S. Senanayake, though opposed to making Buddhism a state religion, had always been known as a devout man. His son Dudley Senanayake also had a high reputation in this respect. He knew his classical Buddhist literature; in personal life he was abstemious and he had advocated prohibition for many years. He was known to be moderate in expression, quiet in demeanor, perhaps even overconscientious in the use of political power. Here was a man whose virtues fitted well the image of the ideal Buddhist in politics. But prior to the election, Mr. Dudley Senanayake had not been willing to remain in the U.N.P. as it was then organized and he had withdrawn. This withdrawal of the "good" man only confirmed the worst suspicions of the party's critics. It lent credence to the argument that "if Dudley couldn't stick it out, there must be something wrong in the party."

As the election approached, Mr. Bandaranaike claimed that 12,000 *bhikkhus*, or 65 per cent of all on the island, actively supported him. Post-election estimates have put the figure nearer 3,000 at the outside, an active minority of perhaps 15 per cent at the most.[35] The high priests of the largest sect on the island called upon their members to refrain from political campaigning and to remain neutral during the election. They were joined by the acting head of the Ramanya sect in the low-country and by the principals of the most important *bhikkhu* training colleges. But the disciplinary powers of the heads of the *nikayas* and the training colleges are limited and each individual *bhikkhu* was in fact at liberty to act in the light of his own best judgment. In the event, during the weeks just before the election, in rural areas, particularly in the Central and Sabaragamuwa Provinces and the interior electorates of Western Province, *bhikkhus* were visibly active, walking the roads in their brilliant saffron robes, conversing with small groups of people, visiting householders. Automobiles with the blue flag of the M.E.P. were seen everywhere, filled with men of the yellow robe. These were usually the younger *bhikkhus*, the older ones remaining in their temples because of their status, in deference to the wishes of the heads of the *nikayas* or because they were less moved by the political excitement than their younger colleagues. Although some of the *bhikkhus* appear to have canvassed for the U.N.P., the message of the bulk of the active *bhikkhus* was reported to be: "a vote for the U.N.P.

[35] The writer's conclusions after cross checking with knowledgeable *bhikkhus*.

is a vote for the Catholics, a vote for the M.E.P. is a vote for Buddhism."

Together the language problem and the threatened state of Buddhism were issues likely to cross caste or class distinctions in the Sinhalese rural areas and provide a way for urban political leaders, rural middle-class people, and peasants all to react together in common resistance to the encroachment of Western values as they came to be identified with the U.N.P. in 1956. The *bhikkhu* was among the experts on Sinhalese who felt that the city man with his English education, often derived from Christian schools, was in many respects a stranger. The villager felt the same way, though those who were above the lower levels of village society might aspire to that same style of life for their children if not for themselves. The *bhikkhu* regretted the non-Buddhist way of life of the governing elite. The village middle-class man and perhaps his peasant proprietor neighbor could sense that the elite was not like a traditional good Sinhalese man should be. Should the *bhikkhu* appeal to him on Buddhist grounds, the villager's sensitivity to Sinhalese national symbols would find a ready response even if he were not an ardent Buddhist himself. As a result, the sources of U.N.P. support in the countryside were in part undermined by active Buddhist *bhikkhus* and laymen.

D. ECONOMIC PROBLEMS

Members of the opposition differed on many things, but they could and did unite on simple economic issues such as the price of rice and a free midday meal for poor school children. Rice accounts for roughly 20 per cent of the Ceylon housewife's food budget. In 1951, the U.N.P. government had increased the treasury subsidy on retailed rice. Caught in the pressure between falling export incomes and the continued high cost of imported rice following the Korean War, however, the government could no longer bear the heavy expense of the rice subsidy. In the spring of 1953 the subsidy was withdrawn. The price of rice rose rapidly by some 300 per cent; there were food riots in which ten men lost their lives, and the prime minister, then Mr. Dudley Senanayake, resigned. Sir John Kotelawala became the next prime minister. Shortly thereafter the world price of rice came down slowly and the rice price was reduced commensurately until it was stabilized at about 50¢ per measure, roughly two times the earlier price. Under the same financial pressure, the free snack of a wheat bun to poor school children had also been withdrawn.

The U.N.P. leadership had anticipated that this issue would be obsolete in the face of the rising enthusiasm for language reform and Buddhist revival.[36] But in the election, the bun became a devastating symbol for the opposition. Wherever the U.N.P. candidates were to speak, there were quantities of wheat buns—strung like garlands, suspended from flags, stuck on long poles like a giant shish kebab. This was so particularly in the areas where the Left was well organized, along the coast in the Western and Southern Provinces and in certain interior towns where both the bun and the price of rice were live issues. The voters—and the U.N.P.—were never allowed to forget which party had been responsible for raising the price of food and eliminating the bun. When some U.N.P. candidates expressed the financier's satisfaction at the healthy state of the country's finances, the opposition could claim that the vaunted budget surplus had been bought at the price of the poor and hungry. This largely economic issue came to symbolize the U.N.P.'s lack of interest in the poor man's lot.

Rice influenced the election another way. Through the guaranteed price scheme, the government purchased at a stable and attractive price all homegrown rice offered. As a result of insufficient government transport and difficulties in village collection organizations there were serious anomalies in the system. The middle man who transported the peasant's rice often received much of the benefit from the guaranteed price. From the peasant's point of view, the government was thus benefiting the middle man rather than aiding the peasantry. Only a much more extensive fleet of government vehicles and an incorruptible public service at the village level would preclude such misdirection of government funds. No doubt the guaranteed price of rice had contributed to improving generally the living standards in many parts of rural Ceylon by inducing the greater utilization of paddy land, but the administration of it was not without its political costs to the ruling party.

Another economic issue which gained momentum as the campaign progressed was the anxious spectre of unemployment. Statistics varied from the 85,000 then registered at the unemployment exchanges to over 500,000 on the basis of a Central Bank Survey of Consumer

[36] Mr. Bandaranaike, too, did not expect that an economic issue would matter much to an electorate considered by many to be highly emotional.

Finances.[37] The opposition encouraged the existing fear of unemployment for electoral purposes and the articulate unemployed students helped to give public prominence to this question.

Underemployment was certainly serious in many rural districts. But it seems unlikely that this issue had much political leverage in the 1956 election, for underemployment in a peasant society is often subtle, lacking the stark outlines of unemployment in the cash sector of the economy. In the urbanized and commercial part of Ceylon, however, unemployment was indeed present, chiefly among those aspiring to white collar jobs, and all signs indicated that it was on the increase. In the absence of adequate statistics it is difficult to define the exact magnitude of the problem. However, more and more people were coming to view the Ceylonese economy as a "stagnant economy," one in which there would be progressively more people competing for a rather fixed number of desirable jobs.

Moreover, the U.N.P.'s approach to economic development did not inspire much confidence among those who were most vocal and critical on economic matters. The U.N.P's program was eclectic, it lacked a clear-cut or easily grasped doctrine, and its gradualist approach to economic development had little appeal to those who looked ahead, anxious over the rapidly rising population. To be sure, the U.N.P. had a "Six-Year Plan," but few measures had been taken to show how this plan was actually working out. Competing slogans of "nationalization," of "a socialist economy" all suggested a more dynamic approach to Ceylon's economic problems. Equally important from the vote-getting view, these slogans carried overtones of a more humane and benign economic arrangement where more equality and less personal privilege were expected to follow from greater government direction of the economy. The U.N.P.'s revised policies in regard to industrialization probably worked against it in the urban areas. The desire for a change, therefore, led some to seek changes in economic management as much as in the political affairs of the country, though the force of this argument was probably limited to the coastal area.

E. OTHER ISSUES

Though seldom mentioned on public platforms, caste played a

[37] Central Bank of Ceylon, *Survey of Ceylon's Consumer Finances*, p. 12. Admittedly this survey was not designed to gather exact data on unemployment. Detailed statistics of unemployment were not available.

subtle, though significant, role. Being of the highest status in the low country with a wife of highest up-country standing, Mr. Bandaranaike had an appeal to the conservative rural man in the Kandyan districts when it was made out that the U.N.P. leaders, though of Goyigama caste, were of lesser status. In the low country, on the other hand, Mr. Bandaranaike was able to win many in the Karava, Salagama, and Durava communities who thought the U.N.P. did not give them sufficient recognition or political opportunity. It will be recalled that the agitation among laymen and *bhikkhus* in the low country was not without a caste element, since the most vocal critics of the up-country, Goyigama sects were mainly of non-Goyigama background.

The issue of constitutional reform was not vigorously canvassed, but Mr. Bandaranaike argued that it was highly irregular for Buddhist Ceylon to acknowledge the Christian queen of Great Britain as its sovereign. He recommended establishing a democratic republic with a president as head of state instead of that role being filled by a governor general as the nominal representative of the British monarch. The Buddhist Committee report also urged a constitutional change so that Ceylon would be a republic within the Commonwealth. India and Pakistan had already cut such symbolic constitutional ties with Great Britain; why could not Ceylon? Particularly in the year of Buddha Jayanti it was important to sever this connection with the Queen who was, after all, "Defender of the Faith."

A more problematical issue during the campaign was the importance of the U.N.P.'s foreign policy. From the beginning the U.N.P. had followed a policy of allowing the British to retain naval installations in the east and an R.A.F. base not far from Colombo in the west as the least expensive way of ensuring Ceylon's defense from any conceivable enemy.[38] Mr. Bandaranaike argued that the continued presence of British bases on the island was a derogation of Ceylon's independent status. Only a complete withdrawal of British forces from the island would make Ceylon independent. Here again, both the Left parties and Mr. Bandaranaike attacked the U.N.P. on the same lines and charged it with being subservient to the Western powers.

Sir John Kotelawala also came under attack for his strong anti-Communist statements at Bandung and his unwillingness to adopt

[38] See Chapter X for a detailed discussion of this problem.

HELP, HELP! I DONT WANT TO BE SAVED!

Courtesy of the *Ceylon O*

Many politicians conjured up fears from which they promised to save the country.

the policy of nonalignment as put forward by Mr. Nehru. Many argued that Sir John's "provocative" differences with India over foreign policy and his often abrupt and public arguments with Mr. Nehru involved Ceylon in unnecessary local friction with the subcontinent to the North. A policy of neutralist nonalignment in the shadow of India had some virtues; close alignment with the Western powers, it was argued, particularly the United States, was full of risks. As if to confirm the worst suspicions of the governing party's critics to the effect that Ceylon's government was a willing instrument of American policy, two weeks after the election campaign had begun the American Secretary of State visited the island following diplomatic discussions in Karachi and New Delhi. Though his visit was brief, it lent credence to the opposition's accusation that the United States was secretly supporting the U.N.P.

Even though the Trotskyists and Communists differed vehemently with one another on their attitudes toward the Soviet Union, they could easily agree that American power was inherently expansionist, "imperialist" and bound to involve its allies in war. For their part, many Buddhists, now considered that Christians had been the source of much of the harm done to Buddhism. They argued that those within the U.N.P. who tended to look to association with Western countries for defense, for economic assistance, or for cultural inspiration disdained Buddhism. Thus, both Marxists and Buddhists could warn against association with Western countries and could use different but converging lines of attack against their common target, the governing party.

Yet, on the whole, it is clear that foreign policy played a relatively small role in the election campaign. The issues that excited the voter were of a domestic, cultural, and even personal nature. In some respects, the election could be looked upon as a plebiscite between two men who were the antithesis of each other. Sir John Kotelawala was a man of action, of blunt words, of quick decisions, one who did not worry if he hurt a man's feelings by what he said. He acknowledged that he spoke first and then thought afterwards, but at least everyone knew where he stood. He was abrupt in debate. He cared little for the conventions of a puritanical Eastern society, but had made his own the secular, uninhibited worldly life of a Western urban society. He had lived abroad on many occasions during the past fifteen years and owned real estate in England.

Mr. Bandaranaike and his wife were of the highest status and had a large family. He had the gift of words in a society that gives great deference to the orator's and the scholar's skills. Few could match his oratorical brilliance in English or Sinhalese; few were more skillful in suggesting nuances of meaning and differences in approach necessary to be the friend of all and the enemy of few. Whereas his opponent had been abroad on many occasions, Mr. Bandaranaike had not been to Europe since his college days. Symbolically he had made Sinhalese his culture, Buddhism his religion, and Ceylon his home. Thus at a time when indigenous language, culture, and religion were on the political agenda, the image of himself which Mr. Bandaranaike was able to project before the public was far more likely to evoke a positive response than his opponent's.

Sir John was known to treat his own workers well on his estates and in his family's graphite mines. But when faced with the labor disorders that precipitated his coming into the prime ministership and, as head of the government ultimately responsible for the continued expeditious handling of the country's imports and exports, he had firmly resisted the political misuse of the trade union movement. But these measures inhibited legitimate trade union organization and thus made it easier for a number of employers to continue unenlightened wage policies. These steps worked to his disadvantage at the hustings.

Mr. Bandaranaike, free from the highest responsibilities, had long made himself the champion of a variety of professional groups and minor elected officials well placed to influence the rural vote. He was one of the few of upper-class background who was mindful of their sensitivities and attentive to their grievances. Although hindsight can now assign proper weight to these elements of Mr. Bandaranaike's rural support, at the time the United National Party's reputation as the party of independence, its links with the traditionally influential, its alleged influence in the public service, and its more visible party organization suggested to most observers that the U.N.P. would be returned again although with a reduced majority.

V · THE CAMPAIGN

In line with British practice, the campaign lasted only six weeks. April is the hottest month in tropical Ceylon, and the physical stamina of Sir John Kotelawala and Mr. Bandaranaike were tried to the limit. Their schedules were so loaded that both candidates not infrequently appeared for meetings over five or six hours late. One group waited for Mr. Bandaranaike from four o'clock until after midnight. Sir John was usually the principal U.N.P. speaker, although most ministers spoke widely in constituencies other than their own. M.P.s generally stayed within their own districts and attempted to nurse their own electorates. Mr. Bandaranaike's responsibilities were heavier than the Prime Minister's, for apart from the Buddhist organizational support in rural areas and uncertain backing of his Marxist followers in the coastal districts, his own organization was no match for that of the U.N.P's. His campaign had the air of improvisation, of a tremendous personal effort to align for himself a congeries of separate group interests.

The leading candidates held large public meetings in the principal towns. Usually the visiting speakers, the local candidates, and notables who supported either the U.N.P. or the M.E.P. were in attendance. Invariably a Buddhist *bhikkhu* would be present to lend the benign aegis of the yellow robe to the candidate, whether it was an M.E.P., or U.N.P., Communist or Trotskyist meeting. Many smaller meetings were held at cross roads and in the villages. A harbinger would go an hour or two ahead of the candidate with a loudspeaker mounted on his car and a collection of Sinhalese recorded music. Microphone in hand, standing on top of his car, the candidate would excoriate his opponent, praise his own virtues, tell all he had done for the constituency already or all he hoped to do when he returned to parliament. Local candidates tended to dwell on local issues, the roads and bridges needing repairs, the schools to be built, and so on. Language, Buddhism, and the need for a change dominated the opposition's appeal. The achievements of the U.N.P., the need for stability and progress, or the impossibility of Mr. Bandaranaike forming an effective cabinet out of his disparate associates carried the burden of the U.N.P. case. The Leftist meetings were well organized in their own districts with large, attentive audiences. The V.L.S.S.P. spokesmen were as harsh on the language issue as they were vigorous on economic issues, emphasizing the incapability of the U.N.P. to solve the country's economic problems. The Trotskyist party argued for communal harmony, they spoke softly of the language problem, but were vigorous on the economic and other issues in the campaign. Like the V.L.S.S.P., they tended to ignore the Buddhist preoccupations though the N.L.S.S.P. warned of a possible theocratic state emerging from new political activity of the *bhikkhus*.

Door-to-door canvassing was common. Many candidates penctrated the remoter areas of their electorates and came face to face with rural or urban reality in a way they seldom experienced except at election time. Representative politics, the great leveler, temporarily turned the tables of influence as the usually important man, his well-protected wife and daughters, or his influential associates solicited the support of his electorate by knocking on doors and chatting with villagers. Jokes and cartoons dramatized the plight of the politician's wife who had to open her home to the prying eyes, and her larder to the insatiable appetites of her husband's prospective voters. Particularly in districts where party organizations were weak, the candidate depended upon such personal solicitations to get out the vote; and in Colombo itself the tireless Communist party leader appeared in many a worker's hut and slum shack for the personal touch.

Pamphlet materials and simple broadsides were used, with a smiling picture of the candidate, whatever his party, and the usual advice to put an "X" in the proper place on the ballot paper. Of particular interest was a devastating poster, reportedly designed by a *bhikkhu* working for the Eksath Bhikkhu Peramuna. A Statue of the Buddha sat under his Bo Tree at one end of the poster and the balance of the cartoon depicted a long parade led by Sir John Kotelawala on an elephant, the symbol of the U.N.P. Sir John was holding a spear pointed at the heart of the Buddha statue. Behind him on the elephant sat one of his reputedly many girl friends. In the parade that followed some were ballroom dancing and drinking champagne, others were waving the country's principal newspapers said to be in the party's pay. In a Buddhist country, to kill meat is abhorrent; to eat it is doubtful practice. In the foreground of the poster came a cart, bearing the carcass of a dead calf to remind the devout of the shocking irreverence committed once by the Prime Minister who himself carved a barbecued calf in full public view. In the background, several Uncle Sams held aloft large dollar signs. The poster was entitled "The fight against the forces of evil—2,500 years ago and now." Underneath ran the caption: "In this year of Buddha Jayanti, rescue your country, your race and your religion from the forces of evil." The allusion was plain. Many temple pictures depict a not dissimilar scene. Mara, the mythical deity of evil, rides on an elephant attacking the Buddha and his followers. And through the power of the Buddha's purity and righteous ways, Mara is confounded, the elephant falls, and Mara is thrown to the ground where he is then helpless. This poster represented an ingenious merging of traditional indigenous imagery applied to contemporary political purposes. The U.N.P. showed no such skill in interweaving traditional cultural modes with their own political objectives.

The press was less sharply partisan in this election than it had been previously, and devoted considerable space to Opposition arguments and campaign speeches. The principal newspaper house, the Associated Newspapers of Ceylon, had been strongly pro-government in two previous elections. The papers of the other large newspaper combine—the Times group—had been more critical of the government, but had supported the U.N.P. ultimately. The Associated

"The fight against the forces of evil 2,500 years ago and now. In this year of Buddha Jayanti, rescue your country, your race and your religion from the forces of evil"—a skillful combination of traditional lore and contemporary politics.

Newspapers of Ceylon especially had given great prominence to the lives and times of the local political figures, the public receptions and travels of the prime minister, the proposals and promises of the government. Although these papers did not invariably give the opposition the space the opposition felt it deserved, editorials were often critical of administrative or policy inadequacies of the government. News stories not infrequently showed U.N.P. politicians—as well as the opposition—in a poor light. In this respect, there was a marked contrast between the English-language press in India and Ceylon. In India the press dealt with Mr. Nehru with great delicacy and circumspection. In Ceylon authority may be deferred to, but it is still quite legitimate to criticize it vigorously. With cartoons and editorials, columnists made a point of exposing the weaknesses and the pretensions of self-important men, whether in the government or in the opposition. Nevertheless, despite the running fire of criticism, it was widely believed that the press associations could naturally be counted on the side of the government. The radio was insulated from the campaign as in previous elections. Foreign governments appear to have remained strictly aloof although there were serious allegations made by the Leftist journals during the campaign.

VI · ORGANIZATION OF THE ELECTIONS

The electoral law called for contests for 95 elected seats in 89 electoral districts.[39] In 1954, to further negotiations with India regarding the status of residents of Indian origin, four seats were to be established by order of the governor general for the separate representation of those of Indian or Pakistani origin who became citizens. But the governor general had not given the necessary authorization and they remained without the vote. In addition, as in 1952, the 400,000 Indians and Pakistanis of voting age did not participate in the election.

A select committee of the second parliament had been appointed in July 1955 to consider the working of the provisions of the Ceylon electoral law in the light of experience gained in the first and second elections. In its report, among other things, the select committee urged that as soon as practicable, the elections should be held throughout the island on the same day instead of on four different

[39] Ceylon (Parliamentary Elections) Order in Council 1946.

days as in 1952.[40] This practice would reduce impersonation and ensure that no one party gained an advantage from the particular day on which its strongest candidates were contesting. It was often argued, for instance, that through its influence on the election commissioner, the U.N.P. was able to run its most prominent and strongest party members on the first day of the election, releasing these men then to campaign for weaker government candidates during the subsequent days. Sweeping victories during the first day's elections were presumed to help the party gain still more votes as the bandwagon started to roll.

The government held to the contrary that since the polling booths had to be manned by government servants, there were insufficient trained personnel available for simultaneous islandwide polling. Three separate days were selected accordingly, April 5, 7, and 10 and the commissioner of elections distributed the constituencies among these three days. Large blocs of adjacent electorates voted on the same day to ease the task of supervision. As if to confirm the charges that three days would be used to the government party's advantage, the prime minister and every U.N.P. cabinet member, but one, ran on the first day; districts where Left parties were known to be strong were nearly all fixed for the second day, and Mr. Bandaranaike himself had to run on the third day.

The supervisory staff of government servants were carefully briefed on their tasks in both writing and in special training lectures organized by the commissioners of parliamentary elections. Supervisors of each polling station, insofar as possible, were upper level public servants. Over 2,400 polling stations were established throughout the island with the aim that no voters should be more than three miles from where they had to cast their ballot. Schools, rural courts, and community center buildings were taken over temporarily. Candidates set up their booths near the polling station so that voters could obtain informal identifying cards from their party and be coached in the proper vote to cast, but the booths had to be more than fifty yards from the polling station. The cards, prepared by party workers, had the name of the person and his number as it appeared on the electoral registers, speeding the task of the electoral

[40] In 1947, the election occupied nineteen days spread over a period of four weeks. *Report of the Select Committee Appointed to Consider the Working of the Provisions of the Ceylon (Parliamentary Election) Order in Council*, Parliamentary Series No. 28, 2nd Parliament, 4th Session (Jan. 1956).

clerk in locating the individual's name and checking it on the register to prevent double voting.

The electoral registers used were English-language registers. There had been considerable agitation prior to the election to have the electoral lists posted in Sinhalese.[41] Lists were translated into Sinhalese and circulated, but the official list used for electoral purposes was that prepared by the Registrar General's office and maintained thus far in English. This list had already gone through one translation, for it was originally taken in Sinhalese or Tamil by local village officials and put into English in the offices of the district revenue officers and government agents. To retranslate these lists back into the vernaculars would have made for serious inaccuracies.

Voting day outside Colombo was quiet and orderly. Everyone but the exhausted candidates appeared in a holiday mood. Free rides were provided to the polls, adding to the carnival atmosphere. This involved a truly remarkable mobilization of the island's vehicles. It was the U.N.P. that held the largest fleet of cars and trucks at its disposal, but the results proved that accepting a ride to the polls no longer puts the voter in debt to a party. Similarly, it appeared as if the majority of the voters in rural districts obtained their identification cards from the U.N.P. booths, but the results revealed that they voted against the party whose label they carried to the polling clerk. The excitement ran higher in Colombo. The decorations were more plentiful, party flags and literature abounded, and large crowds gathered to hear the results.

In 61 of the 89 electoral districts the counting took place that same day, and results began to be known on the first day's elections late that evening. Villagers received the news of the U.N.P. defeat with fewer external signs of joy than the excited crowds in the capital who cheered lustily whenever any opposition member drove up to the office where the results were being counted.

In contrast to reports of previous elections, in 1956 there was little apparent bribery, thuggery, or impersonation. Whereas in 1947, 19 electoral challenges were lodged by defeated candidates or their friends and 21 in 1952, in 1956 only 4 elections were questioned. Of these, only two went so far as to come to trial and only one led to the successful candidate being disqualified. There were few of the horrendous charges of intimidation and tampering with the ballot boxes that marked earlier elections. No accusations were raised

[41] *House of Representatives*, V. 23, c. 1474-1527, for interesting debate.

against police or public servants attempting to use their influence to swing the vote.[42]

Hence, by 1956, the people of Ceylon had an opportunity to express their preferences as between alternative candidates in full and trusted secrecy and without significant corruption or intimidation of the voter. In these respects, a formerly alien political process had thus become thoroughly domesticated, although important side effects raised intractable difficulties.

VII · THE RESULTS

According to the electoral registers 3,464,000 Ceylonese or 45 per cent of the citizens were eligible to vote. Of these, 70 per cent cast their vote, a far higher proportion than is usual in the United States.[43]

Party	*Candidates*	*Seats Obtained*	*Seats Gained*	*Votes*
M.E.P.	60	51	40	1,046,277
U.N.P.	76	8	0	738,810
N.L.S.S.P.	21	14	9	274,204
Federal party	14	10	8	142,758
Communist party	9	3	1	119,715
Ceylon Labor party	4	0	0	18,033
Tamil Congress	1	1	0	8,914
Independent	64	8	7	298,536
				2,647,247

The results were an unambiguous vote of confidence for Mr. Bandaranaike as the fourth prime minister of independent Ceylon. They also gave a clear majority to the coalition that he headed. Indeed, from a statistical point of view, there was a remarkably close parallel between the relative positions of the M.E.P. in 1956 and the U.N.P. in 1952. Whereas in 1952 the U.N.P. held 54 seats and the S.L.F.P. of Mr. Bandaranaike won only 9 seats, in 1956 Mr. Bandaranaike's coalition won 51 seats and the U.N.P. gained only 8 seats. On the basis of the popular vote, the U.N.P. won in

[42] Of course, had the U.N.P. won in the balloting, many charges would again have been levelled against it.

[43] Official figures. The percentage of electors is not comparable to the total votes cast since voters in multimember constituencies cast two or three votes apiece, depending upon the number of seats to be filled. There is some uncertainty regarding the exact number of "Independents" since some ran on ephemeral groupings that do not appear to have survived the election.

1952 with 1,026,005 votes and the M.E.P. won its victory in 1956 with 1,046,000 votes.[44] However, in 1952 the second largest party led by Mr. Bandaranaike, won only 361,000 votes, whereas in 1956 the U.N.P. won 739,000, gaining more than four times as many popular votes as its nearest party rival apart from the victorious M.E.P.

Mr. Bandaranaike's segment of the M.E.P., the former Sri Lanka Freedom Party, numerically dominated the coalition, gaining 41 of the 51 M.E.P. seats. By comparison, the Left parties did less well although their position was strengthened considerably over their record in 1952. The V.L.S.S.P. segment of the coalition raised the seats it occupied from 2 to 5. The N.L.S.S.P. for its part, gained 9 seats in 1952 and raised the number to 14 in 1956.[45] The Communist party with 2 members before the 1956 election added one to its numbers.

In terms of the popular vote, the U.N.P. and the S.L.F.P. segment of the M.E.P. together polled 57 per cent of the votes cast. Together the parties of the Left and the identifiable Marxist members of the M.E.P. polled roughly 22 per cent of the total as compared to 18 per cent in 1952 and 15.6 per cent in 1947.[46] The fact that the number of seats they occupied has more than doubled reflected the concentration of their efforts on relatively sure seats and the elimination of competition between them rather than a commensurate increase in public support. Where they did run candidates, however, they did much better than in previous elections, for in 1952 they polled only 22 per cent of the total votes cast in those constituencies, but in 1956 they obtained 30 per cent on the average. Their greatest accretion of voting strength was in Western Province, the most urbanized part of Ceylon and their traditional seat of strength.

Although Mr. Bandaranaike gained resounding support for himself and the program and special values he represented, for the Marx-

[44] 1952 figures from I. D. S. Weerawardana, "The General Elections in Ceylon, 1952," p. 137.

[45] It lost several members on a split between elections and therefore in fact picked up 9 seats in the 1956 election.

[46] In Western Province they gained nearly 35 per cent of all votes cast compared to 25 per cent in the previous election and won 12 seats instead of the 4 held in 1952. In Southern Province, however, their popular vote declined from 30 per cent to approximately 20 per cent. The significance of these data as indicators of changing public opinion are difficult to appraise along "Right" or "Left" lines, since the issues were not likely to bring out this type of difference.

ists in association with him the 1956 election was of great importance. By adopting a policy of "United Front from Above" for purposes of the electoral campaign and identifying themselves with indigenous cultural and linguistic aspirations as well as offering promise of speedier economic change, one group of Marxists entered the cabinet of independent Ceylon. For the first time, a leader with a following among organized labor and an ambition to transform Ceylon's economy according to Marxist prescriptions gained ministerial powers. Mr. Gunawardena became Minister of Agriculture and Food. A younger colleague, Mr. P. H. William Silva, became Minister of Industry and another erstwhile associate became Parliamentary Secretary for External Affairs. Had the estate workers been able to vote, the Marxist representation would have increased, although it is difficult to say with certainty whether the estate workers would have allied themselves with the Trotskyist N.L.S.S.P., the Communist party, or followed ethnic leadership.[47]

The new cabinet showed greater caste diversity than before. Of fourteen ministers, nine Goyigamas, two Salagamas, two Karavas, and a Muslim gained portfolios. There were murmurings of satisfaction in these communities that at last one of "their" men had attained cabinet rank. The new cabinet also showed a higher proportion of low-country men than previous cabinets. For the first time since independence Tamils were not included.

The election had other important results. Buddhist and Sinhalese values were given greater representation. An important element of the new government was responsive to the demands of the newly organized Buddhist activists. Alcoholic beverages at official functions were replaced by coconut milk and other soft drinks; indigenous dress replaced Western attire for official purposes. Legislation making Sinhalese the sole official language was passed promptly and administrative measures were taken within the government to carry this into effect gradually. Individuals within the public service who had been active in Buddhist and language agitation were moved into responsible positions to effect legislated language reforms more rapidly, and a shift of effective power within the public service could thus be discerned. More official debate in parliament came to be carried on in Sinhalese. Ministers were careful in their public

[47] It seemed unlikely that they would have supported Mr. Gunawardena, who had espoused the Sinhalese nationalist cause in preference to either the Trotskyist or Communist parties which had been more sensitive to Tamil anxieties.

utterances and their private lives not to offend Buddhist sensibilities and to be closer to indigenous ways than before. Agitation for radical reorganization of the educational system continued and was reflected in government policy.

The results in Tamil areas were equally decisive. All Tamils who had been associated with the U.N.P. in recent years were swept from their seats by the tide of Tamil fear of Sinhalese domination. The Federal Party, which had had only 2 seats before the election, gained 10. Whereas in 1952, the Federalists gained 42 per cent of the popular vote in Northern Province but won only 2 seats, this time they won nearly 50 per cent of the votes and took 6. In Eastern Province the debacle of the U.N.P. was most marked. In this area Sinhalese, Tamils, and Muslims are intermingled, although Tamils predominate. In 1952 the U.N.P. polled over half the votes and won 2 seats out of 7. This time no candidates ran under its label. On the contrary, the Federal Party which had gained less than 5 per cent of the votes in 1952 won 4 of 7 seats in 1956, obtaining more than 42 per cent of the popular vote.

It has thus far been characteristic of politics in Tamil areas that more Independents ran successfully than elsewhere on the island. No doubt this is in part a reflection of a firmer social structure, and the fact that there are fewer channels to local prominence than in the south. They appear to be more prepared to rest on their personal popularity or family reputation in their constituencies than to ally themselves with others for a party-oriented struggle.[48] In this election 23 candidates ran as Independents and 4 were returned.[49] Although only one in six was successful, this record is considerably better than the island-wide average where only one in nine Independents succeeded.

The fewer Independents running throughout the island in this election suggested a trend toward the strengthening of parties. Indeed, on the surface the election as a whole came nearer to being a two-party contest than any election in Ceylon's history. In 1947, there were direct two-party contests in only 7 single-member constituencies; in 1952, in only 16. By comparison, in 1956, 32 con-

[48] In 1947, for instance, 28 Independents ran and 6 were returned, a success ratio of 1:4. The island-wide ratio was 1:9. In 1952, the ratio in Tamil areas was 1:3 compared to 1:8 for Ceylon as a whole.

[49] Exactitude here is difficult, since in addition to the Federal Party and the Tamil Congress, two other "parties" entered the field with 7 candidates between them. These were small and proved ephemeral. Those 7 candidates have therefore been counted throughout as "Independents."

stituencies showed simple contests between only two candidates running under competing party labels.

It would be misleading, however, to see in the increase of these simple contests evidence of a growing two-party system along British or even American lines. The competing party labels scarcely concealed the profoundly divergent elements, particularly notable within the M.E.P. Indeed, the most outstanding difficulty of Mr. Bandaranaike at the cabinet level proved to be the unresolved cleavages within his own government. Moreover, once the U.N.P. was brought down, the N.L.S.S.P.'s and the Communist party's no-contest agreement with the M.E.P. had achieved its purpose. There was again every incentive to resume the multiparty struggle as before.

The divisions within the M.E.P. cabinet persisted. Ministers from the two factions disagreed with one another, openly criticizing their cabinet colleagues and taking opposing positions in public and in the house on such matters as land reform legislation, economic development policy, the approach to growing labor union disorders or the problems plaguing the port of Colombo. These open disagreements on fundamental policies hampered cabinet government.

From the time he became prime minister, Mr. Bandaranaike could not contain the communal and religious extremists whose backing had contributed so much to his electoral victory. Many of his erstwhile Sinhalese Buddhist supporters became exasperated by his failure to implement the promises made before the election. The communal disorders of 1956 and 1958 were the direct results of that campaign.

In the spring of 1959, the cabinet split, the Marxists being forced to resign their portfolios. The government remained in power by a slim majority, but it lacked the margin of reliable votes necessary for effective rule. The assassination of the prime minister in September 1959 precipitated another crisis in the political life of the country and opened further divisions within the ruling party. Acts of violence against political leaders had been unknown in modern Ceylon. Ironically enough, the assailant was a *bhikkhu* and a teacher in an *ayurvedic* medical college, symbolically combining in one person two of the very forces that Mr. Bandaranaike had rallied so effectively during the 1956 election.

CONCLUSION

The ruling party that brought independence to Ceylon and controlled the cabinet and parliament for eight years lost the general election in 1956 for a variety of reasons. There was a widespread desire for a change. But this public mood became focused on two key issues—replacing English as the official language with Sinhalese, the language spoken by 65 per cent of the island's population, and improving the state of Buddhism in Ceylon. Both of these issues had cultural implications associated with the search for a national identity and distinctiveness. Career opportunities for the educated Sinhalese and for other identifiable professional groups were involved in the language problem. The threats to Buddhism as defined by an active minority of Buddhist laymen and *bhikkhus* aroused Buddhists in many walks of life and stirred the peasantry. Together, the issues of language and religion provided Mr. Bandaranaike and his followers with a better channel to the mass of the voters than anything available to the U.N.P. The election agitation, in turn, drew into political activity rural professional and middle-class groups which, with the aid of the priesthood, brought into question the traditional influence wielded in the countryside by landowners and rural notables.

Here, two related aspects of the country's tradition—Buddhism and Sinhalese culture—were utilized to challenge another, secular, aspect of that tradition—the influence hitherto understood to reside in the landed old families. These were alleged to have become alienated in a cultural and moral sense from the purity and simplicity of the less educated, less cosmopolitan rural middle class and peasantry who had remained insulated against demoralizing influences from abroad. This rejection by large numbers of the rural voters of the traditionally prominent was perhaps the most significant internal aspect of the election, moving the locus of popular representative power from the hands of the wealthy to the rural middle classes, from the English-educated to the Sinhalese-educated.

The manner of this shift of influence had much to do with one of its results. In previous elections, the U.N.P. had successfully activated the Sinhalese rural masses sufficiently to win their votes. Although fears of Indian Tamils had then been used for political purposes, communal and religious antagonism against Ceylon's minorities had not been sharpened. In 1956, by contrast, Sinhalese rural voters had been enlisted with highly emotional appeals, sometimes explicitly directed against certain of Ceylon's communal and religious minorities.

Economic issues also played a part in the election. The abrupt rise in the price of rice to the consumer, the withdrawal of the free mid-day meal for school children three years before the election, and the growing spectre of unemployment in the present and future served to further undermine the U.N.P.'s following. Economic issues were particularly effective in the coastal belt from the neighborhood of Colombo down to the southern tip of the island and inland as far as Sabaragamuwa, an area where the Left parties have traditionally had their main strength. It was in these areas that the Left parties picked up the bulk of their seats—19 of 22 in all—for the most part from constituencies they had held before the 1952 election. The electorate's responsiveness to the change in the price of rice, already three years past at the time of the 1956 election, suggests how little room for economic maneuver resides in a popularly elected government and how vulnerable such a government is to the changing terms of trade in the world market when signs of economic development are not yet evident.

Although language and other cultural factors were more important, economic difficulties made it easy for the opposition to pin on the U.N.P. a reputation for special privilege and unconcern for the mass of voters. As the moral position of the U.N.P. was being discredited, a new political fact of primary importance surprised many observers. The Ceylonese had had a reputation for personal politics and for ignoring the first principle of party government—the creation of a plausible alternative government. In the previous election, some six parties entered the field against the U.N.P. This time, the opposition forces tempered their own ambitions with a hard discipline. In only twelve constituencies was the U.N.P. faced with an opposition split between competing parties. For the first time, then, the thoughtful voter could foresee an alternative democratic government should the U.N.P. be defeated.

Although such a trend augured well for the development of the two-party system along British or American lines, there was contradictory evidence. In the first place, the M.E.P. itself could hardly be called a "party." The M.E.P. was split in fact into two divergent factions. Unlike the factions in American parties whose frontiers often vary with the issue, the lines within the M.E.P. were all too firmly drawn. One small group in the cabinet and the M.E.P. were "hard" Marxists, talking of the dictatorship of the proletariat, the inevitable victory of Communism in Ceylon, nationalization of estates without compensation, and peasant collectivization. The larger, sometimes led by Mr. Bandaranaike and sometimes without clear leadership, talked of "democratic socialism," "the family farm," and government only by consent of the governed. The "hard" Marxists had effective leadership, their cabinet members were serious, industrious, and had a clear sense of direction. They also had the tacit support of the few Communist party members in parliament although they could by no means count on the support of the Trotskyist party. The democratic socialists, on the other hand, did not have a clear sense of direction or an effective organization, and some of their ministers were not especially industrious. They undoubtedly had a wide, if diffused popular following, for they were able to combine egalitarian "democratic socialist" appeals with the traditional Buddhist and Sinhalese cultural values. Perhaps in the very imprecision there was strength in the countryside even though the urban intellectuals and sophisticates might criticize the vagueness. Such divisions at the cabinet level, however, hampered constructive government. The opposition parties, too, remained splintered.

As with previous elections, that of 1956 impelled many otherwise urban and Westernized individuals, of whatever party, to venture into the deeper countryside or poorer districts to search out grievances and moods, and to sensitize themselves to the needs of the less favored population. Verbal respect for the honorable "Goiya" or upstanding Ceylonese peasant is frequent, but a serious identification with the real needs of the peasantry or urban laborer is rare for those professional and other influential individuals who form the political elite. But there is little doubt that the net effect of the imperatives of assuring the vote was to bring home to the political elite the needs of the mass of the population in the countryside and city. As such, representative elections are perhaps one of the main institutions for rapidly bridging the gap between the privileged and the masses in the city and country.

The 1956 election was remarkably free of allegations of bribery, corruption, and impersonation. The way the voting went was a clear demonstration that the mass of voters believed in the secrecy of the ballot and in their safe, secure right to vote for whomever they pleased.

The communal consequences of the 1956 election were serious. Island-wide issues which tended to transcend the traditional ethnic, linguistic, or religious differences played no essential part in the 1956 election although in 1948 and 1952 they had been of growing importance. For the first time since independence, politics in Tamil areas formed a system without organizational links with the larger parties competing for control in Sinhalese areas. As such, the trend manifest in 1947 and 1952 to absorb Tamil political interests within one or another island-wide party was reversed. Two large parties competed against each other to obtain a parliamentary majority by outbidding one another in Sinhalese districts alone. If such a development is repeated in the future, communal consciousness among the Sinhalese majority of voters is likely to be aroused at every future election. And Tamil interests will be less and less adequately represented.

Perhaps the most urgent and persisting difficulty of the new M.E.P. government after its electoral victory was its inability to determine a course of action to meet the essential aspirations of the Sinhalese community and the basic requirements of the Tamil minority. The loud voices of extremists on both sides set the tone of policy while the gentler voices of moderate men could no longer be heard. The shift of power in Ceylon from the hands of the wealthy gentry to the poorer men of lesser standing, closer to the electorate, is in some ways comparable to the Jacksonian "revolution" in the United States. The new leaders in both countries were less familiar with the proprieties of representative government than their predecessors. In America, however, these men were fortunate to have had a considerable period of national growth during which they learned the arts of governance. The new leaders in Ceylon, it seemed, were not to be so fortunate.

PART THREE

THE SEARCH FOR A FOREIGN POLICY

CHAPTER X · FOREIGN POLICY

"Despite the receding tide of colonialism in Asia, the political, economic and cultural enslavement of millions of Asians and Africans remains one of the hardest and most stubborn facts of our times."—*Times of Ceylon,* December 28, 1954

I · THE PROBLEM OF OBJECTIVES

To PRESERVE and enhance their new-found independence is the principal objective of South Asian statesmen concerned with foreign affairs. They see their independence subject to a variety of territorial, economic, ethnic, and cultural threats. Countering these threats defines a series of more specific policy objectives.

Statesmen have been concerned to protect their territorial integrity—national security in its classic sense. Consequently, considerations of military security familiar to Western statesmen have set the terms for many decisions. The existence of important minorities may be seen as an impediment to effective national unity. Policies designed to deal with minorities at home have had international implications. Independence in the economic sphere has also been an important policy objective. Their highly specialized, often largely export, economies have been particularly vulnerable to changes in world market and supply conditions, and each has lacked a diversity of production to cushion the impact of adverse market fluctuations. Foreign policy, therefore, has had to consider the economics of housekeeping, ensuring entry to remunerative markets, adequate foreign exchange resources for essential imports, and effective access to essential foods and manufactured goods. To meet the growing demand for a rising standard of living, statesmen have had to concern themselves with problems of economic development. These may require fiscal and trade measures with foreign policy implications or the search for capital and technical assistance from abroad on acceptable terms.

The cultural legacy of centuries of colonialism, like the economic legacy, is now condemned. Many people feel that the country's independence is incomplete because of the remaining foreign cultural influences. Perhaps only by holding aloof from certain countries can religious or cultural integrity be ensured. Foreign policy may therefore be influenced by considerations which are far from the tangible matter of European realpolitik.

Relations with the world of distant great powers provided the first set of foreign policy problems. Relations with nearer neighbors also required consideration. Reaction against the colonial past drew all countries in the area away in sentiment from the Western states and toward one another in common Asian consciousness. However, size, minority problems, and other differences promoted a subsidiary system of relationships within the Indian Ocean and Asian areas, where the proper approach to Asian neighbors appeared to require as much attention as did policy toward more distant powers.

As in other countries, too, foreign policy alternatives commended themselves, not only on their merits but also for their utility in the domestic political arena. It has long been a favorite gambit of opposition parties in every country to charge the government with insufficient care for the country's independence. Particularly in South Asia, anxiety over independence is so palpable that this may be one of the better arguments for undermining a political opponent at home. Thus anxieties may be reinforced and the statesman's problems of real foreign policy choices become further complicated.

The geographical, political, and economic setting of Ceylon's foreign policy makers will be examined before specific foreign policy problems will be discussed. In the final chapter the special case of Asian solidarity will be considered.

II · THE FOREIGN POLICY SETTING

A. THE GEOGRAPHICAL ELEMENT

The geographical characteristics of a country set intractable limits to what its statesmen can do, and Ceylon's situation is no exception. The island's position in the Indian Ocean area gives it a focal importance for seaborne trade routes and strategic naval calculations. The Indian subcontinent thrusts down into the center of the Indian Ocean for more than a thousand miles from the ocean's northern shores, and Ceylon is at the tip of India. It lies some 2,000 miles from Aden to the west, 1,500 miles from Singapore in the east, 2,000 miles from Mauritius to the southwest, and 3,000 miles from Freemantle in Australia to the southeast. Ships passing from Calcutta and Rangoon going west to Suez or the Cape, sailing from Bombay and going eastward to Singapore, ships linking the two halves of Pakistan together, and vessels following the principal avenues of ocean commerce from Suez to Singapore or Australia all pass close to Ceylon. In early days, Galle Harbor on the southern shore was the principal port of entry. During the nineteenth century Colombo gained the dominant position as tea exports required a nearer access to the sea and the artificial harbor was developed to give safe berth to vessels too large for Galle.

From the naval point of view, Ceylon has the additional gift of the most spacious natural protected harbor in the central Indian Ocean area. Only Bombay compares to it, but that is nearly 1,000 miles away from the open sea near the Indian Ocean's northern shore. On the east coast, Trincomalee Harbor runs inland some eight miles and the anchorage is large enough to shelter the full fleet of any of the world's great powers.

Newer air routes, too, pass over Ceylon. Flights from Manila in the Far East, or from Australia and Indonesia to the Middle East and Europe use Ceylonese air fields. And because there are relatively few islands in the Indian Ocean as *points d'appui,* Ceylon has an enhanced importance in an age of air traffic.

The Indian Ocean in which Ceylon thus holds a central place has special geographical and political attributes which have played an important part in the history of the area, and these characteristics will probably contribute to future developments as well. The Indian Ocean has been likened to a landlocked sea. By controlling its five gateways and its most important shores for the past one hundred and fifty years one power—Great Britain—held undisputed sway. To the west, she controlled the approaches around the Cape of Good Hope, the entries via the Red Sea at Aden, and via the Persian Gulf by means of the protectorates in Trucial Oman and Muscat. The eastern portals were ensured by the base at Singapore, the Penang settlements, and British control of the Andaman Islands, while the southeastern lanes were dominated by Australia. Moreover, the northern shores of the Indian Ocean, from Iran in the west to Thailand in the east, through Pakistan, India, and Burma were also under the political control of Great Britain. It is fair to say that from the Napoleonic Wars until World War II the Indian Ocean was a British lake.[1] The only exceptions—French, German,

[1] See especially, K. M. Panikkar, *India and the Indian Ocean,* 2nd ed. (London, 1951),

and Dutch holdings—were more beholden to British sea power for uninterrupted access and defense than they were capable of challenging British control.[2]

At the same time, northern land approaches to the Indian Ocean were inadequately organized to pose a real threat. Beyond the Hindu Kush above Afghanistan, over the Himalayas, and beyond Tibet, Russian power during the nineteenth century gradually extended a European kind of government into Kazakhstan through Siberia and on to the Pacific. However, Tsarist administration was not effective and Russian hegemony received a serious set-back from a rising Asiatic nation—Japan—near the turn of the century. China's revolution in the first decade of the twentieth century remained incomplete and the land of the Manchus was never integrated into a reinvigorated polity until the late 1940's. It continued to be the pawn of Western sea powers and of Japan along its coasts and of Russian expansion in Sinkiang and Mongolia. During the time the Indian Ocean was a British lake, then, the countries to the north were immobilized by their own countervailing power or internal weakness. No effective threat from that region materialized, despite recurrent British fears for the Afghan frontier.

The area of ordered relationships and public security managed by British control of the Indian Ocean received one significant challenge prior to independence. During World War II, Japanese armies penetrated the thick jungle to the northeast of India and threatened direct assault through Assam; and more vivid to the Ceylonese, a Japanese naval task force operated deep in the Bay of Bengal wreaking a heavy toll on British and coastal shipping. Carrier-based planes attacked Colombo and seriously damaged naval vessels and installations at Trincomalee, apparently the forerunner of a heavier assault on the Trincomalee area. But because the Japanese were then particularly hard pressed in the Battle of the Coral Sea, they had to withdraw.

The real disintegration of this strategic area was accomplished when the independence movements achieved their goal. After 1947, no one power "enforc (ed) a single command and a unified security in the Indian Ocean. Instead of a single Empire, there (were) a

---

especially Ch. VI; P. R. Ramachandra Rao, *India and Ceylon* (Bombay, 1954); M. Zinkin, *Asia and the West* (London, 1951), Ch. XXII.

[2] The exceptions included French Madagascar, the German territories in east Africa, and the Dutch territories of Sumatra, Java, and the other islands of the Dutch East Indies.

congeries of succession States," each with weak defenses and several with possibly competing interests.[3] The strategic area of the Indian Ocean became "balkanized" and the future role and needs of any one power in the area became commensurately uncertain. At the focal point of sea and air routes traversing the Indian Ocean, Ceylon is a center of attention, a magnet of risks.

In the future Ceylon will no doubt continue to have intimate contact with whatever powers are active in the Indian Ocean. This may be a reinvigorated European sea power based on the British Isles, or a newer sea power from the Black Sea areas of the Soviet Union. Alternately, Soviet Power may be projected directly into the Indian Ocean through the Persian Gulf;[4] American power may enter the Indian Ocean in efforts to forestall Russian or Chinese hegemony over the Eurasian continent; it may be seaborne Japanese power as it was in 1942, or it may be, even, an expanded China, should it achieve hegemony over the Malayan Peninsula and possibly Burma and Thailand, and revert to its early sea-borne tradition under the Ming Dynasty of the fifteenth century.[5] Perhaps, even, it may be Ceylon's neighbor, India. Indeed, from the Indian point of view, if naval forces are engaged in the Indian Ocean, Ceylon's existence as an independent country of great strategic worth has considerable liabilities, not unlike the liabilities to Great Britain of Eire's neutrality during World War II.[6] Indian publicists have pointed out that Ceylon is in fact within India's strategic defense area.[7] If Indian security were threatened from the Indian Ocean, or in a combined attack from the Nepal area and the sea, Indian occupation of Trincomalee would be likely.

For the present the principal external sea power with interests in the Indian Ocean is Great Britain. She is dependent upon assured continued access to the sea lanes and the products of Commonwealth associates in South Asia and Australia, and the latter look upon Great Britain as a large market for their export products and as their principal trading partner. British naval effectiveness in the Indian Ocean

[3] Ramachandra Rao, p. 3.

[4] The negotiations between Germany and the Soviet Union prior to the outbreak of World War II are perhaps suggestive, R. J. Sontag, J. S. Beddie, ed. *Nazi-Soviet Relations 1939-1941* (New York, 1948), pp. 258-259.

[5] Most of these possibilities have been considered by Pannikar and Ramachandra Rao.

[6] Mr. Bandaranaike has drawn the parallel between Ceylon and Ireland from the Indian point of view. *House of Representatives*, V. 12, c. 79.

[7] Panikkar, p. 82; Ramachandra Rao, p. 17.

has been dramatically declining since 1948, but as yet no other great power has taken its place.

Irrespective of what country or countries may at some time in the future become active in the Indian Ocean area, Ceylonese statesmen can count on a lively future. Because of their exposed nodal position in the Indian Ocean, they cannot expect to be ignored unless the Indian Ocean itself becomes irrelevant to world political developments.

The second fundamental geographical fact which confronts her statesmen is that Ceylon is a tiny island country, separated by only a few miles from a massive continental power—India. Nine million people living in an area of 25,000 square miles are inescapably in the shadow of 400,000,000 people living in 1,100,000 square miles. Ceylon's statesmen do not ignore the fact that India has a large industrial potential and that, despite centrifugal political tendencies, the Delhi government appears capable of consolidating India until it may become one of the world's great powers. Even if India should fly apart, a South India independent of Delhi could be a threat to Ceylon, for she has been an area of South Indian expansion in centuries past. Relationships between the two countries are complicated by the existence of immigrants from India who have been living in Ceylon for a number of decades and who form 10 per cent of the Ceylonese population. The standard of living in Ceylon is considerably higher than in India, and a recurrent stream of illegal immigrants remind Ceylonese of population pressures from the north.

B. THE ECONOMIC SETTING

1. *The importance and direction of trade.* Ceylon's economic circumstances set certain limits to what her statesmen are able to do in the international world. Of all the independent countries in the sterling area, Ceylon is an export-import economy par excellence. Nearly 40 per cent of Ceylon's gross national product is accounted for by producing, processing, and handling export commodities. Imports are roughly equivalent to 35 per cent of the G.N.P.[8] Where the import-export sector has such importance in the overall economy, Ceylon's standard of living, like that of most small countries, is closely dependent upon international exchange. Statesmen concerned

[8] IBRD, p. 10 and calculated from p. 139. Only in Malaya, Ghana, and S. Rhodesia does external trade form a higher proportion of the national income.

with foreign policy, therefore, must take economic factors into serious account.

Ceylon's pattern of trade has launched her upon the world's sea ways, willy-nilly. Rice, as we have seen, is the dietary staple, and nearly half of it must be imported. In normal times, rice comes 1,000 miles across the Bay of Bengal from Rangoon, 2,000 miles from Saigon, or 2,500 miles from Bangkok. During World War II these areas were under Japanese occupation and rice had to be brought 4,000 miles from Egypt and nearly half way round the world from Brazil. Manufactured goods come mainly from Great Britain and West Germany, each nearly 8,000 sea miles away. Japan, its nearest large industrial supplier, is over 5,000 miles to the east while the United States is 9,700 miles via Suez or 8,700 by Singapore. Only if India should develop a significant export surplus of industrial goods could Ceylon's basic machine, vehicular, chemical, and other highly processed needs be obtained without regard to the assured use of the world's sea lanes.

To pay for these imports, she needs access to distant markets. Britain, by far the largest single purchaser of Ceylon's products, taking between 35 and 45 per cent, lies beyond the narrow seas of Aden, Suez, and Gibraltar. The most stable item, in terms of quantity and price, is tea, Britain taking nearly 40 per cent and Australia 10 per cent of total tea exports. Future markets for tea are likely to become more diversified as American purchases increase, as consumption grows in presently underdeveloped countries and as Russian buyers enter the Colombo auctions.

The direction of rubber shipments has shown greater variations. Because in most years the United States has been the principal buyer, Ceylon has been the largest single dollar earner of all the independent countries within the sterling area, with the exception of Malaya and Ghana.[9] From the point of view of the Government and its Ministry of Finance, sales to the United States are generally desirable. They provide dollar exchange for import purchases in any market and for reserves, and they give her a certain bargaining power vis-à-vis her sterling area partners. But allowing the United States to dominate the market for one commodity has its risks, for American purchases have fluctuated seriously from year to year, and this has prompt repercussions on the relatively immobile rubber

[9] U.S. Economic Cooperation Administration, *The Sterling Area—An American Analysis* (London, 1951), Table 35, pp. 132-133.

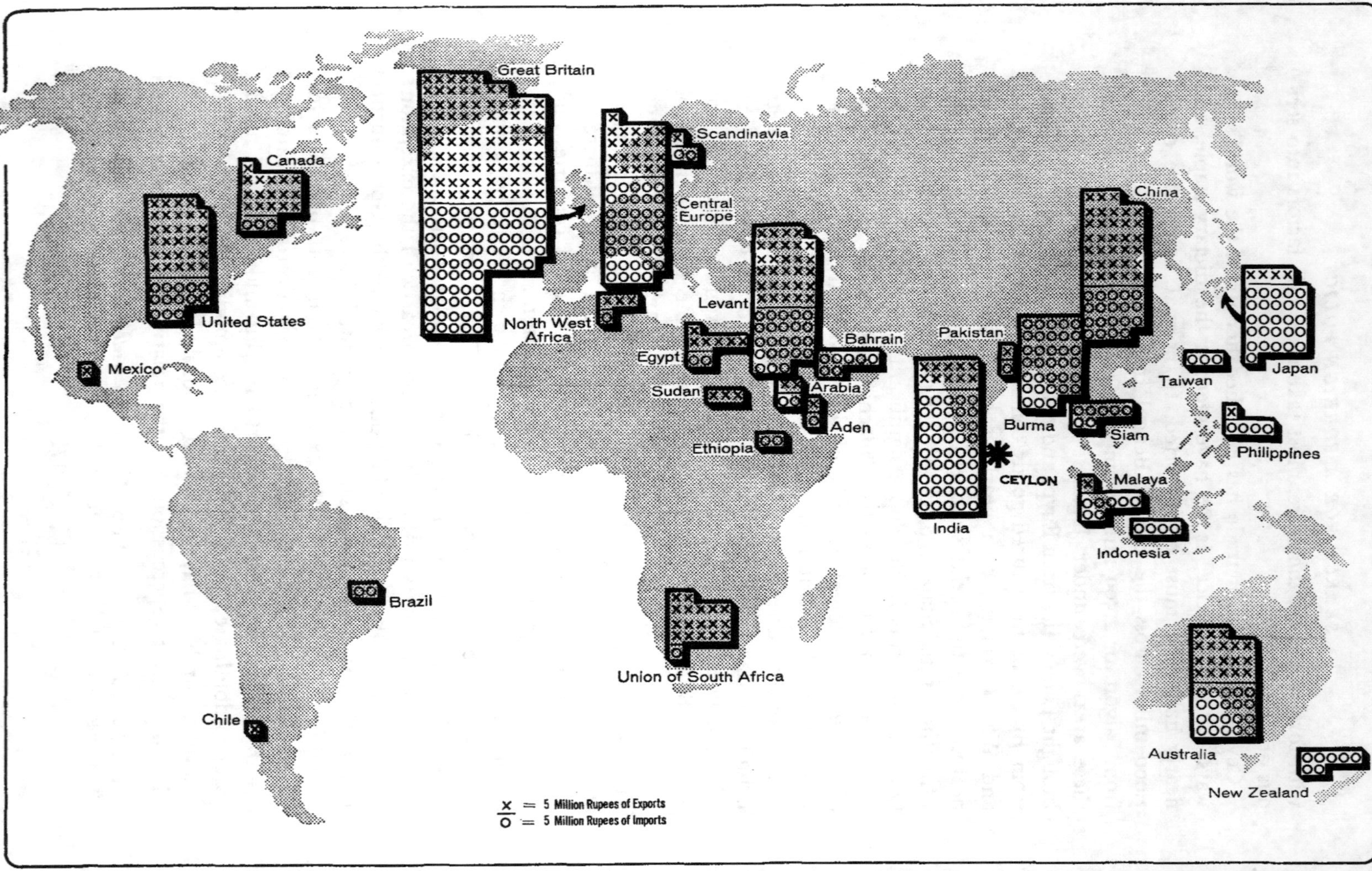

FAR-FLUNG MARKETS AND SOURCES OF SUPPLY

plantation economy. These swings are reflected in the Table below.[10] It is through the sale of tea, rubber, and coconut products that 90 per cent of Ceylon's foreign exchange is earned on visibles. Harbor and chandlering dues and services and tourist expenditure are additional sources of income that also emphasize her dependence upon the sea.

These economic facts raise not only strategic and diplomatic considerations, problems of maintaining access to supplies and markets; they also bring in their train dependence upon shipping lines and those who decide on shipping routes and the rates that will be charged. Ceylonese publicists and business interests are acutely sensitive to changes in freight rates and routes, and an underlying note of frustration and anger is discerned against the international conference that determines and alters shipping arrangements, allegedly without due regard for the interest of exporters, importers, and consumers.

From the mid-nineteenth century until the Great Depression, large amounts of capital flowed from Great Britain to Ceylon resulting in the development of estate and commercial enterprises. Dividend and other repayment obligations have produced a steady flow of payments back to Britain. Since the thirties, fresh capital has been forthcoming in much smaller quantities, and the private capital account has been in deficit. Despite Ceylonese conviction on the matter, Foreign Office policy has often run counter to the interests of British investors. Nevertheless, the network of investment relationships developed during earlier decades has affected the approach of Ceylonese to foreign policy, leading some to lean toward close ties with Britain and provoking others to look upon association with Great Britain as a device for strengthening the privileges of wealthy Ceylonese and allowing the British to further "exploit" the Ceylonese.

2. *Terms of trade.* When such significant proportions of the gross national product derive from external trade, real income per capita

[10] Purchases of Ceylon's raw rubber exports as per cent of total rubber exports by volume, for selected years:

	1925	*1938*	*1942*	*1945*	*1946*	*1949*	*1950*	*1951*	*1953*	*1954*
United King.	26.2	20.3	18.0	8.8	78.7	18.5	17.8	30.6	11.8	11.5
U.S.A.	65.4	47.4	34.7	65.5	5.9	44.3	51.8	20.6	8.7	6.7
Russia	—	—	21.9	17.8	3.0	—	—	—	—	—
China	—	—	—	—	—	1.5	0.1	5.5	62.1	65.3

Liquid latex figures have not been added. They are still relatively unimportant. See *Thirty Years of Trade Statistics*, Table 136.

is bound to alter significantly with the terms of trade. Shortly after World War II, Ceylon had to export 30 per cent more of its commodities in order to import the same prewar amount of goods and services. Trends in world commodity markets have generally been upward since then, but there have been marked fluctuations in the terms of trade since 1946.

An upward trend was evident until 1956, except for the drop between 1951 and 1952, when the index fell from 151 to 109 within a few months, and a less dramatic decline in 1956 and 1957. To escape from such downward fluctuations in terms of trade, while receiving high prices for export commodities, will continue to be a fundamental objective of economic policy. Any country that can offer both high and stable prices for her commodities and, in addition, provide large quantities of essential imports will have an easy passage in its economic relations with Ceylon.

3. *The Sterling background.* Another economic circumstance likely to influence her approach to foreign policy is the fact that not only is the bulk of her trade with sterling area partners, but she has continued to use London as her banker. London provides by far the most convenient nexus of banking relationships for currency exchange, short term commercial and trading credits, and insurance; and she is in touch through a tightly knit network of branch banks and correspondent houses with most of the world's trading centers. Although Ceylonese producers may be annoyed with the short term trading fluctuations in the London commodity markets, they provide easy access to would-be customers, especially in Europe and the Western hemisphere. London banking houses are generally respected in Ceylonese business circles and it is widely assumed that the city's bankers can be relied upon to meet their obligations. Such impersonal confidence has considerable scarcity value in South Asia and has been an important if intangible British asset that was only strengthened by the devolution of power in 1947.

Ceylon has retained in London the bulk of her foreign assets. Prior to World War II, when Ceylon was still a colony and when her banking arrangements were managed entirely by the Bank of England, there was virtually no local governmental control. The colony's assets were held in London and fiscal and other policies followed wider empire policy considerations. During World War II large trade surpluses were built up from sales of tea, rubber, coconut, and graphite to the Allies as well as from troop expenditures in Ceylon itself. These assets were not drawable all at once. Upon the termination of the war, Britain's own financial difficulties made it seem unwise for finance ministers in commonwealth countries to insist on too rapid withdrawals, perhaps precipitating their banker into bankruptcy. Through a series of bargained negotiations Ceylon, like the other creditor countries in the sterling area, agreed with the United Kingdom on a scheduled release of these balances in either sterling or dollars.

In the event, Ceylon's imports from either the dollar or sterling areas were not inhibited by lack of foreign exchange during the early years of independence, though difficulties in 1952-53 and again in 1956, 1957, and 1958 reminded Ceylonese of their dependence on distant financial resources. The direction of Ceylon's trade and the external assets accumulated during World War II formed an economic background to Ceylon's foreign policy once independence was achieved.

C. GOVERNMENTAL AND POLITICAL BACKGROUND

1. *The achievement of independence.* Ceylonese independence came without a dramatic break with the past. In the constitutional, political, and economic spheres, the transition was negotiated so smoothly that, for many, independence was scarcely real. In form the constitution itself was a living reminder of past colonial status. It is not to be found in any single document; it did not emerge after heated public debate in a constituent assembly after the fashion of many democratic constitutions, but resulted from negotiations between the British government and Ceylon's ruling party prior to the grant of independence.

Taken as a whole, the constitutional documents make it clear to all but the hypersuspicious that Ceylon's international status has become that of a sovereign independent state, with all the powers adhering thereto that other members of the Commonwealth exercise. Some symbolic clarity may have been lost, however, when the constitutional documents so regularly revert to traditional commonwealth practice rather than stating explicitly what was intended for Ceylon itself. Britain's friends on the island have not been troubled by these constitutional niceties, but they have given a critical Opposition an otherwise avoidable advantage not within their reach in India.

2. *Foreign affairs powers in the constitution.* Foreign affairs were

brought into the very center of government executive power in Ceylon. The distribution of powers within the constitution is such that the prime minister is explicitly responsible for the portfolio of Defence and External Affairs as well as being first minister.[11]

In British constitutional practice, the prime minister's real, as distinct from his formal, powers in the cabinet depend to a large extent on his personal qualities and the position he cares to assert. Since independence, the first, third, and fourth prime ministers clearly chose to assert their foreign policy powers without necessarily seeking detailed cabinet advice. These prime ministers appear to have successfully maintained a virtually free hand on foreign affairs. The second by temperament and conviction attempted to work in more effective concert with his cabinet colleagues on external matters.

The personal characteristics of these prime ministers played an even more important role in Ceylon's foreign policy than would be the case in Britain under similar constitutional circumstances, for the government has a very small foreign affairs staff. By 1956-57, one permanent secretary, one senior civil servant, six assistant secretaries, and one staff assistant represented the total substantive personnel provided for in Colombo. It would appear as if unofficial advisers and the personal associates of each prime minister had considerable influence over the making of foreign policy. Moreover, there were no precedents and no tradition to give guidance from the past.

The prime minister is thus freed both from cabinet control, if he chooses, and from the weighty influence of a large bureaucracy reiterating traditional policy and the safety of precedents. He is also relatively free from effective parliamentary control. There are no standing committees analogous to the American Senate or House committees on foreign affairs or committees of the French Chamber of Deputies. Appropriation procedures are such as to minimize direct financial control of executive actions. The prime minister, accordingly, has a remarkably free hand in foreign affairs.

3. *Agreements with the United Kingdom.* A set of agreements reached with the United Kingdom as part of the grant of independence formed another element of Colombo's foreign policy environment. Using the classic terms of the Statute of Westminster as a preamble, a defense agreement reiterated Ceylon's status as a

[11] Article 46 (4) Ceylon (Constitution) Order in Council 1946.

"fully responsible member of the Commonwealth, in no way subordinate in any aspect of domestic or external affairs."[12] It obligated the United Kingdom to provide such military assistance for the defense of Ceylon's territory, defense against aggression, and the protection of essential communications as it was in the mutual interests of the two governments to provide.[13] Ceylon's forces were not sufficient for the island's defense against any likely military threat. Her contribution to the "mutual" defense was to permit the British to use naval and air bases, ports, military establishments, and telecommunication facilities. By inference from the document itself and by analogy with relationships between Britain and other dominions, Ceylon had every legal right to terminate these arrangements whenever it saw fit; and Britain, too, could rightfully withdraw if the arrangements did not prove to be to her advantage. There were further provisions for developing such administrative arrangements as they agreed were desirable for the purpose of cooperation in regard to defense matters, and to coordinate and determine the defense requirements of both governments.

The second Foreign Affairs Agreement gave Ceylon access to the system of consultation that is a fundamental feature of the commonwealth association. The government agreed to adopt and to follow the resolutions of past imperial conferences. These, in fact, refer largely to the modes of mutual consultation that have come by convention to be practiced between members of the Commonwealth before any one member takes steps that may affect another. As in the case of earlier members, Britain agreed to undertake diplomatic representation wherever Ceylon did not wish to open its own offices.[14] This second agreement provoked very little public discussion, but from the outset the Defence Agreement was the subject of acrimonious attack from the Opposition members of parliament.

D. THE WORLDWIDE SETTING

The worldwide setting of Ceylon's diplomatic debut should not be forgotten. The constitutional and independence negotiations had been carried forward prior to the sharpening of the Cold War con-

[12] Preamble to the Defence Agreement, February 4, 1948.

[13] For a discussion of these agreements, see Sir Ivor Jennings, *The Constitution of Ceylon*, pp. 137-140, and Part II, Chapter 5.

[14] For a detailed discussion of these conventions and the provisions of the External Affairs Agreement, Jennings, pp. 254-276. Also more generally, Heather J. Harvey, *Consultation and Cooperation in the Commonwealth* (London: 1952).

flict. By the time the independence bills were up for parliamentary debate in early 1947, however, relations between the Soviet Union and its satellites, on the one hand, and the western European and American powers, on the other, were deteriorating. By then the Cold War was sufficiently clear-cut for both opposition and government members to agree that the world was indeed divided into two blocs. They differed on the proper response to this unhappy situation, but they all saw a dangerous world in prospect.[15] For several years the Cold War was to remain far away from Ceylon. Its only local manifestations were the arguments of the Communist and Trotskyist Left. The atomic bomb was not entirely out of consciousness. But not until the development of the hydrogen bomb in the field of military technology and the sharpening of political and military conflict in Indo-China in 1954, did the Cold War come to play a significant role in foreign policy debates.

Nearer home in Asia, independence came at a time when regional neighbors were in the throes of disorder, close to the margin of chaos. Indonesia was only then struggling to independence with a host of grave problems yet to face. Burma was barely thrusting back insurrection from the very gates of Rangoon, and India and Pakistan had hardly bound the wounds left by partition when they were soon at grips with one another in Kashmir. Further north beyond Burma, the new China was just emerging, provoking differing views of the direction she might take. In their midst, Ceylon was the only really orderly and productive economy with long-established, representative institutions. The overwhelming majority of parliamentary spokesmen were well aware of what they had to lose if the surrounding disorder should come to Ceylon, a consideration that contributed to a cautious approach to foreign affairs.

An unknown quantity was the role the United States would play. The United States was young and new. Its economic and military power seemed to grow as the Ceylonese became more aware of Britain's post-war difficulties. Democratic and moderate spokesmen tended to see the United States as a friendly democracy. But from the Left were warnings reiterated that the United States was, after all, the very heart and center of "world capitalist imperialism." Attitudes toward America's role in world affairs would emerge with greater precision only with experience.

Russia was distant, diplomatically inactive in South Asia. Many

[15] *House of Representatives*, V. 1, c. 444.

of the educated considered the Russian revolutions of 1917 the next great surge in the tide of history following after 1789 and 1848. Russia's rapid industrialization was widely admired and the ideal theory of "communism" was morally attractive, although the police and dictatorial aspects of the contemporary regime were repellent where their reality was believed. Ceylonese had not experienced at close range the intimacy between the Soviet Union and the Western Allies during World War II. They were more preoccupied with gaining independence than keeping a close eye on Russia's rigorous efforts to isolate and consolidate its European satellites when the war was over. They were therefore immune to the disenchantment that marked opinion in the West. Although they had had experience in the ways of the Western states during the centuries when there was no effective countervailing power in Asia, the Ceylonese could not be expected to share western European or American concern for the future power of a country whose realm stretched unbroken from the Elbe in Europe to the Pacific. In any case, few expected an active Russian policy in the area and the local Communist party was small. Britain and even the United States were much nearer politically and economically than the Soviet Union. These were among the elements providing the setting for Ceylon's foreign policy problems.

E. THE BALANCE OF FOREIGN POLICY ALTERNATIVES

Within the setting thus defined, Ceylonese statesmen had certain choices available to them. To the doctrinaire, on one end or the other of the political spectrum, it was a matter of hard and fast choice—a clear-cut acceptance of one alternative and an equally clear rejection of another. But as long as international political or military crises remained at a distance, as they did for the first ten years of independence, ultimate choices could be avoided. Many issues could be left abstract and ill-defined. Under such circumstances, it is wiser to describe the choices open as matters of shifting emphasis, of slightly altering the weight of attention, interest, and intimacy in one direction or another.

Those concerned with foreign policy have been explicitly aware of the need to find the proper balance between two competing considerations. They have been traditionally associated with Britain and, like Britain, Ceylon's commerce and economic life depend upon the sea. The cultural life of significant strata of their society is also intimately interwoven with that of Britain and western Europe. Their traditional markets have lain in that part of the world, and they are vulnerable to the application of sea power from whatever distance it may come. On the other hand, they are in Asia; they are an Asian country and their neighbors are Asians. Closer association with Asian countries is culturally and religiously congenial. It may mean greater detachment from Europe's struggles. Yet the Indian Ocean itself is not devoid of its own tides of power. Protection from European storms may be obtained, but perhaps at the price of becoming caught in the Indian Ocean's currents. The central drama of Ceylon's search for a proper foreign policy has been how best to combine these two differing, though not always divergent, ways of viewing and being within the international world.

It is quite possible for strategic considerations, economic policy, and cultural considerations to mutually reinforce one another. It is also possible, when crisis is not upon them, to find these different aspects of domestic life calling for differing approaches to the outside world. Thus, strategic policy may pull in one direction, economic policy in a second, and cultural aspirations in a third. One need not expect a monolithic pattern; in divergence may lie a greater security. On the other hand, eclecticism in such matters may lead to a loss of internal integrity and a sharpening of internal divisions. Domestically competing groups may find their interests better answered by foreign policies that are pulling in opposite directions. They may each find support from competing outside powers. Contradictions can be allowed to develop so far as to incapacitate a country in time of crisis.

During the first years of independence, public opinion and policy judgments were relatively stable and only a small, though articulate, minority put forward alternative policy proposals. Later on, as more views became expressed in domestic politics and the Asian and world setting changed, other alternatives, too, were canvassed and the balance of plausible foreign policy alternatives became significantly altered. In 1952, Ceylon's trade took a new turn; in 1956 a new government sought a different approach to defense.

III · SOME FOREIGN POLICY PROBLEMS

A. THE PROBLEM OF DEFENSE

1. *Britain as the necessary friend.* The intractable geographical terms of Ceylon's defense problem could not be altered, and gov-

ernment spokesmen showed themselves well aware of her difficulties. She was seen as a small, island country, situated at the focal point of commercially and strategically important sea and air routes on which the island depended for its essential supplies of food and other necessities. Mr. Senanayake was no more likely to ignore the massive Indian neighbor just across the Palk Strait than he could forget the island's recent wartime difficulties on short rations. The Indian Ocean was no longer a British lake. The political situation was bound to be in flux for years ahead. Fresh in their minds was the recent memory of the Japanese attack on the island. Mr. Senanayake was keenly aware of the island's military weakness in the face of grave uncertainty. In the first debate on foreign affairs provoked by presentation of the Foreign Affairs Agreements, he put the point bluntly: "I ask honourable Members to be honest with themselves and their constituents. They know as well as I do that we cannot defend ourselves. . . . Let us confess that our defense depends upon someone or other undertaking to help us defend ourselves."[16]

In 1947, India and Pakistan were in the throes of partition, Burma to the east was torn by insurrection, Indonesia was fighting for its very independence. With whom could Ceylon ally? Mr. Senanayake argued cannily that as he looked "around the countries of the world, I see at the moment only one country with sufficient interest to defend us at their expense, and that country is Great Britain." Britain's real interests in the Indian Ocean required her to keep the sea lanes open. "These ships and aircraft carry the mass of supplies which feed and clothe us," just as they carried raw materials to Britain and confirmed the commonwealth ties between Britain, Australia, and New Zealand.[17]

But Britain was considered to be a safe and trustworthy ally for other reasons. The colonial period had not been marked by great strife between Briton and Ceylonese. The Labour Party's long tradition of espousing the cause of colonial peoples in opposition to the imperial policies of the Tories was more than confirmed by the freely given grant of independence when they returned to power after World War II. As one M.P. put it, in justifying the defense arrangements: "Britain is no longer the Britain of the Imperialist period. . . . Today Britain is the ally of the forces of democracy. Britain has learned her lesson. Britain today is the Britain of the

[16] *Ibid.*, c. 445. [17] *Ibid.*

Labour Party. It is the Britain of Harold Laski. I ask the gentlemen (of the Opposition) whether their Socialist friends across the sea would for a moment let them down."[18]

The common World War II experience also contributed to a sense of interwoven defense destiny. British planes and ships had demonstrably defended Ceylon from the Japanese. British authorities had depended upon Ceylonese leaders for many complex responsibilities such as rationing and civil defense, and a sense of mutual respect and equality had been engendered. Although the articulate and politically active often denounced Britain as a power, individual Britons retained a reputation for reliability, hard work, honesty, and fairness. Empirical studies confirm the many desirable social traits attributed by Ceylonese to the British.[19] By and large, Britain's statesmen had acquired a reputation for reliability and, once clearly given, of sticking to their word.[20] This was enhanced by the manner of their handing over power and by their diplomacy thereafter. This reputation contributed materially to the willingness of Ceylonese statesman to work in association with the former "imperial" power.

Another element, not irrelevant to the tie with Britain, concerned the British commitment to parliamentary institutions at home and the potential threat from internal social revolutionary forces in Ceylon. Members of the Left parties talked of the "dictatorship of the proletariat," a concept hardly compatible with parliamentary democratic institutions in a largely peasant country. Prior to independence there had been a series of widespread strikes which appeared to members of the government to have had a distinctly political and disruptive intent. It would therefore not be surprising if the parliamentary leadership saw in the continued presence of friendly British troops a source of emergency strength.[21] British power could be expected to be used in a limited and specific manner in the event of disorder and to be withdrawn upon request. Indeed, Britain's very decline in power was a virtue, for no longer possessing overwhelming power in the Indian Ocean, British officials would not be tempted to misuse the opportunity if they were called upon to help restore order.

18 *Ibid.*, c. 547-548.

19 For example, T. L. Green, "Research on Inter-Group Relations," *Journal of the National Education Society*, Vol. v, No. 1 (Feb. 1956), pp. 1-12, 6.

20 For example, *House of Representatives*, V. 10, c. 931; V. 11, c. 1554.

21 As is to be expected, the Left parties made much of this argument. The government party made no direct reference to it, but its import can be discerned. *House of Representatives*, V. 6, c. 198-199; V. 10, c. 154-255.

Apart from strategic and defense considerations, the government needed "friends" in the broader realm of foreign relations. Ceylonese statesmen were admittedly new to diplomacy. A colonial country was without foreign relations of its own and few of its leaders had had experience in relationships with any other statesmen but Indians or Britons. Only a period of sheltered international relationships could give them practice in diplomacy and develop a sense of confidence in a more versatile approach to the wider world without undue risk to their newly won independence. Hence Ceylon chose to retain British bases on the island and to remain within the Commonwealth.

Membership in the Commonwealth served a variety of purposes. The fact that other countries were part of the association contributed to the acceptability of the British as a defense partner. Australia, New Zealand, and Canada had a high reputation as pioneers of resistance to the more exaggerated presumptions of Britain's colonial past. India, too, remained in the Commonwealth. Actual benefits could be adduced against the critics of the Commonwealth. In the realm of general diplomacy, membership in the Commonwealth ensured Ceylon's statesmen access to a massive flow of information that circulates between commonwealth capitals. Thus the prime minister was in a position to make decisions against a background of knowledge that could be available in no other way. It also ensured prompt representations in London in case Ceylon's interests might be adversely affected by contemplated British action.[22]

In addition to allowing its members to develop through personal conversation a more subtle and truer picture of each other's perspectives on international relations, the periodic meetings of commonwealth prime ministers and other ministers made it possible for Ceylon's statesmen to discuss their problems with statesmen from all parts of the world. Personal relations and conference procedure served to confirm that Ceylon was, indeed, an equal of even Great Britain. When a Ceylonese prime minister returned from London or another commonwealth capital to declare that "they took some notice of what we said," he thereby demonstrated again that his country had fully entered the world of sovereign and equal states.

2. *Arrangements for mutual defense.* The leaders of independent Ceylon could not "think of a better and a safer friend for Ceylon than Britain."[23] The policy of mutual defense between the two

[22] *House of Representatives*, V. 1, c. 443.

[23] *Ibid.*, V. 1, c. 83, 731.

countries took the form expressed in the defense agreement. By administrative understandings the government allowed the British to retain their important naval installations in Trincomalee Harbor. A Royal Air Force base developed during World War II at Katunayake in Western Province was also retained and its facilities improved for the ever-larger planes that came off British and American production lines. It was clear that these facilities were available to the British only so long as the government considered it Ceylon's advantage. There was no specification as to terminal dates nor were the specific terms under which the British used these facilities ever spelled out in any one document. This ambiguity served Mr. Senanayake in two senses. In his relations with the British, it was unnecessary for him to concede to them any facility which he did not wish to concede, given the particular circumstances at the time of the request. It gave to the insistent Left little of a specific nature against which to argue. On the other hand, ambiguity allowed the Opposition parties to inflate the obligations that had been undertaken by the Ceylonese and to accuse the government of a lack of candor in external affairs. In the absence of the specific terms of an agreement, the suspicions of the Opposition could be magnified, so much so that when Mr. Bandaranaike became prime minister in 1956 he appeared to have been genuinely surprised that no secret agreement had specified the terms under which the British used the base facilities.

From the government's point of view, it was fortunate that Trincomalee was on the distant shore, far from the centers of population in the southwestern wet zone. Airport facilities were not so well placed, for the large air base at Katunayake was within twenty miles of Colombo in the heavily populated Western Province. Under Ceylonese prodding, the size of the British military command in Colombo was rapidly reduced after 1949, and was thereafter generally restricted to the areas of the bases. Thus the base personnel managed to be unobtrusive. But for the insistent Opposition propaganda on the matter, most of the population would have ceased to worry about them.

The general policy toward military affairs called for a gradual build-up of trained Ceylonese personnel. During World War II, Ceylon had some 12,000 men in uniform, mostly concerned with service, maintenance, and transport functions. Some officers and men had served in the fighting units attached to the British army. These formed the nucleus of the professional cadre. Early plans put forward in 1949 called for the prompt recruitment of 1,000 men and the gradual expansion to a limit of 3,000. The scheme called for taking over Colombo Harbor defenses first as the British withdrew to the more secluded base areas.[24] Legislation authorizing the government to raise an army, navy, and air force was passed in 1949. As these forces developed gradually, the parallel United Kingdom forces were withdrawn so that by 1951, the United Kingdom had no army personnel on the island.[25] By August 1951, officers were increased to 154 and enlisted men to 1,955. It was considered a great advantage that, because of the presence of British personnel, the Ceylonese forces could be increased gradually.[26] It was also argued that, when the small forces were fully ready under this arrangement, they would be sufficient to "hold an enemy off until we get the assistance of a powerful friend."[27] By 1957, roughly 4,500 men were under arms.

The arrangements for coordinated planning of defense with the "powerful friend" were agreed to in principle in Article 4 of the defense agreement, but no details were issued regarding the working of this arrangement.[28] It appeared to mean that Ceylonese officers met regularly with their British counterparts for planning the defense of Ceylon including the base areas. At the same time, British officers were training army personnel under Article 3 of the agreement, either in Britain or on the island, and Ceylonese officers and men have participated in British naval maneuvers.[29]

Whether these arrangements were judged as the maximum of security available to Ceylon, or whether they were fraught with grave political and military risks as the Left tended to argue, there is no gainsaying the fact that they were extremely inexpensive. At no time prior to 1956 did the defense budget total more than 4 per cent of the government's expenditure, and prior to 1951-52, it was less than 1 per cent! This is a remarkably small sum compared to the diversion of scarce resources considered necessary in India where 20 per cent of the central government's budget went for defense purposes. In Pakistan 35-40 per cent, in Burma 30-35 per

[24] *Ibid.*, V. 6, c. 1482-1483.

[25] *Ibid.*, V. 10, c. 258.

[26] *Ibid.*, V. 10, c. 1840.

[27] *Ibid.*, V. 7, c. 19.

[28] Article 4 specified only that "The two governments will establish such administrative machinery as they may agree to be desirable for the purpose of cooperation in regard to defence matters, and to co-ordinate and determine the defence requirements of both Governments."

[29] *House of Representatives*, V. 10, c. 1843-1844.

cent, and in Indonesia 25 per cent of the governments' expenditures were for defense.[30]

3. *The Opposition reaction.* These defense arrangements provoked vigorous criticism from the Opposition. In the process, both the Left parties and the democratic opposition elaborated their differing underlying perspectives on the world of states and Ceylon's role therein.

(a) The Communist and non-Communist Left. From the outset, the Left opposition parties doubted the genuineness of Ceylon's independence, opposed the Defense Agreements and bitterly denounced the government for allowing Britain to maintain bases on the island. Both Trotskyist and Communist parties had their own familiar Marxist perspectives on foreign affairs. They believed certain actors in the international world were more important than states. They saw two competing camps. The capitalist, imperialist camp centering around Washington, allied with London and Paris, was inescapably exploitative and expansionist, as all "capitalist" manifestations were bound to be. Allied to the capitalist camp were all those owning classes, including Ceylon's "brown capitalists" who, like their overseas friends, exploited the working classes. The Left parties differed, however, in their diagnosis of the "Soviet camp." For the three Communist members, the Soviet Union was the center of the "democratic peoples' " camp, friend of the downtrodden everywhere, mentor and model. For the Trotskyists, the Soviet Union of Stalin marked a degeneration of the original revolutionary regime into a tyrannical, bureaucratic state. Khrushchev's denunciation of Stalin did not automatically exorcise Stalinism, though Moscow's skies were eagerly scanned for signs of a genuine change within the Soviet regime. The Communists particularly, and some Trotskyists, explicitly transposed perspectives on class conflict to the international world, arguing that international relations were essentially class relations and neutrality was as unthinkable in international affairs as it was in class warfare.[31]

Both were agreed that association with the Western camp inevitably meant being "drawn at the chariot wheels" of imperialism,

30 Economic Commission for Asia and the Far East, *Economic Survey of Asia and the Far East 1955*, p. 42.

31 As he put it in 1949, "I do not think there is any neutrality in this matter because what is being fought out today in the arena of international affairs is not a struggle between groups of countries, nor a struggle between nations, but a class struggle. It is a class war that is being fought. In the class war there is not a place for neutrality." P. Keuneman, *House of Representatives*, V. 6, c. 86.

which itself was inexorably being led to international war by its inner conflicts. Hence, allowing the British to retain bases dragged Ceylon into the vortex of imperialism's disastrous course. The Commonwealth was merely another subtle device for ensuring the continued British domination of the island. All proposals for joint action within the Commonwealth had to be opposed.[32]

(b) The Democratic Opposition. Not until Mr. Bandaranaike broke from the United National Party in 1951 was an alternative approach to foreign affairs seriously put forward in parliament by a democratic party, though various Independents had challenged the government's position earlier. For his part, Mr. Bandaranaike looked down from Olympian heights upon the human drama below. He could discern a great transition in progress. Just as feudal civilization withered and died and capitalism took its place, so now capitalism itself was giving way before the rising civilization of "socialism." Socialism need not imply police state totalitarianism of the Soviet variety. He accused the Communists of attempting to "hypnotize people" into believing that the "only conceivable alternative to reaction, imperialism, and capitalism lies alone in the Communist viewpoint." On the other side, he professed to see "the reactionaries" still left in the world, "the imperialists and capitalists who in order to secure their position, point to this horrible bogey of Communism." These two antagonistic ideological camps he likened to Frankenstein monsters, each created out of the intransigence, the presumptions, and the fears of the other. Only by holding aloof from both camps, by pursuing a policy of neutrality—like Switzerland or India—could Ceylon be saved from the disastrous clash between these two irreconcilable monsters.[33]

He, too, opposed the continuation of British bases. He accused the United National Party of depending upon Britain for its foreign policy views, of not developing its own position.[34] He called the Commonwealth a "rather tenuous and nebulous combination." He urged Ceylon to follow India's example, repudiating the Crown and carrying forward an independent policy. He saw the Indian Ocean area as a natural basin for concerted defense and strategic purposes and argued that more attention should be given to closer relations with Ceylon's Asian neighbors.[35]

[32] For further aspects of Communist and non-Communist Left views on foreign policy, see particularly *ibid.*, V. 6, c. 43-46; V. 7, c. 1371-1378; c. 1437-1448; V. 10, c. 270-279.

[33] *Ibid.*, V. 6, c. 280-282; V. 10, c. 1411; V. 12, c. 78-80.

[34] *Ibid.*, V. 12, c. 75.

[35] *Ibid.*, V. 12, c. 76-81.

These perspectives and policies were well suited to Mr. Bandaranaike's own problems in domestic politics. In order to develop his own following he had to differentiate himself from the Senanayake government as well as from the Left. The world-wide analogy of two extremes, each raising the bogey of its opposite, which he originally applied to international affairs, he also used toward domestic politics, accusing both the Senanayake government and the Left of similar false approaches to Ceylon's domestic problems that excluded any third alternative.[36] When the Senanayake government advocated Britain as Ceylon's best friend and the Communist party argued that the Communist countries were Ceylon's natural allies. Mr. Bandaranaike advocated instead "a middle way," associated with neither camp except through the wholly innocuous commonwealth association which bound Ceylon no more than it bound India. His Asian emphasis was likely to satisfy the critics of intimacy with the West, and his strong criticism of Marxism directed against doctrinaires in both Left parties led many non-Leftists to consider that he was a "safe" man.

4. *More recent developments.* It would be incorrect to suggest that Ceylon's approach to foreign policy as a whole during the first decade of independence was entirely oriented toward the British Defense Agreements or the Commonwealth. There was an additional theme—if sometimes insufficiently accented to satisfy the Opposition —of Asian solidarity. The common past of colonial oppression and Asian brotherhood were emphasized. Mr. Senanayake sometimes likened his foreign policy to that of "the Middle Path," a policy independent of the contending world power blocs.[37] The specific efforts to express and demonstrate Asian solidarity involved not merely a different solution to Ceylon's defense problem but also a different conception of sources of threat and safety in the world of states. Details of the successive efforts to accent Asian solidarity will be discussed in the final chapter. It will be sufficient to indicate that the general line of defense policy here described as laid down by D. S. Senanayake continued to direct Ceylon's approach to security problems until the change of government in 1956.

Until 1954-55, there was little public activity on foreign policy. The English-language and vernacular press tended to support the

[36] *Ibid.*, V. 10, c. 1396-1397.

[37] Speech reproduced in "The D. S. Senanayake Memorial Number," *The Ceylon Historical Journal*, v, Nos. 1-4 (July, Oct. 1955; Jan., April 1956) "On the 'Middle Path' in Politics," pp. 110-114.

government's approach. They also approved what steps the government took to knit its relations with Asian neighbors. Toward the end of the U.N.P. regime, particularly The Times group of papers and certain vernacular papers of the Associated Newspapers of Ceylon began to warn against following too uncritically the British or American lead. The S.E.A.T.O. initiative by the United States in 1954 touched a sensitive nerve and awakened latent anxieties of an organized attempt by a Western power to misuse crises in Southeast Asia in order to reestablish Western military power there. Trade unions consistently opposed the base agreements and S.E.A.T.O., and argued for closer links with India and other Asian countries. Only in 1955 and 1956 did Sinhalese cultural enthusiasts and Buddhists become articulate in opposition to the defense agreements as part of their growing activity against the Kotelawala regime. Earlier they had considered the cosmopolitan and anti-religious forces of the Marxist parties their principal enemy. Now they began to argue that cultural and religious integrity were gravely threatened so long as the British held bases on the island.

The electoral sweep for Mr. Bandaranaike and his M.E.P. colleagues brought with it differing ideas of the way to ensure Ceylon's best interests. The preference of Mr. Bandaranaike and his coalition associates for a policy of nonalignment and their criticism of British bases were clearly suggested in the M.E.P. election manifesto. The second proposition concerned foreign affairs: "Our foreign policy must be governed by the paramount need, in the interests of our people, of preserving peace. This object is best achieved by our country steering clear of involvement with power-blocs and by the establishment of friendly relations with all countries. Therefore, no bases can be permitted in our country to any foreign power, and all foreign troops must be immediately withdrawn from our country."

Although foreign policy differences were of secondary importance to the actual outcome of the 1956 election, there is no doubt that this was one of the issues on which orthodox Buddhists, Sinhalese cultural enthusiasts, and Marxists could unite in common opposition to the "capitalists" and the U.N.P. government.

Shortly after the election, negotiations were begun to define the conditions for turning over the bases to the Ceylonese government. Costly dockyard, ship repair, and warehouse facilities were all in question. Somewhat ironically, as the negotiations were getting under way, the London government announced radical changes in its defense plans designed to slash naval effectives at least in half. The failure of the Anglo-French action in Egypt in the late summer of 1956 no doubt prompted a drastic reappraisal of British overseas commitments at a time when Britain's basic NATO strategic concepts were also being revised. The effect of these changes in naval policy was to still further reduce British capacity in the Indian Ocean area. Agreements were concluded between the two governments in 1957 and in November the Union Jack fluttered down and the Sinhalese lion flew from the military bases, making Ceylon's independence, in the words of the prime minister, "at last complete."[38]

Henceforward, Ceylon stood without immediate military associates, dependent upon its own defense resources alone. The withdrawal of British bases increased the likelihood that Ceylon might remain aloof from a conflict originating in western Europe, for the Indian Ocean was now virtually devoid of military installations held by countries from outside the area. Inescapably, the withdrawal of British naval and air power increased Indian naval responsibilities and strategically swung Ceylon more firmly into the Indian orbit. There were few public references to this fact.

It is conceivable that India may in the future be the alternative defense associate now that British military strength has been withdrawn. India has very real interests in ensuring that no hostile power should establish itself on Ceylon. Foreign air strips and naval control of Trincomalee would unbearably expose the Indian peninsula to air and sea bombardment and to assault along her extensive coasts. Indian publicists have argued that Ceylon is within India's defense area, at the very "heart-center" of Indian Ocean defense.[39] K. M. Panikkar read the lessons of World War II as demonstrations that Ceylon: "is for all defence purposes an integral part of India. . . . Ceylon can neither feed herself nor defend herself, nor in respect of any other important matter, stand on her own feet."[40] Events might not go so far as to draw Indian power directly into Trincomalee. But with the termination of the British bases, Ceylon's destiny would again depend upon developments on the Indian subcontinent to the north, as it had for many centuries before the

[38] *Ceylon Daily News*, November 2, 1957.
[39] Ramachandra Rao, p. 17.
[40] *The Strategic Problems of the Indian Ocean* (New Delhi, 1944), pp. 5, 18.

coming of the Europeans. British interests still ran through the Indian Ocean, but Britain's ability to defend them was less sure.

In terms of domestic politics, the absence of a foreign military base removed one useful gambit in domestic political debate and would perhaps sharpen internal social tensions now that a foreign scapegoat was no longer demonstrably present.

B. THE FOREIGN MINORITY AND RELATIONS WITH INDIA

The alternative of drawing closely within the Indian orbit, however, ran up against certain underlying anxieties that were expressed during the debates on the status to be given to immigrants of Indian origin.[41] Negotiations with Delhi on their rights and status have been considerably affected by acute Sinhalese sensitivities. The latter recall earlier views of Mr. Nehru since repudiated by him but nevertheless considered to be still representative of certain of his associates to the effect that "culturally racially and linguistically Lanka is as much a part of India as any province" and political and economic developments "point inevitably to a closer union . . . presumably as an autonomous unit of the Indian Federation.[42]

Leading Indians not infrequently remind Ceylonese that they are part of the Indian cultural area and owe a deep debt to the Indian past from which Ceylon has sprung. Like Americans when their transatlantic forebears remind them of their cultural paternity, the Sinhalese consider such reminders only half the story. As Ceylonese national sentiment is awakened, the Ceylonese prefer to emphasize their own elaboration of what was admittedly an Indian beginning. Indians abroad often present a debonair self-assurance, an air of complacent superiority. Conversations have a noticeable way of dying down when articulate, overbearing Indians are present. But when the "Brahmins" withdraw, life goes on and Burmese or Ceylonese feel free to talk, to joke, and enjoy themselves once more. To these more personal reactions are added the recollection that South India separates the Sinhalese from their benign North Indian ancestors and occasionally an ardent Tamil party in Madras appeals to the Ceylonese Tamils to form a Tamil union.

No one in Ceylon doubts Mr. Nehru's peaceful intentions toward

41 For a detailed discussion of the domestic problem, see above, Chapter VII.

42 Jawaharlal Nehru, "To the Youth of Lanka," October 9, 1945, speech reproduced in *Before and After Independence 1922-1950* (New Delhi, n.d.), pp. 69-70.

Ceylon, but what of his would-be successors? When there is no Nehru, and when India and Pakistan are no longer preoccupied over Kashmir, and India becomes an industrial power, many ask, what then?

This is the wider setting for Ceylon's efforts to find a "solution" to the problem of their large minority of recent Indian origin. This migrant minority is not merely a threat to employment, it does not become assimilated, and frequently supports organizations that oppose the government of independent Ceylon. Its continued presence in the very center of the island, the ties it maintains with South India, and the recurrent flow of illegal immigrants seeking higher living standards serve to remind the Ceylonese majority that only a few miles away live 400,000,000 inhabitants, most of them on a much lower standard of living.

The fear that Indian estate workers will "submerge" the Sinhalese villager is expressed by spokesmen for the Kandyan Sinhalese. Urban workers, too, are susceptible to the threat of destitute workers who will deprive them of their jobs or lower their wages. Though trade unions dominated by Left parties may sometimes have taken a broadly "internationalist" view of the matter, politicians and independent union leaders have found this problem sufficiently vivid in urban districts to use it for political or organizational purposes. Hence, any Colombo government negotiating with India faced a great deal of pressure from Ceylonese interest groups.

In the search for agreement, Ceylonese and Indian governments have negotiated again and again over the status of the Indians in Ceylon. When the Ceylonese government dismissed Indian day laborers from the government payroll and retained Ceylonese workers, or limited the village franchise rights of estate workers, the Indian government protested. As independence approached, negotiations between the Ceylonese and Indian governments resulted in postponing a clarification of the political rights of Indians until after independence had been achieved. Ceylon's legislative measures to define its citizenship and franchise rights were a serious disappointment to the Indians.

The Ceylonese authorities assumed that when they had defined those who should become Ceylonese, the remainder automatically would become Indian citizens. And it would then be possible to negotiate with the Indian government a phased repatriation so that Ceylonese workers could gradually replace Indians. But the Indian constitution also defined the procedures necessary for Indians overseas to obtain their citizenship and, Delhi, too, was cautious in processing estate worker applications for Indian citizenship. In negotiations between Mr. Nehru and Mr. Dudley Senanayake, definite figures were mentioned for the first time in 1953. Mr. Senanayake suggested that perhaps some 400,000 might ultimately be registered as Ceylonese citizens; an additional 250,000 might well be granted Permanent Residence Permits valid for ten years, during which time they could make up their minds to return to India. Finally, some 300,000 Indian residents were to be accepted as Indian citizens and gradually repatriated. These suggestions represented a considerable change of attitude on the part of the Ceylonese government, for it was earlier considered that only an exceptional person would receive Ceylonese citizenship. However, it was not possible for Mr. Nehru to accept the principle that even these numbers should be repatriated.[43] Defining the problem in terms of numbers lent a specific bargaining quality to the discussions which hitherto had been scrupulously avoided. But it served to dramatize for both sides the real magnitude of the problem.

By December 1953 the number of stateless Indians had increased to such an extent that both parties began to accuse the other of bad faith in the matter of registration. In January 1954 Sir John Kotelawala, the new prime minister, and a ministerial delegation went to Delhi to attempt to settle some of the outstanding issues which had poisoned relations between India and Ceylon for many years. In the subsequent Delhi Agreement, the Indians undertook to tighten measures to prevent illicit emigrants from leaving South India. Subject to agreed procedures, they acknowledged Ceylon's right to deport illicit immigrants. Both governments approved administrative and publicity measures to speed the registration of their citizens in order to complete the task within two years. Finally, Colombo undertook to create four special seats in the house of representatives to be filled by representatives elected by those Indians who did become citizens of Ceylon by registration. Kandyans were thus assured that they would not be "swamped" by citizens of Indian origin and the Indian government obtained assurance that Indians would not go without political rights. After ten years, these

[43] For an account of the negotiations, see *House of Representatives*, V. 16, c. 2642-2646.

citizens by registration were to be absorbed into the regular national electoral rolls.[44]

Unfortunately, the Delhi Agreement and the ensuing legislation did not stop the growing numbers of stateless people or the feeling on both sides that the other was not acting in good faith. Technical difficulties were serious. Documentary evidence of previous domicile or intent to remain in Ceylon was difficult to provide. Scanning estate employment rolls was a laborious process. Government officers on both sides appeared to be in no hurry to give estate workers the rights of citizenship. Recriminations were so frequent that the Indian High Commissioner was asked to leave Ceylon because of alleged indiscretions and interference in the affairs of the Ceylonese government.[45] Finally, in order to "induce" Indians to register with India, the Ceylonese government imposed certain restrictions on those who had not been accepted by either country. Individuals not yet registered as Indians could no longer send money to their families, and no travel was allowed except by those who had valid Indian or Ceylonese passports, although simple travel documents had formerly been sufficient.

A new delegation went to New Delhi in October 1954. As distinct from its predecessors, it included not only other prominent members of the ruling party, but Mr. Bandaranaike, leader of the Opposition. In this manner for the first time the "Indian question" was removed from domestic political division. Both India and Ceylon agreed to facilitate travel, and Ceylon agreed that remittances again should be permitted among the stateless, pending final decision. Both expressed their intentions to speed registration, hoping to finish the process within two years, nevertheless recognizing the fact of a "basic difference of approach to the problem of the status of persons of Indian origin in Ceylon."[46]

When Mr. Bandaranaike's party won in April 1956, Indian opinion became optimistic of an early settlement.[47] The Indian press hoped that a new prime minister more sympathetic to India's foreign policy of "nonalignment" would be better disposed toward Indians in Ceylon than Sir John Kotelawala had been. On the other side, many Ceylonese hoped that a foreign policy orientation more

[44] Text of Agreement, *Times of Ceylon*, January 19, 1954.

[45] For some of the technical difficulties, see *Administration Report for Registration of Indian and Pakistani Residents in Ceylon, 1952*, p. 3.

[46] Communiqué in *Ceylon Daily News*, October 12, 1954.

[47] For instance, *The Hindu* (Madras), April 13, 1956; *Times of India*, April 26, 1956.

in line with India's would reduce India's reluctance to accept responsibility for her sons and daughters in Ceylon. Three years of M.E.P. government left the matter as intractable as ever.[48] Each side appeared to assume the other was being "stubborn" and "uncooperative" as a by-product of divergent foreign policy orientations. In point of fact, the issue itself was difficult and left much room for real disagreement. The *Times of India* had earlier observed what many Ceylonese continued to fear: ". . . India is on stronger ground than Ceylon and can afford to wait since Colombo, not New Delhi, will ultimately be burdened with the millstone of the Stateless."[49]

Hence, though both countries came to pursue a relatively similar policy toward world affairs on the global plain, the problem of Indians resident in Ceylon was likely to continue as a source of annoyance. Agreement on wider issues by no means assures agreement on all specific questions where incompatible restricted interests are at stake. Nor, to the contrary, does friction on one issue preclude common foreign policies on other matters.

C. ECONOMIC PROBLEMS OF HOUSEKEEPING—1952-1953: THE RICE-RUBBER AGREEMENT

The defense and strategic arrangements laid down as early as 1947 by the first Senanayake government remained virtually intact until after the 1956 elections. But Ceylon's traditional pattern of trade experienced a noticeable change in 1952 and 1953. The developments in economic policy no longer reinforced strategic and military considerations as they had in the past but tended to pull in the opposite direction.

Specialization in plantation crops for export in exchange for manufactured goods has characterized South Asian tropical economies. Ceylon has perhaps profited most from such trade in the past. Yet like the others, it suffered serious economic dislocations whenever the price for its products in the world market declined because its economic base is narrow and lacks diversity. Ceylon's experience in 1952-53 represents in microcosm the economic malaise that will recur in South Asia whenever prices for their primary products

[48] From January to October, 1956, for instance, the ratio of Ceylon acceptances to rejections was about 1 out of 20, quite comparable to the acceptances of the previous year. Of a total of 235,000 applications received up to December 1956, 132,500 had been rejected, 50,600 *individuals* had been accepted, and 83,400 applications were pending. Editorial, *Times of Ceylon*, November 28, 1956.

[49] *Times of India*, May 9, 1955.

rapidly deteriorate on world markets. And economic difficulties produce visible political difficulties for regimes where public criticism is allowed and interest groups can freely organize.

In 1952-53 the price Ceylon obtained for her rubber was rapidly declining and her sales to dollar countries were falling at the very time that the cost of her principal import requirement—rice—was rising sharply in the world's markets. Rice was becoming more and more a dollar commodity. It was this sharp conjuncture of unfavorable factors on both the supply and demand sides that led Ceylon to enter a field of trading relations not previously explored. For a variety of reasons, Ceylon's traditional Western partners were unable at the time to take prompt measures to meet her economic needs. They should not have been surprised when hard-pressed producers explored new trading patterns.

1. *The rubber situation.* Following World War II, the rubber industry in Ceylon experienced remarkable fluctuations. The world outlook for natural rubber has been uncertain because of improved synthetics becoming more competitive in both quality and price, particularly in the United States.[50] Since 30 per cent of Ceylon's rubber industry is operated by relatively marginal small holders owning on the average 1.3 acres, fluctuations in the fortunes of the rubber crop affect a numerically important section of the population and they, in turn, through their associations and electoral strength carry significant weight in parliament.

The most obvious difficulties affecting the rubber industry came from abroad as world demand declined. This affected adversely the whole rubber industry, but especially the small holders. Extensive unemployment in the rubber districts seemed inescapable. The government, too, was directly affected, since lowered exports meant lowered government revenues, and commensurately less funds available for investment and welfare purposes. Social and political tensions were therefore bound to rise. In 1949 a government commission undertook a detailed study of methods for reorganizing and modernizing the rubber industry at home.[51] The Ceylonese argued that during World War II, when the Western allies were desperate for rubber, Ceylon had helped by supplying at an agreed, noncompetitive price. But now, when Ceylon was having difficulties,

[50] IBRD, p. 237.

[51] See *Report on the Rubber Industry* (Sessional Paper XVIII—1947). Production costs were higher than for neighboring competitors, perhaps by 40 per cent. *Financial Times* (London), June 25, 1949.

Ceylon's traditional consumers were invoking the "law of supply and demand" to justify their unwillingness to pay slightly more than the depressed world price. Nevertheless the same governments were themselves responsible for depressing the world price because of their heavy expenditures on government-sponsored research into synthetics.

The first reprieve for rubber came in 1949 when the Ceylonese rupee was devalued along with the pound sterling. Natural rubber again became competitive with synthetics from the cost point of view. World demand rapidly increased and the price rose from a low of Rs. .46 per pound in June 1949 to Rs. 1.26 one year later. The outbreak of the Korean War added boom conditions once again, the price moving forward within a few months to over Rs. 2.87 per pound.

As the Korean War developed and Communist China entered the conflict in November 1950, United Nations countries engaged in the conflict, began to restrict the shipment of strategic commodities to Communist China. Through export licenses, Britain, for instance, prohibited Malayan rubber from going to China, depressing the Singapore price which was usually accepted as the "world price." Meanwhile, China had been buying small amounts of rubber in Colombo through commercial channels. In May 1951, the United Nations passed a resolution imposing a wider embargo on the export of strategic materials, including rubber, to mainland China and North Korea. To have conformed to this would have meant a return to depressed conditions in the rubber industry. The American government attempted to strengthen the effectiveness of the embargo through legislation known as the Battle Act (Public Law 213, 82nd Congress) designed to prevent any country contravening the embargo from receiving American military or economic assistance. At the time this legislation was being passed, the American administration was negotiating with a Ceylonese mission to Washington to purchase the whole of Ceylon's rubber output for the years 1951-52. The Americans offered the going Singapore price as the usual "world price," but since the Ceylonese traders were still selling some rubber to China, Colombo's price was significantly higher, and naturally enough they insisted on the Colombo price. Negotiations appear to have broken down on this point.

Until then, Ceylonese government spokesmen expressed misgivings about greater trade with China.[52] The Left had kept up a consistent advocacy of closer trade and diplomatic links with China and Russia, and accused the government of playing the American game by not actively promoting this trade.[53] In September Chinese buyers markedly increased their purchases, at prices said to have been considerably above the world market.[54] The American government protested against these sales as contraventions of the United Nations' embargo, but the prime minister replied that he could not help American anxiety. The market for rubber in Colombo was completely free and Americans could buy there, too, if they wished. Discussions between the two governments were resumed in early 1952, but these were cut short by the death of the prime minister, the subsequent parliamentary elections in Ceylon called for May, and election year uncertainties in the United States itself. Before Americans and Ceylonese again took up negotiations, the country's financial difficulties were much more clearly seen by the Ceylonese.[55]

2. *The rice crisis.* In the spring of 1952, the government of Ceylon had increasing difficulties in procuring essential rice imports at reasonable prices. By June, the food situation was serious. No cut was made in the rice ration but stocks were running dangerously low. And American purchases of rubber had fallen off so markedly that Ceylon for the first time was spending more dollars than she earned. A ministerial mission was despatched to London and to Washington to seek assistance.

In London they obtained a release of dollars from the sterling area dollar pool sufficient to purchase 100,000 tons of rice and 45,000 tons of flour in dollar markets. In Washington, the American government agreed to help Ceylon procure rice in the United States, but on the basis of competitive open market bidding which at that time was the only mode of sale for such supplies. Owing to a "sharp and unexpected rise" in the American market price, negotiations were abandoned after only 30,000 tons had been purchased.[56] The American government could not agree to buy rubber from Ceylon at the Colombo price, since it appeared to Washington that the

[52] *House of Representatives*, V. 10, c. 295-296.

[53] *Ibid.*, V. 10, c. 218, 1611, for instance.

[54] *Financial Times*, September 11, 1951.

[55] For a detailed statement of the Ceylon government's view, see *Press Communiqué*, Government of Ceylon, February 25, 1953 in answer to the *Second Report to Congress* of the Mutual Security Administrator on the *Mutual Defense Assistance Control Act 1951* (Washington, 1953).

[56] *Administration Report of the Food Commissioner (Supplies) 1952*, p. 4.

Chinese purchases in contravention of the United Nations embargo had raised Colombo prices out of line with "world" Singapore prices. They were also not then able to assure the Ceylonese of a five-year $50,000,000 economic assistance program under Point Four which the Ceylonese authorities were seeking, for the American administration then had little confidence that Ceylon could be exempted from the clauses of the Battle Act.[57] The impending presidential election in the United States restricted the freedom of maneuver of the American officials and no financial assistance could be promised. They were, however, able to agree to aid the Ceylonese to buy rice in the American market and were willing to buy considerable quantities of rubber at a price higher than Singapore though lower than that then established in Colombo.

As the food crisis deepened, the Opposition made the most of the government's difficulties. Every opportunity was used in parliament to urge a policy of increasing trade relations with China by government initiative. Some time in the spring or early summer of 1952, the Chinese government invited the Ceylonese to send a delegation to Peking to discuss the possibility of a large rice purchase.[58] The government appeared reluctant to do so until every means of purchasing rice outside the Communist orbit had been explored.[59] Other avenues having failed, a mission went to Peking in mid-September. Brief negotiations resulted in a commitment by China to supply 80,000 tons of rice at a favorable price. More important, principles were agreed for a five-year intergovernmental agreement providing for the annual shipment of 270,000 tons of rice to Ceylon in exchange for 50,000 tons of rubber, with respective prices to be negotiated every year. It was explicitly agreed that the price for rubber would be higher than that then current in Singapore.[60] The terms of the exchange were favorable to Ceylon from every point of view. At the current world price one ton of rubber purchased

[57] Under the terms of the legislation, the Mutual Security Administrator could exempt certain countries from the inhibitory clauses if it could be shown that a country's contribution to "mutual security of the free world" more than off-set the harm presumably done to free world interests by shipping prohibited articles to China, Russia, or their satellites. India, Pakistan, and Indonesia had received such exemptions, but not Ceylon.

[58] According to the Press Release of February 1953, the Ceylonese Government knew of the Chinese invitations during the Ceylonese negotiations in Washington in the summer of 1952. The offer was hinted at by Mr. Dudley Senanayake as early as July 30, 1952, *House of Representatives*, V. 12, c. 1732.

[59] *Ibid.*, V. 13, c. 356-358 for efforts elsewhere.

[60] Described by the Prime Minister in Parliament, *ibid.*, V. 13, c. 805-806.

three tons of rice. The Chinese offer, on the other hand, brought in exchange for one ton of rubber over five tons of rice and subsequent negotiations reportedly brought in a ratio of over 6.5 to one.[61] As the *London Times* reported from Colombo: "No Ceylon government could have afforded to accept the American offer on its merits and none would have been able to justify such an acceptance before the electorate in the face of the Chinese offer."[62] When the whole agreement was passed by parliament in late 1952, only one vote was cast against it.[63]

The American government sought other means of discouraging the rubber shipments to China. In early 1953 it was agreed with the United Kingdom that ships of American and British registry would be prohibited from carrying rubber to China and any ships engaging in the trade could not bunker or receive normal port facilities in British-controlled ports, including Singapore and Hong Kong.[64] Sulphur is used as an essential spray to protect rubber trees from blight. Ceylon was among the countries to which shipments of sulphur from the United States were banned.[65] These restrictive measures were serious annoyances, but they had no appreciable effect upon the trade with China that went forward regularly.

The means of administering the sales to China occasioned considerable discussion in Ceylon. Merchant houses that had traditionally handled the rubber export trade since the earliest days of the rubber industry sought to retain the business in their hands. But the government reverted to procedures used during World War II when a government department bought directly from the producers and sold to the foreign purchaser. Subsequently, the rubber trade with China was restricted to the Ceylonese, just as trade with Japan and Germany had been reserved.

3. *Evaluation of the agreement.* Rice began to move fairly promptly from Chinese ports to Colombo, and the shipments of rubber went on as before except that the government gave much closer supervision to the trade and the quantities rose considerably. From the point of view of the rubber producers, the agreement had great

61 *The Scotsman,* December 3, 1952.

62 January 21, 1953.

63 For a detailed and dramatic presentation of the Left argument and interpretation, see S. P. Amarasingam, *Rice and Rubber, The Story of China-Ceylon Trade* (Colombo, 1953).

64 Mutual Security Administrator, *Third Report to Congress, Mutual Defense Assistance Control Act 1951,* First half of 1953 (Washington, 1953).

65 Government of Ceylon, *Press Communiqué,* February 25, 1953.

merit, for it assured price stability for at least one year ahead. The new price stability made it possible to project replanting programs realistically for each year so that the government could plan to rehabilitate the rubber industry.

It was not an entirely unmixed blessing even for the rubber producer, for the Chinese purchased only sheet rubber and did not want the more highly processed crepe. Hence the anomalous position soon developed in which the processed crepe was selling for less than the relatively unprocessed sheet. But, on the whole, it was a boon for the rubber industry.

When they began, the rice imports were a source of great relief to the government and citizens alike. However, within the year, the contract arrangement which had seemed such a blessing during the stark scarcity of the summer of 1952 revealed its other side. Rice granaries throughout South Asia were as bulging in 1952-53 as they had been bare a year before. Rice prices declined commensurately, and Ceylonese buyers were again warmly welcomed in Rangoon and Bangkok. But because of the yearly contract inflexibility, the Ceylonese were obligated to purchase more rice at a higher price in China than they really needed. Hence, there was soon the peculiar situation of Ceylon exporting to Japan rice purchased from China.[66]

Every year the inevitable anomalies of contracted barter arrangements gave rise to some public discussion, but the agreements were not repudiated. In 1954, negotiations were hard-bargained from the Ceylonese point of view. At that time the Singapore price was higher than the contracted Chinese price of the year before and Burmese rice was lower. Then after threatening to break off negotiations, the Ceylon delegation improved the terms of trade in the exchange above the previous year. On the other hand, by 1956, the Malayan and other rubber markets were opening for the Chinese, and Ceylon's bargaining position was relatively weaker.

There was no appreciable increase in the interference of Communist countries in the internal affairs of Ceylon as a result of this agreement. The Chinese presented the best possible appearance to their small and sensitive South Asian neighbors. The Ceylonese government was cautious. It refused to develop diplomatic relations further and allowed only an occasional technical supervisor to see to China's interests in Colombo. Equally fundamental, Ceylon was

[66] *The Hindu* (Madras), November 7, 1954.

not for long dependent primarily upon China for its rice, since bumper crops soon developed in Ceylon's traditional suppliers.

However, the long-run importance of Ceylon's contract with China should not be ignored. This contract represented one of the first steps of mainland China in its diplomatic re-entry ino the wider world of non-Communist states. The fact that China—long the country of gigantic famines—should have been able to export large quantities of rice had an appreciable effect upon the climate of opinion in Ceylon. Naturally the friends of Communist China have not been shy in praising the "tremendous economic achievements of the new China." At the same time, the domestic Left parties gained kudos in the public eye for having long promoted the trade agreement which brought relief to rubber producers and the rice consuming public. It then became more difficult for the opponents of the Left to put them on the defensive as they had during the early years of the Senanayake regime.

The agreement had long-run significance from still another point of view. As the prime minister put it, "These agreements . . . bring Ceylon into a new sphere of trade relations hitherto unexplored."[67] For the first time, large quantities of Ceylon's raw materials went to countries outside the market in western Europe and the Americas. The vision of Asians industrializing themselves or of countries producing raw materials becoming independent of the vagaries of Western markets are the unexpressed but vivid dreams of many in Ceylon and elsewhere in Asia. The fact that only sheet rubber was taken by the Chinese suggests that the interests of primary producers in Asia may be no more adequately met by new Asian consumers than by familiar European customers. Nevertheless, many Ceylonese experienced genuine satisfaction that their rubber could be sold to another Asian country in bulk at stable prices. The fact that Western countries were opposed to it but could not prevent it only added to their satisfaction.

From the specifically Ceylonese point of view, Washington's policies that preceded and followed Ceylon's economic agreement with China left a most unsavory recollection. As the Ceylonese saw it, at the very time when America had drastically reduced its purchases of rubber, Colombo was penalized for selling its rubber to China. Ceylon was the only country to which the Battle Act was applied. A sense of grievance was only sharpened by the realization that,

[67] *House of Representatives*, V. 13, c. 1226.

when Ceylon needed rice, she had to seek it in markets in which dollar buyers were raising the price and converting it into a dollar commodity precisely when American governmental buying policies prevented Ceylon from earning dollars. Finally, instead of allowing Ceylon to earn dollars in the normal way, the Americans were prepared to consider economic assistance, but only after making it clear that Ceylon would be expected to stop her rubber exports to China. This appeared to be an attempt to use Ceylon's economic plight to interfere with the economic self-determination and sovereignty of a small, primary producing country.

There is no economic reason why monsoon Asian producers need choose either one market or the other for the disposal of their goods. They may prefer to hedge by granting long term contracts to the Communist orbit for assured sales at a minimum and stable price while keeping back a varying proportion of total output for maximum profits in a tricky and economically risky world market. By so doing, they will also ensure against undue political interference accompanying a barter or contracted trade agreement.[68] In such market diversity, no doubt, lies the safest course for Ceylon's export policy.

The rice-rubber crisis of 1952-1953 illustrates in dramatic form the housekeeping problem facing the Ceylonese government. It will be recalled that this particular set of difficulties contributed to the impulse to escape dependence upon three estate crops and added to the desire for economic diversification. The financial difficulties precipitated by this conjuncture forced on the government a painful fiscal decision—the removal of the rice subsidy to the consumer. Social and political tensions were so sharpened by this step that the ruling party had to fire on the crowds. These events, in turn, contributed significantly to the ill reputation surrounding the United National Party and weakened popular support for that regime.

D. ECONOMIC DEVELOPMENT ASSISTANCE

Ceylon's foreign exchange position at the beginning of independence was such that her officials felt relatively little need to seek economic assistance or foreign loans. The principal policy designed to increase Ceylon's external resources pressed for a more rapid release of Ceylon's wartime sterling balances. Periodic negotiations

[68] In this connection Ceylonese proponents of bilateral trade agreements with centralized authoritarian regimes would do well to study the experience of Germany's small eastern European neighbors for evidence of the possibilities.

led to agreed schedules of release that balanced, as well as possible, Ceylon's needs for heavy capital and other imports and Britain's concern to prevent too rapid an outflow of sterling.

At the Conference of Commonwealth Foreign Ministers held in Colombo in January 1950, proposals were first discussed to concert the development of countries throughout South and Southeast Asia. The commonwealth countries took the initiative. In Ceylon the Minister of Finance was given much of the credit for the original proposal. It was decided that other countries like Burma and Indonesia who were not members of the Commonwealth would be urged to participate. After considerable consultation through commonwealth diplomatic channels, a further meeting at Sydney in May 1950 agreed that each country should draw up a six-year program of development, training, and investment. In November, the Commonwealth Consultative Committee published a detailed collation of the commonwealth countries' plans and in February 1951 they met once more in Colombo with non-members of the Commonwealth who had agreed to join. In addition to the charter members—Australia, Canada, Ceylon, India, New Zealand, Pakistan, and the United Kingdom and its territories in Malaya and Borneo—Burma, Cambodia, Laos, Thailand, and Viet Nam were also present. The United States, too, had agreed to participate and the International Bank for Reconstruction and Development sent an observer.

Constitutionally, the Colombo Plan "organization" was of utmost simplicity. From the beginning the sponsors of the plan were opposed to setting up a large secretariat or a well-staffed functional organization such as the Economic Commission for Europe at Geneva or the O.E.E.C. in Paris. The new nations were much more sensitive to possible infringements of their economic, political, and administrative sovereignty than were the Europeans. The sponsors, therefore, avoided putting themselves in the position of having to determine in any regularized way priorities between India or Ceylon, for example, as the O.E.E.C. had been doing with Marshall Plan funds. Moreover, it was expected that similarly large amounts of resources would not be forthcoming. It was therefore decided that member countries needing assistance would approach individual possible donor countries and detailed arrangements for determining the types and amounts of aid and the modes of supervision would be negotiated bilaterally between the donor and receiving country.

Hence the Colombo Plan Organization remained in the background. A Council for Technical Co-operation was established, in practice composed of those diplomats of member countries stationed in Colombo. A "bureau" with a small secretarial staff was to coordinate information from the member countries regarding technical assistance requests and likely sources of supply. Requests in the first instance were to pass through the bureau, but when bilateral negotiations had once begun between two cooperating countries, the bureau's task became merely one of keeping in touch, reporting, and general direction.[69] The bureau encouraged more precise definition of requests and through its exchange of information, periodic tours of its director and the meetings it arranged, it helped those concerned with development in different countries to keep in touch with one another and draw what lessons they could from one another's experience.

From the point of view of the Ceylonese government, participation presented no policy problems. The loose institutional framework followed closely the style of the commonwealth association. Since the diplomatic representatives of cooperating countries and not a professional aid staff were responsible for seeing that the aid was well used, there was no risk of such close supervision that it might infringe on Ceylon's sovereignty. Appropriations by donor countries were not publicized as being necessary on grounds of containment or the Cold War. They appeared to be free of any probable political commitments that might conceivably impair Ceylon's freedom of foreign policy abroad.

Although the amount of capital aid forthcoming was not as great as had originally been hoped, the Colombo Plan opportunities for technical training, assignment of experts, and exchange of skills were impressive. Ceylon received large numbers of experts, sent more than 700 scholars overseas for training and received capital assistance to make a total of Rs. 99,000,000 worth of aid up to 1956. Only the far Left considered the Colombo Plan arrangements a threat to Ceylon's sovereign independence.

Not until 1956 was American economic assistance successfully negotiated again after a five-year hiatus. Considerable political controversy accompanied the new agreements; the circumstances for halting the small Point IV program had not been happy. The announcement

[69] For the constitution of the Council for Technical Co-operation, see Cmd. 8080, Appendix 7.

of the new aid program came shortly before the 1956 General Election. Though the agreement had been under negotiation since 1955, nearly a year before the General Election was held, government critics interpreted the announcement of American assistance in March 1956 as an effort to influence the electoral outcome. Dire predictions were heard from the Left that American assistance could only be given with hidden strings that would tie Ceylon inextricably to the "War plans of the Imperialists." There was notable surprise after the electoral defeat of the Kotelawala regime that the United States was prepared to continue an aid program to an avowedly "neutralist" successor government.[70]

American assistance increased rapidly. U.S. appropriations doubled within two years and important quantities of food surpluses were made available in addition to the development of a varied technical assistance program. These came to about $10,000,000 worth per year.

Shortly after the 1956 election eastern European and mainland Chinese intent became more clearly manifest. The Czechs opened a trade fair and offered a low-interest loan to assist in constructing a cement plant. Ambassadors were at last exchanged between Colombo, Moscow, and Peking. In 1958, the Russians offered a $30,000,000 loan at 2½ per cent for capital equipment purchases. Although in 1958 the Chinese negotiated a hard bargain on rice-rubber trading, they agreed to supply $3,000,000 worth of consumer goods, the proceeds from the sale of which were to be used to assist in rehabilitating the rubber industry.

As long as cabinet divisions run along doctrinaire lines and ministers show clear preferences for alternative sources of outside assistance, foreign aid may contribute to increasing cabinet divisions. Critical observers have noticed this possibility. But at least during the early years of these different assistance programs there was broad approval of accepting aid from a variety of sources. This was not merely to accept all that was offered. Insofar as there were lingering anxieties about Western economic aid being used to reconstitute Western economic power in the area, assistance from the Eastern bloc broke a hitherto Western monopoly. For those anxious about the possible political repercussions of receiving economic aid from Communist countries, continued Western aid prevented a monopoly developing from the East. As in Burma and India, there seemed to

[70] *Times of Ceylon*, April 16, 1956. For details on aid programs see Chapter VIII, Section VI.

be emerging a kind of implicit theory, not of the balance of power which was frowned on as a part of European power politics, but of the "balance of aid," whereby the economic independence and political safety of the small or less influential country could be protected by the countervailing and mutually stimulating effect of economic assistance programs mounted by countries from both the democratic and the Communist worlds.

At the end of 1959 it was too soon to assess with certainty the political consequences of economic assistance. The Colombo Plan aid had served to provide many Ceylonese with experience in Western countries that would lead to greater understanding as well as economic and technical skills. The limited supervision of capital assistance contributed to feelings of appreciation without provoking the annoyance that might come with closer supervision though economic results may have been less than originally hoped for. The joint planning, consultation, and mutual assistance under the Colombo Plan drew the South Asian countries into a closer awareness of one another's problems and possibilities. It showed that Western technicians and South Asians could work together on South Asian problems without political considerations distracting them from whatever technical problem was at hand. The quantitatively larger American technical and commodity aid program, and the credit and commodity facilities from the Eastern bloc, brought more technical assistance and investment capital, improved the country's facilities for technical training, and reduced foreign exchange outlays on indispensable imports.

CONCLUSION

All four prime ministers had a relatively free hand in formulating and executing foreign policy. With the exception of pressures arising out of Kandyan anxieties, they did not have to contend with interest groups committed to specific foreign policy programs. Apart from a few individuals in the democratic parties, articulate Marxists, and a handful of journalists, few seriously debated foreign policy alternatives. There appeared to be a notable unconcern with foreign affairs for a people so much affected by developments abroad.

In matters of defense, relations with India in regard to the minority of Indian descent, economic housekeeping, and foreign assistance, Ceylon's governments since independence showed themselves to be independent and pragmatic, ready to experiment but still cautious.

Defense association with the United Kingdom begun with independence did not preclude exploring hitherto untried trading possibilities in the Communist orbit in 1952. Deteriorating free world marketing and supply conditions and the Chinese desire to procure rubber in exchange for rice dramatically affected her trading pattern for a time. Resistance to accepting as citizens any residents of Indian descent raised difficulties with India, but these disagreements did not stand in the way of Ceylon's eventually adopting a position on foreign affairs more in keeping with India's. Commonwealth relations were confirmed by the Colombo Plan's exchange of persons and technical assistance programs and the manner of their administration. But these did not prevent the Ceylonese government from terminating the defense agreement with Great Britain after a new government came to power in 1956.

Even though they were experimental and flexible, a clear, long-run trend emerged. As conditions in Asia changed, as the government gained confidence in foreign policy matters, and as domestic political power shifted from the hands of those who were culturally, educationally, and economically more oriented toward London, the government became less willing to follow the British lead. Weakened defense ties with distant Great Britain presaged closer association with India.

Foreign policy was less important to the outcome of the 1956 election than were domestic questions of language, religion, and socio-economic class considerations. The election results, however, profoundly altered the country's foreign policy. Mr. Bandaranaike's arguments in favor of terminating the base agreements with Britain readily evoked echoes of the pre-independence "struggle against the Imperialists." Marxists, articulate Buddhists, and rural middle-class Sinhalese interest groups, temporarily at least, were united on this issue. There was every evidence to suggest that nonalignment as a general approach to foreign policy was quietly accepted though there would no doubt be grounds for future discussions as to how best to steer a strictly neutral course.

In the early years of independence, the cabinet appeared relatively united on matters of defense, though it became divided sometimes on economic housekeeping and the treatment of minorities. "Nonalignment" requires more decisions and opens new alternatives. At the outset of independence, only the British were diplomatically active. As British influence diminished, first American and then

Russian and Chinese activities increased. India was also more concerned. As more diverse influences play upon the island in the future, differences over foreign policy are likely to be sharpened. But at least opinion may become better informed as controversy becomes keener. Cabinet divisions regarding the proper foreign policy were a marked feature of the M.E.P. government.

Under the new circumstances facing the country, could cabinet agreement on foreign policy free from doctrinaire alignments be achieved? Could a clear party consensus be evolved? Could a broader attentive public develop a view of foreign policy transcending party interests to set a national foreign policy for the future?

One area of the common foreign policy effort on which everyone seemed agreed in principle was that of Asian solidarity, a matter of sufficient interest to warrant separate treatment.

CHAPTER XI · ASIAN SOLIDARITY AND CEYLON'S FOREIGN POLICY

> "Asians now spoke of themselves as 'we-Asians,' as if Asia were an entity, when really it was a huge agglomeration of continents and cultures and races and religions and governments further apart from each other than any European country could be from any other European country. And yet 'we-Asians' gripped the imagination . . . it meant something. There was a feeling of akinness, from Egypt to Japan . . . and all these countries were changing, changing, running the centuries into days, hurrying and scrambling forward at a breathless speed which left European prejudices and platitudes about them as far behind as the buggy horse was left panting after a jet plane. Somehow Europe appeared so staid, stay-behind and unimaginative beside this surging exaltation of Asia."—Han Suyin, *And the Rain My Drink*

I · INTRODUCTION

A PERSISTENT theme in political debates regarding Ceylon's foreign policy concerned the desirability of closer association with Asia and of promoting Asian unity. On ceremonial occasions when good feelings were being promoted, everyone favored closer ties with other Asians. That political leaders in at least some countries in the area continued to evoke the vision of Asian solidarity suggested that it had meaning to their people. Many problems—strategic, economic, and cultural—might be mitigated and some solved if only there were a closer and effective unity among them.

Ceylon and the countries of South Asia face intractable problems in common. No single power now dominates the area as the British once did. A higher degree of unity encompassing India, Ceylon, Burma, Thailand, Malaya, and Indonesia might discourage the encroachment of any new external power.

They all have economic problems in common. They are all vulnerable to fluctuations in commodity prices in the world market. Unlike the United States or Great Britain, mass welfare goals became government responsibilities before the achievement of self-propelled expanding economies. A rapidly growing population bears heavily on limited resources in most countries. Hence, problems unique to this area distinguish their economic experience from that of Western liberal democracies or of Russian or Chinese Communist dictatorships. Many South and Southeast Asian countries have been determined to develop their economies under democratic auspices and avoid totalitarian methods. With a common desire to solve their economic problems in their own way, they may be able to help each other with advice and experience. They may discover other economic interests in common.

Finally, they are still striving to develop their own cultures, to emphasize their own distinguishing characteristics, and rediscover their spiritual and cultural roots as distinct from the culture that many of them took over from the West during the colonial period. They are trying to develop modern indigenous literatures, to strengthen and simplify indigenous languages, to draw their literary heritage into closer touch with the vernacular. They have a further common interest in insulating their developing culture from the less savory elements of extraneous, foreign civilizations. Surely they can learn much from one another and some of these objectives might be pursued by concerted policies. Hence, there are grounds for arguing that a greater degree of unity among South Asian countries would help solve many of their problems.

But the first decade of independence revealed little Asian unity in practice. Some were able to agree in principle on the virtues of nonalignment and toward the end of the decade Ceylon, India, Indonesia, and Burma defined similar policies on many matters. But others did not agree or sought security in another direction. Mutual aid of a concrete nature was inevitably small and they have been unable to support significant forms of economic cooperation. There has been little South Asian cultural exchange. Asian solidarity appeared to have reality insofar as it called upon emotions derived from past struggles or when there was fear that foreign rule might be reinstated again, particularly from the West. It sometimes had reality in a racial sense, where Europeans or whites were excluded. All South Asians were agreed on the necessity of making the voice of Asia heard in the councils of the world. At the United Nations, particularly, South and Southeast Asian countries could often join in common voting on distant issues or where Great Powers—particularly Western Great Powers—were misbehaving. No one statesman could speak on behalf of them all. Critical analysis leads to the conclusion that Asian unity was still limited in political or economic substance.

This should not be surprising. Although western Europeans may presently be setting the pace for effective intimacy between sovereign states, western European nation states required many centuries, innumerable wars culminating in World Wars I and II, and an unambiguous threat from across the Elbe before their common impulses emerged into concrete policy. South and Southeast Asian countries need not take so long, but to assume that effective intimacy could be achieved during the first decade of independent statehood was to expect too much. A close examination of their efforts to reach common policies in their own region should provide some insight into their relationships.

II · SOME BACKGROUND CONSIDERATIONS

A. ATTITUDE BASE

1. *Emotions from the colonial period.* Prior to independence, nationalist leaders realized that progress toward freedom made by any one country benefited the freedom movements in all countries.[1] A sense of a shared destiny proved to be a useful weapon in mobilizing resistance to European rulers. Lacking both wealth and power, Indians and their neighbors excelled the uncouth, scurrying Westerners "in the realm of the spirit." In Ceylon it was possible to remind people that her ancient civilization was in full flower at a time when Britain was still an island of barbarians. In a civilization where age is esteemed and youth is considered thoughtless, the more ancient the civilization, the greater its validity, and the more deserving of admiration. Despite—or because of—the fact that European power dominated these countries and that European techniques held great allure, the ancient indigenous cultures of India, Burma, and Ceylon all deserved respect.

More contemporary elements contributed to a sense of common future destiny. After all, it was the white Europeans who had deprived them all of their independence and had "distorted" their economies to suit the foreigner's pleasure. Traditional political and social institutions had been undermined. The European in all these countries had been triply arrogant. He believed that the white

[1] Werner Levi, *Free India in Asia* (Minneapolis, 1952), p. 16.

race was naturally superior in intelligence, stamina, strength, and creative ability. Racially exclusive, he had considered the "natives" unfit to mix with as social equals. In the upper levels of Ceylon society there was a good deal of sociability between Ceylonese and British. Yet such mixing was not without its incidents and each man bears some scars of a past racial encounter with a European. Social slights or invidious treatment are therefore frequently assumed to be matters of racial concern, and color evaluations are often attributed to social situations which may have no relation to pigmentation.

The white man was religiously arrogant. Christianity—like Islam—presumed that it alone had access to, and knowledge of, the One True God; all other religions were blasphemous, or in error. The Portuguese Catholics and later the Dutch Reformed church had persecuted the Ceylonese in the name of the One True God during the sixteenth, seventeenth, and eighteenth centuries. And during the nineteenth century state assistance was given to Christian institutions. In some of the countries of South and Southeast Asia where religions have been tolerant and are largely personal, private matters, such presumption and organized promotion were greeted with astonishment and incredulity. Active religious emotions can still be evoked by recalling the centuries of religious persecution.[2]

The proud Westerner never let the Ceylonese or others in the area forget that he also considered himself organizationally superior. Indeed, one observer suggests that perhaps the greatest innovation of the Christian missionaries was a totally revolutionary sense of organization which gave to individuals and groups new means of influence in an otherwise tradition-bound society.[3] On the technological and governmental levels, too, Western organizational forms took root, not so much because they were consciously imposed but were developed as the Western rulers attempted to manage in ways they understood the intractable problems with which they were faced. Casual remarks and explicit writings of the Sahibs have revealed that the white man always thought he could do it better than the Asian.[4]

[2] K. M. Panikkar's *Asia and Western Dominance* (London, 1953), particularly Part VII.

[3] Zinkin, *Asia and the West*, p. 20.

[4] That this is no dead issue was demonstrated during the Suez Canal crisis in 1956. One of the arguments in the British case that most annoyed Ceylonese was the implicit judgment that the Egyptians could not run the canal themselves and therefore an international supervisory body was necessary. *Ceylon Daily News*, September 26, 1956.

Three distinguishable groups in Ceylon felt strongly about Asian solidarity. The Western educated elite resented the assumption that Ceylonese were not the equals of Europeans, when by education and social ways the Westernized considered themselves fully as good as the superior Englishman. For those who did not find adequate satisfactions in the opportunities opened to them during and following the colonial regime, Asian solidarity represented one way of expressing their resentment.

The numberless clerks who manned the government services and mercantile establishments, educated through a Western curriculum, blamed the years of Western domination for their career difficulties. Career frustrations, therefore, led many to be susceptible to "anti-imperialist" political appeals, and they frequently followed political leaders who repudiated Western connections in favor of closer ties with Asian neighbors.

A third group of nationalists has grown up since independence who are largely from indigenous educational institutions. Unemployment and limited cultural horizons have made these new nationalists anti-Western in a cultural sense and opposed to Westernized Ceylonese. Insofar as these students go beyond the horizons of village and province, they are among those susceptible to the concept of Asian solidarity as a hope for the future.

Those in the new nationalist group who are also of Buddhist faith—as most of them are—find in their religious philosophy a bond with other South Asian countries, particularly Burma, less so Thailand and Cambodia, to some extent with India, where Buddhism began, and even with China. Hence the idea of Asian solidarity is congenial from a number of points of view.

2. *The revived more distant past.* As long as the Westerner dominated the political and economic systems in South Asia, it was possible for many peoples to feel a sense of shared hostility to the European interlopers. India, Ceylon, and Burma could all be aware of a common destiny in the face of the enemy. Yet, when, as part of their national awakening, these peoples began to emphasize their historical past prior to the Westerner's coming, they found a record of strife and events that would create in the minds of many Asians a sense of mutual distrust. As the Ceylonese explored their ancient chronicles, they realized their cultural and religious debt to India. But they were also reminded of the invasions of the Chola or other empires from South India, or the period when Ceylon paid tribute

to the Ming court in China, thus recalling other dominations from nearer home. The Burmese and Thais have long fought one another, and mutual anxieties persist between these two. National consciousness awakens memories long dormant. These are not necessarily conducive to trust and cooperation.

3. *Minorities.* Throughout the area, indigenous populations feel they have been frisked, outsmarted, and overborne by more energetic, shrewder, and less moral outsiders from neighboring large countries. Ceylonese resent Indian money lenders, businessmen, and hard working estate labor. The Burmese resent Indians in the same fields. In Burma, Malaya, and Indonesia, the overseas Chinese play much the same roles vis-à-vis the more easy-going inhabitants.[5] These minorities are an outgrowth of the colonial era when laborers could move in security from one area to another and repatriate their earnings. But the net effect has been that traditional fears of domination are compounded with economic competition. In each country legislation has been used either to reduce the scope of their competitive ability by excluding them from certain economic activities or to limit the franchise and other political rights of these overly successful minorities.

4. *Mutual isolation.* The mixed attitudes toward each other of the Asian neighbors therefore result from history's contradictory legacy. Moreover, during the colonial period, the division of South Asia into colonies of various European states divided Asia in another way. Individuals in French-controlled areas looked to France; those in British areas looked to Britain, and those in Dutch territory looked to Holland. Only when the old empires withdrew could the peoples again reach out to one another.

During the first decade of independence, there has been a remarkably slight change in this pattern. Colombo's newspaper reporting of significant events in other South Asian countries is very slight. Newspapermen find news on the London ticker more absorbing and relevant to themselves than news from Delhi, Rangoon, or Djakarta. In the past what happened in western Europe was more likely to affect them than what happened in neighboring countries, and they have not yet changed their perspective. Developments at a British Labour Party Congress or the issues of personalities in American elections are given greater prominence than political developments in Burma, for example. Shortly after the remarkable election of

[5] Thompson and Adloff, *Minority Problems in Southeast Asia,* for a discussion.

April 1956 in Ceylon, the A.F.P.F.L. in Burma also held a General Election, but it received little attention. When Prime Minister U Nu resigned later in the year, there was virtually no detailed speculation or informed background information to enlighten a presumably puzzled reader. More surprising, when Ceylon's delegate at the United Nations abstained on a hotly disputed resolution condemning the Soviet Union for intervening in Hungary, Ceylonese papers carried much more information regarding Russian-Hungarian difficulties than they carried news regarding Burma's difficulties on her northern, Chinese border nearer to Colombo by 3,000 miles.[6] This is not because it is technically easier to subscribe to Western wire services and receive news without having to seek it out. Cable service with Rangoon is adequate, and Rangoon has some newspapers with good reportorial staffs. The interest merely is not there.[7]

Most Ceylonese, when they have funds and time for travel abroad, prefer to go to Great Britain, western Europe, or the United States. More recently, tours sponsored by the governments of the Soviet Union and mainland China have been gaining in popularity. Ceylon Tamils may go to southern India for religious and educational purposes. A few Sinhalese Buddhists go to Burma for religious fellowship. But by and large, few travel to South Asia. As yet, there is no notion of the *Wanderjahr* that has done so much to make Europeans aware of one another. There appears to be little curiosity to learn how others live or what they do, and there is a great deal of mutual ignorance. More symbolic than representative was one M.P., subsequently a prominent member of the cabinet in 1956, who refused to believe that China and Burma were contiguous. When told so by the Minister of Finance in 1952, he replied: "did the Honourable Minister of Finance look up his atlas to find out the distance from Burma to China? I am sure it must be over 500 miles."[8]

With a few notable exceptions, it is only in the Left parties that a knowledgeable curiosity regarding Asian neighbors is to be found. The Sama Samajist Trotskyists tend to be concerned with Trotskyist developments in any country, and where there is a Trotskyist party, they become its partisans. The Communist party knits its relations

[6] The summer of 1956. Compare, for instance, *Times of Ceylon*, early November, 1956 on Hungary with October 1956 regarding Burma's border problems.

[7] Indian newspapers, too, have been similarly oriented, devoting roughly 10 per cent of their foreign news space to Asian news, a figure very close to those of leading American papers. See report of International Press Institute meetings in Kandy, *Ceylon Daily News*, November 23, 1957; *New York Times*, November 26, 1957.

[8] *House of Representatives*, V. 12, c. 2211.

with China and the Soviet Union. The Communist leaders have been in Moscow several times, and nearly all the young professional full-time members of the Communist party have been to mainland China within the past few years. This is their one decisive experience outside Ceylon, as the experience of British life and education was for numerous Ceylonese in early years, and is still for many. One can expect, therefore, that unless moderate political leaders and citizens see in South Asia the importance it may well have for the future of Ceylon, few but the Left members will be personally informed.

These difficulties of lack of confidence and ignorance notwithstanding, attitudes favoring greater Asian solidarity are surely more likely to increase than diminish. And domestic political trends are likely to project into the seats of power those less concerned with the outside world and more concerned with immediate and regional matters nearer home.

B. ECONOMIC BASE

The economies of South Asia have much in common. In all of them, highly developed plantation or industrial enterprises exist side by side with a primitive, indigenous agriculture and handicraft production. Although the latter is gradually losing its hold and more and more transactions are entering into the cash economy, it is nevertheless still the economic armature for a rural way of life. They tend to be export-import economies, with the possible exception of India. Roughly 30 per cent of Burma's gross national product is exported; in Thailand, 20 per cent; in Indonesia, 11.4 per cent.[9] Accordingly, they are particularly dependent on exports and imports to maintain their standard of living, and are all vulnerable to adverse shifts in the terms of trade. With the exception of India, they are highly specialized in the commodities they export. In Burma, for instance, approximately 75 per cent of her export values are earned by one commodity, rice. In Ceylon tea and rubber account for 75-80 per cent of her export values. Malaya depends on rubber and tin for 65 per cent of her export values. Cotton and jute account for 77 per cent of Pakistan's exports, while in Thailand rice and rubber account for 65-70 per cent.[10] With the exception of rice, the largest part of these primary commodities of the region have been exported to industrialized countries at the far ends of the

[9] ECAFE, *Economic Survey of Asia and the Far East 1955*, p. 31.
[10] *Ibid.*, p. 32.

world. The only exception to this was China's purchases of Ceylonese rubber in the past few years, although after 1956 these decreased so that even Ceylon tended to return to an earlier pattern where most of its products were exported to Western and industrialized countries.

Taken commodity by commodity, the exports of the countries in the area are mutually competitive. India, Ceylon, and lately Indonesia are competitors in the world tea markets. Ceylon has always sought to have its tea recognized as of better quality than that from India. In the eyes of the island's tea interests, should Ceylonese teas lose their identity and become submerged in Indian stocks, Ceylonese teas would be given second place to the larger Indian supplies. Because of their mutually competitive character India and Ceylon have no longer been able to continue their joint publicity organization for the promotion of tea consumption in overseas markets.

In the case of rubber, Ceylon, Malaya, and Indonesia all compete with one another. As long as political controls in Malaya prevented Singapore rubber from going to China, Ceylon had a favored place, which the Malayan producers could not help but resent. With the relaxation of embargo controls from 1956 on, Colombo's privileged position began to wane. Malayan production is more efficient than Ceylon's, costs being considerably less. Though Indonesian exports have fluctuated as much with internal disorders as with world market conditions, Indonesia and Malaya together largely determine the gross amounts of natural rubber to enter the market. Ceylon's production is less than one-sixth of Malaya's and sometimes only one-eighth of Indonesia's.

Since Ceylon, Malaya, and Indonesia are mutually competitive, it would be logical to expect that they would attempt to divide up world markets or reach commodity agreements to maintain a minimum price for natural rubber sales, such as was attempted with brief success under the Stevenson Plan in the 1920's and 1930's. In the Ceylonese parliament there have been reiterated demands that this be done, but few steps have been taken.[11] The producer countries are up against the intractable fact of government-sponsored synthetic production in the traditionally consuming countries. By 1959 economic pressures had not yet become so desperate as to lead to general acceptance of production controls. The Ceylonese government, or any other government in South Asia, had not shown

[11] *House of Representatives,* V. 6, c. 71; V. 8, c. 1773, for instance.

serious interest in a policy requiring elaborate and sensitive multilateral arrangements. Lack of trust is conspicuous in such matters as trading and business, and to elaborate a safe and sure mechanism which all could count upon appeared implausible. Hence, on commodities crucial to them, Ceylon, Malaya, Indonesia, and India are competitive. And because they are competing in primary plantation products and not in more diversified industrial goods, as are Germany and Britain, a productive interchange and exchange of commodities between them is not likely.

One commodity is an exception to these observations—rice. Both Burma and Thailand produce an exportable surplus of rice and Southeast Asian countries have traditionally been their chief markets. Over 80 per cent of Burma's and Thailand's export trade is within the ECAFE area.[12] Directly after World War II and in 1952-53 when rice was in short supply, many Ceylonese resented the fact that the Burmese charged all the market would bear. Conversely, when rice was again plentiful and Indian and Ceylonese buyers were attentively welcomed in Rangoon, the Burmese considered they drove unduly hard bargains, to the detriment of Burma's development program.[13] Hence, the normal course of international trade does not necessarily serve to draw these countries together.

The countries of South Asia have problems in common with respect to economic development, but they are such that it is difficult for them to help each other except in limited ways. They are short of technicians and skilled engineers, middle supervisors and foremen, men with skilled competence and rolled-up sleeves. They suffer from a lack of sufficient capital and, with the exception of India, they lack the raw materials that are important to a diversified, industrialized economy. They do not have all the information necessary for economic planning. Moreover, they are faced with the pressure of an increasingly articulate populace with vague but pressing demands for a better standard of living. Hence, while they have many problems in common, they do not necessarily have the facilities to help one another meet them.

C. DEFENSE INTERESTS

Analysis of the defense interests of South Asian countries is difficult because there is often no stable consensus among statesmen

[12] These figures include Japan. ECAFE E/EN 11.1/1 and T/92, October 12, 1953, p. 14.
[13] Interviews with publicists and government servants, Rangoon, 1956.

or attentive public regarding the sources of threat and of reliable and trusted associates. Central to the area is India. Her three smaller neighbors, Pakistan, Ceylon, and Burma, live in the shadow of the Indian colossus. It is as hard for Indian publicists and statesmen to believe that India is considered by its smaller neighbors a potential threat, as it is hard for Americans to imagine that Latin American countries should be genuinely anxious about American intentions.

At the pivot where Indian and Chinese influences converge Burma has a double problem. It may be that India and China can agree to a buffer zone between the two regional giants—yet the analogy of Tibet suggests that a buffer is not as yet entirely congenial to the Chinese rulers. An important uncertainty in Mr. Nehru's policy is the degree of Chinese influence in Burma that would be acceptable to India. How far would Mr. Nehru be prepared to allow the radical Left in Burma a free hand to manage as it would? There was evidence that many moderate Burmese believed they would gain little support from India, for India's chief concern, it was said, was not to provoke the Chinese for fear of precipitating a conflict that might throw the Five Year Plan off its precarious base.[14] Moreover, as long as Pakistan remained a hostile element on India's western frontier, the Indian government would be most reluctant to embark on an active defensive enterprise in the direction of Burma. Its immediate defense efforts appeared to have been centered in Kashmir and along the Nepalese and Tibetan frontiers. Though indicative of Delhi's concern for her eastern marches, protracted difficulties in the Naga hills in 1956 suggested there were few resources to spare for an emergency in the direction of Burma. Accordingly, although there is in Ceylon and Burma a real sense of anxiety about the long run future of relations with India, it was clear that there was no immediate threat from that quarter. On the contrary, the Burmese perhaps regretted that India would be unlikely to be active in their direction in case of need.

To the west of India and in the Ganges delta, Pakistan lies divided by India, less than one-fifth its population, greatly inferior in resources and with a much smaller army. As Professor Callard reminds us, "Pakistan was founded on the basis of the vital difference between groups of Asians" and was, in consequence, "less tempted than certain other countries by the concept of Asian (or

[14] *Times of Ceylon*, October 4, 1956.

non-white) solidarity."[15] Preoccupied above all with her Indian neighbor and the disputed matters of Kashmir and water rights in the divided Punjab, her leaders and officials probably saw India as her most intractable defense problem. To the east and north, a weak Afghanistan seemed a poor defense barrier against the militarily mighty Soviet Union. Both the Soviet Union and India on either side of Pakistan were more real than a manifestly disappearing Western imperialism.

Thailand, unlike the other South and Southeast Asian countries was never subject to European control but remained by agreement a buffer kingdom between British Burma and French Indo-China until the Japanese invasion of 1941. No colonial legacy gave emotional strength to calls for Asian solidarity in the face of the remnants of "Western imperialism." Lacking representative political institutions, there were as yet few domestic political incentives for such agitation. The immediate defense preoccupation of Thailand, rather, appeared to be the massive Chinese neighbor to the north and the mounting unrest in Indo-China.

Indonesian interests were uncertain. Indonesia, too, is surrounded by the sea, but unlike Ceylon, no continental country with a massive population is proximate to Indonesia. Its nearest neighbor, Australia. contains less then one-tenth as many people. But Australia is well-organized, its people are vigorous, and it is not enthusiastically supporting the Indonesian ambition to control West Irian. The military struggle for independence against the Dutch, and the difficult political and administrative problems after independence, provided every incentive for anticolonial arguments, with Asian solidarity as their positive symbolic counterpart. In Indonesia there has been remarkably little foreign policy consensus.

Though much of the emotional impulse for closer ties with Asian neighbors came as a reaction against the generations of western European colonial rule, to favor closer Asian solidarity need not inescapably mean being anti-Western in a political sense. Much would depend on how Western power was applied in the former colonial areas of rimland Asia. One of the recurrent issues dividing members of the area was precisely what role should be assigned to Western power. To some, Western power appeared to be less imminent than before. But prudence seemed to recommend voicing anxieties about the now distant and familiar West rather than specu-

[15] Keith Callard, *Pakistan, a Political Study*, p. 321.

lating aloud on other possible and less known contingencies from nearer home. Scattered Indonesia and tense Pakistan were conscious of their own military weakness. Perhaps India, aware of her internal fissiparous tendencies, felt unsure in the face of possible action from Russia or China. More plausibly in the sight of many Indians, the immediate threat appeared to come from Pakistan, particularly after the S.E.A.T.O. was formed. A sense of their individual vulnerability to the military might of the outside world—such a fundamental part of their history—no doubt informed many of their reactions in the face of world events.

But in such considerations, there were certain conventions that were often observed. It was Western and bad form to discuss interstate relations in these terms. To acknowledge anxiety about another country was not done except in private, between good friends. Fears once expressed, might add their deleterious influence to the universal network of cause and effect. To speculate upon the possibilities inherent in geography and relative power was considered to be evidence of the perverse preoccupation with worldly affairs that has always, so it is said, characterized Westerners as distinct from Asians.[16]

During the first decade of independence, there were no real threats to the peace and security of Ceylon. She had been able to define her policy on optimistic prognostications which did not force hard or irrevocable choices. Promoting Asian solidarity insofar as that was possible meant incurring few new risks. Success in the venture might even reduce the risk of Ceylon's being isolated off the shores of a consolidated South and Southeast Asia.

These were some of the elements that formed the background for consideration of Asian solidarity in practice. A discussion of specific endeavors to mark or achieve this objective will make some of these themes clear.

III · STEPS TOWARD CLOSER UNITY

A. MUTUAL ASSISTANCE

1. *Aid to Burma.* When Burma's civil war was approaching its climax in 1949, internal disruption had so interrupted the flow of exports that the government's foreign exchange reserves were desperately low. She appealed to India to see whether, through its intermediary, the commonwealth governments would be able to

[16] The writings of G. S. Bajpai and K. M. Panikkar were exceptions in India.

provide Burma with some form of economic assistance. At the commonwealth meeting in Colombo in January 1950, the prime ministers agreed to the principle of providing what assistance they could to the hard-pressed government. At the time the Left parties in Ceylon vehemently criticized the government for allowing itself to become the tool of British economic interests who were bent on reestablishing their former influence in Burma.[17]

When Dr. Perera carried his criticism against the commonwealth measures to the point of pressing a no-confidence motion, Mr. D. S. Senanayake argued, "If ever it becomes necessary or possible for us to help Burma, we shall certainly give that help to the best of our ability not only for the sake of Burma but for the sake of our own country. Not only are there ancient connections between ourselves, but we depend on Burma to a large extent for our foodstuffs. Peace and order in that country are of the greatest importance to us, and I certainly say that if we can in any way help to maintain them, we shall certainly do so and give the necessary help."[18] Others emphasized that Burma, too, was a Buddhist country, and since Rangoon sought to encourage the development of law and order by promoting Buddhism, there could be no more acceptable way of restoring peace.

The Buddhist theme in Ceylon's foreign relations should be evaluated with caution. Friendship with Burma, Thailand, Cambodia, and China could all be justified on religious grounds, but only with Burma were there close relations. Even so, Ceylonese Buddhists criticized the Burmese for lack of traditional learning, for their unorthodox approach to meditation, or for spending so much on the Peace Pagoda and the Great Cave when the country's economy remained precarious. The Burmese sometimes reciprocated by considering Ceylon unduly influenced religiously and culturally by Western ways. Nevertheless, if any country appeared to be congenial and friendly to the Sinhalese educated masses, it was Burma.

In any event, the Commonwealth Committee for Aid to Burma put forward a concrete proposal and Ceylon's contribution of some Rs. 3,300,000 was in the form of funds from Ceylon's balance in London to be held as backing for Burma's shaky currency. Because these funds were in blocked accounts, they could not be drawn upon by Ceylon in any case. To put them to the credit function of backing

[17] For instance, N. M. Perera, *House of Representatives*, V. 5, c. 2589-2598.

[18] *Ibid.*, V. 7, c. 1404; V. 8, c. 600.

Burma's currency temporarily in no way competed with Ceylon's many claims for improved social services, housing, etc.[19]

Two years later Burma's own hard-pressed trade administrators attempted to use a market shortage of rice for Burma's advantage, and a rather prompt reversal of the supply position favored Ceylon the following year. Thus relationships between Burma and Ceylon were formed of an intricate mixture of sentiment and economic interdependence and in both instances, there were elements that drew the two together and also tended to thrust them apart.

2. *Aid to Indonesia.* When Indonesian forces were in danger from "police action" by the Dutch in 1949, Ceylon prohibited the Dutch from using any Ceylonese ports or airports for military purposes. The prime minister's initiative in taking action against the Dutch was welcomed on all sides with only a few exceptions on the Left. It represented standing in the way of a Western colonial country and it proved at home that Ceylon was not merely following in the wake of Britain but was developing an "independent" policy regardless of British opinion.[20] This step of the Ceylonese prime minister was often referred to in later years by the U.N.P. when the Opposition charged the government with being "tied to the chariot wheels of Western Imperialism."[21]

Once diplomatic relations were established with Indonesia in 1950 the question of whether or not Ceylon required full-time representation in Djakarta was hotly debated in the Ceylonese parliament. The issue was seldom discussed solely on the merits of closer ties with Indonesia, for other matters were also in question. The Opposition charged the government with using Ceylon's limited budget to provide diplomatic posts for its unsuccessful members. From the point of view of Ceylon's wider relations, the D.S. Senanayake government had, along with Britain, early recognized Communist China, but it had never developed closer diplomatic relations. Members on the Left insisted that it would have been far better to establish an embassy in Peking instead of opening a legation in Indonesia.[22] In the end, the representative's appointment to Djakarta was justified on grounds that he had helped prepare Ceylon's and Indonesia's common stand in advance of the Rubber Conference, where the special interest both countries shared in the fate of rubber prices was discussed.[23] Neither the rubber negotiations nor the continued ex-

19 *Ibid.*, V. 8, c. 594.

20 *Ibid.*, V. 5, c. 792.

21 *Ibid.*, V. 12, c. 295.

22 *Ibid.*, V. 8, c. 1773; V. 10, c. 1885.

23 *Ibid.*, V. 10, c. 1885.

change of diplomatic representatives made it possible to achieve an effective agreement on commodity price stabilization.

Indonesian relations received little fresh impetus toward intimacy until the Colombo Powers meeting was called by Sir John Kotelawala in the winter of 1953-54.

B. REGIONAL CONFERENCES

1. *Asian Relations Conference, 1947.* The first significant postwar effort to accent Asian unity was the Asian Relations Conference called by Mr. Nehru in New Delhi in 1947. The living presence of the imperialist powers was still manifest. In Indonesia, the Dutch were actively attempting to re-establish themselves.[24] In India and Pakistan, vast migrations accompanied the devolution of power to a divided India, and negotiations were then still going on between the British authorities and Indian leaders.

Mr. Nehru put his finger on the principal themes of unity. As he welcomed the delegates he seemed to epitomize the sense of fresh strength, of newly discovered unity and the long-anticipated excitement of freedom and independence. New nations, hitherto dormant, were now struggling to rise to their feet. With the end of European rule, "the walls that surround us fall down and we look at one another again and meet as old friends long parted." Only when all nations were free and all peoples relieved of suffering could there be real peace. Hence, the end of imperialist domination and a rapid progress toward economic development were both prerequisites for peace. He ably suggested one of the fundamental purposes of South Asian statesmen when he said: "Far too long have we of Asia been petitioners in Western courts and chancellories. That story must now belong to the past. We propose to stand on our own feet and to co-operate with all others who are prepared to co-operate with us. We do not intend to be the playthings of others."[25]

This new grouping of states was in no way aggressive or against any other country. Mr. Nehru emphasized that the "whole spirit and outlook of Asia are peaceful and the emergence of Asia in world affairs would be a powerful influence for world peace." Although there should be no leaders and no followers in such an association

[24] George M. Kahin, *Nationalism and Revolution in Indonesia* (Ithaca, 1952), for a detailed study of these developments.

[25] "Asia Again Finds Herself," speech before the Asian Conference in New Delhi, March 23, 1947. Reproduced in *Independence and After*, Speeches of Jawaharlal Nehru 1946-1949 (New Delhi, 1949), p. 298.

as this of free and sovereign states, nevertheless, India was the "natural centre and focal point of the many forces at work in Asia." She had synthesized many strands of Asian culture into her own and she had given much of cultural value to other Asian countries in the past. He sketched the flow and interpenetration of cultural currents as they swept through and over Asia and evoked a vision of a civilization with much in common despite its diversity, a civilization stretching from the Middle Eastern Arab and Muslim civilizations through the Ganges Valley on down through to Indonesia. He concluded: "When the history of our present time is written, this event may well stand out as a land-mark which divides the past of Asia from the future. And because we are participating in this making of history, something of the greatness of historical events comes to us all."[26]

But as in all such occasions, the high level at which meetings begin cannot be maintained as members grapple with the immediate intractable problems. Some competition between India and China for the leadership of Asia was already manifest. The Arab States, for their part, were not enthusiastic about developing institutions for closer ties with Asia. They were more deeply concerned over Zionist pressures rising in the Middle East. Because of their Muslim faith and the efforts of their coreligionists to set up a separate Pakistan, they could not be expected enthusiastically to embrace Mr. Nehru's vision of the future. The Muslim League in India boycotted the meetings, considering them "a thinly disguised attempt on the part of the Hindu Congress to boost itself politically as the prospective leader of the Asian peoples."[27]

The smaller nations also showed anxieties over the possibility of being dominated by an Asian power at the very time that independence had been obtained from the Western countries. Both Burma and Ceylon expressed fears of being overwhelmed by a growing Indian population.[28] To the Ceylonese, having in mind their Indian minority, the most important discussions were those concerning migration and the rights of migrants. All representatives were against discrimination of any kind, but it was agreed that each government had the right to determine for itself the composition of its national population. They admitted that there was considerable *de facto* dis-

[26] *Ibid.*, p. 299.
[27] *Times of Ceylon*, despatch from New Delhi, March 20, 1947.
[28] *Ceylon Daily News*, March 31, 1947.

crimination against the Indian minority in administration and public life, but these matters could be solved by long-term measures, such as education and social contacts which would speed assimilation.[29]

Nothing came of discussions setting up a permanent organization to facilitate cultural interchange, exchange of scholars, and for the closest possible economic relations compatible with national sovereignty.[30] In the end an eight-man committee was established to plan for the next meeting, which was to be held in China in 1949.

The meetings brought together statesmen who were struggling at home with the tremendously difficult though exhilarating problems of newly acquired independence. Internal difficulties of each country were then infinitely more pressing than each one's need for the other. It was a time for halting explorations toward new associations with awakening neighbors. The older opponents, against whom they had all struggled and whose very existence had given them their primary political purpose, their vocabulary of political polemic and, in many ways, their followings at home, were fast withdrawing from the area. New modes of political life were now necessary. To explore together these new horizons no doubt gave courage to each one there. Conferences within the Commonwealth are productive of few concrete results, but are considered sufficiently worthwhile for prime ministers and foreign secretaries to journey half way around the world to one another's capitals. But the mutual understanding that comes from tentative and personal discussions brings each a clearer conception of the other's problems, possibilities, and personality, and helps define more clearly the limits of cooperative action. This was particularly important where the participants lacked precedents and experienced foreign affairs staffs, and where the political leader had a preponderating weight in determining foreign policy.[31]

2. *The Indonesian Conference.* The next common effort came two years later in January 1949 during the "second police action" of the Dutch in Indonesia. Mr. Nehru called together members from eighteen countries to protest against Dutch attempts to suppress the

29 *Ceylon Daily News,* March 28, 1947.

30 *Times of Ceylon,* March 26, 1947.

31 For contemporary evaluations, see Virginia Thompson and Richard Adloff, "Asian Unity: Force or Fiction?" *Far Eastern Survey* XVI (1949), pp. 97-99. Werner Levi, "Union in Asia," *Far Eastern Survey* XIX (1950), pp. 144-199. Gerald Packer, "The Asian Relations Conference," *Australian Outlook* I, No. 2 (June 1947), pp. 3-8. Nicholas Mansergh, *The Commonwealth and the Nations* (London, 1949), pp. 98-120. Werner Levi, *Free India in Asia,* Ch. III.

new Republic. Here indeed was an issue on which common views could be expected. A colonial power par excellence was attempting by force to re-establish its rule after having broken agreements regarding the devolution of power to the struggling Indonesian Republic government. Leaders of the Republic had been jailed and military forces were again in action against the forces of the emergent government. New independence was felt to be a shaky, uncertain thing, and all the delegates sensed a common danger. Mr. Bandaranaike, the Ceylonese representative, made the common view explicit. "In regard to Asia, this is a particularly flagrant and provocative attempt by the Dutch to re-assert the principles of imperialism and capitalism. If it succeeds it is bound to have damaging effects on other countries that have recently obtained their freedom from colonialism."[32]

The issues were sufficiently clear-cut for there to be no serious disagreements. No one wished to defer to the other in taking the initiative in being anti-Dutch. Prior to the meeting, Mr. D. S. Senanayake had already taken the lead by prohibiting the Dutch from using Colombo Harbor and Ceylon's airfields for the transport of men and material to the fighting in Indonesia. At that time, commonwealth members were somewhat reluctant to stand up too obviously against Britain's efforts to find a formula to save Dutch face while ensuring the final devolution of power to the Republic. Nevertheless, the resolution they agreed to charged the Dutch with being aggressors, called on them to withdraw immediately from the Republican capital they had recently occupied, and to withdraw progressively to the lines they had held before the recent attacks. They also insisted that the ministers and political leaders be freed and that the Republic be again allowed to negotiate freely for the specific terms of independence.[33]

Under the circumstances, the resolution, though mild, reflected an impressive unanimity of opinion expressed by the Asian governments. The British Foreign Secretary, Mr. Bevin, for one, acknowledged its importance. In discussing affairs in the Middle East, he declared in parliament that "the recent Asian Conference in New Delhi (was) a phenomenon which it would be very unwise for (the United Kingdom) to ignore. This group of countries looks west to Arab lands as well as east to Indonesia. . . . Our vital in-

[32] *Times of Ceylon*, January 18, 1949.
[33] Resolution as reported in *Ceylon Daily News*, January 24, 1949.

terests spread through the whole area and we have to remember this when we are considering the whole problem of our foreign relations."[34] No doubt it strengthened the hands of those in the State Department and Whitehall who saw that through facilitating the transition to independence they had a better chance of continuing a beneficial association between the Western countries and South and Southeast Asians. It contributed in this way to induce these and other members of the United Nations to press more insistently for a strong Security Council action that speeded independence for Indonesia.[35]

Nothing like such unanimity could be achieved again by the Asian statesmen until the British and French attempted to reassert their power in the Suez Canal dispute of 1956 on the other side of the Indian Ocean.

3. *Colombo Conference, 1954.* Between the conference on Indonesian Independence held in 1949 and the Colombo conference held in 1954, events on a wider stage altered the setting within which the South Asian countries could draw together. India was rapidly consolidating its position at home, although India and Pakistan continued to struggle over Kashmir. Indonesia was now fully independent. The Korean War, far to the north on the further side of China, had brought American troops to fight on the continent of East Asia. Nearer to hand, in Indo-China, Viet Namese nationalists, under Communist leadership, and French forces were locked in the final throes of that protracted struggle. In December 1953, Sir John Kotelawala took the initiative in inviting India, Pakistan, Burma, and Indonesia to meet in Colombo.

They had many things in common. They were united in expressing opposition to the remaining manifestations of Western colonialism in the Indian Ocean or Southeast Asian area; they had all experienced European rule; they all sought, with greater or lesser singleness of purpose, economic development. They all hoped to have a larger voice in world affairs, to develop relationships of equality and self-respect with the hitherto dominating powers from western Europe or with the United States, Russia, or mainland China. Most of them were seriously attempting to consolidate representative regimes in areas that had had very different political traditions.[36]

[34] *House of Commons*, V. 460, c. 928.

[35] See, for instance, William Henderson, *Pacific Settlement of Disputes—The Indonesian Question 1946-1949*, Woodrow Wilson Foundation, 1954, p. 51.

[36] Although as yet Pakistan had not had an election.

The outlines of the interests that divided them were also clearly discernible from the beginning. India's leaders apparently feared that her smaller neighbors desired to mediate in the Kashmir dispute.[37] Mr. Mohammed Ali of Pakistan had to reassure his followers and opposition that the meetings were not going to result in India's becoming the leader of an Asian bloc.[38] He was particularly concerned to exclude from the conference any discussion of the bilateral military arrangements he was then negotiating with the United States.[39] The Indonesians hoped that the countries present might help to bring peace between India and Pakistan.[40] They also sought to add to the Muslim contingent representatives of Nasser's Egypt. Even though representatives of additional states were not invited, Mr. Sastroamidjojo carried his desire for a wider conference into realization later, at Bandung.

As the Colombo meeting approached, the crisis in Indo-China deepened, the French became more hard pressed and American military assistance to the French increased. One week before the Colombo Powers met, apparently without detailed preliminary consultations, the American government publicly proposed that the countries of Southeast Asia join together in a defense organization with American and British participation similar to the NATO in Europe. A few days later, the European powers, the United States, Russia, and mainland China met in Geneva to reach an agreed settlement in Indo-China.

These events as seen in Colombo were characteristic of "the Great Powers." The American proposal appeared to many publicists in the area as still another example of Westerners using local disputes as an excuse to once again bring Western armed power to bear in Asia. Moreover, the Western Powers, Russia, and China were deciding in Europe the fate of Indo-China—a Southeast Asian country—without seriously consulting the South and Southeast Asian leaders. The *Times of Ceylon* was probably representative of articulate opinion when it editorialized: "But Mr. Dulles does not trouble to find out how Asia's repugnance to communism might best be utilized in the cause of world democracy, with Asia's consent. He is in a hurry and, with bland arrogance, imagines that because Free Asia abhors communism it will automatically embrace any made-in-

37 Interview with one of the early proponents of the conference in Ceylon.

38 *Dawn* (Karachi), February 6, 1954.

39 *Dawn* (Karachi), January 14, 15, 1954.

40 *The Hindu* (Madras), March 12, 1954.

Washington scheme for liberating Asia in spite of the Asians. . . ."[41]

Both India and Indonesia were opposed on principle to military blocs and pacts, and had been developing a theory of "nonalignment." They feared that weak Asian countries in intimate military association with strong powers from whatever part of the world would inescapably become the pawns of their more powerful allies. The story of the British conquest of India gave historical plausibility in their thought to this dangerous possibility. Too poor to pursue simultaneously urgent economic development and costly defense programs on their own, they would become completely dependent on the wealthy outside power who assisted them to strengthen their military stance. The S.E.A.T.O. proposal appeared to be a particularly distressing example of such a policy. How could Thailand or the Philippines, for instance, be expected to follow an independent policy in association with the large, wealthy, well-organized and energetic United States? If Pakistan joined the S.E.A.T.O., that association would then become the channel for arms that Delhi feared would be used against the Indians. This would add anxiety to the argument on principle against such military organizations. They feared that "alignment" on one side or the other of the Cold War would only bring Russian-American rivalry nearer to an area that above all others in the world required peace if even its minimum subsistence needs were to be met. If all of South and Southeast Asia remained aloof from either bloc, an area of peace would be extended. Worldwide tensions would be reduced, since the efforts of both blocs to woo the uncommitted would place a premium on moderation and peaceful behavior by both protagonists in the Cold War. This would contribute to lessening tensions and thus reduce the chances of World War III. In their eyes, any country in the area that associated with outside powers was thereby risking the tranquility of all and weakening their influence for pacification between the American and Russian giants.

The smaller powers in the neighborhood of China and India, however, had a somewhat different perspective. The Pakistanis were prepared to accept direct defense agreements with the United States, either against Communist aggression, as many Pakistanis maintained, or with hostile intent against India, as the Indians claimed. The Ceylonese prime minister was outspokenly anti-Communist. Less demonstrative, the Burmese were nevertheless aware that almost

[41] *Times of Ceylon*, April 20, 1954.

all of Burma was only an hour away by plane from China. They were all cautious about the American initiative, but they did not necessarily accept Mr. Nehru's interpretation of events.

India's was the broadest vision at the conference, concerned not so much with inter-Asian relations as with the storm in Indo-China. Before coming, Mr. Nehru had put forward a six-point proposal as a basis for solution, and he pressed for its adoption by the whole conference.[42] The Pakistani, persistently contrary to Mr. Nehru, argued that until local South Asian issues were solved, there was little value in attempting to solve more distant peoples' difficulties. Sir John, like Mr. Nehru, urged a settlement of the Indo-China imbroglio, but he pressed for a conference resolution finding that "aggressive communism" as well as "the attempt to perpetuate colonial rule" was an additional threat to democratic freedom.

All were agreed that China should be admitted to the United Nations. American refusal to recognize the manifest fact of mainland China appeared as one more example of Westerners' inability to recognize reality when dealing with Asians. All sought the end of atom-bomb tests, liberation of French North Africa, and increased aid to Arab refugees. A resolution expressing opposition to colonialism was easily passed.

A parallel resolution condemning "international Communism" presented serious difficulties. Pakistan and Burma reportedly supported Sir John Kotelawala's proposal, while India and Indonesia demurred. The latter states argued that to condemn Communism was to condemn Russia and China—aligning oneself on one side of the Cold War; the former argued that both "colonialisms" were dangerous. In any event, the old colonialism was a disappearing menace and Communism was a growing one.

Meanwhile in Geneva, Mr. Eden had been able to postpone discussions there for a few days, it was understood, in order to give the Colombo Powers time to forward their recommendations. This confirmed the publicists in their faith that Britain, at least, took the voice of Asia into account even if the United States did not.[43] Mr. Eden went further and invited the Asian premiers to set up a Southeast Asian body to administer the transition government in Indo-China should China, France, Great Britain, and the United States accept an immediate ceasefire.[44]

[42] *New York Times*, April 25, 1954.
[43] Editorial, *Times of Ceylon*, April 28, 1954.
[44] Sir John Kotelawala, *An Asian Prime Minister's Story* (London, 1956), p. 120.

Though pressed to play a part in the settlement, the conferees were unable to accept. Understandably enough, the statesmen were reluctant to undertake responsibility for administering an agreement whose terms were not yet known.[45] Personnel to supervise a settlement were not readily available. Indonesia and Burma could spare no troops because of continuing disorders at home. Ceylon had none to send. And at that time it was inconceivable that India and Pakistan could jointly participate in the same administrative and policing enterprise. As a group they therefore reluctantly had to return to others the responsibility for administering a solution on the periphery of the Southeast Asian area.

In the end, the Colombo Powers urged an immediate ceasefire in Indo-China, prompt negotiations between the combatants, an irrevocable commitment by France to grant full independence to Indo-China, and an appeal to China, the United Kingdom, the United States, and Russia to reach agreement on the steps necessary to prevent a recurrence of hostilities. Eventually, only India sent officers to assist in supervising the fulfillment of the armistice agreements.[46]

The conference also was ultimately able to agree on a formula regarding communist and colonialist "intervention" in others' affairs. The Burmese delegate appears to have played an important part in pressing the view that it would be meaningless if the French withdrew from Indo-China, only to have them replaced by others. The Indians and Indonesians reportedly feared that other Westerners would replace the French—namely the Americans whose concern was being daily more manifest—but the Burmese, Ceylonese, and Pakistanis appear to have feared the Chinese more.[47] In either case, the conferees declared their "unshakable determination to resist interference in the affairs of their countries by external Communist, anti-Communist or other agencies. They were convinced that such interference threatened the sovereignty, security, and political independence of their respective States and the right of each country to develop and progress in accordance with the conceptions and desires of its own people."

Mr. Nehru emerged as the public inspirational figure of the con-

[45] *Ceylon Observer*, May 9, 1954.

[46] Royal Institute of International Affairs, *Survey of International Affairs 1954*, pp. 41, 65.

[47] *The Hindu* (Madras), May 6, 1954; *Ceylon Daily News*, May 4, 1954. Text, *Ceylon Daily News*, May 3, 1954.

ference. The crowds in Colombo welcomed him with great acclaim and the essentials of his view had been accepted on Indo-China. But neither Pakistan, Burma, nor Ceylon were yet prepared to accept Mr. Nehru's interpretation of a proper international response to the Cold War or the "Communist threat." Their agreement on this matter remained on the level of ambiguous verbal formulae. They did not discuss Kashmir nor Ceylon's difficulties with the residents of Indian origin. Concrete steps for closer economic or political relationships in the area were not taken.

Yet, the Colombo conference marked one more step in reminding the Western world and Russia that new states were emerging whose voices had to be heard. Their knowledge of one another had been increased. And they had for the first time faced as a group the difficult problem of combining good advice in world affairs with possessing adequate means for carrying out in practice their best judgment. No doubt it was sobering to have had responsibility thrust upon them and to have had to turn it away.

4. *Bandung, 1955.* Carrying forward Mr. Sastroamidjojo's idea, the Colombo Powers decided that another meeting should be arranged, composed of a much larger number of Asian and African countries. The overall purpose was quite clear. They were at one in believing that now that these new countries were coming to independence in areas outside the traditional centers of world power, they had a right to be listened to with greater attention. They were at one in protesting against what they considered a Western inclination to make important decisions affecting their area without consulting them. They were concerned about the mounting tension between China and the United States in the Far East focusing on Formosa. They hoped, by drawing China into closer relations with their countries on the basis of self-limiting principles, to loosen Mao's ties with Russia, to sensitize Mao's government to the fears and aspirations of China's southern neighbors, and to discourage the Chinese from supporting local Communist parties in the South Asian countries.[48]

They differed on many more detailed matters. Mr. Nehru reportedly sought a selected grouping of states which would endorse his "Panch Sheela," or "Five Principles" of good international behavior. In the

[48] Interviews in Colombo and New Delhi. These arguments defining the basic purposes parallel closely Kahin's reporting. See his very detailed discussion, *The Asia-African Conference, Bandung, Indonesia, April 1955* (Ithaca, 1955).

course of negotiations with India over the future of Tibet, Chou En-lai had committed himself also to follow them. To cast these unexceptionable principles of state behavior in the term "Panch Sheela," brilliantly merged traditional Buddhist cultural style with contemporary international politics and no doubt had considerable resonance in Asian public opinion.[49] Mr. Nehru hoped that the more explicitly all states committed themselves to these principles, the less likely would the large countries—including China—project their power into South Asia.[50] Indonesia sought a large Muslim contingent from the Middle East and Africa, in part to promote her aspirations toward West Irian. Sir John Kotelawala reportedly hoped to gain the conference's endorsement for a strongly worded resolution condemning communist "colonialism" as much as the traditional Western variety.[51] The sponsors met in Bogor, Indonesia, in December 1954 and issued thirty invitations, of which twenty-nine were accepted.[52]

The Colombo Powers had met the year before at a time when events in Indo-China appeared to be approaching a clash between Chinese and American arms in the lowlands of the Tonkin Delta. The meetings at Bandung were conducted against a background of sharpening tensions between these countries over the Formosa Straits and the small islands of Quemoy and Matsu off the shore of mainland China.

The twenty-nine nations that met at Bandung had almost contiguous frontiers stretching all the way from Japan in the North Pacific to the Gold Coast in the South Atlantic. They represented half the world's population who together commanded less than 10

[49] They were (1) mutual respect for each other's territorial integrity and sovereignty, (2) non-aggression, (3) non-interference in each other's internal affairs, (4) equality and mutual benefit, (5) peaceful co-existence. For the full text of the Nehru-Chou En-lai statement, see "Communiqué on talks between Mr. Nehru and Mr. Chou En-lai, 28 June 1954" in *Documents on International Affairs 1954, R.I.I.A.*, pp. 313-314. Details on how these principles received their popular label are to be found in a letter from Mr. Nehru to Professor R. H. Fifield, reproduced in his *The Diplomacy of Southeast Asia* (New York, 1958).

[50] Kahin, particularly p. 8.

[51] For preliminary discussions, see *Times of Ceylon*, December 27, 1954; *Dawn* (Karachi), December 28, 29, 30, 1954; *The Hindu* (Madras), December 28, 29, 1954.

[52] The countries that attended were: Afghanistan, Burma, Cambodia, Ceylon, Mainland China, India, Indonesia, Iran, Iraq, Japan, Jordan, Laos, Lebanon, Nepal, Pakistan, the Philippines, Saudi Arabia, Syria, Thailand, Turkey, North Viet Nam, South Viet Nam, and Yemen in Asia. From Africa came Egypt, Ethiopia, the Gold Coast, Liberia, Libya, and the Sudan. For discussions of who should be invited, see *Times of India*, December 28, 1954; *Manchester Guardian*, December 29, 1954; *The Times* (London), December 30, 1954.

per cent of the world's national incomes. Every one had known the presumption of the European and within each country new groups were thrusting forward to assert their right to play a more important part in public affairs.

The procedure of the conference was informal, modeled on the periodic commonwealth prime ministers' meetings, where the agenda was ill-defined and maximum opportunity was provided for personal exchanges. Mr. Soekarno's opening address alluded to their common opposition to colonialism, the poverty they shared, their desire to avoid involvement in other people's wars, and the responsibility they felt to use their independence to prevent a new war.[53] He appealed to the delegates to avoid fear and despite the admitted religious, racial, and cultural diversity in Afro-Asia, to live in peace and harmony, tolerance and friendship with one another and with those from outside Afro-Asia. Other delegates echoed these ideas. Sir John Kotelawala even cited Buddhist apothegms regarding the proper way to deal with fear and hostility. "Not at any time are enmities appeased through enmity, but they are appeased through non-enmity. This is the eternal law."[54]

Iran, Iraq, and Pakistan in the west alluded in veiled terms to the "new colonialism" manifest in eastern Europe, the Baltic countries, and Turkestan. Cambodia and particularly Thailand expressed concern over their proximity to a China whose peaceful intentions and genuine commitment to "Panch Sheela" still remained to be proved. These were muted and careful references, politely but clearly put.

Mr. Chou En-lai was well within the overriding spirit of the meeting when he spoke on April 19. He quietly stated that different ideologies must not be allowed to divide. Each country had a right to its own way of living and governing itself. He sought to emphasize how much he had in common with South Asian countries, for China's struggle against colonialism had gone on for more than one hundred years. How could Chinese want to interfere in others' affairs when they had always been against others interfering in theirs? It was not the Chinese who were interfering in their neighbors' affairs, but there were other people setting up hostile bases all around China. His suave and gentle response to outspoken criti-

[53] *Times of Ceylon*, April 18, 1955.

[54] Text in *Times of Ceylon*, April 18, 1955. To those who knew him it was incongruous, to say the least, to hear Sir John talk in this vein, for if ever there was a man in public life who enjoyed a confrontation of forces and a blunt and vigorous exchange of political blows, it was he.

cism of Communist methods skillfully turned others' criticism to his own account, for he thus appeared to be the most pacific of them all. He was also at pains to allay anxieties that emerged from the heritage of overseas Chinese in Southeast Asia who had hitherto claimed dual nationality.[55]

A lengthy discussion of Western colonialism proceeded in an orderly atmosphere until Sir John Kotelawala asked whether, since they were all against colonialism, they should not also take note of the "new colonialism" of the Soviet Union in eastern Europe, and "openly declare our opposition to Soviet colonialism as much as to Western colonialism." Immediately after this statement, Mr. Chou En-lai left the conference hall and Mr. Nehru was reported to have taken Sir John to task.[56] U Nu urged that Sir John be conciliatory. Whatever prompted Sir John's initiative, many other representatives were ready to take up the question, including Pakistan, Iran, Iraq, Turkey, and Lebanon in West Asia and the Philippines, Thailand, and Cambodia in the East.[57] After much discussion, a resolution was agreed to which condemned "colonialism" in all its manifestations as an evil to be speedily brought to an end.

Another note of discord came from India's other neighbor, Pakistan, who stressed again the right of collective self-defense. Pakistan's nostalgically entitled principles—"Seven Pillars of Peace"—were much like Mr. Nehru's "Panch Sheela" except that the Pakistan proposal approved of regional and collective self-defense arrangements. Mr. Nehru's reaction was rather intemperate.[58] According to the Indian view, Pakistan's association with a power from outside the area brought the Cold War nearer, into South Asia. It reduced the unaligned area of the world and therefore consolidated the division of the world into two irreconcilable blocs. Questions of self-esteem and pride were also involved. "It is an intolerable humiliation for any Afro-Asian country to degrade itself as a camp-follower

[55] He gave private assurances to the representatives of Thailand, Cambodia, and negotiated on the spot an agreement on the matter with Indonesia.

[56] It was reported in Ceylon that Mr. Nehru went up to Sir John and declared: "Sir John, you should have had the courtesy to let me know that you intended making a reference to Soviet colonialism." Sir John is reported to have replied: "Why should I consult you? Do you tell me when you intend raising something at the conference?" *Ceylon Daily News*, April 26, 1955.

[57] Kahin speculates that Sir John decided to raise the question after Chou En-lai reportedly refused to give Sir John adequate assurances that Ceylon's Communists would receive no more help from abroad, p. 18. Many in Ceylon believed Sir John was merely reaching for the headlines. Others argued he simply did not want Mr. Nehru to dominate the conference.

[58] Kahin, p. 23.

of one side or the other among power blocs."[59] Mr. Mohammed Ali protested against the inference that Pakistan was a mere "camp-follower" of its defense associates. He argued Pakistan was indeed sovereign and had adopted its approach to the Cold War after its own independent analysis, which differed from Mr. Nehru's. Others, too, argued that because their countries were much smaller and less able to stand alone than India, they had to seek their security in association with other countries—an imperative India did not experience.[60] In the end, a resolution was included approving regional collective defense arrangements so long as they did not mean that any country in the area was to be used to serve the particular interests of any of the big powers.[61]

The Bandung conference was important in many ways. In the first place, it gave Chou En-lai an opportunity to show himself as a moderate, reasonable, and responsive statesman. The fact that he responded quietly and even politely to Sir John's attack on the "Communist colonialism" enhanced his reputation.[62] He capped this air of quiet moderation by declaring toward the end of the conference that he was prepared to talk with the United States about easing tension in the Formosan Straits.[63] Only later, after the headlines and news broadcasts had carried this final example of moderation to the world, did he indicate that naturally these talks would in no way affect China's right to "liberate" Formosa—one of the fundamental issues in the dispute.[64] Mr. Chou may have come away with a clearer vision of China's long-run interest in reassuring her southern neighbors.[65] He confirmed his adherence to principles of

[59] As reported in *Times of Ceylon* and *Ceylon Daily News*, April 23, 1955.

[60] *Ibid.*, April 23, 1955. Lebanon, Iraq, and the Philippines also argued Pakistan's case.

[61] At home Sir John argued that the Bandung conference in effect approved of Ceylon's defense agreements with Great Britain. *House of Representatives*, V. 20, c. 4182.

[62] Kahin, p. 25. See also Sir John's own reaction as reported to parliament, "I must say that although we do not share his political views he discovered himself to be a reasonable man who was prepared to respect the views of others." *House of Representatives*, V. 20, c. 4180.

[63] Reported in *Sunday Times* (Colombo), April 24, 1955; *Ceylon Daily News*, April 25, 1955.

[64] *Ceylon Daily News*, April 25, 1955; *Times of Ceylon*, April 25, 1955. Before the delegates separated to travel homeward the news was posted that the United States had rejected Chou's offer. Thus, Chou appeared to be the reasonable one, the United States the intransigent party. Both Sir John and Mr. Mohammed Ali were reported as believing the United States had made a serious mistake in not meeting Chou half way. *Ceylon Daily News*, April 25, 26, 1955.

[65] Kahin, p. 14.

noninterference in others' affairs.[66] Bandung may have seen the high-water mark of good feeling between China and her southern neighbors.

Second, the Bandung conference showed that at least in April 1955 there were other issues of great importance to the countries of Asia and Africa in addition to "colonialism," and they were not at one in their view of these issues. They were not agreed on the problem of Communist aggression; they did not all see the United States as "capitalist imperialist," and they were not all in favor of Mr. Nehru's approach of nonalignment. On the economic side, the Bandung conference reached little agreement.[67]

Third, the differences between the Colombo Powers unfortunately became sharper as a result of the Bandung interchanges. Pakistan, Ceylon, and Indonesia were all antagonized by what they regarded as the patronizing attitudes of Mr. Nehru and Mr. Krishna Menon.[68] Mohammed Ali and Sir John had both been particularly unwilling to accept Mr. Nehru's lead. This discouraged the Colombo Powers' initiatives for the future.

Fourth, differences in approach to the Cold War were most clearly transcended on the issues of independence for French North Africa and the inclusion of western New Guinea in Indonesia. They were agreed that membership in the United Nations should be universal and that Asia and Africa were underrepresented at the Security Council. They were at one in accepting the United Nations Universal Declaration of Human Rights and in deploring racial segregation and discrimination. They appealed for a reduction in armaments, and the prohibition of production and testing of nuclear and thermo-nuclear weapons.[69]

Fifth, the conference served an important function in acquainting all members with the special problems, aspirations, and anxieties of one another. The categories hitherto used to classify states and describe their purposes and attitudes had proved too simple. As U Nu summed it up: "This Conference brought home to us the practical realization that there is a world outside our own borders; a world even in Asia and Africa of diversity—diversity of belief, tradition, background and outlook. We learned that problems which

[66] *Ceylon Daily News*, April 26, 1955; *House of Representatives*, V. 21, c. 166.

[67] As was clear from the final communiqué, they also discussed such matters as commodity agreements, regional shipping and a regional payments union and common exchange facilities. However, no concrete measures were agreed to.

[68] Kahin, p. 36.

[69] *Ibid.*, pp. 32-33.

to us appeared simple and straightforward had a different appearance to our friends, and we learned the need for taking into account their attitude and feelings, and to make adjustments."[70]

Finally, the Bandung conference produced another formulation of principles of international conduct. To Mr. Nehru this may have been the most significant accomplishment of all. He has attached great importance to an agreed code of international behavior of universal application. "Panch Sheela" was one, and the Bandung Principles formed a second statement. It was believed that statesmen committed to these principles would thereby be inhibited from interfering in others' affairs. If they did go back on their commitment and later actively promoted subversion or other forms of interference, their insincerity would be manifest and it would be relatively simple then to mobilize opinion for action against them. Moreover, "Panch Sheela" and the Bandung Principles have had about them a special aura of being a characteristically "Eastern" contribution to world affairs. Numbered clusters of precepts for good conduct were a familiar part of Buddhist, Taoist, or Confucian tradition. They therefore were considered familiar, appropriate, and right.

Whatever their origin, they seemed to demonstrate that Asian countries were now in a position to play a creative role in world affairs. No longer could it be taken for granted that the Western Powers and Russia alone set the tone of world international relations. Countries in monsoon Asia, too, had a right to make their views known. Through their collective efforts they could now assert the propriety of certain principles of behavior. They had been confronting Western values and ways of doing things for too long and always on the defensive. Now they had been able to assert their own individuality as a body of opinion distinct from the Western environment, at last giving advice to others.

Bandung also defined the limits of their unity, for the distribution of power in the area is unequal and their interests differ. The small powers in the shadow of larger states sought some measure of security by continuing an association with the larger countries outside the area. They were not prepared to risk losing their own small identities in the larger Asian matrix even though as a group they sought to assert their individuality vis-à-vis the West. So long as these smaller states considered it more in their interests to continue association with states outside the region—and so long

[70] *Ibid.*, p. 35.

as the large states in the area allowed them to continue these ties—there would be competing pressures of influence. Bandung demonstrated their drive for common identity and its limitations. It confirmed the view that within South and Southeast Asia there was a subordinate system of state relations with a dynamic that was then largely independent of the major conflict between the communist and non-communist powers.[71]

On his return to Colombo, the Ceylonese prime minister was subject to vigorous criticism from his domestic political opponents for having "disrupted" the Bandung conference. A motion of no-confidence placed before the house by Mr. Bandaranaike was strongly pressed by him and the Left leaders.[72] Sir John was charged with having talked of Asian solidarity when he called the Colombo conference but of using the meetings to press his own "pet views" on Communism, to obtain international publicity for himself, and to curry favor with the Americans in order to obtain American assistance. Others, while averse to accepting without question Mr. Nehru's interpretation of international events, were nevertheless aware of Ceylon's small size and were rendered anxious as well as embarrassed by Sir John's "irresponsible" disagreements with the widely respected Indian leader and the less familiar Chou En-lai. At the voting in the house, Sir John carried the day, but a number of his party members were not present.[73]

5. *The Simla Conference.* Meanwhile, the American government had been seeking acceptable ways of providing considerably larger grants of economic assistance to South and Southeast Asia. It was believed in the Washington administration that one source of Congressional reluctance to allocate larger funds was the multiplicity of countries that made their competing requests directly to the American government. With western European experience in mind, aid administrators reasoned that some kind of concerted assessment of needs, programs, and priorities by governments in their region might induce greater economic cooperation among them and simplify the administrative and decision functions of the American Mutual Security Administration. Accordingly, they encouraged a meeting of South, Southeast Asian, and Far Eastern countries to

71 For a discussion of the subordinate international system in the Middle East, see Leonard Binder, "The Middle East as a Subordinate International System," *World Politics*, x, No. 3 (April, 1958), pp. 408-429.

72 *House of Representatives*, V. 20, c. 4309-4365.

73 *Ceylon Daily News*, April 28, 1955.

consider the most appropriate methods of administering American economic assistance. The Indian government took the initiative, inviting members to Simla in May 1955, only a month after Bandung. The Americans were not present in the hope that the consultations would be frank and full.

Coming hard on the heels of the Bandung meetings, Simla evoked relatively little interest. It may be that the meetings were hastily conceived and the parties came together before a thorough exploration of possibilities within their own governments. Some South Asians felt they had been rushed into it by Americans more used to dealing with European than Asian governments.[74] The amounts likely to be forthcoming were expected to be small in any case. The Ceylonese and Burmese did not attend, not only because they were not receiving American assistance at that time. In the case of Ceylon, some saw this conference as an Indian initiative primarily designed to promote opportunities for Indian industrial and commercial interests in the outside world.[75] Though the Karachi papers warned of this Indian initiative, the Pakistani and Indian technicians cooperated at Simla as their prime ministers met once more in Delhi to seek a settlement on Kashmir. Indonesians apparently feared that Japan would use the occasion of American regional aid to reconstitute its economic strength in the archipelago.

To the surprise of observers accustomed to polemic warnings against American aid being used to interfere in their internal affairs, the conferees appeared to prefer continuing bilateral arrangements with the United States to establishing a regional intermediary.[76] The Simla meetings were a disappointment to proponents of Asian solidarity and discouraged the Americans and Indians from further efforts to develop regional arrangements for economic assistance.[77]

6. *Suez Canal crisis of 1956.* The British and French effort to regain control of the Suez Canal in 1956 on the western edge of Asia evoked greater agreement than had been seen since the Indonesian conference of 1947 which had been called to consider events on the eastern edge of Asia. It was not surprising that the Ceylonese should have been sensitive to developments in the Isthmus. Perhaps 65 per cent to 70 per cent of their exports and 45-50 per cent of their im-

[74] Interviews in Colombo.

[75] "Conference on American Aid," *Thought*, April 23, 1955; *Ceylon Daily News*, April 23, 1955.

[76] *The Hindu* (Madras), May 14, 1955; *Times of India* (New Delhi), May 12, 1955; *New York Times*, May 13, 15, 1955.

[77] *Times of India* (New Delhi), May 11, 1955; *The Hindu* (Madras), May 14, 1955.

ports passed through the canal.[78] Import business houses and government ministries dependent on uninterrupted supplies, were all acutely aware of ships moving toward Colombo from western European and east coast North American ports. Use of British troops in Egypt in 1951-52 when Egypt abrogated the 1936 Treaty with the United Kingdom had been closely followed, particularly by the Opposition critics of the government who professed to see there a foretaste of what they could expect should Ceylon seek to terminate the British base agreement.[79] During the 1956 election campaign, Mr. Bandaranaike had argued his own intention of withdrawing the British base rights and of associating more closely with his Asian neighbors should he be elected. Colonel Nasser's bold initiative touched sympathetic Asian chords as the Egyptian leader stood up to Western influence and demonstrated his independence. Ceylonese experienced no indignation when Colonel Nasser nationalized this enterprise on Egyptian soil. To doubt the legitimacy of the Egyptian move would raise the question of the future right of the Ceylonese to nationalize the tea estates. The British themselves had set a precedent earlier, nationalizing the coal, steel, and transport industries at home. Many considered the abrupt American repudiation of the Aswan Dam proposals on which so many hopes for Egypt's economic development had been pinned as sufficient provocation for the Egyptian move designed to bring the Egyptian treasury a larger proportion of Canal income.

Other Asian countries, too, approved Colonel Nasser's step well before he became the target of military action by Britain, France, and Israel. He confirmed his reasonableness in their eyes by not molesting British or French nationals, despite the vigorous British and French protests, and canal traffic continued uninterruptedly despite dire warnings from London and Paris.[80]

Ceylonese publicists at first considered the "vested interests" challenged as those of the European stockholders whose incomes would be reduced.[81] Promptly, however, voices warned of the possible con-

[78] Calculated from ECAFE, *Economic Survey of Asia and the Far East 1956*, Table 5. Exports to and imports from North America could go via Pacific or east coast ports, no distinction being made in the data. Seventy per cent of India's export trade and 60 per cent of her imports passed through Suez according to *The Hindu* (Madras), November 15, 1956.

[79] *House of Representatives*, V. 11, c. 1724; V. 12, c. 337.

[80] Approving editorials and comment *Morning Times* (Colombo), August 8, 1956. Mr. Chou En-lai approved Egypt's move on August 6, 1956 and other Arab states including Iraq did so on August 7.

[81] *Ceylon Daily News*, July 30, 1956.

sequences to Ceylon's economy of a disrupted Suez Canal passage. A national vested interest in the continued free passage of the canal became apparent, though Colonel Nasser's success in continuing uninterrupted passage appeared to prove that his management posed no immediate problem, at least in the short run. Ceylon's dependence upon the shipping companies was dramatized when certain British and French shippers began to by-pass Colombo altogether in their Australian service. But other traffic continued as before.[82]

The attack on Egypt profoundly shocked the Ceylonese and others in the area. Britain had acquired a high reputation for justice and for taking Asian opinions into account. The November events in Suez appeared to contradict the entire bent of British policy since World War II. Deep emotional springs were tapped. *The Statesman* in India stressed the "sense of injury in Asia over the humiliation of military invasion inflicted by two Western Powers on a member of the Asian family."[83] The *Observer* in Ceylon argued that the "moral leadership" of Britain, the foundation of the new Commonwealth in which the "colour-line was suddenly and wonderfully transformed," was now destroyed. Having shown itself once more willing to indulge in military attack where its own interests were at stake, what was there now to stop Britain from doing whatever it pleased with the "militarily ineffectual Asian members of the Commonwealth?" Could Britain be trusted any longer as Ceylon's banker? Closer ties between Pakistan, India, Ceylon, and other Indian Ocean countries were necessary now that the Commonwealth had been "shattered."[84]

The tension was heightened by simultaneous events in Hungary when Russian forces put down what many considered to be a popular rebellion against the Communist regime. Whereas the Suez events were thoroughly reported and touched familiar sensitive nerves—western Europeans using superior force against an Afro-Asian people only recently come to independence—Russian action in eastern Europe was hidden by the Iron Curtain and called for novel responses. Perhaps only the Trotskyists knew their own reaction. Those attempting to define for Ceylon the new policy of "nonalignment" were inhibited by the thought that to criticize the Russian intervention in Hungary would be tantamount to aligning themselves

[82] *Ceylon Daily News*, September 15, 1956.
[83] *The Statesman* (New Delhi), November 13, 1956.
[84] *Ceylon Observer*, November 4, 1956.

with the United States and others in the West who were most vehement in their criticism of Moscow. The Ceylonese press, however, was outspokenly critical of the Russian move. Mr. Nehru himself drew a distinction between events in Egypt and Hungary, responding clearly to the first and at the outset temporizing on the second on the grounds that full information was not available. Debates at the United Nations General Assembly showed that while all the Afro-Asian countries were agreed on the appropriate stand to take on Egypt, there were differences over the Hungarian events. Some Indian and Ceylonese publicists were quick to see with Jayaprakash Narayan what they considered to be a "double standard" among Asian countries, responding with whole-hearted indignation to events in Egypt and with careful restraint to developments in Hungary.[85]

Under Indonesian encouragement, the Colombo Powers were invited to Delhi in mid-November to consult on a common response to these highly dramatic events. Divisions between the Colombo Powers had been lessened by these developments. To those who accepted nonalignment, both Suez and Hungary demonstrated the liabilities of allowing foreign bases on home territory, a clear confirmation of the virtues of their own basic perspective. Mr. Bandaranaike's electoral victory in Ceylon brought to this meeting of four of the five Colombo Powers a leader publicly committed to a policy akin to Mr. Nehru's. The Pakistan prime minister was already consulting with Muslim and Arab countries and Turkey regarding a concerted Middle Eastern demand for the withdrawal of foreign troops from Egypt. Having already agreed to discussions in Teheran, he was unable to attend the Delhi meetings, removing another likely critic of Delhi's approach.[86]

Agreement on the Egyptian events was easy, but there appears to have been a great deal more discussion of how best to express disapproval of the use of Russian troops in Hungary. In the end, they approved of the steps already taken at the United Nations to induce a cease-fire in Egypt and to establish an international force to help separate the belligerents. They welcomed the promise of the Israeli, French, and British governments to abide by the United Nations resolutions and urged them to withdraw their troops forth-

[85] *Times of Ceylon*, November 13, 1956; *The Statesman* (New Delhi), November 11, 1956; *Ceylon Observer*, November 14, 1956.

[86] *Dawn* (Karachi), November 16, 1956; *The Hindu* (Madras), November 9, 1956.

with. They had "watched with deep distress" the events in Hungary, asserted the right of all peoples to determine their own destiny, and "were of the opinion that the Soviet forces should be withdrawn from Hungary speedily." They saw both sets of events as action by larger countries against smaller ones and they viewed with great concern the "revival of the spirit and methods of colonialism . . . whatever form it may take."

A new departure for the Colombo Powers, they concurred that military pacts and the stationing of troops on foreign soil were a cause of fear and international tension—a danger to world peace. Instead of arming, they appealed to the large and wealthy states for economic assistance to raise standards of living everywhere.

As to concrete steps to be taken by the Colombo Powers to ensure their circumstances for the future, little was said. Mr. Bandaranaike had hoped for an enlarged Colombo Powers' organization to be established in Colombo to voice jointly their common concerns and to coordinate shipping, supply movements, and policies toward fiscal difficulties bound to arise in a future emergency.[87] The suggestion appears to have received scant attention at the conference, although India apparently expressed her willingness to help Ceylon with certain supplementary food and medical supplies during the crisis.

After the Delhi meetings on the Suez Crisis in November 1956, no initiative was taken by the South and Southeast Asian governments for further meetings until the spring of 1959, when Mr. Bandaranaike pressed for fresh discussions on common economic problems. Indeed, the center of interest in promoting Afro-Asian meetings shifted from Delhi, Colombo, or Djakarta to Cairo as eager Arab spokesmen, following well-worn organizational patterns developed in Moscow, organized a series of conferences for students, professional men and women, and parliamentarians. Although many were alert to some of the influences that appeared to be behind the meetings, the delegates learned more of one another and came to see their own problems in a broader perspective. The governments of South and Southeast Asian countries appeared cautious in their approach to these initiatives.

During 1958 and more markedly in 1959, a shift of mood among neutralist countries could be discerned. Those most closely in the shadow of mainland China, particularly Burma and important ele-

[87] *Morning Times* (Colombo), November 13, 1956; *Times of Ceylon*, November 14, 1956; *The Statesman* (New Delhi), November 15, 1956.

ments of Indian opinion, became more anxious about the awakening giant to the north. During the autumn of 1958, for example, in Burma and even in Indonesia, statesmen privately approved the firm American stand in the Formosa Straits although they remained committed to a policy of nonalignment.

In India, there were growing numbers of individuals prepared to express anxiety about the rising power of China. China's refusal to respect the autonomy of Tibet in the spring of 1959 appeared to produce much the same concern in Delhi as Chinese border pressure had produced in Rangoon several years before. The popular reaction in other Buddhist countries was strongly critical. This, together with China's subsequent incursions into Indian territory and arrogant diplomatic style, appeared to undermine the reputation for moderation which Chou En-lai had been at such pains to create at Bandung.

These developments suggested that there might be emerging a clearer awareness of a common security threat besetting all the countries on China's periphery. Whether this would lead to concerted local efforts to form a common front or would induce each to seek his separate accommodation with Peking remained to be seen. In Ceylon, public opinion was stirred by these events, but danger seemed more remote since Ceylon was, after all, separated by India, Burma, and the Bay of Bengal from direct pressure from mainland China. Ceylonese were much more concerned with growing political difficulties at home.

CONCLUSION

In these explorations of differing manifestations of Asian solidarity, certain points stand out. Naturally enough, agreement was easiest in familiar situations, i.e., where Western power was applied on the periphery of Asia against the will of local inhabitants, as in Indonesia in 1949 and in Egypt in 1956. No doubt solidarity among the countries of non-Communist Asia could be most effectively promoted should Western power again return unasked in force to that area. Trade fluctuations emphasized their common dependence upon favorable world marketing conditions, but combined action to remedy this widespread difficulty was not effected. The foreign policy results of the 1956 election in Ceylon demonstrated that the fortunes of Asian solidarity are linked with the movements of domestic politics within each country. The impulse for greater regional solidarity, therefore, comes from a variety of sources.

When the immediate defense interests of members were in question at Colombo in 1954 and Bandung in 1955, smaller countries often interpreted differently the dangers besetting them than did the larger states. Differences of perspective crystallized in divergent responses to S.E.A.T.O. India, Indonesia, and Burma publicly protested; Ceylon remained aloof though it continued to permit the British to use the island's bases. But Thailand, the Philippines, and Pakistan were ready to strengthen their own defenses in association with a power from outside the area—the United States.

Efforts to create regional organizations did not meet with success, apart from the clearly apolitical United Nations agency, the Economic Commission for Asia and the Far East which provided a research service for the region and opportunities for ministers and technicians from different countries to consult together. Colombo Plan organizational informality fitted well the needs of the area during the first decade of independence, where personalities and direct, face-to-face relationships were of the essence and institutional structures were held to a minimum. The effort to do more at Simla was a failure. Joint economic endeavors or efforts to mediate particular conflicts between the countries in the region were not undertaken by regional bodies.

From this brief survey it is clear that on most issues of foreign policy, there was no single Asian view but a variety of special perspectives defined by the geographical location, economic needs, and differing interpretations of the outside dangers that threatened each country. Despite the variety of views on specific matters, their efforts to define their common perspectives and to present an Asian front have already brought their needs more effectively to the attention of the Great Powers outside the area than would have been true had they not sought to concert their efforts. Their statements of good conduct in the world of states represent efforts to deal with their massive Chinese neighbor and are a symbol of their newfound—and therefore particularly precious—right and capacity to have their voices heard and to define standards by which their own and others' conduct may be judged.

Toward the end of the decade as British power became less decisive in South Asia, fewer spokesmen found it expedient to argue in public in favor of continued close ties with Western countries.

Indian influence inescapably increased in areas where Chinese power was not yet marked, and nonalignment as a policy became more widely approved. As mainland China sought to demonstrate its growing capacity for economic and political influence, near neighbors became publicly more respectful but privately anxious at the growing Chinese colossus to the north.

The long-run future of the South and Southeast Asian state system remained uncertain. It may be that one country within the area or from outside it will come to be seen as a manifest threat to all. Mainland China's growing power and its policies toward Tibet and the Indian frontier may provoke the countries of the area to merge their views and actions in closer effective unity. Perhaps some one dominating country will gradually encompass them all before they have time to concert their efforts. Alternatively, perhaps the South and Southeast Asian state system will continue much as it has evolved thus far, with states drawing together on certain issues, dividing on others, in constant motion and adjustment to their neighbors and more distant fellow-members of the world state system. During the first decade of independence, it was clear that the wider world tension between the Communist bloc of states on the one hand and the United States and its associates on the other was not their primary foreign policy preoccupation. Problems nearer home were more important.

CONCLUSION
AN ASIAN POLITICAL SOCIETY

IN 1958 at the end of the first decade of independence, the government and people of Ceylon could look back upon many real accomplishments. Political power was successfully transferred from British to Ceylonese hands without public disorder. There was no partition, such as on the Indian subcontinent, no insurrection as in Burma or Indonesia. Three general elections between 1947 and 1957 were held and in an unintimidated expression of the popular will, a group of leaders, who had ruled since well before independence, was peacefully replaced by a new coalition of political forces in 1956. During the period, governments were formed, cabinets reached policy decisions, proposals were debated, and a wide range of legislation passed. The apparatus of government functioned without interruption. Apart from trade union violence in 1953 and communal outbreaks in 1956 and 1958, the Ceylonese managed many intricate problems in a decade of relatively orderly government.

Some of the glaring economic and social inequalities existing at the time of independence had been mitigated by governmental policy. The scourge of malaria was all but mastered. Extensive social welfare legislation had been passed; heavy expenditures to improve health, education, and insure a minimum diet for all inhabitants were undertaken. Economic development generally kept pace with a rapidly expanding population. New trading relationships were opened with other countries in an attempt to make the economy less dependent upon the fluctuations of the free world market. The Ceylonese gained more control over their own economic affairs. Political independence in the world of states was consolidated and the country's representatives played an active role in regional conferences and at the United Nations. These accomplishments take on a greater magnitude when placed beside the variety of tasks that faced the country's leaders and people.

When national leaders took the reins of power from British hands and sought to carry forward representative political institutions, the privileged position of certain groups, particularly the more Westernized, was bound to change. The desires of some to modernize the country and extend egalitarian welfare standards contrasted with the social and economic conservatism of others. There were inevitable stresses between the traditional assumptions that a man's social standing derived from his family's status and the democratic principle that governmental authority was vested in individuals by the process of elections. The apprenticeship of nearly all the political leaders had been marked by reiterated criticism of the colonial ruler. Now, those in the government were faced with the necessity of managing the country's affairs and members of the opposition had to decide upon their political tactics with the thought in mind that some among them might one day have to form a government. Many of the problems were the legacy of four hundred years of colonial rule; and some could be traced to persisting social ways and modes of production that antedated the coming of the Europeans.

On the basis of this intensive study of a single country, it is possible to describe one type of Asian political society. The following model is consciously simplified in an effort to stress those characteristics which Ceylon appears to have in common with its neighbors.

THE PLURAL SOCIETY AND POLITICS

There has always been a marked social and cultural distance between the ruling elite and the mass of the people. The elite that accomplished independence is distinguished by its assimilation of many European political values and ways of life. There are few individuals in intermediate classes comparable to the large middle class in Europe. Members of the Westernized elite are particularly dependent on political intermediaries between themselves and the masses because of their social distance from the electorate and the electorate's tendency to retain traditional affiliations based on family, regional, religious, or linguistic community loyalties.

The modern Westernized elite is not itself homogeneous. Politicians, administrators, professional and business men stress differing aspects of Western culture and have differing career needs. Politicians in the Westernized elite compete with one another for a following among the mass voters in order to acquire or retain the right to rule. The politicians are themselves divided along ideological lines, holding differing convictions regarding political goals, the proper constitution, and the legitimate means of political competition. Electoral politics therefore may threaten the unity and stability of the institutions that make elections possible.

Since the mass of voters tend to retain their affiliations within the plural society, their political behavior is defined more by the group to which they traditionally belong than by their action as individuals in response to specific issues of policy. Even though the growing urban population may join industrial and commercial trade unions, it still remains susceptible to many old loyalties. In consequence of the persistence of these communal and ethnic ties, there is little capacity to identify themselves with those who are not in their own community, and mutually exclusive demands characterize political debate.

Traditional identifications, though profoundly important, usually lack well-developed organizations to express and protect their interests in a regular fashion. Unexpressed needs may lie dormant for years; but when awakened, these latent aspirations may overwhelm whatever more formal and visible affiliations individuals may have. Thus, political practitioners are peculiarly uncertain of their real strength and both government and aspiring opposition leaders must experiment and improvise in their search for unpredictable support.

The characteristics of the leaders who acquire power at independence are of fundamental importance. The most successful are well-acquainted with representative, constitutional ideas and institutions. Outstanding leaders synthesize Western and indigenous values and are able to identify themselves with the mass electors. They have grown beyond parochial divisions into an awareness of a country-wide patriotism which they are able to symbolize to the wider, diverse public. They are aware of the incipient divisive potentialities and are able to lay stress upon the common aspirations of numerous particular groups, drawing them together in support of a legislative program at the cabinet level. These special qualities appear to be necessary to counter the fissiparous tendencies of the plural society.

POLITICAL INSTITUTIONS

Political parties are loose, personal associations rather than organized parties. They lack orderly and accepted ways of changing or confirming leaders, for sounding out membership opinion, or for resolving internal differences. There are few opportunities for younger members to experiment with new responsibilities. Personal identification with individual leaders is usually a more important determinant of party affiliation than are the actual policies adopted. Such parties can moderate the contradictory desires of their constituent groups so long as support rests on a personal rather than on a policy basis, and so long as the inner circle of prominent individuals can compromise their differences among themselves. This is often difficult. When a leading political figure dies, family and personal rivalries especially are likely to become intractable. When party support begins to be based on policy considerations, the parties are often inadequate instruments for promoting a consensus on behalf of a program because they are still without recognized channels for resolving internal conflicts.

The cabinet tends to reflect the country's diversity at the outset, for included in it are representatives of the different communal elements of the society. The absence of strong parties means that diverse and often competing interest groups seek direct access to the cabinet as the center of government policy-formation. The Westminster principles of cabinet unity and collective responsibility are very difficult to apply effectively. Directed government policy-making is impeded where cabinets must themselves perform the role of party moderators.

The parliament, characteristically, shows a very loose governing coalition facing a splintered opposition that poses no real threat to the government. There is therefore little incentive for government solidarity. This does not prevent considerable legislation from being passed on a broad range of government matters. However, the emergence of an "alternative government" is impeded, with the result that the voters cannot foresee a real choice among the parties in advance of a hasty electoral coalition which may lack cohesion as well as clear alternative policies.

Despite the numerical preponderance of the ruling majority, the splintered opposition has ample opportunities in parliament to express public criticism and to challenge the ruling party. This is so because of the latter's inner divisions and because at the outset, at least, the established practices of British parliamentary procedure were well-understood by the political leaders of all the parties and are supervised by a neutral speaker in parliament. The country's communication system is also sufficiently open to give considerable circulation to the content of the debates beyond the precincts of parliament. The result is more likely to prevent the abuse of power and to discredit the rulers than it is to encourage the development of effective, well-directed government.

During the colonial period, careers in politics brought prominence and high status. It is widely assumed that the country's problems can be solved only by parliamentary decision carried out by the public service. The government is looked to for a broad range of services and activities. Comparatively little is expected of individual initiative or of organized endeavor at the community level or by volunteers. Though often accused of being domineering and distant, the public service is nevertheless widely considered more just and equitable than business or volunteer organizations which tend to be associated with special privilege. Positions in the public service are coveted above all others and have higher social and dowry status than the professions or careers in business. Accordingly, both politics and the public service are given greater prominence in the country's life than they normally receive in Western countries.

It proves relatively easy for the public administration to establish procedures necessary to ensure unintimidated elections and for politicians to abide by the rules. More difficult is the task of developing those restraints and inhibitions which deter politicians from raising issues that are bound to exacerbate communal or other tensions. In the course of successive elections, politically neutral supervision becomes progressively more effective. Election challenges and charges of bribery, intimidation, and impersonation decline; the conviction grows that the ballot is secret. The electoral process requires the urban politicians to move closer to the rural population. In Ceylon, eight years after independence, the leaders of the democratic opposition, by seeking out and enlarging grievances within the majority community, displaced the men who acquired power at independence. The result is a government closer than its predecessors to the mass voters in the majority community. In the process, minority interests are ignored and intercommunal hostility reaches a new height. Accordingly, elections allow a peaceful change of leaders, but one byproduct may be a noticeable increase in social conflict.

The new government that succeeds in displacing the men who achieved independence is less sure of its sources of political support. It is more dependent on the shifting attitudes of a newly aroused rural electorate strongly influenced by lower middle-class interest and professional groups. The newly influential are less sensitive to the inhibitions implicit in parliamentary practice and less attached to the constitutional forms and practices than their predecessors. In the face of communal discord and growing unrest, the nature of the constitution is open to repeated review and question.

CULTURE, RELIGION, AND POLITICS

Colonial rule generates a reaction against European culture and those who most clearly represent it in the indigenous population. This reaction may be delayed, however, because during much of the colonial period, foreign values and ways of life are at a premium in the upper levels of society and those who are most adept in the foreigner's ways gain the best opportunities and are the most influential. The leaders who acquire power at independence have stressed the importance of indigenous cultural values, awakening group consciousness in order to enlist support for themselves against the foreign ruler. Pride in past achievements offsets the arrogance of the Westerner. After independence is attained, these same leaders can be challenged on cultural grounds, for they are peculiarly vulnerable to the charge of being unduly Westernized. Those who wish to rule in their place are therefore likely to use cultural values as a way of undermining the men who first gain power at independence.

Expanded education in the vernaculars brings a largely liberal arts curriculum to the many, a curriculum hitherto reserved to the few. As there are insufficient career opportunities of proper status for these graduates, students become discontented. Rapidly expanded vernacular education also activates self-consciousness among the groups in the population who speak different languages. In consequence, a growing communal awareness develops more rapidly than identification with a set of over-all, unifying national symbols. Hence, educational policy increases the numbers of those whose ambitions outrun available opportunities and augments communal self-awareness that can be easily turned into resentment against competing members of other communities.

As Westernized political leaders seek support among the non-Westernized, matters of language policy become of great political importance. Two sets of grievances emerge from language differences—traditional competition between ethnic communities and resentment against the clearly privileged position of the Westernized. After English is regarded as dethroned from its high estate, language antagonisms between majority and minority groups become sharpened. The vexed question of the official language of state becomes a key election issue, demonstrating the political importance of cultural values. Language controversy leads to bitter communal riots, further deepening the fissures dividing the plural society.

Religious considerations also become significant in politics. After independence is achieved, religious spokesmen attempt to give indigenous religions a more prominent place in national life than they occupied during the colonial period. In Ceylon, because there are four different religions, the leaders at independence adopted a secular state as the appropriate model, and they are reluctant to give special state support to the majority's religion. But their position is ambiguous because during the colonial period many of the best-equipped and most influential schools were managed by Christian institutions and many influential individuals were Christians. Hence, from the point of view of many Buddhists, the early leaders appear to prefer maintaining the privileged position of the Christians rather than help Buddhists to overcome what they consider to be the disadvantages inherited from the colonial past.

Because Hinduism and Buddhism have traditionally dispensed with institutions comparable to "the Church" in medieval France or Germany, a confrontation between church and state along European lines does not take place. Religious spokesmen, however, seek greater state support for religious education and for reforms designed to consolidate the organization of the majority's religion. State support for these religious activities is part of the ancient tradition. The reluctance of the modern ruling elite to meet their desires is taken by the devout as evidence of indifference to the majority's religion. Laymen and *bhikkhus* combine to form new interest groups, define these religious grievances, and press for their correction.

As indigenous religious virtues receive greater public deference, political leaders begin to be measured by their ability to live up to the traditional image of the virtuous ruler. Assimilation of European ways may then become a political liability where once it was of great advantage.

THE ECONOMY AND POLITICS

The plantation-peasantry economy provides relatively few satisfying opportunities to the ever-growing numbers of educated youth. With rare exceptions, only the wealthy or their relatives have access to managerial opportunities on the estates. As yet, few are drawn toward new businesses and the openings are limited. The educated tend to disdain agriculture and other directly productive activities. The public service, the goal of so many, cannot possibly expand rapidly enough to satisfy all the hopes that focus upon it. Consequently, many articulate individuals tend to be frustrated in their ambitions, a likely source of political unrest.

Egalitarian conviction as well as political expediency promote a large expenditure for food subsidies and for health, welfare, and education. These in turn help many more people to survive who must be fed, and increase the numbers and ambitions of the educated. Together with the costs of a growing public service, these expenditures absorb the bulk of the government's budget. There is therefore a relatively limited margin of savings for development investment.

Dependent on the level of world market prices for only a few export commodities and importing large quantities of indispensable foodstuffs, the economy is liable to abrupt changes in its terms of trade. This specialization has permitted the economy to profit from comparative advantage in the past. But uncertain world prices for these commodities mean unstable returns, and modern welfare commitments are hard to reduce when revenues decline. It is difficult for elected representatives to retain the good will of the populace when interest groups have become so well organized that they can promote unrest and disorder if welfare allocations fall off markedly. The temptation is therefore very strong to reduce capital investment expenditures instead. Accordingly, in an export-import economy, subject to sharply fluctuating terms of trade, the position of elected leaders is vulnerable and the pace of economic development unsteady.

The government is assigned an important initiating and operating role in economic development, but the results are disappointing.

There is insufficient consensus among the politically articulate elite as to immediate goals and proper policies. There is a great shortage of middle-level technical supervisors, foremen, and adequately trained farmers. Educational curricula are difficult to alter from liberal arts to a more immediately vocational and economically productive course of study. Tradition frowns on the man with rolled up sleeves and dirty hands. The distance between the Westernized elite and the rural masses impedes the communication of new techniques. Capital for investment is limited and is subject to unexpected changes, so that steady allocations are difficult. Talk of "nationalization" that has its political utility discourages individual investment. The public service is already overburdened with many complicated tasks. For these and other reasons, economic development does not keep pace with the expectations of the articulate. Representative institutions provide the means for publicizing and spreading criticisms. The government's position is therefore weakened when the economy fails to develop as rapidly as hoped.

Elaborate political strategies tend to be attributed to those who propose alternative economic development policies. The allocation of development funds may be influenced by communal calculations. Identifiable communities may be won or angered by investment policies that are thought likely to affect the distribution of coveted opportunity. Competition for access to new land developments may sharpen communal conflict. Allocations of development funds may affect—as they are likely to reflect—the relative influence of different cabinet members. In the long run the direction of economic development will affect the channels to positions of influence and therefore the prospects of different political leaders and groups. These considerations are of greater interest to large numbers in the elite and are seen by them as more immediately important than the problem of productivity itself. Accordingly, economic development, by its very nature, cannot in practice be considered apart from its political context.

Economic development is demonstrably difficult in a newly independent South Asian country. Yet without an expansion of the country's real product at a rate faster than the population grows, and without more numerous new opportunities becoming available to the growing numbers of educated and ambitious, communal and class conflicts are bound to increase. This can lead to a disruption of production, a further decline in welfare and opportunities, and therefore mounting social conflict. Economic development cannot in itself assure greater social peace or durable representative government, but it is one of the indispensable conditions.

FOREIGN POLICY AND POLITICS

Foreign policy is generally the concern of the few. Interest groups are not oriented toward foreign policy, except regional spokesmen fearing migrants from the large neighbor, certain business interests concerned with export-import activities, and, on occasion, Marxist trade union leaders familiar with the outside world. Foreign policy is therefore not the result of a widely canvassed public consensus but reflects the judgment largely of the inner core of the cabinet and a few personal advisers of the prime minister.

Among those concerned with foreign affairs, a sense of weakness in the world of states is acute. The country's relative size, exposed position, and its poverty are well understood. Military preparations are seen as a dissipation of scarce resources more usefully spent in other directions. At the outset, the World War II experience of the Japanese attack from the sea provides the principal assumption of the type of threat to guard against. Intimate defense association with some other, larger country seems prudent. As an island off the shore of a large continent, historically the recipient of large Indian migrations and periodic military invasions from South India, Ceylon looked upon Great Britain as the best associate.

In domestic politics, expressions of hostility toward the former colonial and other Western countries and symbolic policies demonstrating independence from the West can be expected. These may be essential ingredients in a leader's attempts to consolidate a country's plural diversities. They also serve to help bridge the gap between the Westernized leaders and the masses; by criticizing the Western, non-Asians, political leaders demonstrate their solidarity with the rising non-Westernized levels of their own societies. Accordingly, it can be a political liability to elected leaders if they stand up and are counted on the side of the former colonial countries or their associates. As a byproduct, public arguments opposing association with Western countries may confirm old or create additional anxieties about intimacy with the West, adding further limits to the actual range of foreign policy choices open to the leadership.

The area's past encounters with European empires raise doubts about continuing close trading ties with Western countries. The past has taught that there has been a close connection between economic and political power. Rigorous efforts are believed necessary to ensure that Western economic enterprise will be under adequate control and economic assistance will not be misused in order to forward peculiarly Western political interests. Foreign business enterprise tends to be distrusted, though particular arrangements for sharing capital and management responsibilities with local entrepreneurs are in fact developed, bringing both capital and technique into the economy. Since economic and political activities are believed to be still combined in Western foreign policy and trade practice, many believe there is no greater political risk in trading with Communist countries than there is in the more traditional trading arrangements with the West.

Because of the vulnerabilitiy of the economies of these countries to sharp fluctuations in their terms of trade, there are mounting pressures to reach bilateral trade agreements that promise at least some degree of stability in export prices. Ceylon has established economic relations with Communist countries where state control facilitates intergovernmental trading. So long as sharp price fluctuations characterize the free world markets, government-to-government trading is likely to become more attractive.

Efforts to achieve solidarity among the ex-colonial countries of Asia produce only limited results. As European countries withdraw from the area, a subsidiary system of state relations develops quite apart from the Cold War or relations with either the West or the Soviet bloc. China and India are the two large powers in the area. They are seeking to industrialize; their populations are big and they have been the source of large and energetic migrations in the past. There are three characteristic responses to this situation: some identify themselves with a chosen outside power who acts as military supplier and adviser and potential defender in case of aggression. A second seeks to exist quietly in the shadow of the two giants, hoping that each will regard it as a buffer not to be interfered with by the other. A third may seek to detach itself from association with a former colonial country, increase its dependence on one of its large neighbors, and articulate a closely parallel foreign policy. In the shadow of two great powers, the multitude of smaller nations seek their own roads to security rather than follow unquestioningly the lead of any one or combine in a united regional system. On the other hand, efforts to achieve closer cooperation among states in

South, Southeast Asia, and the Far East will no doubt continue to be made.

These various elements of public life have their differing impacts on political developments. The plural social background accentuates divisive political tendencies and increases the potentialities for social conflict. Representative political institutions placed in the plural society are more successful in allowing a variety of voices to be heard than they are in carrying out effective policies on the basis of a broad and stable consensus. Religious revival and cultural awakening help to diminish the distance between elite and masses and contribute to a greater sense of freedom from European rule and Western ways. When national and cultural independence is more clearly experienced, it is accompanied by growing internal conflict. Although economic development cannot itself assure social peace or representative institutions, it is one of their indispensable conditions in a society with a rapidly growing population and expanding educational system. The legacy of the colonial era and recurrent fluctuations in foreign exchange earnings impede intimacy with the West. Nonalignment becomes a more appealing answer to the security dilemma facing many of the small states, but a growing awareness of China's rising power calls forth new uncertainties from an unfamiliar quarter.

On all these fronts—social, political, economic, cultural, and in foreign relations—the leaders and people of Ceylon aspire to independence. Out of their own history and the centuries of foreign rule they are attempting to evolve institutions and practices appropriate to their own genius. The sensitive among them see with anguish the relative poverty of their people. They understand what life is like in other countries in the twentieth century, while every day around them they must face the harsh reality of inequalities and the slow pace of technological and economic growth. They want to modernize their country without destroying the fundamental values of their own traditions, for these are the source of their consciousness of self and their originality. They aim toward a government that is both effective and representative. They seek greater control over their own resources and above all are chary of involvements that once again might threaten their independence, whether the threats come from the West or from larger neighbors nearer home. In the international world, their leaders wish to participate in an economy insulated against sharp fluctations. They seek equality of status and treatment. They ask of both camps in the Cold War and of the uncommitted countries the expected rights due a free and sovereign people—freedom to follow what course they will and to choose their friends.

It is as fallacious for outsiders to assume that these aspirations are irrelevant to the course of events as it is for the Ceylonese to equate the wish with the achievement.

BIBLIOGRAPHY

I. PUBLIC DOCUMENTS

Central Bank of Ceylon. *Annual Reports of the Monetary Board to the Minister of Finance,* Colombo: 1950-1958.

Central Bank of Ceylon. Department of Economic Research. *Survey of Ceylon's Consumer Finances.* Colombo: 1954.

Government of Ceylon. *Administration Report of the Commissioner for Registration of Indian and Pakistani Residents for 1952.*

———. *Administration Reports of the Commissioner of Labour for 1946, 1955, 1956, 1957.* Colombo: Government Press, 1947, 1956, 1957, 1958.

———. *Administration Report of the Director of Agriculture for 1956, 1957.* Colombo: Government Press, 1957, 1958.

———. *Administration Report of the Director of Education for 1955.* Colombo: Government Press, 1956.

———. *Administration Report of the Director of Industries for 1955, 1956, 1957.* Colombo: Government Press, 1956, 1957, 1958.

———. *Administration Report of the Food Commissioner (Supply) 1952.* Colombo: Government Press, 1953.

———. *Correspondence Relating to the Citizenship Status of Indians Resident in Ceylon.* Sessional Paper XXII—1948.

———. Department of Census and Statistics. *A Report on Paddy Statistics.* Monograph no. 9. Colombo: Government Press, 1956.

———. Department of Census and Statistics. *Census of Agriculture 1952: Part I - Tea Plantations.* Colombo: Government Press, 1956.

———. Department of Census and Statistics. *Census of Agriculture 1952: Part II - Rubber Plantations.* Colombo: Government Press, 1956.

———. Department of Census and Statistics. *Census of Agriculture 1952: Part III - Coconut Plantations.* Colombo: Government Press, 1956.

———. Department of Census and Statistics. *Census of Agriculture 1952: Part IV - Agriculture.* Colombo: Government Press, 1956.

———. Department of Census and Statistics. *Census of Ceylon 1946* (2 vols.) Colombo: Government Press, 1951.

———. Department of Census and Statistics. *Census of Industry 1952.* Colombo: Government Press, 1954.

———. Department of Census and Statistics. *Preliminary Report on the Economic Survey of Rural Ceylon 1950.* Sessional Paper XI—1951.

———. Department of Census and Statistics. *Report on the Census of Government and Local Government Employees 1951.* Colombo: Government Press, 1952.

Government of Ceylon. Department of Census and Statistics. *Statistical Abstracts for 1955-1957*. Colombo: Government Press, 1956, 1957, 1958.

———. Department of Commerce. *Thirty Years of Trade Statistics*. Colombo: Government Press, 1956.

———. *Final Report of the Commission on Higher Education in the National Languages* (Sinhalese and Tamil). Sessional Paper x—1956.

———. Ministry of Finance. *Economic and Social Development of Ceylon (A Survey) 1926-1954*. Colombo: Government Press, 1955.

———. *Economic Survey of Rural Ceylon 1950-1951. Final Report*. Sessional Paper xi—1954.

———. *Estimates of the Revenue and Expenditure of the Government of Ceylon for the Financial Year 1st October 1956 to 30th September 1957*. Colombo: Government Press, 1956.

———. Gal Oya Development Board. *Annual Report 1954-1955*. Colombo: Government Press, 1956.

———. Ministry of Finance. *Government Policy in Respect of Private Foreign Investment in Ceylon*. Colombo: Government Press, July 1955.

———. *Parliamentary Debates. House of Representatives*, Vols. i-xxviii.

———. Planning Secretariat. *First Interim Report. National Planning Council*. Colombo: Government Press, 1957.

———. Planning Secretariat. *Six-Year Programme of Investment 1954/1955 to 1959/1960*. Colombo: Government Press, 1955.

———. *Press Communiqué, February 25, 1953*.

———. *Report of a Commission on Immigration into Ceylon*. Sessional Paper iii—1938.

———. *Report of the Commission of Inquiry on the Working of the Commercial Sector of the Port of Colombo*. Sessional Paper ii—1957.

———. *Report of the Commission on Government Commercial Undertakings*. Sessional Paper xix—1953.

———. *Report of the Commission on Local Government*. Sessional Paper xxxiii—1955.

———. *Report of the Commission on Tenure of Lands of Viharagam, Dewalagam and Nindagam*. Sessional Paper i—1956. Colombo: Government Press, 1956.

———. *Report of the Committee on Utilization of Crown Lands*. Sessional Paper iii—1953.

———. *Report of the First Delimitation Commission*. Sessional Paper xiii—1946.

———. *Report of the Joint United Kingdom and Australian Mission on Rice Production in Ceylon—1954*. Sessional Paper ii—1955.

———. *Report of the Kandyan Peasantry Commission*. Sessional Paper xviii—1951.

———. *Report on the Rubber Industry*. Sessional Paper xviii—1947.

———. *Report on the Rubber Replanting Subsidy Scheme 1953, et seq.*

———. *Report of the Select Committee Appointed to Consider the Working of the Provisions of the Ceylon (Parliamentary Election) Order in Council.* Parliamentary Series no. 28, 2nd Parliament, 4th Session. January 1956.

———. *Report of the Select Committee on the State Council on Sinhalese and Tamil as the Official Languages.* Sessional Paper XXII—1946.

———. *Report of the Special Commission on the Constitution.* Colombo: Government Printer, 1928.

———. *Report on the Survey of Landlessness.* Sessional Paper XIII—1952.

———. *Report of the Taxation Commission.* Sessional Paper XVII—1955.

———. *Reports of a Commission appointed to Inquire into the Working of the Buddhist Temporalities. Ordinance no. 8 of 1905.* Sessional Papers XXIV—1920; XII—1923.

———. *The Final Report of the Official Languages Commission.* Sessional Paper XXII—1953, and five preceding Interim Reports.

———. *The Independence of Ceylon.* Sessional Paper XXII—1947. Colombo: Government Press, 1947.

Great Britain. Colonial Office. *Ceylon: Report of the Commission on Constitutional Reform.* Cmd. 6677. London: His Majesty's Stationery Office, 1945.

———. Commonwealth Consultative Committee. *Reports on The Colombo Plan for Co-operative Economic Development in South and South-East Asia.* Annual Reports 1950-1958. London: His Majesty's Stationery Office.

Government of India. Council of States Secretariat. *Parliamentary Debates.* Vol. VI, No. 5. February 19, 1954.

———. Ministry of Information. *Independence and After: A Collection of the More Important Speeches of Jawaharlal Nehru.* New Delhi: 1949.

International Monetary Fund, *Staff Papers,* Vol. VII, 1 (April 1959) 41-74.

United Nations. United Nations Economic Commission for Asia and the Far East, Research and Planning Division. *Economic Surveys of Asia and the Far East* for 1954-1958. Bangkok: 1955-1959.

United States Government. Economic Cooperation Administration. Special Mission to the United Kingdom. *The Sterling Area—An American Analysis.* London: 1951.

———. Mutual Security Administration. *Second Report to Congress—Mutual Defense Assistance Control Act 1951.* Washington: Government Printing Office, 1953.

II. BOOKS AND PAMPHLETS

Almond, Gabriel. *The Appeals of Communism.* Princeton: Princeton University Press, 1954.

Amarasingam, S. P. *Rice and Rubber: The Story of China-Ceylon Trade.* Colombo: Ceylon Economic Research Association, 1953.

Ariyapala, M. B. *Society in Medieval Ceylon.* Colombo: K. V. G. de Silva, 1956.

BIBLIOGRAPHY

Arts Council of Ceylon. *Art and Architecture of Ceylon-Polonnaruva Period.* Colombo: Arts Council of Ceylon, 1954.

Bailey, Sydney D. *Ceylon.* London: Hutchinson's University Library, 1952.

Bailey, Sydney D. *Parliamentary Government in Southern Asia.* New York: International Secretariat, Institute of Pacific Relations, 1953.

Bareau, Paul. *The Sterling Area; What It Is and How It Works* (Pamphlet). 2nd edition. London, New York: Longmans, Green, 1950.

Barua, B. M. *Asoka and his Inscriptions.* 2nd edition. Calcutta: New Age Publishers, 1955.

Bennett, G. (ed.). *The Concept of Empire: Burke to Attlee 1774-1947.* London: A. and C. Black, 1953.

Berkes, Ross N. and Mohinder S. Bedi. *The Diplomacy of India: Indian Foreign Relations in the United Nations.* Stanford University Press, 1958.

Bowers, Faubian. *Theatre in the East: A Survey of Asian Dance and Drama.* New York, Edinburgh: Nelson and Sons, 1956.

Brown, Donald Mackenzie. *The White Umbrella: Indian Political Thought from Manu to Gandhi.* Berkeley: University of California Press, 1953.

Buddhist Committee of Inquiry. *The Betrayal of Buddhism.* Balangoda: Dharmavijaya Press, 1956.

Burtt, E. A. (ed.). *The Teachings of the Compassionate Buddha.* New York: Mentor Books, 1955.

Callard, Keith. *Pakistan, A Political Study.* New York: Macmillan, 1957.

Calvocoressi, Peter. *Survey of International Affairs 1954.* London, New York: Royal Institute of International Affairs, 1957.

Carrington, Charles Edmund. *The British Overseas; Exploits of a Nation of Shopkeepers.* Cambridge: Cambridge University Press, 1950.

Catholic Union of Ceylon. *Education in Ceylon according to the Buddhist Commission Report: A Commentary.* (Pamphlet). Colombo: Colombo Catholic Press, *n.d.*

Ceylon Daily News. *Parliament of Ceylon 1947.* Colombo: Ceylon Daily News Press, 1947 (?).

Ceylon Daily News *Parliament of Ceylon 1956.* Colombo: Ceylon Daily News Press, 1956 (?).

Codrington, H. W. *A Short History of Ceylon.* London: Macmillan, 1947.

Collins, Sir Charles. *Public Administration in Ceylon.* London: Royal Institute of International Affairs, 1951.

Conze, Edward. *Buddhism: Its Essence and Development.* Oxford: B. Cassirer, 1951.

Cook, Elsie K. *Ceylon, Its Geography, Its Resources and Its People.* London, Madras: Macmillan, 1951.

Coomaraswamy, A. K. *History of Indian and Indonesian Art.* New York: E. Weyhe, 1927.

Cottrell, Leonard. *Lost Cities.* New York: Rinehart, 1957.

Crane, Robert I., and Burton Stein. *Aspects of Economic Development in South Asia.* New York: Institute of Pacific Relations, 1954.

de Silva, Colvin R. *Ceylon Under the British Occupation 1795-1833.* 2 vols. Colombo: Colombo Apothecaries, 1953.

de Silva, Colvin R. *Hartal!* (Pamphlet.) Colombo: Lanka Samasamaja Star Press, September 1953.

de Silva, Colvin R. *Outline of the Permanent Revolution,* an "Outline Proof of the Theory of the Permanent Revolution," A Study Course. Colombo: L.S.S.P., January 1955.

de Silva, Colvin R. *Their Politics—and Ours.* (Pamphlet). Colombo: September, 1954.

Desai, Maganbhai P. *Our Language Problem.* Ahmedabad: Navajivan Publishing House, 1956.

Dutt, Nalinksha. *Early Monastic Buddhism.* 2 vols. Calcutta: Luzac, 1941.

Dutt, Romesoh C. (trans.). *The Ramayana and the Mahabharata.* London: J. M. Dent and Sons, 1953.

Emerson, Rupert. *Representative Government in Southeast Asia.* Institute of Pacific Relations. Cambridge: Harvard University Press, 1955.

Farmer, B. H. *Pioneer Peasant Colonization in Ceylon.* London: Oxford University Press, 1957.

Ferguson's *Ceylon Directory 1956.* Colombo: Ceylon Observer Press, 1956.

Fifield, R. H. *The Diplomacy of Southeast Asia, 1945-1958.* New York: Harper and Brothers, 1958.

Folliot, Denise (ed.). *Documents on International Affairs 1954.* London, New York: Royal Institute of International Affairs, 1957.

Frankel, S. H. *The Economic Impact on Under-Developed Societies.* Oxford: Blackwell, 1953.

Franks, Oliver S. *Britain and the Tide of World Affairs.* London: Oxford University Press, 1955.

Geiger, W. and C. M. Rickmers (trans.). *The Culavamsa.* 2 vols. London: Published for the Pali Text Society by Oxford University Press, 1929-30.

Geiger, Wilhelm (trans. and editor). *The Mahavamsa or The Great Chronicle of Ceylon.* Colombo: Ceylon Government Information Department, 1950.

Goonewardene, Leslie. *Differences between Trotskyism and Stalinism.* Colombo: L.S.S.P., 1954.

Goonewardene, Leslie. *L.S.S.P. Manifesto.* (Pamphlet.) Colombo: L.S.S.P., 1951.

Goonewardene, Leslie. *The Third International Condemned.* (Pamphlet.) Colombo: L.S.S.P., 1940.

Han, Suyin (pseud.). *And the Rain My Drink.* London: Jonathan Cape, 1956.

Harvey, Heather J. *Consultation and Cooperation in the Commonwealth.* London: Oxford University Press, 1952.

Henderson, William. *Pacific Settlement of Disputes—The Indonesian Question 1946-1949.* New York: Woodrow Wilson Foundation, 1954.

Humphreys, Christmas. *Buddhism.* London: Penguin Books, 1954.

International Bank for Reconstruction and Development. *The Economic Development of Ceylon.* Baltimore: Johns Hopkins Press, 1953.

Jayasuriya, A. P. *Sri Lanka Freedom Party—First Anniversary Number.* Colombo: December, 1952.

Jayewardene, J. R. *Buddhism and Marxism.* (Pamphlet.) Colombo: M. D. Gunasena, 1950.

Jennings, Sir W. Ivor. *The Approach to Self-Government.* Cambridge: Cambridge University Press, 1956.

Jennings, Sir W. Ivor. *The Commonwealth in Asia.* Oxford: Clarendon Press, 1951.

Jennings, Sir W. Ivor. *The Constitution of Ceylon.* 3rd edition. London: Oxford University Press, 1953.

Jennings, Sir W. Ivor. *The Economy of Ceylon.* 2nd edition. London: Oxford University Press, 1951.

Kahin, George M. *The Asian-African Conference, Bandung, Indonesia, April 1955.* Ithaca: Cornell University Press, 1955.

Kahin, George M. *Nationalism and Revolution in Indonesia.* Ithaca: Cornell University Press, 1952.

Kautsky, John H. *Moscow and the Communist Party of India.* New York: John Wiley; London: Chapman and Hall, 1956.

Keuneman, P. *The Fight for Left Unity.* Colombo: Communist party, 1951.

Kondapi, C. *Indians Overseas 1838-1949.* New Delhi: Indian Council of World Affairs, 1951.

Kotelawala, Sir John. *An Asian Prime Minister's Story.* London: Harrap, 1956.

Kularatne, H. de S. *The Essence of Buddha-Dhamma.* Galle: South Ceylon Youth Council, c. 1955.

Kundra, Jagdish C. *Indian Foreign Policy 1947-1954: A Study of Relations with the Western Bloc.* Groningen: J. B. Wolters, 1955.

The Lanka Bauddha Mandalaya. *An Event of Dual Significance.* (Pamphlet.) Colombo: Ministry of Home Affairs, 1956 (?).

Lanka Samasamaja. *The F.I. and the U.S.S.R.: Theses of the Fourth International.* (Pamphlet.) Colombo: Star Press, September 1956.

Lee, Douglas H. K. *Climate and Economic Development in the Tropics.* New York: Published for the Council on Foreign Relations by Harper, 1957.

Levi, Werner. *Free India in Asia.* Minneapolis: University of Minnesota, 1952.

Lewis, William Arthur. *The Theory of Economic Growth.* London: Allen and Unwin, 1955.

Livingston, George. *The Tamilians in Ceylon and a Federal Constitution* (Pamphlet). Colombo: Ilankai Tamil Arasu Kadchi, n.d.

Ludowyck, E.F.C. (ed.). *Robert Knox in the Kandyan Kingdom.* Oxford University Press, 1948.

Mahajana Eksath Peramuna. *Joint Programme of the M.E.P.* Colombo: March 1956.

Mahanayake Thero of Malaya and Singapore. *Mangala Sutta Vanna.* Penang: Mahindarama Temple, 1956.

Mansergh, Nicholas. *The Commonwealth and the Nations; Studies in British Commonwealth Relations.* London: Royal Institute of International Affairs, 1948.

Mansergh, Nicholas. *The Multi-Racial Commonwealth.* Proceedings of the Fifth Unofficial Commonwealth Relations Conference. Lahore, Pakistan, 17-27 March 1954. London: Royal Institute of International Affairs, 1954.

Mende, Tibor. *South East Asia Between Two Worlds.* London: Turnstile Press, 1955.

Mendis, G. C. *Ceylon Today and Yesterday. Main Currents of Ceylon History.* Colombo: Associated Newspapers of Ceylon, 1957.

Mendis, G. C. *Ceylon under the British.* 3rd edition. Colombo: Colombo Apothecaries, 1952.

Mendis, G. C. (ed.). *The Colebrooke-Cameron Papers, Documents on British Colonial Policy in Ceylon 1796-1833.* 2 vols. London: Oxford University Press, 1956.

Mendis, G. C. *The Early History of Ceylon.* Calcutta: Y.M.C.A. Publishing House, 1954.

Morgan, Kenneth (ed.). *The Path of the Buddha: Buddhism Interpreted by Buddhists.* New York: Ronald Press, 1956.

Murphy, Gardner. *In the Minds of Men.* New York: Basic Books, 1953.

Namasivayam, S. *The Legislatures of Ceylon, 1928-1948.* Vol. v in the series *Studies in Colonial Legislatures.* Edited by Margery Perham. London: Faber and Faber, 1950.

Nana Dicca, Venerable U. *The Thirty-Eight Blessings for World Peace—Maha Mangala Sutta.* Rangoon: Burma Buddhist World Mission, 1955.

Narada Thera. *Buddhism in a Nutshell* (Pamphlet). Bambalapitiya: Vajirarama Publication Society, 1954.

Narada Maha Thera. *The Buddhist Doctrine of Kamma and Rebirth* (Pamphlet). Bambalapitiya: Vajirarama Publication Society, 1955.

Nyanatiloka. *Fundamentals of Buddhism*—Four Lectures. Colombo: Bauddha Sahitya Sabha, 1949.

Nyanatiloka. *Path to Deliverance.* Colombo: The Bauddha Sahitya Sabha, 1952.

Oliver, Henry M., Jr. *Economic Opinion and Policy in Ceylon.* Durham, N.C.: Duke University Press; London: Cambridge University Press, 1957.

Panikkar, K. M. *Asia and Western Dominance.* London: Allen and Unwin, 1953.

Panikkar, K. M. *India and the Indian Ocean.* 2nd edition. London: Allen and Unwin, 1951.

Panikkar, K. M. *The Strategic Problems of the Indian Ocean.* New Delhi: Indian Institute of International Affairs, 1944.

Perera, Father S. G. *History of Ceylon for Schools.* Colombo: n.d.

Pieris, Ralph. *Sinhalese Social Organization—The Kandyan Period.* Colombo: Ceylon University Press Board, 1956.

Pieris, Ralph (ed.). *Some Aspects of Traditional Sinhalese Culture.* Peradeniya: Conference on Traditional Cultures, Ceylon University, 1956.

Political and Economic Planning. *Colonial Students in Britain—A Report.* London: P.E.P., 1955.

Ponnambalam, G. G. *Presidential Address, First Plenary Session, The All-Ceylon Tamil Congress.* Colombo, November 27, 1944.

Radhakrishnan, Sarvepalli. *East and West: Some Reflections.* London: G. Allen and Unwin, 1954.

Radhakrishnan, Sarvepalli. *The Hindu View of Life.* London: G. Allen and Unwin, 1927.

Rahula, W. *History of Buddhism in Ceylon: The Anuradhapura Period.* Colombo: Gunasena and Company, 1956.

Rao, P. R. Ramachandra. *India and Ceylon: A Study.* Indian Council of World Affairs. Bombay: Orient Longman's, 1954.

Rhys-Davids, T. W. *Buddhist India* (First Indian Edition). Calcutta: Susil Gupta, 1950.

Rhys-Davids, T. W. (Trans.). *Sacred Books of the Buddhists.* Vol. III. London: Frowde, 1910.

Rossi, A. *A Communist Party in Action.* (Translated by W. Kendall.) New Haven: Yale University Press, 1949.

Rostow, W. W. and M. F. Millikan. *A Proposal.* New York: Harper and Brothers, 1957.

Rustow, D. A. *Politics and Westernization in the Near East.* Princeton: Center of International Studies, 1956.

Ryan, Bryce. *Caste in Modern Ceylon. The Sinhalese System in Transition.* New Brunswick: Rutgers University Press, 1953.

Ryan, Bryce. *Sinhalese Village.* Coral Gables: University of Miami Press, 1958.

Sarathchandra, E. R. *The Sinhalese Folk Play and the Modern Stage.* Colombo: Ceylon University Press, 1953.

Sarkar, N. K. and S. J. Tambiah. *The Disintegrating Village.* Colombo: Ceylon University Press, 1957.

Selznik, Philip. *The Organizational Weapon.* New York: McGraw-Hill, 1952.

Smith, F. Harold. *The Buddhist Way of Life.* London: Hutchinson's University Library, 1951.

Smith, Vincent A. *A History of Fine Art in India and Ceylon.* Oxford: Clarendon Press, 1930.

Sontag, R. J. and J. S. Beddie. *Nazi-Soviet Relations 1939-1941.* New York: Didier, 1948.

Staley, Eugene. *The Future of Underdeveloped Countries; Political Implications of Economic Development.* New York: Published for the Council on Foreign Relations by Harper, 1954.

Story, Francis. *Buddhism Answers the Marxist Challenge.* Rangoon: Burma Buddhist World Mission, 1952.

Tambiah, Henry W. *The Laws and Customs of the Tamils of Ceylon.* Colombo: Tamil Cultural Society of Ceylon, 1954.

Tennent, Sir J. Emerson. *Ceylon: An Account of the Island—Physical, Historical and Topographical.* 2 vols. 2nd edition. London: Longmans Green, 1859.

Thani Nayagam, Xavier S. *Tamil Culture* (Pamphlet). Colombo: Tamil Cultural Society, 1955.

Thompson, V. and R. Adloff. *Minority Problems in Southeast Asia.* Stanford: Stanford University Press, 1955.

Tinker, Hugh. *The Union of Burma: A Study of the First Years of Independence.* London, New York: Oxford University Press, 1957.

Underhill, Frank H. *The British Commonwealth; An Experiment in Co-Operation Among Nations.* Durham, N.C.: Published for the Duke University Commonwealth Studies Center by Duke University Press, 1956.

United National Party. *The Manifesto and Constitution of the United National Party.* Colombo: 1947.

UNESCO, World Art Series. *Paintings from Temple, Shrine and Rock.* New York: Graphic Society, 1957.

Vaidialingham, A. *Samasamajism.* (Pamphlet.) Colombo: L.S.S.P., 1940.

Vijaya-Tunga, Jinadasa. *Island Story.* Bombay, N.Y.: Indian Branch, Oxford University Press, 1949.

Vijayavardhana, D. C. *Dharma-Vijaya (Triumph of Righteousness) or the Revolt in the Temple.* Colombo: Sinha Publications, 1953.

Vittachi, Tarzie. *Emergency '58; The Story of the Ceylon Race Riots.* London: A. Deutsch, 1958.

Wallich, Henry C. *Mainsprings of the German Revival.* New Haven: Yale University Press, 1955.

Weerawardana, I. D. S. *Government and Politics in Ceylon (1931-1946).* Colombo: Ceylon Economic Research Association, 1951.

Weerawardana, I. D. S. *The Senate of Ceylon at Work.* Colombo: Ceylon University Press, 1955.

Weerawardana, I. D. S. and M. I. *Ceylon and Her Citizens.* Madras: Oxford University Press, 1956.

Weiner, Myron. *Party Politics in India: The Development of a Multi-Party System.* Princeton: Princeton University Press, 1957.

Wickramasinghe, Martin. *The Buddhist Jataka Stories and the Russian Novel.* Colombo: Associated Newspapers of Ceylon, 1956.

Wickremasinghe, S. A. *The Economic Crisis.* Colombo: Communist party, 1953.

Wickremasinghe, S. A. *The Way Ahead: An Economic Policy for Ceylon.* Colombo: Lanka Press, 1955.

Wijesekera, N. D. *The People of Ceylon.* Colombo: M. D. Gunasena, 1949.

Wijesekera, O. H. de A. *Buddhism and Society.* (Pamphlet.) Colombo: Bauddha Sahitya Sabha, n.d., c. 1954.

Wijesekera, O. H. de A. *Buddhism and the Moral Problem.* Colombo: Buddhist Brotherhood, 1945.

Wilson, Christine. *The Bitter Berry.* London: Hurst and Blackett, 1957.

Wint, Guy. *Spotlight on Asia.* London: Penguin Books, 1955.

Wittfogel, K. A. *Oriental Despotism: A Comparative Study of Total Power.* New Haven: Yale University Press, 1957.

Woodward, F. L. *Some Sayings of the Buddha, According to the Pali Canon.* London: Oxford University Press, 1955.

Woolf, Leonard S. *The Village in the Jungle.* New York: Harcourt, Brace and Company, 1926.

Zimmer, Heinrich. *The Art of Indian Asia.* 2 vols. (Joseph Campbell, Editor.) New York: Pantheon, 1955.

Zinkin, M. *Asia and the West.* London: Chatto and Windus, 1951.

Zinkin, M. *Development of Free Asia.* Fair Lawn, N.J.: Essential Books, 1956.

III. ARTICLES AND PERIODICALS

A Beachcomber's Diary. "Conference on American Aid," *Thought* (Delhi) VII, no. 17 (April 23,1955), 5.

"A 'People's Government': Social and Political Trends in Ceylon," *World Today,* 12, no. 7 (July 1956), 281-291.

Almond, Gabriel. "The Comparative Study of Interest Groups," *American Political Science Review,* LII, no. 1 (March 1958) 270-282.

Bajpai, G. S. "India and the Balance of Power" in *The Indian Yearbook of International Affairs,* Vol. 1, Madras, 1952.

Bandaranaike, S. W. R. D. "Why I Became a Buddhist," *The Buddhist,* v, new series (May/June 1934).

Binder, Leonard. "The Middle East as a Subordinate International System," *World Politics,* x, no. 3 (April 1958) 408-429.

Bunker, Sydney K. "Some Reflections on the Jaffna Family System," *The New Lanka,* I, no. 4 (July 1950), 29-33.

Ceylon Historical Journal, *Special Issue—The D. S. Senanayake Memorial Number,* v, Nos. 1, 2, 3 and 4 (July/October 1955, January/April 1956).

Cullumbine, H. "An Analysis of the Vital Statistics of Ceylon," *Ceylon Journal of Medical Science,* Section D, VII, pts. 3 and 4 (December 1950).

Das Gupta, B. B. "The Theory and Reality of Economic Development," Central Bank of Ceylon *Bulletin,* v, no. 11 (November 1955), 5-10.

de Silva, Dudley K. G., "A Rural Teacher's Life," *The Ceylon Journal of Education,* III, no. 4 (May 1945), 83-90.

Ellepola, D. B. "Changing Trends in Village Ceylon," *Proceedings of the Tenth Annual Session of the Ceylon Association for the Advancement of Science* (Presidential address, delivered 26th November, 1954) Colombo: Colombo Apothecaries Co., *n.d.*

Green, T. L. "Culture and Education in Ceylon," in R. Pieris (ed.) *Some Aspects of Traditional Sinhalese Culture.* Ceylon University, 1956.

Green, T. L. "Education and Social Needs of Ceylon," *University of Ceylon Review,* x, no. 4 (October 1952), 297-316.

Green, T. L. "Education and Society in Ceylon," *The Educand* (University of West Australia), 2, no. 3 (November 1956), 49-65.

Green, T. L. "Looking for Status Rather than Work," *Manchester Guardian,* October 4, 1954.

Green, T. L. "Social Education for Teachers in Ceylon," *The International Review of Education,* II, no. 2, *n.d.,* 200-214.

Green, T. L. "The Social Significance of Science Education in Asia," *Teaching* (September, 1956), 1-6.

Handy-Perinbanayagam, S. "Principal's Address of Welcome to the Prime Minister," in Kokuvil Hindu College *Annual 1954.*

Jennings, Sir Ivor. "Additional Notes on the General Elections," *Ceylon Historical Journal,* II, nos. 3 and 4 (January and April 1953), 193-208.

Jennings, Sir Ivor. "Nationalism and Political Development in Ceylon," *Ceylon Historical Journal,* III, nos. 1-4 (July, October 1953), 62-84, 99-114, 197-206.

Jennings, Sir Ivor. "Politics in Ceylon Since 1952," *Pacific Affairs,* XXVIII, no. 4 (December 1954), 338-352.

Jennings, Sir Ivor. "Race, Religion and Opportunity at the University of Ceylon," *University of Ceylon Review,* II, no. 142 (November 1944), 1-13.

Jennings, Sir Ivor. "The Ceylon General Elections of 1947," *University of Ceylon Review,* VI, no. 3 (July 1948), 133-195.

Lanerolle, J. de. "The Future Official Languages of Ceylon," *University of Ceylon Review,* IV (November 1945), 35-43.

Levi, Werner. "Union in Asia," *Far Eastern Survey,* XIX (1950), 144-199.

Malalasekera, G. P. "Buddhism in Ceylon," *2500-Buddha Jayanti Souvenir.* Colombo: Lanka Bauddha Mandalaya, 1956. 129-136.

Mendis, G. C. "The Causes of Communal Conflict in Ceylon," *Ceylon Historical Journal,* I, no. 1 (April 1943), 41-49.

Morgan, Theodore. "The Economic Development of Ceylon," *The Annals* of the American Academy of Political and Social Science, 305 (May 1956), 92-100.

Murphey, Rhoads, "The Ruin of Ancient Ceylon," *The Journal of Asian Studies,* XVI, no. 2 (February 1957), 181-200.

Nehru, J. "To the Youth of Lanka," *Before and After Independence, 1922-1950.* New Delhi: Indian Printing Works, *n.d.,* 69-70.

Packer, G. "The Asian Relations Conference," *Australian Outlook,* I, no. 2 (June 1947), 3-8.

Pye, Lucien W. "The Non-Western Political Process," *The Journal of Politics,* XX, no. 3 (August 1958), 468-486.

Rasaputram, W. "Gross National Product of Ceylon at Constant (1948) Prices," Central Bank of Ceylon, *Bulletin,* 6, no. 1 (January 1956), 8-16.

Rippy, Fred J. "Trinidad and Ceylon, Two Profitable British Colonies," in L. W. Shannon, *Underdeveloped Countries.* New York: Harper and Brothers, 1957.

Rostow, W. W. "The Take-Off into Self-Sustained Growth," *Economic Journal,* 66, no. 261 (March 1956), 25-48.

Ryan, Bryce. "Primary and Secondary Contacts in a Ceylonese Peasant Community," *Rural Sociology,* 17, no. 4 (December 1952), 311-321.

Ryan, Bryce. "The Sinhalese Family System," *The Eastern Anthropologist,* VI, nos. 3 and 4 (March-August 1953), 143-163.

Ryan, Bryce F. and Murray A. Straus. "The Integration of Sinhalese Society," *Research Studies of the State College of Washington,* XXII, no. 4 (December 1954), 179-227.

Sarkar, N. K. "Population Policy in Ceylon," *Population Studies,* IX, no. 3 (March 1956), 195-216.

Senanayake, D. S. "On the 'Middle Path' in Politics," *The Ceylon Historical Journal,* V, nos. 1-4 (July/October 1955 and January/April 1956), 110-114.

Siriwardane, C. D. S. "The Buddhist Problem Today," *Law College Buddhist Annual 1955-1956.* 2-6.

Stein, Burton. "Problems of Economic Development in Ceylon," *Aspects of Economic Development in South Asia.* New York: Institute of Pacific Relations, 1955. Reprinted in *The Ceylon Historical Journal,* III, nos. 3 and 4 (March/April 1954), 286-330.

Straus, Jacqueline H. and Murray A. "Suicide, Homicide, and Social Structure in Ceylon," *The American Journal of Sociology,* LVIII, no. 5 (March 1953), 461-469.

Straus, Murray A. "Childhood Experience and Emotional Security in the Context of Sinhalese Social Organization," *Social Forces,* 33, no. 2 (December 1954), 152-160.

Straus, Murray A. "Cultural Factors in the Functioning of Agricultural Extension in Ceylon," *Rural Sociology,* 18, no. 3 (September 1953), 249-256.

Tambiah, S. J. "Ethnic Representation in Ceylon's Higher Administrative Services 1870-1946," *University of Ceylon Review,* XIII, nos. 2 and 3 (April-July 1955), 113-134.

Thompson, Virginia and Richard Adloff. "Asian Unity: Force or Fiction?" *Far Eastern Survey,* XVI (1949), 97-99.

Weerawardana, I. D. S. "General Elections in Ceylon 1952," *The Ceylon Historical Journal,* II, nos. 1 and 2 (July, October, 1952), 111-178.

Wignaraja, P. "Some Relationships Between Population Growth, Capital Formation and Employment Opportunities," Central Bank of Ceylon, *Bulletin,* 6, no. 11 (November 1956), 8-11.

Wijesekera, N. D. "Dynamism of Traditional Culture," in R. Pieris (ed.), *Traditional Sinhalese Culture.* Peradeniya: Conference on Traditional Culture, Ceylon University, 1956.

IV. NEWSPAPERS

Buddha Jayanti (Colombo) Vols. I-III (1954-1956).
Ceylon Daily News (Colombo).
Ceylon Observer (Colombo).
Dawn (Karachi).
Financial Times (London).
The Hindu (Madras).
Manchester Guardian.
Morning Times (Colombo).
New York Times.
Rodaya (Colombo).
The Scotsman (Edinburgh).
Sunday Times (Colombo).
The Times (London).
Times of Ceylon (Colombo).
Times of India (Bombay).
Wall Street Journal (New York).

V. UNPUBLISHED MATERIAL

Green, T. L. "Sinhalese Children's Stereotypes of Sinhalese, Tamil, Burgher and English."

Green, T. L. "Studies in Stereotypes Held by Ceylonese; Group Attitudes of Adult University Graduate Teachers."

Green, T. L. "Tamil Stereotypes of Sinhalese, Tamils, English and Burghers."

Tambiah, S. J. "Kandyan Marriage Customs." (Paper read before the Ceylon Association for the Advancement of Science, November 24, 1956.)

INDEX

INDEX

GPSR Authorized Representative: Easy Access System Europe - Mustamäe tee 50, 10621 Tallinn, Estonia, gpsr.requests@easproject.com

www.ingramcontent.com/pod-product-compliance
Lightning Source LLC
LaVergne TN
LVHW052213200926
848481LV00001B/91